The Works
of Patrick
Branwell Bron

GARLAND REFERENCE LIBRARY OF
VOLUME 1238

THE WORKS
OF PATRICK
BRANWELL BRONTË
AN EDITION
VOLUME I

EDITED BY
VICTOR A. NEUFELDT

GARLAND PUBLISHING, INC.
NEW YORK AND LONDON
1997

Library of Congress Cataloging-in-Publication Data

Brontë, Patrick Branwell, 1817–1848.
    [Works. 1997]
    The works of Patrick Branwell Brontë : an edition / edited by
Victor A. Neufeldt.
          p.   cm. — (Garland reference library of social science ;
v. 1238)
    Includes bibliographical references and index.
    ISBN 0-8153-0224-X (alk. paper)
    I. Neufeldt, Victor A. II. Title. III. Series.
PR4174.B23 1997
828'.709—dc21   97-11630
                                                  CIP

Printed on acid-free, 250-year-life paper
Manufactured in the United States of America

To Audrey

CONTENTS

ACKNOWLEDGEMENTS

It is with pleasure that I acknowledge the cooperation and assistance of the many persons and agencies without whose generous help this work would not have been possible.

For their generous financial assistance in the form of research grants I wish to thank the Social Sciences and Humanities Research Council of Canada and the Office of Research Administration of the University of Victoria, and for its generous secretarial assistance, the Department of English at the University of Victoria.

For their support during my very pleasant term as a Visiting Fellow at Clare Hall, University of Cambridge, I wish to thank Gillian Beer, President, and the staff of the Hall.

For their permission to reproduce the texts of manuscripts, transcriptions, and letters held by them it is my pleasure to acknowledge the following libraries and individuals: the family of the late C. K. Shorter; the Council of the Brontë Society; the Brotherton Collection, the Brotherton Library, University of Leeds; the British Library, Department of Manuscripts; the Houghton Library, Harvard University; Special Collections Division, University of British Columbia; William Self.

For their assistance in locating and making available materials and answering numerous queries, I wish to acknowledge the assistance of the following individuals: Juliet R. V. Barker; John Beer; Jane Sellars, Kathryn White, Ann Dinsdale and Tracy Messenger at the Brontë Parsonage Museum; Christopher D. W. Sheppard and staff at the Brotherton Collection, University of Leeds; the Keeper and staff, Department of Manuscripts, British Library; Richard Wendorf and staff, Houghton Library, Harvard University; the staff of the McPherson Library, University of Victoria; and colleagues John Fitch, Peter Smith, Lisa Surridge, and Ted Wooley. I wish also to thank Juliet Barker, Christine Alexander, Jane Sellars, and Margaret Smith for the assistance they have provided with the timely appearance of their recent publications.

Finally, for their unflagging help in preparing the manuscript and the annotations, I wish to thank Monika Rydygier Smith, Scott Swanson, Robin Cryderman, and my wife, Audrey, who declines to be listed as co-editor.

LIST OF ABBREVIATIONS

Alexander CB	*An Edition of the Early Writings of Charlotte Brontë*, vols. 1 and 2, ed., Christine Alexander, Oxford: Basil Blackwell, 1987 and 1991
Alexander EW	*The Early Writings of Charlotte Brontë*, by Christine Alexander, Oxford: Basil Blackwell, 1983
Alexander Magazines	*Branwell's Blackwood's Magazine*, ed., Christine Alexander, Edmonton: Juvenilia Press, 1995
Alexander & Sellars	*The Art of the Brontës*, by Christine Alexander and Jane Sellars, Cambridge: Cambridge University Press, 1995
Barker Brontës	*The Brontës*, by Juliet Barker, London: Weidenfeld and Nicholson, 1994
BL: Ashley	British Library: Ashley Collection
BPM: Bon	Brontë Parsonage Museum, Bonnell Collection
BPM: BS	Brontë Parsonage Museum, Brontë Society's Collection
BPM: SG	Brontë Parsonage Museum, Seton Gordon Collection
Brotherton	Brotherton Collection, Brotherton Library, University of Leeds
BST	*Brontë Society Transactions*, 1895-1992
Butterfield	*Brother in the Shadow*, by Mary Butterfield and R. J. Duckett, Bradford: Bradford Libraries and Information Service, 1988
Dembleby	*The Confessions of Charlotte Brontë*, by John Malham-Dembleby, Bradford: Privately published, 1954
De Quincey	*The De Quincey Memorials*, 2 vols., by Alexander H. Japp, London: William Heineman, 1891
Gaskell CB	*The Life of Charlotte Brontë*, by Elizabeth Gaskell, London: Smith Elder & Co., 1857

Gérin BB	*Branwell Brontë*, by Winifred Gérin, London: Hutchison & Co., 1972
Gérin CB	*Charlotte Brontë. The Evolution of Genius*, by Winifred Gérin, Oxford: Oxford University Press, 1967
Grundy	*Pictures of the Past*, by F. H. Grundy, London: Griffith and Farrar, 1879
Hatfield Papers	The papers of late C. W. Hatfield at the BPM, containing notes, transcriptions, and correspondence
H L	Houghton Library, Harvard University
Leyland	*The Brontë Family, with Special Reference to Patrick Branwell Brontë*, by Francis Leyland, 2 vols., London: Hurst and Blackett, 1886
Leyland Letters	*A Complete Transcript of the Leyland Manuscripts Showing the Unpublished portions From the Original Manuscripts*, by J. Alex. Symington and C.W. Hatfield, Privately printed, 1925
Neufeldt Bibliog	*A Bibliography of the Manuscripts of Patrick Branwell Brontë*, ed., Victor A. Neufeldt, New York: Garland Publishing Inc., 1993
Neufeldt PBB	*The Poems of Patrick Branwell Brontë*, ed., Victor A. Neufeldt, New York: Garland Publishing Inc., 1990
Neufeldt PCB	*The Poems of Charlotte Brontë*, ed., Victor A. Neufeldt, New York: Garland Publishing Inc., 1985
SHB LL	*The Brontës: Their Lives, Friendships, and Correspondence* (The Shakespeare Head edition), ed., Thomas J. Wise and John Alexander Symington, 4 vols., Oxford: Basil Blackwell, 1932
SHB Misc	*The Miscellaneous and Unpublished Writings of Charlotte and Patrick Branwell Brontë*, (The Shakespeare Head edition), ed., Thomas J. Wise and John Alexander Symington, 2 vols., Oxford: Basil Blackwell, 1936 and 1938

Shorter 1923	*The Complete Poems of Charlotte Brontë*, ed., Clement Shorter, with the assistance of C.W. Hatfield, London: Hodder and Stoughton, 1923
Shorter EJB 1910	*The Complete Works of Emily Jane Brontë*, 2 vols., ed., Clement Shorter, London: Hodder and Stoughton, 1910
Smith Letters	*The Letters of Charlotte Brontë*, 2 vols., ed., Margaret Smith, Oxford: Oxford University Press, 1995
Symington Papers (BPM)	Correspondence, news clippings and other materials, mainly concerned with the publication of the SHB
Winnifrith PBB	*The Poems of Patrick Branwell Brontë*, ed., Tom Winnifrith, Oxford: Basil Blackwell, 1983
Wise Bibliog 1917	*A Bibliography of the Writings in Prose and Verse of the Members of the Brontë Family*, ed., Thomas J. Wise, London: Privately printed, 1917
Wise Collection	The Stockett-Thomas J. Wise Collection, Special Collections Division, Library of the University of British Columbia, containing, along with works by and about Wise, Hatfield's proof copy of Shorter 1923, and correspondence concerning the Brontës by Hatfield, Davidson Cook, Alice Law, and J.A. Symington

INTRODUCTION

Of one, too, I have heard,
A brother—sleeps he here?
Of all that gifted race
Not the least gifted; young,
Unhappy, eloquent—the child
Of many hopes, of many tears.
O boy, if here thou sleep'st, sleep well!
On Thee too did the Muse
Bright in thy cradle smile;
But some dark shadow came
(I know not what) and interposed.

(Matthew Arnold, "Haworth Churchyard")

"But some dark shadow came . . . and interposed." Even if, in 1855, Matthew Arnold did not know the cause, his lines clearly imply the effect: Branwell had squandered the gifts he had been granted and had failed to fulfill the promise of the Muse's bright smile. Of course, Arnold did not know that Branwell had published at least nineteen poems[1] between 1841 and 1847— eighteen of them before the publication of *Poems By Currer, Ellis, and Acton Bell* in May 1846. All but one published under the pseudonym "Northangerland," these poems appeared in the *Halifax Guardian*, the *Bradford Herald*, the *Leeds Intelligencer*, and the *Yorkshire Gazette*. Being published in these Yorkshire newspapers was a significant achievement; it placed Branwell in the company of poets with established reputations,[2] and his poems enjoyed a wider initial readership than the volume published by his sisters, which had sold only two copies by June 1847.

---

[1]   Juliet Barker argues for an additional unsigned poem—see Barker Brontës, 933, n. 18.

[2]   These newspapers were very proud of their poetry columns, and published poems not only by local worthies, but also by Wordsworth, Tennyson, Shelley, Southey, Hood, Leigh Hunt, Thomas Campbell, and Longfellow among others. The *Halifax Guardian*, in which Branwell published the largest number of his poems, welcomed gifts of 'Original Poetry' but did not hesitate to reject material which it considered beneath the high standards of which it boasted, and printed stinging rebukes to poor souls who had presumed to send in 'feeble' verses for publication. For further information on the publication of poetry in newspapers, see Neufeldt PBB, xlvi, and Barker Brontës, 371.

Arnold's judgment has, with few exceptions, remained the accepted view
of Branwell's achievement. Branwell himself gave credence to such a view with
his deathbed comment, "In all my past life I have done nothing either great or
good" (Barker Brontës, 567). And certainly it was the view fostered by his sister
Charlotte, by some of his friends, and by those who created the Brontë legend
after her death.

Charlotte had begun to express her vexation at her brother's failure to
achieve success as an artist or a writer in letters to her close friend Ellen Nussey
long before Branwell's dismissal from Thorp Green in 1845 and his subsequent
decline into alcoholism and drug addiction. When he accepted the position at
Sowerby Bridge as "assistant clerk-in-charge" on the Leeds and Manchester
Railway in October 1840, she wrote to Ellen mockingly:

> A distant relation of mine, one Patrick Boanerges, has set off to seek
> his fortune, in the wild, wandering, adventurous, romantic, knight-
> errant-like capacity of clerk on the Leeds and Manchester Railroad.
> Leeds and Manchester, where are they? Cities in a wilderness—like
> Tadmor, alias Palmyra—are they not? (Smith Letters, I, 228).[3]

When Branwell transferred to Luddenden Foot as clerk-in-charge, on a much
higher salary, in April 1841, Charlotte wrote to Emily, "It is to be hoped that
his removal to another station will turn out for the best. As you say, it looks
like getting on at any rate" (Smith Letters, I, 251).

After Branwell's dismissal at Thorp Green and the revelation of his
involvement with Mrs. Robinson, his employer's wife, Charlotte vehemently
expressed her bitterness and contempt for her brother in her letters to Ellen
Nussey, whose brother Joseph was also an alcoholic. The two friends, noting the
parallels in the behavior of their brothers, commiserated with one another:

> You say well in speaking of Branwell that no sufferings are so awful as
> those brought on by dissipation—alas! I see the truth of this
> observation daily proved—Ann and Mercy must have a weary and
> burdensome life of it—in waiting upon their unhappy brother—it
> seems grievous indeed that those who have not sinned should suffer so
> largely (Smith Letters, I, 441-442).

The sense of martyrdom implicit in the final sentence is further evidenced in
Charlotte's refusal to take up Ellen's invitations to Brookroyd or to allow Ellen
to visit Haworth: "Branwell makes no effort to seek a situation—and while he is

---

[3] "Boanerges" means "sons of Thunder," the title Jesus gave to his disciples
James and John; the name "Brontë" means "Thunder" in Greek; and Tadmor was
a city built in the wilderness by Solomon. See Mark 3:17; II Chronicles 8:4.

at home I will invite no one to come and share our discomfort" (Smith Letters, I, 420).[4]

On October 2, 1848, the day after Branwell's funeral, Charlotte wrote to W. S. Williams (her reader at Smith Elder):

> The removal of our only brother must necessarily be regarded by us rather in the light of a mercy than a chastisement: Branwell was his Father's and his Sister's pride and hope in boyhood, but since Manhood, the case has been otherwise. It has been our lot to see him take a wrong bent; to hope, expect, wait his return to the right path; to know the sickness of hope deferred, the dismay of prayer baffled, to experience despair at last; and now to behold the sudden early obscure close of what might have been a noble career.
>
> I do not weep from a sense of bereavement—there is no prop withdrawn, no consolation torn away, no dear companion lost—but for the wreck of talent, the ruin of promise, the untimely dreary extinction of what might have been a burning and a shining light. My brother was a year my junior; I had aspirations and ambitions for him once—long ago—they have perished mournfully—nothing remains of him but a memory of errors and sufferings—There is such a bitterness of pity for his life and death—such a yearning for the emptiness of his whole existence as I cannot describe—I trust time will allay these feelings (SHB LL, II, 261).

These views Charlotte passed on not only to Ellen Nussey and W. S. Williams, but later also to Mrs. Gaskell and Harriet Martineau. The latter, on receiving the news of Charlotte's death, published a tribute in the *Daily News*, 6 April 1855, beginning "Currer Bell [Charlotte's pseudonym] is dead," in which she drew the outline that, as Juliet Barker points out, Mrs. Gaskell would embellish in her Biography two years later: "Most of the half-truths, misconceptions and downright untruths which would give such lurid colouring to the story of Charlotte's life were already evident here: a father who was 'simple and unworldly' and 'too much absorbed in his studies to notice her occupations'; an older brother 'a young man of once splendid promise which was early blighted'; a home among the 'wild Yorkshire hills . . . in a place where newspapers were never seen.' " (Barker Brontë, 775).

Thus was the Brontë legend created and with it the (mis)conception of, to use Charlotte's own words, "the emptiness of [Branwell's] whole existence." This conception was given immediate reinforcement by Matthew Arnold's lines,

---

[4]   For a fuller discussion of Charlotte's attitude toward her brother, see Barker Brontës, 366-67; 470-72; 568-69, and Smith Letters, I, 17-18, 412, 418, 426, 432, 444.

quoted above, published in *Fraser's Magazine* in May 1855.[5] It was further reinforced by the family's seemingly complete ignorance of his literary achievements. In the letter to W. S. Williams cited above, Charlotte goes on to state:

> My unhappy brother never knew what his sisters had done in literature—he was not aware that they had ever published a line. We could not tell him of our efforts for fear of causing him too deep a pang of remorse for his own time misspent, and talents misapplied. Now he will *never* know. I cannot dwell longer on the subject at present—it is too painful (SHB LL, II, 262).

Juliet Barker is sceptical about Branwell's complete ignorance of his sisters' publishing activities (Brontës, 487-89). Whatever the case, *there is no evidence that Charlotte or any other member of the family was ever aware of Branwell's publications.*[6] Nor is there any suggestion of such publications (with the exception of "THE AFFGAN WAR" in the *Leeds Intelligencer*) in Gaskell CB or in Leyland's much more sympathetic treatment of Branwell's achievements, nine years later. Indeed, Mrs. Gaskell's description of Branwell's lack of achievement is even harsher than Charlotte's (see chapter xiii), and it established the view that persists to this day. Branwell the published poet (except for the one poem on the Afghan War) did not exist until 1961, when Winnifred Gérin (BB, 186, 209) indicated an awareness of six poems, although she identified only five. In his 1983 edition of Branwell's poems, Tom Winnifrith identified six (pp. xxxii-xxxvii, 287, 291, 297). In 1989 Selwyn Goodacre increased the number to

---

[5] In these lines Arnold seems to question the very existence of Branwell, for he asks "Of one, too, I have heard/ A brother—sleeps he here?" then again "Oh boy, if here thou sleep'st, sleep well!" In fact Arnold labored under the misapprehension that Charlotte and her family lay in the churchyard at Haworth, when in fact they were buried in the vault under the church, and was vexed to discover that reality was not in accord with his artistic construct. He wrote to Mrs. Gaskell in June 1855, "I am almost sorry that you told me about the place of their burial. It really seems to me to put the finishing touch to the strange cross-grained character of the fortunes of that ill-fated family that they should even be placed after death in the wrong uncongenial spot" (Barker Brontës, 968, n. 5).

[6] When Joseph Leyland advised Branwell in 1842 to publish his poems "with his name appended, rather than the pseudonym of 'Northangerland'" (Leyland, II, 25), Branwell replied "Northangerland has so long wrought on in secret and silence that he dare not take your kind encouragement in the light in which vanity would prompt him to do" (Leyland Letters, 15). Branwell persisted in using the pseudonym to the end. He used it not only for 18 of his 19 published poems, but also for 7 other poems, all of which were intended for publication.

eleven;[7] in 1990 my edition of Branwell's poems identified fifteen and in my 1993 bibliography of his manuscripts I increased the number to nineteen.

Yet, as recently as 1993, despite the available evidence of Branwell's literary achievement, a prominent scholar, in a review of Robert Collins' edition of two previously unpublished prose tales, could still write:

> Branwell revealed an early gift for art, music and literature, dreamed of becoming a great writer, and between the ages of 12 and 17 penned around thirty assorted tales, poems, dramas, journals and histories, all written at fever pitch. He wrote more than the sum total of his sisters' output, though without a particle of the talent. But he was already slipping out of the Parsonage to the Black Bull rather too regularly, a youth of sizeable personality and minuscule character . . . . London had confirmed what he already suspected: that he had meglomaniacal ambitions and no practical interest whatsoever in achieving them.[8]

The rest of the review's account of Branwell's life focuses on his supposed debauchery and embezzlement at Sowerby Bridge [*sic*] and his affair with Mrs. Robinson, concluding "with the law breathing down his neck for unpaid debts, Branwell took to his bed, scrawled his final document (a begging note for gin) and died in his father's arms." Nowhere is there any mention of his publications or of his success as a translator of Horace's Odes. Old myths, it seems, die hard, and a just, informed assessment of Branwell's achievement will not occur until all of his work has been published.

This review illustrates the tone of dismissive scorn that has bedeviled Branwell scholarship to this day. Aside from the personal biases possibly involved, that scorn is frequently the result of readers having read only the fragmentary bits and pieces of Branwell's work available in print to date, with little knowledge or understanding of how the bits relate to the larger context and purpose of Branwell's work. As recently as 1982 Barbara and Gareth Evans quite rightly complained:

> There is no one complete and accurate edition of all these MSS . . . . Some have been transcribed and editions published, but by no means all of them, particularly in the case of Branwell's writing. Moreover, what has been published is not always easily accessible. Some volumes are either out of print or so large and expensive that they are beyond the pocket of the ordinary book-buyer. Some that have been reissued or

---

[7]   "The Published Poems of Branwell Brontë," BST, 19, 361.

[8]   Terry Eagleton, "Angry 'Un," *London Review of Books*, 8 July 1993, p. 16. Eagleton's figure of "thirty assorted tales" is quite inaccurate; it should more accurately read "forty-nine."

republished are, sadly, not updated in the light of more recent knowledge and are often unreliable, with material omitted, misdated or misread. There are also references to some manuscripts, by title, that seem no longer to exist at all—or are being held back, wittingly or unwittingly, their location and/or history of their acquisition shrouded in mystery. As there is, therefore, no single complete and accurate source for the scholar or the interested amateur to go to and browse through, it has not yet been possible to feel the full impact of the vast amount of writing that Charlotte and Branwell accomplished during their early childhood and teenage years.[9]

Christine Alexander's edition of Charlotte's early writings, when the third volume is completed, will provide such a source for Charlotte, and this edition, when the three volumes are completed, one for Branwell. In fairness it must be pointed out that until the publication of the bibliography of Branwell's manuscripts in 1993 it was virtually impossible for a reader/scholar to know how much Branwell had actually written, how fragmentary and unreliable the published texts were, and how all the bits fit together. As a result, all biographical treatments and studies of Branwell's work predating Juliet Barker's 1994 biography have to be approached with caution. Hers is the only study so far to make use of Alexander's work on Charlotte, my editions of Charlotte's and Branwell's poetry, and my bibliography of Branwell's manuscripts.

These three volumes will contain all of Branwell's known writings, excluding his letters. Volume One covers 1827-1833, when Branwell was aged nine to sixteen. Volume II will cover 1834-36; volume III, 1837-47. The first volume focuses on the creation of the Glass Town Confederacy and on the emergence of Rougue/Alexander Percy/Ellrington as Branwell's chief character. Only the first two items in this volume are not associated with the Glass Town saga. Volume II will focus on the creation of Angria, and the conflict between Percy and Zamorna. Volume III will cover Percy's defeat and decline, and Branwell's writings after he abandons the Angrian saga in 1839.

Early attempts to list Branwell's manuscripts, such as Clement Shorter's "The Early Brontë Manuscripts," *The Brontës: Life and Letters*, 1908, II, 430-34 and Thomas J. Wise's *A Bibliography of the Writings in Prose and Verse of the Members of the Brontë Family*, 1917, are not only very incomplete, but also often incorrect in matters of text, title, authorship and dating. Mildred Christian's "A Census of Brontë Manuscripts in the United States," *The Trollopian*, II and III, 1947, is out of date, and offers only a very partial listing of Branwell's manuscripts because the bulk of them are in the United Kingdom. More recently, the *Index of English Literary Manuscripts*, vol. iv, 1800-1900, eds., Barbara

---

9   *Everyman's Companion to the Brontës* (London: J. M. Dent and Sons, 1982), p. 154.

Rosenbaum and Pamela White, New York, 1982, while listing all the manuscripts of the three sisters, surprisingly ignores Branwell entirely. One has to suspect that the dismissive scorn mentioned earlier may have been a factor.

The manuscripts currently known to exist are scattered over thirteen libraries and private collections, though the great majority are held at the Brontë Parsonage Museum and in the Brotherton Collection at the University of Leeds. The manuscripts contained in this first volume are largely intact, most of them more or less fair copies in the form of magazines, newspapers, dramas, volumes of poems, bound prose tales, and notebooks of collected poems.[10] Nevertheless, the manuscript of **The Travels of Rolando Segur** (p. 10) has disappeared; there is good reason to believe that Branwell did produce Blackwoods Magazines for February through May, which have disappeared; and three items—the **History of the Rebellion in My Fellows** (p. 2), the July **Blackwoods Magazine** (p. 21) and **The Fate of Regina** (p. 203)—all have pages missing.

The Brontë canon is now well established and questions about authorship are minor, pertaining mostly to the early magazines on which Branwell and Charlotte collaborated. Although the magazines were begun by Branwell in January 1829, the editorship passed to Charlotte in August 1829, with Branwell promising to assist and to contribute "now and then" (see p. 30). Collaborative efforts from the magazines Charlotte edited, signed "U T" or "W T" (usually interpreted as "Us Two" or "We Two") have therefore been included in this volume; although they are usually in Charlotte's hand, the initials indicate that Branwell was involved in their composition. I have also included three poems which Christine Alexander attributes to Charlotte. Although two of them appear in BLACKWOOD'S YOUNG MEN'S MAGAZINE edited by Charlotte, I believe all three are more likely by Branwell. Two are signed "Young Soult," Branwell's pseudonym, and the subject matter of all three suggests Branwell rather than Charlotte.[11]

The same dismissive scorn and neglect has also characterized the handling and publication of his manuscripts from the beginning. When C. K. Shorter was negotiating the 1895 purchase of Brontë manuscripts from Arthur Bell Nicholls, the latter wrote on June 18, "There are a large number of Branwell's manuscripts but I don't suppose you care to have them" (Nicholls-Shorter Correspondence,

---

[10] At least twenty of the items in the table of contents of this volume are works "published" in Glass Town. The same is probably true of another seven, but they are missing their title pages.

[11] The three poems are **"High minded Frenchmen"** (p. 33), **"What is more glorious"** (p. 35), and **"Interior of A Pothouse"** (p. 36). If one takes the comments on Alexander CB, I, 74 at face value, however, these poems are by Charlotte only. See also Alexander CB, I, xxi.

Brotherton Collection). On July 3 he wrote that he would be sending Branwell's manuscripts in a day or two, yet he obviously did not send them all, for Sotheby's sales of the second Mrs. Nicholls' effects in 1907, 1914 and 1916 contained at least eighteen of Branwell's manuscripts. Both Shorter and T. J. Wise (on whose behalf Shorter had purchased the manuscripts from Nicholls) passed Branwell's manuscripts off as Charlotte's or Emily's when it was advantageous to do so. On 6 June 1895, Nicholls wrote to Shorter, "I send a number of manuscripts of Emily and Anne Brontë"; underneath the statement Shorter penciled, "they turned out to be Branwell's." Yet in Shorter's 1910 edition of Emily's works, twenty-five poems and verse fragments are, in fact, Branwell's. Of these, thirteen are facsimile reproductions—nine duplicating printed items; of the printed items, several are fragments from the same poem, and one item consists of lines from two different poems. However, Shorter's volume also contains facsimile reproductions of Emily's verse manuscripts, and the difference in the two hands is readily apparent. Thus, despite Shorter's assertion that "seventy-one new poems are taken from original manuscripts that have passed through my hands," and that "the new poems . . . have been carefully collated by me and that these are unquestionably Emily's work as she left it in the rough manuscript" (Shorter EJB 1910, II, vii), it seems likely that he had simply accepted T. J. Wise's attributions, for he also comments that the facsimiles were "reproduced from the Original Manuscripts in the possession of Mr. Thomas J. Wise and Mr. Walter Slater" (Shorter EJB 1910, II, 417). I have discussed elsewhere some of Wise's attempts to pass off Branwell's manuscripts as Emily's or Charlotte's,[12] but it is worth noting here that there exist four volumes of manuscript fragments, bound and labeled as Emily's by Rivière for Wise, which contain eighteen items belonging to Branwell. Since all of these appear as Emily's in Shorter's 1910 edition, it is clear that Wise had put together these random collections of manuscript leaves before 1910.[13]

I have also detailed elsewhere (Neufeldt PCB, xxv-xxvi) how Wise "prepared" manuscripts for sale, and how he used unbound leaves for exchanges or gifts. Materials he felt were too insignificant for major sales or to be used as gifts, he disposed of through minor London booksellers, among them Herbert Gorfin. In 1899, four years after Wise had acquired them, Gorfin sold twenty-one Branwell manuscripts to the Brontë Society for £5.50.

Wise's negative attitude toward Branwell's manuscripts remained consistent to the end. While C. W. Hatfield was assisting Wise in the preparation of his 1829 Brontë Bibliography, he wrote three times (17, 22 May, 2 June—Symington Papers, BPM), warning Wise that "The Wanderer" was not

---

12 See Neufeldt PCB, xxv-xxvii; Neufeldt PBB, xxvii; and Neufeldt Bibliog, xxiii, n. 14.

13 For a more detailed discussion of Wise's activities, see Neufeldt PBB, xxvii-xxviii.

Emily's, but an early draft of **Sir Henry Tunstall**, and pointing out that large portions of the poem had been printed as Branwell's in *De Quincey*. Yet the Bibliography appeared with the poem ascribed to Emily, with a note acknowledging that it was an early draft of the poem in *De Quincey*, but suggesting that either Branwell had pinched the work from Emily or she had transcribed it for him.

The subsequent publication history of Branwell's work suggests a similar history of neglect, but also of sporadic, unsuccessful attempts to redress that neglect. After Branwell's death, part of one poem appeared in Gaskell CB, one in Grundy's 1879 volume, and twenty-seven items in Leyland's two-volume biography (1886), written to counteract what he felt was an overly negative portrayal of Branwell by Mrs. Gaskell. Unfortunately, in assessing Branwell's literary achievement, Leyland was limited to the manuscripts his brother Joseph had accumulated; the rest were with Nicholls in Ireland. Two more poems appeared in 1891 and 1897. The Shorter/Wise 1895 purchase of Brontë manuscripts did not lead to the flurry of publications that appeared for Branwell's sisters between 1896 and 1923. Wise published only four of Branwell's poems; Shorter, twenty-five items as Emily's in his 1910 edition of her works, and three as Charlotte's in his 1923 edition of her poems. In the same year, however, John Drinkwater produced a privately printed edition of Branwell's translations of the odes of Horace to demonstrate his considerable ability as a translator, and in 1927 C. W. Hatfield reproduced the Luddenden Foot Notebook in the BST. Additional items appeared in the BST in 1919, 1920, 1927, and 1933; in *The Bookman*, 1926; and in catalogues in 1927 and 1932.

Other editions containing Branwell's writings, such as A. C. Benson's 1915 edition of the poetry of the Brontës, merely reprinted items already published. In doing even that, Benson felt he was breaking new ground; he comments in his Introduction: "It has been customary to omit all mention of Branwell's work. The catastrophe of his life was so deplorable, and the wreck of a charming and attractive nature, through self-indulgence and morbidity, so tragical, that he has been hurried out of sight."[14] Ten years later, C. W. Hatfield, in a letter to Davidson Cook (9 January 1926, Wise collection) reiterated the continuing lack of interest in Branwell's work:

> I was two or three years in preparing a book of his poems which I completed a short time ago, and am hoping that Hodder and Stoughton will issue it towards the end of this year . . . . But Branwell Brontë, unlike his sisters, has no literary reputation to back him up, and although the quality of his poetry is higher than that of Charlotte's or Anne's I doubt whether the publishers will consider it of a high enough

---

14 *Brontë Poems* (London: Smith, Elder & Co, 1915), p. xviii.

standard to justify them in incurring the expense of producing the volume.

In the end, Hatfield's edition was never published. He sent the manuscript to C.K Shorter for submission to Hodder and Stoughton, with whom Shorter had close connections, but Shorter fell ill, and Hatfield wrote to Cook, 29 October 1916 (Wise Collection): "It has never been sent to the publishers and if I do not succeed in getting it back again there will be two years wasted . . . . I feel annoyed when I think of it, for Mr. Shorter lost my first typescript volume of the poems of Charlotte Brontë. What became of that volume I never learnt, and in order to get the poems published I had to prepare another volume for the printers." His manuscript was finally returned in December by Mrs. Shorter after her husband's death, but by that time Hatfield had become involved in other Brontë projects, and he never got around to doing the revisions he felt the volume needed before it could be published.

J. A. Symington saw the proposed Shakespeare Head edition of the works of the Brontës as a means of redressing the disparagement of Branwell's work. He wrote to T. J. Wise, 23 March 1931, "The distinctive feature will, of course, be the Branwell section"; to Basil Blackwell on 26 June 1931, "I think we shall cause a little sensation when we publish the remaining volumes of the edition by being able to prove that many of the works attributed to Charlotte by Shorter, are none other than the writings of Branwell, and that Branwell will come into the full share of his credit" (Symington Papers, BPM). His optimism reached its zenith in an interview in the *Yorkshire Evening News*, February 3, 1932, announcing the publication of the Shakespeare Head edition:

BROTHER OF THE BRONTËS
VINDICATED IN NEW WORKS

An authoritative vindication of Branwell Brontë, so generally regarded as the irresponsible and philandering brother of the famous Brontë sisters, will be one of the features of a new edition of the Brontë works, part of which is to be published this week . . . . The aim of this edition is to achieve finality[15] on the subject, for probably all the existing

---

[15] Ironically, the call for "finality" was first issued by T. J. Wise. Initially Symington and Blackwell considered omitting poetry entirely from the proposed edition. Wise responded in a letter to Symington (6 April 1931—Symington Papers, BPM):

I cannot understand your suggestion to omit the Poems. To do so would in the first place be to render your edition incomplete, and thus deprive it of one of its chief attractions, and one of its greatest claims. Your war-cry should surely be "The Final, and only Complete Edition of the Writings of the Brontë Family." If you fail in this, sooner or

material of value has been accumulated after 10 years of research by the editors . . . . 'The results may well prove,' said Mr. Symington to a representative of the *Yorkshire Evening News* today, 'that the great esteem in which Branwell was held by his family was justified and that, indeed, he was the dominant factor in the early literary life of the sisters.'

Branwell will be revealed not as the 'bad lad of the family,' but as a well-read and scholarly young man. 'Actually, he was a tutor in a clergy-man's family for nearly three years, which proves,' said Mr. Symington, 'that he had some attainments worthy of his job.'

It will be shown that it was not till after he had done his best work, and in the last year or two of his life, that he really gave way and weakened, but that was due to love affairs.

Unfortunately, these high expectations were at best only partially realized because, as Symington's later letters reveal, once he actually confronted Branwell's unpublished manuscripts, he found himself "getting into a maze trying to ferret out some key to their construction" (5 December 1932).[16]

---

later, probably sooner than later, some other publisher will take the wind out of your sails. With all the new stuff you can add, you are in a position to bring out an absolutely definite and final edition; under such circumstances every copy is bound to sell; it is only a question of time, for the Brontës are classic, and no competition could by any means be introduced into the market (Symington Papers, BPM).

Despite being named co-editor and offering "to assist the great undertaking in any way I can," Wise contributed very little to the preparation of the edition, constantly pleading illness of one kind or another in his subsequent letters of 1932-34. Although he supplied Symington with some transcriptions, he was at times unable to find manuscripts and/or transcriptions that were supposed to be in his library.

[16] Symington's bafflement over how to fit all the bits together is wonderfully expressed in his letter to Wise of 22 November 1932:

I got home quite safely with the treasures, and have been working at them ever since. The more I get into them, the more I am convinced that C____ & B____ worked on a fixed plan for the construction of the stories. Maybe it was the political history of their time which they reconstructed from the local press (newspapers)—The Duke of Wellington was made Prime Minister in 1828, and the great days of the Reform Bill, The Abolition of Slavery, the Catholic Emancipation, and the African exploration of Walter Oudney, Hugh Clapperton, Denham Dixon and Richard Lemon Lander all seem to have a bearing on the interpretation of the Angrian stories. I often wonder whether old Nicholls ever heard the secret behind these writings, as there surely

Manuscripts were incomplete and confused; existing transcriptions suspect;[17] the whereabouts of manuscripts needed to check them against unknown; and the task of reading the minute script daunting. In the introduction to the 1934 volume of Charlotte's and Branwell's poems, Symington hinted at the difficulties he was beginning to encounter, difficulties that were already dampening the enthusiasm he had expressed two years earlier. In the end, he resorted to facsimile reproduction of many pages of manuscript in the two volumes of Miscellaneous and Unpublished Works (1936 and 38), and expressed his reservations about the reliability of the edition in his "Conclusion" to the 1938 volume.[18]

In the end, the three Shakespeare Head volumes containing material by Branwell included 65 poems and verse fragments of which only 23 were wholly new; four complete prose manuscripts and 8 fragments, all previously unpublished; one complete prose manuscript and eleven fragments in facsimile, all previously unpublished. Since then, 75 items have been added to the Branwell canon, 72 of these since 1983. Ironically and entirely in keeping with the

---

must have been a set key and plan on which C____ & B____ wrote their different sections (Symington Papers, BPM).

[17] Before Wise arranged, bound, and sold the manuscripts, he had many of them transcribed in part or in whole. The quality of these transcriptions is apparent from Shorter's description of them as "rough typewritten copy" and Hatfield's comment that "none of them is in the handwriting of either Mr. Shorter or Mr. Wise. They are in half a dozen different kinds of handwriting and it is clear that some of the scribes exercised great care and that some were careless and inefficient" (Letter to Cook, January 9, 1926, Wise Collection). Shorter, who also made some transcriptions, seems to have been more conscientious. After obtaining transcriptions of Charlotte's **The Search after Happiness** from both Shorter and Wise, Hatfield commented: "That from Mr. Shorter is almost an accurate trancript of the manuscript in the possession of Mr. Wise, while the transcript from the latter contains so many differences that it seems impossible for it to have been from the same manuscript" (Letter to Cook, December 10, 1925, Wise Collection). Not only were Wise's transciptions full of errors, but there were also blank spaces for words and phrases his scribes had been unable to decipher (Hatfield letter to Cook, January 12, 1926, Wise Collection), and in some instances manuscripts were only partially transcribed (Hatfield letters to Cook, January 25, February 19, May 18, 1926, Wise Collection). Even worse, in some cases the scribes had conflated manuscripts. Hatfield wrote to Cook that he was "particularly pleased to get the photograph copy of Arthuriana because I knew the transcript I had was incomplete and I now find that it also includes one poem which is not in the manuscript, and does not include one of the poems that is" (July 25, 1927, Wise Collection).

[18] For a more detailed discussion of Symington's reservations and his strange omissions, see Neufeldt PCB, xxx-xxxii, and Neufeldt PBB, xxxiii.

publication history I have described, in 1954 John Malham-Dembleby added parts of three new items to the Branwell canon in his attempt to prove that Charlotte had written most of the work ascribed to Branwell, Emily and Anne.

All the poems in this volume have been published previously in my 1990 volume of Branwell's poetry. Of the thirteen prose items, four (totaling approximately 63,000 words) are published here in their entirety for the first time.[19] Of the other six items (totaling approximately 94,200 words), one was printed in Gaskell CB, four in SHB Misc I, and two in more recent publications.[20] Only Barker's transcription of **The Battell Book** retains Branwell's original spelling, punctuation, sentence structure and paragraphing. The other texts not only have been normalized, but also contain significant misreadings, "revisions," and omissions.

Branwell's script and punctuation have obviously created difficulties for would-be editors. Almost all of the manuscripts through 1839 are written in a minute printed script, which in many cases must be read through a magnifying glass. His abandonment of the minute print in 1839 coincides with his abandonment of the Angrian saga. While he used the tiny pages for which the Brontë children have become famous only through 1832, then fairly consistently used pages taken from notebooks measuring approximately 9 x 15 cm., 11 x 18 cm., or 18 x 24 cm., Branwell continued to cram as many words as possible onto a page, up to approximately 2500 on an 11 x 18 cm. page, making reading extremely difficult and interlinear additions or revisions almost impossible to decipher. Added to these difficulties is Branwell's erratic punctuation. Essentially, the only punctuation he uses in the prose manuscripts is the full-stop, which, while scattered liberally throughout his prose, is seldom used to signify the end of a sentence.[21] Nor does he always capitalize the first word of a sentence.

The intention of this edition, therefore, is both to correct the effects of "misreadings" and "improvements" and to provide the reader with the actual text Branwell produced. All of the texts in this edition are based on my own transcriptions of the manuscripts, or, where the manuscript is unavailable, on the most reliable text available. It has not been possible to retain original page breaks, or the original lining in the case of prose works, except for title pages, contents pages and advertisements. In all other respects the text offered is the text as Branwell left it, except in the matter of his revisions, where only major

---

[19] The four items are **The History of the Rebellion in My Fellows** (p. 2), **The Liar Detected** (p. 92), **The Politics of Verdopolis** (p. 333), and **An Historical Narrative** (pp. 365 and 406).

[20] See pp. 1, 118, 137, 170, 180, 191, 210, 230, 239, 250, 266, 296.

[21] Sometimes it serves as a comma or other type of natural pause, but frequently it serves to indicate nothing more than Branwell resting his quill when trying to think what the next word(s) should be.

canceled stanzas or passages have been reproduced. In the case of uncanceled variants, the latest variant is given in the text; other variants appear in the notes. Editorial insertions have been added in square brackets where necessary for the sake of clarity. Doubtful readings due to manuscript deterioration, blotting, or the impossibility of reading the minute print writing appear in <   >. Titles in square brackets are ones indirectly supplied by Branwell.

The items appear in chronological order; however some placements are problematical because Branwell sometimes worked on items simultaneously, and in at least one instance provided both a fictional date and a real date only months apart (see p. 179). The order, therefore, is based on when Branwell actually completed the item. Thus, for example, in this volume, **Letters From An Englishman**, volume II, dated at the end "March 18, 1831," is placed after **The History of the Young Men**, dated "May 7th 1831" at the end, because **Letters** is also dated "real date . . . June 8, 1832" at the end. Similarly, although volume IV of **Letters** is dated "August 3, 1832" on the title page, it is dated "April 19, 1832" at the end, and is therefore placed before **The Fate of Regina**, dated May 1832. On the same basis, **Letters**, volume V , is placed before the poems on pp. 222 and 227.

As noted on p. xxi, n. 10 above, many of the items in this volume were "published" in Glass Town. In short, from the age of eleven on Branwell saw himself as a published author/editor. The reproduction of the text exactly as he left it allows the reader to trace clearly both Branwell's adoption of various authorial personae—magazine/newspaper editor and publisher, travel writer, poet, dramatist, critic, newly-arrived observer, historian, military man and chronicler, for example, in this volume—and his "mode" of composition.[22] Doing so increases the difficulty of reading the text and might lead to a wish that Branwell had written less and more carefully. It should be remembered, however, that the poems and chronicles until well into the second volume were never meant for actual publication. They are the result of childhood play and adolescent fantasy, often written in the headlong rush of fevered composition. In his poetry, Branwell consciously experimented with various forms and metres, more adventurous and more self-critical than Charlotte early on. Thus the quality of his work is uneven, yet the subsequent volumes will also reveal a Branwell who, when at his best, carefully revised his poems (up to four versions of some are extant) to achieve his goal of becoming a published poet, a goal accomplished five years earlier than his sisters achieved it. This edition serves as a record of that growth and development, and, it is hoped, will help to dispel some of the myths and misconceptions that have become associated with Branwell's name.

---

[22] The practice of standardizing and "correcting" the grammar, punctuation and spelling of the original script has created a false impression of childhood writing much more sophisticated, polished and carefully written than it was in reality.

Battell

Book

P.B. Bronte

March 12

1827[1]

the Battle of Washington was fought on [th]12 <Sep> between the British and their Allies 2.21000 men and by United States and their Allies 3.04000 British comanders Sneky and <Wellington>

---

[1]   Branwell's earliest extant manuscript, a hand-sewn booklet of eight pages (5.8 x 6.8 cm) in blue paper cover cut from a sugar bag, in the BPM: BS 110. The title, signature and date are repeated inside the front cover and on the first page. Pages 2-5 contain pencil and watercolor sketches: soldiers in red and blue uniforms with cannon and standard bearers (entitled "Battell of Wshington"); map of north and south America; soldiers with a blue flag; a castle (entitled "Bandy castle). Branwell then turned the book upside down, began with a color sketch of a moated castle with blue flag on p. 7, followed by the broken off fragment above on p. 6. The final page contains several variants on the phrase "Sneaky was afterwards," suggesting Branwell may have been planning to write a story about him (Alexander Sneaky). For more detail on the sketches, see Alexander & Sellars, 284-86.
    The battle actually took place in late August 1814, and is described in "Campaigns of the British Army at Washington, &c," Blackwood's Magazine, ix (April 1821) 181-83. See also Gérin BB, 34-35.

HISTORY OF THE

REBELLION

IN: :

MY FELLOWS[1]

1828[2]

---

[1]   Hand-sewn booklet in grey paper covers (11.2 x 12 cm) of eight pages written on lined music paper (but one leaf—pp. 5-6—is missing) in BM: BS 112. For the relationship of this manuscript to the Brontë's "Our Fellows" play, based on Aesop's *Fables*, see Alexander EW, 40-41 and Alexander CB, I, 6.
[2]   Branwell's dating is somewhat confused. The beginning of chapter one is dated "Sept. 1 to 5 1827," and includes an internal date of "third of September 1827," changed from January; the beginning of chapter two was originally dated "Sept. 5 to Oct 9 1827," then altered to 1826, but contains an internal date of September 1827; the beginning of chapter three was originally dated "Oct 9 to Nov 22 1827," then changed to 1826; the beginning of chapter four was originally dated "Nov 27 to Jan 1 1820," then altered to Dec 31, and to Dec 1 1827.

Chap 1—Begining *from Sept. 1 to 5 1827*[3]
A Number of Goodmans[4] forces, do of mine

Page 1   Battle, of Lorraine End
                        Goodman was A Rascal and did want
                        to Raise A, Rebellion and so He got
                        together A number of disafected spir[i]t

                        _____

                        in number 16000 with wich he
                        intended to Force Lorraine A Town
                        in Sheperds, county About 800 miles
                        from carroin[5] he, was then About
                        02 miles From Lorraine, in the meanetime
                        I Asembeld About 10,000 men, to stop this
                        progres, but when he got before the walls
                        of Lorraine hi[s] Army Amounted to 02000
                        Foot And 5000 Horse, he began
                        operations on <three> of September 1827[6]
                        seeing my force would be inadequat

Page 2   to the thing I orderd Boaster,[7] to Raise 02000
                        more! he did so and they marched to
                        Lorraine, Goodman having disposed his
                        Army in wings the Right
                        comanded By muleman & Left by Himseelf
                        *ABs was Fo[r]med in the same way Right by,
                        Himself Left by carter the Battle Began with

_____

[3]   All italicized material is in script rather than print in the original.
[4]   Charlotte's character—see Alexander EW, 41. The name may possibly be
borrowed from Sir Steven Arthur Goodman (d. 1844), who as a Major-General
took his regiment to the Iberian Penninsula and commanded the light companies
of Hill's division at the Battle of Talavera (July 27-8, 1809).
[5]   The town of Carrion and the river are located in the north of Spain. In 1808,
during the Peninsular campaign, Marshall Soult was stationed at a bridge on
the Carrion River, from which position Napoleon tried to orchestrate the
invasion of Galicia as part of his plan to subjugate Spain. Although Branwell's
"history" is fictional, the reference to Carrion suggests that it was inspired by
his reading on the Napoleonic wars in *Blackwood's Magazine*, and perhaps Scott,
as indicated in the subsequent notes.
[6]   January is crossed out. At the bottom of the manuscript page is a tiny
sketch of a fortified building—see Alexander & Sellars, 287.
[7]   Boaster is based on a character in Aesop's *Fables* —see Alexander CB, I, 4-6
and CW, pp. 40-41.

A Furious onset By Goodman And on our Part it
was as furiously withstood, G^{d}man prresed
Forward And Broke the First line But the 10th
Regement of Horse, made him Fall Back
he Rushed on Agane, and Defeated the 1 line
And Rushed Against the 2 line & Drove it of the Fiel[d]
Everything was in Disorder the Army Fled
with the utmost Percipetion & G^{d}m, lost
1000 killed &, 2000 wounded we lost 2000 killed And
3000, wounded this event proudced much
They were comman[d]ed
by Advising Boaster—.

* the AB stands For
Advising Boaster.
P3 consternation in the capital, / Funds rose 2 percent

Page
3

2 Chapter 3 Page—
Raising of my army
—goodmans Letter from Sept. 5 to
—siege. of Loo^8—End——*Oct 9*
1826

soon After this *Battle. I Raised
A Army of 100,000, Horse 200000, Foot.
Too opose his progres, 05000 Horse, 100000 Foot
in the north. And the same Number & in the south
GM, collected 30000, more, his Force now <Araouned>
to 40,000 Foot And, 11 000, Horse. He marched to
Loorain and wrote me this, Letter, it is in his Handwritin[g]
Sept 1827 I will go to war with you
littele Branewell.   Sept[e]mber
1827. to littile
Branewell—
Signed good
=man

*wrong
it should, be to

Page 4

no Answr was. returnd *Boaster*

---

8   Presumably the Seige of Lorraine, which Branwell spells "Loorain,"
below—see his heading for Chapter Three.

around 3000, men. to be sent to Loo
to force the city. But this force being
found insuficent 10,000. were sent
marching. 10,000 foot. and 3000 Horse—
these. marched to Loo. and attacked
Goodmans. forces. amounting to 10,000 foot
and. 3000. Horse. they took the
city after 2 weekes. Siege. this mad[e]
up for, the Disastrios termination
of the Battle of Lorrain. it
Being Goodmans Capital.
       funds lowred 1 per. cent

Chapter. 3. 4 Page—

from
Oct 9
to
Nov   *Begining. Embasy to Charllotes*
22   *Country. suc[ce]ssful. Battle*
1826   *of Parimont Negocitions. End—*

I saw that this would not do
so I sent an Ambasador to Charlottes
country while this was doing G. man[9]

Chapter. 4 Page 7

                                        Dec 1
peace. Refused. peace agane Acepted   *from Nov. 22*
invaacon. of my contry by <it> wished   *1827*
            by people

GM. agane, proposed termes of peace
but as they were the same as the other
I would. not agrre to them at last he came to
such terms as I wished. namly. 1 that he should
lay down is arms. 2 and pay homage—to me—
these terms he agrred to. I asked Charllote
if she. would & let her troopes. stop some
time longer. she concented & thus peac. was at last
con<ci>led. I now Began to set things. to right
I conferd upon AB. the title of Ducke of. Barno,
& upon, AN.ᵗ the title. of Ducke of. Parimont
things were all. now put Right so that

---

9   A leaf of the manuscript is missing at this point.

I began to govern quietly. when the wickid
people. landed near Brochies, to the Amount
of 10000 men. however I sent. A
fleet of 5 ships of the line and 2. frigats
they Ran they Ran to there ships. and put
out to sea. and my ships saild

t AN   Back
stands for
Adderman

now. all. Being at peace I began to fortify
my country I built. c[h]urches. castles and
other publick Buildings. in abundance

PBBs Concluding Remarks
against me

Chap 1   the forcing of Lorrain was productive of
against   very evil consuquense it gave good man the
me   possibite of building ships and ca<nno>ns. stores
              to his Army for there was A forest. near it—
              the raising of my army amt 10,000000£ by wich I was
              obliged to levy taxes wich made the people Disconten[t]
Chap 2   the seige of Loo. was productive of many Advantages
for me   1. it made me Master of a large city 2 I could by it get
              abundance of money
              I was obliged to send the embasy to Charllote
Chap 3   Because I could [not] pay <my own unles> I raised taxes
for me   wich would make the people much be disconted
              wich would make them turn to good mans
              side the Battle of Parimont ended the war
              wich was a very good thing <   > the war
              was. ended. very Dearly. Bought by the losses
              of so many Brave felows. the
              peace now Being concluded I Began to
              attend to my Afairs when the <   >
              people began thoug[h] happily no Blood
              was spilt I made 100 castles for Defence
              of my kingdom
                    Fines [sketch]*t* previous <   >10

---

10 A tiny sketch of a fortified building with two words beside it—see
Alexander & Sellars, 288.

MAGAZINE

January 1829[1]

NATural History
O Dean [2]
—Kairail—
—Fish—

---

this fish. is generaly found from 80 to 100 Feet Long it [h]as large scales
The back blue belly & sides white spoted with Red fines yellow—

[diagram of the fish][3]

it is chiefly Prized on account of its skin and horn
the skin makes exelent Leather and the horn which is of a a beutiful Gold coulor
and is TRansParent for for ORnament & in Chemistry the horn is 20 or 30 Feet
lond[4] & is hooked at the End
When they cacth it they Never kill it for the skin Only incumbers it and its horn
will grow in the space of an hour
the m[e]thod of catching it is this a Ship and six long boats of this shape

[diagram of the long boat]

are provided the boats are to be 100 Feet long
2 boats are to be laid along side one another in this way

[diagram of two boats
with a fish between them]

---

1   Hand-sewn booklet with covers of grey letterpress fragment (5.4 x 3.8 cm)
of ten pages (two blank) in HL: MS Lowell I (8). No title page.
2   The heading has been read as "O Deay" and "O Dear," but I believe it is "O
Dean," linking it to Charlotte's "The Origin of the O Deans," Alexander CB, I,
6, and to the play "Our Fellows"—see p. 2, n. 1. Barker Brontës, 159, 864,
argues for "O Dear."
3   See Alexander & Sellars, 289.
4   Branwell sometimes writes a "d" instead of a "g."

with a strong net 1 side bound to 1 boat and one [to] the other the under part in the sea and the top above open at one end and shut at the other the fish enthers at the open side which is then shut up and hual[ed] out of the sea so as to be tight betwen the 2 boats
the skin &c. are then took of the fish and then it is let go &c

P B Br—t

—Poetry—

Oh May America
Yeild to our Monarchs sway—
 And No more contend &
May they their interest see
With England to agree
And from oppression frre—
 All that amend[5]

This was sung at the ["young mens" canceled] our oratiorio and was much approved) CT[6]

Bany do ought Not to Punit de Doung móaned For having rebelled against do For dhey did dier Duty

Good[7]

—Travels N⁰ 1—

Preparations set out for
Mons & w—s[8]
Island maners
Laws

---

[5] The poem is an adaptation of the British National Anthem. See also Alexander Magazines, 36, n. 3.
[6] Captain Tree. The following page is blank.
[7] The Goodman of p. 2, speaking in the "old young men tongue" Branwell invented: "Yorkshire dialect spoken by holding [the] nose between finger and thumb" (Alexander EW, 35). The statement refers to the rebellion on p. 2.
[8] Wamons. Branwell first wrote "Stumps island," then changed his mind.

Sept. 3 1818 I had a mind to visit Mons[9] I walked to the Harbour in the Glasstown and asked if any ship was going of the young Man a vessell of 1500. tons. was goind of I Instantly got 355 158£ together with 3000£ in silver and copper & 80.000£ in Paper & Pocket money for to Trafick with and ran into the ship paid my fare and went into the Cabin—in a little time the ship set of it was a Fine Pleasent mornind and the sea quite calm as the ship Glided down the huge harbour slowly I had time to Observe every thing North the city with its houses Palaces Cathedrals and churches Glittering in the sun before us the sea in a little time every thing vanished from our veiw Nothing was see[n] but the wide south Atlantic Ocean—in the Afternoon some Dim *Mountains* were seen it was KLUKS Maantin—in Mons and Wamons wich they think the high[e]st mountain in the world and which is the high[e]st in thier Iilands

at 6 we arrived!!! at Tieps Taan after a Delightful Passage of 250 miles in 12 hours the city was extremly Neat and pleasent and so were the In[h]abitents the men were generaly Dressed in a 3 cornerd hat Red waistcoat Blue coat white breeches & Tawny stockings and Black shoes—women white cap borderd with a Red Riband Red waist Blue gown & White Apron—[10]

---

[9]   Branwell originally wrote "Stumps Island," then changed to "Mons"; in renaming the islands he was obviously having fun with the "old young men tongue."

[10]   The following page is blank; p. 10 contains a diagram of a large human figure labeled "Kluks," beside which stand a male and female (and a dog) dressed as described. See also Alexander CB, I, 230, n. 4, and Alexander & Sellars, 289-90.

THE TRAVELS OF ROLANDO SEGUR

Comprising his Adventures Throughout
the voyage, and in America, Europe, South Pole, etc, etc,

By
PATRICK Branwell
BRONTË —

Author of Townslaw Book Journey to Leeds —
Young Men's Magazine — Tragical Book,
Newspaper, &c &c &c — Volumn I — Begun
April The fifteenth — Ended May Twenty seventh
1829 Δ Θ H '[1]

---

[1]   The manuscript is untraced and untranscribed. The title above is provided by
John Malham-Dembleby (*The Confessions of Charlotte Brontë*, Bradford:
Privately published, 1954, p. 31), who claims to have borrowed the manuscript
from the London bookseller, Walter T. Spencer. Hatfield (Hatfield Papers)
confirms its existence: he describes it as in two volumes, with paper covers,
10.2 cm x 6.4 cm. A possible source for Branwell's title is Philippe Paul
Compte de Ségur, *History of the Expedition to Russia, Undertaken by the
Emperor Napoleon in the Year 1812.* 2 Vols., London, 1825. This title appeared
in *Blackwood's Edinburgh Magazine* under its "Monthly Lists of New
Publications" in May 1825. Ségur is also cited in Scott's *Life of Napoleon*.

BRANWELLS
BLACKWOODS
MAGAZINE=[1]

P
B
Genius
Cheif[2]

CHEFE GLASS
TOWN

Printed & sold by—
Sergt Tree
& & & & &

CONTENTS
MAGAZINE
P B JUNE 1829

<table>
<tr><td>1 Dirge of the Genii</td><td>-1-</td></tr>
<tr><td>2 The Enfant part 2</td><td>-2-</td></tr>
<tr><td>3 Letter of Bud</td><td>-4-</td></tr>
<tr><td>4 Journey to Mons &</td><td>-6-</td></tr>
<tr><td>5 The Nights part 1</td><td>-7-</td></tr>
<tr><td>6 The Nights part 2</td><td>-11-</td></tr>
<tr><td>7 Advertisments</td><td>-16-</td></tr>
</table>

Charlotte[3]

[1]   Hand-sewn booklet with covers of grey letterpress fragment (5.2 x 3.3 cm) of seventeen pages in HL: MS Lowell I (7). There is no title on the cover.
[2]   Lettering is inside a colophon.
[3]   Charlotte's signature is in longhand, whereas the rest of the booklet is in the usual minute print. It appears to have been added by Branwell. Below the list of contents appear the words "cloud," "Clouds," and <"pour">, probably related to the note at the end of the next item.

Glass town
Printed by Searg^t Tree

MAGAZINE. PBB
———————
DIRGE OF THE GENII—
———————

THUS I begin my song—
The Genii all are gone—
Theyre gone gone gone—
Gone for ever gone—

The sky is blackning—
+Its rain pours down—
Its tears for the Genii—
while we are dancing rond

<while> we are dancing <rond>
tonite the merry bagpips <sound>
answer to our triping feet
above below around—

So hurra O ye Genii—
Ye have got your maches now
Alas once to your Feiry eye
all all the earth did bow—

but now O ye Genii—
ye are laid in your graves
& above below around you
do dance the merry knaves

thus I do end my song—
the Genii all are gone—
there gone gone gone—
gone for ever gone—

———————————————————————————

+should be The sky it is &c
The clouds porus down

THE ENFANT
Part 2. by Charlotte B—te[4]

---

he related to the Intendant all the circumstances. poh poh said the intendant this is much too trivial a matter for me to interfere with go about your bussniss dont come troubling me with such nonsense MH[5] then bent his way towards the Thuillierys[6] when he arrived there he addressed himself to a little page who introduced him to the chamber of presence—there sat the great Empreur. who had made all Europe to tremble surrounded by his great Marshalls and officers of state—at any other tim[e] M H. would have been awed by all this state but he felt a love for the Enfant for which he could by no means account this emboldened him to address the Empreur with some degree of confidence therefore throwing himself on his knees at the feet of the empreur he recounted the whole affair

Soult[7] said Napoleon order a party of Gendearms to go instantly to this fellows house the Tavern of the Castle bring hither Pigtail and the Enfant

your order shall be obeyed replied Soult & he quitted the apartment. the Empreur then asked H. if he had any childern I had but it was stolen from me answ[e]red H. and the tears gushed from his eyes as he spoke. Well praps this may be yours replied the empreur it may it may shouted H. and he began to jump like a madman for joy—

moderate your transports said the empreur had it any mark by which you may know it yes it had the mark of an adder bite in its left arm returned H. just at this moment the genedearms enterd with P. and the E. H imeadeatly snacthed up the Enfant and uncovering its left arm gave a scream for joy for there was the identical mark of the adder bite the enfant was not less rejoiced when it found that H was its Father and the 2. leaped abut. half frantic in the mean time Pigtail took the oppertunity of leaping out of the window to contintue his misterious wanderings—at length when H. and the E. had recovered some degree of composure the Empreure gave them 2000000 livers. with which Moses Hanghimself purchased a beautiful estate in the fruitful province of languedoc where he now lives with his Enfant one of the happiest and most contented mortals alive

Charlotte Bronte

---

4   The text and signature are, however, in Branwell's hand. Part one presumably appeared in the May issue, now lost. For a complete later version, see Alexander CB, I, 34. See also p. 174 of this edition.

5   Moses Hanghimself.

6   Before it was destroyed by arson in 1871, the Tuileries Palace was the French royal residence adjacent to the Louvre in Paris.

7   Marshall Soult, Wellington's opponent in the Peninsular Campaign and at Waterloo under Napoleon—see p. 369, n. 13 below; later a character in the Glasstown/Angria saga—see the Glossary.

TO THE EDITOR
Glass Town
June 1 1829

SIR

I write this to accwaint you of a circumstanc which has happend to me & which is of great importance. to the world at large On May 22 1829 the Cheif Genius Taly came to me with a small yellow book in her hand

she gave it to me saying it was the POEMS of that Ossian[8] of whom so much has been said bout whose works could never be got—upon an attentive perusal of the above said works I found they were most sublime and exelent I am engaged in publishing an edition of them in Quarto—3 Vols—with notes commontrys &c I am fully convinced that it is the work of OSSIAN who lived 1000 years ago—and of no other there is a most intense anxiety prevailing amongst literary men to know its contents in a short time they shall be gratified for it will be published on the first of July. 1829.

> I remain
> yours &c &c
> Sergt bud Jun
> T S C

to the Cheif Genius Bany

Journey TO THE
MONS and wamons
N2—Islands by P B B—te

One Morning I went to the key to see the departure of 10 boats for the Harvest of the Glasstown and its environs—and to go with them myself. I need not truoble the reder with a discription of what he has seen so often.—Sufice it to say that I departed with them & after 9 hours prosperous sailing arrived at the Glasstown. after an absence of 1 week & 5 Days

B
END — P
B

---

[8]   The Brontë family's copy of *The Poems of Ossian* by James Macpherson, London, J. Walker, 1819, is in the BPM. Branwell is obviously aware of the debate about the authenticity of the poems. See also Alexander Magazines, 38, n. 19.

NIGHTS[9]

SCENE I
A LARGE ROOM IN
BRAVEYS INN
Night—candles lighted bottles on the table

Caracters
DUKE OF WELLINGTON
Bravey. Bady[10]
GRAVY.
CAPTAIN. PARRY
ANDREW JACKson.
Epimanondas Johnson
Cicero Stephenson
YOUNG SOULT
LUCEIN Bonaperte[11]

---

[9]   Modeled after the "Noctes Ambeosianae," in *Blackwood's Magazine* from 1822 on.
[10]   Sir Alexander Hume Bady (or Badey), based on Dr. John Robert Hume, surgeon to the Duke of Wellington from 1808.
[11]   Sir William Edward Parry, the arctic explorer who had just returned from his expedition to reach the North Pole and Emily's hero—see p. 155 and the Glossary. His expeditions were featured in *Blackwood's Magazine* for 1818, 1820, and 1821. Andrew Jackson (1767-1845), U.S. military hero and seventh president of the United States inaugurated in 1829, the first U.S. president to come from the west, and the first elected though direct appeal to the mass of voters. With Epimanondas, Branwell is referring to Epaminondas, a Theban general and statesman who defeated the Spartans at Leuctra about 371 BC, and was killed at Mantinea, 363 BC, in a battle against the Lacedaemonians. Andrew Johnson (1808-1875), before he became the seventeenth president of the United States (1865), was a radical Jacksonian who had achieved political prominence in Democratic politics by the 1830's. The Roman statesman and prose writer, Cicero (106-43 BC), was elected Consul, but refused to join Caesar's triumvirate, and following Caesar's assassination presented his "Philippics," attacking Mark Antony and urging amnesty from the Senate for the conspirators. For this, when Antony and the second triumvirate came to power, Cicero was tracked down and murdered. George Stephenson (1781-1848) engineered the first locomotive in 1814, pioneering the use of steam motive power. Lucien Bonaparte (1775-1840), brother to Napoleon, was largely responsible for Napoleon's election as consul on 19 Brumaire (November 1799), but, disenchanted with his brother, fell into disfavor and left for the U.S.; captured at sea by the British, he was temporarily imprisoned in England. Returning to

Duke of Wellingto[n] by the fire with Bravey Soult & Parry Lucien in a corner
writing
GRavy pacing up and down the rome in agitation & the Americans in a corner
talking about wool and such stuff—Bady drinking as hard as he can

---

Duke of Wellington
Bravy what Newspapers do you take
    Bravy
Why the young Mans Intelligencer the Oppesishion. the Greybottle—the
Glasstown Intelligencer the Courier Du Francais—the Quatre Deinne. &c &c &c
Rings the bell   enter waiter*[12]
    Bravy
are the newspapers come
    Waiter
Yes   brings them in*
    PARRY
taking the young mans Intelligencer
When you here this you will not bear the Genii much longer. reads
PROCLAMATION wheras Bany wants some cash he reque[s]ts 500 000000£ if
this is not complied with he will let the Genii upon the world signed by order of
Bany—LIGHTNING—did you ever hear of anything more Rascally—
    Omnes—
        starting up from their seats*
we never did we never did
    —Wellington
What of the bill for the supression of the Faction Du Manege[13] has it past or
Not
    Parry reads

France, he offered Napoleon help during the Hundred Days (1815), stood at his
side in Paris, defended Napoleon's prerogatives at the time of his second
abdication, then spent the rest of his life in Italy. His publications include an
epic, *Charlemagne; or, The Church Delivered* (1814), *The Truth About the
Hundred Days* (1835), and *Memoirs* (1836).

[12] Asterisked stage directions are in longhand.

[13] The Faction Du Mange, also referred to by Charlotte, is glossed by
Alexander as "[p]robably imaginary," although she notes that it may allude to *le
parti du manche*, "based on the expression *être du côté du manche*, literally 'to be
on the right side of the broomstick' (presumably those in power)." (Alexander
EW, 119). See also Alexander Magazines, 39, n. 27. The bill is likely a
reference to the passage of the Catholic Emancipation Bill in April 1829. For
Charlotte's comments on the passage of this bill, see Alexander CB, I, 100.

The house then divided and there appeared for the bill 293. against the bill 207
Majority 86.
  Duke
I could hardly have expected so much
  Lucien
nor I either—
  —Young Soult sings
the bill it [h]as past
at last at last—
it has past like the sun in his glory
in my mind I cast
that it would not have past
or else two[u]ld have pased gory
  DUKE
our motto should hereafter be
    love liberty in great Animation
    Hate the Genii
  GRAVY
we sho[u]ld never hat[e] anything
  Jonson
President welleslly hows [the] wool trade geting on[14]
  Duke
striving to supress his anger*
hem hem hem I dont know
  Bady
Dooog kill hin him Kill him
  Jonson
a recken what kill me for

SCENE 2
Additional Persons
MARQUIS of Douro[15]
LORD CHARLES welleslly
Sergt. BUD—junr—

---

14 The Brontë children followed activities in the American Colonies in the
newspapers and magazines. The *Leeds Intelligencer* of January 1, 1829, for
example, carried a full account of John Quincy Adams' speech to Congress on
December 2, 1828 regarding free trade, duties and tariffs. Compare with
Charlotte's depiction of Andrew Jackson, Alexander CB, I, 83-85.
15 Wellington was given the title Marquis of Douro (based on the River Duero
in Portugal) in 1812.

Scene 2
supper on the table—all siting around with the 3 new persons

———————————

———————

Badey
Soult do give us a song
    Omnes
Yes do yes do begin
    Soult
Very well Gentlemen I will he he hem
    SINGS
    —Soult—
If you live by the sunny Fountain—
if you live in the streets of a town
if you live on the top of a mountain
or if you wear a crown—
    —The Genii meddle with you

Think not that in your graves
you will be quiet there—
For Genii come with spades
To dig you up they dare
    Genii will meddle with you

even if in your palaces—
among your courteir[s] there
The genii meddle with you—
For mischief is there care—
    Genii must meddle with you

Come Britons then arise—
and let your swords be bare
of wich the geniis blood—
let them be covered fair—
    —They shall not meddle with you
    OMNES—with the exeption of the Americans
Hurra Hurra Hurra thats a brave fellow. a capital song that
Hurra Hurra Hurra
    MARQUIS of Douro
Gentlemen I arise to propose a toast which I think you will drink with great
pleasure the whish which is contained in that toast would if accomplished prove
of imensce benifit to the world. what are you now but the Slaves of Slavery then
you would be freedoms sons—the toast which I mean is—THE DOWNFALL of
THE GENII—
Drunk with nine times Nine—and Thunders of Applause*

Marquis of Douro
  aside to Charles*
Charles arnt you glad that we came to Night
  Lord Charles wellesly
Yes Brother I am very glad
  ANDREW Jackson
Gentlemen its my turn to Propose a toast none of you have said anything of
Liberty that cause which raises up so many ste[a]m engines and such Inventions
as those—American Liberty.
loud Hisses with cries of well not drink it well not drink it
  Stephenson
I reckon that thats vile
  GRAVEY
Gentlemen I disire that you propose no more Toasts
  BADEY
but we will Gentlemen I propose a toast wich is good—The prosperity of
GROG
Drunk with 3 times 3 by a few
  Young Bud. junr
You have heard of Ossians poemes
  DUKE
I have
  lord charles wellesly
one should very much like to see them
  Bud
very well to make a short cut the Genius TALY has made me present of it
  Lucien
has she no doubt it will contain some <Elegunt> passages worth remembering
  Bud—junr
It does I will read a few parts
reads—at the end of one of his battles is this—T[he] Groan of the People spread
over the hills. it was like the thunder of Night when the cloud bursts on Cona
and a thousand gohsts shriek at once in the hollow vale. and another troubled joy
arrose in her mind like the red path of lightening on a stormy cloud. Another
Father of heroes O Trenmor high dweller of eddying wind were the dark red
thunder marks the throubled cloud what think you of these[16]
  Omnes
exelent exelent
  end

---

[16] Bud's first passage is taken from Book III of Macpherson's "Fingal"; in
addition to changing the punctuation Branwell has altered "wind" to "vale." The
second is from "Oithona"; Branwell has altered "on" to "in." The third is from
the opening lines of Book II of "Temora"; Branwell has changed "winds" and
"clouds" to the singular.

ADVERTISMENTS

SHORTLY will be published
BY Searg^t BUD
Ossians poems with Notes
and Commentary in
3 Vols Quarto
Glasstown   Searg^t Tree &c &c

ADDRESS
to the world by Capt Leg
in 1 volumn Oct
Glasstown printed by
Seargt Tree

TO BE SOLD
300 Barrels of prussian Butter.
& 80 bags of WHITE flour[17]
by Moses ride on the back of an ass

---

[17] Prussian Butter is made with prussic acid (hydrocyanic acid, or cyanide in liquid form), a colorless, extremely poisonous liquid obtained from Prussian blue, a ferrous-based dye. White flour, also sold as "white bread," is made with arsenic, a highly toxic poison, and oil of vitriol, the name given to hydrated or liquid sulfates such as sulfuric acid. See also pp. 31, 173 and Alexander CB, I, 87; II, Part I, 133.

JULY
1829[1]

BRANWELLS
BLACKWOODS
MAGAZINE =

P
B
CHEIF
Genius[2]

1829 JULY
CHEIF GLASS
TOWN

Printed and sold
by
Searg^ت Tree. &c &c &c

CONTEN[T]S--

Glasstown
Printed by Tree
Glasstown

---

[1]   Hand-sewn booklet with covers of grey letterpress fragment (5.2 x 3.3 cm) of twenty-one pages (plus at least one missing leaf), in HL: MS Lowell I (9). The date appears on the inside of the cover.

[2]   Lettering is inside a colophon.

THE NIGHTS
NO. II = = =

<u>PBB</u>   <u>1829</u>

SCENE 3—

_____

CARACTERS . . . .

NAPOLEON BONAPART
Duke OF WELLINGTON
SIR EDWARD PARRY
CAPTAIN ROSS[3]
YOUNG SOULT
CAPTAIN TREE
SIR A. BADEY
GRAVY.
Serg[t]. Bud. Junr
CAPTAIN BUD
J. MURAT[4]
A. SOULT[5]
GENIUS
BRAVEY

_____

[3]   Sir James Clarke Ross (1777-1856) who had accompanied Parry on his expeditions (see p. 15, n. 10), and Anne's hero—see the Glossary.
[4]   Joachim Murat (1767-1815), one of Napoleon's most celebrated marshals, was responsible for instigating street slaughters in Madrid during his stay in Spain. For services to France, he was rewarded with marriage to Napoleon's sister and appointed king of Naples (1805-15). As King, Murat broke up Naples's vast landed estates and introduced the Napoleonic Code. In 1812, he took part in Napoleon's Russian campaign; but, although left in charge of the Grand Army during its Russian retreat, he abandoned it to try to return to his own kingdom, Naples, where he was assassinated while attempting to recover the city from its former Bourbon rulers. See also pp. 52, n. 12; 378, n. 27.
[5]   Marshal Soult was Wellington's opponent in the Peninsular War and at Waterloo, under Napoleon. See p. 169, n. 13.

SCENE

the Duke Parry Ross Bady and Bravey with Murat & Soult sitting round the
table drinking. NAP struting about the room young Soult. Tree. Bud & Searg[t]
Bud. and Gravey walking abut talking
Night Candles lighted
Room in Braveys Inn

Enter Newspapers
GRAVY
takes up the grog bottle and after reading for <some> time excl[a]ims*[6]
I can no longer bear this Newspaper it is the very esscenc[e] of wickedness
Bravey why do you take it
BRAVEY
Hem Hun Hem why because there are men Pothouse master villains &c for
whose use it was first Instituted. often comming to my house they ask for a
newspaper I give it them & if it is not this thell not take it—
GRAVEY—
A preety reason to be sure
MURAT
Since you dont like it give it me
GRAVEY
I Shall Not.   flings it at back of the fire*
Murat & Soult
heh hih hih heh he-e-e
BRAVEY
You villains   takes up the paper
instan[t]ly the chimney puffs*
DUKE
who was siting close to the fire
Fuff Fuff Fuff—look look the chimney Puffs Bravey what[7] it filling we shall be
all suffocated
ROSS—
If I dont Declare its a genius the villain
Omnes
You rascal you Dog you villain
GENIUS
Na Na Ye have Flung yer Newspaper on the top of my Food which I was atin at
boack of fire[8]

---

6   Asterisked stage directions are in longhand.
7   "watch" obviously intended.
8   These words are in the "old young men tongue."

BRAVEY

Its all <cause> of you Gravey

GENIUS

Prepare to DIE

Omnes

well not well not of villain of of to your hole

Soult

cooly flings a bottle of Odours on the Genius who goes cracking and splitting to his hole again

PARRY

Thats right

Omness

Hurra Hurra Hurra thats right

TREE

Well seargt Bud what of ossians poems

Seargt Bud

Gentlemen sho[u]ld you like me to read some part of my book. or commentary

Omnes

Yes Yes

Young Bud

very well hem. m. Hem Part of the Beggining of the First book of the poem of Fingal by Ossian

Cutthullin sat by Turas walls by the tree of the rustling sound and His spear leaned against the rock His shield lay on the Grass by his side Amid his thoughts of mighty cairbar a hero slain by the cheif in war[9]

Cutthulin[10] or Cotholion one of Ossians cheif heroes and gen eral of the Irish tribes during the minority of Cormac the young King of Scotland	Mighty Cairbar Cairbar was tyrant and usurper of the kingdom.of.Ireland till Fingal came to rescue it he was slain and it was rescued after a furious contest between Fingal and Caibairs bro
Turas.wall Tura the dwelling of	ther Cathmor who took the quarr el up after Cairb

---

9   The quotation from the opening lines of Macpherson's "Fingal" is accurate except for the deletion of punctuation, some changes in capitalization, "wall" altered to "walls," and the addition of "and" after "sound."

10   The commentary is Bud's.

Cuthulin it	ars. death.
is by some	The cheif in war
thought to be	Ossians son Oscar
a cave by others	<wen> in killing
a castle. in	Cairbar was slain
those times	but he was reven
their greatest	ged and Cairbars
chiefs lived in	army cut to peices
caves very often	Ossians generations
and to have a	Trenmor
rock and grass	Trathal
just by a castle	Comhal
is not very like[ly]	Fingal
I think is is [a] cave	Ossian
	Oscar[11]

Well what think you of that.
    DOURO
Ossian is sublime the commentary is in many parts very good sound and Just
but that which relates to Tura is unjust in the extreme
it says that Tura is a cave whereas by your own account. it must be a castle for
Ossian says Cuthullin sat by Turas WALL. no cave could have a wall. A castle
could nay must have walls can you answer
    BUD junr
owaow <oh> no o o Im shure its very bad
    Douro
ha ha he hih ha
    NAPOLEON
Come come dont quarrel but settle all with a song
    Old Soult
Come son of mine sing
    Capt Bud
I Never saw such a good arguer as the Marquis of Douro he will be like his
Father your Grace.
    DUKE
rousing himself from sleep.*
heigho what
    BUD
your son Il. be like you
    DUKE
Pshaw nonsense.   sets to Drinking*

---

11   Branwell's citing of generations is accurate. *The Poems of Ossian* lists
Trenmor as great-grandfather to the hero Fingal, Trathal as his grandfather, and
Comhal as his father. Fingal's son, Ossian, is father to the fated Oscar.

NAPoleon
young soult Marquis Douro & loord charles Wellesly come sing a song each
take a verse by turns come come
    CHARLESES
No thank you
    DUKE
somewhat <heated> by Wine[*]
but you shall Or Else
    Omnes
yes do come do[12]
    YOUNG SOULT
why the one for May had two or three peices of poetry in it[13]
    TREE
one by you.
    BUD
and one by you Tree
    Omnes
young soult give us a song
    SOULT
very well   begins

One day I went out a walking
and I saw a sheet of fire
hovering oere the mountain
kindled was my are

It blazed upon the mountain
and upon the castle wall—
It blazed upon the Ocean—
& the distant coast of Gall[14]—

then suddenly it flew afar
over Africs. desart sand
till it seemed like the even star
I saw it streech. its wand—

upon a caravan of Araps—
I saw him streech his hand

---

12 At least one leaf is missing here.
13 Presumably a reference to **Branwell's Blackwoods Magazine.**
Although no longer extant, we know it existed because it contained the first part
of Charlotte's "The Enfant"—see p. 13.
14 i.e. "Gaul."

so that they every one did die
by the stroke of his great wand

I saw it was a Genius now
so that I ran away—
For fear that he should let me know
if this was my last day—
    Omnes
Hurra Hurra Hurra
    NAP.
Gentleman I propose the health. of Young Soult the Rhymer
Tremendous Applause[*]
    Young Soult
thank you
    Tree[+].
the health of the Marquis of Douro & lord charles wellesly
    DOURO
gentlemen I return thanks in behalf of myself and my brother charlie for the
honour you have conferred upon us both this day
    Omnes—
Hurra Hurra Hurra

[+]drunk with great applause

    DUKE
Gentlemen I propose that the cupboard of this house be now cleared
    Omnes
It shall it shall.   Mon
                                               end
      C Bronte[15]

REVEIW of BUDS commentary on Ossian
29. vols Folio. 2 edition

One day being out of employment we took up in Trees shop a volumn of this
work & sat down by the fire and asked Three for the whole set of volumns he
gave us 28. we were dismayed. but however we sat down and began to peruse
them the preface ouccupies 1. vol. folio. Introduction 1 vol folio. Introductory

---

[15] Charlotte's signature, in longhand, appears to have been squeezed in later,
probably by Branwell in acknowledgment of Charlotte's participation in "The
Nights."

dissertation 3 vols folio Ossian with commentarys 23 vols. folio & the Appendix Index &c 1 vol folio[16]

beginning of Catholda the first poem in all Ossian.

> A tale of the times of old
> why thou wanderer unseen
> thou bender of the thistle of lora
> why thou breeze of the valley
> hast thou left mine ear
> I hear no distant roar of stream
> no sound of the harp from [the] rock[17]

a tale of the times of old a usual begining with Ossian	evry stormy scene No sound of Harps Harps were almost the only I[n]strum
the thistle latin Carduus Greek σκολνμος a prickly weed abounding in Scot land & cheifly grow ing in cornfields	ents of music in those days as we learn from the Old Manuscript found in the ruin \<Marchesran\> \<0 X 7 π π 2 r
roar of streams Ossian uses this very often the roar of a stream is not very loud in gene[ral] yet he very freq uently and rather \<ingeneously\> makes them	∂ 2 oo π o I S X 2 † 2 to π 1 ∏ 1. X 5 f r 2 I I 7]. 2 7 I 7 > X 5 a 2>[18]

---

16 The actual one-volume edition owned by the Brontës contains "A Preliminary Discourse," "Preface," "A Dissertation concerning the Æra of Ossian," "A Dissertation concerning The Poems of Ossian," and "Dr. Blair's Critical Dissertation on The Poems of Ossian" before the actual poems.

17 The quotation is accurate except for the deletion of punctuation, some changes in capitalization, "streams" altered to "stream," and "the" omitted from the last line.

18 My imperfect rendition of Branwell's "imitation" of ancient script, probably intended to be Greek.

the principal.

<   >

this is one of the most long winded Books that have ever been printed we must now conclude for we are dreadfully tired.

July 1829.   P B B

THE MADMAN A Tale
by Capt Bud—

One fine & sultry evening in the Month of July. 1829 as I was walking through the Meadows. on the North of the glass-Town I was accosted by a Man. very wild and mad looking he ran up to me & without introducing himself &c &c. said in a tone and manner which showed that he was MAD

you Dog look hes coming hes coming I see that I must let this world know that it is not me that wil[l] any longer remain in its clouded Atmosphere—Why whats the Matter. said I

My Destiny is as clouded as yonder sky the day was just now fine Now it is dark and lowering so is mans life at one time burst[ing] upon you bright and seemingly everlasting rays. then suddenly it is ore cast with Black <u>clouds of despair</u>. Ah Ah Ah yewew I must DIE

by this time we had Neared an old ruind building in wich I knew their was kept a good tavern the Owner of which was M.[19] if hes sober he shall be made to sup if hes drunk he shall live under a flag.[20] we both stept in and called for a Glass it was given and we sat down I desired this Madman to tell me his story. after much howling and yelling he began

Woe be to the day in which I first saw the light of the sun woe woe woe there was a time when I in youth went to find glory in other lands but that time is flown by like a first ray & shall not return I was wandering by the banks of one of the veins of this world in other climes under a <u>broiling sky</u> when I saw One coverd when I saw one coverd with sunny scales folding coiling in bright waters In gazing eagerly one its many colours I slipped down the banks of <st[r]enght> gave way & in I fell that scaly glory caught me in its folds and on we plunged through blood or earth with the swiftness of light till we got into other worlds beneath oceans from here that scaly coiling <folder> brought me to the mighty Prescence of a Formless <u>indistinguisable</u> one clothed with thunders jet skys and rolling orbs darting fire of clouds here were others clothed with scales of light.[21] That formless one bent down and I was <u>put in black darkness</u> there I remained howling yelling and crieng out woe to the day in which light entered my eyes woe woe woe untill rolling years expired untill at last I was allowed to veiw the

---

19 "M" is probably Moses Hanghimself—see p. 13, n. 5.
20 i.e. the flag of defiance—nautical slang for being drunk.
21 Probably "Bany Lightning" as the dark Genius and Taly, Emmii and Annii as the "others" clothed in light.

sun for the space of a day this is the day I was bid to enter black stormy regions—this Night I must go—so may you Fare well I must begon

Instantly he darted out of the door and away was gone. The Tavern began to get very dark and I heard muttering of Distant thunder I lookt out at the door to see what it was and what did I see but the Madman standing on the top of a Hill. a Bright flash of Lightning darted through the sky and folding him in it Flew again through the air this was followed by such a Dreadful peal of Thunder as made me start

I looked round & lo and behold there I was at my own fireside with a bottle and glass on the table beside me the truth was That I had had a drop to Much + and my wife coming in had given me a good thump as she was wont to do on such occaisions

| July 1 | | Captain |
| 1829 | | BUD |

+ and the[n] gone to sleep

THERE is a new work going to be published—it is POEMS by young Soult the Ryhmer with notes and commentarys by Moses Chateaubriand.[22] in 1 volumn Quarto—it will probably be published on the 1. of October 1829[23]

PB Brontë

CONCLUDING
ADRRESS.

to my Readers   P B B—te

We have hitherto conducted this Magazine & we hope to the satisfaction of most. (No one can please all) but as we are conducting a Newspaper[24] which requires all the time and attention we can spare from ot[h]er employiments. we have fouund it expedient to relinquish the editorship of this Magazine but we recomend our readers to be to the new Editor as they were to me the new one is the chief Genius Charlotte she will conduct it in Future tho I shall write now and then for it. Δ Θ H'[25]

July 1829   PB Brontë

[22] See p. 47, n. 3.
[23] See p. 47. The rest of the manuscript page following the double line contains a canceled "Advertisement," written upside down, for the new volume of poems by Young Soult.
[24] See p. 250.
[25] This Greek tag, like the ones on p. 10 and at the end of **Caractacus** on p. 117, seems to have no discernible meaning.

ADVERTISMents

To be sold
100. pair of Fine shoes
by M walk 20 miles a hour.

To be sold 17. Pounds of
Prussian
Butter by
<how to> kill 20 folk a day

To be sold
The 9 Quart Tavern
Tip staff lane cheif
Glasstown
by Corporal drink <some>

The Tiplers
a Talk
by M Chateaubriand
M De la Pack
Paris

Sir[1] it is well known that the Genii have declared that unless they.[2] "perform certain arduous duties every year of a mysterious nature all the worlds in the firmament will be burnt up & gathered together in one mighty Globe which will roll in lonely Grandeur throug[h] the vast wilderness of Space inhabited only by the 4 high Princes of the Geni till time shall be succeded by eternity" the impudence of this is only to be parall[el]ed by another of their assertions namely "that by their magic might they can reduce the world to a desert the rivers to streams of livid poison & the clearest lakes to stagnant waters the pestilential vapours of which shall slay all living creatures except the Bloodthirsty Beast of the forest and the ravenous Bird of the rock But that in the midst of this desolation the Palace of the Cheif Geni shall rise sparkling in the wilderness and the horrible howl of their war cry shall spread over the land at morning at noontide & night but that they shall have their anual feast over the bones of the dead & shall yearly rejoice with the joy of victors I think Sir that the horrible wickedness of this needs no remark & therefore I haste to subscribe myself yours &c

                                                        July 14 1829 UT

---

[1]   One-page manuscript (6.5 x 8.2 cm) in BPM: Bon 79; possibly intended as a letter to the editor of the **Young Men's Magazine.** The original signature has been erased and replaced by "U T." "U T" presumably means "Us Two," indicating a collaboration—see, however, Alexander CB, I, 74.

[2]   The Young Men presumably.

High minded Frenchmen love not the ghost[1]
who rides on the clouds of war
with the eye of an eagle he views your hosts
and grins with delight from afar

———————

For the time in his powerful mind he sees
when like a slave before him led
the kingdom of France shall bow at his knees
& gloryfy him as its head

———————

Though at this time his brow ma\<y\> not lour
he looks to the future with Joy
when from his high embattled tower
in his terrible might he shall cry

———————

Kingdom of France I bid thee beware
at the storm which is drawing nigh
Look at the troubled & darkening air
Look at the wrath in mine eye

                    Young Soult July 17 1829
                         C Bronte

———————————————

[1]   Part of a manuscript leaf, 12.1 x 6.7 cm, the ninth of twelve manuscripts
randomly bound in red morocco by T.J. Wise at the BPM: Bon 80 (9); the poem
follows a fair copy of Charlotte's "The Enfant," originally published in
Branwell's Blackwoods Magazine, May and June 1829— see p. 13.
Alexander (CB, I, 34) suggests that Charlotte is either using Branwell's
pseudonym (Young Soult) or transcribing a poem by Branwell. The subject
matter and the use of the pseudonym would suggest that Branwell is the author,
but the fact that Charlotte's signature appears at the end of the poem, though
lower on the page and separate from the poem's signature, and the marked
improvement in poetic quality over previous items in this edition, suggest that
the poem may well have been a collaborative venture. However, in contrast to
"The Enfant," which is in the usual miniature print writing, the poem is written
in longhand, and the number of errors and corrections suggests it is a first draft—
see Neufeldt PBB, 361 for further information. Both Charlotte and Branwell had
been reading Sir Walter Scott's *The Life of Napoleon Buonoparte*, Edinburgh,
1827, at this time—see Alexander CB, I, 28.

O when shall our brave land be free[1]
When shall our castles rise
in pure & glorious liberty
before our joyful eyes

How long shall tyrants ride in state
upon the thundercloud
the arbiters of Englands fate
and of her nobles proud

Thou sun of liberty arise—
upon our beauteous land
terrible vengeance rend the skys
let tyrants feel they hand

let tryants feel thy hand we cry
& let them see thy gaze
for they will shrink beneath thy eye
& we will sing thy praise

the song of vengeance shall arise
before the morning sun
illuminates the arched skys
or its[2] high course doth run

the song of venegeance shall not cease
when midnight cometh on
when the silver moon shines out in peace
to light the traveler lone

July the 24   U T

---

[1]   Part of **Blackwoods Young Mens Magazine** for August 1829 (HL: Ms Lowell I [6]), the first of the miniature magazines edited by Charlotte—see Alexander CB, I, 54. In the magazine's table of contents it is entitled "a song," and it constitutes the "Poetry" section of the magazine. The tyrants are the four Chief Genii —see p. 153.
[2]   The authors first wrote "mighty," then changed to "high."

what is more glorious in nature or art[1]
than a bottle of Brandy clear
there's nothing I like so well for my part
it rids you of evry fear

it raises your spirits on stillest night
it carries you lightly along
it wings you away from this pitiful sight
& disposes your min[d] for a song

for a song like mine it makes you wish
& it keeps your eyes from a doze
unless you are dull as a kettle of fish
then't sends you of to repose

I hope high Duke that you like my song
which for your pleasure I chant
as it is beautiful & not long
your approbation grant

                                        [July/August 1829]

---

[1]   Part of "Military Conversations" in **Blackwoods Young Mens Magazine** for August 1829, edited by Charlotte (HL: Lowell I [6]). It is sung by Sir Alexander Hume Bady; after this drunken performance the Duke of Wellington orders that Bady be taken to the triangle. While Alexander attributes the song to Charlotte (CB, I, 60), the subject matter and the quality of the verse suggest Branwell as author.

Interior of A Pothouse By Young Soult[1]

the cheerful fire is blazing bright
& cast[s] a ruddy glare
on beams & rafters all in sight
& on the sanded floor

the scoured pewter on the shelf
glitters like silver <pure>
& all the ware of stony delf
doth like to Gold allure

and where this fire so magical
doth spread its light around
sure many scenes most magical
are acted on that ground

about that oaken table
in the middle of the floor
are sat those who are able
to play one card or more

and now behold the stakes are set
now watch the anxious faces
of all who have laid down a bet
scarce can they keep their places

but see the teller holds the card
above the silent crowd
look at his meagre visage hard
& list' his accents loud

he says the card is number one
look at that fellow there
I think he has his buisness done
Behold his ghastly stare

---

1   Part of the September 1829 issue of **Blackwoods Young Mens Magazine** (BPM: SG 95), edited by Charlotte. See Alexander CB, I, 62. Although signed "Young Soult," Branwell's pseudonym, the poem was originally signed "U T" at the beginning and end, and is listed as by "U T" in both the magazine's table of contents and in Charlotte's "General Index" to the magazines she edited. The number of cancellations and corrections suggests a first draft. A pot-house is a low public house. Compare with Alexander CB, I, 82-83.

now he has drawn his sword
and plunged it in his side
look at his dying struggle
while <g>ushes forth the tide

of red & streaming blood
the current of his life
pouring a crimson flood
while all within the strife

of racking pain of body
& torturing pain of mind
doth rend his heart in peices
& will no freind mos[t] king[2]

wipe from his brow the calmy[3] swet
& cheer his dying hour
promise to aid his orphans dear
with all within his power

no there they'll alway let him lay
& pass unheeding by
unless the[y] find him in their way
when theyll kick him all awry

or tearing up a flag[4]
in the neatly sanded floor
theyll throw him in & leave [him] there
& think of him no more

& now I've done my verses
you may read them if you choose
or throw them in the fire
as Ive nought to gain or lose
                    Young Soult
                    August the 21 1829

---

[2]   "kind" obviously intended.
[3]   "clamy" obviously intended.
[4]   i.e. a flagstone.

The Glass Town by ~~CB~~ U T
the Glass Town[1]

1

tis sunset & the golden orb
has sunk behind the mountains far
& rises now the silver moon
& sparkles bright the evening star

2

but in the west an crimson light
above the horizon glows
tinting all nature with the bright
gay colours of the rose

3

and over all the eastern sky
the robe of twilight gray
is heaving up the heavens nigh
while the pale milky way

4

goes clearer still & clearer
as vanishes the light
till it arches all the firmament
like a rainbow of the night[2]

but the sound of murmuring waters
from distance far I hear
like the rushing of a cataract
it fall[s] upon my ear

tis the roaring of the multitude
within those mighty walls
whose noise is like to rageing
or rushing waterfalls

---

[1] Also part of the September 1829 issue of **Blackwoods Young Mens Magazine**, edited by Charlotte (BM: SG, 95). The first line of the title appears at the bottom of a manuscript page with the blotted initials "CB" before the initials "U T," followed by a canceled line: "tis evening and the glorious sun." The second line appears at the top of the next manuscript page. The poem is also listed in the magazine's table of contents as by "U T"—see Alexander CB, I, 69.
[2] What is now the final stanza of the poem originally followed this stanza, then was canceled.

tis that great & glorious city
whose high ruler doth defy
the might[i]est of the a[r]mies
who their strength against her try

O may he ever reign in glory
may his glittering sword be dyed
in the life blood of his enemies
though on the clouds they ride

O may he bring them to the <earth>
with fearful scorn and shame
may they bow their heads before him
& dread his mighty name[3]

but now the roaring sound has ceased
the city is sunk to sleep
& oer the world nights curtain falls
mid silence still & deep

but yet the silver moon shine[s] out
& the <bright> sparkling stars
are wheeling down the firmament
their shining pearly <rays>

no sound doth break the silence
save the merry nightingale
as it pours its sweet warbling
dow[n] the still and lonely vale
                    U T August the 25 1829

---

[3]   Line 36 is followed by the canceled signature and date, "UT August 25 1829," and ten canceled lines, suggesting that the poem was originally to end here. The ruler is the Duke of Wellington.

on seeing A beautiful statue
& a rich golden vase full of wine lying
beside it in the desert of Sahara[1]

---

see that golden goblet shine
decked with gems so starry bright
crowned with the most sparkling wine
casting forth a ruby light

Emerald leaves its brim encircle
with their brilliant green
and rich grapes of saphire purple
twined with these are seen

near a majestic statue
of purest marble stands
rising like a spirit
from the[2] wilderness of sand's

but heark unto that trumpet swell.
which soundeth long and loud
rivailing the music.
of the darkest thundercloud

tis the signal that from hence
we both of us must go
so come my brother dear
let it be even so

U T Sep[t] 2 1829

---

[1] Part of the October 1829 issue of **Blackwoods Young Mens Magazine**, edited by Charlotte (HL: Lowell I [5]). See Alexander CB, I, 70.

[2] The authors first wrote, then canceled "dry and barren." This stanza is followed by a canceled stanza which reads:

but see a flash of lightning
has darted from that cloud.
now listen to that thunder peal
so crashing long and loud

THE SONG OF THE ANCIENT
BRITON'S
ON LEAVING THE GENILAND by U T[1]

Farewell O thou pleasant land
rich are thy feild's and fair
thy mighty forest's they are grand
but freedom dwells not there

thy rugged mountains rise sublime
from thy[2] barren desert wild
and thou wouldst be a pleasant land[3]
if freedom on thee smiled

Our hearts are sad as we turn from thee
and thy pleasant smiling shore
to think that not again shall we
Behold thee ever more

ere many day's are passed away
the sea will between us lie
and when in freedoms land we dwell
for thee we'll heave a sigh

because that oer thee triumph
those tyrant's of the air
who dwell in halls of thunder
& robes of lightning wear

but now we're bound afar off
to our fathers land we go
swift foaming billows roll us
and winds of heaven blow

---

[1]   Part of the November 1829 issue of **Blackwoods Young Mens Magazine**, edited by Charlotte (HL: Lowell I [4]). See Alexander CB, I, 78-88. For a description of the ancient Britons' habitation in the land of the Genii, see Alexander CB, I, 7-8, and **THE HISTORY OF THE YOUNG MEN**, Chapter 1, p. 139 below.
[2]   The authors first wrote "the," then "thy"; neither is canceled. They also wrote "wild wilderness," then changed to "desert wild."
[3]   This line originally read "soft and propitious is thy clime."

there rises freedoms palace
like a tower of burning gold
around it roars the ocean
with its world of waters rolled

up to the glorious castle
where mighty freedom dwells
while round her like a tempest
sea music sweetly swells
U T
Sep^t 7 1829
But now were bound afar [off]
to our father's land we go
swif[t] foaming billows roll us
and winds of heaven blow
U T
Sep^t 7 1829

ON seeing the Garden of
A Genius by U T[1]

How pleasant is the world
where mighty Geni dwell
like a vision is the beauty
of wild forest stream & fell

their palaces arise
from the green and flowry ground
while strains of sweetest music
are floating all around

their castles of bright adamant
all mortal strength defy
encircled round with geni
towering like rocks on high

& now behold that verdant plain
spa[n]gled with star like flowers
watered by purest silver lakes
& crowned with emerald bowers[2]

---

[1] Also part of the November 1829 issue of **Blackwoods Young Mens Magazine**, edited by Charlotte (HL: Lowell I [4]). See Alexander CB, I, 78-88. Between stanzas four and five are two canceled stanzas (followed by "Sep[t] 7 1829") which were taken directly from the previous poem (stanzas 7 and 8). There is also a canceled, undecipherable final stanza, with the alternative version added at the bottom of the page, following the table of contents.

[2] Two canceled stanzas follow which read:
> there rises freedoms palace
> like a tower of burning gold
> around roars the ocean
> with it world of waters roild
>
> up to the glorious walls
> were <mighty> freedom dwells
> while round her like a tempest
> sea music loudly swells
>   UT
>   Sep[t] 7 1829
See stanzas seven and eight of the previous poem.

in the midst appear[s] a palace
of yellow topaz bright
from which streams forth a glory
of sunny golden light

O if the dwellers in this land
heeded their dreadful name
how all the mortal world would sing
that bright & quenchless Fame

But now the eye of hatred
follows whereere they go
in the sea or in the firmament
it trys to work them woe

they may robe themselves in darkness
themselves with lightning crown
they may weild the sword of venegeance
but to them well not bow down

they may frame in the dark ocean
high palaces of pearl
mid the silver orbs of heaven
their dragon wings unfurl

& throned on the star's of night
while thunder rolls around
may bid the earth to wait on them
but vain shall be the sound
                    U T
            Sep^t 9 1829
how pleasant is the world
where mighty geni dwell
like a vision is the beauty
of wild forest stream & fell &c &c

Found in the Inn Belonging to you[1]

Thou art a sweet & lovely flower
planted in a fairy's bower
cherished by a bright sunbeam
watered by a silver stream

Thou art a palm tree green & fair
rising from the desert plain
thou art a ray of silver light
streaming o'er the stormy main

When the mighty billows mix
with the hanging cloud
when the light[n]ings flashes
& the thunder roaring loud

Then when some pale star sends out
a gentle pearly ray
the mariners all hail it
as the herald of the day

When the sun shall rise in splendour
ting[e]ing the coursing foam
with the colours of that gorgeous bow
Which arches heavens dome

When the rocking ship shall rest
on the glassy ocean calm
its red flag stirred by the gale
whose breath is sweetest balm

Blowing from Britan's shore's
& her roses red and white
O'er Scotia's thistle wild
and Erin's emerald bright

---

[1] One side of a single leaf bound in green morocco in the library of William Self, Studio City, California. For the other side of the leaf, see p. 70. The size of the leaf and the subject matter suggest that the poems were intended for **Blackwoods Young Mens Magazine**, but were either never included or were part of a lost issue that has been dismembered. The "Inn" may refer to Bravey's Inn—see Glossary.

While the music of the harp
and the music of the song
are borne upon the passing wind
in solemn strains along.
                    U T
                    Sept 28. 1829

YOUNG:
SOULTS
POEMS WITH
NOTES::

IN II VOLS QUARTO
VOL I. [1]

A
COLLECTION OF POEMS
by Young Soult
the Ryhmer[2]
ILLUSTRATED WITH
NOTES =
AND COMMENTARYS BY:
MONSEIUR
DE LA CHATEUBRIAND[3]
Author of Travles in Greece the
Holy land &c the state of
France reveiw of the
Empire &c &c &c

Sept. 30   ———————   AD. 1829.

---

[1]   Hand-sewn booklet with grey paper covers (5 x 6.4 cm) of 18 pages (1 blank) in BPM: BS 114.

[2]   Branwell may have derived the name from the seventeenth-century poet and critic, Thomas Rhymer, but a more likely source is Thomas the Rhymer in Scott's *Tales of a Grandfather*, of which the Brontë family owned a copy.

[3]   François-René, Vicomte de Chateaubriand (1768-1848), French essayist, travel-writer, and diplomat, left pre-revolutionary France for America and then Britain. He returned to France in 1801, became a diplomat, and was later Ambassador to Berlin, London, and Rome. Although Branwell invokes Chateaubriand as his model and Gérin suggests he read the *Travels* in an 1812 translation at Ponden Hall (BB, 43), the number of notes in the *Travels* is, in fact, very modest, and they either are explanatory or indicate historical uncertainty. Branwell's actual model is more likely Macpherson's *Ossian* with its copious notes—see the "REVIEW OF BUDS Commentary on Ossian" on p. 27. He was also familiar with the copious notes that sometimes accompanied poems in *Blackwood's Magazine* —see, for example, ix (May 1821) 187-91 or xxiv (September 1829) 365, which cite Chateaubriand's *Travels*—and the poems of Scott. Barker suggests that both here and in the commentary on Ossian, Branwell is doing a satirical send-up of the learned commentaries he had to read for his classical studies (Brontës, 164).

PARIS
Published by M D LA Pack
le eleve M De Brunnete &c
Cheif Glass Town.
Seargeant Tree Corporal Bull
Captain legwind &c &c &c &c
Twemys Glass Town Capt leg.
Parrys glass town Col Wind
Rosses glass town Seargt Snow

THE AMMON TREE
Cutter a poem by young Soult the Ryhmer[4]

O Miserable man
who to the injury of thyself
and others leadest a wretched life
of pain and sorrow not one drop of joy
O think how many thou hast made lamen[t]
even untill their last and worst day
I tell thee think and leave thy wret[c]hed life
Or die by the Remor[s]eless land of Law
wich spareth not nor knoweth how to spare
those wretches who to Dare it do pretend
Think when thou hearst the sentence of the jud[ge]
thou wretch thou art by law condemd to die
then Bound then Mancled thou art led
unto the yawning bloody guilotine

Ammon Cutter- - - - -	or make stools of
or Ammon Skinner	their bones- - - - - -
these are most a dang	O vile amon tree cutter
erous class of men--	thee I will slay
Inhabitants of Paris	and fling thee in the gutter
and its environs they	that thou may rot away

4   I have been unable to find a source for the almond tree cutter. The opening line appears twice as a line of poetry in a review of Robert Southey's *All For Love, or a Sinner Well Saved* in the July 1829 issue of *Blackwood's*. The description of Paris resembles that in John Malcolm's "A Trip to Paris," *Tales of Field and Flood* (Edinburgh, 1829, p. 179), a work Charlotte was reading in September 1829 (Alexander CB, I, 89). The initial "O" is ornamented.

go out in the Nights--
and cutt down all the
Ammon Trees and---
burn all the vineyards
of those against whom
they have a spite. and
If they can catch the
owners they flay them
allive-- and then tie--
them to a tree with
their skin as an--
umbrella

O vile Ammon tree cutter
thee I do hate
and some day. wen. I see thee
Ill dash thy dismal pate
                Culvin<gton>[5]
                    vol 3.325

Guilotine- - - - - - -
A instrument used in--
France instead of the--
Gallows- - - - -

O leave thy wicked life when thou dost hear
what I am going to say tis for thy good
in Paris in that most famous city
though it is oft. convulsed by horrid wars
their lived a Man by nature feirce & high
also proud and disdainful. rich he was.
but with low villains meetin[g] they did strip
him of his riches and did leave him poor--
Desolate and fo[r]lorn he wrung his hands--
he stamped he raved he tore his hair--
but all for nought for they s[t]ood looking on
with the utmost composure hah thou poor
Deluded man. he could not brook all this
but forth with out he ran and for a long time
nothing of him was heard- - -
            End of the First Book   Sept 1.
    PBB.   1829

In Paris that most & c
PARIS a city and - - -
capital of Frenchyland
situate on the River—
Siene. 50 miles of the
open sea it is a glassto
wn. and very large it is
thus de[s]cribed by Capt
Tree - - - - - - - - - -
O Paris I approach thee
thou world in minature
full of Wickedness.

abodes of misery wide
spacious streets little
dirty narrow lanes - - -
            Travles. vol 2
                p. 355

with low villains - - - -
this alludes to a Tavern
the most horrid
places imaginable for
an accurate
discription of one see
Discription of a Tavern

---

[5]   Probably Branwell's invention.

| Rioting Idleness & Grandeur thou hast Tembles[7] reaching to the skys the abode of Grandeaur holes in the groung[8] the | Branwell's Magazine March 1829[6] - - - - - - - by M Chateubriand |

The Ammon tree cutter —
BOOK 2

One moonlight stary Night along the side
Of the clear lake which semed another sky--
I slowly walkt. thinking upon those times
when europe was involved in dreadful war
and wild dest[r]u[c]tion raised her standard high
I saw a shining light burst from the Trees
calld Ammon which their heads did statly rear--
and O that light did shine so briliantly
that it seemd like the sun on Oceans wave
Into the grove I walked to see that light
which did shine with such splendour on the lake
that it did serve ins[t]ead of the pale moon
which then enwraped in clouds did hide itself
I went and Oh wat met my aching sight
The very man of whom I spoke before--
his face was haggard and his sleeve tuckt up--
a knife which reekd with blood was in his hand

| When Europe was &c the time of the late French Revolution-- in which all the Nations of-- that qua[r]ter of the globe acted and took the part | fruit called Almonds |
| Amonn. tree- - - - - of Almond tree is a tall and sta[te]ly tree | like the sun on oceans &c this passage may seem obscure at first but after a little reflection people will see that it is a just simile for the sun set ing on the sea causes a long Train of light to shine over the sea-- this may well be compa |

---

6   Probably a reference to the poem **Interior of A Pothouse** (p. 36), though if it is, Branwell is mistaken about the date.

7   "Temples" obviously intended.

8   "ground" obviously intended.

| which produces the | red to the rays darting
from some <su[r]fess after>
bright light <streams> |

He trampled upon a victim skinnd
Who writhd about in dying agonies
Onward I rushed on the Murderer.
I seized him by his throat & cried forbear
forbear thou Wretch from slaugthe[r]ing this man
He stared at me then with a fearful cry
Away he dashed leaving part of his flesh
with me such was the fearful wrench he gave
I He[s]itated to pursue for he--
did run like leopard bound oer the plain
And now the morning came with swiftest wings
The sun arisen. brightend all the feilds
and gladned Natuere sung her song of joy
as on to <Paris> I did bend my way
          Eend of the Second Book   Sept 6
PBB.   1829.

--The Ammon Tree Cutter
BOOK THIRD

What do I hear--
Is it the sou[n]d of multituds--
Or the mighty cataracts roar--
Yes tis a Roaring Rushing multitude--
that Horrid Instrument the guilotine
which doth before them gapind[9] bloody stand

| A victim skinned
alluding to the mann
er in which they
treat the masters | of the Amon trees[10]
see <Note> page 1--
the <   >
see <Note> page 1-- |

before the judge whose is seated on high
their stands a wretch in whom I recognise
that very Murderer who flayed alive
that man in the dark grove of Ammon tre[es]
handcuffed and bound and pale he was

---

9   "gaping" obviously intended.
10 These two notes are heavily blotted and virtually unreadable.

and haggard was his cheek deep sunk his eye
but still a sterne and frowning look had he
<Taws>[11] he who once was rich who Now was poor
Sternly he eyed the Judge who thus began--
Villain thoust dared the Mighty Empreurs laws
In killing his great Marshall Peirre Marmont
Thy punishment is Death by th[e] guillotine
The villain raised a Horrid wailing cry
Ha Ha you vile partial Judge Murat[12] - - -
I am then doomed to die the Dismal death
Yes but before I do Revenge is Mine
Revenge Revenge Revenge so saying he flew
On the Judge Murat and like a madman
Tore him in peices saying Revenge

The Mighty Empreur Napoleon Bonaparte Empreure of the-- French	Judge Murat Napoleons Brother in Law a savage man-- who would not care
great Peirre Marmont the famous Marmont or Marma. as he is-- sometimes calld he is a mortal enemy to younng soults-- Fathrer Marshall Alexander Soult--	for the death of his own son more than that of a Rabbit--his Name at full lenght is Jean Joachim- - - Murat. Mayor of the City of Paris Chateaubriand.

the soldiers and police did now rush on--
like to the waves driving against a rock
to take him from the dead Jean Joachim
who was torn peicemeal in a thousand bits--
and lay in his last agoneis on t. floor--
Stern the villain stood his sword was lifted high
and the first that came up his skull in tow[13] was clef[t]
another and anothe[r] followd him--

---

[11] "Twas" obviously intended.
[12] The inclusion of Marmont and Murat suggests Branwell's reading of Scott's *Life of Napoleon Bonaparte* (1827) which Charlotte refers to in June and September 1829 (Alexander CB, I, 28 and 90). Murat was governor (not Mayor) of Paris in 1804. Marmont's Christian name was Auguste Federic-Louis rather than Pierre. Neither meets the fate described here. See also p. 376, n. 24 on Marmont and pp. 22, n. 4; 378, n. 27 on Murat.
[13] "two" obviously intended.

but at the last the Murderer was took
they flayed him then coated him with salt
then laid him on a gridiron to roast alive
and Oh the Horrid yells that burst from him
was like the roaring of the wind mid trees
and rocks and mountains in a misty Isle
untill at last they slowly died away
unto a low hoarse mourmer then were gone
and nought was heard but dripping of the fat
into the raging fires which blazed around
THE Multitude Movd of and left him there

concluding observations on the
Poem of the Ammon
Tree Cutter.

The Ammon tree cutter is certanly one of the best
of young Soults productions and also one of th[e]
longest it is said the reason why he wrote
it was one of them had been spoiling his
Fathers trees. in this poem he evidently
makes fun of Murat as any person will
see who reads it. some will wonder
why he speaks of persons living after
they are skinned alive and it to them
(especially those living in England)
seem[s] impropable[14] and arroneous--
but it is neither for it is known how
Hard Frenchmen are to kill some--
cant be killed for a day others for 2
days and Pigtail. cannot be killed--
for 3-days!!! certainly these
cases are not often but a vast--
Number will live 12 hours afte[r]
they are skinned alive or their--
Hearts cut out. but No. Frenchman
or Englishman or any other man--
can remain alive after their Heads are
cut of
　　　Frenchmen can live when their heads are on
　　　Frenchmen can live when their Hearts are gon
　　　Frenchmen cant live when their heads are of

[14] "improbable" obviously intended.

& Frenchmen cant endure a scoff
                              Tree. vol 2 p 11
this saying of Captain Trees is very jus[t]
For Frenchmen can never endure a- - -
Scoff. or Taunt or Bitter joke they--
either will fly out into an ingovernab
le--feury or go and hang or poison--
themselvs without more ado- - - - - -
                              CHATEAUBRIAND

Visit to the ruins--ColdaiDuh--[15]

THE golden sun had long gone down
had sunk beneath the azure sky
when I from Vina journ[i]ed on
    To see the ruins of coldaiai

Along I travlled many a mile--
    over the bleak and dseart[16] plain
    wher nought was seen but high mondile
And the far distant stormy main

I travlld till the Moon arose--
    I travlld till the Night was gone
    I travlld till the Midnights close
I travlld till the Morning sun

In his high splendour did arise
    to drive the clouds afar away
    to reedn all the arched skys
    To promise a fine Harvest day

when before me what did their stand
but the ruins of great coldaiduh
still stood his eastern tower grand
but of its other ruins few--

coldaiduh	Vina

15   Coldai Duh, Vina, Mondile, Dalcos and Farsas throne would all seem to be Branwell's inventions, and possibly refer to the settlement of the Ancient Britons in West Africa. See **The History of the Young Men**, p. 137.
16   "desart" obviously intended."

a misterious castle on the Genii Desart built by the Anceints	a town near the desar[t]
	Mondile a mountain on its— border

Now still remain to show what was
   The glory once of the whole world
   For by the mighty cheif Dalcos
it from its powre was hurled

I sat me down upon a stone
   and thought of the days gone by
   but the sudden screech of Farras throne
And the blackning cloudy sky

And the moaning wind which blew arou[nd]
were warnings of a mighty strom[17]
   and soon there was a Dreadful sound
   of trumpets and a heideus form

Appeared striding upon a cloud
red lightning flashing from his eye
what dost thou here he asked proud
what dost thou here for thou mus[t] fly

Fly or red lightning from a cloud
Shall thee prusue[18] away I went
and was far from this Genius proud
Ere he his dreadful lightning sent

Dalcos a famous British or Gaulic Prince who fought agains[t] the Prince of Coldai & overthrew him &	Farras throne a misterious build[ing] or tower whenev[er][19] it screeches <there> is shure <to be a> storm
burnt his palace & city the ruins of which I now went to see- - - -	This poem < > red in < > Branwell < >

---

[17] "storm" obviously intended.
[18] "pursue" obviously intended.
[19] These notes have been largely obliterated by a piece of paper glued over them to repair a tear in the manuscript.

Ode to the cheif Genius
BANY

O thou mighty Genius
Thou ruler of the world
Take care lest from thy power
Thou shouldest soon be hurled

Thou ridest on the Thunder cloud
above all here below
Take care lest from thy height so proud
Thou art humbled low

O look at the planets
look at the bloody moon
and then thou wilt see
that thy time will come soon

O look at the storm clouds
hear thunder rumbling slow
O look at the Dreadful
starry Archers bow

O thou mighty Genius
Thou Ruler of the world
Take care lest from thy Power
Thou shouldest soon be hurld

Starry Archers-- One of the 12. signs called Sagitories	This poem is short & irregular it is an address to Bany chief Genius

ON seeing the ruins of
The tower of Babylon---[20]

Ah what is that peeping above the hill
Towering to the sky

[20] Possibly a reference to John Martin's painting "The Fall of Babylon" (Alexander CB, I, 97). See also pp. 65 and 70 below.

it is reflected in this rill
which far from it doth lie--

whichever way I turn my eyes
No mortal can I see
For in this Mighty Desart
There is No one but me

To gaze upon this tower--
Raised by the hand of Man
which Defieth the Geniis power
For down with it who can

it is reflected in the rill which far from it doth lie This may seem un meaning. to many but it is not so for anything which is at a great distance must be emensly high to be reflect 20 miles distance from it- - - - - Chatueab	Tower of Babylon or Babel a tower founded in the earlyest ages of the world and after wards repaired by-- Nebuchadnassar King of Babylon it is Now in ruins-- the dwelling place of all manner of- - - monsters &c &c

Thy name great Tower is Babylon
Once the abode of kings
Ah now the Vulture doth not deign
In thee to spread her wings

Thou risest in lone grandeur
Above the Desart Plain
thou seest the sun roll oer thee
but no king thee doth claim

But now to other scens I turn
And leave thee desolate
My heart doth for my country burn
And for her pending fate

The Desart Plain The Tower of- - -	fo[r]lorn O Babylon thou that

Babylon is situate
in a plain which
though once fert
ile is now Desert
ed save a few- - -
wretched villiages
of mud hovels--
belonging to the--
Arabs- - - - - - -
Buds Travels vol 2.13

once was the abode
of kings now liest
humbled
in the dust thy
sun [h]as sunk
thy glory is forever
gone- - - - - - - -
    Luciens[21] speech
or. oration on the ret
urn of the men sent
to explore Babylon

But no king thee doth
claim
Alluding to Babylon
once being the abode
of kings but now
she is Deserted

My heart doth for my
country burn
Alluding to the faction
Du Mange[22] and the
troubles caused by it

Ode to Napoleon----

O great Napoleon son of storms--
Whose Heart in Dreadful Battle warm
              Mild in peace
              Just when War
Raises her Death shout from afar
              To thee I raise
              my tuneful lays
Ruond me play the glorys of thy star

how many victorys thou hast won
My mind cannot take nor yet my pen
              Thy star flew
              Through the span
Of the blue arches to meet the man
              who is the one
              that thee has Done
Because all of thy Followers ran

---

21 Probably a reference to Lucien Buonaparte, whom Scott describes as a distinguished orator, "Scarce inferior to his brother in ambition and talent." See p. 15, n. 11.
22 See p. 16, n. 13.

round me play the glorys of thy star Bonaparte believs that their is a ruling star to direct him for he is very supers titious	To meet the man This means the Duke of Wellington and the whole verse alludes to the Battle of Waterloo at which the General is sore Displeased and
my mind cannot take nor yet my pen This is not right for it should be- - - - my mind cannot th ink. nor yet my tou nge-- think tounge	when he first read it he said- - - - - This is hatred under the mask of freind ship & if this fellow-- writes any more such he shall be guilotined

At Austerlitz Bright Laurels crowned
thy head and round thy Temples bound
     Swords were Red
     victims hair
was dyed with blood by sabers bare
     and the wild cries
     from soldiers rise
that Victry Victry crowns our Emprair

Russia Russia was the cry--
and to it all thy Liegones fly--
     but the Ice
     made them cold
And they sore mangled left their hold
     but Empruair
     you did stare
and of you ran through Poland old

Then to Elba Frances Eagle flew
And Ah Napoleon if thou knew
     thy dire fate
     thou would not fly
to Waterloo wheron to Dye
     the feild with blood
     Thy soldiers stood
strong gainst th[e] opposing Eneimy--

At Austerlitz-- the battle of Aust	Then to Elba-- Bonaparte was sent--

erlitz- - - - - - | an exile to Elba a little
Russia Russia was the cry | before the battle of
the war with Russia | Waterloo

but thou wast beaten and thou did fly
to under Africs burning sky
Helena--
was the Isle
where prisoned thou wast to live awhile
Thou ran away
from hellena
and of to France thou sailed full a 1000
mile away

but now Napoleoon I have done
my story which of the[e] makes fun
I hope that
Thoult pardon me
for all I uttered was in a spree
I have finishd
and have diminishd
Thy most splendid height and grate glory

For all I uttered was in | passion for the Emp
a spree | reur had decided
spree is a low cant-- | against him in some--
term for fun. vide | cause or other- - - -
Boyers Dict[23] p. 322 | but however young--
THIS poem is an ex | Soult was tried and
cedingly rambling | sentenced to be fined
and irregular | 1100£ which he
meter and contain | in 3 weeks time- - -
s--a great many | paid but he promisis
things for which he | es that he will- - -
ought to be punish | not write anymore
ed Young Soult-- | against the
<I> wrote it while-- | Empreur- - - - - - -
drunk and under | S//Chateaub.[d]
the influence of |

---

23   Abel Boyer's, *The Royal Dictionary, French and English, and English and French*, which by 1819 was in its twenty-third edition. However, it contains no such definition.

THE PROPHECY —
By young Soult TR

I saw a flame which shot along the sky
And then I heard a peal of thunder loud
The rain came down in torrent I did fly
for there did stand a genius on a cloud

In his right hand he held a flaming sword
and in the other a trump whose dreadful blast
made the earth shake he loud as thunder roared
O faction Du Mange thy glory is past

thou art gone thou art gone like morning Dew--
before the glorious rising sun- - -
thy insolence thou shalt forever rue
For now in th[e] scale of parties thou art gone--

Soon as the genius had said those words
A peal of Dreadful thunder <underground>
I fell upon my face when it I heard
but in the pale blue sky the Genius had <gone>

I saw a flame- - - This means a flash of Lightning- - -	bill for suppressing the faction Du Ma nge in the chamber
thourt gone thou art gone like the morning Dew Before the glorius rising sun This passage is very similar to one used by Rarras[24] in the 2 reading of the	of Deputies- - - - Make your enemies Die away like Mist on the hill before the Glorious rising sun It appears to be so similar that I think <it> is took from it- - - Chateaub[d]

APPENDIX

This volumn of poems was written [by]
young Soult the Ryhmer with notes

---

24 Seemingly Branwell's invention.

and commentary by M D Chateaubriand
         The Poems are six in number
                    - Namely -
The Ammon tree cutter--3 books Blank
verse with 14. notes & a commentary
A visit to the ruins of ColdaiDuh with
6 notes and a commentary (regular
verse. 10 verses- - - - - - - - - -
ADDress to the Cheif Genius Bany- -
with 1. note & a comment[a]ry 5 verses
irregular
On seeing the Ruins of the Tower of Babylon
with 5 notes and a commentary 6 verses
irregular verse
To Napoleon Bonaparte. with 7 notes
and a commentary 7 verses regular
The prophecy--with 1. note & a comm
entary regular verse. 4 verses- - -

         In the whole—
there are 6 Poems 35 verses and- -
30 notes & commentarys- - - - - - -

===================

PS
This is the only compleat edition of an
number of the works of young soult
the Ryhmer excepting the Octavo one
of his Ryhmes--by Cuvier[25] which is
not compleat having no notes wich it
very much needed--(Chateaub.

September 30
AD 1829
Patrick Bra
nwell Bronte
[figure of justice][26]

---

[25] There is no evidence of a volume of Young Soult's "edited" by Cuvier; it is
probably Branwell's invention, especially since he is likely referring to Baron
Cuvier, the famous French naturalist. See also Alexander & Sellars, 162-63.
[26] For a detailed description, see Alexander & Sellars, 292.

YOUNG:
SOULTS
POEMS WITH
NOTES::
IN II VOLS QUARTO
VOL II [1]

A
COLLECTION OF POEMS
By Young Soult
the Ryhmer:

ILLUSTRATED WITH
NOTES
And COMMENTARYS:
BY
MONSEIUR
CHATEAUBRIAND
Autor of Travels in Greece,
the Holy land, state of
France, reveiw
Of the Empire,
&c &c &c &c:
Sept 30 AD 1829
PARIS
Published by MDL Pack

---

[1]   Hand-sewn booklet with grey paper covers (5 x 6.4 cm) of ten pages (1 blank), in BPM: BS 115. See Alexander & Sellars, 292-3, for a description of the sketches on the inside of the covers.

Contents
I   Adress to the Genius &c
II The shipwrecked mans complaint
III Song 1
IV Song 2
V   Address to the Genius of War
    There ar[e] 11 notes   P B Bronte

=========

Preface
This volumn is a continuation of the First--
It contains the productions of leisure hours
of young Soult every trifle of a great
genius is worth preserving
signed ‖ Shateubriand

[Adress to the Genius &c]

Onward thou rushest in glory and might
Onward thou rushest all men to affright
Onward thou rushest black clouds are lowering
Onward thou rushest lightning is pouring

and far of stands that mighty tower
Over whose top the cloud doth lower
lightning steams upon its side
which but for it the storm would hide

Thou ridest on terrific clouds
and beneath thee are firghtend crowds
fleeing like sheep arcross the plain
but ah thoult soon upon them gain

And far of stands that might tower the Tower of ALL NATIONS which is a Immensely high tower built on the plan	which but for It the storm would hide meaning. The storm would hide the side of if it was not that the Lightning darting up

of the tower of Babyl[2] on it is situate in the Cheif Glass Town- - - Belongs to the Cheif Genii & is the highest in all the Glass town	on it enlightens it- and beneath the[e] are fri ghtend crowds alluding to the crowds of the people fleeing away from under the Genius

Onward thou rushest a flood & a storm
Onward thou rushest a Terrible form
while low at thy feet hunderds do lie--
Or else afar from thee the cowards do fly

Onward thou rushest Destruction thy name
Onward thou rushest companion of fame
Onward thou rushest ally of war
Onward thou rushest of famine the star

while low at thy feet hunderds do lie	companion of- - - fame- - - - - - -
In the painting there are represented many people are liying beneath the cloud on which the Genius is riding- - - -	of famine the star alluding to war all ways occasion a drea dful famine in the cou[n]try which [h]as lat ley been its seat--
Destruction thy name alluding to the name of the painting which is The Flight of the Genius of Destruction[3] over the glass town	This poem was com posed after soult had seen the paint ing from which the engraving of the--
companion of fame meaning that Destru cton being closely all ied to war and war being akin to fame Destruction must be the-	Flight of the Geniu s of Destruction over the glass town published in the Acts of the Genii (engra vings) by PBB & CB[4]

---

[2]   See pp. 57-58; 70.
[3]   May refer to John Martin's "The Fall of Ninevah," reviewed in *Blackwood's Magazine*, July 1825.
[4]   If the "Acts" ever existed, it is no longer extant.

[The shipwrecked mans complaint]

We ride upon the rageing sea
And soon from our veiw fair land
Thoult Die
we go to make all nations free
Over the stormy waves we fly

Soon will the world in Darkness be
For the glorious sun is going Down
his gold rays glimmer oer the sea
and on thy palaces O town-

On our vessell a flood of light
comes beaming from the sky
tis a sign that we shall conquer
and make the rebels fly

well emulate those heroes
who for their country died
over the billowy ocean
well like an arrow glide

O now the trump is sounding
Of glory & renown-
Over the sea were bounding
Far from our Native town

| fair land thoult Die | on thy palaces O town |
| or thoult vanish | the glass town |

[Song 1]

W[h]ose that who ridest on the storm
Swiftly oer the sky he glides
it is a genius hideos form
but in his hieousness he prides

See now he strides upon a cloud
and blows his trumpet strong
Ah tis the dreadful note of war
Tis loud impetuos--long--

He says ye Nations listen
A war is coming on--
Already Deaths bright met[e]ors glisten
and dance the sky along--

See there they are in clusters
dancing around the sky
See there they are their bright green forms
are leaping shooting high

Around around me meteors
Around around me fly
My name is wars dread messenger
I am a genius high--

When the Genius had said these word[s]
He flew into the air
And I bid you O Nations--
For a dread war prepare

[Song   2]

O those Days wich are long gone by
Which have fled like a morning beam
O those glorious days whe[n] I
Did hear the Falcon scre[a]m

Did climb up those rocks towering grand
to take the Hawks nest which stood there
And when I in my own Native land
Did rouse the Moor cock from his lair

And when when the storms blew around
And lo[u]d thunder rolld through the air
homeward oer the Heath I Did bound
As gaily as if [i]t. had been fair

Those days of my childhood are past
They are fled forever away
Ah now on a shore I am cast
where Despair must end my day

Im cast on a land where th[e] keen
and Pitiless winter winds blow

where the gay summer never is seen
& where nought but the Iceicles grow
O those days they have long gone by
They are fled like a morning beam
Those glorious days when I
lived by brawling Carrils stream[5]

[Address to the Genius of War]

Roll Roll o ye Thunders
And you ye Lightnings fly
Rush on Rush on ye black cloud[s]
And Deluge the sky

while on the Bleak Mountain
I am sitting fo[r]lorn
looking on this Tempest
with deris[i]on & scorn

in the glens & plains below m[e]
There hunderds do lie
benumbed & chilld with horror
unable to fly--

while the rolling Darting rushing
Thunder lightning rain
Are around me around me
but to me they give no pain

Rocks & mountains are tumbling
From the Tempest riven Sky
And the people wild are screaming
At the wrack which is on high

Roll Roll o ye Thunders
And you ye lightnings fly
Rush on Rush on ye torrents
And Deluge the sky

---

5   Refers to Carril, Cuthulin's bard in "Fingal," *The Poems of Ossian*—see p.
24, n. 9.

Appendix
This volumn was written by
Young Soult edited by Mr
De la Chateaubriand --
   =the poems are 5
   = in number

<u>The genius of destruction</u>--
5 verses. and 20 lines--
8 notes and a commentary

———   ———

The shipwrecked sailors--
song 6 versees 24 lines

—————

Song. 6 verses 24 lines

—————

Song 5 verses 20 lines
2 Notes - - - -

—————

To the genius of war 6 v^s 24 1^s.

Addressed to 'the tower of all nations[1]

O thou great thou mighty tower
rising so solemnly
o'er all this splendid glorious city
this city of the sea

thou seeme'st as silently I gaze
a pillar of the sky
so lofty is thy structure
so massive & so high

the dome of heaven is oer thee
hung with it's silver star's
the earth is round about the[e]
with it's eternal bars.

& such a charming dogge[re]l
as this was never wrote
not even by the mighty
& high Sir Walter Scott
U T October 7 1829

---

[1] One side of a single leaf bound in green morocco in the library of William Self, Studio City, California. For the other side, see p. 44. On the 'tower of all nations,' see pp. 56, 64-65 and the Glossary.

On the great Bay of the glass Town [1]

1 tis pleasant on some evning fair
  after a summers day
  when still the breeze & calm the air
  & seawaves gently play

2 to veiw the bay o'er whose still breast
  white sails do softly glide
  how peacefully its waters rest
  like to a sleeping child

3 when the blue concave of the sky
  is clear without a stain
  & the bright arch of heaven on high
  imparts to the wide main

4 its beautiful & saphire glow
  while the suns golden light
  makes all the western sky to glow
  with fair streams like ruby bright

5 then like fair piles of burnished gold
  those marble pillars stand
  palaces of imortal mould
  & castles towring grand

6 while mur'm'ring sounds of pomp & mirth
  rise from the mighty walls
  & wildly mingleing sweep forth
  like thund'ring waterfalls

7 till softened into echo's tone
  on the calm sea they die
  or rising with the <drearest> moan
  on winds of heaven fly

8 to play with them amid the strings
  of harps whose magic voice
  in the lone dark'ned forest sings
  while fairies round rejoice

---

[1]   Part of the first number of **BLACKWOODS YOUNG MENS
MAGAZINE** for December 1829 (BPM: BS 10). See Alexander CB, I, 91.

9 as through tall trees the wild winds moan
& silver moonbeams glance
the harp peals forth with triumphs tone
& spirits mirthful dance
U T November 2
1829

**lines spoken by a
lawyer on the occasion of
the transfer of this magazine**[1]

All soberness is past & gone
the reign of gravity is done
frivolity comes in its place
light smiling sits on every face

gone is that grave & gorgeous light
which every page illumind bright
a flimsy torch glare in the stead
of a bright golden sun now fled

Foolish romances now employ
each silly senseless girly & boy
O for the strong hand of the law
to stop it with its powerful claw

at night I lay my weary head
upon my sofa or my bed
in the dark watches of the night
does flash upon my inward sight

visions of times now pass'd away
when dullness did the sceptre sway
then to my troubled mind comes peace
Would those bright dreams did never cease

thus sang a lawyer in his cell
when suddenly the midnight bell
rang out a peal both loud & deep
which told it was the hour of sleep
                              W T Nov 20 1829

---

[1] Part of the first number of **BLACKWOODS YOUNG MENS
MAGAZINE** for December 1829 (BPM: BS 10). See Alexander CB, I, 91. "W
T" signifies "We Two." Charlotte's table of contents lists the poem as by "U
T." The lawyer referred to in the title is probably Sergeant Bud. See Alexander
CB, I, 95, n. 7 for possible sources for ll. 15-16; l. 18 recalls Pope's *Dunciad*.

**lines by one who was tired of
dullness upon the same occasion**[1]

Sweep the sounding harp string
all ye winds that blow
let it loudly swelling
make sweet music flow

let the thundring drum roll
gladness fly around
merry bells peal & toll
ringing trumpets sound

let the mighty organ
play & peal & swell
roll its floods of sound on
till echos every dell

sweetly sweetly breath[e] flute
pour thy gentle strains
let thy music rise lute
no more Dullness reigns

sweep the sounding harp string
all yee winds that blow
let it loudly swell & ring
make sweet music flow

in your splendid cloud halls
princely Geni dance
till from the vapour walls
bloody lightnings glance

your music is black thunder
therefore let it sound
tear the earth asunder
shake the sky around

---

[1] Part of the first number of **BLACKWOODS YOUNG MENS
MAGAZINE** for December 1829 (BPM: BS 10). See Alexander CB, I, 91.
Charlotte's reply to Branwell. This and the previous poem point to the
differences of interest and emphasis that had arisen between Charlotte and
Branwell, and mark the end of Branwell's involvement with the magazine,
though he obviously regarded the changeover as deleterious. Line 16 recalls
Pope's *Dunciad*.

fair[i]es of the greenwood
Sing amid the trees
pour of joy a bright flood
dance upon the breeze

drink from the bright flower
crowned with crystal dew
<burnish> with the green bower
buds of snowy hue

no longer hid your name is
ye spirits of the air
for now your mighty fame is
set forth in coulours fair

sweep the sounding harp string
all ye winds that blow
let it loudly swelling
make sweet music flow
                    U T
              Nov 21 1829

HARVEST IN SPAIN[1]

Now all is joy & gladness, the ripe fruits
Of autum hang on every orchard bough
The living gold of harvest waves around
The festooned vine empurpled with the grape
Weighed to the ground by clusters rich & bright
As precious amethyst, gives promise fair
Of future plenty. While the almond tree
Springs gracefully from out the verd[ant] earth
Crowned with its em'rald leaves its pleasant fruit
and waveing in the gentle Fragrant breeze
which sweeps o'er orange groves mid myrtle bowers
& plays in Olive woods drinking the dew
which falls like crystal on their tufted leaves
hid by luxuriant foliage from the beam
of the great glorious sun which shines on high
In bright & burning strength casting its rays
to the far corners of the mighty land
enlightning & illuminating all
making it glow with beauty and with joy
& raising songs of gladness and of praise
To God the Father & the king of all

December 9 [C. Bronte deleted] UT 1829

---

[1]   Part of the second number of **BLACKWOODS YOUNG MENS MAGAZINE** for December 1829 in BL: Ashley 157. See Alexander CB, I, 113. The poem is likely more Charlotte's than Branwell's, as indicated by the fact that Charlotte first signed the poem with her own name, then changed to "U T." The change from quatrains to blank verse quite possibly reflects Charlotte's reading of Milton—see Gérin CB, 24.

LAUSSANE
A TRAJEDY
≡|BY.|≡
YOUNG SOULT
In I VOL Octavo
PBB::[1]

LAUSSANE:[2]
A:
DRAMATIC POEM
BY
YOUNG SOULT
The Ryhmer
I VOL
Octavo::
Price 12s
ANNO DOMINII
1829:

---

[1] Hand-sewn booklet with grey paper covers (5.5 x 9.2 cm) of 16 pages (1 blank) in BPM: Bon 138. This is the first of three "dramatic poems" Branwell composed in 1829 and 1830—see also pp. 98-117 and 125-36. Alexander (EW, 21) suggests Byron as a source for Branwell's interest in poetic drama in 1829/30. For another possible source, see the "Horae Germanicae" series in *Blackwood's Magazine* from 1819 on.

[2] Originally the title page began "VALOISE & LAUSSANNE," but "VALOISE" is canceled. The play does not seem to be based on any specific historical or literary incident. Laussane had been a bishopric well before 1423; thus a Count of Laussane would not have existed. The English-French mixture of "John de Valence" is equally problematical. In fact, Branwell may well have borrowed names from Charlotte's *The Swiss Artist* begun in 1829; initially set in the south of France, then shifted to Switzerland—see Alexander CB, I, 92-94; 115-17)—it contains among other characters "Jean de Valence" and "Compte de Lausanne." The Brontë family also owned Scott's *Tales of a Grandfather* (Edinburgh, 1827-28), in which Sir Aymer de Valence chases Robert the Bruce, and Abbé Lenglet Du Fresnoy's *Geography for Youth* (Dublin, 1795). The city of Valence, on the Rhône River, is well known for involvement in battle during the Wars of Religion (1569-98), and for its later association with Napoleon who, on his return to France in 1791, was appointed first lieutenant of the 4th regiment of artillery, garrisoned at Valence.

Paris Printed and
Sold by M^r D'La Pack
Glass town
Seargaent Tree
and
by all
Other booksellers
[figure of Justice][3]

PBB   Page 3

A DRAMATIC POEM BY
YOUNG SOULT
Dec 18   ≡IN THREE ACTS   AD 1829
— PROLOGUE

The scene is laid in France in the year 1423. ALBERT
Count of Laussain in France ofends
another count named John of Liliard
Count Liliard attacks him in his castle drives
him out of it and the count of lausainne
is obliged to fly to Spain and while siting on
the sumit of a Hill near Toledo says and
does as follows

= ACT FIRST
— Scene Ist

Laussaine

My Native Land, no more shall I Behold.
Thy hills, with Castles crowned; thy fruitful plains
No more the splendid scene arrests my gaze
Of Trampling Horses & the gorgeous Train
Of livered servants. To my high command
Obiedient. At my sight no more shall bow
Atennding vassals, but why am I scornd?
Scouted. & weeded From my rightful Land?
By low born rascals? I will rise & go
Will fling the Firebrand of avenging war

---

3   For a description of the figure, see Alexander & Sellars, 293.

Upon the Monsters head! Oil on my soul
Is poured to kindle up the <sa[c]red> flame
Wich soon shall rise; upon his haughty towers
The Beacon blaze; of my returning Fame!
But whose yon stranger?

                                                      A Hermit—*
              HERMIT   startled at seeing a man
                                            in arms[4]

Art thou a Traveller?

              Laussane

Be not afraid I am but who art thou?

              HERMIT

I am a Hermit who. where younder light
From mongst those trees doth gleam lives
                    far retire[d]
From noisy haunts of men where only pain
And vice; and folly; hold their dreadful reing.[5]

              Laussaine

Thourt right. & I have felt their Iorn rod.
Hast thou?

              HERMIT

If thoult go to my Hut then thou shalt hear
The story of my pleasures & my woes
For num'rous as the stars that sparkle high
In the blue Firmament. or as the Leaves
wich clothe the tree in springs heart glading time
both pleasures & my woes have been
But now they both are few as sunny days
when winter wraps his sonwy[6] robe around
all th[e] wide creation wilt thou go or stay?

---

4   Stage directions and lines marked with an asterisk are in longhand.
5   "reign" obviously intended.
6   "snowy" obviously intended.

Laussaine

I will & tell thee mine for both had I

They Depart to the hermitage*

SCENE 2

They both having arrived at the Hermitage
sit down & the Hermit begins his
story

PBB
Dec 18 1829   HERMIT   evening sunset

How changeful are all sublunary things[7]
One day the sun shines bright all Nature smiles
Another & the sky is wrackd with storms
The Thunder rolls the vivid lightning flys
rending the Hardest rocks
                    One time you stand
On the high sumitt of th[e] abode of joy
Another & youve falln in the pit of woe
IN me you see a lonly Hermit who
In woods doth live from Humankind retir'd
I was not always so 3 winters now
Oer me have rolld since I was Blythe & gay
As th[e] merry streamlet wich with jocund Din
Doth gaily rush through meadow & through grove
Dashing its spray upon the sun gilt stones
Under Count Liliard I served—

Laussane

Under Count Liliard, ah ah thou Villain!
may fire & vengeance on thy gui[l]ty head
Fall like the cataract! & crush thee down
To the vile Dust from whence thou like a mist
or pestilential fog arose to slaughter
But thou shalt perish! with thy Tale go on

---

7   This line, combined with the references to the Wheel of Fortune on pp. 111
and 140, suggests Branwell already knew something of medieval philosophy—
perhaps Boethius's *Consolation of Philosophy.*

Hermit—

What means that storm of passion which has <burst>
From thee? & what these words so vehement?

Laussaine

I soon will tell thee but go on. go on

HERMIT

Under Count Liliard I serv'd, & laburd
To serve him single hearted, but alas!
Capricious man! his anger on me Fell
With thunder & with lightning crashing loud
Just at some fellow servants envious tale
He then not hearing as in Justice bound
Defence or prayer for pardon. hurld his lightnings
At me. and Drove me far from his domains:
Though I one day had saved his life in hunting,
Had been his trusty steward many a year.
Waiting for my reward. he left me now
like some old oak wich stands alone & Blasted
By stormy winds. where once it rose on high
the pride of all the smaller throng of Bushes
And of the other Trees. how diff'rent now!
long time I laboured with the pelting storm.
Untill at last. resolved to lead a lonely
And quiet life knowing that amongst all mortals
There is No Happiness I here retired
Now the account of all my woes & sorrows
I've finished, tell me thine.

LAUSSANNE

And dost thou not remembe[r] Count Laussaine?

HERMIT

I Do. I Do. remember him with pleasure,
For he one time seeing me lying frozen
In the cold night in Dark Decembers time
Ordered his servants to recover me.

LAUSSANE

Well I am He[8]

HERMIT

And art thou He can I believe my senses!
And how art thou reduced to this low ebb?

LAUSSANE

This base. vile. envious man the Count of Liliard
Seeing that I was powerful as himself
Forg'd letters to th[e] intent that I my sovreing[9]
Intended to Dethrone & showd them to him
Who to to credulous believ'd the wretch
And frowning on me blasted all my Fire
Forcing me From my native land to Fly,
here I now wander like the frighting[10] hare
Startled at evry wind that Blows—

HERMIT

Thou Trat'rous villain! now thy deeds unfold
Their Bloody leaves to keen inqur'y's sun!
Whose Beams shoot through them bringing to the world
Thy foul thy Base thy cruel slaug[h]trous deeds!

LAUSSANE   after some silence

I have a project

HERMIT

What Ist

LAUSSANE

To morrow thou shalt know

---

8   Preceded by two canceled lines which read:
         And are you He! Can I believe my senses!
         And how art thou reduced to this low ebb?
9   "sovereign" obviously intended.
10   "frightened" obviously intended.

HERMIT

Thou mayst want food?

goes & gets some
they sit down and
eat after wich
they both retire
to rest*

PBB   SCENE ≡
Dec 21 1829.   THIRD.   Morning—sunrise

LAUSSANE.

I will Die!
rather than that Count Liliard should go on.
                    What sayest thou?

HERMIT

the same:
Why should he send his lightnings & destroy
Why should he roll his torrents & overwhelm
                    Whoere he pleases?

LAUSSANE

Then let us to his castle go with minds
Low'ring and Bloody
                    Bent T'e'nwrap in flame
His castle, & that castles inmates, too.
Ill see my native hills again. but I
Will Die them. with the blood. of slaughterd men
Liliar[d] thy aincent house is falling down.
Tumbling to ruins. Thy last hour hath come
Swift as the mornings beam. or swifter still.

HERMIT═══

Ill join thee at the peril of my life lets go

They Both Depart for the

Count of liliards castle a
distance of 200 miles*

ACT SECOND

PBBronte   Scene First   Dec 21 1829.

— INTRODUCTION —

The Count of Laussane and the Hermit
having arrived at the domains of Count
Liliard lodge in a deserted building in a tolerable
state of repair. this scene is laid in that build
ing at 5 oclock in the morning the Hermit alone the
Count of Laussane having gone out to procure per
sons to enter into the conspiracy against Liliard the
Hermit soliloquises thus

HERMIT

Liliard thy star doth sink in tears
Behind th[e] Horizon. & thy years
Are fast approaching to their end.
And down that pathway thou must wend
Where the black mists enwrap thine eyes
Which from thee hide the world its sighs
Its joys its sorrows & its Fame
And more than earthly Tongue can name
O when thou seest that gateway wide
Through which dim ghosts & shadows glide
I fancy I can hear the crys
Which thou will give when to thee flys
A skinny form besmeard with gore
With scythes & arrows covered oer
Round thee I see him wrap his scaly form
And roar with joy like some wild northern storm
Then through the gloomy gate he drags thee on
And thou for ever from this world art gone

Enter Laussane
with 10 more men the chief
of whom are John De Valence
Richard De raymont Albert Fres
noy &c &c &c*

Laussane   with a bitter smile

I fancy that we have got our helpmates here
to crush the haughty Liliard who this day
Shall grovling bloody in the splashy mire
Whith his last breath groan out how am I falln

Fresnoy

Een the degraded gibbet were too good
For him so black and dark his caracter

VALENCE

Enough of him how shall our deed be done

LAUSSANE

You have appointed me. I must command
Silence therefore!

They now sit
down to eat wich is done in sil
ence after they have finished
Count Laussane rises & says*

LAUSSANE

My friends you see that golden Orb wich oer
Yon hill doth rise rejoicing in his strenght
Determined to fulfill his Task. like him
What you have thought of Do & do it well
Like him go on in glory & in joy
Like him shower good around you & like him
By men be reverencd, But now my Friends
We must proceed to overthrow the towers
And all the pride of Liliards bloody count
Now let us go like bloody lions or
like yon bright glorious sun. WILL YOU <DINE>

Omnes   with a loud
shout*

We will we will Now Liliard is your hour

They all depart for liliards
castle*

SCENE THE
SECOND =

PBB Dec 21 1829   The Afternoon =

Count Liliard seated in a Hall in his palace surrounded
by his retinue of knights squires &c &c an
Attendant enters announ[c]ing that 10 men wich
to speak with him

LILIARD

Order them in

Laussane
the Hermit and their followers
enter disguised as Italians*

LILIARD

What want ye Fellows

LAUSSANE

Most Noble Count. we are your humble slaves
The Land of Italy's' our native home
By sad Disasters from that home were forc'd.
like a dark thunder cloud. wich oer the plains
A while doth hover & then on them bursts
with forked lightnings scattering ruin round
So Count Laussan
whom you for ever banished from yo[u]r sight
Came on us drunk with Black & Foul Revenge
He burnt our dwelling & in bloody spite
Oourselves would have destroyd if we had not
Fled blasted exiles from our Native land
And he prusues[11] us like the scorching wind
Which rages in Arapias[12] desart land
To thee most Noble count weve come with pray'res

---

[11] "pursues" obviously intended.
[12] "Arabias" obviously intended.

That thou would have compassion

                    LILIARD   coldly*

Whithout a cause I never steer through whirlpools

                    HERMIT

Most Noble Count we are your slaves & this
Is your Estate therefore—

                    LILIARD

How! my Estate? Then may my anger fall
ON Count Laussane before the Iinquisition
As Heritic he shall be branded and
Fire round him like a snake shall coil
Till all his bones do hiss his muscles crack
And down he falls a worthless blackned coal

                    HERBERT VALOISE   one of Liliards
                                                        Knights*

Ev'n as our count hath said
So shall it be

                    RAYMONT

This moment is the Traitor within sight
of these High tow'rs

                    LILIARD

Treason! arm arm yourselves my gallant
Knights

                    LILIARDS Knights   starting up
                                                        in great anger*

We will! we will!

                    LAUSSANE   drawing his
                                                sword his
                                                followers do
                                                the same

Monster I stand before you
I am Laussane

LILIARD

My Knights go to Deluge this Hall with Blood
blood of these traitors

Liliards Knights
Attack Laussanes followers
who also attack them
Laussane rushes
upon Liliard throws him down
and says*

LAUSSANE

Foul Monster! thou art overthrown
Now bloody mayst thou loudly groan
O were I humble & obscure
O that my Heart & mind were pure
Then should I have escapd this flash*
Which now it[s] might doth on me <lash>*
O then with heart as free as wind.*
Id leave these wiked senes behind*
leave me O leave me just one hour*
I would not were it in my power
howere thou groan howere thous sigh
If tears of blood stream from thy eye
I would not spare thee die then die!!!

prepares to stab him*

LILIARD

My life ebbs out apace & I must die
but O Laussane if pity dwells in thee
have pity oh have pity on my child
To him be has[13] a father & a friend

LAUSSANE

My heart relents I cannot strike the blow[14]

---

[13] "as" obviously intended.
[14] From here to the end, everything is in longhand.

liliard wilt thou amend?

LILIARD

I will I will Lassane

LAUSSANE

Then I relese thee

Liliard

my bright & glorious blessing
<beam> on thee
henceforth Ill walk amid
the pleasant paths
of pure & shining virtue
I give thee back thy lands[15]
and all that thou desir'st

They all desist
from fighting

Liliard

I order I proclaim a sumtous feast
for you Lassane & you his followers
Till such time as your castles ready

THE CURTAIN FALLS

PB Bronte begun
December 1^t ended Dec
ember 23 A D 1829

Young Soult TR

---

[15] This and the next line seem to have been added later and are in the minute print writing.

One eve as through a Darksome lane[16]
I lonely walked Mid scenes of Pain
Before my eyes thick as a wood
A herd of lean parisians stood
And in the Middle of this throng
There stood a youth lank pale and long
A Ballad in his hand held
Which when he read full soon dispelld
All sorrow and in joy they yelled
While on his seat he sung and dirld
As if that day hed' gained the world
Thus oft within his wiry cage
The Ape doth chat and spit and rage

But now the night with dusky wings[17]
Flys on the world & darknes brings

Dŏnavĭt Me, Tŭlliŭs Mŏriĕns[18]
Hŭjŭs Tĕserae, Āit. "Ō Silvĭus
Hujus Donavit me, Tullius moriens
Portia Tesserae, Dicens, "O Silvius!

---

16   The first of three fragments on the last two pages of the manuscript booklet
of **LAUSSANE**, appearing after the signature at the end of the verse drama.
17   The second of three fragments at the end of **LAUSSANE**.
18   The third of three fragments at the end of **LAUSSANE**. These lines seem
to consist of preliminary sketches for a piece of Latin verse composition, a
series of attempts, suggests the late Everard Flintoff of the University of Leeds,
to work up a few detached lines that could be read as Latin poetry, explaining
why the same words appear over and over and are shuffled about. Despite the
obvious problems in grammar and spelling, the heavily Virgilian vocabulary
suggests how much Branwell by the age of twelve had already steeped himself in
the Virgilian epic. At the beginning are seven canceled lines which read:
     Marcius Moriens Donit Dic Hic
     Reserva Hic in Memoriam tu pater
     Dum Habes tu crescam quam candidus flos Agris
     Marcius Moriens donit Donavit Me
     Partus Hujus Tesserae Ait "O Silvius
     Ego dono tu Hic Tessera
     Dum habes tu crescam quam <candidusque>
     Portius   <Hujus> <   >

Tu pater Memoriam hic in Reserva
Dum habes crescam que candidus agris
——————————— Tu quam flos floris
vos   in cruenti
O Romanos ruite Bellum O splendidus Tonitrus
velox quam Fulgor Nubem Jubarque
Terribilis qam Dii qui Regunt in <Caeli>
Laelux quam illic Sul in Caelum <   >[19]
Ei quam stellae quae ardeant in Noctibus
Multis
Sic Ruite vos que
luceamini Aut Expirate
vincite
O vos Romanos ruite in cruenti bellum
Velox quam fulgor Nubes

Ruite bellum in cruenti O vos Romanos
In cruenti O vos Romanos ruite bellum
Volitate quam tonitrus Fulgor splendidus <   >
tonitrus quam Nube
Regunt quam dei terribilis in celi sublime
Cealum in ardens <dire> sol illic quam Italus
que noctius Multi
Et stella quam Ardeant
Vinicte que ruite sic vos aut expirate

Ruite in bellum Romanos O vos cruenti nos

---

[19] The page is badly blotted.

THE

LIAR DETECTED

BY:

CAPTAN JOHN BUD

I VOL QUARto[1]

The Liar unmasked. by Capt Bud
June 19 1830

CHAP I

IT [h]as always Been the Fortune of Eminent Men in all ages and every country to have their lives their actions and their works traduced By a set of unprinciple[d] wretches who having no caracter of their own to support and being to indolent to work vilely employ ther days in spitting their venom on every author of Reputation within their reach Homer had his Zoilus Virgil his Meavius and CAPTAIN TREE his wellesly[2] all these were & are alike contemptible in character and Influence and like vipers can do no more than bite the heels of their Enimies OF Wellesly this new recrurit in their troops I shall give a small account as many of My reader[s] Have propably Not before heard of

---

[1]   Hand-sewn booklet in grey paper covers (5 x 6.4 cm) of 14 pages in BPM: Bon 139. Bud is one of Branwell's pseudonyms. On the inside of the front cover appear several fragmentary pencil sketches and on the inside of the back cover a pencil sketch of a male figure—see Alexander & Sellars, 297.

[2]   Zoilus was a sophist and grammarian living in Amphipolis, 259 BC, whose acerbic criticisms of Plato and Homer made his name proverbial as a malignant and captious critic. Lemprière's *Classical Dictionary*, which the Brontës owned, records that Zoilus was known as *Homeromastix,* or "the chastiser of Homer"; that he apparently met a violent end as a result of his unpopular criticisms; and that "the works of this unfortunate grammarian are lost." Maevius was likewise "a poet of inferior note in the Augustan age" whose attacks on Virgil and Horace earned him his only fame. According to Lemprière, "[h]is name would have sunk into oblivion if Virgil had not ridiculed him in his third ecologue and Horace in his tenth epode."

As a sometime member of the eighteenth-century Scriblerus Club, Parnell wrote *The Life of Zoilus: And His Remarks on Homer's Battle of the Frogs and Mice,* a satire on the pedantic interpretation of texts.

him he was born in England or Ireland I know not which. Sometime in the year 1815. and while yet a Bantling was remarkable for remarking on and spitting at the visitors to his Fathers house and For wich he w[as] often severly reprimanded but this would not do. so I believe he wa[s] sent in the 10 yer of his age to th[e] college of Eton from this place he was soon after removed to Africa his father having gone there It was then he heard of CAPT Tree And though but 15 years of age pushed himself in to all company presented to put forth his "I thinks" and his "I believes" upon him and others for a year or so. rather pitied & despised than otherwise till some ti[me] latley when he put forth a small book of verses this often delighting the ladies of fashion being quoted in the young Misses letters and so forth was swept into Oblivion another and another followed they sharing the same Fate till quoth he. "forshooth I'm the greatest man in the world and thes[e] ladies the best judges" And so he st[r]uck up a little Magazine to instruct them It was now considered high time <to> quash him therefore Tree put o[ut] a small tract for that purpose. instantly the Magazine was stoped the poems ceased to be quoted and the little stock of reputation <had> withered before the breath of that <g>reat man though still the little Author strutted about skleped[3] and barked round the feet of his destroyer like a puppy dog with its tail cut of and to complete the sum of his petty villainy—he vomited forth a dose of scandal and self importance in the shape of an octavo volumn this was published June 18. 1830[4] it is this work that I am to confute for. however mean and paltry it be. the lies it contains are to daring to pass unoticed The little reptile has stung or endeavoured to sting no less than 15 Individuals[5]

Brock	1	Maggrass	8
Bobbadil	2	Bady	9
BUD	3	Douro	10
NAUGHTY	4	Lofty	11
Laury	5	ROUGE	12
Tree	6	Y ROUGE	13
S Bud	7	S Tree	14
		S Rouge	15

3   The *OED* provides no entry for the word "skleped," but Branwell may have intended to use a form of the medieval "clepe," meaning to cry or call out. Alternatively, he may have been using a version of the term "skelp," common to northern dialects. In Lancashire, Northumberland, and Durham, "skelp" means to slap or strike violently, particularly on the breeches or the cheek. In Scottish usage, it has the additional meaning of bounding quickly along.

4   See *AN INTERESTING PASSAGE IN THE LIVES of Some Eminent Men of the PRESENT Time*, Alexander CB, I, 170-76.

5   All these characters appear in an unflattering light in Charlotte's story. Bobadil is based on the boasting, cowardly soldier in Ben Jonson's *Every Man in His Humour*. See also pp. 123; 353 below and Charlotte's **The Poetaster**, Alexander CB, I, 179-88.

CHAP. II

The accomplished and Noble author begins his work by stating that their are no Men in the universe with whom he is so familiar as grooms valets & footmen This he states in a manner which might lead one to suppose that they were Ministers of State Noblemen and Soldiers Now we all know that these persons are proverbial for their lying propensities. Therefore is not this a firm foundation to begin his Fabric of Truth and candour? but it is now time to see what his accusations are. The Footman who told him this budget of Information begins with the interveiw of Capt Tree and Leiut Brock and in Process of the Narrative states that while he was in the Avenue he slipped over a hedge how could that be? a hedge in a covered avenue! is not this sufficient to set the Book and its author down as a lie and a liar! but to proceed again he Mentions the librarian being dressed in a cloak and a Mask. and he (the footman) directly knew who it was. but stop young Boy—how could a footman know one dressed in a cloak and mask & that to in the dark? Impossible! But no[t] content with this our author procceds into the same error the very next page. not yet satisfied the young lad mention[s] that Magrass opened the gate of the cemetry to them now we can prove that Maggrass was then in stumps Island wither he went to attend at the opening of a will and is not yet returned in a few pages after mentioning their 2d visit to the cemetry he states that Sir A H Bady. Edward laury and young Man Naughty slided down a perpendicular wall of smooth Marble 100 feet high this is indeed beyond the bounds of probability unless he could prove that they like flys were possesed of feet with which they could slide down Marble or even glass. he says Tree was a great coward. now could that Man be a coward who [h]as Fought in 8 battles. and in all was covered with wounds blood and glory.

8th error. He makes Hume know the books buiried in the cemetry at a glance. now we concieve Hume no great reader. and Few could tell not only what the books were but to whom they belonged in deep Midnight

9th. He presumes to represent the Marquis of Douro. as being in company with a Monkey an Insolvent & sikly lawere. a sour old gentleman 3 coxcombs & an Idiot. what company for [a] Good Marquis the son of a King!.

10. This learned author say that Racking leaves on[e] whole as befor but a little stretched we deny this for it puts ones bones out of Joint and frequently kills.

11. he Impudently. (and we suppose to highten his own dignity) represents t<he> Marquis of Douro as being a gre<at> freind of his. even calling him Charles love.

12. He now proceeds to a scene which no doubt he think[s] no poet or prose writer can equal for sublimity and grandeur. the Ocean roaring the trees and streams of the vale wich were in all concience far enough of[f] murmering. &c &c. O how I fancy I can see the yong Author brimfull of himself after having finished this passage rise up take the Manuscript in his greasy hand rubb his

head stick out a his shirt frill give a few hems pop into Popes homer[6] to see if
their was a passage their equal to it then sit down his self esteem no way abated
and fag away like one on a wager
But we have now despatched the little shop boys volumn in Blue morroco back
with. :lt edges. in truth a fit present for. Miss M. H—me.[7] or any of her
hysterical and delicate crew. therefore we must proceed to see the crimes for
which this Jupiter [h]as fulminated his thunders at us.[8] They are as follows

Brock	Felony & Treason
Bobbadil	An ugly count[e]nance
BUD	Conivance at theft
BADY	Body snatching
Douro	keeping bad company
Laury	Body snatching
Lofty	puppyism
Magrass	conivance at theft
Naughty	body snatching
Rouge.	Extravagance
S BUD	Folly
S ROUGE	Idiotism
S Tree	Felony and treason
Tree	Felony and treason
Y Rouge	Coxcompry

CHAP. III

On[e] Day latley as I was siting in my study I recieved a note to be Present. at A
dinner given by Lord L—d. that day. to several of the nobility Gentry & C. in
the glasstown I Accordin[g]ly made my appointment and came at the time
perfixed. when I arrived I found a large company among whom were the little
puppy C Wellesly. Fine Furniture an excellent dinner. &c. After the dinner was
done we set to our bottles and <then we> talked about Politics. the state of
France. Poachers Parrys government &c. the women about the Fashion town

---

[6]   Although there is no evidence that the Brontë family owned a copy of
Pope's translation of Homer, Branwell seems to have had access to a copy—see
p. 166.
[7]   Marian Hume.
[8]   By the mid-nineteenth century, *The Times* was known by the nickname
"Jupiter Tonans" or "the Thunderer," an allusion to a phrase used by the assistant
editor, Edward Sterling: "We thundered forth the other day an article on the
subject of social and political reform." Compare to Alexander CB, II, Part II,
221.

news & we enjoyed our selves for sometime till the Ladies and amongst other[s] this Wellesly withdrew. and shortly after he was of the master of the house remarked what a foolish lad he was to have so many monkeys about him

Young. R— answered. but I believe he is delighted with [them] as a baby with its doll. I suppose [it] does not indeed cannot give him the return of affection

CAPT T— well enough for him well enough for him it diverts him from deluging the world with his paltry tracts

Young S—t. what do you think of Lord Charlses "VISION"[9] Is it not a capital performance?

Young R—e. very so so I believe

Capt T It is no more than a repitition of a former work of His I forget the name. wich indeed was not worthy of Remembering But his whole works are of the same stamp light trifling foolish & giddy without one redeeming exelence to Rescue them from that Oblivion. into wich they must inevitably Fall.

Old R— yet he seems to consider himself an admirable writer

Capt T— he does as do many others I mean not to Include Young S— and the Marquis of D—ro. their writings show mind thought and Poetry his is but empty Bombast

Young S— gentlemen you seem to hard upon him I must beg leave to differ from you in all respects as it regards him

YOUNG B— why you yong S— are patronised by his Father and Brother therefore in the First place you—

YOUNG R— Oh Sir do grant us a respite from your First Second and third places

YONG B I conceive sir that their is no Article in law which authorizes you to stop my conversaiton therefore —

LORD L— come come dont quarrel

CAPT T— what do you think of his general character?

Lord L— a rather silly but amiable young Man

YOUNG R— amiable! indeed! does he not Fight and attend rows every day of his life have I not seen Ned L— go to the palace and request him to attend a Battle between two Factions and did he not with the greatest alactrity join him?

YOUNG S— I believe sir you have a little overcharged the picture

CAPT. T— not at all I my self have seen him do these things and more also but what think you Capt BUD of his caracter?

MYSELF I am sorry to say I entertain no very Favourable opinion of him. But the contrary he is I think a Boy uterly destitute of all common understanding Foolish and Inconsiderate in the extreme But with a few small marks of some sort of a genius

CAPT T— I myself do think that he is a child utterly without Talent or genius of any sort spit[e]ful to the greatest exess presumptous lying and vain add to these Foolish Fanciful and Ridiculeus. then I think you have his character.

---

[9] See Charlotte's poem, "The Vision: A Short Poem" (13 April 1830), Neufeldt PCB, 32.

The party now seperated for it was near Midnight and I went home to think on the I may say public voice given as to the character of Charles Wellesly

---

CHAP IV

Now Charles Wellesly I have given you the voice of the public and I myself Praising and dispraising of you I have reveiwed faithfully and candidly your last Publication I have corrected your errors I have discovered your Falshoods And without Malice or spleen I shall now give you my Advice attend to it and profit by it "You have hitherto been been Fanciful and giddy to exess And no one not even your Father [h]as ventured to stop the torrent of Impetousity which you are I hope unmeanly bringing on your future prospects in life If you Charles conduct yourself in life with a caution and dignity worthy of you you may rise to eminence and Flourish in greatness a[nd] prosperity. on the other hand if you continue in your present course Poverty Shame despair and their attendant evils will over take your shortly and tossed on the ocean of human existence with out and anchor or compass. you will at last be consigned to a prison or brought to the Block or die an outcast from all human society[10]

S‖ CAPTAIN. J. BUD,—

WORKS BY. BUD

A Treatise on political Economy in 3 vols
quarto. 3$^£$ 3^s

2
Discourses on the Eelements
10 vols quarto. 10$^£$ 10^s.

---

[10] For Charlotte's response to this attack on Charles Wellesly, see **The Poetaster** and **Conversations**, Alexander CB, I, 179-96; 234-39.

CARACTACUS[1]
A DRAMATIC ≡
≡ POEM BY ≡
YOUNG ≡
Ξ SOULT
IN §SSSSSSSSS
I
VOLUMN Ξ
§ QUARTO

§ CARACTACUS.
A DRAMATIC POEM.
BY PATRICK Branwell
Bronte.
IN
ONE ≡
VOLUMN §§
§§ QUARTO
B
Y
YOUNG (TR)
SOULT

Cheif Glass Town printed and sold
by ≡ ≡
≡ SEARGEANT TREE
DUKE of Wellingtons
Glasstown. S. price & Co
CAPTAIN E PArrys
Glasstown S. Jenrills
CAPTIN J. Ross's
= Glasstown & Caleton

"In Dramatic Poetry the passions are the cheif thing and in
"Proportion as exelence in the depicting of these is ob
"tained so the writer of the poem takes his class am

---

[1]   Hand-sewn booklet in grey paper covers (13.2 x 10.5 cm) of 20 pages,
including 3 pages of battle statistics at the end, in the Brotherton Collection,
University of Leeds.

"ong Dramatic authors."

C. BUD'S Synopis of Dra[2]
matic writing Vol I. p 130.
JUNE 26. A D 1830.

CHARACTERS≡

I	CARACTACUS _____	16 Times mentioned
II	MUMIUS ____ Fabulous _____	23 _____
III	CARTISMANDUA_____	8 _____
IV.	CLAUDIUS_____	6 _____
V.	CARAUSIUS __ Fabulous _____	3 _____
VI.	ICENUS _____ Fabulous _____	4 _____
VII	BRIGANTES___ Fabulous _____	1 _____
VIII.	OSTORIUS_____	4 _____
IX	CAPTN of the GAURDS _____ Fabulous	2 _____
X.	BARDS _____ Fabulous _____	1 _____
XI	PEOPLE OF ROME_____	1 _____
XII	BRITONS _____	2 _____
—	XII. _____	72._____

PREFACE

Of The events recorded in this poem, those
which are not ficitious are took from the early
English History. And the truth stands thus
"When the Romans under the command Ostorius Scapula
AD. 51. Invaded Britain Caractacus a British King under
took to defend his country and therefore put
him self at the head of a large army of
Britons. with these he retired to the Mountains.
of Wales perpetually harrassing the Romans for
Nine years. till at last being obliged to
come to a descicive Enggagement. wherein
he was defeated. but however he fled to Cart
ismandua Queen of the Brigantes who basely

---

[2]   Compare the very similar comment on the title page of **The Revenge**, p. 125.

delivered him up to the Romans. he was with
Other prisoners carried to Rome when he was
Brought there nothing could exceed the curiosity
of the people to behold a man who for Nine
years had braved their choicest legions on his
part he testified not the least sort of dejection
and while the other captives were meanly
beggeing their pardon Caractacus stood
before the Tribunal with an Intrepid air
And seemed rather willing to accept pardon
than meanly sollicitous of sueing it
And in consequence of his manly and heroic
behaviour. the Emperor Claudius gave him
and them full and Immediate LIBERTY.

   This is the true history of Caractacus
But whatever deviations I have made must
be ascribed to the Nature of the Poem not
Myself. which allows far more Latitud in this
respect than I have given it, but I now
Leave the work to my readers let them
who are Impartial judge me and my work
Not the base and snarling critics who having
No exelence of their own employ themselves
In underating those of Others[3]

---

[3] Although Lempriere's *Bibliotheca Classica* notes Tacitus' *Annals* as the source for Caractacus, it is not the source for Branwell's Preface. The Preface may well consist of notes compiled from various sources, including William Mavor's *Universal History,* 25 vols., London, 1802-4, a work Charlotte recommended to Ellen Nussey in 1834 (SHB LL, I, 122). Some similarities with phrasing in VI, 167-77 suggest Branwell had read Mavor, yet the Preface contains details not included in Mavor. Branwell's "deviations" are in fact considerable. The characters he identifies as "fabulous" (Mumius, Carausius, Icenus, Brigantes) bear no resemblance to the originals. The Iceni and Brigantes were tribes defeated by Publius Ostorius. If Branwell took the names Carausius (whose name also appears in *Ossian*—see "The War of Caros") and Mumius from Lempriere, he changed their characters completely. Lempriere describes Carausius as "a tyrant of Britain for 7 years," and Mumius as a Roman consul who destroyed Corinth, Thebes and Chalcis by order of the Senate but "did not enrich himself with the spoils of the enemy . . . . He was so unaq[u]ainted with the value of the paintings and works of the most celebrated artists of Greece . . . that he said to those who conveyed them to Rome, that if they lost them or injured them, they should make others in their stead." Thus Mumius' treachery and his conversation with the Queen in Act I, scene i, as well as the whole of Act I, scenes ii and iii; Act II, scene i; and the final dialogue between Mumius

Paris June 28.   Young Soult
Anno Dominii 1830.   P B B

ACT, FIRST.
P B Bronte June 26.≡
AD 1830. AD.
SCENE
I

The palace of Cartismandua. the queen seated on her throne
Caractacus Brigantes and Carausias k[n]eeling before her
The Druids &c standing round

≡ ≡CARACTACUS

O Queen a humble suppliant kneels before you
Caractacus my Name once high in Power
But late there came to desolate my land
The Romans keen in war and eagle eyed
They Drove us from our homes and native forests
They burnt our towns and ravaged all our lands
Long I withstood but Fortune on them shone
And we were worn with famine plagues & care
Like billows rushing onward to the shore
Even so they came in thousands after thousands

---

and Claudius are Branwell's inventions. The comments concerning critics are
aimed directly at Charlotte, part of the literary rivalry that had developed between
them (see p. 73, n. 1, and Alexander EW, 65-6).

Caractacus withstood the Roman army for nine years before being defeated
and escaping to Brigantia (Yorkshire) to request aid from Carthismandua (or
Cartimandua), a Roman matron married to the Chief of those parts. Caractacus
was also known by the Britons as Caradoc (or Cradoc), a king of Welsh origin
whose exploits were recounted in various early histories, folktales, and ballads.
Caradoc was also mythologized as a knight of the Round Table in several
Arthurian legends. Drayton mentions Caradoc being led naked to Rome in
Polyolbion (1612). In 1809, Byron alludes to the "spectacle" of *Caractacus*
produced by Thomas Sheridan at the Drury Lane Theatre, a version of
Beaumont's *Bonduca* minus the dialogue: "And Beaumont's pilfered Caratach
affords/ A tragedy complete except in words" (Byron, *English Bards and Scotch
Reviewers*).

T'oppose were vain. So slowly we withdrew
And wandered Exiles. till amid the woods
We saw to cheer our souls these rising towers
And now O queen I kneel before your throne
A suppliant not for my life but my country's

CARTISMANDUA

Arise Caractacus I know your deeds
Your Wars your exploits fame round all the earth
Has blown them In my Palace rest your selves
Till from these clouds the smiling beams of Fortune
Burst forth And show the way to glorious victory

CARACTACUS

O[4] Queen your name for this in after times
Shall brightly shine "the Helper up of Britain"

MUMIUS a Druid

Will th[e] Romans give rewards to those who take you?

CARACTACUS

Yes! For my head they offer crowns and kingdoms
And heaps of gold

CARTISMANDUA

Proclaim a splendid Feast
To receive a King with Honour worthy of Him
Go now Caractacus you needs must want
Sweet rest for 'tis the Balm of every pain
28*[5]

CARACTACUS and his Fol
lowers depart leaving the
queen alone with her
Druids and a cheif
named Icenus.

---

4   The opening words of these two lines are written across a sketch of a ship
under sail—see Alexander & Sellars, 297.
5   Asterisked numbers are Branwell's.

Druid MUMIUS
Cheif ICENUS

MUMIUS

Queen herest thou what he said? Crowns kingdoms gold
are offered for him   Ill would it beseem
One so renowned for wisdom not to seize
That way to power shown to thee by the Romans.

CARTISMANDUA

What say you! Shall I act so base a part
As to deliver up a stranger, one who fled
To me for shelter? rather would I die!

MUMIUS

Stop queen! The gods require not such a strict
Performance of the rights of Hospitality
They offer to thee riches glories honour
Why should thou slight these offers?

CARTISMANDUA

                             Slight them! yes!
They are no gods who offer these to me.
To yeild a stranger to the mercilless fury
of the ferocious and cool blooded Romans!
T'were not the act of Human creatures rather
Of the most savage & the wildest beasts

MUMIUS

No one shall know the deed thou needest but tell
The Roman General thou hast seized Caractacus
In He will enter like a noiseless River
And seize the wretch among his silent waters.
Icenus what sayest thou?

ICENUS.

                             Nought but what thou sayest
For what else should I say? seize him O Queen!
Or else Thou wilt repent when in the dungeon
Thou liftest up thy eyes and sees him seated

High on thy throne thy scepter in his hand
King of thy country having seized thy power
Who to securly trusted him.

CARTISMANDUA

I waver. shall I? no the—

MUMIUS

                    away the thought!
The rights of Hospitality! away! away!
Icenus go thou to the Roman general
He's not far distant

ICENUS

        Yes and quickly to!

                        Departs*6

CARTISMANDUA

Stop O Icenus stop—what can I do
T' avert the storm wich hangs upon thy head
Caractacus. Mumius I am a queen
Remember that. how dare you—

MUMIUS

                Kill me Queen
But if thou dost the vengeance of the gods
Shall fall upon the[e] like some dreadful Tempest
Wich rushes on the plain with Horrid noise
Sweeping away whole woods and villiages
Into Eternal everlasting ruin.

                        All depart*7

---

6   Asterisked stage directions are in longhand.
7   The margins of the manuscript page contain various attempts at spelling the word "grief."

SCENE. 2D.

Night a Hall in Cartismandua's palace. CARACTACUS. and his companions in misfortune CARAUSIUS and BRIGANTES seated together conversing

BRIGANTES

What unexpected changes oft the Gods
Give to us It is like a lowring sky
Black clouds and Tempests overcast its surface
While we despair of all but storms and waters
But Lo the clouds Break up a Beam of sunshine
Shoots through the Hazy mist to cheer our souls
The flowers lift their heads the wild birds sing
And all is joy and
ightness so our state
Lately the Romans with a bloody fury
Oerwhelmed us drove us from our native soil
But now we find releif and joyous comfort
Protected by this queen

CARACTACUS

                    Tis so my friend
But Hope not thou to higlly[8] damp forbodings
Now chill my soul I feel a surety
We have not yet passed through our hardest journey
Sawst thou that Druid hoary white with age
Who stood beside the throne sawst thou his frown
His eye which shoot upon us with a Radiance
Which showd that Death was brooding in his heart
For though I fear him not. yet still Ill heed him

CARAUSIUS

Fear him! no!

> Enter
> Ostorius Roman general
> Mumius the Druid
> with soldiers

MUMIUS

---

8   "highly" obviously intended.

Now we have caught the lion in the coils!

CARACTACUS

Stand back! what want you here?

MUMIUS

Come soldiers bind him
CARACTACUS

Stand back or die! What you O Roman here?
Think on my power on the well fought feild
Of Cambria when the rivers red with blood
Ran rolling to the main Think on my power
When with my sword I forced your Men to yeild
And made my way through lanes of slaughtered foes!

OSTORIUS

I know you Briton then you conquerd me
But now your turn is come or yeild or perish!

BRIGANTES

100*
What! yeild to you Foul Roman? no I would not
Even though I stood with thousand enimies
On all sides round me with uplifted swords

MUMIUS

Rush on them soldiers bind them with these chains
Kill those who dare oppose you

CARACTACUS

Old Man what say you
Die first thyself!

rushes on MUMIUS
who flies off

CARAUSIUS

O Brave and valiant man!

The Roman[s] rush
on & seize
all but Caractacus
who stands still
menacing them with
his drawn sword

CARACTACUS

Come on ye Romans is a wall before me?
What hinders you from rushing on me? Come!
How ist that you before whose conqring Eagles
Whole kingdoms tremble kneeling to adore you,
How ist that you are held at bay by one?
One only man and he a wandring exile!

Ostorius

Give thyself up

CARACTACUS

Take me I stand before you

Ostorius

Rush Soldiers bind him fast with Iron chains

ROMANS

we dare not!

CARACTACUS

as a rock I stand around
Whose base the billows dash and loudly murmur
Striving to shake it but amid the clouds
It soars unmindful of their din

MUMIUS again enters
surrounded by guards
and trembling—

MUMIUS

Gold Romans

Gold will I give you this shall be your pay

holds out a purse of gold—

CARACTACUS

advancing towards them

I now myself surrender. keep thy gold
Old man for all the world is not like thee
All prize not gold as the cheif human god

They take him

MUMIUS

Now burn him on the Altars of our gods

OSTORIUS

Thy gods old man. But know the Romans care not
For god[s] like thine. Caractacus thou goest
To Rome Imperail Ceaser their shall judge thee

Him & his companions are led of—

SCENE, 3D. s̄ s̄

A another room in the palace of Cartismandua. MUMIUS
and Cartismandua herself. with Bards.

MUMIUS

Well I have executed half my purpose
I've set my face against the least compassion
Like some vast Rock its stony front opposing
To all the rage of warring elements
But still tis not accomplished yet the villain
Must go to ROME th' eternal city there
To meet the scorn and the reproach of thousands
For having braved so long their choicest armies

CARTISMANDUA

To meet the scorn and the reproach of thousands!
O Mumius could they scorn the man who waged
A war of Nine long years against all their force
The force of ROME?

MUMIUS (aside)

    Ah! does the queen still thwart me
But she shall suffer.

           Enter Icenus—
           with the reward
           given them by the
           Roman general

ICENUS

    Here is the reward.
Of all our Bloody deeds I now repent
What have we done! the thought like peircing lightning
Strikes me we have betrayed a confiding stranger

MUMIUS   eagerly snatching
               at the money

What now Icenus? Why so womanish
Call up your spirits like the new fledged Eagle
Lo here is gold enough to buy a kingdom
Half's for my self & take the rest to thee
And to the queen for I—I have worked the Hardest

CARTISMANDUA

No Mumius and Icenus take your gains
I will have none I wash my hands of all
Your foul and murdrous and base conspiracies.

             (She departs)

MUMIUS

Icenus! how she thwarts us let us kill her
For she'll not let us rest till in the tomb
She lies

ICENUS   starting back

Ha! villain! Murdrer! base conspirator!
What having kill[ed] thy guest at least nigh killed him
to kill thy Queen!

MUMIUS

Soft softly speak Icenus
Or elese the Bards will here our plots and darkness
Icenus now I feel an Inward dampness
A horror in my soul tis guilt guilt guilt!
Sing Bards It may divert my Melancholy

BARDS

sing this
song

1   UNTO our Fathers in the sky
                This joyful song we raise
         Round the whole earth their fame shall fly
                Born by our tuneful lays

2   If, on the Billowy ocean
                Like misty clouds they sail
         Or on the Tempest howling loud
                Or on the rageing gale

3   Or If in distant kingdoms
                They pour the storms of war
         Upon the cursed Inhabitants
                In civil hate and jar

4   Or if in Desert Halls they
                Sit like giants hoar
         Our gladdning and our tunful songs
                Into their ears well pour

5   Like sweetly murmring waters[9]
                Which through the meadows flow

---

9   In the margin is a sketch of a wall with two animals, one on top and one at
the bottom, and a waterfall and river below.

Or like the loud and passing wind
　　Which mid the forests blow

6　　And when thou diest O Mumius
　　　　Thy fame shall swiftly run
　　From the rising to the setting of
　　　　The chariot of the sun

7　　Unto our fathers in the sky
　　　　Our joyful songs we'll raise
　　Round the whole world their fame shall fly
　　　　Born by our tuneful lays

End of the
FIRST ACT P B B
June 26 1830

ACT, THE, SECOND
SCENE FIRST

CARACTACUS having been conveyed to the City
of Rome is seen seated in a dismal Dungeon Lighted by
A glimmering lamp and the Moonbeams which stream through
the small grated window.

CARACTACUS

Fortune how ficle and how vain thou Art[10]
One hour thou smilst upon th' unhappy wretch
Who is deluded by thy tempting offers
The next struck by thy withring frown he falls
In to the Black abbyss of hop[e]less woe
Just so the sky unspotted by a cloud
Fortelleth not the Dark and coming Tempest
All is serene but lo above the brow
Of yon high Mountain thick and gloomily
It comes oershadowing all the wide stretched plains
Feirce lightning flashes from its sides and Thunder
Mixed with the Rain rolls round the darkned world
And where so late was calm and joyous sunshine   200*

---

[10]　See p. 80, n. 7; 140, n. 11.

Now stretches wide a bleak and stormy region
For thus O Fortune hast thou been to me
Who late in Britain braved Romes choicest legions
But thou and fell Adversity conspired
To throw me from mine eminence, Adversity!
Who enters in the Roofs of king and peasant
All men are subject to its visits all men
Have seen its haggard features, feirce as Lightning
It hurls the Monarch from his throne the Proud man
I[t] makes to bite the dust in wild despair.
Exepting Hope naught can allay its terrors
HOPE which een in the Dungeon lights the eye
Of the poor criminal and bears him up
When tossed upon lifes wide and stormy Ocean
And the Huge billows of Adversity break oer him
And now while in this damp and darksome cell
O HOPE I cast my lingring eyes upon thee
Thou art my Lamp whose bright but glimmering rays
Do light me on my way when oer Adversitys
Thorny and darksome wilderness I travel.
Nor wilt thou leave my footsteps till I gain
That Broad and stormy torrent which no man
Has eer oercome. "DEATHS loud and billowy waters—"

Enter MUMIUS the
British Druid
who
wis[h]ing to see Car
actacus'es death
has come to Rome
to see it. and also
Guards.
to take him
before the Em
pror Claudius

MUMIUS

Rise up thou wretch and make obeisance to me
Is not thy spirit broken yet?

CARACTACUS

No Mumius
Nor ever will be tis a Giant Oak
Which winds and storms do not oerthrow but strengthen

MUMIUS

Wretch Villain know that like a criminal
Thourt to be dragged before the Roman Empror
And there to die amid the shouts of thousands
Look here is my reward for taking thee

                                                    Holds out his gold

Do you not Envy me my riches villain?

CARACTACUS

No Mumius I do not but here this
Not all the gold and wealth of Rome would tempt me
To do the like to thee or such another
Would I betray. A wandring exiled stranger[11]
Who trusted I wo[u]ld save him from the fury
Of the Merciless Romans! never Mumius never!!!

CAPT^N of the GUARD.

CARACTACUS come to await the judgement
Of Romes Imprial monarch, as to you
Old Briton know we Romans do not Revrence you
So scoff not at th[e] oppressed & Desolate
Though He must die yet not a better fate
Awaits you, Rascal.

MUMIUS

O Valiant Roman if youll get me pardoned
This gold is yours.

CAPTAIN

Ah! Ah! vain man nor gold nor all thy tresure
Could get thee pardoned if it were decreed
That you should die but t'is not yet commanded

MUMIUS

O Valiant Roman much I thank you for
Your generosity to me your slave.

---

11   In the margin appear the words "Touton Tetrarch Tou Tetra."

gladly
puts up his
purse
All Depart.

SCENE. 2.

The Ampitheatre. Claudius the Empror seated on his throne surroundy[12]
by his attendants &c Ostorius his general with several others
on his right hand the British Cheifs
Brigantes and Carausius. with other minor Britons
Before him. and Immense crowd of Romans &c looking on—

CARAUSIUS.   kneeling

Spare us great Empror spare us yet a little
We do Implore thee O august and mighty
Claudius before whose golden Eagles fly
Whole kingdoms and before whose awful frown
Their Monarchs fall we in the Dust for pardon
Repentant beg, And never more against thee
Will we uplift our vain and feeble arms

BRITONS

O King we echoe these our cheiftians prayrs

CLAUDIUS

Where is Your King CARACTACUS go Soldiers
Go bring him hither

SOLDIERS

Yes but lo! he comes

CARACTACUS
Enters surrounded
by soldiers with
Mumius who very
officiously has come
with them

---

[12] "surrounded" obviously intended.

CLAUDIUS

Art thou the king of these ferocious Britons
Who hast for Nine long years braved all our Legions?

                    CARACTACUS   Advancing forward
                                                  And standing intrepidly
                                                  before the Emprour

Yes I am he. I glory in my deeds
And if I had the power this glorious city
Should soon be one wide waste of tossing flames!
And you O King should Perish by these arms!
What did I do? defend my Native country
From desolation from the Merciless fury
Of you O greedy and destructive Romans!
Ah! how is it that you O mighty Romans
Possesed of such Magnificence. these Temples
Whose glittring domes shine like th' Meridian sun
This wide spreads city and whole hills of gold.
Whose glory fame has spread round all the world!
How is it possible that you should envy
Me a Barbarian in my Native forests
A peacful cottage and unharming people!
But such you are—can never rest content
Without the world lies prostrate at you[r] feet
But King your victorys resound as much
Unto your honour as to my disgrace
For had I given up the war as hop[e]less
When first it shed its lurid beams upon us
Then neither my dishonour nour[13] your glory
Would eer have drawn the thunders of applause
Which now I hear from these your Mighty subjects
Not then would all this hight of Human granduer
This Pomp these golden Eagles and these chariots
And high Triumphal Arches had been planned
But softly stealing waters of Oblivion
Had flowed on you Ostorius and on me
But Roman now I stand allone before you
Not with my armies and the storms of war
But a poor pris'ner bound with Iron chains
I'm at your mercy if my life be spared
I shall remain an everlasting monument

---

[13] A variant of "nowhere" (*OED*).

Of Roman clemency and moderation

CLAUDIUS

Caractacus thou now hast shewn thyself   300*
An Enimy worthy of the Roman arms
Thy Air thy stature and thy kingly dignity
Do give thee title to complete forgivness
SOLDIERS RELEASE THERE BONDS.

Roman People

Long live the Empror!

Britons

We thank they with our hearts most mighty Claudius

MUMIUS   throwing himself
before the Empror

Hear me O Empror hear me of thy clemency
This villain whom thou now hast rashly pardoned
Thinks to dethrone thee nay he has already
Planned his design. Then let the executioner
Send him a victim to the shades below!

CLA[U]DIUS

Old Man! who art thou!

CARACTACUS

Great Empror this his he
Who has betrayed me to your conqring legions
With such a malice has might well befitt[14]
One whom I'd persecuted and destroyed
His House and all his wealth with wasting flames

CLAUDIUS

Hence with him give the wretch that recompense
His guilt demands go soldiers go behead him

---

[14] The word "! CLAUDIUS" appears at the bottom of the manuscript page.

MUMIUS

Mercy O Empror! Spare me yet a little!
Grant me a day of Life and all my gold
My choicest treasurs I will yeild to thee
For but a hour one only hour of Life
I cannot die!

CLA[U]DIUS

Wretch thinks thou that thy gold
Can buy thee Life no! to the scaffold with him

MUMIUS

Then must I die! O Life fly swift away!
I Hate the sun! I sicken at the sight
But yet I dare not no I will not die!
Despair now seizes me I feel the flames
Of guilt of opened guilt CARACTACUS
I have betrayed the[e] and now thou'st conquerd
Little did I expect this thunder bolt
This peir[c]ing arrow this unmoveable sentence!

He is Hurried
of to excectut
ion by the
soldiers and
followed by the
shouts of the
Romans & Brit
ons.

T
KE≡[15]   330 lines

CURTAIN FALLS

Young Soult.

Begun June 26. Ended. June 28.
AD 1830 therefore I have finished It
In 2 days Sunday wich happened between
being left out

PB Bronte[16]

---

[15] See p. 30, n. 25.
[16] Following the play are three pages of tables of battle statistics, with the word "Military" in both lower case and upper case Greek letters at the top of the first page.

LeTTERS
From
An Englishman
I VOL 8tvo
PB B—te
FIRST SERIES[1]

LETTERS::
FROM
An Englishman to his Relative
IN::
LONDON:::

[Figure of Mercy and Justice][2]

C^t Ross's Glasstown
Printed
and
Sold by
Seargt, Windlass.
= cheif Glass:=
= TOWN =
SEARGT Tree &c &c &c
: Patrick Branwell Bronte
September
6th
Anno Domini
1830[3]

---

[1]   Hand-sewn booklet with grey paper covers (5.5 x 9.3 cm) of 18 pages (one canceled) in the Brotherton Collection, University of Leeds.
[2]   See Alexander & Sellars, 206.
[3]   The date is in longhand.

Preface

I shall not in this place say wether these Letters or the Incidents contained in them are true or false neither shall I mention my name but here I issue it forth into the world Let candour and Justice judge for me

Signed
CAPT F—[4]

Rosses Glass town =
September 6th
Anno Dominii
1830[5]

Letter the
I

Glasstown Sept 2
An Dom 1830

My dear Freind
    Truely this is a wonderful country when at England I had as adequate an Idea of it as you would have of the Pyramids of Eygipt were it told you that they were larger than nutshells wherever we go we meet with something new something to arrest the attention Mills with rooms nearly a mile long towers a mile high Palaces unlike anything however grand to be seen in the whole world besides street[s] as wide as a valley and to crown the whole that wonderful structure the Tower of Nations where shall I find words to express any Idea of that amazing Building It disdaining all aquaintaince with this lower world
    "Soars from the vale & midway leaves the storm"[6]

It leave[s] clouds tempest and lightnings at its base and seeks the aquaintance of the skys alone by Itself it seem[s] some vast Formless and Incomprehensible remains of another world and when looking on it we are struck with so great an awe that we could bow before it as the ruler the Director of All But I must now leave it to accquaint you with some Few adventures since my arrival in this Magnificent city with the account of my Landing I will not trouble you suffice it to say that when I gained the shore I went to an Hotel where I stoped for the night next morning I went out to enquire for some of my old Friends whom I knew resided their—'ay' said one man from whom I enquired of them Ay lad youll never hear of them again and if you dont be off my rare man youll share a bite of their cake this news astounded me for from it and judging by the cruel

---

4   Captain Flower. The Preface is in longhand.
5   The date is followed by the initials "J et M."
6   Oliver Goldsmith, "The Deserted Village," l. 190.

caracter of these monsters I concluded that they must have slain them At last however I found your Freind MacDougal and Mr Law These men served to cheer the solitude in which otherwise I should have been in. alone amid 20 millions of human beings! what a thought! but however I must now haste to my subject and Pass over the many events which happened to me the First 3 weeks of my residence here and also what I have heard and seen These I will treat of to you in another letter but I will now relate to you the Following Incident which happened to me

ONE Night, on the 2d week of my arrival I was determined to take a walk about the city Therefore taking my directory and guide book I sallied out after strolling through several spacius and Magnificent streets lighted like the rooms of a fine Palace I stopped by the shop door of the great bookseller Tree while I was standing there up comes a young Lad apparently 19 years of age most gaily dressed and his manners from what I could see of him were most light and giddy[7] some times he was laughing and sometimes scolding every body he met in the most virulent and abusive manners then flitting abut like a butterfly which seemed in all respects a Fit emblem of him

"Well" said he staring at me with his large blue eyes (the likes of which I have never seen in our country) well, you fool what are you gawking at here get along with you and behave at least like a sensible beast young man said I I am seeking for a guide to show me the city Well he answered you couldnt Find a Fitter person than me Ill show you every Nook from Braveys inn to Tom cuteheads Pothouse of from the Tower of Nations to Dick Scavengers pigstye come along with me and trot a little Faster you liverless Englishman I was you may guess now glad to find shuch an agreeable Cicerone and quickly followed him where he chose to lead me we thus went on he showing me the beauties of the city and also the various person[s] whom we saw saying who they were and expatiating on their characters in the most lively and agreeable manner possible till I was quite delighted with him as any would have been however morose and of however Impenetrable feeling and Indeed I was wholy taken up with listning to him, and admiring the City and its occupants who passed by with the noise of a torrent by thousands nay millions a resistles Ocean of Humanity

never ending still begining[8]

At last however having rambled about for nearly 5 hours which rolled by with the speed of lightning of a sunbeam we arrived at a spacious and magnificent but rathe[r] gloomy palace which frowned over the whole side of a street here my young conductor stoped and lightly leaping up the steps of the great door beconed me to follow him I did so concluding that this was his Fathers house He then opened the door himself not waiting for porter or servant And led me into a large room where was a blazing Fire and Supper on the spacious and well furnished Table At one end was seated A Man or Brute which shall I call him?

---

[7] Lord Charles Wellesly.
[8] Dryden, "Alexander's Feast," l. 99.

He was more than 6 feet high corpulent and exceedingly ugly Out of his red brutish Face peered forth 2 sharp grey eyes and the muscles of his Face were puckerd up most ridiculously about the nose The moment I entered he accosted me with "Pliz whit are you dwing here are you kim tuh be mid a sibjict iv I was startled and knew not what to reply to this unintelligible jargon till my young conductor answered for me "Oh no Hume[9] mind your puddings And Beef Ive picked the yellow faced consumptive out of the street as I thought some one Might have took him for a dried cane and so ran of with [him] Bud Im in sid wint iv e sibjict he answered and mist iv win cim aling you stinking riskil Doctor Hume sit down And at least try to make yourself appear possesed of common sense if you have it not in reality said a person whom till then I had not particularly observed[10] He was a tall young man very handsome and with an Air of Melancholy in his countenance wich however did not detract from but rather heightned the expression of his Feathurs his hair Fell on his Forehead in brown curls like a cluster of grapes his eyes were large and of a clear dark blue and his Figure rather slight and slender

Sir he said then addressing me You had better take your seat by me I had till [then] Been sitting near the Brutish Fellow just spoken of

Au no I kin do with him hes A viry plisint Kimpiniin Answered Doctor Hume with A sneer but however I did not heed him but took my seat by the gentlemanly person above spoken of we were now going to begin supper in silence when my young conductor starting from his seat said well Brother why have not we got Miss Hume here do you intend to make her a nun? but Ill go and call her. and so saying he jumped up and was of before any body could call him to stop In a short time however he returned with a young lady about his age and so like him in person and manners (though not quite so giddy) that I thought she was his sister they came in laughing and talking to each Other but no one could hear what they said till at last they Both sat down with the rest to supper when it was ended Eeach one retired to their rooms except the tall young Man before mentioned who ordered his carriage [and] drove of at the Instigation of my young Friend Doctor Hume allowed me to sleep in his house therefore I with the rest retired to a room provided for me

                                                        yours truly &c
                                                        Adam Scott

To Mr Bellingham
     London England

---

9 Dr. Hume Bady.
10 Arthur Wellesly, Marquis of Douro.

LETTER THE
IId..

Londem Sept
ember 2 1830

My dear Friend
        You in my last letter left me I believe in bed at the Palace of the great
Doctor Hume Bady for shuch he was when in my room I had leisure to think
upon the events of the day I was quite astounded to think I had seen one of those
12s who passing over a wide and stormy Ocean and over coming inumerable
difficultys had founded and made laws for this magnificent city and whose glories
now resounded over every sea and through every land spreading An awe and
admiration of their Genius and virtues wherever their name was spread And one
of these Heroes I had now seen! who the other two young men were I could not
tell I knew they must be something out oF the ordinary line but still I could not
find any great men corresponding to their age among all of whom I thought or
could bring to my memory exept the Marquis of Douro and Lord Charles
Wellesly But not for a moment did I think that it could be them Reflecting upon
these things I Fell asleep how long I continued In that state I can not tell but
when I awoke the First Red beams of the now rising Sun were bursting into my
Apartment tinging every Object visible with a crimson Light exepting the
corners of the room which were dim and hazy It was now 5 o'clock therefore I
rose dressed and was preparing to go down when as there were 3 doors in my
room and I had Forgot by which I entered the preceeding night I knew not by
which to get out Fearing I might enter where I had no buisness but however at
last I tried one It led me down a dark Flight of stairs where was no light however
I still went on untill I came to a large Iron door where I heard men muttering
inside whose there" cried one in a loud voice."The Englishman whom you have
so kindy entertained" replied I. "Ah The sweet tones of an English man are
pleasant But step" in cried the same person in a sneering manner I therefore
opned the door but the moment I did so such a tremendous smell slatued[11] my
nostrils that I steped back quite stund "Come in you lazy lout and dont phay
such theatrics" cried a tremendous fellow as he rushed forward and seizing me by
the collar dragged me in he then shut the huge door and brought me before my
host and enimy Dr Hume And a tall Genteel supercilious sneering & merciless
looking Frenchman "Deer gentleman hes neer Fayntin he moost let his blood
Fly Forth" said he with a laugh "Thats rare" cried the man or rather giant who
took me prisoner and whom I remembered to have seen before he was 7 feet had
a crownless and broad brimed Hat on his head From underneath wich peeped
Forth the most Ferocious and weatherbeaten Face I have ever seen his dress
consisted oF a ragged coat made after the manner of those worn by Poachers (of
which Fraternity he seemed to be) and also a pair of breec[h]es much in the same

---

[11] "saluted" obviously intended.

style These with two huge stockingless and shoeless legs and feet enough to
have dismayed Hercules himself formed his grotesque but tremendous figure
"My rare lad its grand that youve come here what a subject youll have my rare
Men" cried he in tones of thunder at these words knowing I was to be dissected
alive I shrieked out and fell into a swoon when I recovered I found myself lying
bound to a large Oak table which as well as the Floor of [the] room was covered
with d[r]ied blood The walls were unplastered and thickly coated with spiderwebs
the beams of the roof Broken And rotting in many places while one small Iron
grated window served to admit a feeble light just serving to make
"Darkness visible"[12]

The Great door was open while at its entrance stood a man whom I concieved to
be of no ordinary authority he was 6 feet high rather sparly formed but very
broad shouldered his countenance, his firm and <decided> eyes grey sharp and
peircing his air expressive of command and himself dressed in Military costume
with large Hessian boots to his Feet[13] at his side stood my young conductor his
blue eyes bright with anger his fingers applied to his nose and uttering the most
abusive language his vocabulary could afford on Dr Hume and the giant who
both stood with their heads hanging down and in the most submissive manner
possible while (Horresco referens) Laury the Frenchman was shuffling a coffin
and dead body out of sight into a large receptacle which he had just opened "What
are you doing there Laury" enquired the tall man just entered in a loud voice "Oh
hes only just puting away a few provisions your grace" answered the
Frenchman—"look Father its the body of Old Bobbadil"[14] cried the young
cicerone
"Bady—aw no its only jist a deed min git frim the Hispitls
    Tall Man dont I see you rascal, who it is. Ned laury go this moment and
carry Dr Hume and the Frenchman to prison.
Ned Oh rare!
Tall Man go this instant Fellow!
Ned laury now took them both by the collars and dragged them of notwistanding
the frequent cries of Hume "Eem inisint eem inisint" and the obstinate resistance
of the Frenchman.
The tall man and the young one now came up to me asking how did I come
here?. The young Fellow not leaving me time to answer said Oh Father this [is]

---

12 *Paradise Lost*, Book I, l. 60.
13 The Duke of Wellington.
14 See p. 93, n. 5. Both Branwell and Charlotte were fascinated by the famous
Hare and Burke case. Hare and Burke murdered and robbed their victims, then sold
the bodies to the surgeon Dr. Robert Knox for dissection. Hare turned King's
evidence and Burke was hanged in January 1829. Knox was attacked for his trade
in human bodies in the "Noctes Ambrosianae," *Blackwood's Magazine*, March
1829. See Alexander CB, I, 82-83; 172-75.

the English man of whom I just told you Theve brought him here to dissect him
as I heard Dr Hume threaten last night
Tall Man Is it charles. well get up and thank your stars for ever geting out of
this hole"
I now got up and was thanking them for their kindness when the young man
Interrupted me with "Stuff no[ne] of your bowings and scrapings here who do
you think we are liverless rascal mind this Im lord Charles wellesly and heres
my Father the Duke of Wellington"
I was for some time struck Dumb with astonishment but after I had recovered
my suprise I expressed my gratitude in the most ardent terms and went home to
my Hotel filled with wonder and admiration at the disposition of the Grandees of
this city

yours truly &c &c &c
Jame[s] Bellingham.[15]

To Adam Scott Esqr London
PB Bronte Sept 6 AD 1830

---

[15] The signatures of Bellingham and Scott were originally reversed, then corrected.

THE REVENGE[1]
A
TRADGEDY
BY YOUNG SOULT.
II VOLS:
VOL, I.

THE REVENGE
A
TRADGEDY IN :
3 Acts by
: YOUNG SOULT
IN
TWO volumns[2]
QUARTO
P B Bronte S S S

In dramatic poetry the cheif thing to be attained
Is an excellence in describing the passions and in
proportion as this exelence is attained so are we
To judge of the merits of the peice
                            J BUDS synopis of
                            The Drama Vol I p 130[3]

GLASS TOWN
Printed and. sold by S Tree
PARIS
M De La Pack
December
18th

---

[1] Hand-sewn booklet in grey paper covers (8.8 x 10.2 cm) of 14 pages (3 blank) in BPM: BS 116.
[2] Volume II, containing Act 3, seems never to have been written. In the existing manuscript, the text covers twelve pages (one blank), the next two pages have been cut out, and the final two pages are blank.
[3] See the similar statement on the title page of **Caractacus**, pp. 98-99.

ACT THE I,::
SCENE the I

John a prince of Germany in the 14th century[4] having alienated
his subjects from him by ecsessive tyranny a conspiracy is formed
against him having Count ALBERT THURA at their head This scene
represents Albert alone in a dark room of an old building or watch tower now
deserted waiting for the rest of the conspirators who had promised to meet
him there. P B Brontë Nov 23. AD 1830.

ALBERT

ALBERT Tyrant thy course is stopt no longer now
      Shalt thou relentless desolate the earth
      All things devouring in thy rapid vortex
      Thousands have falln before thy bloody throne
      And yet vain hope thou thinkst that thousands more
      Shall shortly bite the dust beneath thy footstool
      And roll in agonies before thy eyes
      Fond man thou little thinkest what a tempest
      Shall shortly burst on thy accursed head
      Thy Honours all are blasted ravving Fortune
      Vails her bright countenance in clouds and tempests
      Soon shall this strong right arm and faithful sword
      Destroy thee King or thou destroyest me
      Yet as the sun has set and the pale moon
      Rolls up the vault of Heaven her silver car
      Ill wile away the eve with songs of venegeance
      And tune my harpstrings Tyrant to thy downfall

        He sings:

      O ye departed spirits Fallen
      By the tyrants bloody hand
    Oer him fulminate your thunders
        Desolate his land
      Though now he sit upon a throne
      Though kingdoms now beneath him groan

---

4   Although Branwell places the play in fourteenth-century Germany, it does
not seem to be based on any readily identifiable historical event or literary
source. Indeed, the content is more typical of German/British Gothic than
medieval German literature and suggests a knowledge of Goethe and Schiller—
see p. 77, n. 1 and 2.

Though he be robed in kingly state
Though daily flatterers round him wait
Yet see the cloud of venegeance nigh
It shades his land it blots his sky
    It darkens round his throne
His kingdom glories power and fame
What are they but an empty name
    His Honours all are gone
    I had a son but slain by thee
He now lies lonely in his watery grave
And oer him loudly roars Old Norways wave
    From earthly sorrows free
Never Ah never to return
    Then shall a Father cease to mourn
    To vow for venegeance on the slain
    And dye his sword in blood again
Yes I will rise though age benumbs my arm
    Though not now as of yore
Runs through my veins the lifeblood red and warm
Yet I will rise and steep my sword in gore
    Prepare now tyrant for thy doom
    Thy sun has set in deepest gloom
Soon mangled and deserted shalt thou lie
Exposed to chilling blasts and winters stormy sky
    Not one shalt shed a tear
Oer the[e] laid silent on some desart moor
Where Ghosts and wolves shall round the[e] moan and roar
    Unwept neglected there

                                          a loud noise
                                          of men entr
                                          ing is heard

Hark! now they come! Tyrant thy fate is sealed!
This days the last which thou shalt have to live

        A band of Robbers enter to deposite their booty
        They discover Albert

        CAPTAN of the Robbers

What! ho! whose this? seize him companions seize him.

        ALBERT

Come at your peril seize me and you die
Back villains!

CAPTAIN

Why delib'rate rush upon him
Bind him with chains convey him to our cavern
There to abide my judgment and his fate

They rush on
and seize him.
All depart

SCENE, II.

The Robbers cavern Albert standing bound before the captain
Robbers armed and ranged round the sides and entrance

CAPTAIN

Now pris'ner tell thy name thy rank thy fortune
What brought thee to that ruin? Why so lonely
In the dark hour of night? Thou seemest not
If I from thy appearance may conjecture
A humble sheperd or some way worn traveller
Wandring among these wilds and cloudy mountains

ALBERT

Cease ye these vain conjectures and intreateis
I am count Albert Thura and a subject
Of John our Tyrant for no better name
Methinks that man deserves who slew my son
And me he would have slain but feared to do it
He sent him exiled to old Norways shores
And there twas said he fell destroyed in secret
While I his Father since that Fatal day
Have cherished up my venegeance, Like the miner
Who digging secret saps the strongest wall
Ra[i]sed from its deep foundations even thus
I silent sapped his throne the Fatal hour
has come when with a band of strong conspirators
Men injured like myself we had appointed
To give him his reward for all his deeds.

CAPTAIN

kneeling before
him (ie Albert)

Father I am thy son!

ALBERT

What do I hear!
Art thou indeed that son for whom I greived?
And thought for ever snatched from these old eyes?
And comst thou now to cheer thy Fathers spirit,
And waken all my fainting energies   the captain a[rises]
Into-new life? arise! my son arise!
Little-thought I this morn when stung with sorrow
With sorrow for thy loss little I thought
That fortune ere should croun my aged head
Whith Joy like this with such allcheering beams!
Yet she bright Godess showers on us her Favours
When least expected and when most desired
Yet now the transports oer relate O Werner
Thy dangers since that dark that Fatal day
Had snatched thee from my sight I am Impatient
To know how thou could scape from his red Fangs

WERNER[5]   The late captain of Robbers and Alberts son

Wer Thou knowest O Father how on False conviction
       Of Traitrous designs against his throne
       False as the Tyrants heart He had condemned me
       To exile on Old Norways desart shores
       Swift from the port the Gallant vessel darted
       Which should convey me with afflictions
       To the far distant land when lo the Heavens
       With murky clouds surcharged muttered dull thunder
       Big drops descended from the reddning sky
       The air was still as death and the green billows
       Rolled dull and hevily on the dark sea
       Silence reigned through the ship the saddend sailors
       Raised hurried glances to the gloomy Heavens
       Then fixed them on the labouring waves below
       Yet for myself I felt no fright or terror
       Reckless willing to die not caring how
       When soon a broad red flash shot from the heavens
       And the big thunders rattled through the air
       Loud roared the winds and with inconstant blast
       Swelled the dull waves to vast and raging billows
       The sea was one continued roar with heads

---

[5]   Possibly named after Byron's tragic hero, reviewed in *Blackwood's
Magazine*, xii, 1822, 10-19; 782-85.

Hoary and white the waters rushed upon us
The huge ship heaved and groaned the cables cracked
The sails were rent The tall masts broke asunder
While the dread Genius of the gloomy tempest
Rode on a thunder cloud and from his urn
Poured down his blasts his Fires his rushing torrents
Man after man was by the billows snatched
From the rent ship. and tossed on the dark Ocean
Found there his executioner and grave
But now the maddning billows bore us on
To certain death for frowning oer our heads
Towered a huge rock blackned with fires and tempests
Now seeing certain death before my eyes
I frantic plunged in the dark world of waters
And the storm bore me on the shaking strand
And there O Horrid sight I saw our ship
Sturggling in vain to brave the ravenous ocean
When lo a billow swifter than the lightning
Relentless dashed her on the frowing rock
One cry I heard one loud despairing cry
Which echoed in the Heavens Then all was oer
And the white waters curled above their grave
All Night the thunders through the aerial hall
Continual rolled while tempests shook the heavens
And Ocean raged inccessant oer his prey
While I Fo[r]lorn upon this dreary shore
Heard the shrill seamews voice and cormorants cry
But lo when morn with wing of rosy hue
Suffused the Heavens with light the storm departed
And left the azure vault cloudless and calm
Whith the suns golden beams all Nature smiled
And Ocean slumbring seemed another sky
But I nor smiled nor cast a gladdened eye
Upon the rosy East. no, worn with sorrow
I cast myself upon the sea beat shore
There all the live long day I lay bewailing
My adverse Fate. torn from my native country
By a relentless Tyrant and surviving
My lost companions drowned in the waves
But to perish by a more dreadful fate
But when the second Night rolled oer the heaven
And covered all with tenebrific gloom
Twas then frantic with sorrow cold and hunger
I called on Frowning Fortune with these words
"O thou soul withring power call down thy vengeance
"This moment strike me to the stygian gloom

"Hurl yon black cliff upon my sorrowing head
"And bury me at once in blank Oblivion
"Ending at once my hope and my despair
"Or roll the clouds from of thy shining throne
"O burst upon me with renewed splendour
"Give me ah fond vain hope! to see my country
"And all I once held dear let me oh let me
"Hurl the dark Tyrant from his bloodstained throne
"And satisfy my thirst with his hearts gore"
When I had ended this vain Imprecation
I cast my eyes around the swelling sea
And lo! all dim upon the Far Horizon
Oh Happy sight I saw a small white sail
Bending its course full to the fated rock
On wich I stood what joy then filled my heart
Joy mixed with thoughts of vengeance till the morn
I stayed Impatiently straining my sight
To see If twas a flase[6] Inconstant vapoure
But no It held Its rapide course till Heaven
Glowed with the rising sun then Full beforeme
The ship like lightning passed I called I shouted
For help for succour did the[y] hear my voice?
did they regard me? breathlessly I waited
THEY DID! the pilot turning round the helm
Full to my sight displayed a mighty vessel
Glowing Majestic to the rising sun
Soon they received [me] on their welcome deck
And swift we sailed to the German coast
And after many perils many dangers
We landed on my countrys wished for shores
Where bent on vengeance on the Tyrants head
Gathered a band of strong and bold assasins
Him to destroy the rest you Father know

                    ALBERT

I do my son. but now my friends are waiting
For me to join and to assault our King
Now with thy followers join thy own Avengers
And me thy Father to destroy thy Thyrant
Let us begone. yet how my strenghts renewed!
High beats my heart elestic bounds my step
My youth returns at sight of thee returned

---

6   "false" obviously intended.

WERNER

Yes Father I will go Id go alone
This only Arm should make his lifes blood flow
If You commanded come my Follower[s] come!

Albert and
his recovered
Son Werner
depart with
the Robbers--
followers of Wer
ner to meet--
the rebels at
the old ruin

:ACT, I,I,:
SCENE, I.

An Apartment in the palace of John the Tyrant--
His Knights and Retainers conversing

RAYNER, a Knight.

Lodbrog knowst thou the reson why our prince
With such a company of men prepares
To visit Albert Thura's castle?

LODBROG. a knight and the favourite of John.

Rayner!
Why askest thou to know our princes secrets?
But wilt thou promise never to reveal
What I shall tell thee?

RAYNER.

Yes I will, go on!

LODBROG.[7]

Hark Rayner then! Twas me and not our prince
Who exiled Alberts son the brave young Werner!
For seeing his large possesions waving woods
Fit haunts for regal deer his golden Harvests
And wide spread medows and his towring castle
I saw and envied and resolved to have them
Therefore I forged a paper in the name
Of Werner Alberts son its purport was

---

[7] A King of Denmark, contemporary with Charlemagne.

Our sovreign to dethrone and also murder
And give the kingdom to Count Alberts hands
This to our prince I showed and he beleived
Grey headed Fool and Dotard as he is!
Aught wich I tell him he'll directly credit
He me empowered to send young Werner exiled
To Norways shore and there tis thought he died
This gained I had removed the strongest barrier
Twixt Alberts lands and me twas no hard task
Farther t' unbend our sovereigns doting mind
I showed to him how powerful Albert Thura
Was now becoming and that Fame had spread
Some some darkling hints that he and other Nobles
Were leagued to kill him and usurp his Kingdom
This struck the final blow our prince was feared
For life his sceptre and his crown he appointed
This day to visit Alberts lordly castle
With a strong retinue of knights and vassals
And under the pretence of hunting there
To seize the count and here to murder him
And best of all to grant me his estates!

                    RAYNER. in great Anger.

Foul villain! Cursed art thou! cursed John our sovreign!
Neer shall my hands be stained with sucha deed!

                    LODBROG. dissembling his anger at Rayner.

Nay hush thee Rayner! For our King is coming!

                                                    Enter John
                    JOHN.   the King follow
                                                    ed by many
Now knights prepare to visit Alberts castle   vassals
Come and let us begone!

                    LODBROG. kneeling before John

                    My lord my sovereign
How can I go? seeing we have among us[8]

---

8   Between this line and the next, upside down and canceled, an earlier draft of
Act I, Sc I, ll. 1-15 reads:
        Tyrant! thy course is stopt no longer now

A Faithless Traitor! one who cursed his king!
And me thy knight He cursed

JOHN

                    Who! Where! Which is he?
Bind him in chains! behead him!

LODBROG

                    This is he
This is the Traitor Rayner is his name[9]
The dark the Bloody monster Take him Guards
Bind him and when our sovreign doth return
Triumphant laden with his just renown
Then lead him out behead him throw his carcase
To the Feirce wolves and to the keen eyed Ravens
To whom shall his estates be giv'n?

JOHN.

                         To thee,

LODBROG.

I thank thee prince thy humblest vassal thanks thee!

          Shalt thou relentless desolate the earth
          All thing[s] devouring in thy rapid vortex
          Thousands have falln before thy bloody throne
          And feasting yet thou feasts thy mind with thousands more
          Which soon thou thinkst shall bite the dust before thee
          Rolling in agonies before thy footstool
          No now thy torrent stops and favring fortune
          Now veile they countenance in clouds and tempests
          Ye shades of those who died at thy command
          Departed spirits now I do ajure you
          Call down your vengeance & fulminate your thunders
          On his accursed and <reviled> head
          But lo the sun has set and the pale moon
          Rolls up the vault of Heaven her silver car

9   Squeezed in at the bottom of the same manuscript page, following this line, appears the uncanceled trial line "But <cheifly> traitor thou art doomed to feel steel"—see Act II, ll. 75-76.

RAYNER.

Unjust! Tyrannical! O! Lodbrog! Lodbrog!
Heaven shall reward thee for--

LODBROG Hastily

Of with him Of!
Why wait to hear the babbling wretch of with Him!

Guard c[arries]
off Rayn[er]

ATTENDANT   Enter An Attenda[nt]

My lord a man wrapt in a sable Robe
Desires to speak with thee in private

JOHN

Order him
To enter.   Exit Atte[ndant]
                             Enter an [Ast]
                             rologer--
                             He bows to [the]
                             King

ASTROLOGER

King before thee I appear
And from the Fates this message I declare
A storm there comes from Norways billowy
Even now I hear the distant thunders roar
On high sits death a black and gory form
On thee O king he wreaks the avenging storm
Eere yet again the sun enrobed in gloom
Silent descends the Fates have fixed thy doom
But cheifly Lodbrog thou are doomed to feel
The peircing vengeance of the shining steel
Now to this Hour the course of life thoust run
But here thy journey stops the Fates decrree tis done
Full many a flower blighted by thee now lies[10]
Exposed to winters blasts and stormy skys
From many a heart thoust wrung the bitter groan

10   See Gray's "Elegy Written in a Country Churchyard," l. 55.

And now thy life must for thy crimes atone
Perhaps my head is do[o]med your rage to feel
Perhaps through my heart youll drive the shining steel
I heed you not my message I declare
Fate wings its way towards you prepare O King prepare

Lod-brog and the king stand confou
nded and unable to speak. at length
Lodbrog hurridly exclames

LODBROG

Villain! what now how what meanst thou by this
Thou dampst my (recovers himself) But whith wine my heart is flushed
I know what Im saying hence thou vagrant
Guards take him bind him bind him in the dungeon
And if we come not by to morrows dawn
Release him if we do then drag him forth
To see the end of all his false predictions
And die himself

ASTROLOGER

Freely I give myself
Into your hands knowing my life is certain

Exit
Astrologer
to the prison

JOHN

Come knights let not this vain Astrologer
Oercast your mind with such a gloomy cloud
Bring wine to cheer our souls let us be merry
And drown all gloomy thoughts in songs and feasting
Then let us go to haughty Alberts castle.

Exeunt
Omnes

297   300 line

THE
HISTORY OF
THE ι.

YOUNG MEN : ι :

FROM
Their First Settlement
To

The present time=ι
COMPREHENDING AN ACCOUNT OF ASHANTEE
FROM THE EARLIEST PERIOD TO THEIR ARRIVAL[1]
∴ BY :
JOHN BUD ESQ'R
CAPTAIN IN THE :
≡ 10 REGT OF HUSSARS
VICE PRESIDENT OF THE ANTIQUARIAN SOCiety
FELLOW OF THE LITERARY SOCIETY : •
FELLOW OF THE ASSOCIATION FOR ≡ ~
THE REWARD OF LEARNING—
CHEIF LIBRARIAN TO—
THE ROYAL GLASS—
TOWN LIBRARY—
&c &c &c &c
IN   VOLUMNS :[2]
VOL I .

"It IS my TASK
"TO Explore the Dark recesses of the past
"And Bring to light the deeds of former ages"
Marquis Douro's
School of Learning v. 139

---

1   Hand-sewn booklet in grey paper covers (15.8 x 19 cm) in 18 pages (2 blank) plus a double-page map of the Glass Town Confederacy with various sketches on the back, in BL: Ashley 2468. Compare with Charlotte's account in Alexander CB, I, 7-18.
2   Although the blank suggests that Branwell was not sure how many volumes he would produce, there is no evidence of additional volumes.

[Pen-and-ink sketch of a figure labeled "Mentor"]³

1831
Great Glass town Printed and sold by Seargent Tree

INTRODUCTION.
TO THE
HISTORY OF THE YOUNG MEN
Dec 15th Anno Dominii 1830

It⁴ was sometime in the summer of the year AD 1824 when I being desirous to possess a box of soldiers asked papa to buy me one which shortly afterwards he procured me from Bradford They were 12 in number price 1s 6d and were the best I ever have had Soon after this I got from Keighly another set of the same number These soldiers I kept for about a year untill either maimed lost burnt or destroyed by various casualities they
"departed and left not a wreck behind!"⁵

Now therefore not satisfied with what I had formerly got I purchased at Keighly a band of Turkish musicians which I continued to keep till the summer of AD 1825 when Charlotte and Emily returned from school where they had been during the days of my former sets I remained for 10 months after they had returned without any soldiers when on June the 5th AD 1826 papa procured me from Leeds another set (those were the 12s) which I kept for 2 years though 2 or 3 of them are in being at the time of my writing this (Dec 15 AD 1830) Sometime in 1827 I bought another set of Turkish Musicians at Halifax⁶ and in 1828 I purchased the Last Box a band of Indians at Haworth Both these I still keep. here now ends the catalogue of soldiers bought by or for me And I must now conclude this Introduction already to long with saying, that what is contained in

---

3 See Alexander & Sellars, 299 for a description of the double-page map and the figure.
4 In contrast to the usual miniature print writing, the Introduction is written in longhand.
5 See Shakespeare's *The Tempest*, IV, i, 155.
6 Bradford, famed for its manufacturing and woolen industries in Victorian Britain, is located about eight miles west of Leeds and twelve miles east of Haworth. Keighley, a thriving market town, lies to the northwest of Bradford, five miles north of Haworth. Leeds, approximately twenty miles east of Haworth by the river Aire, was a major textile, manufacturing and commercial center during the nineteenth century. Halifax, an ancient clothing and manufacturing town by the river Calder, is located approximately twelve miles south of Haworth.

this History is a statement of what Myself Charlotte Emily and Ann realy
pretended did happen among the "Young men" (that being the name we gave
them) during the period of nearly 6 years though in some places slightly altered
according to the form and taste of the aforsaid young men It is written by
Captain John Bud the greatest prose writer they have among them.

P B Brontë
Haworth December 15 AD 1830

HISTORY
OF : THE : YOUNG, MEN
BY;;
CAPTAN JOHN BUD, F.A.S. M.R.L.S.A. P.S.C.&c.

P
B CHAPTER
B

I.	From	‖ AM 2000
contents	To.	‖ AD 1761

I The Ancient Britons and Gauls 2. The English settlement of 1500.
Guinea or Ashantee[7] is a large country or rather a number of countrys extending
1700 miles from East to West and 500 from North to south it is bounded
eastward by the Immense desarts extending far into the Interior of Africa to the
Westward lies the north Atlantic sea on the South It is bounded by the Gulf of
Guinea and on the north by the far extended range of the Jibbll Kumai or
Mountains of the moon When and by whom this part of Africa was first peopled
cannot at this distant period of time be fully ascertained But the most likely
conjecture seems to be that its first Inhapitants were the Ancient British and
Gauls who some time about AM 2000 came over to the country And peopled the
South Eeastern parts of it what became of them is not now known some assert
And among this number is the Author of the "Romantic Tale"[8] published

---

[7] Ashanti, a west African state active in the slave trade of the eighteenth
century, occupied what is now southern Ghana. It unsuccessfully resisted British
penetration in the nineteenth century. During the Ashanti Wars of the 1820's,
which were reported in the press during Branwell's youth, the Ashanti managed
to defeat British forces (1824), but made peace in 1831 and avoided conflict for
the next thirty years. The Kingdom of Ashantee appears on the map of West
Africa in J. Goldsmith's *Grammar of General Geography*, 1823, owned by the
Brontës, and a source of Branwell's map referred to in note 1. For another
possible source, see "Geography of Central Africa. Denham and Clapperton's
Journals," *Blackwood's Magazine*, June 1826.

[8] See Charlotte's **A Romantic Tale**, Alexander CB, I, 7-8.

between 20 and 30 years ago. That after continual and ferocious wars among themselves which lasted for many years they returned again to their native countrys. while other Authors state that for the noble and daring spine they showed in resisting the cruel and Infamous oppressions of the Genii they were for ever rooted out and destroyed by those Heartless Monsters which of these Traditions may be correct it is usless at this time to determine for who in AD 1830 can pretend with exactness to state what happened in AM 2000? All we now now is that they once did Inhapit Ashantee But that they have long ceased to exist After the departure of the Britons and the Gauls the Natives took possesion of the country which they with few interruptions from the Romans inhabiting Carthage[9] and the other Governments in Africa kept for more than 3000 years. IE. till AD 1500 About which time A colonoy of English settled on the south coasts where they continued for 30 years till harrashed by the natives and Tyrannised over by the Genii they determined to depart which They accordingly did and sailed for England on August, A.D. 1537. Several Buildings erected by them still remain the most considerable of which are Killdenny Hall the seat of JOHN GIFFORD Esq cheif Judge of the Glasstown and President of the Royal Antiquarian Society a man to whose Laborious and well directed researches I owe much of what I have written respecting the early state of this country[10] There is also another fine specimen of their style of Architecture about 30 miles east of the Glass town. it is a large and strongly Built castle supposed by Gifford and Leaf to have been the residence of their Governor besides these there are many other Castles churches Houses &c scattered about the coasts of Ashantee. wich The space I have alloted to this part of my History will not permit me to mention But now after Their departure the country again relapsed in the hands of the Barbarians whose Monarchs reigned here in undisturbed Glory and prosperity the acknowledged Emperors and Arbiters of all Southern Africa for 220 years But the Wheel of Fortune never ceases to revolve and bears alike kingdoms and men with it now on the height of Human Grandeur the next moment in the darkest and most hopeless despair[11] And thus it proved with the Ashantees For at a time when they thought themselves secure from all danger and the Admiration of the whole world a more terrible overthrow and

---

9   Carthage, an ancient city and republic of Africa, was reputed to rival Rome. It flourished for 700 years, at its height under Hannibal. It maintained three wars against Rome (the Punic Wars), finally being destroyed during the third war in 147 BC. On its defeat, the city was set on fire by the Romans, burning for seventeen days. The Emperor, Augustus, subsequently planted a small Roman colony on the ruins of Carthage, which was partially rebuilt by its new settlers who remained in Carthage (renamed Hadrianopolis) until it was reconquered from the Romans by the Vandals in 439.
10   Gifford is possibly modeled on William Gifford, first editor of *The Quarterly Review*, famous for his conservative criticism, and satirized by Byron in *English Bards and Scotch Reviewers*.
11   See p. 80, n. 7.

which should more utterly humble them than Any other wich they had yet experienced was preparing to burst over their unsuspecting heads (P B Brontë Dec 15th AD 1830) *End of Chapter the first.*

CHAPTER·:
IID:,
contents

| | From | ‖ Jan 7 AD 1770 |
| | To | ‖ June 5 AD 1770 |

I List of the 12S   2 Their characters   3 set out of the Invincible   4 death of Stumps   5 destruction of the dutch   6 arrival at Africa   7 concluding Observations

In the Begining of the year AD 1770 there set sail from England A Ship named the Invincible It was Bound for Ashantee Its crew consisted of 13 Men All strong healthy And in the highest Spirits Imaginable Their names were

— BUTTER CRASHEY Captain   aged 140 years　　　?
— ALexander CHEEKY surgeon　---　20　　　　　?
—⁺ARTHUR WELLESLY Trumpeter--- 12　　　　40
— WILLIAM EDWARD PARRY Trumpeter 15　　40
— ALEXANDER SNEAKY Sailor 17　　　　　70
— JOHN ROSS Lieutnant 16　　　　　　　15
—⁺WILLIAM BRAVEY Sailor 27　　　　　70
— EDWARD GRAVEY sailor 17　　　　　　60
—⁺FREDERICK GUELPH sailor 27　　　　　=
— ═STUMPS　　　12 Middy　　　　　46
—⁺═MONKEY　　11 Middy　　　　　52
⁺═ TRACKY　　10 Middy　　　　　45
— ═CRACKEY　　5 Middy　　　　　20

But before I proceed with this part of my History it will be better breifly to describe the characters of these 12 Founders of our city and Fathers of our Nation. CRASHEY the captain was a patriarch full of years and full of wisdom CHEEKY was the most stout hearted man in the ship it is true neither his face nor his mind were such as to preposses one in his favour But to his bravery need their be a higher testimony than the Author of The Romantic Tale who says when describing a storm *"even* the heart of our cheif doctor quailed"[12] The character of Arthur Wellesly was that of a bold and brave young lad Ardent for all

---

[12]　See Alexander CB, I, 10.

military glory and fame and though only 12 years old would have shamed many older Men than himself in his patience under fatigue & coolness in the hour of danger W E PARRYS caracter was that of a Brave sailorlike young man differing from Mariners in general in one respect only that of being a little too fond of subterfuge but alas! how are the Mighty fallen![13] A Sneaky was Injenous artful deceitful but courageous J Ross frank open honest and of A Bravery when in battle sometimes a-proaching to madness W Bravey was of a character similar to Ross But his countenance and habits seemed alike to say Give us good cheer eat drink dance and be merry Different from these was the character of EDWARD GRAVEY he was Naturally Grave and Melancholy and his temper was still furthur soured by the sneers and laughter which the rest raised against him but like the rest he was daring and brave Of Frederic Guelph Duke of York and afterwards king of the Glass town we now very little nor is our present stock of Information likely to be much added to for he being now dead and The 12s never very loquacious respecting affairs connected with their early history are absolutely dumb to all Inquires respecting him but from what we can gather from Leaf and other early historians he seems to have been Generous brave and commanding. of the other 4 midd shipmen I need not speak particularly suffice it to say that like other middys they were Merry thoughtless liked sport and cared not for the future but I must now conclude this digression and haste on with my narative. Every thing being got in readiness and the wind being fair for their voyage these Intrepid Heroes set sail on February 5th AD 1770 and after bidding a Farewell to England which Many of them were never more to see they Glided rapidly down the CHANNEL and the Misty and wave circled Isle of England departing from their veiw presented to their eyes the sunny and fertile plains of France

"Stretched like a golden line along the wavy sea"

young Soult[14]

On the 11 they touched on the coasts of Spain where they land[ed] and took up a supply of provisions From thence The wind drove them in a south westerly direction on the Island of Trinidad where they met with a violent storm but however they refitted their ship and set sail again for the coast of Africa and touched at Ascension Island then in possession of the Dutch[15] it was during this

---

[13] Branwell here echoes 2 Samuel 1: 19-20.

[14] Presumably Bud is quoting from one of Young Soult's works, but the line is not from his existing works.

[15] Ascension Island, a small island of thirty-four square miles in the south Atlantic Ocean, was discovered along with the island of St. Helena, lying 700 miles to the southeast, by the Portuguese navigator Joao da Nova Castella in 1501. The Dutch occupied St. Helena from 1645-51, but although Ascension Island was regarded as a dependency of St. Helena, it was not inhabited until 1815 when Napoleon took residence on St. Helena, and the British occupied

part of their voyage and on the 18th of May that STUMPS died. Himself Arthur Wellesley and F GUELPH had been sent on shore for water which they soon found and were returning to the ship on their way they were met by a party of 8 Dutch soldiers belonging to the garrison who enquired what they were doing on shore without the permission of the Governor to this they returned no answer whereupon the dutch fired on them and the first shot struck STUMPS to the Ground he only called out "REVAUNGE MOY DAUT"[16] and then expired this A Wellesley and F Guelph did in earnest for with a good aim they brought down 3 of their enemy who seeing This fled towards the fort But the English after Giving them another salute which killed 2 quickly retreated toward the ship When the crew heard of this affray and the death of STUMPS they immediatly called a council of war to deliberate upon what they should do Gravey showed to them the utter foolishness of 12 young men or rather Lads presuming to attack a strong town with a Garrison of 400! he therefore advised them to set sail immediatly "What" cried Bravey "and leave my son to be buired like a dog by the rascals" SNEAKY counselled them take the enymy by suprise First to send 6 men to the Governors Castle on pretence of setteling the affair they were to keep the Garrison of their guard till dead of Night at which time 3 men should be dispatched from the vessel secretly in to the town were they were to massacre and burn every thing they met with while the remaining 3 in the ship should sail into the Harbour and commence cannonading the town When things were arrived at this crisis the 6 ammbassadors were to set upon and massacre the Governor and his attendants and then joining their comrades complete the victory A WELLESLEY next rose with his proposal He said that as the first expedient of flight was cowardly and that of Treachery was mean he saw no way but to Face the danger openly had not they set out from England with a determination to accomplish thing[s] which none ever had done before? and were they then to fail and shrink from the First opportunity? No rather than commit so base an action he would rush into their town and fall a victim to the exasperated Dutch He would ask were the Father Uncle and Brothers of the murdered Stumps to retreat without firing one shot evincing one desire to revenge his death? he would now conclude with stating that the best and most Honourable way of Procedoure would be to proceed with the vessel into the Harbour and immediatly Bombard the town till it was reduced to ashes. I[f] necessary also they might send a party on shore to engage the enemy the assembly having divided on the 3 proposals there appeared for

GRAVEY'S	——	1
SNEAKY'S	——	4
WELLESLY'S	——	6
Majority in favour of Welleslys proposal —— 2		

Ascension; British ships however, had been using it since the latter part of the seventeenth century.

16   Old Young Men's tongue—see p. 8, n. 7.

Thus the proposal having received the consent of the meeting and the approbation of CRASHEY, was immediatly carried into effect Firstly the long boat was sent out with 4 men under command of F GUELPH (these 4 were Wellesly Tracky Bravey and Monkey[17]) to attack the Dutch forces on land while the ship proceeded on its course to the Harbour. during the time that these things were passing on board the ship the 3 remaining Dutch soldiers had arrived at the governors whose name was VAN HAALEN,[18] hearing what had happened he sent a detachment of 10 men down to the shore while not knowing of what force the ship might be he ordered the Inhabitants to be on the watch and put the fort in a state of defence, when the party had arrived at the shore they were suddenly received by a sharp fire from behind the rocks which killed 1 man and wounded 3 others instantly they rushed to the spot from whence the volley proceeded But the English had retreated to a sand bank on the other side from whence they opened another brisk discarge which *extinguished* 4 more the remaining 2 were now about to fly but were intercepted by Tracky and Monkey who darting from their hiding place stabbed the 2 fugitives and thus put an end to the entire party while they all having come forth from the rocks were congratulating each other on the success of their expidition a Rocket sent up in the air (it was now night) and a low thunder of cannonry followed by repeated and sharper discharges of Musketry from the town (about a mile distant from where they then were) told them that the engagement between the ship and the garrison had commenced. "Come then lads" said Frederic in high spirits "lets of to the town we'll give them a bit more light than they have" and the party marched up to the aforsaid part of the Island for the purpose of seting fire to the houses and massacering the Inhabitants but we must now leave this Heroic little party to relate at what happened meanwhile at the other point of battle the ship having entered the harbour and moored opposite the town prepared to fire. but suddenly PARRY exclaimed "Hallow! Dear! Oi tee troy bowt's cawming oup tow us" (ie Hello there! I see 3 boats coming up to us) Well point the cannon to them and take your aim True answered Leiut Ross Yes an' we'll give them a taste of our quality cried Parry at that instant a stream of Fire followed by a tremendous crack that made all hearts jump from the foremost of the Dutch boats announced the commencment of the battle any Damage done there asked Ross with the utmost sangfroid no replied Sneaky the gunner and at the same moment he answered the boat with 2 or 3 long 30 pounders which dashed through its bottom and sides sinking it like a cracked egg shell thats brave! and now for another resounded through the ship but before they had time to fire again a good broadside from the Fort struck down the top of the Mast and laid Ross and Cracky sprawling on the deck with the one his arm pretty well smashed and mowing of the legs of the other This was answered by a volley from the ship and now the fight became

---

[17] Among those honored by Napoleon for valor during the Battle of Valoutina (1812) was Captain Moncey. His name also appears in Scott's *Life of Napoleon*, VI, 203.

[18] There was never, in fact, a Dutch governor of the island.

very hot [and] dangerous the 2 remaining Dutch boats were soon sunk they having imprudently ventured close under the ship with intent to board it soon however Gravey and the mast went together into the sea struck by a feirce broadside from The Fort and now matters were becoming Desperate with only 4 men on board and the ship quite disabled how could they hope to stand a battery of 13 cannon from the Fort continualy kept up against them? but while in this embarrassment they were suprised to see the Firing from the Fort discontinued a loud noise was heard in the town while a bright red glare as of Fire had diffused itself over many parts of the town As they now had no doubt but that the land party had entered the town victorious and were burning and massacring all before them CRASHEY commanded the boats to be put of and knowing that they were none to molest the ship in their absence he ordered that all the remaining crew (ie Cheeky Parry & Sneaky) should with himself row with all possible expidition toward the town to help their comrades when they arrived there The First thing which met their eyes was a band of 30 dutch soldiers and Inhabitants fleeing with the uttermost consternation through the streets and falling houses, many being killed by the roofs Fires and Timbers continualy percipitated on them by the exasperated English when they saw this new reinforcement from The ship they set up a loud cry for mercy for panicstruck with terror they knew not the small number of the English. but imagined them a ligon of Ghosts and demons let loose upon them like an overwhelming torrent "Yes loves we'll give you mercy" cried Cheeky Parry & Sneaky at the same time rushing on and destroying them without distingtion of age sex or condition they now with CRASHEY at their head continued to scour the streets killing burning and destroying all before them till they came to The town hall in front of which they saw Guelph Wellesly Bravey and Monkey massacring a few wretched people who had fled there to avoid their fury when the Ship Party saw them they set up a loud shout which was answered by the Land Party with a still louder one "Well lads" cried Guelph "how've you fared as for us we've got Tracky slaughtered but nobody else" an' with us Ross Cracky and Gravey have departed this life" answered Cheeky. They now all formed into one company consisting of 8 men CRASHEY being at their head and with continual cries of "Revaunge Revaunge" proceeded to attack the Fort which was fortified and prepared for their reception by 130 men!!! as soon however as they arrived in front of The building They were saluted by a smart fire which struck the venerable CRASHEY on the arm laying [him] sensless on the ground at this infamous proceeding the party were enraged beyond measure and swearing that if they took the place they would leave alive neither man woman or child they boldly rushed on to storm it with Guelph at their head soon the[y] mounted the parapet scaled the battlement and were preparing to enter the powder Magazine for the purpose of blowing it up when the governor at the head of 90 soldiers rushed up to dispute their entrance and now a most desperate conflict was commenced between the English breathing Revenge and the Dutch actuated by despair! Wellesly with 2 men had mounted a heap of ruins and kept up an incessant fire upon the crowded ranks of the Dutch while a party of 3 more under Guelph made incessant and desperate sallys with their long and sharp bayonets now however unresisted by the Dutch who constantly endeavoured to keep of and destroy them. but now in the heat of the conflict the Governor anxious to end it by one Decisive blow rushed upon Guelph and attempted to inflict a death wound on him which through The blindness of his foury failed and Guelph stabbed him in the neck while Parry and Sneaky coming up at the same time ended his life with one or two deep gashes on the Head with their broad sabres Now the English prepared for another attempt on the Magazine and each grasping a peice of Blazing Timber they rushed forward through the entrance door Here the Dutch rallied again and with a smart salute laid Monkey and Bravey dead on the spot but now the cry resounded among the Dutch of "Flee Flee for all is over" and in a moment after a most awful and tremendous explosion followed by [a] vast white sheet of fire which shot an emmense hight into the Nightly sky announced that the Magazine was blown up. This dreadful report was succeeded by deep and awful silence every man stood motionless in the posture which he happened to be as if suddenly they had been changed to stone but soon this stillness was broken by the stones beams and fragments of the building plunging into the sea hissing and rattling on the ground and falling in showers among the Dutch they killed or wounded almost every surviving man [19]The English had now little else to do than seize the prisoners which they did collecting every one soldier man woman or child both in the Town and Fort and cramming them all in number 180 into a small room in the cas[t]le the English then laid themselves on the ground to sleep worn out with the fatigues of the day. When Morning came, Guelph Wellesly Parry Sneaky and Cheeky the survivors of the desperate struggle deliberated upon what they should do with the prisoners and at last came to the resolution of blowing them up with the castle in which they were confined This may to some seem monstrous and cruel in the extreme but let us recollect that these people had wounded CRASHEY and after this who would think of sparing them? after this act of justice and vengeance had been performed they gathered the bodies of Crashey Ross Bravey Gravey Monkey Cracky and Tracky. which they soon <u>made alive</u> by the usual means though after the most diligent search the remains of Stumps could nowhere be found they therefore the town being burnt down and the Inhabitants destroyed left the Island on the 20 of May with their renovated companions 12 in number but all true Heroes. after they had continued sailing for 23 days on June 2 Monkey who was in the shrouds cried out I see land instantly all where on deck gazing with eager eyes for the long sought long wished for termination of their pilgrimage the coasts of Ashantee and soon the far of and indistinct Mountains of the Interior and the low sunny coast of Guinea burst full in their veiw and after 2 days farther sailing they landed a[t] what is now called the Glasstown Harbour now the most splendid one in the world then a deserted stormy and reed choked bay it was at 6 oclock in the morning of the 5

---

[19] Branwell's description of the battle, including the blowing up of the magazine, was much influenced by the "Campaigns of the British Army at Washington, &c," *Blackwood's Magazine*, x, 1821, 180-87. Scott's *Life of Napoleon*, III, 40-41 also describes a powder magazine explosion.

of June AD 1770 that they anchored their vessel and the first act which they did was to throw up a small camp for the better preservation of themselves and their effects from savages or wild beasts in this camp the[y] remained during the day, proposing on the morrow to elect a king and then to march of for the purpose of exploring the company.

We have now arrived at the conclusion of this astonishing voyage we have conducted these 13 more than Heroes through innumerable perils and difficulties during a pilgrimage of many thousand miles we have seen them surmount all these dangers and though often plunged into gulphs from wich less daring and Noble minds would have despiared of extricating themselves they reached their long sought and desired haven crowned with all the Honours encircled with all the glories which human acheivements can ever obtain we have seen all these things and now will it now be desirable to know what charm or enchantment or power enabled them [to] steer through the tempest and reach the highest seat in the temple of Fame Was it those mighty and mysterious beings the Chief Genii who since the formation of the universe have watched over and have been considered the presiding DII of of the land of Ashantee though why they have chosen this spot for the Throne of their power no mortal can ever hope to know was it that they resolving among themselves to establish this country as the seat of all Grandeur Fame and Glory. Fixed upon these 13 men long before they were in being. to carry this their project into execution and instigated them by a kind of Fatality to this seemingly hopeless enterprise look at the subject in all its bearings consider the mysterious silence of the 12s on every thing conected with their history at the proceedings of CRASHEY that mighty and venerable patriarch and above all look at the Glasstown its tremendous tower its mighty Harbour the enchantment by which it was built and will not every wise and rational person lean to my opinion?

**CHAPTER,
III.
FREDERIC,
THE FIRST.**

From	June 5 AD 1770
To	June 9 AD 1770
	Year of the 12s I

I The meeting to elect a king II copy of the proclamation III Expidition to explore the interior of the country IV The [e]ncountre with the Genii V concluding observations. Capt. Bud January the 10th AD 1831[20]

[20] A sketch of what appears to be a bridge is on the right-hand side of the page.

When the morning after their arrival had come CRASHEY called a council of all the 12s to deliberate on the expediency of electing a King in a tempory hall when all had assembled He arose and made the following speech (NB the account of this meeting is translated from Leaf who wrote in the old young men toungue with a little alteration to make it intelligible to those of the present day)

"Young men, we have now, after a long and perilous voyage from our country arrived at the land of our hope. something with in me says we were not brought here to lie idle No No beleive me when I say that we shall have far greater trials far more dreadful dangers to go through ere we reap the Fruit of our labour. You are all young ardent impetous you are divided among yourselves one desires one thing and some other immediatley calls out for another in this state your counsels will never prosper your expeditions will fail and shortly you will be forced to return from whence you came covered with disgrace & infamy thus situate you will cry what shall we do to attain unity? I answer elect a king soberly consider among yourselves who is the fittest person to fill that high and ardous office and elect him whoever he be as for myself I will stand aloof from all your smaller conserns consult me when matters are too difficult for you to manage then I will direct them for you"

This speech from their wise and venerable leader was received with deep and reverential attention and after Due pause Edward Gravey arose and said

≡ ! ! GRAVEY "After what our Father has said it may be deemed presumtous in me to add anything relating to our electing a king but certainly my Freinds I will own that what I have to state shall not be advice to you as to the way of proceeding in this case of that our venerated leader has sufficiently informed you nor methinks would it be proper in a young man of seventeen to dictate to an assembly what they should do in a matter of such vital importance the cause then for which I adress you is to state my opinion as to whom is fittest to hold that high office I have attentively observed the maxim communicated to us by our great Father I have cast my eyes round ammong you I have pondered your characters deeply in my mind and the results of my deliberation is that of all this assembly JOHN ROSS is the person best calculated to weild our sceptre and direct our counsels in him you see all the advantages of outward appe[a]rance he is tall strong Manly but shape and comleyness do but little make the caracter of a king therefore to these he adds a soul firm determined and cool he is brave undaunted in the hour of peril unshaken amid the thunders of war elect him my companions and you shall go on conqring and to conquer slight him in[21] the sun of Hope has sunk from you for ever henceforth the portion allotted to you shall be Danger and Famine and desolation and Infamy without end"

SNEAKY Halt my good friend not so fast in your wording nor so sweeping in your sentence every man is not of a mind You may think that with out this perfect Apollo this concentration of all wisdom. we shall cease to exist but rely on my word lad that there is none other in this assembly who behold in him the

---

21 "and" obviously intended.

perfection you imagine therefore though I myself shall propose none I intreat some more rational person to rise and oppose the proposal of this addlehead but if none do rise I shall certainly propose myself

WELLESLY What now! have you so soon forgot the advice of our ever to be venerated leader that we should keep unity among ourselves? do we not see one among us rise to propose his choice and another immediatly stand up to ridicule and oppose it? do you rebel against our leader thus to act so contrary to his precepts? Not my freinds that I in any way intend to applaud or sanction the choice made by our companion Gravey when he rose up I expected to hear sentiments at once wise eloquent and just but oh what was my suprise to hear of the proposal of King John the second! surely a worse choice could not have been made among us and therefore I shall not lose time in showing his defects as a king which we are all aware of But as the sun is far advanced in the heavens and we must soon proceed on our investigation of the country I shall immediatly name him who of all here present best deserves the crown. let me then my Freinds propose to you Frederic Guelph Duke of York and second son of his majesty George III after due investigation I can see no one who can claim an equal right with him to our throne are we not Englishmen is he not the son of the King of England in whose dominions we were born and whose subjects we latley were? [h]as he not bravely fought for us and headed our troops at the conflicts on the Ascension Island? propose him then and . . . .
The rest of the speech and meeting is lost from Leafs manuscripts nor is any MSS yet descovered supplied [which] the chasm but however after some deliberation the meeting elected F GUELPH. whom we shall hereafter denominate the Duke of York or King as the King of the 12s as the original proclamation of this is in my possesion and being both courious and valuable I shall insert a facsimile and Translation

FAC SIMILE	TRANSLATION
PROCLOMAUTUR	*proclamation*
WOURAID YA MOTTIN AUCIN BONIR	*Whereas a meeting having been collected*
CULAUCKTED TOU ILE...A KAUNG	*to elect a king it was proposed that*
AUT WAUD PRUPOD DAUT GAULF TAU	*GAULF (Guelph) was to be king and it*
BO KAUNG ON AUT WOD CAGID.	*was carried*

FAC SIMILE (continued):
'≡AUTANTOII. L. | GOLU XVIII
S. | AUNNO DOMINII
| MDCCLXX
BEU≡CRASHEY

TRANSLATION (continued):
Ashantee L | *GOULOU (July)18th*
S | *Anno Dominii---*
| *1770----------------*
| *BUTTER CRASHEY*

When this buissness was finished A Wellesly, W Parry, A Sneaky and J Ross, under the command of the king prepared to march on an expedition for discovering the interior af[t]er having recieved the advice and benediction of their great leader they set off their rout for the first day was over a luxuriant but uncultivated plain with not the least sign of an Inhabitant but about the middle of the 2d day Stumps who had been hunting for the support of the expidition came running up to the king almost breathless crieng out that he had seen in a little dell about 2 miles of the print of footsteps which measured 14 feet from the heel to the tip of the toes and innumerable other which extended from 2 to 3 feet. on hearing this suprising relation the[y] all repaired to the spot and while buisly engaged in looking at the monstrous footmarks the sky which till then had been blue and clear was suddenly covered with black and tempestous clouds which hurried to and fro as if in some great and awful convulsion The atmosphere was hot still and suffocating save that now and then loud and howling blasts passed through the air while thick and sulphrous clouds of smoke where continualy rolling from the west Terrified at this awful change the whole party stood still and waiting for the Issue The[y] had not long remained there when they beheld advancing from the west an Immense and terreble monster his head which touched the clouds. was encircled with a red and fiery Halo his nostrils flashed forth flames and smoke and he was enveloped in [a] dim misty and indefinable robe around this dreadful figure were many lesser monsters similar to himself who when they saw the party of young men stand bound to the spot with terror and astonishment rushed up and whith hideous yells and ferocious gestures prepared to devour them but ere they could do this the bigger one grasped all the young men in his huge hand and immediatly flew away after a short time however he alighted at an immense palace which he entered and conveyed them into a hall of inconceivable extent and splendour at one end of the room were seated three beings of much the same height as himself wraped in clouds and having flames of fire round their heads when he entered they all stood up and enquired "Have they come?" "Yes" he answered at the same time <placing> them down before them instantly the taller of the 3 new monsters seized Arthur Wellesly the next seized E W Parry and the last seized J Ross For a long time they continued looking at them in silence which however was broken by the monster who brought them there he saying "Know you then that I give into your protection but not for your own these mortals whom you hold in your hands" at hearing this, Wellesly Parry and Ross each set up a doleful cry thinking that they were forever to be separated from their king and companions but the 3 monsters after expressing their thanks to their benefactor. assured them that they would let them go immediatly but that they would watch over their lives and as their guardian demons wheresoever they might go the Monster first seen then seized hold of Sneaky saying "Thou art under my protection and I will watch over thy life" for I tell you all that ye shall one day be Kings"[22] when he had uttered these words he he waved his hand thrice in the air crying DEPART! and immediatly the whole party found themselves standing in the little hollow dell the sky clear and unclouded all nature sleeping silently under the red beams of the just setting sun when they had recovered from their astonishment they immediatly agreed instantly to return to their companions and aquaint them of

---

[22] Possibly adapted from Shakespeare's *Macbeth*. This whole passage is, of course, another version of Charlotte's account of each of the sisters' claiming one of Branwell's toy soldiers (Alexander CB, I, 5). Sneaky, it must be remembered, is Branwell's soldier.

these strange procedures accordingly early the next morning they set off homewards each man pondering within himself the prophetical words "I tell ye that you one day shall all be kings"

And now before I conclude this chapter I will make an observation on the bold and daring courage of these Mighty Heroes. Where I ask could we now find 12 men who would of their own accord go forth from their native country to a savage and unknown land and when arrived there though surrounded by demons desarts and a feirce and mighty nation of barbarians hating them and determined to destroy them where could we find any who in such circumstances would think of building towns exploring countrys and setting their Foes at defiance there never has been nor will be such another instance of human courage skill daring and success.

The End of the third chapter P B Brontë January the 25 AD 1831

CHAPTER:
IV.
FREDERIC 1st continued.

From		June 7 1770
To		November 4 1779
year		
of the		
12s		7

Contents

I Building of the 12s Town II return of the party of discovery and mysterious departure of Crashey III Death of Kashna Quamina IV Battle of Rossendale Hill[23]*and Death of Frederic the first V Inscription on his tomb*

WHILE matters were thus proceeding with the party on Discovery those left with the ship had not been inactive for though they *might* (and probably others similarly situated would) have delayed to build a town till the arrival of their Freinds yet their ever vigourous minds hating and disdaining Idleness led them Promptly to begin the erections soon the firm and massy walls rose before them then the neat but humble cottages and within a week after digging the foundations. the new town firm complete and able to resist all intruders greeted their anxious and delighted eyes a little creek or harbour was dug surrounded whith walls wherein they might store the ship and keep her safe from the barbarians and now when all things were completed CRASHEY their venerable

---

23 The Forest of Rossendale lies just south of Burnley, near Todmorden, in West Yorkshire.

director gave a feast to all the Builders namely Cheeky Bravey Gravey Monkey Tracky and Cracky in the public hall. hardly had they sat down or tasted the first mouthful of food when to their utter suprise the door opened [and] in stalked the party of men who had been sent out to explore the country headed by the king and seemingly in great agitation without previous salutation or answer to the questions repeatedly made why they had returned so soon the king directly informed them of the strange adventure they had met with and of the predictions of the dreadful monsters who had so strangely avowed themselves their protectors while he was relating this Crashey was observed to look anxiously round and in a short time to arise and depart from the hall This at the time was not taken notice of and they continued the Feast till night but when morning came and he had not returned they began to be uneasy and determined to send out a party of 4 men to seek for him and to attempt his rescue if he had fallen into the hands of savages accordingly the king chose for this purpose Sneaky Bravey and Monkey commanded by J Ross they set out with the first light of the morning and before they had proceeded many miles just as the sun was rising the[y] observed advancing from a distance a large party o[f] savages the first they had seen in the country they were tall strong well made and of a black or copper coulor their garments were skins and their arms spears bows and sheilds their number might be about 40 or 50 and at their head marched a tall young man seemingly cheif or king when the young men observed them Ross ordered them to fire they did so and laid six savages on the ground dead or dying when the Ashantees for such they were heard the noise and saw so many amongst them fall dead without any assignable cause they stood motionless with astonishmesnt another volley was made which killed 4 more for the young men are admirable marksmen and now [the] savages knelt and lay on the ground crying and praying to their gods for mercy not being able to tell from whence their destruction proceeded but the young men party suddenly rushing up sabred or made them all prisoners they then questioned the cheif as to his name country and motives for coming theere but he hautily refused to answer their inquirys Ross then ordered the party to return whith their prisoners to the town and when the savages refused to proceed his threats of shooting them he soon made them submit and they proceeded homeward and here let me stop to remark the boldness and courage of these men who though only 4. in number could think of attacking a force ten times as many. and succeding in their attempts they soon arrived at the town when they conveyed the prisoners bound to the castle and then deliberated in the great hall what further means should be taken to rescue CRASHEY while sitting together in the common hall and as the unknown author of the Romantic Tale graphicly says "The wine cups standing upon the round table filled to the brim"[24] the air suddenly darkened the hall shook and streams of fire continualy flashed through the room followed by long and loud peals of thunder while all were standing pale and affrighted at the unusal phenomenon a dreadful Monster similar to those first

---

[24] See Alexander CB, I, 11.

seen or indeed one of the same[25] entered the room with Crashey in his hand he
placed him down and said in a loud voice "I am the cheif Genius Brannii with me
there are 3 others she Wellesly who protects you is named Tallii she who
protects Parry is named Emmii she who protects Ross is called Annii those
lesser ones whom ye saw are Genii and Fairys our slaves and minions we are the
Gaurdians of this land we are the guardians of you all, revere this man Crashey
he is intrusted with secrets which you can never know I prophecy unto you that
ye shall one day become a great and mighty nation and rule all the world Be not
afraid go on as you have done Adiu ye shall see us again" after thus speaking he
spread out his dragon wings and flew away and immediatly the thunder ceased the
darkness rolled of and the setting sun streamed in a red flood of light through the
large Gothic windows Of what followed for some time after this memorable
interveiw we know little or nothing exept that A party of Natives came to the
town about a month after the capture of the former party and brought a ransom
for the prisoners which was accepted and they accordingly all departed and now
for 8 years the 12s enjoyed uninterrupted tranquillity for confident in their
strength and courage and the protection of the Chief Genii they feared nothing
and the Ashantees under the government of their mild old king Cashna traded and
communicated amicably with them But such happines was not doomed to last
long for on the 3rd of [August][26] AD 1779 died after a long and happy reign of
46 years and aged 90 years CASHNA QUAMINA King of the
Ashantees....were I to dwell sufficiently on the many virtues of this
venerable king it would occupy a larger space of my History than could
conveniently be spared I will therefore pass on after saying on the authority of
every Historian of those times now extant that he lived as he died a pattern for
all king[s] who wish to be thought Fathers of their people and happy would it
have been both for his own country and the 12s if his son and succseasor had
possesed some portion but an iota of his many virtues but it was not fated so to

---

25 PBB's notes at this point:
    NOTE I The truth of this respecting the Monsters is when I first saw them
    in the morning after they were bought I carried them to Emily Charlotte and
    Anne They each took up a soldier gave them names which I consented to
    and I gave Charlotte Twemy (ie Wellington) and to Emily <Pare>(Parry) to
    Anne Trott (Ross) to take care of them though they were to be mine and I to
    have the disposal of them as I would--shortly after this I gave them to them
    as their own—PB Brontë
    NOTE 2] This town here mentioned is not the the Great Glasstown but was
    built 10 years previous to it its name was the Twelvestown and was burnt
    down at the duke of Yorks death the Glass town was erected. ie. AD 1780
                                                              JOHN BUD
    NOTE 3] The Ashantees were small nine pins which were brought from
    Leeds at the same time with the twelves one of them remains at this time ie
    January AD 1831 PBB
26 "August" is crossed out, but no substitution has been provided.

be for Sai Tootoo Quamina[27] was young headstrong and revengeful. I have forgot to mention that the cheif who was taken prisoner by Ross was this Sai Totoo. and Ever after he cherished an eternal hatred and rancour against the 12s and all conected with them and though he dared not show it openly during his Father[s] reign yet now when he came to the throne he determined on the first opportunity openly to avow it and the more readily as since the landing of the 12s they had accuired the use of fire arms accordingly when shortly after the Death of the old King the 12s sent a deputation of Sneaky Ross and Wellesly to "snuff the wind" under pertence of condoling with him he refused to admit them into his presence and ordered them to depart from his Dominions immediatly the deputation accordingly returned breathing anger and revenge when they arrived at the town they communicated to the King their reception From him it passed to the rest and now all the 12s were filled with anger they assembled in front of the Kings house crieing out for instant war and revenge declaring they would never lay down their arms or sheath their swords so long as a single Ashantee remained alive the King who was in reality as much enraged as any yet chose to conceal it replied that he would send Crashey to speak to the Genii and accordingly Crashey departed into the evil desart for that purpose after 2 weeks abscenc he returned, saying that the Genii had given the following answer to him *(translated from Leaf.)*

"Twelves go up to battle Fear not for we will help you though terrible
dangers await you yet shall you conquer in the end"

Inspired by this prediction and never pausing to think what these "terrible dangers" might be they leaving their town quite empty commenced their march for Comasiee the Ashantees capital[28] on November I AD 1779 For 3 days the[y] proceed[ed] up the country meeting nought but a few deserted houses. and their Heroic minds undaunted by the terrible rains which deluged the face of the country or the barren wilderness over which they were passing or the length of the journey mighty armies which they knew were prepared to take vengeance on them when they arrived at Coommasiee yet undaunted by all this they marched on and the morning of the 4 ushered in their arrival within sight of the city they now by command of the king took position on a step hill which overlooked the surrounding country and after fortifiing themselves with falln trees trenches &c

[27] Osei Tutu, leader of the Ashanti during the 1670's, crushed opposition from neighboring states through a series of military campaigns, following which he was installed as king of the new, expanded Ashanti empire. After his death in either 1712 or 1717, he was succeeded by Opoku Ware, under whom the Ashanti Empire reached its fullest extent within the African interior. The Ashanti defeated a British force in 1824, but made peace in 1831 and avoided conflict for the next 30 years.

[28] Under King Osei Tutu, Kumasi was named the capital of the newly formed Ashanti state. For a possible source of information on Sai Too Too and Quamina, and the capital Coomassie, see *Blackwood's Magazine*, v, 1819, 175-83; 302-10.

they determined to await the assaults of the Ashantees an army of whom amounting to 13000 commanded by the king Sai Tootoo were preparing to attack them. the post which the 12s occupied was a small meadow behind which rose tall cliffs covered with wood before them ran a deep and rapid river scarcly at that time fordable by the rains and on all sides round an[d] in Front of this meadow there sloped an exceedingly steep ascent covered with rocks falln trees and rubbish in such wise as to render it immpossible for cavalry and nearly so for Infantry to mount to the brink of the torrent In such a situation it would be very possible for a force of one thousand or even of 600 men to defend themselves against an army of 12 or 13000 men But not in this world could their be found 12 men save these undaunted heroes who would think for a moment of opposing alone and unassisted in howsoever advantageous a position the assault of 13000 furious and valiant warriors. And now while the 12s were thus waiting impatiently for conflict they heard the faint flourish of Trumpets and soon beheld the plain covered with myriads of warriors who bent their way to the foot of the mountain on which they were situate. For a moment I have it on the confession of several of them their hearts died within them at the seeming immpossibility of sustaining a single assuault for a moment but no more and roused anew to the utmost pitch of their superhuman courage they welcomed with a loud shout the appearance of the Ashantees who headed by the king and confident of success marched boldly up the ascent. which was about a quarter of a mile in length but I have forgot to mention that the Duke of York had with great pains constructed a sort of sluice gate by wich he could turn the river from its natural channel down the hill side full on the ashantees now therefore after the enimy had got nearly to the top of the hill he called out to his men "turn the river" immediatly they executed his command and down rushed an immense volumn of water with a sound of thunder sweeping rocks trees earth and every thing wich opposed it[s] way full upon the front of the <amazed> and terrified Ashantees hurling hundeereds of them along with it into a small lake at the foot of the declivity which however by reson of the immense quantities of rocks trees earth dead bodies &c &c washed into it soon over flowed its banks and burst like a deluge over the whole plain breaking and destroying the rear of the Ashantee army in an instant The confusion among them was now indescribable the torrent rushing on their front the shreiks and cries of those born along by it to certain death and the ravings and despair of the remainder were indescribable Indeed the greater part of the Ashantee army thinking that the 12s were Gods and not men immediatly turned back and fled down the steep to the plain where yet many having escaped death from the torrent above were fated to be slain by the deluge below But still there remained a formidable body of 700 cheifs and soldiers of the more courageous sort who ralling round their king boldly forced their way in the face of the rocks and waters which with headlong fury were continualy thundering on them up to the natural platform on which the 12s stood Dauntless as lions and commenced a most furious attack upon them. Now indeed there ensued a scence utterly unparrarelled in the annals of the world and to which my pen is inadequate to do the least justice The battle of Marathon[29] and the conflict at the pass of Thermopylae[30] are not to be compared to this insomuch as there their enimies deserved not the name of men but here 12 young soldiers had to cope with 700 furious and desperate warriors of their own nature courageous and often tried in many dreadful wars

When the King perceived how matters stood he ordered Monkey Cracky and Tracky commanded by Arthur Wellesly to station themselves on a high rock there to single out and fire upon All the leaders and most courageous men in the Ashantee army while the remainder of his men froming themselves into a compact circle himself being at their head stood with their pikes and bayonets bristling forth on all sides and froming a hedge of steel to all who should oppose them meanwhile the Ashantees surrounding them on all sides Rushed with one accord and yelling like tygers on this noble handful of men who stood unmoved as a rock laying multitudes dead at their feet charging upon them in scattered bodies then rallying in a circle round their king and when wounded placing one knee on the ground while the other supported their buckler and in this manner stabbing with their long pikes every one who opposed them and if any one happened to be dangerouly wounded two or three would unite holding their targets over him and defending him to the last. nor were the Ashantees inactive for though many of their cheifs were slain by the unerring balls of the little band stationed on the rock yet they threw themselves with a blind and headlong fury on the cool but desparate 12s continualy endeavoring to slay Guelph the King who at the head of his men fought with a strength and courage more than human in this state the conflict continued for more than an hour till at last anxious to end all by one desicive blow Quashia Quamina a great cheif and brother to the King flew on Guelph with his huge sabre and aimed a blow at his head which would have separated it from his body had not he parryied it with his target and grappleing with the chief threw him on the ground here a deadly struggle commenced between them they rolled over on the ground stabbing and and attempting to <throttle> with each other till at last having got uppermost the Ashantee cheif wrenched the pike from guelphs hand and plunged it in his heart though the next moment he himself fell dead peirced with and infinite multitude of balls from the band stationed on the rock. The conflict was now for the body of the King all the 12s rallyed over it those from the rock descended and joined. while the bravest of the Ashantees rushing on with the fury of that torrent which so latley had well nigh ruined [them] attempted to over-whelm the determined

---

[29] Marathon was the site of a decisive battle (490 BC) during the Greco-Persian wars; in the course of this battle, fought over a single day, the Athenians repulsed the attempted Persian invasion of Greece.

[30] The pass of Thermopylae from Thessaly to Locris, only twenty-five feet wide at its narrowest part, is famous for its heroic defence by 300 Spartans and 700 Thespians who defended the pass in 480 BC for three days, although vastly outnumbered, against Xerxes's Persian host. On the subject, see Branwell's poems in volume II or in Neufeldt PBB, 90 and 165.

12s many were [the] acts of superhuman courage which signalized the death of the King many were the victims devoted to his shades the conflict for the dead body of Patroclus on the shores of Troy[31] must sink to nothing before the actions of this memorable day but now their leader be[i]ng slain the 12s no more acted with that coolness which had before saved them from so many enimies though furious and courageous as ever yet the[y] fought blindly for Crashey who might have supplied Guelphs place was laid wounded amid the heaps of Ashantees who had fallen by his hand and shortly there remained only 5 of the 12s spent with fatigue stiff with wounds and over powered by numbers in this state they kneeling under a rock for the[y] could not stand the[y] implored the Genii to help them and their prayer was not disregarded for suddenly the heavens darkend the wind blew a hurricane and torrents of rain accompanied with thunder and lightning announced the approach of the cheif genii who all four suddenly appearing over the heads of [the] ashantees cried out with a loud voice "Arise Twelves arise we have renewed your strength Faint not within sight of the goal" and then suddenly dissapeared. The remaining 12s having new strength poured into them now charged on the amazed and terrified Ashantees giving no quarter but massacering them without mercy and that with comparitive safety to themselves for their enimies being as it were stunned with fright could offer no resistance. If we may exept the King Sai Tootoo Quamina who with 60 men the remainder of his army once amounting to 13000, after the surviving 12s had made an end of the Ashantees, they *resuscitated* or "*made alive*" their companions who had been slain the[n] threw the dead Ashantees into the small lake before mentioned and having dug a grave or vault in the ground they with great greif and lamentation buried therein FREDERIC GUELPH. DUKE OF YORK AND KING OF THE TWELVES, and raised [a] pillar over his tomb bearing on it the following inscription

≈ TAVCRED TW ≈
DE MAVMERV
WF,
FRAVDRIC GWVLF.
KING.
OVF DE TWAVLVES ≈
HWV WAVD TLWIN HERE AT
DE BAVTLE
OF ROUDAUNDOYLE HILL
NOVAUMBER IV
MLCCLXXIX ≈

SACRED TO
THE Memory
OF
FREDRIC GUELPH
KING
of the TWELVES
Who was slain here at
the battle
OF ROSSENDALE HILL
November 4
AD 1779 ≈

---

31   According to Homer's *Iliad*, Patroclus, beloved companion of Achilles, was killed by Hector while wearing Achilles's armor. According to rights of battle, Hector had claim to his opponent's armor and to the trophy of his head; but Ajax and Menelaus intervened to save the body of Patroclus from this indignity, and were able to bear the corpse back to to the Grecian camp.

Ever since this battle it has been the custom of many to make a pilgramage to this monument from all parts of the 12s land and many offerings are offered at a small temple near to it[32] and now after they had performed the last duties to their departed Monarch there arrived at the camp a deputation from the Ashantees praying for peace on the terms highly advantageous to the conquerers but for some time the Twelves would not listen to them until CRASHEY expostulated with them showing that it was not possible even were it right to exterminate the inhabitants as they wished and that these terms were exceedingly advantageous to them adding that they had avenged the death of their king as it became them and now they should seek to elect another and return as the articles of peace stipulated back to their town this wise and prudent advice was not to be slighted and therefore the terms offered by the ashantee King were taken and the twelves immediatly returned unmolested to their city on the coast

Thus ended a champain unparlleled in all history alike for it[s] design execution and end[ed] a champaign in which 12 young soldiers in the midst of a foreign country the inhabitants of which were decidedly hostile to them yet maintaned themselves against an army of 13000 courageous warriors and in the end forced them to submitt to their power And thus too ends the reign of Frederic the First a Prince in his life time loved respected and venerated by his noble subjects and at his death lamented by them with a deep sorrow deep though I cannot say lasting for the hearts of these heroes were not formed to receive many tender immpression[s] when they sorrowed they sorrowed not for the man but for the mind IN person FREDERIC GUELPH was very tall Leaf says 6 feet 7 inches and another MS. 6 ft. 9 In He was well shaped strong and muscular his countenance was open frank and noble his whole deportmen[t] kingly and Magnificent IN disposition he was generous to the last degree, ready to pardon but severe in punishment in battle his courage was ardent but he was cool and quick in observation ever ready to take advantage of the least favourable position of the ground as may be well observed in the battle of Rossendale. Throughout the whole of his reign he was redy to reward slow to punish just in all his actions and in his whole conduct anxious for the good of his people insomuch that I will venture to affirm that he was the best Monarch that ever sat on the throne of the 12s

But befor I enter upon the next reign I must speak a few words on the laws and customs of the 12s at this period of their history Though the lights which we possess on this subject are scanty indeed there being none save Leafs history which is much mutilated and a few records inscriptions and. scraps of

---

[32] PBB's note at this point:

NOTE The reason why we let GUELPH be killed so as he could not be got alive at this battle is that at the time we let this battle take place (ie in the beggining of AD 1827) The real Duke of York died. of a mortification and therefore determined that he should die so as that he could not be got alive the which however was unusual among us

P B Bronte April 28 AD 1831

Manuscripts. as to the 12s themselves as well might we ask of the Pyramids to declare who built them as seek for information from them

Their Monarchy appears to have been elective at the death of one king another being to be chosen not for his power but his merit and method which is in my opinion far preferable to hereditary monarchy in which we may be obliged to submit at one time to Tyranny at another to profligacy at another to avarice Their king was rather despotic than limited yet he had his bounds his office was I To have the sole command of the armies and to have the privilege of making war and comanding peace when he pleased II decide the punishment of criminals III levy taxes call counsels and to jud[g]e in cases of law—Thus far he was despotic but not farther He had not the power of life and death in his hand he could not confiscate his peoples property or infringe their rights nor could they abridge his power and consider him as a cipher everything was as it should be the king was every inch a King yet the people were Free IN their customs and manners the 12s were simple and primitive they had not titles but the Military ones a custom which still pervails among us to a great degree in their affluence property &c one person was nearly equal to another their dress for occassions of state was curious if we may judge from the statues Bas releifs and illuminations remaining to this day it consisted of A high black cap with several hierogliphical figures on it the meaning of which is unknown their coat or rather jacket was shaped after the manner of a sailors and was in colour a light scarlet. They also wore tight pantaloons of the same colour but their shoes were the most curious part of their apparel. This shoe, for each man wore only one! was like a round flat cake wit[h] two holes in the middle into which his feet were inserted as in a stocks. many have been the attempts made to find out how this shoe could possibly be used, and many the volumns writ on the subject. all of which are improbable and many impossible. The only guess which I conceive to be near the truth is that suggested by my learned freind Proffesor Gifford. R.A.S he thinks and with great appearance of truth that they were composed of some tough substance like Indian Rubber which might be stretched almost any length and yet not break and that they used it to bring themselve[s] to a good method of walking in which they much prided themselves in but this dress and shoe was only used for particular occasiones such as a Counsel or solemn ceremony The common dress was regimentals somewhat like what we now have[33]

---

[33] PBB's note at this point:

NOTE. The state dress here spoken of was what my First soldiers (ie the 12s) were realy carved and painted in the curious shoe was the little stand which each soldier had to keep him from falling.

PB Brontë
April 29. AD 1831

CHAPTER THE VTH,	FROM	NOVEMBER 30 AD 1779—
FREDERIC, II.	TO	August 3. AD 1782—
	Year of the 12s	9.

CONTENTS

——————

——————

WHEN the Twelves had arrived at 12s Town they shortly called a council. on Dec 3, to elect a new King and while in the midst of debating on the subject a hollow tomblike voice from without the hall cried out. "CRASHEY CRASHEY" The venerable patriarch immediatly rose and departed And shortly after returned with a ghastly sceleton like figure clothed in tarnished regimentals CRASHEY ascended the throne and thus addressed his auditors who pale and speechless with astonishment sat quite silent

"YOUNG MEN him whom you here see is FREDERIC STUMPS who was so basely slain And whose death you so gloriously avenged at the conflict on the Ascension island after long and suprising adventures both by sea and by land He has regained our country though in what condition you here see. Young men Elect him for your king know his courage coolness integrity ability you know how he resembles in his mind our late lamented king and by electing him you will show your respect for the memory of Frederic the I who before his death often said that were he himself to die the person whom he would like to be his successor should have been Frederic Stumps but he thought Stumps to be irrecoverably slain therefore he but wished it—

This speech was received with loud cries of long live King Frederic the second nor did one dissentient voice speak against his nomination The crown of their late monarch was placed on his head and after he had given them a relation of his adventures the meeting separated. What these adventures were is not now know[n] though I and several learned freinds are making diligent search after a manuscript reported to be preserved in some one of the great libraries. which contains an account of them. This manuscript if it is in being and can be discovered I shall insert either in my appendix or in some future edition of this work

For three years the reign of Frederic 2 was quiet and without war but on July AD 1782 the storm [which] had so long been hushed broke out againe with doubled violence for Sai Tootoo and his subjects having recovered from the fright and confusion [into] which the battle of Rossendale hill had thrown them immediatly assembled an army of 5000 men and as is the custom with barbarous nations without open declaration of war marched down on the 12s town who totaly ignorant of their approach were quietly enjoying themselves with hunting games in wrestling boxing running &c. as was their custom in times of peace and leisure The first who had intimation of their approach was Arthur Wellesly He had been with his gun to hunt on the mountains near the city and having climbed a rock to look for game he saw the Ashantee army moving along the valley instantly he seized his gun and darting with the rapidity of an arrow reached its gates in much less than half an hour. having run the whole distance of 6 miles in that space of time! when he had arrived he instantly alarmed the rest who had scarce time to bar the gates and mann the walls before the Ashantees came on the city like an overwhelming torrent but before I proceed with my narrative I must give some account of this army of Ashantees. They were all with trifing exceptions Natives of Acrofcroomb a city and province of Ashantee. Their leaders wer[e] 10 brothers the eldest was named Sai Quarenqua and they had all vowed to eat the flesh and drink the blood of the 12s should any fall into their hands. when therefore they arrived at the foot of the city walls they commenced a furious bombardment with shells flaming brands bombs and so forth and proceeded to undermine the foundations of the walls but the young men were far from Idle For they returning the compliment with the same missiles made dreadfull havoc among the thickly crowded ranks of the Asshantees this mode of fighting continued for 4 days but on the 30 of July the enimy having made a breach in the wall rushed furiously into the city and in one moment filled every street the 12s now retired to the tops of the houses where they continualy poured stones tiles rafters &c to crush the enemy all save J Ross who with a long pike in [34] [his hands] rushed fearlessly among the thickest of the Ashantees stabbing and slaying all he met untill covered with wounds he fell dead amid the heaps of slaughtered enimies Inspired by this feat of Heroic bravery superior to that of Isadas the Spartan[35] A Wellesley W Bravey and A Cheeky each with a spear in his hand rushed forward the same and after scattering terror and destruction among the ranks of their adversaries. were obliged to retire wounded and covered with glory to their companions but Cheeky was taken by the Ashantees to be reserved with Ross for their Cheifs banquet But now after 3 hours valiant fighting the Remnants of the 12s ie Crashey Wellesly Sneaky

---

[34] PBB's note at this point:
NOTE I The Acroofcroomb cannibals here mentioned were ninpins whom we let fight just such a battle as is here mentioned and also kill their <prisoners> & eat them PB Bronte
NOTE 2 The reason why we realy let Stumps be king was he was the same wooden soldier which the Duke of York had been PB Bronte April 30 AD 1831
[35] Isadas, when he saw the Thebans entering Sparta, stripped himself naked and engaged the enemy with spear and sword, for which he was rewarded with a crown.

Parry Monkey and Tracky together with the King. were obliged to retire to the great Magazine where blocking themselves up they bade defiance to all the attacks of the Ashantees. who taking with [them] the killed and wounded 12s ie Cheeky Gravey and Cracky. retired to a small distance from the capital and there horrid to relate roasted and made a feast of them (the place where they were eat is still shown) When the 12s heard of this dreadful banquet they were filled with rage. "This" said the King "this far more demands vengeance than the death of Guelph he was slain with fair dealing and honour but such atrocitys as this must not go unpunished cast then of all thoughts of Defence think but of revenge or death. To this speech his men replied with loud shouts of approbation and when Night came on they march[ed] slowly and cautiously to the Ashantee camp with a bravery like that of Diomed[36] and Ulysses[37] or Nisus and Eurayalus[38] They penetrated in to the very midst of the sleeping barbarians killing hundereds without waking the rest till they came to the decaying embers of the fire were lay the mangled and half eaten bodies of their friends at this horrid sight they could not be prevented from exclaiming aloud "Not A man shall escape for this dee[d]" which roused the ten Ashantee cheifs but the 12s were to much for them the[y] killed six and would have slain the rest but the Ashantees awaked by the noise came rushing on them in hundereds and thousand insomuch that the 12s forming themselves into a phalanx stood with their spears opposed to their enemies determined to conquer or die. hundered[s] of Ashantees were soon laid bleeding on the ground and Sneaky and Tracky on the 12s side were slaughtered But these godlike heroes soon made the Ashantees give way who after an hours hard fighting made a confused and dishonourable retreat leaving behind them 1500 men dead on the feild of battle and their 5 remaining cannibal cheifs prisoners in the hands of the 12s the other 5 having been slain. without turning

---

[36] Diomedes, reputedly one of the bravest of the Grecian chiefs in the Trojan War, successfully engaged in battle with Hector and Aeneas, obtaining military glory by repeated acts of valor. He became Ulysses's companion, helping Ulysses to steal the Palladium from the temple of Minerva at Troy, and later accompanying him into the Thracian enemy camp, where he assisted Ulysses in killing Rhesus, the king of Thrace, and slaughtering the Thracian soldiers.

[37] Ulysses, the king of Ithaca, was especially renowned for his exploits with Diomedes—see note above. For eminent valor at Troy, he was universally lauded by the Greeks and rewarded with the arms of Achilles, thus being honored over and above the famous hero Ajax.

[38] According to the legend recounted by Lemprière, Nisus travelled to Italy with Aeneas, where he distinguished himself by his valor against the Rutulians, into whose camp he and his companion, Euryalus, the Peloponnesian chief, entered in the dead of night. Leaving the camp victorious after much bloodshed, they were spotted by a group of Rutulians who attacked Euryalus. Although Nisus came to the rescue of his companion, the two, greatly outnumbered, were overcome and killed. The deaths of these companions were lamented by all Trojans, and their great friendship became proverbial.

ife—

to pursue the routed army the 12s immediatly dragged the cheifs to a huge oak growing hard by and hung them in chains as victims to those who were slain next Crashey Implored the Genii saying "O Cheif Genii Guardians and defenders of our city who have promised to make us lords of all. we implore you now to make your promise good give us to root from the earth these infamous monsters who have so horridly slain and feasted on thy favoured warriors descend with the spirit of life on these who are stretched pale and mangled round these fires which witness the Atrocity of the Ashantees" Instantly the dead and wounded twelves with [the] half eaten victims to the Acrofcroombers started from the ground living vigorous and free from wound the rest of the 12s also felt new spirit and strength breathed into them and all now seized their arms[39] when Wellesly cried. "let us before we enter our city before we taste a morsel of food or take a minutes rest. rush after these infamous monsters and prusue them into the heart of their country event to the city of Acrofcroomb and let us rase that city to the ground so that no stone may remain to tell where it stood" This animated advice was immediatly taken and of the whole 12 rushe[d] on the retreating Ashantees like Tygers bounding on their prey. For three days and nights they prusued them without a moments stop untill either slain by their spears or drowned in crossing rivers or dead of fatigue or dispersed into wood caves &c not a vestige of the Ashantee army remained but still the Twelves were not satisfied for marching with their king at their head and scattering desolation werever they came. they arrived at Acrofcroomb here they set fire to the city murdered the unresisting Inhabitants and then returned to their own town laden with honour and glory after a journey of 200 miles performed in 3 days.

CHAPTER VI.	From—	August 30 AD 1782
FREDERIC II. continued	To—	November 30th AD 1790
	Year of the 12s	12

Contents

---

[39] The nickname of the 2nd. Battalion, the regiment of Arthur Wellesley (later Duke of Wellington), was "The Immortals." This nickname dates from the Marāthā War of 1803-4 which Wellesley fought in India, and originates from a story current among the Indian forces that the regiment were immortal, because of the number of soldiers wounded in action who subsequently recovered and reappeared in the fighting ranks.

We are now in the course of our History approaching times pregnant with events wonderful in their causes operations and effects times to which there is no parrarel in the history of the world. Events in which we behold a nation from consisting at first of twelve young men becoming at length a nation the greatest most powerful most warlike and most magnificent in the whole world a nation before whom Persia Greece Rome and England must hide their diminished heads and to which the whole world pays homage and is subject to but before I begin to write of these events I must first relate of several things which happened in Europe and which though not to a superficial observer at all connected with them. yet are in realty closely interwoven with their whole substance IN AD 1769 the French rose In insurrection against their government[40] and compelled their Monarch Louis the XVI to accept the crown on conditions calculated to lower his athority and raise theirs (ie the *mobs*) higher. But he having attempted to escape was soon entirely dethroned and beheaded the French now instituted a republican government the leaders of which committed the most unheard of cruelty and butchery on all in the least suspected of disaffection. This together with the murder of their monarch roused all the principal monarchs of Europe and a bloody war took place. but in 1779 Napoleon Bonapartè a victorious French General having raised himself up by his arts and abilities to high honour and favour. now seized on the supreme power and proclaimed himself in 1782 Emperor of France and King of Italy.[41] it was at this period, no general. or army either of the Prussians Austrians or Russians being able to withstand his ability and courage. that all Europe looked upon England as the only country which could have a chance of successfuly oposing the French and Bonapartè But even England amid her many heroes found not one equal to the task. Therefore having heard of the wonderful prodigies of men which spread such terror and destruction through Africa. Pitt and the ministry[42] determined to send a deputation to Ashantee for to pervail on one of them to come over and assist his native country for this purpose they fixed upon the celebrated JOHN LEAF Esquire then a private Gentleman though since know[n] and admired through Africa as the Author of that noble energetic learned and Eloquent work "The acts of the Twelves"[43] A ship was hired and Leaf set sail from England on his Mission. October 12 AD 1782 The first intimation which the 12s had of such a thing being in contemplation was the arrival of the ship itself in the port. on landing

---

40 The storming of the Bastille, which came to symbolize the inauguration of revolution in France, took place in July 1789, not 1769 as Branwell has it.
41 Branwell's date is again not accurate. In 1802, after further victories in Europe, Napoleon was voted First Consul of France for life, and, after promoting the formation of an Italian Republic modeled on the French, was nominated president of the newly formed Italian Republic. In 1804, when the Empire was proclaimed, Napoleon assumed the title of Emperor.
42 William Pitt (1759-1806) was the British prime minister during the French Revolution and the Napoleonic Wars, from 1783-1801, and again from 1804-06.
43 Perhaps borrowed from "The Acts of the Apostles."

Leaf was introduced to the King were he explained his mission. Frederic then ordered all the 12s to be called in "and never" says Leaf in one of his works "never was I struck with a body of such Gigantic noble looking and muscular men Each seemed of himself able to overthrow an army" On the nature of the mission being explained to them each eye brightened with pleasure and to a man they all steped forward as willing to undertake all required that they might gain fame and glory—rank and riches they spurned for after their services were no longer requisite in Europe they determined to sail again to Africa. Unable to decide wich should go from among so many CRASHEY was sent to the desart to enquire from the genii. in two days he returned saying the Genii had given him [a] certain rod saying "Take him whose height shall answer to the length of this rod" (The rod is now kept in the great Museum of the glass town) Arthur Wellesly was the only one to suit it and he was accordingly chosen. On the morning of January 1 AD 1783 he took a farewell of his freinds and the city and embarked in the Royal George for England. but I have forgot to mention that. JOHN LEAF. having took the hearts of the 12s they earnestly requested him to supply the place of A Wellesly. Therefore leaving his First Lieutenant Dorn to accompany A Wellesly to england he gladly accepted the opportunity now given him to observe the manners and cultivate the acquaintance of men to whom. all other men were but as "dust of the earth"[44]

For several months after the departure of A Wellesly the "Champion of Europe" as my highly Talented freind Capt Flower has styled him. the 12s enjoyed comparative peace and quietness. Though the Ashantees often made incursions. and many bloody fights were the consequence among themselves reigned entire unanimity. save on a few occasions. one of which I will describe as it is celebrated and affords a good specimen of the *private* demeanour good *manners* and politeness of these noble heroes

An Election was taking place at the public hall. Leaf does not inform us what this election was of And the King arose to harangue the 12s who were all assembled. Ross and Bravey liked not his speech and both at the same time rose to reprove him in a most convincing manner enforcing their arguments by addressing their monarch in such epithets as "Baundy legged" (Bandy legs) "Stumpois" (Stumpy) "taump haud" (Tump head) and the like royal and respectful language. on this Crashey arose and remonstrated with them. when they not daring to answer him retired into a corner like two sulky children. and began fairly to weep aloud the other more loyal subjects addressing the two "taulky wans" (sulky ones) by the most opprhrobrious languae their vocabulary could sujest but the mischeif did not end here—for while Parry had lain himself on the ground to rest Tracky in a most gentlemanly manner came and unceremoniously sat upon him whereat Parry jumped up and stamped upon him

---

[44] A phrase from the Anglican burial service, used to denote absolute mortality. It is founded on scriptural texts such as *Genesis* 3: 19: "dust thou art, and unto dust thou shalt return," and *Ezekial* 27: 18: "I will bring thee to ashes upon the earth in the sight of all them that behold thee."

But the Chief Genius Tallii now coming in seized and protected Tracky And the Ch—Gn—Emii took up her favorite Parry. But from this time forward a great hatred has subsisted between the two heroes. and also between Ross, or Trott as the King called him. and his monarch. For some months the peace of the community was disturbed by constant fighting between Rosses Faction and the Kings Faction which was however ended by the Kings taking Ross prisoner in single combat and hanging [him] to the Triangles

But something was now coming on which was to divert their attention from these petty [strifes] to other [of] more importance for the King of the Ashantees had assembled an immense Army of what number Leaf does not tell us and in the spring of 1785 marched on The city like an overwhelming torrent. The 12s now drew out to oppose him which they did for some time but at length exausted with fatigue and wounds they retired into The city wither the Ashantees pursued them and would have massacred the whole number had not a legion of Genii been sent to assist them who rushed on the Ashantee army filling them with a panic terror insomuch that many of them leapt into the great bay and the rest fled to their own country This is all the account I am able to give of this battle for Leaf who is my cheif light in these times is much mutilated hereabouts after this engagement the 12s under the government of a good king enjoyed uninterrupted Tranquillity for the space of 5 years. ie till the return of Arthur Wellesly of whom I must now speak after having so long wandered from him. his voyage to England where he landed June 5 1783 was calm and unproductive of Adventure on his arrival at London he was dignified with the title o[f] General Sir Arthur Wellesly. and dispatched with an army of 20000 British soldiers to Spain and Portugal which the French were then desolating. I need not say how gloriously he fought and beat them how he confounded Bonapartes best Generals and in the end [after] 4 years hard fighting changed the seat of war into the heart of France. But while engaging them in their own country news arrived that by the combined forces of Austria and Russia Napoleon was beaten and driven an exile to the Isle of Elba all Europe now rejoced at being delivered from his tyranny. But their joy was turned into Terror when they saw this man so latley abjectly driven from his country return gather his "comrades in arms" and dethrone the rightful king Louis XVIII. Seating himself on the throne as securly as ever Sir Arthur Wellesly was now again called on and after having been promoted to the rank of Feild Marshal with the title of DUKE OF WELLINGTON was sent over to the Netherlands with 30 000 Brithish Forces most of them his veterans from Spain and Portugal to endeavour again to quash Napoleon Bonaparte. with these forces aided by 35000 foreign troops he met the Userper on the celebrated plains of Waterloo—all the world knows the proceedings and end of that battle suffice it then to say that for a long time

> sat doubtful conquest hovering oer the feild
>
> Pope's Hom I i.[45]

---

[45] Actually Book XV, l. 361. See also p. 95, n. 6 above.

Neither party being able to conquer the other untill after fighting the whole day a large Body of Prussians headed by Blucher came up rushed on the French and with the assistane of the British drove them of [the] Feild pursuing them as far as Gemmape[46] with immense slaughter, This battle ended Bonapartes hopes to the throne of France and he fled to the sea shore with the intention of escaping from the country but here a British squadron intercepted him and he was conveyed to England. where the Government ordered [him] to be banished to the Island of St Helena. he was accordingly carried thither July 1. AD 1790[47] As for the Duke of Wellington soon After the battle of Waterloo he returned to England where he met with a reception due to the counquerer of Bonaparte. The Government loaded him with honours and bestowed on him a large estate in the Neighbourhood of England.[48] but all these praises gifts and flatery pleased not the Duke. he sighed to be with his companions in arms on the coast of Ashantee. he therefore requested an audience with the Prince Regent. and when introduced he thus addressed him

"The states of Europe are now freed from war and the Tyrant Napoleon is in exile I Therefore humbly conceive that my presence in this quarter of the globe is unneccessary. Your Majesty may believe how I must feel in a country the innhabitants of which have few ideas or associations which are congenial to me I therefore humbly intreat your Majesty to grant me permission to return to the coast of Ashantee. a country in which I have passed nearly the whole of my life and where abide the men whom only I could call freinds and companions. of all I have seen in the world I mean not a disrespect to the people of England they have treated me nobly honourably far more so than is due to my humble merit. but if I remain here I must remain inactive and a state of Inactivity is of all states the most foreign to my nature. If your Majesty or the countrys in this part

---

[46] The Battle of Gennape took place June 18, 1815.

[47] After one year of exile on the island of Elba, Napoleon returned to France (March 1815) for the so-called "One Hundred Days." It was during this period that he engaged with Wellesley's British forces at the Battle of Waterloo, where he was finally and decisively defeated. Following this defeat, Napoleon abdicated for a second time and was sent to his final exile on the remote island of St. Helena, a British dependency in the south Atlantic ocean. Napoleon was confined on the island of St. Helena from 1815 until his death in 1821.

[48] The historical Arthur Wellesley received many honors for his military actions, especially in the course of the Peninsular War. In 1809, for services to his country, he was rewarded with the title of Viscount; in 1812, he was granted an earldom; then later that year, in recognition of his defeat of Marshal Marmont at Salamanca and for his occupation of Madrid, he was given a marquessate and a grant of £100,000 for the purchase of an estate. After winning the decisive battle of the Peninsular War in 1814 he was made Marquis of Douro and Duke of Wellington. After the Battle of Waterloo, Wellesley was given £500,000, and granted the estate of Strathfieldsaye in Hampshire.

of the globe at any time may need my humble assistance I shall be ready as I have been to come over and lay myself at your feet"

To this noble and independent address an adress worthy of one of the 12s the Prince Regent replied that however sorry he must be to part with such a true hero yet he could not in justice refuse his request and he intreated him [to] make known any other wish he might have for if he could not of himself grant [it] yet he was certain that the country would. To this the Duke replied

"My mind knows not dissimulation therefore I will aquaint your Majesty with a wish not originating in me but in those brave soldiers who have fought with me the battles in Spain Portugal and Waterloo. They all to a man humbly intreat your Majesty that they may be permitted to sail with me to Ashantee and there to abide with their children after them"

The Prince Regent aquainted the parliament with this and it was unanimously agreed to therefore a large fleet of ships was prepared at the docks of London and on the 1st of. October. AD 1790 there sailed from England the Duke of Wellington and 30000. Brave veterans being all who survived the wars in which the Duke commanded They were all of them the strongest finest looking and Bravest men in the British Islands. and to this circumstance is mainly owing the wonderful size strength &c of the present Inhabitants of 12s land of whom indeed these make a part they set out with a fair wind and the applauses and good wishes of a concourse of 300000 persons assembled to see them depart Their voyage to Ashantee was like most other voyages a compound of calms storms fogs and foundering. I will therefore pass it over to give an account of their arrival at the 12s Town

in the Evening of November 30 AD 1790 as Leaf was standing on the castle tower hoisting the flag up. he saw over the sea something black moving towared land as it continualy increased in size and proximity to the shore he soon saw it was a fleet of ships on this he ran down from the tower in to the public [square] where the rest of his companions were and cried out "Theyre come" "Who are come" asked the astonished 12s in a breath. but before he could answer a loud blast of trumpets was heard on the shore 'To arms lads' cried the King and with bayonet in hand they rushed into the streets to welcome the newcomerers either as freinds or enimies but what was their suprise and delight to find the first thing that met their ey[e] sight the Duke of Wellington. at the head of many thousand English soldiers and a large fleet at anchor in the bay they all sprang toward him criyng Oh Arthur how glad we are to see you. we little thought to have that pleasure on his part he testified no less delight at once more beholding the freinds and companions of his youth The 12s had laid in an Immense stock of provision in case of a siege. Therefore they immediatly a feast was prepared[49] on a large open space of ground near the city. where all the newly arrived soldiers and the 12s and Duke of Wellington enjoyed themselves the soldiers happy to arrive at the end of their voyage the 12s happy to behold their companion again

---

[49] Branwell first wrote "they immediatly ordered a feast to be prepared," then crossed out "ordered" and "to be" and added "was."

whom they never expected to see. at this feast the Duke gave them an account of every thing that had passed in Europe since his departure and how he had defeated the Conqueror of Nations. At the conclusion of his recital, the King arose and taking the crown of his head placed it on that of the duke of Wellington saying "I am not worthy to rule this man he is your king" Instantly the whole assembled multitude cried out long live king arthur and though against all his endeavors they carried him in triumph to the great hall where he was formally installed "King and ruler of the 12s town and of all its inhabitants"

Thus ends the reign of Frederick II. a reign which will long be remembered in the annals of the young men. he was a good king though his qualitys were not shining yet they were of sterling worth. and were the concluding act of his reign only remembered it would justly entitle him to take a place among the BEST Monarchs that ever reigned—.

Here ends
THE I, VOLUMN *of,*
The
History of the Young Men
Begun December 15th AD 1830
Ended MAY 7.th AD 1831

John Bud

[Figure of Justice][50]

Note These soldiers were the second box wich I bought after the box of 12s— For wich vid Introduction P B B—rontë May 7. 1831

---

[50] See Alexander & Sellars, 300.

LETTERS
FROM AN
ENGLISHMAN:
VOL II
PBB::

2D SERIES[1]

LETTERS
FROM AN
= ENGLISHMAN =
TO
HIS FREIND IN =
LONDON
BY
= CAPTAIN JOHN FLOWER
VOL II[d]
[Figure of Justice]

C'T' ROSS'S GLASSTOWN.
Printed and sold by
= SEARGT WINLASS.
JUNE =

PATRICK BRANWELL
BRONTE
June 8.th AD 1831.
[ornamental figure][2]

---

[1] Hand-sewn booklet with grey paper covers (5.7 x 9.1 cm) of 16 pages (1 blank) in the Brotherton Collection, University of Leeds. On the back of the title page appear the words "ma chere frère vous l'avez ecris tres bien je croyais non vraiment vous n'avez pas. Ma foi que vous étes un mauvais garçon et vous serez un choquant homme"—Juliet Barker suspects Emily is responsible (Brontës, 179).
[2] See Alexander & Sellars, 300.

VOL
II

LETTERS,
FROM
AN ENGLISHMAN
BY C Flower
P B Brontë March 10. 1831:

LETTER. III.

MARCH 16. 1831[3]

Sir,

After having remained for nearly 3 months in this magnificent city surrounded by persons whose habits manners and customs are totaly dissimilar to those of my native island all my senses bewildered by the stupendous undertakings the splendid buildings the Tumult confusion and dangers of a people whose rising and greatness is attended by such suprising and supernatural event[s] and who now rule with a power before whom all opposition is usless not only [in] the vast tract of Africa but the whole world after having continued a quarter of a year in such a city and under such circumstances conceive if you can how rejoiced I was when the Marquis of Douro (with whom I have the great honour to be accuainted) arrived at my house a few days ago with proposals for my taking a journey with him across the Twelves land to his Father the Duke of Wellingtons Glasstown on the river Gambia miles to the west of the Glass town I read[i]ly accepted his proposal, and after I had adjusted the affairs of my firm we set off in his Lordships chariot accompanied by Young Soult the celebrated poet and my gay young freind Lord Charles Wellesley The morning of our set out was clear warm and pleasant the sky with out a cloud and our party in the highest spirits imaginable rapidly we rolled out of the city and beheld it[s] smoky chimmnys and lofty towers lessen behind us spire after spire successivly sinking behind the hills till at last the Tower of Nations alone remained rising majesticaly above The clouds vapours and smoke wich obscured its base like a misty and indefinable robe and backed by the vast Atlantic Ocean before us lay stretched an enchanting and fertile valley bordered on each side by Romantic and picturesque hills robed in dark green woods and yellow cornfeilds here and there diversified by the extensive parks and noble seats of the Nobility of the city while from the summitts of thes[e] hills occasionally rose bare rocky peaks towering to an immense hight in the heavens and at a great distance in front rose the vast forms of the Jibbel Kumrii seeming like the terrible but undefinable phantoms of a dream to threaten the plains at their feet with instant destruction their summits glittering with the accumulated snows of 4000 years the sides and base robed in a black indefinable mistiness but I have forgot to mention a

---

[3]   Originally dated October 1, AD 1830.

striking feature in our veiw namly the broad glassy waters of the Guadima which rolled its smooth and silvery current through the middle of the valley reflecting the sky hills and every thing on its banks as distinct as the objects themselves with here and there a white sail gliding rapidly by

"To the rendesvous of Nations and queen of
The globe"[4]

For a long time the Marquis of Douro and myself continued gazing on the scene silently forgetting in our excess of admiration that we were in a chariot or were any other than alone till we were startled out of our reverie by the noise and bellowing of an immense drove of Mountain cattle which were going toward the city the road which was a noble width being one hundered yards across was choked up with them to the distance of a qua[r]ter of a mile and as the Bulls were remarkably feirce the drivers were all mounted on horses and armed with a long and sharp lance to goad such as were refractory I had often before heard the Bulls of this country praised as the finest in the world and now had an opportunity to judge of their excellense. For you to do so I will give you a discription of one wich rushed past our chariot and a little farther on tossed and killed a driver who endeavoured to stop it. its length from the snout to the insertion of the tail was about 12 feet it[s] hight to the top of its back was nearly 6 feet its neck was immensely st[r]ong and thick its head wa[s] short broad and curly on its forehead was the resemblance of a white star its eyes were feirce lowring and malignant its horns short and exceedingly strong it[s] hoofs broad it[s] tail very large and its whole appearance was that of amazing muscular strength and a perfect model of a noble bull after gazing some time at this magnificant animal the Marquis directed my attention to the head driver and seemingly the owner of the drove saying "Do you observe that man Mark him well for he is one of the most celebrated men of our countries." I immediatly turned my eyes toward him but instantly started back with an exclamation of Horror and suprise. He was nearly 9 feet high! lean bony and ill built yet bearing the marks of extreme strength his legs wer[e] long and crooked his feet huge mishapen and flat his arms were of an exccessive length his hands like those of an orangoutang or some othe[r] equaly hideous ape—his "carcase" was lank and "ill favoured" But his counten[an]ce was the most horridly ugly and savage of any which I could before think of. Describe it I cannot nor could you have even an idea of it unless you could see the man but rather than leave you utterly in the dark about it I will *attempt* a description. it was deformedly long and narrow the cheek bones rising up to his eyes and then protruding from the skin like long ears his nose was large and shapless his jaws I cannot call it mouth was wide and turned up his lips thick and black his eyes sunken grey peircing and of an express truly horrif[y]ing but coverd by immense hanging eyebrows his beard and hair wich he had suffered to grow untouched was[5] black long thick and clotted with filth—and his garments wich were all

---

4   No source has been found; the line may well be Branwell's composition.
5   A partial sketch of a face appears here at the bottom of the manuscript page.

dirty and tattered consiste[d] of a dark lead colour[ed] coat waist coat and the remnants of a pair of once gold laced breeches such was the dress and appearance of the celebrated PIGTAIL the champion of Frenchmen when this horrible monster came up to us I observed the Marquis to whip on his horses and as well as his brother and young soult to look apprehensively while the Giant laying hold of the side of the chariot. and stopping it!! such was his incredible strength—roared out in a hollow tomblike sound and in the French *dialect* "Stap whuth hm hll huv 'm yit" (ie stop with him he'll have them yet) whereat the marquis drawing forth his sword aimed such a blow at his huge hand that it chopped it of in an instant and the monster ran of howling between rage and pain when we had got from among the drove of cattle at my request the Marquis gave me the following short history of Pigtail

"This man was originally a snug shopkeeper in Paris and one of the buisest men in those turbulent times for it was at the period when the Faction Du Mange[6] troubles were at their height but when the Great bill was passed which crushed the hopes of that ferocious party he along with others falling into the suspicion of the severe "Empreur" (Napoleon) had his goods confiscated and was himself proclaimed an outlaw made furious by this he entered a "Tavern" where he continued drinking Brandy and eating "white bread and prussian Butter" for a whole year never during that period once rising from his seat save when having taken an undue quantity of the above mentioned articles he was now and then carried forth to be buried at the expiration of this year he rose and killed his landlord "Monseiur who lives and who dies" (you know the ridiculousness of French names) and took upon himself the managment of his Tavern which soon became the most notorious in Paris Pigtail was the greatest vender of white bread and Prussian Butter

Here I stopt the Marquis with "I confess I do not quite understand the terms"

MARQUIS "not understand them! but I'll aquaint you then fore if it were know[n] that you did not you would be sent to Coventry by all your freinds and aquaintances as the greatest dunce existing. "White Bread" is a composition of Arsenic and oil of Vitriol Baked into the form and consistence of singll loaves "Prussian Butter" is prussic acid Transformed by a process with which I am not accuainted in to the colour and consistence of very yellow butter! What think you of men eating this fine composition as cooly as you would a good slice of the true "staff" but to return to my story "Pigtail being famous for making and vending these delightful articles to such an extent as almost to thin the good city of Paris was very properly sued before the Empreur for his Life but in the midst of the trial Napoleon being seized with a "catalepsy" Pigtail first driving with a poker every one out of the room, walked toward the Fire lifted up the top of the Mantel peice which was an extremly large one. laid himself down in the holl-ow within and shutting it down lay hid there for 2 weeks no one knowing where he was. at the end of that time while the Empreur with a large party were dining in the room out bursts Pigtail from his confinement—springs to the window. leaps

6   See p. 16, n. 13.

onto the ground from a hight of 30 feet a pretty smart jump I can assure you! and entering a Tavern satisfied his fortnights fast stole a large balloon[7] and advertised that he would fly to the sun as soon as he could get any young men to join him I suppose you will think it would [be] long enough before any one would trust themselves with *him* on such an errand but you are mistaken for many young Fellows of the first consideration among whom were Myself my brother then only 5 years of age And young Soult having a mind for a freak went with him. but I will pass over this part of his History I cannot reveal the horrid crueltys and hardships we endured from him and this was the reason why I just now on seeing him approach towards us urged on my horses and looked so apprehensivly after this exploit he took for his companion Monseiur Sheckleton (or Sceleton) and they both performed a journey to the mountain of Nawhalgerii in India it is now about a year since they returned from that memerable expidition and during this period they have been wandering about together through hurricane and calm winter and summer without any end other than that of picking up stray children called by them *Enfants* or *Aungfaungs* and selling them to the owners of mills or torturing them to death to amuse themselves in their solitary rambles[8]

MYSELEF how! is it then that this Pigtail is possesed of such a large drove of cattle?

MARQUIS How! Why he has picked them up out of the feilds on his road and probably his companion is behind with another as large or larger than this to speak in plain language they steal them and driving them to the great Glasstown sell them there at what price any body chooses to give!

CHARLES Yes and once I saw this Pigtail sell to my Father some [of] our own cattle and my Father knowing the[y] were his did not say anything but paid him a penny a peice for them knowing that he would be quite content with that sum thus he recovered the beasts at 3 pence while had he gone to law or arrested the brute he would have had to pay 30 or 40£.

Thus we beguiled the time away by conversation both pleasing and to me edifying as it informed me of all the manners and customs of so wonderful a people and fited me better to travel through these countrys But our attention was now diverted to the appearance of the landscape which began to assume a widly different garb From the pleasant and delightful country we had just left no trees appeared or if any some huge black Scotch firs in clumps by the roadside here and there small patches of heather were observed on the summits of the hills the ripe corn was exchanged for brown furze the fresh green grass for swamps and rushes the while once or twice I observed[9] a moorcock to spring from the road side and after a few minutes further riding we found ourselves entering on an

---

7 For the Brontë children's first-hand knowledge of balloon flight, see Barker *Brontës*, 145.

8 See Alexander *CB*, I, 34, and p. 13 above.

9 The phrase "while once or twice I observed" is repeated at the bottom of the manuscript page and at the top of the next page.

immense moor which to the eye presented nothing but a ceasless sea of heath
not a single object to enliven the dreary waste but now and then a flock of red
grouse or a savage and gigantic poacher travelling over the heath who whith his
high crowned and broad brimmed hat leather belt and long Spanish gun well
harmonized with the scence But to complete the sum of our misfortunes Night
was rapidly rolling down and over the face of the sky which had hitherto been
clear immense black clouds were continualy rolling along portending a violent
storm shortly Lord Charles whose theeth began to chater exceedingly. expressed
whishes to get to "Scroveys cottage" The Marquis employed himself in lashing
on his horses to as great a speed as possible I like a true Englishman prepared to
encounter the tempest by buttoning on a ample greatcoat and taking 4 or 5 folds
of a silk neckcloth round my throat while Young Soult after the manner of a hair
brained poet. sat motionless conversing whith the planet Mars which still
look[ed] throug[h] the gathering tempest in such raphsodies as the following

O Mars who shakest thy fiery hair
Portending desolation blood and arms
Thee I address O lord of war
Who wakest the world to glorys charms
Oft on some mountains lofty steep
When all creation's laid asleep
I thoughtful stand alone
And see the lightnings round me sweep
And hear the thunders loud & deep
Roll over heavens high dome
While mid the dark tempestous night
Thou shinest flickering red and bright
The Genius of the storm
Nor can the clouds thy brightness hide
Which hurry o'er heavens concave wide
Nor thee beddim those fires which glide
Athwart the gloom filling thee minds of men
With dire alarm

but he was silenced in the midst of this bombast by a loud squall of wind which
sweeping full in our faces carried of every mans hat into a pool on the road side
This was the signal the trumpet blast for the storm to begin for now a relentless
torrent of hail and rain poured continualy up-on us like shot from a battery The
wind blew a hurricane while broad red flashes of lightning continualy blazed
through the air followed by peals of thunder which seemed to crack the earth. but
while in this situation when drenched with rain and shivering with cold we all
despaired of gaining shelter that night Lord Charles suddenly exclaimes I see a
light we looked eagerly and indeed there was a cottage hardly a stones throw from
us in the interior of which we conjectured that something "merry was agoing" at
least it seemed probable tremendous noise of laughing stamping etc but to cut
the matter short we rode up to it alighted and the Marquis knocked at the door it

was opened immediatly by a gigantic fellow who bolted forward and collared him. "Naughty, its me my brother and two friends we want admission. exclaimed lord Charles at this the monster letting go his hold said "I hope your fathers not here." and after looking round apphrehensively let in the Marquis and his brother As for you my grand dogs he said putting himself between young Soult myself and the door As for you I know a place that 'ud much fairer become you than this so along with me"

Now Naughty behave as you should do these 2 are my freinds. replied the Marquis at this the giant allowed us to enter but not without much grumbling and discontent when we were in he placed seats for us beside the fire till supper was ready which time I employed in looking about me the room in wich we were seated was of considerable extent and its walls hung round with guns and other *peaceable* instruments From the rafters depended a number of lion leopard and bear skins together with inumerable braces of moorgame partridges hares &c but the most remarkable feature in the scene was the occupants these were 5. The first was a man nearly 8 feet high. bony haggard and lean his nose and chin where hooked like the beak of an hawk his eyes small deep sunk and of a sinister malignant expression. his face was covered with tremendous scars particularly one which had almost cloven his chin in two this however was partly covered by a pair of huge Mustachios and thick bushy beard This was the Famous TOM SCROVEN. the owner of the cottage in which we then were

The second was a tremendous fellow of 8 Ft. 6 In. high and by far the most muscular man I have ever seen indeed his strength was such that were I to recount some of his displays of it you would set me down as an infamous liar. he was rather stout not owing to fatness but the size of his muscles his countenance was such an one as you could not long gaze at for two sufficient reasons in the first place you would turn tail and strive to get as far from such a terrible physiognomy as possible secondly If he saw you looking at him he would cleave your scull in the twinkling of an eye for it is among the poachers accounted the height of ill manners to look a man in the face his age judging from the greyness of his hair was about 65. his eyes were very small of a greenish grey and bright as lightning though sometimes covered by huge bushy and frowning eye brows his mouth was commpressed and scornful and the character of a ruthless ferocious bloody and revengful desperado darkned his whole countenance This was YOUNG MAN NAUG[H]TY the champion of the poachers.

The 3 person was exceedingly tall and straight his face was remarkably fine looking but with [a] ridiculous expression of a brutish melancholy about it this was NED LAURY the rival of Naughty

Besides these worthies there were 2 other poachers each 6 feet high whose only dress as were Scroven Naughty and Laury a leather breeks cross belts and steel boots but my attention was now diverted from these to the supper which was now laid on the table. it was all of a peice with the cookers. consisting of a quarter of beef 6 stones of potatoes an immense plum pudding and numberless braces of various kinds of Game together with 2 dozen pints of the "savour of life" ie Irish whiskey. We all now sat down without ceremony and whith sharp

and unsophisticated appetites to this ample and excellent repast but here let me
stop to remark the truly noble disposition of the young men here I beheld a
Marquis and a lord both sons of a King sitting down with the utmost ease and
affability among a set of what we insolent English would style "common
people" and these "common people" not degrading themselves by servile flattery
and obsequiousness. but showing a due respect to their rank and title
When the dinner was finished Tom Scroven our host called out to clear the room
and have a dance This was no sooner said than done but as the Marquis Charles
and myself declined to be active partakers in the amusement we stood to look on.
The cracked fiddle struck up to the celebrated tune of

Cannikinn clink

Drink boys drink[10]

and immediatly they began Their style of footing it was tremendous he who
could jump highest and stamp loudest was thought the best dancer Laury was
remarkable for his leaps and the ceiling being rather low he had an adroit method
of "shortning" himself as he ludicrously termed it that is doubling his knees up
to his chin. when he had neared the roof young Man Naughtys footing was
beyond what I thought any human being could have done for every stamp
sounded almost like the report of a musket The others each danced with immense
agility and stamping but where completly thrown into the background by
Naughty who at the close of the dance wishing to "end with a thumper" gave
such a powerful stamp that as every one expected the floor gave way beneath
him and we immediatly found ourselves snugly lodged in a gin celler underneath
the house Naughty after he had recovered his feet broke out with
   "You rare dog Scroven you catstail why did you make us an egg shell to
dance on you dog tail you—
SCROVEN. Im not going to be called in that fashion by sichlike bears heads as
you and—and—and (his voice broken by sobs and tears) you'll be pleased to peal
wont you
hold your beastish toungue answered Naughty and immediatly put himself into
fighting attitude as did Scroven also I was very curious to see how two such
herculean Giants would fight. and had my attention riveted to the spectacle They
both showed themselves complete masters of the art and went to work in
slashing style The first blow was aimed by Scroven but his antagonist parrying
it with his elbow deleivered him a most tremendous stroke on the forehead which

---

10   *Othello*, II, iii, 64. See also *Blackwood's Magazine*, xxiv (Dec 1828), 739,
where the lines appear as part of an old catch in a story about three Cornish
brothers working in an underwater mine:

Cannikan, clink

Drink boys, drink

Under the sun

There's no such fun

As to sit by the cask and see the tap run,

With a brown loaf and a rasher well done.

covered him with blood and then following this up by other blows in quick succsession so bewildered him that he fell almost senseless on the ground Brandy was given to him upon which he rallyed laid on Naughty in good style giving him a stinger on the throat apple and one or two black and red patches on the eye closing up one peeper but this was only provoking his fate for Naughty rendered furious by the blows flung himself on Scroven with his whole force and a most desperate struggle enseud between [them] For allong time it was doubtful which would get the victory untill Naughty delivered his antagonist a closer on the collar bone which smashed through the skin and caused the blood to stream on the ground in torrents[11] all now cried out for them to stop lord Charles raved at Naughty young Soult shuddered an shut his eyes while I fell down almost ready to swoon and the Marquis drawing his sword stepped in between the antagonists cooly saying that "If either of you attempt another blow I will run this sword through whoever be the aggressor." This firm and well timed threat pacified them sooner than all the entreatys in the world could have done for each after a little necessary grumbling shook hands and parted Naughty though bearing marks of sore punishment was by far the freshest of the two. Scroven was indeed nothing but a mass of blood And bruises but Night was now coming on therefore we all retired to sleep except Naughty Scroven & Laury who were engaged in council about something important which though we did not then know it will soon be seen what it was

LETTER IV.

The next morning at 5 o clock found us again in the chariot rolling over the wide moor and whiling away time in conversation respecting the country and its inhabitants. which was not interrupted by any thing animate or otherwise.[12] Till we saw the blue head of a far off mountain the first we had [seen] since we entered the moor rising above the sea of heath as soon as the Marquis his brother and young Soult observed it they immediatly took of their hats and made a profound bow I asked them the reason of this The Marquis answered. "That hill sir whose summit you now see is ROSSENDALE HILL on which our first King Frederic Guelph was slain in the glorious and ever to be remembered battle with the Ashantees and it is the custom for the young men when the[y] see it to bow You may easily conceive that when I heard this I did the same, We now continued our journey for some time gazing silently and with feeling of awe & veneration at the spot on which the great founder of the Nation died fighting gloriously for his country, till gradually the tops of other hill[s] appeared above the horizon, and at last we bid farewell to the Glass town moor and entered a

---

[11] For Branwell's interest in boxing, see p. 294 below, Alexander EW, 128-29 and Barker Brontës, 196, 229.

[12] A canceled passage of 19 lines follows here.

delightful plain in the middle of which rose ROSSENDALE HILL surround[ed] by woods meadows and villages. It is a noble mountain about the height of Pendle hill in England[13] & very much of its shape. at its foot is stretched a beutiful little lake the one into which the Ashantee army was percipitated and rising above the groves on the plain we saw several of the towers of Coomassiee Majestic in their ruins for the city which once numbered 500000 inhabitants and ruled over all southern Africa is now desolate & inhabited by tygers and owls. The sensations which rose in our minds were all of a pleasing and soothing nature unlike the turbulent delight I felt in seeing the Great glass town But as our horses were fatigued and we ourselves after. 4 hours hard riding wanted refreshment we drew up at the inn of a little villiage at the foot of the mountain and 40 miles from the Great glass town where we found entertainment both good and abundant We stayed in this villiage all day and night proposing on the morrow to visit Comassiee and Rossendale hill but early the following morning as we were in the travellers room ready to set out on our little jaunt a chariot dashed up to the inn door the horses covered with sweat and dust. and soon entered the room 2 men The [one] a tall military looking middle aged man with broad shoulders eagle eyes aquiline nose and lantern jaws this I immediatly knew to be his grace the DUKE OF WELLINGTON The other whom I did not know was a very young and han[d]some man with bright eyes hair parted on his forehead as is the fashion and exeedingly gay both in his dress and manners. They both seemed in great Animation and talked loud and passionatly (not angrily) with each other. before they entered the room the Duke first stepped forward and putting on a cool countenance said,

"Arthur I have come here for the purpose of telling you that your prescance is required at the great glasstown we are on the point of a revolution Alexander will tell you the rest as for me I have to go 30 miles farther to W Bravey's and E Trackeys country seats to warn them of the danger and to concert for the removal of it so saying the Duke left the room and shortly shortly after we heard the rumbling of his chariot as he set of on his journey directly after the Duke had gone the young man beconed the Marquis in to another room and while they were absent I enquired of Young Soult who he was "he is" said the poet Alexander Wilkin Sneaky a son [of] Alexander Sneaky and king of Sneakys land." While we were talking however the Marquis and the young king again entered both with Faces glowing with animation The chariot was ordered to be got ready immediatly and we soon all found ourselves rolling back to the glasstown with our new and interesting companion Alexander Wilkin Sneaky.

<u>March. 18 1831</u>

real date, PB Brontë, June 8th 1831

---

[13] The Lancashire borough of Pendle on the eastern boundary between Lancashire and Yorkshire takes its name from Pendle Hill (1831 feet), an area famous for its association with the Lancashire witch trials of the seventeenth century.

LETTERS
FROM AN
ENGLISHMAN
VOL III
PB B—te
2D SERIES[1]

LETTERS:
FROM AN
ENGLISHMAN TO
HIS
FREIND IN.
LONDON:
BY:
CAPTAIN JOHN FLOWER:
VOL III.
[Figure of Justice]
C'T ROSS'S GLASSTOWN
Printed and sold by
SEARGT WINDLASS

———————

BY PATRICK BRANWELL
BRONTE
June 11th AD 1831

[ornamental figure][2]

---

1   Hand-sewn booklet with grey paper covers (5.5 x 9.4 cm) of 20 pages (3
blank) in the Brotherton Collection, University of Leeds.
2   See Alexander & Sellars, 301.

LETTERS
FROM:
AN ENGLISHMAN
BY Captain
Flower F L S S &c
P B Bronte June 9. 1831

LETTER 5

Great glass town

On our entering again the great Glass town on March 15 1831 a scene presented itself which a common observer would perhaps feel disapointed to witness but to my mind it conveyed more fully than ever the horrors and gloom of an approaching revolution. The din of the Factories was silent the shops were shut up the Theatres closed the markets empty not a single woman or child to be seen in the streets no apparent bustle was seen anywhere but the persons whom I saw walked along silently with slow steps and thoughtful countenance This was the scene in the public streets in the alleys and pothouses it was quite different here you beheld knots of 300 or 400 of poachers & "rare lads" gathered together reading the newspapers and conversing with an animated voice on the proceedings of the government but no arms no manifestations of violence appeared. if we except at the barracks where throngs of armed soldiers were stationed and at the Iron Forge and gun shops which were all at work & crowded with customers. Our chariot drew up at the Marquis's residence. where were Col. Grenville[3] and lord Lofty waiting for him to accompany them to the house of Representatives which was. just about to sit. he accordingly in a short time drove of thither accompanied by these two friends and myself I stationed myself [in] the gallery to observe the proceeding which promised to be highly animating and important
CHrasheys speech having been read and the accounts of expenditure made Alexander [Rogue] rose amid cries of down with the demagogue he said
"Several of the members of this misnamed honourable hous[e] (*order*) have accused me of turbulence and sedition but I here declare that I have never have been so turbulent as they now show themselves to be who (puting on a feirce look) who I ask accuses me of being a demagogue bring him forth an[d] let him prove it if he can Is to be injured despised ruined thwarted by the Government to be an outcast from society to appeal for redress and to have that appeal refused is

---

[3]   Lord William Grenville (1759-1834), on Pitt's death (1806), became Prime Minister of the Coalition "Ministry of All Talents," and offered Wellington his first seat in Parliament. He actively supported Fox on the abolition of the slave trade.

this to be a demagogue? if you can prove this I confess myself to be one (cheers and hisses) but gentlemen your excessive decorum and your gentlemanly behaviour have quite driven me out of my course I had risen to offer a reply to CHRASHEY'S speech These are not days for mincing the matter therefore I will throw of the mask of Flattery and show myself in the simple clothing of Truth I say gentlemen that this speech will do more to agitate the minds of men than any speech that I have ever made (encreased uproar and cries of Turn him out order &c) yes (with a furious look) yes you do indeed require to be called to order and if you do not order your selves I know who both can and will (here several members got on the[ir] legs to answer Rouge but he with his loud & furious tone drowned their voices so that only he was heard he went on) I will proceed in spite of you. Crashey begins his speech by saying that he beleives us on the verge of a Revolution that in this city their is a feirce and enterprising populace whose interests lie opposite to those of their rulers and that they are led on by a demagogue whom he will not name. will not name no he cannot name him (here the confusion rose to an alarming height several members drew their swords and others taking theire hats departed saying they would hear no more such wickedness silence having been in some measure restored Rogue went on) He knows not of whom he speaks. but we need not wonder at that for every man must some day fall into dotage (here Col Grenville the chairman rising said) "This language shall not here be permitted with impunity Officers take this man out and shut the doors." Three officers immediatly laid hold of Rouge who resisted not and conveyed him out of the house The doors being again shut the chairman moved that a committee should be formed to enquire into the conduct of Rogue. This was immediatly done and the commitee consisting of Marquis Douro JOHN Sneaky Arthur Parry Captain Flower and 6 others retired after and in a short time returned saying that they thought him no longer fit to sit in that house. he was accordingly expelled! by a large Majority. The house then seperated. Thus ended this stormy debate a debate which will I think end in some tremendous convulsion before tomorrow night.

March 16 This morning I was in the delightful company of Marquis Douro JOHN and Wilkin Sneaky Edward Tut Ross and Arthur Parry 5 of the gayest most agreeable and most rational young men I have ever seen Marquis Douro seemed the most learned John Sneaky the coolest Wilkin Sneaky the gayest Tut Ross the most open and Arthur Parry the most daring. They had all being military men come to town for the purpose of gaining Glory in the approaching revolution they[4] declared Ambition at present and they did not care who knew it I said ambition may be some times a laudable motive. upon the ruling motive of their minds Arthur Parry starting up said. "Sir it is alwa[y]s a laudable motive The world [h]as long been in the dark about it. Was man formed to lie idle and inactive" To this they all cried "No you say right Arthur" but while we were thus talking the loud report of a cannon followed by a sharp fire of musquetry made us all start up What ever is that said Wilkin let us see what it is answered

---

4   "their" obviously intended.

the Marquis and immediatly they all grasped their swords put on their military caps and rushed with one accord into the street and a fine appearance they made as they darted along with the speed of 5 young greyhounds. as soon as they were gone I ascended a tower of one of the cathedrals to obtain a veiw of what was doing[5] in the city and there I saw a dense mass of armed men blocking up the whole of St. Georges Street. Their number could not be less than 300000 These men were engaged in a desperate conflict with the military who were with sabres and bayonets trying to disperse them but with no avail after great hesitation a tremendous fire was opened upon them from the castle battery which over looked the street This mowed down thousands at once shaking the houses and breaking the windows of the whole quarter of the city volley after volley followed so quickly and with such effect that the immense mob first began to stagger and at length fled in good ernest pursued by a body of 3000 Lancers who charging on while they were flying so completed their overthrow that in half an hour not a man of them was to be seen. When the dredful affair was over I descended from my eminence into the street where the battle had taken place here the heaps of dead and wound[ed] [were] lying pile[d] up in masses 4 or 5 feet high while at every [turn] I observed persons washing out the blood from their ho[u]ses in to which streams of it had run. through the spaces under the doors The stones of the pavement weres all broken and shattered in peices and the stree[t]s were all ploughed and absolutly ripped up by the cannon balls This scene of blood and horror however soon sickened me and I repaired home and returned home where I found a messenger waiting to conduct me to the 4 Kings who as I was the richest banker in the city requested to see me on particular buisness. I instantly obeyed overwhelmed as I was with confusion at being called into the prescence of the 4 greatest men in the World when I entered the room of Braveys Inn where they they were all engaged in writing & poring over several immense maps wich lay on the table they seemed much harrased with fatigue and watching having travelled for 3 days and nights together [and] never slept for the whole week. Parry was a very tall man swarthy and and spar[e]ly formed his hair was brown and his eyes glassy and searching Ross was short broadshouldered and exceeding muscular his "coal black hair shorn round and close set of his sunburnt face" and his general appearance was frank bold and sailor like Sneaky was as tall as Parry with a sly dark looking countenace and peircing eyes The Duke of WELLINGTON'S appearance I have already given (see Vol I p 15 and Vol II p 18)[6] therefore I need not give it again behind the kings were a crowd of Noblemen and Officers conversing with each other on the subject of the revolution When I had entered Sneaky rose and questioned me in the following manner

SNEAKY   are you the rich English banker whom we have sent for?

MYSELF   I am

SN—What is your capital?

---

5   A small pen-and-ink portrait appears in the margin here.
6   See pp. 123 and 179.

MYS—100000000£

SN—Indeed. and are there others engaged in the concern besides yourself?

MY—6 others (I here mentioned their names)

SN—You are the principle I suppose?

MY—I am

SN—Co[u]ld you in the name of your firm give a loan of 13 millions to the gove[r]nment of the great Glass town to be paid up by them at the close of this affair which we are about?

MY—Yes

SN—Then sign this bond

I did so and having settled the affair departed

MARCH 17. every hour a grand movement of the Requesists is expected. for Rouge Naughty Scroven Lawless Scavenger and O'Connor set of early this morning at full speed into the country. For what purpose is not know[n]. immense bodies of soldiers from Sneakys and Ross countrys principally cavalry are continualy entering the city The whole number of them at present in the city cannot be less than 130000. but this is nothing to what there will be. all the twelves with their splendid equipages fill the great Hotels and in short nothing can be more imposing than the present state of the great glass town a sight of it would be enough to fill any man with an ardour for military glory I was at the Marquis of Douro's residence this morning for I am become a person of great consequence while there he told me that a force of 1200000. men would scarcely be sufficient to defend the city alone and the great struggle was expected in a very few days for Rouge was assembling immense bodies of men around the city to corroborate this he accompanied me to the dome of St Michaels Cathedral. where I saw extending along the whole horizon from North east to south west the forces of Rogue and I observed numbers continually comeing up to reinforce them

While we were looking at Rougues forces we observed all the roads in the south as far as the eye could reach covered with myriads of soldiers who seemed moving to the Glass town When the Marquis perceived them he exclaimed "yonder troops are my Fathers and Captain Parrys Oh how rejoiced I am that they are come But I must go immediatly and accuaint my Father" he according[ly] darted down the steps of the tower and in a short time I who remained above saw him on his horse rattling through the streets below toward the duke of Wellingtons residence after I had remained above 2 hours on the dome I descended to my house from which however I was soon called by the tremendous bustle and confusion which I heard in the city. This as I found proceeded from the Duke of Wellingtons and Capt Parry[s] troops entering the city (Rosss & Sneaky's had entered as I have said vid p 4) to the immense number of 300000 men but this was only the van guard of the incalculable numbers which were to follow. For the whole day and night the city was kept in incessant agitation and tumult by soldiers who poured in at every gate unceasingly accompanied by thousand[s] of cattle baggage and store waggons cannon &c so that not one I beleive in all this immense city closed their eyes during the whole of this stormy night about ten o'clock at night meeting Arthur

Parry and John Sneaky at Braveys hotel I asked of them how the kings could possibly defend the city which is 30 miles in diameter. Why he answered. The kings have divided the city into 4 quarters and they are each to have care of one. and they have so ordered the plan of defence that no confusion can result from it.

While we were thus speaking however we were startled each to his feet by such a roar of cannonry as I never heard before it continued incessantly with[out] a single stop. and so stunned me that I [k]new not what I was doing. [and] now thought the city is taken by storm and we are all lost. I therefore flew to my house to see if all was safe there on my way I met the Duke of Wellington and Captain Sneaky galloping down the street at their utmost speed They told me that I had better keep in my house or I should have my head blown of my shoulders. I took their advice and remain close in my room all night but was hardly able to keep from fainting so great was the concussion an[d] shaking of the room and so terrific and astounding the roar and thunder of the cannonry what it was about or who was gaining the victory I knew not For I never stirred from my room all night warned by the crash of houses and the sound of balls which fell on every side. Toward morning the noise and horror rather increased than diminished. and when it was daylight I mustered courage to go out into the street to see what was the matter but I had hardly stepped a foot on the pavement when I started back with an exclamation of horror and suprise every house round the walls of the city were thrown down or wrapt in one sheet of fire wich extended as far as the eye could reach on every side. Thousands of wounded soldiers were moving slowly along the streets some with legs some with arms lopped of or wounded in some other manner. nothing was to be heard any where but the incessant roar of cannonry the tumbling of houses the shreiks of the wounded or the shouts of the conquerers and it was with the greatest difficulty that I gained Braveys hotel where I met Capt Ross with his arm bound up in a sling [and asked] what there was to do. "What there is to do" he answered "why the Roguetes to the amount of 2800000 men are attempting to storm the city on all sides and we to the amount of 1900000 men are attempting to stop them we in the middle of the city are quite safe yet but how long we shall be so I am not quite certain" he added if you are afraid retire into the very middle of the city and there you will not here or see anything of the danger unless the enemy conquer but thats unlikely" But alas! I saw that there was not a great chance for the Twelves so immensly superior were the numbers of the enimy. but however I took the advice of Ross and retired to the great square yet here though 10 miles from the scene of warfare I could not hear a person speak nor see any one at the distance of a few yards so great was the roar of the cannonry and so dense the smoke from the burning houses and the gunpowder used in the fight For the whole day the firing continued incessantly and to the alarm and and terror of everyone it was rapidly nearing the centre of the city Whole troops of wounded soldiers were continualy flocking into the great square and now crash after crash of the batterys and rattle on rattle of the falling houses told us that it had come to within a mile of the centre towards evening the fire and fighting was trebled for for it had been do[u]bled long before what it would come to at last none of us poor wretches who not daring to fight had gathered together in the square could tell. and while we were expecting to be blown up into the sky every crack. the firing suddenly ceased about 9 o clock in the evening having raged incessantly for 30 hours The ceasing of the fire was followed by a shout which echoed through the whole city. and on looking out of doors to see the cause of it. to my horror and dissapontment and to the same of every one around me I saw the Revolutionist banner waving on the highest tower of the citadel despair now took possesion of everyone nothing was heard but. raving yells and curses as the remains of the Twelves army fled in the greatest confusion from the city gates leving the great glass town wholly to the mercy of Rouge and his blood thirsty associates but I must now subscribe myself with

tears and lamentations

James Bellingham
March 18th. 1831

LETTER VI

Great glass town
Cheif prison
March 19

Oh my Freind! We are in a horrid condition Rogue has ordered—but I will inform you regularyly of the course of events the morning after the 12s had evacuated the city I and thousands more went out to look at the scene of the battle I first reparied to what once was the great gate This gate with its posterns 150 feet in hight was blown to atoms and not one stone rema[in]ing on another every house around it was also battered in peices or consumed by the flames as far as I could see both within and without the walls the ground was covered with heaps of dead bodies and riven and rent open as if by an earthquake every gutter and fissure ran with streams of blood arms cannons horses and men lay piled up in ridges two or three hundered feet long This was the scene throughout every street in [the] whole city a. city 30 miles in diametre it is calculated that 60000 peices of artillery and 5000000 men were engaged in the conflict. The number of slain on the 12s side amounted to 1000000 on the side of the Roguites to 800000 From this meagre statment you may judge somewhat of the terrific nature of the combat but unless you saw with your own eyes and heard with your own ears not all the fine language not all the Rhetoric nor all the vividness of painting that the world can afford could give any thing like an adequate idea of the Horrors of the 17 and 18th of March[7] but I must now hasten on to relate of

---

7   The existence of "unspeakable" horrors is a consistent refrain of the reporter of "The Subaltern—A Journal of the Peninsular War," *Blackwood's Magazine*, xvii (March 1825), 294, who declares that scenes of battle and their aftermath are "such as no powers of language are adequate to describe." In describing the Great Rebellion, Branwell drew on accounts of the 1830 revolutions in Paris,

other things as soon as Rogue had fairly secured himself in the city he formed what he styled a provisional government. till the city was restored to order This infamous government consists of himself as the head. Y M Naughty on the war department Col O Connor Capt Lucius Carey Capt Charles M Carthy and a host of other wretches patterns of himself form the other branches of government The first decree of this worthy set was su[i]table to their characters it was to order the city to be given up to pillage The 2d was just of a peice with the first by it he ordered that all persons suspected of dissafaction to the present gov should be instantly seized and confined in the great prison to take their trial & be punished. These two infamous mandates were immediatly executed and immediatly the city was one scene of plunder and violence while troops of supected persons were constantly hurryed to the prisons by thousands at once As for myself while I was sitting in my room meditating on the state of thing[s] in stalks two of Rogues minion[s] one of them said "My rare dog are'nt you Mr James Bellingham the great English banker?" "yes" I answered "I am" "Then come and follow me" he said at the same time pulling from his coat pockets a pair of strong manacles which the other immediatly putt on my hands They then hurryd me of to certain death at least so I felt and do still feel for there is no chance for me. I am now while writing to you confined in a large dark damp dungeon in which are 600 of my fellow prisoners. and the door of the room is continualy opening and shuting either to take out to execution or to bring in to the horrid apprenshions of execution some unhappy victim.—But oh! what shall I do? I am undone a messenger has sent for me to take my trial their is no hope for me I must die Farewell

March 20] = I now resume my story I was conducted from the prison to a large open area which was covered with blood and dead carcases which several persons were engaged in carrying away. This area was crowded with people and at one end of it at a large table which was covered with papers sat Alexander Rogue and several members of the provisional Government before them was placed on a blood-covered scaffold a block and 2 executioners. I was conducted up to this horrid tribunal where Rogue questioned me as follows.

ROGUE. You are I suppose James Bellingham, the English Banker?
MYSELF I am
R. It is reported that you favour the 12s answer me do you or not?
M I do favour the 12s and likewise I abbhor and detest you as the most wicked cool blooded and inhuman tyrant that ever existed!
R. This is enough is it not Gentlemen
COUNSEL'S.   it is it is
R. Executioners do your duty
The executioner immediatly dragged me onto the scaffold placed my head on the block and was about to lift up the axe when a tremendous shout of "The 12s are coming hurry, the 12s are coming" was heard through the city & instantly the

Belgium, Poland, Germany and Italy, and on the unrest in Britain over the proposed Reform Bill (Barker Brontës, 180). See also Alexander CB II, Part I, 98 and 301.

executioners jumped from the scaffold Rogue and his company sprang out of the yard and in a short time all were under arms and jumping from the scaffold in an ecstasy of delight I sprung to the gate of the area but it was locked for the multitude being in to great haste to open it had jumped over the walls a feat which I being an Englishman could not perform Therefore I climbed on to the platform in an agony of despair and hope resolving to wait either till the 12s conquered & gave me with the with the other prisoners liberty or till Rogue should return victorious and order my death. While I was thus situated a tremendous roar of cannonry announced the commencement of the Battle. The conflict was not for glory or for a few miles of land—it was on both sides for existence. accordingly they fought more like gods than men but as I saw none of it being confined in the horrid Execution yard. saw none of it I will therefore refer you for details to the Newspapers &c suffice it to say that after the conflict had raged furiously and with doubtful success for 3 hours. a splendid triumphal car drawn by 10 horses dashed into the midst of the battle. in it was seated the venerable CRASHEY who rising from his seat cried out "O my sons spare yourselves I intreat you What have you done? What are all these slaughters and desolation for? little did I think the the young men whom I have so long watched and presidoed over would have thus attempted to destroy one another" Instantly both the Armies dropt their arms and weeping implored his pardon. "Yes" he answered "yes I grant you my pardon but Rogue and you his followers you deserve it not Why have you done thus" at this Rogues party simultaneusly cried out that they would never transgress his commands again and both sides mingling togehter entered the city with Crashey at their head Oh how sublime and affecting a spectacle to behold a great and mighty nation moved by one impulse actuated by one feeling and thus obeying the voice of their venerable Patriarch I have forgot to mention that every prisoner and among the rest myself was immediatly released Peace is completely restored all are uniting to make alive the dead and to repair the city

Postscript. March 23. 1831.] I have just now returned from the first day of the Celebration of the Olympic or Great African games[8] where I have witnessed a scene which I think will serve to expand your Ideas of the young men (this is only by way of postscript) The assembly in number perhaps 5. or 6 millions being seated. the orchestra of 10000 performers on the Organ trumpet flute and clarionet these being the only instruments allowed to be used began An Ode to the praise of the Twelves in a solemn strain of the sublimest music that ever I heard Handel Mozart and all those who till now I considered the best Musicians in the universe sunk to nothing before it. it began by a single flute which was scarcly heard through the building but which seemed to float on the air like the music of a fairy This was in time joined by a trumpet then 2 or 300 instruments and at last the whole orchestra of 10000 joined in the chorus To give you an idea of its sublimity I will tell you that through the mysterious influence of music on the soul not a dry eye was seen in the whole assembly and rare lads and

[8]   See p. 222 below and Alexander CB, I, 342.

poachers present absolutly wept aloud for we all-ways see the unsophisticated common people more affected than the more refined higher orders not to say that they were so in this case for the higher orders here are much less artificial and *refined* than in England but the common people shewed it more To me the delight at last became to great for pleasure and I felt as if I should be choked and wept copiously as the Majestic music thrilled and trembled through the arched roof and lofty walls of this Mighty building The following is the Ode sung on this occasion

ODE IN PRA[I]SE OF
The Twelves
Sung at the Olympian games

O Fathers of our glorious land
Who oft avert the Geniis dreadful hand
And when they leaning from the stormy sky
Oer us extend their flaming swords on high
Do sheild unweariedly thy chosen band
Ye have raised those mighty towers
Over who[se] heads the flying hours
have past unnoticed by
While moveless as yon Mountains vast
Which oer us frown bleak drear & waste
They seek their kindred sky
Ye who long woes and toils have born
And from your home and country torn
have fought mid feilds of gore
Who now have seen your glorious name
Born on the eagle wings of fame
To every clime and shore
We now repentant kneel before your throne
And all our crimes and our transgressions own
What though by angers whirlwind born
We have ourselves relentless torn
Though we in ruins have our city laid
And have destroyed the works ourselves have made
Yet oh withdraw these gloomy clouds
Which now from us your glory shrouds
And shed your brightest rays
Shine on us as in times of yore
And sheild us with your mighty power
Through all succeding days
I Remain yours &c
James Bellingham

Glass town March
the 23. AD 1831

===============================

P B Bronte June 11th AD 1831[9]

---

9   Pages 19 and 20 following are blank except for a column of figures on p. 20 totalling 134.

LETTERS.
FROM
A N
ENGLISHMAN..
.VOL. IV.
IIId series
PB B—te[1]

LETTERS From.
AN.~
ENGLISHMAN TO.
His Friend in
LONDON.
BY
CAPTAIN JOHN FLOWER.
.VOL. IV.

[Figure of Justice][2]

CT. ROSS'S GLASS TOWN.
Printed and sold
By Seargt Winlass.

═══════════════════

BY PATRICK BRANWELL
: BRONTE
August. 3. 1832:

[ornamental figure]

---

[1]   Hand-sewn booklet with grey paper covers (6.2 x 9.9 cm) of 20 pages (two blank) in the Brotherton Collection, University of Leeds.
[2]   See Alexander & Sellars, 301.

LETTERS FROM AN
ENGLISHMAN

===============

VOL
IV.

THIRD SERIES

===============

LETTER VII

Sneaky Gl^{ss} T^n. March 3d.
1832.

You may recollect that early Last year I set out with the Marquis of Douro on a journey to the Duke of Wellingtons glass town but was called back before I had proceeded 100 miles by the bursting out of the Rebellion. A fortnight ago how[ev]er the Marquis resumed his thought of taking the journey with me, not to the Dukes country but to Sneakys Glass Town & the great Greygarach Mountain he aquainted me with his design and I readily and joyfully agreed to it. we accordingly set of on our expidition March the 1st. 1832. In his Lordships own chariot. accompanied by Young Soult the Ryhmer. By the Marquises suggestion we also provided ourselves with a bottle of a most valuable Medcine for the prevention of Hypochondria and all other cares and sorrows. Of this medcine you will naturally desire to know something as it would be of inestimable benifet to our freinds in England who are eaten up with such affections. But I am sorry to inform you that it can only be procured in the Glass town. it is called Charlie Wellesly and is in great vogue with the "rare apes" I beleive that I need not describe to you the scenery for the first 100 miles of the road which as it lay through The delightful Glasstown Valley you will find described in the 2 Vol. of my letters. Through This magnificent vale we continued our course for 2 days till we arrived at Freetown a considerable place seated at the junction of the 2 great arms of the Mighty Niger and 150 miles from the Great Glasstown. here our road changed and a new scene began We left the valley of the Glasstown behind us and entered a realisation of that [picture] poets have conceived or Arabian writers have depicted of Egypt in its most fertile and flourishing state it was a plain perfectly level extending as far as the eye could reach on every side it was so entirely covered with flowers of all sorts and the most beautiful coulors that every inch of green grass was hidden The edges to the roads and feilds were composed of the finest orange trees all of them covered with loads of golden fruit and snowy blossoms Figure to yourself such a plain as this with here and there large groves of statly plam trees shooting up their tall and gracefull stems covered with long broad fan like leaves, and mixed with grape trees twining round their trunks & hiding them in a veil of purple fruit. Let the Mighty stream of the Niger more than a mile wide, be seen shining along amid these palms and flowers its calm surface reflecting every tree on its banks and every sail on its waves till after glittering and winding like a vast lake all along the horizon it is lost in a bright golden haze let a most delightful and aromatic perfume be diffused through the whole air. let this landscape so beautiful and this majestic river be all flooded with a rich yellow and dazzling light continually pouring down from a cloudless and blazing sky which seems to the beholder from east to west, one continued and unshaded sun. Figure to yourself all this and even more enchanting ideas and yet you will fall short infinitly short of this glorious and fairylike scene

While we were travelling over this beutiful plain the Marquis related to me many things concerning the young men highly courtous and instructive. and while he was speaking I could not help smiling at the difference between him and some young English Marquis's.

Among other things he observed that—

"The Mountain of Aornos whith Rossendale hill the Lake of Hyle and indeed the whole co[u]ntry for 50 miles round constitute the Classic land of our Hystory Mount Aornos is our Olympus[3] the abode of the Cheif Genii and the lord of the Jibbel Cumraii Rossendale Hill is sacred to the memory of the tremendous battle in which our King Fredric Guelph was slain. The vast and stormy Lake Hyle[4] is the the place of many wild and wonderful recollections in our History on an Island in it is the tomb of our Thucydides Capt Leaf and above all on the northwest shore of the lake and at the foot of Aornos rise the grey and Noble ruins of Coomassie. the Troy of the Glass Town Countries[5] This part of the land is also on[e] of the wildest and Grandest in appearance its scenery is composed of Magnificent lakes [which] stretch their bright waters in the midst of rude moors. old Gigantic fir trees. vast grey Rocks and gloomy caverns Magnificent though shattered ruins and bold Black Heathy Mountains rising one

---

[3] Aornus, a towering, rocky peak that makes for an impregnable natural stronghold, is located in modern Pakistan a few miles west of the Indus. This was the site of the great Seige of Aornus (327 BC) which took place during the invasion of Asia by Alexander the Great. Although the name derives from the Sanskrit word for enclosure or fortress, the Macedonians interpreted it to mean "the place to which no bird can rise" in recognition of its virtually inaccessible height. In Greek mythology, the entrance-place to Hades was named Aornus because it was fabled to be birdless as a result of the noxious gases rising from the underworld. See also the Glossary.

[4] See, for example, Charlotte's poems, Neufeldt PCB, 102-04.

[5] The references to Olympus, Thucydides and Troy reflect Branwell's study of classical literature. Ironically, given the supernatural agency involved in the founding of the Glasstown Confederacy, Thucydides' history of the Peloponnesian War looks to human agency rather than supernatural forces to explain events. The razing of Coomassie (named after the African City, Kumasi, which was the capital of the Ashanti empire in the seventeenth century), is recorded in **The History of the Young Men.**

over the other on all sides in a frowning chaos And crowned with the white shining peak of the immense Aornos. Though undoubtedly those who seek for Nature in her wildest & and most terrific garb will find her even in higher perfiction than this if they dare venture into the unexplored solitudes round the Mighteir Elymbos. which in my opinion exeeds any spot on earth for. this the noblest species of scenery not exepting Grey-Garach.

When the Marquis had finished his speech I On looking up beheld the sun just setting behind the west of the delightful plain. The sky was perfectly clear and cloudless save for one very small cloud which lay to the NW. its appearance was remarkable for though overwhelmed and surrounded with the bright beams of the sun it glittered like a rock of fire or the Evening Star which indeed I for a moment thought it was. I pointed it out to the Marquis. who simply smiled and said "a very *substantial* cloud I think." yong Charlie and Soult were about to exclaim but he nodded to them to be silent. We neither of us said anything more respecting it till about half an hour afterward when the Marquis again said. See "the cloud still keeps its place." I looked up and beheld it exactly as before save less bright. I asked what in the world did such a cloud as that mean. he answered. "Your bright speck which you believe to be a cloud is in reality the summit of GREYGARACH." "Nonsense" I replied "would you have me believe that we could see Greygarach when near 300 miles from it?" "Yes I would" he answered "take the Telescope and see for yourself." I did as he directed me and with the glass plainly perceived it to be the summit of a Mountain covered with snow. I laid by the glass and we all gazed at it with silent Awe and wonder till the twilight increasing hid it from our sight

As it was now Night we stopped at an Inn by the Banks of the Niger. and early next morning set off for Sneakys Glass Town. Our route continued through the same delightful plain as before. so that I began to change my Ideas of Sneakys country. I had hitherto beleived it to be a wild cold heathy and mountainous highland far elevated above the sea level but I here beheld an enchanting & fairy like plain level as a carpet and without a single hill or rising round the whole Horizon. I remarked this to the Marquis who answered Dont come to rash conclusions you have scarce seen the country yet I returned. "but here we command a very wide Horizon of 70 or 80 miles diametre. and yet not one poor hillock will appear even in the farthest distance. though the day is so clear He answered nothing but lashed his horses to a very smart trot. and we rolled gaily on for 2 or 3 hours. he conversing on various interesting topics to keep my attention from the scenery at the expiration [of] which time he drew up his horses and and told me to observe the Horizon I looked round and saw toward the west a long pale blue line exhib[i]ting vast undulations like the waves of the sea with other lines stretching away at the back of this till lost in the distance in a short time I saw also this same chain continued to the north but higher and bolder and more distant. the plain also on which we were was beginning to lose its level character and to swell into long low ridges. about 50 or 70 feet high The Marquis asked me wether I had retracted my hasty conjecture I owned that I did he said Yon hills which you see are 50 or 60 miles of. They are the beginning or the roots of the great Hig[h]lands which stretch up as far as the

Lake of the Genii and the the vast Chain of Mountains called Dimdims Throne. many hundereds of miles from hence

I now found by the goodness of the roads the incresed number of houses and the immense crowds of passengers and carriages that we were nearing the capital of Sneakys country and began to look out for some signs of it. Toward evening the tops of spires and chimney canopied by clouds of blue smoke appeared over a long hill in our front and at about 10 o clock at night we found ourselves rattling along the stone pavement of Twelves Street Sneakys Glass Town. We alighted among thousand[s] of Gas lamp oil lamps lanthorns and every species of light at the Great door of The Northern Hotel were we rested that night. intending on the morrow to explore the city and its inhabitants

Yours ever &c

J Bellingham Esq[r]

LETTER THE
VIII.th.

Red River
March 8th.
1832

Next Morning the 3th of March[6] the Marquis young Soult Ld C Wellesly and myself set out in his Lordships chariot on the aforesaid excursion But ere we had drove 100 yards it struck us that every thing seemed in a desturbed state no Buisness appeared to be doing in the markets the shops were closed and the streets empty however after riding a little farther on the mystery was cleared we were proceeding down a long dark alley when on turning a corner we saw before us a vast and compact body of "RARE LADS" gathered in complete arms round a platform of boards and Barrels on which stood severl men above the common stamp. one of whom in particular was standing in front and adressing with vehement gestures the multitude who listened to him with deep attention. he was a tall Man with a pale countenance. worn into wrinkles with care and anxiety. his appearance evidently once handsome seemed broken down by hardships and depraved habits I fancyd that I had seen him before but the matter was at once explained by the Marquis whispering "he is Alexander Rouge." we instantly pressed through the crowd in order to hear his speech which partly from the Newspaper reports and partly from my own recollection I shall here give

"Fellow country men! Banished from all places hated by all men Persecuted by my superiors and maligned by my inferiors I have here sought that Refuge and attention which has been refused to me every where before. When Enimies have taken and wasted the plains and sea shores the last refuge of the conquered has always been the inaccessible rocks and sterile hills. here too have I thought

---

[6]   The date should be March 5th; Branwell initially wrote "6," then changed it to "3."

and O! may I still think so here to among these wild Mountains Boundless Moors will Justice and Truth take shelter now that Pride and Bigotry Slavery and deceit Fraud and Violence have conquered the open and effeminate plain My freinds you know how, lately when in the Glass town countries the freinds and upholders of Liberty made a last noble stand against the encroachments of the tyrant Twelves (I will speak out) you I say have heard how by the force of overwhelming numbers and infamous treachery they were beatend down slain or expelled from their native country by those infamous men I perceive my freinds that many of you will be shocked at my severe language but I will ask you what have the Twelves or their misguided crew done for us. you may answer by appealing to the sack of Acrofroom and the battle of Rossendale hill but I here declare that it appears as plain as the light of that sun now shining on us that all these actions were done for the aggrandisment of their own peculiar ambition and that nothing was farther from their thought than your welfare. but you will say the Duke of Wellington brought our fathers from England to this land. Ah but what did he bring you over for? here is a little secret for you why my Lads he I am credibly informed brought you over for no other end than to be the instruments of his vengeance in rebelling against and destroying the other 12s which he would have done had not Frederic the 2d by a timely sacrifice resigned the crown to him Now what think you of this will you own alleigance to the 12s one moment longer will you any more respect them obey them or revere them? No will you rather hate despise and abjure them will you not rise up in an universal mass and rushing at once with the force of the united streams of a hunderd hills will you not for ever annihilate them and their detestable rule. Yes my freinds now Now is the time for action now is the moment of your freedom I behold it coming over these mountains like the rising Sun and as that from its prescence drives away all the weak but glittering stars so shall Freedom drive away the as weak and glittering 12s. I propose to you that we instantly and quickly march up to the western mountains. their to deliberate on the best measures for effectually securing to us the invaluable blessing of Liberty"
This speech though grownded on such an evident and wretched falshood. was yet in consequence of its great Eloquence and plausible language received by the deluded Multitude with loud and vehement cheering. and universal enthusiasm seized them and they all prepared to begin their march immediatly Rouge descended from the platform for the purpose of giving some orders but as he passed by he observed the Marquis and us among the crowd he gave on[e] withering look at us and then passed on in a moment however we were all seized thrown down and bound hand and foot before we knew what we were about resistance was vain we could not move Rouge came forward and ordered them to cut our heads of directly. They refused to do so for the Marquis and Young Charlie are exeedingly well known and liked by the rare lads. Rouge frowned but ordered them to convey us to the rear of the troops well guarded This was soon done. The signal was given to march and the whole body moved of in perfect silence. utterly unobserved by the city for such was Rouges masterly arrangement. we departed out by an old gate and soon entered into a wild flat but rugged moor The scene was awful and immpressive for the men in number

30000 and upward were arranged in three narrow lines of immense length & under many commanders. They all carried long spanish guns. with swords pistols and knapsack and wore Blue scarfs, Banners of the same colore were waving about every where. perfect silence was observed but the grim look And grotesque appearance of the men made that stillness more awful than the loudest tumult night was coming fast on for the forms of the men at a little distance. were so mingled by the darkness with the surrounding herbage that a troop marching along seemed like a vast black shadow on the ground. The Marquis young Soult and myself were driven along in the rear fast bound and guarded by 8 gigantic fellows the very personifaction of Ruthless daring and cool blooded cruelty as for Charlie. he being an especial Favorite of the Rare lads sat mounted on the shoulders of one fellow. like a little Monkey chattering and laughing at all around him. and creating simils[7] or rather grins on the face[s] of the sternest rare lads in the company. for such is his happy temprament that no danger or distress however imminent can stop one moment his exessive flow of spirits and animation To return however we almost knew that we were going to certain death. The night was cold wet and dark as a dungeon. The wind kept constantly sughing along the heather with a loud moaning howl. while we were in walking constantly falling among peat haggs or splashing up to the knees in water. Morning seemed as if it would never appear and when the first crimson streak of returning light began to dawn under the heavy wet clouds. we found ourselves 50 miles from the Sneakys Glass town. in the midst of a boundless moor which stretched on every side to the farthest Horizon. Broken everywhere into vast undulations. which 20 miles in front of. us began to assume the appearance of high bleak dreary hills nothing appeared to relieve the solitariness and uniformity of the scene save the advancing troops of this Banidts[8] like army and the Great Red River. which now and then appeared glittering among the distant heath as an instance of the ruling passion strong in death I may state that though drenched with rain and fainting with fatigue and hunger my love of Geographical and tophographical Knowledge continued so strong that I could not pass this Noble stream without gaining some account of it from those around me I learned that it rises in the wild regions of Robbers hill. from thence it runs 30 miles eastward to the Bloody Lake amid scenery remarkable for its desolate grandeur Flowing out of this Lake it proceeds in its course to the same point. till it receives the Silsden. a river 90 miles long which runs from the south reinfor[c]ed by it it glides for 86 miles along the bases of Arthurs peaks to the Large City of Fidena. below which. it receives the Fidenaz flowing from Greygarach. From hence it takes a South East direction to its junction the fine River Denard nearly 200 miles long They two united run rapidly for 40 miles in to the all absorbing NIGER. its whole course is 352. miles & where we saw it (300 miles from its source) it was of the noble breadth of 900 yards. we arrived at its bank at sunrise having travelled 60 miles without a stop I and young Soult were nearly dead we

---

7   "smiles" obviously intended.
8   "Bandits" obvioulsy intended.

dropped down on the heath and declared we could go no Farther. But our conductors had no sympathy for us as every one of them was able to walk nearly twice that distance. They were therefor just going to force us to get up with the points of their lances when a horseman galloped up from the van whom I knew directly to be Lieut. L. Carey. Rouges Minion he cried out to the army to halt and rest by the River side. and then galloped of toward his quarter. every one immediatly set up a shout of joy. Some began to dig trenches for the camp others to collect ling[9] for firing while numbers of the most expert took their guns and sallied of onto the Moor to collect stags hares and birds for food. The Marquis Young Soult Myself and Charlie. also though prisoners had no reason to complain for we were allowed a fire and plenty of provisions to[g]ether with a bottle of the waters of life which Charlie had dexterously wheedled from one of the men. We therefor soon despite our uncertainty wether we should die next day or get of clear before another hour. began to be as merry as any around us. and entered into brisk conversation. in the course of which. the Marquis to whom we look for all information informed us that he knew from sertain signs not to be mistaken that fighting was not so far of as one would think who knew that Sneakys Government the very day before had known nothing of the Insurrection. such were Rougue['s] masterly mesures he also told us to notice. the excellent place which had been chosen for the encampment. an unfordable river formed one side of the camp so broad also that the Army could not be annoyed by Musquetry from the opposite bank. a deep ditch and impassable Morrass. formed the other boundarys while the whole country being full of steep hills and sudden holes and rocks would render cavalry of no avail against him and provision and Firing was in abundance by reason of the quantity of Heath Game and River water We thus continued to amuse ourselves. till noon at which time I have sat down to inform you of the events which have happened. it is now wearing late. and I need some repose there fore I must conclude to morrow I shall continue this letter if we have not to march of which however there are few fears

March 8 I now proceed with my narrative. When I arose this morning I found the camp in a state of extreme bustle and excitement but what occasioned it we (the prisoners) knew not. till about 9 o clock AM. The matter was in a manner cleared up by a herd of 300 of Sneakys soldiers with many cattle and baggages being driven in to the camp fast Bound and goaded along with the points of the Rebels lances. it was evident that Rouge had suprised and captured a division of some advancing army or perhaps a garrison of some Neighbouring town.

The prisoners were made to halt in a large open space near were we stood. in a short time a dozen horse men galloped up they were Rouge and his Aid de Camps he stopped and looked at them a moment with his eyeglass. and then said "Take out the Officers and march them to head quarters." The Officers 30 in number were immediatly separated from the privates and marched off into the rear Rogue nodded saying "Thats well now draw the rest up in-to a square and give them a few rounds of grape shot." I shuddered and shut my eyes for this cruel

---

9   "ling" is a common term for a type of heather.

command was said in his usual cool collected manner and his countenance changed not in the least from its usual sneering Ironical expression The poor Fellows were stationed as he ordered with out a word. being spoken and several cannon being brought were placed oposite. Rouge cried "Fire." and after a few mourderous disc[h]arges the whole number were laid dead and dying in a heap I turned sick at the sight but Rougue after exclaiming "Thats well now take and throw them into the river" turned round and trotted off conversing with his infamous minions in a totaly unconcerned manner But I must now leave off for dinner.[10]

EVENING Surely something very extraordinary is taking place. Since noon when I left off wrighting. not 10 minutes have passed without Bodies of 50 or 100 prisoners being driven into the camp or large troops of the rebels marching off we (the prisoners) know not where But I listen and I tremble whilst I write it. every one of the prisoners. who are all Sneakys soldiers. are shot the moment they arrive and then thrown into the Red River, red indeed may it be called, for while I write, a gutter of Blood is running close by my feet into it. at dinner the Marquis on giving his opinion said that. the sole reason why Rouge had not killed *us* long before now was that himself and Charlie being sons of the Twelves he feared that the Rebel soldiers might dislike their death and mutiny against him. especialy as he (the Marquis) and his brother CHarlie were so well liked by the rare lads. he wound up this delightful speech with the consoling advice that "we had better take care lest we should die by poison" But I hear a great bustle in the camp I must go out to see what it is. . . . .
. . . . The tumult I heard was occasion[ed] by 2 things Firstly a Force of 8000 fresh rebels arriving to Rouges help—all Fierce Fellows fresh from the Highlands. so that as near as I can learn Rougues army now consists of the large number of 42000 men all well equipped and organised. The second reason is, that orders have been issued for the army immediatly to prepare with all haste for Marching. and from what I perceive it will be a[n] exceedingly long and forced one of course where we go not a man in the Army knows save Rouge himself. who keeps his secrets as close as Wellington did Truly he is a very great General. his look and manner shows it. I see him now. on his horse ([h]e has never been 10 minutes off him this day) with a telescope in one hand & map in the other. now eagerly looking over the country. and chart then clapping his glass to his eye and looking intently at the bare moor around him and then with a quick keen glance looking round on the army to note if they are all doing things in order. if he sees the smallest neglect in any thing he quickly calls out "Sir" or "Fellow why is not that done as I ordered" or "Make haste or to the triangles" and he is instantly obeyed for he is vigorous and prompt in his punishments. and at the same time condescending to his soldiers in the utmost degree indeed I never saw or read of a general who had such an excellent method of making them obey him But as to real love or mercy I

---

[10] Such an execution of prisoners by means of artillery is described in Scott's *Life of Napoleon*, III, 43. See also p. 379 below.

beleive he has not an atom in his constitution he is dead to every feeling but that of hate revenge and ambition.

But I must now conclude for the camp is breaking up and the trumpets and Bugles are sounding I must prepare to depart with my 3 fellow prisoners. We expect an exceedingly fatiguing march How in the world can *I* bear it.

Farewell

Yours &c.

J Bellingham.

LETTER
IX.

Near Fidena
March 9th.
1832

I continue my story. a minute after I had written my last. I was called of to join the army. We (the 4 prisoners) were station[ed] in the middle of Careys company wich I perceived the Marquis did not like for Carey and he are declared enimies. and as Young Soult told me have once fought a duel. Charles as usual is allowed by the rare lads to go among them where ever he pleases and he avails himself of this kindness to its utmc . latitude he is everywhere. one moment I saw him perched on the head of a fellow close by me and the next seated on the shoulders of a man. many companys distant. he is constantly chattering and laughing. but I am running out of my subject. at 8 oclock at night the Army began to march in one compact mass over the moor. Bodies of horse were flung out of the lines to many miles distance as scouts to note the appearance of the country and wether there were enimies in sight. but nothing was to be seen and no interruption having delayed them the Rebels gained the edge of the moor before morning having travelled from the red river camp 30 miles in 8 hours which with any regular army would have [taken] 16 hours I and Young Soult now began to be dreadfuly fatigued we begged to have a horse This request though without Rouge or Carey knowing it the rare Lads granted. and we began to entertain hopes of marching the rest of the way in tolerable comfort though we had. yet 30 or 40 miles farther to go.

But now haveing forsaken our old companion the heath we entered on a rugged half cultivated region sloping down before us and after having marched 9 miles over this we came upon a delightful plain. full of trees and green Feilds. watered by the magnificent Red river and speckled with innumberable white houses and villages This scene reminded me so much of the South of England that I could scarce believe that I was not actualy among the shades of Windsor and that in that river I beheld the Noble Thames Here war the same verdure and the same luxuriance, But as a rising breeze began to roll away the clouds which had hitherto hid the Horizon an occasional glimpse wich I caught of Black Mountains with bare hoary peaks shooting over these and vast snowy sumits still towering above them. effectualy dispelled the illusion. and told me that I was still wandering a prisoner among the wild and wonderful scenes of Twelves Land in Africa. But an object now appeared in veiw which caught the attention of my feirce companions much more than the woods and verdure of the plains or the snows of the mountains it was the noble city of FIDENA.[11] gleaming in the distance its tall monuments and shining domes rising high above the dark shady groves wich surround its wall it lay about 8 miles from us evidently in utter unconciousness of the Fate preparing to overwhelm it But it was soon doomed to be undeceived Rouge galloped in front of the line and commanded the army to halt instantly a hundered Bugles sent forth their inspiring music and a thousand voices with shouts joined in the chorus each man unslung his musket: there was nothing but an incessant snapping of cocks and sharpening of swords heard in [the] army. ROUGE mounted an eminence and begun. "The Goal is now before you the course is clear and easy gain Fidena and you will gain Africa. That citadel is the throne from which we shall receive the obeisance or command the death of all the dominions of the 12s when one arrives [at] the summit of a Mountain the path is downward on every side. so when we shall have conquered Fidena our difficultys are over. you may henceforth think of rest and power. it is seldom that great acheivments are performed without great labour but here is an exception. in those white walls you behold your only obstacle crush them and you may sheath your swords for soldiers their are none in the place. then you may sheath your swords and grasp your firebrands yes burn destroy and exterminate all before you should one finger be uplifted by the meanest wretch those walls contain to oppose your progress, severity is necessary for should we spare this our first conquest. those citys which we shall storm hereafter will laugh at us as a parcel of Women and protract that Fate which assuredly will be doomed to them Now let Careys Mackenzies and Doms regiments be drawn out in line with Bayonets fixed give each man a glass of Brandy and bring my black charger directly. we will then set of to take possesion of the town" all was done as Rouge had commanded with the utmost promptitude and he, with 3000 chosen men at his heels marched quickly down the plain on their murderous errand with their long Bright bayonets glancing in the sun and their scarlet flags waving in the air, when the[y] had gone the rest of the army sat down on the hill side in the form of a crescent to take their dinner and watch the progress of the fight. it is while they are observing Rouges troop marching over the plain that I have sat down to write you [a] short account of what has been going on since my last letter. I must now conclude as I hear a loud shout in the direction of Fidena. and must haste to observe the action. when all is over I will continue my letter.

Yours &c
James Bellingham

PB Brontë April. 19. AD 1832.

---

[11] Fidena was the name of a town in Latium, conquered by the Romans in 435 BC. See Alexander & Sellars, 303.

P.S. I have forgot to inform you that hitherto. we (the four prisoners) have been kept fast chained. and under close surveillance. but early this morning several Officers entered [our] place of confinement. with orders to allow us full liberty to walk about &c. provided the Marquis of Douro should promise in our name. not to attempt and escape This the Marquis refused to agree to unless. they provided that. it should not be considered a breach of his word of Honour. If he or the others attempted to escape should they be treated with any harshness. confined. or put into. a severer restriction. than the Officers of the rebel army. Not being able to get from us our promise under severer restriction. and not daring to desplease the army by killing us. and yet determined to prevent the Marquis in particular from escaping to the other party where he might be such a powerful help. Rougue at length. reluctantly agreed to his proposals. we are now in a comparitivly easy condition. The Marquis tells me that though he is determined to keep his word. to the very letter. yet should the Rebel leader slacken in the slightest from his part of the agreement I Young Soult and Charlie must. prepare to fly with him to the. Snekean Army. instantly. As it is. he continued. I can scarcley bear to look on Idly here unable to take. any part in the. action. but I know that had I stretched the string one pull tighter had I asked proposals one jot more lenient Rougue would jump into the other extreme and ordered our heads to be cut of regardless of consequences. I did the best I could and. I hope that we shall soon be at liberty. by Rougues attempting to break his word That is some comfort

[The Fate of Regina][1]
[Book 1st.]
[330 lines]

While round the battlements and round the plain
    The swift scouts note O'Connors coming train.
    The din tumultous ever rattles round,
       And the proud Coursers snort, and the loud trumpets sound
But here I stop to tell each Leaders name[2]
And show their Actions and their souls to fame.
First rises Arthur; who in days of yore
Through every Land the English banners bore,
Before his look his stricken foes would fly,
Stern is his mind and Eagle like his eye.
Next [to] him stood Alexander, bold and wise
No art of war was hidden from his eyes:
Edward, and John, in the last order stand[3]
Brothers in arms and valiant hand to hand.
All these had fought in the same feilds of yore
And had together swept the seas and shore;
And now to crown their honours and their fame,
Their sons were worthy of their fathers name.
    Meanwhile O Connor down the Mountains brow
Pours his feirce warriors on the plain below;
Whose far off bugles, with a solemn wail
Foretell Reginas fate a melancholy tale.
Mixed with the clash of arms, whose sudden light
Breaks oer the hills and blazes on the sight.
And hark yon shout, through all the city sounding!
And from its mighty walls and towers rebounding;
"They come! They come!" all seize their glittering arms

---

[1]   The first of five poems in a hand-sewn notebook, without covers, (18.5 x 23.7 cm) in longhand, in the BPM: BS 117-5. The five poems in the notebook are fair copies. Originally 28 pages, but the first four containing ll. 1-166 of this poem are missing. The poem is dated May 1832 in Branwell's table of contents at the end of the notebook in volume II.

[2]   Although the verse form is reminiscent of Pope's translation of *The Illiad*, Branwell was clearly also influenced by Milton's description of the war in heaven; he was reading *Paradise Lost* as early as September 1830, when he quotes from Book I—see p. 123, n. 12.

[3]   Arthur Wellesly, Alexander Sneaky, William Edward Parry, and John Ross, the four kings of the Glass Town Confederacy, respectively. The battle described here is clearly another version of Rogue's insurrection in Glass Town, described in volume III of **LETTERS FROM AN ENGLISHMAN.**

And each bold soul for death and danger warms;
Determined thousands, at the Eastern gate
With burning hearts O Connors warriors wait;
Whose brazen bugles near and nearer blown
Strike on the ear with sad foreboding tone.
With iron throats the black Artillery lower
On every battlement and every tower,
Battery, ranged high oer battery, gun, oer gun:
Doomed soon to shake the heavens and shade the sun.
    But now the first deep roar with crashing sound
And burst of thunder rapid rattles round;
Thick wreaths of smoke blot out the rising sun!
And black, and dense, declare the Battle is begun.
Now crash on crash and roar succeeding roar[4]
Shakes the vast heavens and echoes round the shore,
Above, the smoke mounts heavy to the pole:
beneath bright lances gleam and cannons roll:
While all around the shouts of conflict rise,
And the loud tumult mounts and thickens in the skys.
At every gate the storm increasing roars,
While oer the rout Mars wrapt in terror soars,
He shakes his lance and bids the mighty fall
Gashed oer with wounds round the contested wall.
    But cheif the Eastern Gate withstood the shock
Of Connors Warriors; like some mighty rock,
Which, towering high above the stormy main,
Defies the waves which round it rage in vain.
Still frowning oer the deep with ages grey
While boiling round its base the white foam breaks to spray.
Thus stood the Gate amid the mortal jar,
Thus backward rolled the fiery tide of war:
There Arthur firm amid the tumult stands,
And hurls his thunder gainst the rebel bands:
High on his foam white charger, forward flying,
Victorious, trampling oer the dead and dying;
Though oft a mighty weight of steel clad foes
Bursts furious on and round his warriors close,
Yet, when his glittering sword he waves on high,
Scared by the flash, they start recede and fly;
On bursts he then his white plume waving far
Now seen now hidden as mid clouds a star.
Not less O'Connor towers amid the fight,

---

[4]   A small sketch with the letters "PTAB" and a pen-and-ink portrait appear in the right-hand margin of the second page of the manuscript.

Feirce in his mein, his eye in vengeance bright,
With savage Gordon[5] on he mows his way
Like a fierce tyger thirsting for his prey.
This[6] all the day, the storm of battle roared;
While on each side red Death the slaughter poured
Rank; ranged gainst rank; they fight and fall and slay
While clouds of smoke and dust obscured the fatal day.
Thick the red flames around the city stream,
And through the streets with baneful lustre gleam.
The cannons thunder, and the towers around
With hunderd echoes rattle back the sound.
Thus hours on hours unoticed rolled away,
Till on the Horizon hung the setting day;
And yet though evenings shades fast close oer all
The battle rages round the blood bathed wall,
Still at the gates are heaped the mangled slain,
And still the gory torrent stains the plain;
But yet Reginas Kings refuse to yeild
Though their dead warriors strew in heaps the field
Though Gordons troops impetous on them pour;
Though gainst the wall fast beats the Iron shower;
Though bands on bands fresh pouring round them close
Yet still they keep their gates and stand the charging FOES.
But Mars no more will brook this long delay,
He bids the fates to clear the doubtful day:
They with new force the rebels hearts inspire
And with the hope of conquest sets their souls on fire.
But cheif, O Connor at the eastern Gate
Ranged his black Cannon; marking it for fate:
Loud roared the guns, forth shot the Jets of flame,
And the loud chrash the posterns fall proclaim,
Mid clouds of dust the mighty portals fell;
And seemed to ring Reginas funerall knell.
With shouts of joy which drowned the cannons roar
On, through the breach the furious rebels pour,
On, like a cataract, man by man impelled
One mingled blaze of arms rolled swiftly through the feild.
Still to the gate they rush a yelling throng,
While shouts of "Victory!" break from every tongue.
But lo! all stop amid their full career
And stand with look aghast and straining ear;
For while the shades of Night fast viel the sky

---

5   George Charles Gordon: George Gordon was Byron's Christian name.
6   "Thus" obviously intended.

High oer the cloud they hear a mighty cry,
First burst it forth in shrill heart freezing tide,
Then wailed oer heavens vast arch, and in the distance died
Now, not till now, despair the Monarchs know
Frozen is each heart, cold sweat stands on each brow,
For with that yell and in that dreadful hour
Despairing fled Regina's guardian power.
But Gordons troops, emboldened by the sound
Makes heavens high arches to their shouts rebound;
Still furious onward through the breach they fly
While rent on either side the walls wide yawning lie.
Their foes before them heaped on thousands fall
And block their passage with another wall.
High oer the rest amid the shock of war
Their mighty leaders every danger dare,
Here, savage Gordon spreads destruction round
And heaps with arms and slain the groaning ground,
There, furious Connor to his warriors crys
To bring the fires, and bids the flames arise.
Then first blazing beam the cheiftain took,
And high in air the giant torch he shook;
His soldiers now with his example vie,
And soon the flashing fires glare through the reddening sky
Oh! who can paint the horrors of that Night,
When bloody terror ruled with wild affright;
Wher ere the wretched fugitive can fly,
Death, in some form is present to his eye;
If here, the fires mount aye with bloody light,
If there, the battle glitters to his sight;
If hid in night he hopes to escape his doom
The foemans sword still flashes through the gloom.
Reginas Kings, while arms or strength remain
Still nobly fight, but fight alas! in vain.
But, when they heard the sad foreboding cry
Which warned them from their native homes to fly,
When they beheld the clouds of smoke and fire
Born by the wind to heaven's black arch aspire,
Their own ancestral mansions wrapt in flame,
And their high temples but an empty name,
Then, then, hope leaves them! sinking on the ground
All heedless of the battle roaring round;
To Heavens tempestous vault they raise their eye
And mournful to their guardian Genius cry
"O ye! who brought us to this far of shore,
And gave us glory by your mighty power,
Now! now, if ever, oer us raise your sheild

And give us victory in this battle feild."
They ceased, a voice within them cried "depart."
And rising mournful with despairing heart,
Unknown, unnoticed through the wars red tide
They bent their course to Nigers sedgy side,
And lay on earth with care and sorrow worn,
To wait the rising of another morn.

The fate of Regina
Book. IId.
100 lines

Again, black night oer vast Regina falls,
And shades her giant towers and hoary walls.
But oh! how different from the former night,
Now rage, revenge, despair, and pale affright,
Stalk through her streets, no Moon shines forth on high
But frequent storms traverse the cloudy sky:
While the Heavens tremble and the deeps resound
To the rough thunder loudly roaring round:
The blast impetous howls along the plain,
And sweeps across the waste in showers of sleet & rain.
Black ocean boils through all her thousand caves:
And round the rocks all horrid howl the waves:
The trembling stars have hid their beams divine,
No light through all the gathering storm can shine,
Save yon fast reddning fires, which blaze on high
And burst in showers of sparks amid the cloudy sky.
How fast the fire flakes round the city rise
And in their roarings drown the shrieks and cries
Of dying and wounded men now equal all
Alike the vanquished and the victors fall
There by the unsparing sword or lances die
Those mangled neath the oerwhelming bulwarks lie
From every opening glares the wasting blaze
Through every street are shed the lurid rays
High oer the citadel at length they rise
And shake one vast white sheet against the troubled skys
Its broad walls tottering in the furious blaze
Stand black and huge against the fiery rays
While the high towers with dun smoke circled round
Stand like the guardian Genii of the ground
Till down they fall impetous from on high
While to the thundring burst the ruins round reply
But still O Connor through the city flies

And bids the towers to fall and flames to rise
Still savage Gordon Joyed these sights to see
Alike slays those who fight and those who flee
Nor fires nor ruins stop his fell career
Nor flying or fighting foes essaye his spear
His warriors follow where their leader flys
And maddning fury fills their hearts & eyes
Though scorched with fire and bathed in sweat and gore
Though scarce their weight their tottering limbs can bear
Yet still through smoke and fire they force their way
Nor can the feircest blaze their headlong passage stay
    But now when towers and halls in ruins lie
When scarce one hapless foe remains to die
When sleep the stiller of the human breast
Flys with soft wings to give the passions rest
The bloody swords the rebel warriors stay
And in the royal square wait for returning day
There mid the fires which flickering round them shine
They warm their wearied souls in feasts and wine
While riot rout and revelry and song
The silent gliding hours of Night prolong
    Mean while forlorn within a desart cave
Between whose rocks the echoing surges rave
That the four Kings with wounds & care oprest
Their countrys woes lay rotting in their breast
Now frantic hope now dark & deep despair
Breaks on their hearts with never ceasing care
They view their city blazing to the skys
They hear their foemens shouts th[e]ir subjects dying cries
Greif nerves their hearts they seize their arms of war
And forward rush resolved the worst to dare
With death before them and despair behind
On toward the town they rush on wings of wind
    But when they reached the gates twas silence all
No sentries paced around the battered wall
Nought heard but streams of blood which trickling ran
And groans of anguish from some dying man
Onward they marched amid they blazing halls
But saw no foe through all the wide spread walls
Untill they reached where drunk with foaming wine
The Rebel warriors lay in sleep supine
Which mid their circling warriors there they found
Connor & Gordon stretched along the ground
Now Wellesly with greif and rage oprest
Plunged his bright sword in Gordons traitrous breast
Inspired by him next Alexander stood

And drenched his falchion in O Connors blood
Then Edward blew his horn the rebels round
Start and their Kings amid them standing found
While at their foot all weltring in their gore
Lay their two cheifs their wars and conquests oer
Advancing forward Alexander cries
Rebels submit and tame your haughty pride
Behold your Leaders stretched along the plain
Confess your Kings and live in peace again
He ceased the armies loud applauses rise
And the glad shout reechoes through the skys
  But now the gloomy night is changed to day
And the tempestous clouds are rolled away
The rising sun illumes the gladdened morn
And the bright dew the opening flowers adorn
While in the joyous city all unite
To bind the wounded of the former fight
The fires to quench the ruins to repair
And Nature breath[e]s at length from those feirce storms of war

LETTERS
FROM AN.
Englishman.
VOL. V.
IIId. Series
PB B—te[1]

LETTERS FROM.
AN.
ENGLISHMAN.
To His Freind
In
LONDON:
BY
CAPTAIN JOHN FLOWER
VOL. V.

[Figure of Justice][2]

C^t ROSS'S GLASSTOWN
Printed and sold
Seag^t Winlass.

══════════════

BY PATRICK BRANWELL
BRONTE
August 3. 1832

[ornamental figure]

---

[1]   Hand-sewn booklet with grey paper covers (6.2 x 10.4 cm) of 18 pages (one blank) in the Brotherton Collection, University of Leeds.
[2]   See Alexander & Sellars, 302.

LETTERS. FROM AN
ENGLISHMAN.

Third Series.

VOL. V.

The LETTER. X.

Fidena
March 11.

That shout of which I spoke in my last letter was not as all expected the signal
that Rougue had commenced the storming of Fidena. but proceeded from a very
different cause it appears that Sneakys Government having awoke to a sense of
their danger had roused and ordered forth an army under the command of John
Sneaky to march after attack and destroy the army of the Rebels. This Force after
many forced marches. had come in sight just as Rougue with his 3000 men were
rushing forward to charge the gates of Fidena. Sneakys horse to the number of
7000 men instantly gallopped in between Rougue at Fidena and us on the hill
thus in a masterly manner separating the two parts of our army. This happened
just as night was comming on and therefor we knew nothing of the state of our
commander. but were in a dreadful state of suspense and anxiety. This was not
however the case with the Marquis young Soult and myself whose only hope lay
in the defeat of the rebels [whose] Commander in Rougues absense was Colonel
Arthur O Connor a man orginally of lofty and superior In[t]ellect but degraded by
low and wicked company into a stern ruthless determined and stone hearted
villain perpetually plunged in dissipation and play. at this moment he happened
to have had an ill run and lost much money he therefore came out in a storm of
passion and ordered every man to stand instantly to arms. and directed that all
absent. should when they came back be instantly shot and flung into the Red
River. but when it was told him that about 9000 soldiers were out foraging and
diverting themselves in the country he became as if mad he stood for a moment
and then with many violent gestures. ordered the whole body present to retreat
instantly. of course none could contradict this insane command by wich they
were to desert and leave to perish their Leader and above 13000 troops gone with
him or despersed over the country. For O Connor is much feared by the army
They all therefore in number 30,000. well armed men with out the slightest
reson for despair but merely by the coommand of one half frantic general rushed
down the hill and through the woods with out any order but each man pushing
over the other as he best could The army on a sudden were seized with a
compleat panic They they took not the lea[s]t consideration of the madness and
folly of their retreat They knew not from what they were flying or to whom they

were going but merely rushed along headlong over everything nothing was to be heard but shouts cries and cursing. The Night was quite dark & the sky pouring down torrents of rain and to increase the horror of the scene the old and gigantic trees of the wood where everywhere groaning and cracking in the wind. The prisoners were hurried along in the midst of this torrent hatless shoeless and our cloaths torn into rags among the press I was ready to faint with the pressure of the crowd for whenever a gust of wind came more violent than usual or a large tree fell in the hurricane the crowd in thousands rushed back from the spot whence it proceeded beleiving it to be the enemy. and pressed upon the other bodies with their whole force hundereds were trampled down and killed in the mire. we at last came to a rugged and nearly perpendiculary descent at the bottom of which was a deep marsh here the scene was horrifying for the men in the dark mistaking it for level ground rushed down in bodies of thousands at a time and gaining force as the[y] went down at length lost all power over their motions and rolled to the bottom in vast heaps of dead and living here those who remained were destined to new dangers for rising and preparing to run forward the first step they made plunged them together up to the waist in reeds & mire. here they floundered about over each other shouting and screaming till either spent with fatigue and fright or swallowed up in the b[o]gg they had all expired a horrible silence now ensued for a few minutes untill a new body rushed down the precipice and began the same scene of terror and tumult over again and also met with the same fate at the quagmire below [3]This state of things continued for some time untill those remaining seeing it impossible to escape that way all stood still for a moment. on the brink here having a small time to reflect they began to be sensible of their ridiculous Folley in retreating at all they therefore unanimously with shouts prepared to return but how were they to get back through that horrible wood in such a dark and stormy night many hours had yet to elapse before daylight. and stopping still were they stood was out of the question For as is often the case in Africa the night was intensly cold and in their drenched condition motion only could preserve them from death. They therefore rushed backward with but little order and that little. soon became none

---

[3]   Grotesque as this episode seems, Branwell may well be drawing on his reading of "The Subaltern—A Journal of the Peninsular Campaign," in *Blackwood's Magazine*, xvii (March 1825), which presents a similar episode, though it is staged in the context of an attack, not a retreat. Chapter Three of the journal, describing the assault on the coastal town of St. Sebastian on the River Gurumea, refers to the carnage effected in the following terms:

[t]he enemy having reserved their fire till the head of the column had gained the middle of the stream, then opened with the most deadly effect. Grape, cannister, musketry, shells, granades [sic] and every species of missile, were hurled from the ramparts, beneath which our gallant fe ows dropped like corn before the reaper; insomuch, that in the space of two minutes, the river was literally choked up with the bodies of the killed and wounded, over whom, without discrimination, tne advancing divisions pressed on (293).

and in a short time the advance became as dreadful as the retreat describe it I cannot for I had very little recollection of the circumstances being myself not far removed from the state of those on whom I every moment trod on. When the first faint Twilight began to show objects not far of in a dim manner we found ourselves still in the midst of the woods but knew by the footsteps of advancing men that we were discovered in a few minutes a faint glancing of armour was seen among the trees Then an universal click click click all along the borders of the forest This was followed by a great blaze of light and one simultaneous burst of sound louder than the loudest thunder We were intirely surrounded by many thousands of Sneakys soldiers who had levelled a murderous disc[h]arge among us. which had the effect of recalling the spirits of men into the bodies of the Rebels The[y] awoke as if from a horrid dream into a pleasant reality rallyed immediatly together as well as the nature of the ground would allow and stood presenting a formidable, no, a terrible front of pikes to their enimies, who not in the least daunted by their resolution, fixed their bayonets and with a loud shout rushed to the contest. I had once before in the Great glass Town rebellion seen a horrid and wholesale butchering with 200 or 300 cannon disc[h]arged at a time in the style of Bonapartes battles[4] But had never beheld any real fighting of man to man. untill now when I saw such a specimen of it as I shall not soon forget not one man in either army showed the slightest disposition to fling from his work not one was there that did not glory in it There the rebels stood like a vast broad compact wall with their bright pikes jutting dreadfully forth before them. and there too opposite were placed a parrarell wall of Sneakys Soldiers with there correspond ng front of Bayonets firmly fixed for the charge. a narrow lane ran between stretching away quite to a point in the distance. but in a moment this lane vanished as if by majic and in place of it was seen nothing but a bright and confused assemblage of shining steel and a struggling tossing and swaying on all the vast numbers of men mixed with shouts screams and a confused clashing of weapons This scene continued for some time untill the foremost of Sneakys rank fell back in confusion. and disclosed what before was pleasant green turf. a black, trampled soil drenched in blood and covered with huge heaps and rows of arms and men heaped one over the other struggling groaning and shreiking horribly but again Sneakys soldiers at once charged forward with irresistible violence and again this dreadful scene began with renewed force neither side would give or take an inch for each army was composed of men cast exactly in the same mould all were from the poachers and rare lads, but in the midst of this fighting the Marquis's experienced eyes b ne' some indication in Sneakys left wing that all

---

4   Napole   as a strong believer in the use of artillery and came more and more to substitute massed firepower for tactical expertise as his battles continued. His ideal artillery ratio was five guns per thousand men, but he rarely succeeded in having more than three per thousand. He fired massed concentrations at Friedland (1807), Wagram (1809), Leipzig (1813), and Waterloo (1815). As the close-range effect of cannister or grape was murderous, such massed gunfire was indeed "horrib!

was not going on right he pointed out to me its undulating motion as if the hinder troops were pressing forward on the van in a short time a sharp fire of musquetry was heard in that direction Sneakys troops began to give way and presently fled in confusion from the wood, disclosing to us the cause of this sudden rout in a large body of rebels newly come down from the Northern Mountains and under the command of Young Man Naughty who arriving at the rebel camp and hearing there how we were situated had marched up into the wood and attacked the Sneakyan soldeirs unawares We all now hastened out of the wood toward our camp. anxious to learn how Rougue meanwhile had got on at Fidena but on coming within sight of it we beheld it vast clouds of smoke rising from the place where it stood yes that noble city which we left last evening with the setting sun shining brightly and calmly on its white walls and marble houses. we now beheld a vast heap of ashes and blackened reeking ruins. for Rougue taking advantage of the darkness & stormyness of the Night had divided his small body into two parts of 1500 men each with the one he under cover of the rain and hurricane entered silently the enimies camp where breaking suddenly into a loud shout. he so effectualy discomfited them that though so immensly superior in number they fled were prusued with immense slaughter far over the plain and when left were rapidly retreating to Sneakys Glass town The other body perc[i]pitatly throwing themselves into Fidena in like manner suprised the Inhabitants who though like lions for courage were rendered defencless for want of their arms They were all or nearly all massacred the town was instantly set on fire and in the morning we beheld its ashes. The statements of the numbers and losses of the conflicting armies is as follows

Rebels,		Number.	Losses
At the camp & woods	—	30000	13000
Straggling in various parts	—	9000	-- --- --
At Fidena with Rougue	---	3000	600
Reinforcment of Naughty	—	28600	2000
Rebels. Total	—	70600	15600

SNEAKYS				Number	Losses
Before Fidena	—	—	—	14000	4900
At the woods	—	—	—	22000	11050
Inhabitants (men) of the city			—	48540	31000
Sneakys Total			—	84540	46950

This will show at once the sanguinary Nature of the battle or rather series of battles But I have forgot to mention that the prisoners Rougues has taken (including the inhabitants of Fidena) amount to 15928. persons. all these are doomed to death. and now while I write this letter in one of the unconsumed

houses in the city. I hear nothing but the volleys of musquetry fired on bands of these wretched beings. But I must now conclude. expect more hereafter yours &c
James Bellingham.

LETTER. XI.

Fidena
March 13th
AD 1832.

Dear Friend
    I you see, am still in the land of the Living. to continue to you my prec[i]ous narratives To go on—The whole army of Sneaky Being completely routed and driven away Rougue has been employing himself in murdering his 31000. prisoners and when these were disposed of he ordered into the great room of the Town hall one day. Colonel Arthur O Connor—all knew what was about to be done therefore vast numbers hurried there I among the number to witness the trial for dereliction of duty. When we entered Rougue was standing at a table at the upper end of the hall. with his hat under his arm talking with young Man Naughty and Captain Carey his face bore exactly the same sneering Iron[i]cal and determined expression as when I last saw him when making his speech near Fidena not the slightest expression of joy or sorrow anger or pity was to be observed in it though the present occasion, one would think would have called forth some passion in his dry stony frame For O Connor his his near relation has passed his life with him, shared his victorys and defeats and been his constant companion in his dissipations and gambling so much for the compassionate side of the picture Taking it one the other veiw he was appointed to a vast trust in the army This trust he betrayed in the most miserable manner by his drunken rage. being the cause why victory was delayed the great part of the army destroyed. and Rougue himself put in the most imminent danger surely I thought this would produce some impression on the demagogues contenance but no. The moment that O Connor entered bound and led by two men. Rougue without turning his face said "sit down sir" and continued talking with Naughty for ten minutes longer at the end of wich time the Giant took his seat with the other officers. Rougue then turning toward the prisoner. said. "Of course Sir you own yourself to be the person whom I left in c[h]arge of the army. on the 9th of March?" Connor made no reply. "Sir don't you mean to answer?" asked Rougue Still Connor spoke not a word Rougue then speaking to the officers. said well gentlemen since the Colonel out of kindness wont speak in order to shorten our debates. let us follow up his beginnings .and decide immediatly how we must resign his existence Shooting is the manner in which we annihilate common soldiers beheading is the death of civilians and as I am anxious for the honour of my relative I beg leave to submit to your consideration the *gallows* as the most dignified manner of terminating so honorable a career it certainly is the most

exalted death. I can think of what think you gentlemen?" he had scarcly finished when Connor starting up exclaimed "Wretch! Villain! I will never suffer such a death I will die like a soldier." So saying he snatched a pistol from the table and directing it to his heart fired and fell The room was instantly a scene of confusion till Rougue ordered "Silence." he then stepped up to the fallen O Connor. and said The colonel I am glad to say has not yet terminated his honorable and useful career he has kindly held his hand up to my face. in the attitude of boxing to remind me of the pleasant. "Mills" we have often fought together, it is therefore expedient. to 'exalt' him as soon as possible that he may *feel* the benifit of a change of air in a higher region Guards Take him to the gallows in the yard" Rougues commands were instantly obeyed The wretched man was born out groaning and bleeding profusely Rougue and the rest followed and I was left alone in the room. too sick with what I had seen to wish to see more of it.

Night. Mar. 12. I have just witnessed a scene Both curious in itself and doubly so to me as exemplifying the character of the young men. This evening about sunset we the 4 prisoners (or rather 3 as Charlie was of with Naughty) were sitting together in a room with many of the Rebel officers Rougue himself among the number, when we heard in the camp a loud sound of howling and crying and shouting, had we heard it in an European camp we should have thought that the enimy had suprised us but all knew that the "rare Lads" never make sounds of *Woe* on such an occasion we therefore started up to see what was the matter we had not much time to think for the door soon opened and In entered Old Young Man Naughty. the Giant blubbering like a child. he made his bow and stood still staring wildly about him at his back were a hundered others all to appearance as greivously afflicted as himself in a short time indeed the whole camp were round the doors crying and howling dismally. We (the Officers) began to laugh at the odd spectacle and Rougue. asked Naughty what was the matter were they all mad? as soon as the veteran could get the mastery over his fright & tears he sobbed out "Oh rare apes y^r honours whats the matter oh what shall we do as how we were a going into the woods to shoot rare beasts and sich like un un oh rare dogs I can't tell what to do un un un we seed som'at. we seed him come skelping from a rare villain of a tree and he he had fire in his eyes and and and nay rare beasts I can tell what to say." of course we could not tell what to make of this speech. Rougue exclaimed. "Speak out you Old Fool *what* did you see?" Naughty began to answer but. on a sudden a shrill whooping was heard in the distance. followed by the yells and cries of the soldiers They screamed out "He's coming its coming" and each fellow scampered of with all his might. we saw them rushing past the windows in hunderds at a time young man Naughty and those at the door burst into the room nearly frenzied with their fear. at their backs followed a being. the nature of which it puzzled us to tell. It was about four feet high lean meagre and covered with filth. in coulour it was dusky and. in shape

> "If shape it might be termed which
> shape had none."[5]

It bore the most resemblance to a starved monkey or the "Dwarf" in The Lay of the Last Minsterl[6] Its hair was thick and abundant in quantity but tangled with thorns and matted with filth. while its deeply sunk eyes gleamed sometimes with an Idiotic stare and often with the most Malignant expression conceivable The moment It saw us it burst into the room with a loud whoop and threw itself on the floor where it lay grovelling and rolling about muttering constantly in a guttural manner "Grildrugh. Glomdalclutch. glimmering Bridge or sounds to that effect. varying them occasionaly with a shrill whistle which made most present start. The first who dare touch it was yong Charlie who advanced to seize it but the moment it saw him it stared and giving a loud grunt of joy seized his hair and dragged him down on to the floor here they commenced a deadly struggle. fighting with teeth and claws like two rats however Charlie at last by the superior strength of his opponent was quickly giving way and would have been killed had not the Marquis his brother ran in a[nd] tore him away The Imp now seized on Arthur biting scratching and screaming most vehemently till several Officers coming up laid hold of him, but were glad to lett it go Rougue at last caught the creature and dashing it on the ground placed his foot on it but it twisted itself up and bitt through [h]is boot in an instant making the blood run profusely. The Demagogue enraged at the pain drew out a brace of pistols and applying on[e] to each of its ears fired and shot it through the head as it now lay quite motionless and apparently dead sever[a]l present took it up and began to examine it when suddenly, as if inspired with new life it jumped from their hands out of the wind[ow] and dissapeared among the woods
It was Lemuel Gulliver!!![7]
This wretched creature has never been seen. since the Departure of the Genii Inns about 40. years ago. except once in 1801. some Rare apes who had gone into the glens of Elymbos on an hunting expedition saw him among the heath. more they could not tell for of course a general scamper was the order of the day.
This incident may serve to show you the character of the rare lads bolder than lions when opposed to. something of which. they know the nature however great and terrible. But more timorous than childern. before a fancyd Ghost or "Boggard."[8] Even this wretched and Dwarfish maniac literaly drove before him

---

5   *Paradise Lost*, Book II, l. 667.
6   The London 1806 edition owned by the Brontës is in the BPM.
7   See Alexander CB, I, 61 for an indication that the Brontë children were reading *Gulliver's Travels* as early as the summer of 1829.
8   Boggard: a word of popular usage in Yorkshire, Lancashire, Cheshire, and the North Midlands. It is evidently related in dialectal use to "bogy," a word designating a spectre or goblin supposed to haunt a particularly gloomy spot or scene of violence.

for 2 or 3 mile[s] several thousand Men whom a whole legion of Tygers could not move from their post[9]

LETTER. XII.

March 14.
Fidena.

Dear Friend.
On the morning after the date of my last Numbers of scouts came at full speed into the city. with intelligence. that the Snekeyan Army. had rallied. and was marching up in 3. great divisions. from the capital. the Wareham road. and from the direction of Fort Niger. It was stated moreover that. it was supported. by. powerful reinforcements under the command. of. Captain Parry Fredric Stumps. and the Duke of WELLINGTON. I was in the room. when this was announced to Rougue. When the last leaders name was mentioned I looked at his face to see wether the news would make any external impression on him. But no his face preserved the usual. stern Ironical. sneer. he. flinched not in the least.. but only asked. what was the force of the enimy. on one scout naming 100000. and another 300000. he laughed and. bowed them out of the room I went out with them On my entering the street. a scene of Bustle and tumult presented itself. such as I expected. from the nature of the news. What suprised me was the universal air. of confidence and joy which seemed to diffuse itself on every on[e]. present. I asked Naughty. what grounds they could have. for hope to bear up. against the overwhelming numbers and admirable leaders they would have to encountre. The Giant pointed to the huge line of hill. rising to the west of the city. He said "you rare brute thats our ground we expect some folk from there this evening you oaf. of an Englishman" From this I understood that they expected to beat them by the Mountaineers. which were understood to be about to join them from their inaccessible dwellings.
The remainder of the day passed on without anything important taking place but In the evening after sunset a report ran through the city that the reinforcements had arrived from the North. numbers ran from all sides to witness their entry I was among them. I stationed myself at the inner entrance of the great NW. gate and there beheld a long troop of men marching up the city hill. These were not the men you or I have hitherto been accustomed to see. They had come not from merely the "Mountains" as others whom I had seen had done but. from the wildest most savage and barren regions in the Glope[10] From the shores of the Great Lake of the Genii from the sides of Elimbos Elboros and the Geniis throne. These were the Inhabitants of that Immense and lofty chain of black untraversed mountains called the "Brannii Hills" stretching from 2. to 300 mile[s] beyond the most northern city town or villiage in the country and truly

---

9   A leaf with writing on both sides has been cut out.
10 "Globe" obviously intended.

these men were worthy of their abode. They came trooping up file after file dark Gigantic, Savage, Beings more like Genii than men. I saw not one of them much lower than 7 feet. several reached the enormous height of 8 or 9 feet!! They were magnified and exaggerrated resemblances of the most northern Highlanders of the 17th century. like them their rough long ragged and matted Hair hung over their shoulders and visages mixing with as rough and ragged a Beard But not so as to conceal a pair of huge dark glaring eyes. which wandered about from every objet. with an expression of ferocious delight and wonder natural to all savages Their complexions were copper colour and their shoulders as is usual with all the men of our countrys were of an uncommon breadth. Their dress startled me from its strange appearance it was universaly a sort of short "plaid" or frock of bear skin with the fur outward. The cheifs or leaders wore a crown of feathers from the Eagles wing none of the rest had any covering to the Head or feet what-soever Their arms were huge. Iron lances which I was unable to lift from the ground. vast clubs of the same metal and long Spanish Guns. several troops also bore. Bows 8 feet long. These were the strongest and most terrible men in the Army. indeed you may conceive they would need strength to weild such a weapon. I am anxious to see how they use it. To this miserabley feeble an[d] prolix description I will only add that their number was estimated at from 60 to 70 thousand!!![11]

I saw the leader of this strange tribe He is termed the "Ape of the Hills"[12] according to the usual ludicrous language of the "Rare lads." excepting CRASHEY I never beheld so striking and venerable a figure. though more than 100 years old he. is still as erect as his own spear. and his enormous hight and shaggy black garment. crowned. with Hair and beard of a snowy whit[e]ness give him the appearance of one of his own. majestic Mountains. He seemed the Genius of Elimbos. He was born more than a century ago. in one of the wild Highland glens which stretch round the. base of Ben Nevis.[13] here he spent the

---

[11] A canceled passage follows this sentence:
Their leaders name is the "Son of the Mist" He was a Gigantic man. with Snowy. Hair and Beard. and aged. more than 100 years He can trace his descent from The Time when the ancient Britons ruled over these countrys. For remember. not to confound. these men whom I have been describing with the Twelves. or Rare Lads. They Are in no manner related. to them saveing that they both derive from the same stock These are the DESCENDANTS OF THE ANCEINT BRITISH. They can boast of an uninterrupted line of Ancestry. reaching back to a period of 4000 years. and for that immense period of time they have preserved their habits intirely free from all corruption. They are still the genuine "Briths". Their language is the Old. British or Gaelic. slightly tinctured however with a few African phrases and Idioms.

[12] See also Alexander CB, II, Part I, 182-83.

[13] Britain's highest peak, Ben Nevis, is located in the West of Scotland, standing at 1343 feet.

first 40 years of his life. in the way then customary with the most savage of the Highlanders. in the day time pursuing either deer or men over the rocks and mountains and in the night resting his head on a pillow of mountain snow. about the middle of the 18.th century he had a vision on the top of "Loch-in-y-gair,"[14] in which a little old man with a red head. appeared to him. and told him to go over the Cheiviots into the country of the "Saxons" and. there proceed to the Sea shore where he would. learn what should befall him. he. rose up. and departed from Scotland immediatly. when he reached the sea side in Northumberland he saw coming toward the shore a copper cauldron with the little red man. in it whom he had seen in his dream.[15] The old man made a sign for him to get in. the Hig[h]lander did so. They sat. opposite each other and continued tilting over the wave[s] for many days without a word being spoken on either side. after a long time. the Highlander saw blue hills rising. over the sea. One summit kept rising up after the other then the green shore appeared. They soon dismebarked from their strange vessel. and landed at the Glass Town. here the little Red Old man motioned. to him to go forward. into the city. while he himself. took the huge Cauldron on his head with the utmost ease and. walked. into the sea. (This Old Man was the Genius Brannii) The rest of the story is soon told the Gigantic Hig[h]lander soon found favour in the eyes of the Twelves he accompanied them to the seige of Accrofcroomb and the storming of

---

14 There is an isolated spot on the coast of Western Scotland near the island of Aran called Loch Gair.

15 In an early biography of the Brontë sisters, *The Life and Work of the Sisters Brontë* (1900), Mary Ward draws attention to the "mixture of Celtic dreaming with English realism" in the Brontës' character, claiming that this mixture "gives value and originality to all [the Brontës] do." Celtic influence, however, seems to be most apparent in Branwell's work—not surprisingly, perhaps, for Branwell's name (Bran/well) links him directly with one of the most powerful figures of Celtic folklore, Bran the Blessed, guardian of the cauldron of plenty, and in certain of his manifestations, prototype of the Fisher King. Branwell's recounting of the episode of the Highland Chief's vision, with its dwarfish figure (or "leprechaun") riding the ocean in a copper cauldron, has numerous precedents in the Celtic mythologies of Ireland, Scotland and Wales, as well as in their literary descendants, the medieval romances. The Celtic dwarf normally has extravagant powers, possessions, and appearance, combining great strength with striking features, either beautiful or ugly, and may be entirely hostile or beneficent. He is frequently associated with magical objects, especially the cauldron of regeneration, and is typically associated with the color red. For example, in the Irish tale of Fergus, the dwarf Iubdan, whose voice is "sweet as copper's resonance," and whose cheek is "like the blood-coloured rowan-berry," gives Fergus shoes of bronze which travel on land and sea alike; in another tale, the hero Cuchulainn plucks a little man from a boat of bronze; while in the story of Herla, king of the ancient Britons, a noble dwarf-king sprouts "a red beard so long that it touched his breast."

Coomasseii where he performed acts scarcly inferior to their own. When the Duke of Wellington came over with his veterans from Europe and Africa was conquered he choose the 42. Regiment of Highlanders and. settled in the most Northern Mountains of Ashantees There he has scince remained the Cheif and King for they like their Fathers in the British Islands scarcly own the government of their lawful Sovereign Sneaky

These terrible men had join[ed] Rougue merely for the sake of fighting (they cared not for what cause) and getting plunder. The moment they have obtained sufficient booty Rougue may cease to recon on them. They will then return to their native hills and Fastnesses,

NB. to morrow we expect the allied armies to appear in sight There will be some hot work that day and the following If I am not much mistaken. You shall hear the result. but I must give up the pen for the present Good Night

Yours &c.
James Bellingham

PB Bronte June 16th. AD 1832

IIId. ODE.
on the.
Celebration of the Great
AFRICAN   GAMES[1]

---

177. Lines

Once again bright Summer now
Shines on Afric's scorched brow
Once again the vales appear
In the new glories of the year
Once again! yet Once again!
Sunlike towering oer the plain
Rises in light the Immense Olympian hall
Back casting from its front grey twilights dusky pall
      Then rise ye thousand Nations rise
      Lift to the east your joyful eyes
      Lo oer the deset drear and grim
Floats widly sounding the triumphal hymn
      Its parched and barren sands rejoice
      In the sound of human voice
      Let the heavens and earth and seas
         Hail with Joy the coming morn
      On the widly wafting breeze
         Let the tidings round be borne
      Let every Nation now rejoice
While mighty Genii with an answering voice
      Re echo back the song
      While you ye woods and Mountains grey
      And thou O everlasting sea
      The joyful notes prolong
      Come thou stern Monarch Lord of war
      Come from thy chosen land afar
      That land where forests huge and hoar
Stretch their black shadows to the western shore
      While Gambias stream with glittering pride
      Pours through those vales her winding tide
      And on her rocky margin sees
Halls towers and towns of men rise oer the shady trees
      King of the North arise and come!

---

[1]   The second of five poems in BPM: BS 117-5—see p. 203, n. 1. Despite Branwell's indication of 177 lines in both the title and the table of contents, there are only 175. For additional information on the African Games, see volume III of **Letters to an Englishman**, p. 188 and Alexander CB, I, 342.

Down from thy wild and mountain home
Where Caseputh hugh and Dimdim grey
Frown beetling oer the Genii's sea
Where hills oer hills rise black and high
Eternal clouds! they shade the sky
Their serried peaks by thunder riven
And standing gainst the vault of heaven
    With an eternal frown
While from their summits bleak and hoar
Oer craggy rocks the torrents pour
And onward with unceasing roar
    Rush hoarsly thundering down
Thy freeborn sons O King attend thee now
From Morven's[2] snowy heights and Dimdims cloudy brow
And thou O sunny smiling plain
    Where Ardrahs stream unfettered glides
    Sloping from vast Nevadas sides
    Toward the glassy main
Like Nigers waves your thousands pour
From every hill and every shore
Haste onward haste your coming feet
While brightest joy appears your footsteps here to greet
As when the sailor on the sea
Tossed by the force of storms away
    Beholds the Heavens all hushed in gloom
While the black Ocean stretching round
In long dull waves without a bound
With a drear melancholy sound
    Seems destined for his toomb
Slowly the vessel Labours on
As slow the black waves glide along
    Her streamers drooping hang on high
    Still sleep the clouds in the Iron sky
    Nature seems turned to stone
When sudden bursts upon thir sight
A little Island shining bright
    Girt by the foaming sea
All fair and green and broad it lies[3]
In mists the blue hills statly rise

---

[2]   The name is taken from Macpherson's *Ossian*. See pp. 27-29 for Branwell's
reading of *Ossian*.
[3]   Two following lines have been canceled:
    Its blue hills peircing through the skys
    Whith <aspect> bold and free

Their tall tops peircing through the skys
    With aspect bold and free
A sudden breeze sweeps oer the main
Up start the waves to sight again
From thir high tops they shake the spray
And whiten with surf the merry sea
The statly Vessel mid sheets of foam
Glides swiftly through her watery home
Shrill scream the winds in her sailyards high
    And her streamers long and gay
Wave proudly in the summer sky
    As she plunges upon her way
All Heaven bursts forth in sight again
Brights shine the clouds and bright the main
Even thus time silent passed along
    Nor left one flash to mark the circling year
      Nature herself seemed turned to stone
And the great world rolled round a ruin dark and drear[4]
    When as if sent from Heaven the Olympian Hall
      Sudden erects its pillared wall
      It dawned upon the eyes of men
      And gave them Light and Life again
      All thought dead Greece restored once more
      Afric seemed the Achaian shore
      Mid sandy plains and burning skys
      A greater Athens seemed to rise
      Again Olympus towered above the plain
    But looked not on the sunny Grecian sea
Where mid a thousand isles the light waves sported free
    No round it roared the immense Atlantic main
    Cradle of tempests and the whirlwinds reign
    Not awful Jove not golden Juno here
      With bursting splendour fills the air
      Not here does Great Athenia shine
      Nor Phoebus spread his beams divine
      No here dim forms involved in gloom
    Like—Spectres rising from a midnight tomb
      With winds and tempests fill the air
        I see I see appear

---

4   Two following lines have been canceled:
      It dawned upon the eyes of men
      And gave them light and sight again.

Awful Branii gloomy giant[5]
Shaking oer earth his blazing air
Brooding on blood with drear and vengeful soul
He sits enthroned in clouds to hear his thunders roll
Dread Tallii next like a dire Eagle flies
And on our mortal miseries feasts her bloody eyes
Emii and Annii last with boding cry
Famine and war fortell and mortal misery
All these the blighters of the varied year
All these and more than these before my eyes appear
Yes more far more a horrid train
Rising like clouds above the main
Meagre and black and thin
Round their huge jaws the red foam churning
Their souls for blood and battle burning
And though from conflict still returning
Yet still again impatient to begin
These not the golden Deities of Greece
These are the powers that rule our Land
Nor can we hope their fetters to release
Or quench their scorching brand
Then where oh where must Mortals turn their eyes
Not to the Genii throning hills or tempest giving skys
No to the Twelves. O Fathers of our fame
O Fathers founders of our glorious name
To you we look our latest hope
Our great Defenders and our common prop
Led on by you we force our way
Oer every land through every sea
Yes the vast Atlantic main
Shall oppose her waves in vain
With all the loudest winds of Heaven
Full against its surface driven
Let its billows rage and rave
We will dare the stormiest wave
If you upon us shine
Let it be our common grave

5   When Charlotte returned home from Roe Head School for Christmas
vacation in 1831, the four children decided to dissolve the imaginary kingdom
they had created, and she recorded the dissolution in her poem, "The trumpet hath
sounded" (Neufeldt PCB, 150), but in this poem Branwell seems to be trying to
resurrect the four Chief Genii, giving "Awful Branii" pride of place, perhaps
because the poem is dated on his birthday. His frustration over the failure of his
attempt is recorded in "A FEW WORDS TO THE CHEIF GENII"—see p. 250.

If you hide your light divine
But why thus cloud one glorious day
With these sad thoughts O pass away
Away ye tempests of the north
Let the sun of hope shine forth
Bursting bright on earth and sea[6]
Gilding the Olympian Hall with splendour gay
And you our Fathers now descending
Glorious in your chariots ride
While your children round attending
Hail in you their countrys pride
Let us onward hasten all
To the vast Olympian hall
Now let the trumpets loud and shrill
Awake the Falcon on the rocky hill
Let the Heavens all tremble now
While the majestic Organs blow
While you[r] assembled thousands raise
One universal song of praise
Haste oh haste your coming feet
Joy appears your steps to greet
Haste upon this day of Gladness
Drive away the voice of sadness
And of Grim Despair
To the Olympian Hall arising
Your bewildered eyes surprising
On all cares of Life despising
Haste oh haste rejoicing there

PB Bronte
June 26th
A D 1832

---

6   The line originally read: "Bursting forth in glorious day."

**Ode to the
Polar Star**[1]
87, Lines.

Lord of the Northern feilds of Heaven
May Light like thine to me be given
　　While I thy praises sing
Let sordid flatterers cringe and wait
Before the rich mans open gate
And bow beneath the glare of state
　　And there their offerings bring
But on some rocks tremendous steep
High hanging oer the hoary deep
　　Let me be seated lone
And while the tempests round me fly
Howling across a midnight sky
Behold thee shining bright and high
　　And silent and alone
Star of the pole amid the sea
How many now may look on thee
　　And bless thy light divine
How often doth the sailor pray
When tossed by tempests far astray
That thou wouldst guide his wandering way
　　And on his vessel shine
How often from the abyss of air
Hast thou heard the sailors prayer
—Lo yon tall vessel labring amid the storm
—But vainly struggling 'gainst his giant arm
With shattered masts with sails all rent and riven
Tossed from the gulphs beneath to the black clouds of heaven
　　Lo! the night increasing shrouds the sky
　　While upward burst the waves on high
　　Oer unseen rocks they rage and roar
　　Whitning with surf the shaken shore
High oer the ships tall bows they break away
　　And fill the air with showers of spray
　　Black clouds vast billows drive along
　　And as they drive she hurries on
　　Now on the secret quicksands dashed
And Girdled round with foam

---

[1]   The third of the five poems in BPM: BS 117-5—p. 203, n. 1. Again,
Branwell has miscounted the number of lines.

Then from her rocky harbour washed
And hurled upon the main mid its huge waves to roam
    Then then how droops the s[a]ilors soul
    Hopeless he gazes toward the pole
    For tossing on an unknown sea
    How may he hope to look on thee
    But Lo the clouds all rent and riven
    Have to the winds a passage given
    Forth breaks upon his upward sight
    The dark blue concave of the night
    Its thousand stars all fixed on high
    And twinkling in the silent sky
    High throned in Heaven he sees thee shine
    Well know[n] to him thy Light divine
        He sees thee and adores
    Unheeded now may rage the sea
    Secure in thy directing ray
    He learns to avoid the rocky way
        And seek his native shores
            But not alone to him
            Who doth a wanderer oer the Ocean roam
            Wilt thou bestow thy beam
And guide him toward his home
The Traveller oer the desert drear
Gazes on thee his heart to cheer
Though waste on waste expands before
Nor can his eye a bound explore
Though far behind his native valley lies
Though unknown scenes his wildered sight surprise
    Yet as he folds his mantle fast
    To guard him from the bitter blast
        Swept from the unclement sky
    Unmindful of the gathering night
    Upward to thee he strains his sight
    Where he beholds thee shining bright
        His Guardian in the sky
Blesser of Mortals! Glorious Guide
Nor turning ever from thy course aside
    Eternal pilot while Time passes by
        While Earthly guides decay and die
            Thou holdst thy throne
            Fixed and alone
In the vast concave of the nightly sky
        Kingdoms and states may droop and fail;
            Nor ever still abide
        The Mighty moon may wax and wane

But thou dost silent there remain
  An everlasting guide!

      P B Brontë
      June 26th.
      A D 1832

LETTERS
FROM AN.
Englishman. . .
VOL VI.
IIId series. . .
P B B—te[1]

LETTERS FROM
AN:
ENGLISHMAN.
To his Friend.
.IN LONDON.
BY
CAPTAIN JOHN FLOWER
VOL: VI.

[Figure of Justice][2]

Capt Ross's Glass town.
Printed and sold
By Searg[t] Winlass
By Patric Branwell Brontë
.August, 2d. 1832.

---

[1] Hand-sewn booklet with grey paper covers (6.1 x 10.3 cm.) of 20 pages (four blank) in the Brotherton Collection, University of Leeds.
[2] See Alexander & Sellars, 301.

LETTERS FROM:
AN ENGLISHMAN

Third Series.

VOL. VI.   LETTER
                                            XIII

The dawn of this morning has brought with it the first appearance of the Allied
army. about sun rise. ie. 5 o clock. This Important fact was announced to
Rougue by the Scouts and watchmen. The moment I heard of it I with the
Marquis of Douro and Young Soult repaired to the principal steeple of the noble
cathedral where elevated. 300 feet above the city and 700. above the river. we
enjoyed a wide and undisturbed prospect of the country for many leagues round.
We had looked with our glasses on all sides without being able to discover any
thing for some time when suddenly the Quick eye of the Marquis was attracted
by the appearance of a faint line which seemed to move along. (but. from the
distance nearly imperceptabley) over the hieghts beyond. Haslingden.[3] about 13.
miles south East of the city We looked intently toward that quarter & in a short
time observed. another line. rising behind it and a third. stretching away toward
the direction of Summerfeild We had observed these for about 10 minutes. when
happening by chance to cast my eyes toward the South. what was my suprise to
find every hill and road in that direction covered with moving undulating lines
evidently of armed men. I thought at first that they had risen from the earth. so
suddenly and without any warning had they appeared They kept increasing and
spreading forward giving exactly the idea of a mighty torrent rolling on toward
us. destroying everything in its way. on looking at their immense numbers I
could not help sighing to think of the seemingly utter impossibility. for any
force to stand against them.
As for the Marquis. It was pleasant to see the fire that lighted up in his eyes as
he stood intently observing. their movements. He looked like a young Eagle.
perched on a hundred fathom cliff. surveying the thou[sand] Floocks and herds in
the plains an[d] valleys below. and deliberatting on which of the countless
victims at his disposal he should first dart down and infix his sharp and hungry
talons. But alas! the simile is scarcely applicable here. The Marquis was rather as
a chained Eagle. veiwing what he once could revel. in but. what now was denied
to him I shall not easily forget the manner with which he turned round to us and
said "Oh. for my own sake how much rather had I have suffered myself. to be
bound confined despised. treated in the worst possible manner hitherto might I
have some chance at least now to attempt to free my-self and join those ranks

---

[3] Haslingden, a market town, is located by Haslingden Moor, near Blackburn
in Lancashire.

yonder. I hope Rouge may take it into his head to order me to be hanged before this night then I should be free to try an escape. As it is I can do nothing"

But to return from this digression. We contin[ued] observing the March of the allied Armies from 6 o clock. till 12 during all which time they seemed to be advancing nearer without the slightest opposition and were rapidly nearing the large and well fortified town of Haslingden. which is the principal pass to Fidena. But at the time of noon. our souls, "Fatigued

"In that celestial colloquy sublime
Dazzled and spent sunk down & sought repair[4]

The repair of a substantial dinner. which we accordingly hasted to partake of. descending from our lofty eminence into the commonplace every day. world. while passing through the streets we observed unusual bustle. and tumult for it was understood that a powerful detachment of Mountaineers were to be marched down to Haslingden there to oppose the progress of the Rebels.

I dined with Rougue and his principal Officers. The Demagogue did not seem at all concerned or alarmed at the tremendous hazard of his situation he neither ate more or less than usual. nor. did he seem more or less thoughtful or more or less cheerful. There was no sign by which you could tell that he knew any thing of the enimy. After dinner was dissmissed. YM. Naughty came in to say that. the forces for Haslingden. were ready for marching. Their numbers were.

22,000 —	Mountaineers under the command of The Ape of the Mist.
3000	Horse. from the east plain led by Carey
9,000	Lancers commanded by Capt C Dorn.
Total — 34,000 men	

Besides these. 16,000. mountaineers were ordered to cross the Red river to Marchtown and Spalding Hill. 10,000 to Clifton Fort and Castleton[5] and another 10,000. along the banks of the Red River. The total of the force expected to be called into immediate action was 70000. men Rougue soon ordered his horse to be brought. he mounted him and rode to the southern gate where the troops were stationed. I and thousands of others followed, the appearance of the Army was very martial. The Mountaineers especialy looked. so terrible that as I before wondered how. Rougue could bear up against the Allies so I now wondered how the Allies could bear up against Rougue but I was inexperienced. and knew no better, The first corps under the Ape of the Hills began their march about 6 o clock in the evening with loud yells and blowing of Bagpipes. They moved of without baggage or Artillery at a running pace with their vast 12 foot lances fixed before them in the attitude of charging the enimy, The 2 corps of horse with Carey departed with these. which order occasion[ed] great confusion

---

4   *Paradise Lost*, Book VIII, ll. 455-56.
5   There are several Castletons in Britain. The nearest one is in North Yorkshire.

for the Horses becoming much entangled with the choleric Mountaineers great altercations ensued in some places increasing to blows and indeed close by me—I saw a feirce Highlander. lift up his huge lance and strike it through a trooper. who fell dead instantly.[6] Next followed the 3 corps under Dorn. These were the lancers the finest soldiers (excepting) the Mountaineers) in the Army They marched out with with their colours flying and Bands playing as if to certain victory. Night began to close in before all these could pass through. And Now another scene of vast tumult. began. The 4th corps of 16000 Mountaineers and the 5th of 10000 Lowlanders by some unluky mischance. began to pass through at the same time. Their fiery spirits refused to give place to each other Both endeavoured to force themselves through the Gate ways and one side drove the other back again no orders from the Officers could be heard amid the roaring and tumult. They themselves were born along with the throng. and the darkness of the night for no moon had risen. added to the horror of the scene in a short time I began to fear that we should have a repitition of the memorable retreat. from the hill camp a fortnight ago. every thing was fast verging upon it. lances and swords were now drawn on both sides and a dreadful fight began between these untamed beings The superior numbers of the Mountaineers were rapidly driving back and crushing the lowlanders when their fellows the 6ths and 7th corps (20000 men) cried out they would not suffer their comrades to be beaten by a set of insolent savages and they stand cooly looking on, They actually fixed their bayonets and rushed forward pell mell. upon the Mountaineers who received them on their portended lances. Still neith[er] party prevailed till YM Naughty who had shamfully joined in this disgracefull quarrell instad of endeavouring as a commander to supress it. ordered several of the Houses near the Mountaineers to be set on fire. This was done, In an instant a clear red glare of fire shot up into the sky. showing the scene in all its deformity. The Noise and danger was now becomeing horrible. I felt sick and trembled violently. But Rougue who had hitherto stood coolly looking on. now sent his Aid de Camps in every direction. to gather the rest of the army from all parts of the city to hem the Insurgents round. he himself galloped to the castle I knew not for what reason till. startled by a terrific noise and a bright flash as if the Citadel was being blown up into the sky. the dreadful screams and numbers dropping down on all sides of me. announced that He had ordered a disc[h]arge of Artillery to be fired from the Ramparts full in the midst of the insurgents to prove if that could settle their disturbance. it had the desired effect. They saw the folly and madness of contending and destroying one another while. in that situation. They soon

---

[6]   "The Subaltern—A Journal of the Peninsular Campaign," *Blackwood's Magazine*, xvii (May 1825), makes note of traditional military rivalries: "[p]erhaps I need not tell the reader, that between the infantry and cavalry in the British army, a sort of natural antipathy exists" (373). However, although "curses not loud but deep" are exchanged, and although some soldiers are "wantonly jostled," expressions of rivalry are reported as being actively limited to such minor incidents.

seperated to different sides of the streets and after settling into their ranks commenced marching out. (the Mountaineers first) over the dead bodies of their fallen comrades. Though scarce half the army had passed through it was now midnight. I therefore trembling with fright wended my way as well as I might toward my lodgings w[h]ere I have sat down to inform you of the events of the day. you may easily perceive that this disagreement may produce the most unhappy consequences in Rougues army Its effects cannot be eradicated from the minds of the feirce Soldiery and their jealousy may again break out at a time when it may ruin Rougue and his companions—

Good Night—

LETTER
XIV.

I was awoke that Morning by the Sound of firing in the Direction of. Marchtown. it was loud and incessant. I hastily dressed and went into the street to gather news. but few persons were stirring. it was yet very early. probably 3 o clock The air was cool and raw. the sky covered with. dark masses of clouds which thickened. rapidly. but lay as if asleep in the Iron heavens all [a]long the Horizon was spread a a pale line of light flushing the clouds for a little way up with a crimson glow, I listened but could hear no sound. except the deep dull bursting sound of the cannon. severll miles distant. whose repeated and measured discharges. suggested to me the Idea. of a funeral bell tolling the death of one of the great Armies about to engage in fight before me I shall not forget that morning There was I standing alone in the Dawning twilight in the middle of a wide ancient street the hoary. half hidden Cathedral. rising before me and high black houses piled storie ofer story. Up the castle hill. before me. the still gloomy appearance of the Heavens threat[n]ing a tempest and heavy rain before noon the answering character of the earth. in its portentous gloominess. threat[n]ing a tempest also. but oh far more dreadful in effects to mortals. and then all this hightend by the circumstance of while listening to the cannon on Spalding hill. my hearing on a sudden. one loud long prot[r]acted roar, "Take up the wonderous tale"[7] from the direction of Haslingden and in a quarter of an hour after the same thick heavey shaking sound burst from every point of the compass. Now I thought Fidena and the whole country round will be taken by storm. My first Impulse was to seek the Marquis notwithstanding the early hour. (4 o clock.) but I recollected that He had. by permission set of last night with the Corps destined for Marchtown against which it was thought his Fathers troops would be opposed. and where he hopeed to be taken prisoner by him and set at liberty to fight with him against the traitor Rougue. Then I thought of

---

[7]   Addison, *The Spectator* no. 465, Aug 23, 1712. Ironically, Addison's poem, containing the line, "the Moon takes up the wondrous Tale," is based on Psalm xix.

going to the Cathedral. to survey the battle from thence. I. ran up the steps of
the tower. and soon had the country spread below me like a map. A tremendous
spectacle here presented itself to me. Just at my feet lay the widly spreading and
strong walled City. every street filled with soldiers. and every rampart Bristling
with cannon—in its environs too every road and house was crowded with
marching troops and Mountaineers. The red River for 3 miles on its south bank
was lined. with. armed men. in close rank. on Clifton hill[8] there could not be
less than 8000. yet they seemed nothing in comparison with the enormous
bodies round them. Thus far all was peacable. no tumult and smoke and thunder
of Guns could be perceived their. But. looking straight southward the scene was
different
The whole country in the S. direction below Marchtown was covered with
thousands of [marching troops] The Duke of Wellingtons Army ranged opposite
To the Mountaineers. long lines also Branched of from Fountains castle.[9] the
Headquarters towards Spalding and Marchtown Castle for what purpose I could
not tell. certainly there was no enimy in sight there. about the town. there
appeared most fighting. The cannon discrharged. continualy their tremendous
volleys but without receding or advancing an inch. It was evident that the
Mountaineers kept firm. But the Battle or series of Battles was by far the hottest
round the large town of Haslingden. This place. is strongly fortified. and is the
key. of Fidena once gain it and you have gained all. Rougues utmost endeavours
were to strengthen this place he had last night sent there 34000 men he now
agmented it to 60000. but the force of Snekeyans and Parrys army ranged against
it amounted. to 100000 men. When I looked thither they had gained by storm
Archer Hill overlooking the place and River From thence they were pouring
tremendous vollies of grape shot upon the town and Rogues lines. in little
while. dense columns of. smoke. proceeding from the houses. plainly showed
the effect of their fire. on taking a birds eye veiw of this enormous feild of
Battle. it on the whole seemed evident to me that. the allied army would soon
overwhelm their opponents but when I cast my eyes. downward. into the streets
of Fidena and saw the vast bodies not yet in action. ready to be called. up at a
moments notice by their General. Rougue It. I the issue of the contest appeared
doubtful but enough of this. I now feeling the calls of appetite (with an
Englishman a most imperative call) descended from my lofty eminence into the
streets of Fidena and at the. Northern Hotel. attacked a tremendous sirloin of beef
and entirely defeated. it taking several huge slices prisoners on my plate
after Breakfast hearing a great tumult in the city I hastened to know what was the
matter. it proceeded from a large column of. Lowlanders. who had been driven
from the bridges on the Red River and were flying in the utmost confusion,

---

8   Cliff Hill (approximately 400 feet) is located outside the village of Clifton
in the West Riding of Yorkshire, close to Halifax.
9   Fountains Abbey, in the West Riding of Yorkshire near Ripon, was attacked
and partially destroyed during the Reformation. Its ruins are now preserved by the
National Trust as an historic site.

They averred. that the Duke of Wellington who had attacked that point was pushing forward at the head of 40000 men and would soon be within cannon shot of the city. The man who communicated this news had scarcly finished when a ball struck him to the earth covered with blood thus sealing the authuenticity of his intelligence After this repeated and tremendous charges of cannonry from Clifton announced that the enimy were attempting to storm that place. Rougue and his Aids de Camp galloped about every where urged. several regiments of Reinforcement. forward and. pushing them one on the other through the narrow gates leading toward the clifton road. as fresh files kept coming up before otheres had gone out, the passages were blocked up and irretreivable confusion. began to appear. but at length the vast tide ebbed and slowly dissapeared. all was now quiet for about the space of an hour. when their entered into the city from. opposite quarters the 15000 Highlanders with the Ape of the Hills and about 13 or 14000 Lowlanders or rare lads. with YM. Naughty. These were returning from an ineffectual attack on the lines of Sneaky and Parry at. Haslingden and where the same who so small at time since. engaged in the desperate struggle at the great gate. They met opposite each other in the great square. I was in the Castle Hall. when this news was brought to Rougue. When he heard it his face instantly turned. deadly pale. he laid down his wineglass with a trembling hand. and stood as if he saw some dreadful Apparition. This was the only time I had seen him display any emotion. however he with an effort cleared it off And. commanded the two divisions to be posted in intirely separate divisions of the city. on this the messenger left the room but he had scarce gone when a loud shout rung through the city Rougue. nodded as if to intimate that all was over and immediatly left the room. I with many others ran out after him to see what might be the matter. Here my *historic* relation of this rebellion terminates herefter I can only relate a *narrative* of things in which I was immediatly concerned. to go on. The moment that I steped into the street I was hurried along in the overwhelming crowd through many streets in the direction of the Great square. The twilight was fast coming on and a dismal gloom pervaded every thing. I Half breathless was born forward amid deafning cries. and firing of guns till we reached the great square. here I beheld thousands of Mountaineers and as many lowlanders engaged in feirce conflict around and before me Lances and spears flashed on all sides and showers of balls whizzed constantly through the air a spent bullet struck me I fell amid the feet of the crowd. a torrent of people rushed over me and I fainted. I must have lain their a long time for when I awoke and looked up it was black night The whole of the square was in one vast glare of fire which shone terrificly on the wild figures and countainances of the Mountaineers who were rushing on all sides after the flying lowlanders and killing them in numbers. Vast heaps of dead lay round and the light of the burning houses was reflected in a hundered pools of gore smoking in every hollow and gulley at one glance I perceived that this dreadful ruin was occasioned by the two parties of Mountaineers and lowlanders who had fought last night meeting by ill luck in the great square both hot with rage and malice. here they had had a pitiched battle. What I saw was the result The reason of Rougues despair. may soon be guessed at. he saw that dissension having once broken out among such fiery spirits it would be impossible ever to quench it and he and his army would be irrevocably ruined. The recollection of the dreadful consequences of enmity among the Jews flashed on his memory. I heard him as he went out of the room cry out "O Jerusalem!"[10] But the end was not yet The moment I had recovered my feet a vast body of new lowlanders entered the square in support [of] their fellows The scene of death began again and continued. till a vast roar of cannonry and terreific crys all round the wall of the city announced the prescene of a common enimy the allied army. Rougue rushed into the square on foot and bare headed. he cryd out "O unhappy men you have ruined me and yourselves What fury has possesed you thus to tear in peices your own flesh and lapp your own blood had you remained united we should have beaten them now it is to late you must fight not for victory but for bare life!" on hearing this these madmen stopped the work of mutual slaughter and stood bloody with smoking arms irresolute between rage fear and shame. but not a moment. had elapsed when bloody with spurring fiery hot with haste shouting and tearing up the ground beneath their feet a vast body of cavalry headed by Sneaky himself rushed into the square and commenced hacking and hewing with their sabres on every side at this moment I beheld a number of men dragging along the Marquis of Douro young Soult and Charlie. all bound and bloody as they went by they seized me tied me and hurried us all into the thickest of the conflict Their the[y] placed us together, Rougue at this moment rode up and said now you 4 wretches I'll punish you I could not before but youve got it now. he then departed The Marquis said nothing but "Feind" and stood motionless his eyes flashing fire and his face as pale as death. The crush and hurry around us was terrible lances and bayonets were constantly darting round us multitudes were falling like Hail at our feet in a short time a ball struck Young Soult. he sunk on his knees gave a groan and. fell a showere of dead and dying hid him immediatly from our eyes. directly after directly after a ball hitt Charlie he cried out "Arthur save me" clung to his brother for a moment but was soon knocked of by a dead body falling on him and lay motionless. I shall never forget the expression of Arthures countenance at this moment his eyes strained as if the[y] would burst and blazed with a mainacll lustre. The sweat started to his cold forhead he clenched his teeth & muttered, "Yes I will save you." with one mighty effert he broke his bonds. like packthreads seized the first sword he found with an energy that made the blood spring out at his finger nails and threw himself. on the thickest of Rougues troops he whirled his sword round with force of resistless lightning at every blow some man dropped he espied Rougue at a little distance. I saw him dart forward spring against against his Horse with such a forc[e] as to throw him on his knees and lifting his sword whirl it and himself to full in the front of the demagogue, all three fell at once together I saw no more for a ball at this moment struck me a mist came across my sight and I fell

It was again my fortune to recover from this shot. when I recovered from this swoon. I found myself in bed. in a large lighted room I for a moment thought all

---

[10]   Possibly a reference to Matthew 23: 37.

that I had witnessed was a dream. but the bandages and plasterrs round my head soon convinced me to the contrary. in beds oposite to me were laid. young Soult and Charlie both still senseless. for they moved not. I sat up in bed and undrew the curtain. of the window and looked out The night was cold and rainy. before me lay a vast yard surrounded by high gloomy houses. partly unroofed and shattered with balls. This vast yard or square was filled with human beings in the middle was an empty space floored with black cloth and the Paling round it covered with the same. dead silence and utter motionlessness pervaded the vast assemblage below me till a swaying two and fro among them announ[c]ed the approach of some one. it was the Kings Sneaky Wellington Parry & Stumps who with their attendants ranged themselves on one side of the open space next followed 10 soldiers with muskets guarding a tall man dressed in black with a countenance as pale as death. I fell back on the bed breathless for it was Alexander Rougue. when I looked again. he was standing erect at one end of the area with a white handkercheif in his hand The soldiers were ranged opposite. about 12 paces distance with their peices levelled all was silence you might indeed have heard a pin drop at length Rougue called out in a firm clear but sepulchral tone "Gentlemen FIRE" My head grew dizzy. The soldieirs fired. I saw a bright flash and loud crash. He fell dead.

Alexander ROUGUE
was no more

═══════════════

PS. before morning Y Soult & Charlie awoke. from their swoon and the surgeons entering pronounced none of us three dangerously hurt. Afterwards the Marquis entered he looked dreadfully exhausted from efforts of the night before. for this night was not the night of the battle but the one after he stated that. when he attacked Rougue his sabre broke through his helmet and stunned him so he immediatly seized him and dragged him to the Kings, I knew the rest. Good night I myself am dreadfuly exhausted and can write no more

Ever yours
J Bellingham

P B Brontë August 2. A.D 1832.

═══════════════

THE PIRATE

A TALE.

By Captain John Flower

I. Vol.

PB Brontë.   February 1833.[1]

════════════

---

1   Hand-sewn booklet in grey paper covers (11.5 x 18.5 cm) of 16 pages
(1 blank) in BPM: Bon 140.

THE PIRATE.

A Tale by

The Author of Letters from an
Englishman.

Great Glass town printed by Seargt Tree.

PB Bronte Feb 8. 1833

CHAP. Ist.

PB Bronte
January
30. 1833

Alexander Rougue[2] has just returned from no one knows where He has bought a fine house in Georges Street where He lives in the utmost style of Magnificence. But what are his *means*. or from whence he draws his evidently princly income no one can guess This is well known that every acre of his paternal possesions has long long ago bid adeiu to him. Having several times in the course of my life been brought in to collision though much against my will with this singular and Mysterious character I Fancied I might without offence pay him a visit of congratulation upon his arrival in the city ordering therefore my Carriage I drove of for Georges Street and alighted at the door of his splendid Mansion upon delivering my card I was ushered by a foreign servant through many noble passages and up a grand staircase to his study I entered with the usual compliments he was seated allone on his sofa but before I describe the master let me glance rond the apartment it was spacious as most drawing rooms the ceiling painted in Arabesque and the walls lined with books 2 fine bay windows curtained with velvet lighted the apartment and opened a gorgeous veiw of the vast glasstown harbour with its endless shipping crowded quays and mighty expanse of blue water stretching away till one might fancy they beheld towering over its horizon the hills of Stumps land and the towering hights of Monkeys Isle over the rich Persian carpet were scattered a vast number of Naval maps plans and charts the table groaned beneath a profusion of Atlases and Treatises one Navigation while round the room in rosewood stands and cases were placed

---

2   Unlike Frederic Guelph, who was "killed so as he could not be got alive" (p. 158, n. 32), this is not the case with Rougue. In **The Foundling** Charlotte provides the details of a deal struck with Branwell: if the Marquis of Douro is to be resurrected, then so too must Rougue be (Alexander CB, II, Part I, 116). This is Branwell's first full-scale story about the figure who has become his hero, and begins the transformation of Rougue into Elrington and Northangerland. See Barker Brontës, 188-89; 873, n. 68 for a discussion of Byron, Scott, Milton and Hogg as possible sources for the character and career of Branwell's hero.

the rarest and most valuable curiositys from every shore and Ocean in the midst of this princly confusion sat Rougue upon his sofa intently perusing a Folio of Maps and sipping incesantly from a bottle of the most fiery liquers the moment I entered he started hastily but recovering himself arose and welcomed me forward with his usual insidous and serpentlike smile

How much was I shocked to behold the ravages wich I know not what had made upon him since I last saw him True his tall and statly form still stood as erect as ever but his hair once a bright Auburn now looked thin and even grey his eagle eye gleamed dully and glassily under his pale high forehead now covered with scars and wrinkles his cheeks were hollow and bloodless while as he shook my hand his felt cold and clammy he trembled constantly and started at the slightest sound or motion he bade me sit down and himself taking a seat began as follows in his usual carless scoffing manner "Well Freind I have taken you see to the navy since you last saw me why man Ive been on my voyages ha! Ive turned Merchant you see no not so I [am] an Admiral. But Ive not hit it yet Im more Im Rougue I Im all three Im Three in one you know ha. dont you? look my man If youve money and want it in safe hands (here he took a long pull from a flagon of claret) I say if youve money and love it let me have an hand on it and it'll stick to you for ever. yes I tell you Im not one of your pitiful land. louping Merchants who when they send out there vessels can never make sure of being able to send them back again no no Bankruptcies and tempests and losses can never hurt Rougue ha! nor *piracys* neither ha! (here he drank again and turning suddenly round he fixed his eyes upon me I feared he would fall into some fit but he continued) Sir Sir I say did you ever know of a man whose wealth was in danger of being lessened by the very means he used to get wealth you dont understand me how should you (he paused) its all long of this (laying his hand on his forehead) I say sir Im as near foundering as Life can be be I say Im a Perfect wreck why (drinking again largly) why I could'nt keep body and soul together if it wasnt for this Body and soul did I say. Fool who in the name of nonsense ever heard of two things seperating that were never together? ha. Now sir Ill lay 10 to 1 that I cannot walk without help from this fire to the door. (he tried but stopt at the window where he stood ernestly gazing on the sea. and apparently forgetful of my prescence began soliloquising to himself. in such words as these) Oh how I wish they would heave in sight surely with him on board they could never either founder [or] strike no He promised me a dozen prizes and (pulling out his watch) this is the hour in which he vowed to bring theire goods in Let me see theres Grenvilles 2 Luckymans 2 Macadam 2 Bellingham and Co 4. Cotterell 3. in all 13.[3] Oh how I wish they would heave in sight If he deceives me! (The reader may guess how I was suprised to hear him mention the name of My Firm and Myself in these suspicious Transactions. I started involuntarily. at wich he recollecting himself turned hastily round and looked at me keenly but with evident embarrasment as if to see. whet[h]er I guessed his meaning or heard his words I Feigned a careless inattention and

---

3   All Glass Town residents.

appeared to gaze upon Warders Atlas.[4] at this moment. several vessels bore up the Harbour he lighted up and took a vast draught from a bottle of Raw Brandy then going again to the window stood silently watching them unload, in about a qua[r]ter of an hour the study door opend without notice being given or servant appearing a little old Man entered of decrepid Figure and wearing a vast slouched hat over his brow a much worn great coat on his back and a stick in his hand, without any salutation he began First Fixing his little keen grey eyes upon me as if he would read my inmost soul "Rougue Rougue do you doubt me now? "Oh" he answered "I cant tell yet you are an eternal deceiver Ill wait till I see and handle the. the you guess what" Why dont you name them? returned the old Man Why dont I name you? asked Rougue. you dare not. he replied. "Why" answered Rougue again "an you begin your impudence Ill blow your brains out. If you take me and light me like a match just after sit down and heres the waters of life. drink drink" The old Man drew a chair to the table and commenced drinking glass after glass of Raw Brandy with the utmost indifference as if it had been cold water. Rougue stood against the Mantle peice eying him with looks of mingled scorn hatred contempt and slavish obedience the old man shutting his eyes continued drinking with an uneart[h]ly smile upon his haggard Features. at this Moment the ponderous knocker rung below. and some one was announced by a servant he was ordered to be admitted. There accordingly entered the study a stout little Old Man wrapped in a military surtout and wearing a cocked hat on his head he bowed politly to the company and with; his hands placed behind his back began to pace rapidly round the Apartment he seemed agitated Rougue smiled but put on a behaviour of the utmost politness The stout little man. stopping suddenly short looked Rougue Full in the Face and with much grimace broke out as Follows

"What in the name of wonder. is he about What does he mean Why is *he* to be insulted and defied by Such a robber as him is[5] the name of L Empreur. The terror of Europe to be set at naught and scorned by him he tells him that Talleyrand[6] has informed of the loss of 3 ships of the French Nation which were reported to be taken by a Pirate carrying scarlet colours which he is informed are those carried by the Ships. belonging to the firm of Rougue and and. he knows not what but it does not matter The circumstance is reported to your Government and he shall see what will follow." The Emporer Napoleon for him it was here turned round and without speaking another word left the apartment. <Shortly> we heard his carriage depart from the yard. when he had shut the door behind

---

4 Although most of the publications Branwell mentions are based on actual titles/authors, this work seems to be fictitious.

5 "in" obviously intended.

6 Talleyrand (1754-1838), a French ecclesiast, statesman and diplomat renowned for his dissipated life, was most notable for the political machinations which underwrote his capacity for political survival. Talleyrand managed to hold continuous high office through the French Revolution, under Napoleon, at the Restoration, and under Louis Phillipe. See also p. 369 below.

him Rougue burst out into a loud laugh and takeing a full glass of spirits said turning to the little Old man. "Well, Mr 'Sdeath what now think you" Why returned Mr Sdeath if such was his title "I think him a bigger fool than yourself" At this moment the knocker rang again. and another visitor was announced he entered a tall Military looking Man plainly dressed with Eagle eyes and Aquiline Nose The Moment Rougue beheld him his Face turned as black as death. but preserved its usual effrontery it was the Duke of Wellington! his Grace bowing to me and biting his lip at Mr Sdeath. adressed Rougue thus Sir I have this Morning received information from several persons that a number of armed Vessels carrying scarlet colours have been recently infesting these Seas and committing the most violent and wanton aggressions upon the vessels carrying the Flags of this Nation as also upon those of France Parrys Ross's and my own. Now I have also learned that the ships employed by the concern of "Rogue Sdeath and Co" of which you are a member carry a scarlet flag and report avers these to have been the indentical vessels which comitted the piracys. Now I am not qualified to judge upon this buisness but Sir you must know that your characters does not stand perfectly free from reproach in the opinion of most Therefore it is incumbent upon you to Free yourself if possible from. this new stain laid upon it. Seargent Bud (here a sharp thin Lawyer like looking young man entered) I request you to make out a writ calling upon Alexander Rougue to present himself to morrow before the court of Admiralty to clear up some aspersion[s] which at present rest upon his character." The writ was executed in a twinkling and ready for Rougues signature who as he took up the pen said "I am sensible your Grace that I have many enimies and it is these who have raised and propagated this infamous slander upon my own character and the honour of my firm however to morrow I shall not fail to clear those both in the eyes of the world and to my own content." His Grace then saying very well Sir. bowed to me touched his hat to Rougue and departed. I also took my leave. having more calls to make and much buisness to do.

CHAPTER. II.d.

That Night as I was sitting in my Study looking over our clerks accounts and musing upon the strange news I had gathered that morning relating to Rougue and his preceeding news both strange and unpleasant to me [I] liked not the mention of four of our vessels among the number of those he mentioned to himself as having [been] taken. there suddenly burst into my apartement 6 tall <stout> men wearing black cloaks swords and visors without a word being spoken on either side they siezed & bound me. Then taking me upon their shoulders they hurried out of the house and plunged into a set of dark narrow alleys or Lanes. after rapidly threading these for some time they stopped before the back door of a large house where they gave a peculiar whistle thrice repeated the door was opened and they hurried me up a flight of stairs breathless and unable to speak into a large lighted apartment which I was astonished to find was that identical Rougues study which I had left that morning He himself I saw walking with hasty strides through the Apartment his hat and gloves on and with a sword under his arm around him. were 9 or 10 tall dark looking men armed and like himself equipped for a Journey The Old dwarf Mr Sdeath was seated at a sideboard taking a long drink of his favorite liquors. The moment I entered the reason for my forcible capture flashed accross my mind I cried out in a fit of Terror. "Oh Rougue let me go and I will never divulge what I heard this morning I never will" Rougue answered drinking of a glass of brandy "Well sir Its all as one. divulge or not divulge I have you. Come Gentlemen Follow me our time is almost out." They all prepared to move taking me with them. But Mr. Sdeath cried out in a passionate Screech Owl voice "Dogs stop till Ive finished fools What are ye so slippery for" They waited with great deference till he had drained of the contents of a stone bottle of distilled waters then they forcing me allong with them moved down the steps. Mr. S'death following. reeling along and muttering curses to himself we plunged at a running pace down a narrow lane till we arrived at the great quay of the Harbour here lay a long suspicious looking vessel with unfurled sails and grinnning port holes we all Rougue and S'death taking the lead mounted on to the deck where the crew received us in the utmost silence. at a signal given by Rougue the Cables were loosed the Anchor drawn up and the vessel pushed of from shore gliding swiftly down the Harbour into the open sea all this was the work of a minute and done almost ere I was aware of being on board. The moment I found the vessel was at sail I flung myself on a heap of cables and gave vent to greif in a fit of groans and weeping. I could scarcly credit my senses to think that I in the space of a few minutes. had been dragged from my quiet home thro[ugh] half the city. at the command of a merciless and cruel man and without the slightest show of reason thrown bound on board this unknown and suspicious vessel. probably a pirate or a privateer there perhaps die a violent death or be carried and sold in foreign lands. my second thought was to inquire of myelf what could possibly be the reason why I was thus treated. in a little while the result of my cogitations left me no doubt. that this was the truth of this cruel transaction. Rougue had probably for some time past been in the habit of scouring the Glasstown seas with vessels armed and manned by his dependant desperadoes. and with these assaulting and capturing all the unarmed and laden merchant vessels he could meet with by this means he had amassed those riches and obtained that splendid house wich I had just left. when he had gained money enough by this illegal system to procure that palace he resided in it and under the Title of the "Firm of Rougue S'death, and Co." continued to send out these armed vessels as if for the purpose of peaceful trading and on their return sell the goods taken by them. as if they were those lawfuly bought by the ships of his company. This practice he had continued till it got wind and was rumored [through] all the glasstowns. This morning. when I visited him he was in suspense expecting the arrival of the ship I was now in. and while gazing for it in a fit of abstraction had uttered some sentences in my hearing which were to plain for me not to guess their meaning. This joined with my being present at the conference between him the Duke of Wellington and the Emperor both of whom had heard of his conduct. determined him at once to take me prisoner and stop me from reporting what I had heard by

violent means. The circumstance of the Dukes commanding him to prove his
innocence to morrow at the Admiralty where Rougue knew well he could never
prove it determined him upon decamping that very night on board one of his
vessels and conveying me along with too probably to sell as a slave in a foreign
country while he commenced anew his acts as a pirate while employed in these
conjectures and lamentations I took no notice of anything but lay down upon the
cables on the deck unheeding and unheeded when therefore I lifted up my eyes
again what was my anguish to find myself far out upon the rolling sea. no trace
of the Glasstown remaining save the great Tower of Nations standing black and
huge against the long red lines of light wich stretched in the west betokened the
early dawn. The fast receding shores looked dark and gloomy in the Twilight
while a cold raw breeze swept over the Ocean. raising long undulating ridges of
waves and howling with a mournful cadence amid the lofty masts and cordage of
the gallant ship the crew were all asleep and only the solitary watch remained
pacing the deck with monotonous footsteps. With a mind and body exhausted by
the events of the day and my eyesight lulled by the dead calm of nature I at
length fell into a deep sleep

When I awoke it was midday the Tropical sun glared hotly from a blazing
sky shooting his beams perpendicularly down upon the dancing and glancing
waves a thousand fish of the brightest and most varied dyes were playing and
wallowing [in] the bows of the glowing vessel. The crew tall stern dark looking
Fellows from the Northern Mountains were all either lolling under the shade of
the oil cloth awnings. leaning over the bows of the ship were basking in the
sunlight, But all this as nothing to me I continued groaning on the deck in
cababal of excertion and wishing myself "packed in my own grave a 1000
fathom below the keel of the pirate vessel I passed the day in execrating Rougue
and his ruthless crew. and heaving heavy groans as I saw one point of land after
another sink beneath the horizon, untill at Sunset Africa had vanished and I
beheld one melancholy waste of waters heaving and rolling all round the sky, 3
days I passed in this miserable state on the fourth Rougue came up and
commanded my fetters to be knocked off. and assigned me a hammock in the
steerage giving me liberty to roam where I would about the ship. This was no
act of charity he saw that I could neither escape nor do harm without a freind or
succour for 300 miles round for we were now within an equal distance from the
Glasstown and Monkey Island toward which we were evidently tending. This day
toward evening the man from the mast head cried out that he saw a strange sail
standing to westward. Rougue took his telescope but it was too distant to decide
with certainty its identity. he however affirmed it to be a large Vessel from. the
Glass town it was gradualy coming towards us but the darkness soon wrapt it
from. sight. Rougue Sdeath and Carey were up all night consulting with each
other. when the Morning again revealed the vessel. it was seen coming up with a
great pres[s] of sail while its sides bristling with cannon and its crimson colours
showed it to be a fine Glass towne Frigate of the First class. Mr S'death came
upon deck in a Captains Uniform. and winked to the men who evidently
understood what he ment They all went below. stripped their daggers & cutlasses
coming up again. transformed into. plain merchant seamen with blue jackets.

and seal skin caps instead of their red pirate handcercheifs on their heads. I observed that the scarlet flag had been taken down in the darkness while the green colours of Wellington were waving aloft in their stead. Rougue appeared not as usual on deck. but Old S'death often went into his cabin. and after communing with him som[e] time came out with a malignant grin adorning his withered features. It was evident some infernal plot was on foot against the ill fated vessel when she had hove up within speaking distance. an Officer appeared upon her Deck and commanded us to shorten sail. Our sailors obeyed with the utmost alacrity and stood to, The ship then lowered her boat and placing about 20 men with an Officer in it. came on our deck. showing a warrant. signed Wellington and Grenville for the apprehension of Alexander Rougue to answer for high crime and misdemeanours. and authorizing those bearing that warrant to search any or every vessel for his body or information conserning him the Officer accordingly demanded to see our Captain, Mr S'death came up, he showed him his document after glancing over it. our sham captain making a profoun[d] bow. said he was most happy to inform him that he was at present in possesion of the person he sought for. disering him at the same time to step down into the cabin where he would both see the prisoner and learn how he had been captured." The Officer suspecting nothing expressed the utmost joy and accompanied by his men proceeded toward the cabin I sighed involuntarily to see these poor fellows going to certain destruction but S'death turning roung gave me a horrid look touching at the same time the hilt of his knife. They dissapeared into the room, 20 of the pirates were beconed in after them. by the new Captain. in a few minutes I beheld with the utmost horror our sailors come out one after the other each with the head of one of these devoted victims in his bloody hand Rougue. in a genteel suit of black and with a smile of satisfaction on his countenance led them up the ladder and placing them in a row on the deck before the unhappy vessel his crew raised a tremendous shout of "Rougue and Victory" when their ill fated comrades beheld this spectacle they for a moment stood in mute consternation and then all ran to their guns. before they could fire Old S'death snatching up his Musket took aim at their Captain. The ball whizzed true to its mark and that Officer fell dead from his deck into the sea. Rogue cried out to your guns & the pirates gave a tremendous broadside This was returned with vigour and many on each side rolled on the decks wounded and dying our vessel gave another broadside. whith fatal effect. every ball told, The contending ship was nearly dismasted and being struck between wind and water appeared rapidly sinking still her crew fought with determination but Rougue commanding his men to form with their pikes in hand. run his vessel straight under the prow of the enimy and placing himself at their head the[y] lept on to its deck a scene of dreadful confusion followed. and the sinking vessel became the scene of a most bloody conflict, The superior skill and ferocity of the pirates soon prevailed Their enimes lay dying round them and then each man seizing his prisoner lept again on board their own vessel. They had scarcely done this when the Magazine of the Glass towner. blew up with a horrid roar and the ill fated vessel went to the bottom almost drawing us along with her in the whirlpool occasioned by her sinking This was followed by one loud yell from the dying wretches and all for a moment was silent again

For a while the pirate crew stood on deck astonished at the speedy and decsicive nature of their victory. This astonishment at length vented itself in rude jests and bursts of savage laughter, As for Rougue, he continued a while pacing the deck in silent abstraction And S'death betook himself with vast zeal and fervor to the keg of Rum, untill he fell grovelling and cursing on the floor like a crushed worm, in the space of half an hour Rougue ordered the deck to be cleared. and the prisoners brought onto it They were led up bound and pinioned 30 in number all fine stout hearty Fellows my very soul groaned for them, They shook hands with each other as they were placed in a square by themselves. They knew what would follow, A select number of the pirates were placed before them with loaded Muskets, Rougue with his usual stern sneering look commanded them to fire, They obeyed, The thirty prisoners all fell dead or dying on the deck At this moment Old S'death rushed forward with A large knife in his hand advancing to the bloody heap he plunged it into the hearts of all those yet allive and then wiping his nose with the cuff of his coat looked round with a screech owl laugh. I saw All the crew at this action cast upon the Old wretch a look of detestation even Rougue hardened as his heart is to compassion, giving him a glance of scorn and hatred cried "Get down below you ugly brute I did not tell you to do this" Old S'death gnashing at him his toothless jaws. and muttering curses to himself. obeyed his leader and retired in to the cabin, The dead bodies of these unhappy men were now taken up one by one and thrown into the hungry ocean without a groan or tear. The scarlet coulours were replaced on the Mast head the sails unfurled to the breeze and of flew the conquering vessel with its ferocious crew. over the foamy billows towards its far off bourne.

:CHAPTER. IIId.

PBB
Febry.
8th. 1833

Two days we continued sailing after this dreadful event on the morning of the 3d. Another strange Sail hove in to sight The priates by their leaders command again played the old tricks transforming their ship into a peaceful glass town Merchantman, but I observed that this time our sham Captain was Carey and not Old S'death who since the hateful part he had played in the last bloody Tradgedy and the reproof he received from Rougue. had continued. sulky and intoxicated muttering to himself all manner of curses and execrations, The strange vessel. on heaving to was observed to be a small ship carrying the Glasstown Flag. and bearing on board the Earl of Elrington and his family on a visit to Stumps Island. When Rougue knew this he swallowed a vast bumper of Claret and ordered the long boat to be launched. in it he placed Carey with 30 armed men bearing a Warrant forged from the one. brought by the unhappy crew of that former vessel. stated to be for the apprehension of Rougue. with this. the. 30 men hailed Elringtons vessel and having all stepped on its deck Carey proceeded to show his warrant and while the Master and the Earl were assuring him they had no such person on board his pirate followers rushed forward seized the guns and disarmed the crew whose scanty numbers could offer no defence In spite of their offered resistance the groans of the Earl the cries of the young Elringtons and the Remonstrances of Lady Zenobia[7] they were all led but with the utmost civility and respect from their own ship into ours Rougue received them with an elegant dress and his best looks. and bowing to the Earl and young ones he offered his hand to Zenobia. leading them all into the best cabin here they remained for some time when he appeared again and calling for the Captain of the Captured vessel. held a long conference with him garnished with a seasonable bottle of wine. the result of which was that the Elringtons appeared again on deck with by no means the same expression which they First trod it I thought that Lady Zenobia especialy seemed changed in her thoughts for the better. Rougue with that winning easy gentility which he well knows how to assume when he thinks it worth his while conducted them all on board their own vessel. as they passed I heard Lord <Fideana> remark "Sister what a courtship" I and our crew were amazed to see the two vessels. both tack round and sail back to the Glasstown side by side, The matter was soon guessed at and ere Night by their frequent interchanges of compliments and "substantilitys" the crews of both vessels were "roaring drunk" and merry. as for myself I soon had an inkling of the matter But how it was brought about I knew less of. I had often heard Rougue declare that of all the women in the world he most admired Zenobia Elrington. her too I had not less often heard say that she thought Alexander Rougue in her mind in spite of his conduct had the form & spirit of a Roman Hero I must now for a moment turn to another incident, My cabin lay between those of Rougue and S'death That Night as I lay awake musing on the incidents of the day. I heard an unusual stumbling and muttering in the passage between the beforementioned rooms suspecting I knew not what I jumped up opened the door silently and peeped out I there beheld Old S'death with his great knife between his teeth (the way he usualy carried it) stealing softly toward Rougues room muttering "I'll do up with him for what he did to me" he opened the door

---

[7] Zenobia, a third-century warrior queen of Palmyra reputedly descended from Cleopatra, was an adversary of Rome, leading her people in a war of revolt against the client-rulers of Rome. She is described enthusiastically in Gibbon's *Decline and Fall of the Roman Empire* (a copy of which was available to Branwell in the Keighley Mechanics' Library) as "the most heroic of her sex." She was proficient in Latin, Greek, Syrian and Egyptian, and familiar with Homer and Plato, having studied under Longinus. Charlotte's Zenobia is referred to as the Verdopolitan Madame de Stael, a reference to Anne Louise Necker, Baronne de Stael-Holstein (1766-1817), a noted intellectual who received, in her Paris salon, on the eve of the Revolution, the most progressive elements in French society. She was exiled by Napoleon and met Wellington, whom she regarded as a heroic liberator, in 1814. For Lady Zenobia Elrington, see the Glossary.

and clenching his weapon in his hand as he saw Rougue before him sprung on him with a feindish yell. I ran in after him The old Dwarf was striving to strike his knife into Rougues heart who was grappling with him They were both on the floor in my hurry I seized a poker and running up dashed it at the head of S'death This stunned him Rougue then snatching a pistol from the table clapt it to his head. and fired the skull was blown in peices and the brains scattered round the room Rougue without speaking motioned me to take hold of his feet and himself seizing his shoulders we proceeded silently up the steps to the deck here Rougue crying "I have done with thee thou wretch" took the ugly heap of mortality and hurled it into the sea

   when it touched the water a bright flash of fire darted from it it changed into a vast GENIUS of immesurable and indefinable height and size and seizing hold of a huge cloud with his hand he vaulted into it crying "and I've done with thee thou fool" dissapeared among the passing vapours.[8] Ere he departed 3 vast flashes of fire came bursting a round They were the Cheif Genii TALLI EMII & ANNII He that. ere this little hideous & bloody old Man was the CHeif Genius BRANNII. I stood petrified with fear and astonishment. But Rougue who all the time knew well who he was laughing said "Well Ive settled this buisness however. now Bellingham. for your generous assistance of me Ill set you free on the spot. Why man Im going to settle down and become Alexander Rougue Viscount Elrington and husband of the Lady Zenobia Elrington the bonniest lass in the Glasstown." I fell on my knees and thanked him fervently for his generosity, and we both returned to our rooms no one save ourselves knowing what had happened

when morning arose both vessels were ploughing their course back to the Glass town. where we arrived in two days Rougue instantly proceeded to the residence of the Duke of Wellington where in the presence of the Marquis of Wellesly Captain Sir E Parry Lord Lofty Col Grenville and myself he offered full recompense to all parties for the damage he had done as a pirate on condition of being that moment pardoned [for] his offences. This was immediatly agreed to and settled. he then stating his approaching marriage. invited all present to attend they gave him their warmest congratulations This morning I attended the wedding of Lady Zenobia Elrington with Alexander Rougue now Viscount Elrington. I must break off for I have to attend this evening at a grand feast given at Elrington Place by the Old Earl in honour of the occasion were will attend all the Nobility and gentry of the Glasstown.

PB Brontë February
the 8th. AD 1833.

———

Haworth

———

[8]   A canceled line here reads: "I stood petrified—it was the cheif Genius BRANNII."

No. I.st.   **The Monthly** [Figure of Justice] **Intelligencer**[1]

From March 27. AD 1833. to. April 26th. Great. Glass Town P Bronte. March 27.

A Few words to
The Cheif Genii

When a Parent leaves his children young and inexperiences. and without a cause absconds. never more troubling himself. about them those children according to received notions among men if they by good fortune should happen to survive. this neglect and b[e]come of repute in society are by no means bound. to believe that he has done his duty to them as a parent. merely because they have risen. nor are they indeed required to own or treat him as a parent. this is all very plain. and we believe that 4 of our readers will understand our aim in thus speaking

A child of the. G-ii[2]

A VISIT TO
Elrington Hall. by A.B.C

One day last week. I received an invitation to a grand dinner about to be given by Alexander Rouge. "Viscount Elrington. on the occasion of his recent marriage on the appointed evening my carriage drew up in front of his regal. Mansion on stepping out I was ushered. immediatly into the Great Hall a most noble apartment. blazing with light and hung with gold and velvet. everything around me was conducted upon such a scale as nothing but the most princly fortune could keep up upon my entrance I found that as yet but few of the company had arrived nor had our Host and Hostess made their appearance the first person whom I recognized was little Charlie Wellesly squatted under a chair and playing

---

[1] Four-page newspaper (two leaves folded, 18.5 x 27.7 cm), written in four columns, in the BPM: BS 117. It was likely modeled on the *Leeds Intelligencer*, to which the Rev. Patrick Brontë contributed a number of letters to the editor. For Charlotte's references to Branwell's newspaper, see Alexander CB, II, part I, 98 and 210. For a description of the Figure of Justice, see Alexander & Sellars, 303.

[2] The signature is in longhand. Juliet Barker suggests that the editorial is Branwell's response to Emily and Anne's desertion of Glass Town to set up their kingdom of Gondal (Barker Brontë, 193).

with a huge dog not being able to extract any[thing] rational from him I passed
on to where stood my old freind Capt Bud. his hands in his pockets and his eyes
now cast sorrowfully upon his fair round paunch and anon hopefully surveying
every door in expectation of the long delayed. dinner having entered in to
conversation with him we were joined by a long lean anatomy ancient and
bookworn. with hanging eyebrows and the smell of decayed cheese Bud
introduced him to me as the thrice celebrated John Gifford. at the sound of this
name a hideous army of dusty and cobwebs ponderous tomes & rusty armour
attacked my defenceless imagination I decamped leaving them both engaged in a
profound disscussion upon the blade of a Roman knife which had been lately dug
up in Buds garden and which when I left them he was just hauling from his
pocket for a more rigid scrutiny However before I had proceeded many yards a
most deathlike groan from Gifford. announced some dreadful discovery I turned
round and beheld Bud standing with eyes and arms uplifted in unutterable
mortification. while Gifford was reading "as it were his neck verse"[3] the word[s]
marked upon the rusty blade "Swashing Tom, Cutler G G Town, 1823." leaving
this distracted pair I steered immediatly toward the principle table where were
standing divers groups o[f] visitors admiring the various and costly works of art.
under which it groaned. before one party lay spred the magnificent nay glorious
work. De Lisles "Verdopolita delineata." a vast Elephant. Folio of perhaps the
most splendid engravings of the most splendid Architecture which ever existed.
Others were examining the five quartos of Dundees Scenery of the Glass town
countrys[4] others a profusion of the most richly bound richly engraven and costly
works which could be conceived. Apart from those and far retired stood the two
men of Millions Luckyman and Grenville debating together upon the affairs of
Empires and bargaining away the wealth of Ages Joyous bursts of laughter now
alloured me to the fireplace round which were gathered Young Lofty the
Elringtons and a whole host of the sprouts and spirits of the Glass town
boasting and telling feats of their dogs horses chariots and themselves—Thus
like the Bee I wandered from group to group gathering sweets from every <u>Flower</u>

---

3   "Neck verse" refers to the first verse of Psalm 51, because it was the trial-
verse of those who claimed exemption from criminal jurisprudence through
benefit of clergy. If a prisoner could read this verse, he was said to read like a
clerk ("legit ut clericus") and could thus literally save his neck, being burnt only
in the hand and then set at liberty. "Letter nor line know I never a one/ Wer't my
neck-verse at Hairibee"—*The Lay of the Last Minstrel*, I, 24.
4   Both De Lisle and Dundee were eminent painters in Glass Town—see
Alexander CB, I, 64, 113 and 129; II, Part I, 154. De Lisle may have been based
on Guillaume Delisle (1675-1726), a French mapmaker who led to major
reforms in the science of cartography. He produced about 100 maps and wrote on
mensuration and ancient geography, becoming chief geographer to the king in
1718. Dundee was possibly based on an amateur painter, Captain Dundee, who
was active from 1818-1854 and sent five landscapes (views of England, France
and Germany) to the Royal Academy.

till the door flew open and there entered Our Host and his Lady with the Marquis and Marchioness of Douro. all eyes were turned toward them. and truly it puzzled one to judge which of the four in appearance held the preference the contrast to was so striking between. them. Rougue advanced tall and statly. with a stern aristocratic expressio[n] upon a countenance. which though shattered and worn with care and dissipation. yet presented an expression astonishingly noble and intellectual, mixed it is true with something so secret cold and sarcastic that the spectator felt on beholding it an involuntary awe and creeping of the flesh. The Marquis on the contrary entered the room with a cheerful though noble aspect his bright eyes beaming gaity and congratulation. to all around him and his firm an[d] upright figure presenting all the strength and vigour of a joyos and. unharased youth. Between Lady Zenobia and the Marrchioness of Douro there existed as striking a contrast the one so high and haughty with an air so freezingly exclusive the other so young gay and merry. that the the humblest and poorest being on earth. would feel delight and confidence when speaking to her, of the beauty of either it is needless to speak. Company now began to flow fast in a [moment] great rattleing carriages were heard at the door then a great bustle in the hall and soon the door being flung open there entered followed by a train of attendants 4 men of the old days tall stern. built as if of iron with frank yet peircing aspect and ornamented with many scars on their lofty forheads every one stood up and bowed with the greatest reverence to these the four KINGS of ASHANTEE Sneaky Wellington Parry and Ross dinner was now announced and we were all ushered into the dining hall a room still more spacious and splendid than the one we had. left it was the summum bonum of magnificence. of the dinner it is sufficient to say that it comprised all the dainties of winter summer Autumn and spring gathered from America Asia Africa and Europe. and [the] gorgeous display and the number of guests equalled anything that had ever been seen among us. dinner being now over and the ladies with the younger and more courteous gentlemen withdrawn to the sitting room. the "rum 'uns" and "old 'uns" had drawn the chairs round the fire and were busy in disscusing. the great comfort of life. ample justice was done to its qualitys and bottle after bottle dissapeared with such vast rapidity that I feared we should have a new edition of the < >[5] scence Rougue sat upon his Throne and. lord of the feast set a laudable example to every one by empt[y]ing with the most perfect steadyness (i<mean> steadyness of supply not steadyness of hand) glass after glass and bottle down his well-in-those matters-tried throat the Kings. on their elevated seats smiled at the follies and frolics of their childern in the midst of this joyous scene Captain Tree who <was busily> engaged in the <convivialities> cut of summut above leaped from his seat over threw the table and cutting a caper near three yards high uttered such a peircing scream that all thought his soul was leaving its clay. he continued leaping about in convuslsions of fright and agony. shouting Oh my leg my leg my leg all for a moment were in consternation at the strange spectacle till a shrill and well known laugh from under the table

---

5   The name is illegibly blotted.

unravelled the whole mystery and out crept young Charlie. brandishing an immense pin in his hand. and uttering peals eldri[t]ch laughter ran up to to Tree who when he espyed him became perfectly incontrollable. running about in every direction pursued by the young elfin rougue. at this odd sight we all burst out into a yell of laughter. while Rougue. springing from his seat ran after. Tree and caught him by his coat tail Tree frantic with fright. sprang at Rougue but missing his aim hit Bud in the face Bud darted at Tree and Sergeant Tree fastened <Bud> others joined they fray became general and outrageous each man struck his neigh[b]our and his neighbour felled him down went tables and bottles and pictures and hanging[s]all trampled under foot in the universal tumult. lamp after lamp was extinguished untill except for the blazing fires the room would have been left in darkness. at this time the noise had become so outrageous. that the ladies in the other room gu[e]ssing what was the matter rush<ed> in. in a body headed by Zenobia herself. parted the combatants the shrill and awful sound of the female voice struck instant terror into the hearts of the warriors. the fight instantly. ceased. and the whole array of combatants with. blackened faces bloody noses blind <eyes and>. torn coats marched behind their silken sovereigns into the supper<room>   March. 1833.

===============

PARLIAMENTARY
INTELLIGENCE
Great Glass town March 20
Meeting of the
GENERAL SENATE.

[The Day of] March 18. 1833 was the one fixed by proclamation for the first meeting of the Grand General Senate of the All Glass town countrys for many days past all the principle hotels have been occupied by the different Members from. each country the whole city was full of animation for a vigorous campaign is expected. all hope it may not be a bloody one the doors being opened at 1 o clock. pm. the members and spectators began to assemble in the hall. shortly after 2. the venerable CRASHEY. arrived he took his seat on the throne. their Majestys Wellington Parry and Sneaky being seated on his right and Ross Monkey & Stumps on his left. hand the Members being arrived and the Hall filled. all in silence expected the opening speech CRASHEY. rose and all being uncovered. spoke as follows. with a vigorous and energetic tone. of voice and manner—
My Childern
The last time 2 years since when I opened this parliament it was under circumstances mournful to you and disagreeable to myself the kingdoms seemed all shaken discontent pervaded all men and society itself seemed disorganized. Feeling this I. in my speech made upon that occasion pictured to you a prospect

for the future which presented few features calculated to fix admiration or to excite feelings of pleasure succeeding events justified these prophecies and bad as they were yet infinitly exceeded them in dangerousness. through providence after a long and dreadful struggle. these threatning clouds were dispersed and much of the elements of discord being spent in the tempest all things seemed to promise a renewed and lasting peace. impressed with these hopes I here again am permitted to adress you and to again open your assembly for deliberation upon the affairs of your nations. yet forgive old age forgive my infirmities if. I confess that I cannot yet. be so sanguine as others on looking at the prospect. of future affairs disturbances may have been quelled but the cause of those disturbances has not yet been rooted. out. the tempest is quiet but there are yet materials for another Two years have elapsed scince that civil discord[6] to which I have all along alluded. during the first year suceeding it. in consequence of. the unsettled state of affairs no parliament could be called another year has now passed away and a parliament is at length convened. you are assembled armed with vast power excercise that power judiciously. you meet to make laws for the nations make just and appropriate ones you are composed of two ranks the nobles and the commoners legislate then for these two ranks. and do not let partiality enter into your councils. the argument lately used against you the complaint wich raised the rebellion was that you did not legislate. impartially that all your deeds were for the advancement of the Aristocracy and that the people had neither a voice in your council nor a place in your hearts wipe out by your future conduct this dreadful aspersion redress all the greivances which can be redressed. and where you meet with those which cannot. teach the Nations to bear them patiently As for me I am aged and infirm. I hold a feeble life by the gracious will of the Genii though without the fire and vigour of youth. without the strength and firmness of manhood having only left me the feebleness caution and. infirmity of hoary age. yet will I so long as I live. continue to watch over your welfare to unfold to you my experience to teach you the will of the Genii & to the utmost of my power I will guide you all with my hand and place you in the fair and open way of an enduring prosperity (Here the whole assembly knelt while Crashey standing up and stretching his hands over them cried) Now. may the awful Genii the guardians of our kingdoms and sole disposers [of] Mortal man. continue to protect you. hertofore as they have hitherto. O mysterious Beings. Shine upon these thy servants stretch your hands over your favorite city give strength to our arms wisdom to our councils show us the path of happiness sheild us from harm

All now rose standing in reverential Silence. while the venerable. Patriarch led by the four Kings. departed from the Hall and mounting his chariot. proceed[ed] to his hall in the Tower of Nations—the Senate then adjourned, to meet again on Wednesday the 20. of March.

---

6   See pp. 181 ff, for Rougue's rebellion.

March. 20.th. 1833   PB Bronte
The. House of Commons

Upon our entering the Hall at 1 o clock few Members had yet Arrived but we observed a sign of the times[7] far from favorable to peace and harmony. which was. that all the Movement members with Rougue at their head. were present and activly engaged disscusing in groups upon the politics of the day We saw among the new members. many of that formidable phalanx which in times of strife aid Rougue with toungue and sword bearing him through Every contest. among these men we apprehend that Capt Carey Mr Dorn and Mr O Connor. will prove powerful aids. to his party
At 2 o clock many being assembled buisness was commenced by. the Election of a president for this year. the. Candidates were Coln Grenville. and. Mr Flower. which after a warm but unimportant discussion terminated in the Election of the former to that Office. Crasheys speech being. read. ROUGUE rose[8]
        Gentlemen. it has allways. been the custom. of speakers upon their rising to mention the many and powerful feelings under which they labour now this practice laudable as it is I have never as yet followed. but upon the present occasion. I must deviate from my general rule. and for once avow. that at this moment my very heart is torn in peices between embarrasment greif and anger. For many years past it has been my fortune to hear the speeches of. our Patriarch. and I have always marked the day upon which I have heard. them with a black spot in the tablet of Memory I came sir determined to be satisfied. determined. to feel pleased & the moment this speech was read all my good resolutions dispersed to the winds and nothing remained to me but feelings of grief and discontent It was in vain that I argued that our patriarch must know best. must see fullest in to futurity and must therefore predict most accuratly but when I looked to his remarks upon what has happened when I see the the what shall I call it Gentlemen? the strangly distorted view taken of many late events the misrepresentations (order silence) when I saw his crooked notions of things past I began to doubt the accuracy of his remarks upon things to come (*loud uproar*) Silence gentle men silence. upon the speech we have just heard I cannot

---

[7]   Carlyle's 1829 polemic about the dire state of the newly emergent "Mechanical Age" of the nineteenth century, entitled *Signs of the Times,* popularized this term in the early part of the century; but its use derives from a general concern with what writers widely referred to as "the Spirit of the Age." Indeed, by 1830 an anonymous writer for *Blackwood's* complained about the way "that which, in the slang of faction, is called the Spirit of the Age, absorbs, at present, the attention of the world."
[8]   Branwell imitates the verbatim reporting of parliamentary debates in the newspapers of his day. See Barker Brontë, 112.

make one other remark it is intirely composed of vague lament and a still more vague hope the complaints are general and the advice is as general But there is one little paragraph which shines forth from among its Fellows. I mean that one in which he mentions the complaints. which raised the late commotions avers that if the disturbances are suppressed. the cause of them is not removed and in fine exhorts you to enquire. into those causes to redress. those greivances to legeslate for the many and not for the few. Now upon this passage I dwell with delight though you perhaps will look on it in gloom I consider it the first light of the morning you perhaps may fear it portends the fast approach of evening you all ask me what we complain of and first telling us you are ready to redress them next silence our complaints and threaten our bodies (*partial cheering*) what do we complain of? what does the chained captive complain of. (*cheers and hisses*) What when condemned unheard and unjustly sentenced when torn from his home and family and adjudged to the monotonous misery of a floating prison when guarded by hearts of iron and bound by fetters of iron what does the Galley slave complain of He complains Sir in short of being made a man yet cannot enjoy the feelings of men to wish for the free air of heaven and to have the damp pestilence of a dungeon. to desire the social converse of man and to have. the rude growlings of demons to have been made free and to be a slave. now Sir what he complains of we complains of. We the people the great body of your nation the strength. the sinews of the country—

THE PRESIDENT

Lord Elrington ought not to deal in such vague assertions it is against the rules of this house keep to your subject. sir.

ROGUE Keep to my subject sir? Yes Yes this is <always> the conduct always adopted by you oh oh oh Your whole aim is to quash disscussion but you cannot Sir you cannot (*partial cheering*) the people enslaved as they are have ears and understandings But the Night is fast waning and I must bring my speech to a conclusion I must be silent upon many topics which otherwise I should bring forward & enlarge upon fully. But sir if the people find in you carelessness and injustice. they shall find in me an unflinching. undaunted advocate The more sirs you threaten me the stronger I shall be supported. and let me tell you that Alexander Rogue backed by a million heroes is at least as powerful as Patriarch Crashey supported by 11 old men (tremendous uproar intermixed with partial cheering) The honourable Member waited until it had subsided and then continued) Thank you gentlemen thank you my lord! you have expressed your opinion most emphaticaly and. in a manner worthy of those opinions swine will grunt. and asses will bray (general uproar). Silence! I am not to be interrupted thus. Gentlemen I shall on the evening of Monday March 25. bring in a bill framed for the purpose of a redress of those greivances of which our people complain, (*loud uproar and disapprobation mixed with partial cheering*)

The House then. adjourned to Monday April 25

APRIL. 25 1833 =
House of Commons

This evening the house was crowded almost to suffocation and an immense mob blocked up the doors and passages all armed with. guns spears or bludgeons. Rougue on his entrance was greeted by them with tremendous cheers. the president being seated. Rougue rose with. an aspect. which showed. his determination to carry his measure either b[y] force or by argument. his partizans in the house hailed his rising with. immense. applause which was echoed and re-echoed from the passages to the doorways and in the streets reverberated with tenfold vehemence he smiled and begun. ROGUE

My[9] lords and Gentlemen I appear here before the bar of an a[u]gust and important tribunal. to plead the cause of an oppressed. and injured country. The Kingdom of the Glass town is my client. and pride? Ignorance and tyranny are her lawless oppressors now if the Genii have not. withered in you every flower of freedom if they have not. quenched in you every spark of patriotism if in leaving you the forms of men they have also left you the hearts of men I upon my knees entreat you impartialy to hear my cause and impartialy to judge it. you are the nation of the Glass town and therefore it is your parent then Oh! shall I appeal to a son for his father and shall that appeal be in vain Long Sirs and perseveringly have I endeavoured. to bring our complaints before you and as often and perseveringly have. a hundered. misfortunes prevented me. from bringing them before you meanwhile when in the depth of misfortune or amid the hurry of combat we. could not find. time to speak you have. filled up eve[r]y pause with the cry "Of what do you complain" Of what. do we complain? Of what do all men in misery complain. of what when condemned unheard and unjustly sentenced when torn from his home and. family and doomed to the damp misery of a dungeon when severed from every earthly friend and surrounded by every earthly enimy of what does the chained captive complain? We Sir complain. of hopes excited and. hopes withered, of promises made and those promises never performed we complain of having asked an empire and of receiving a chain What? and. is this your greivance do. you cry out for impossible blessings do you repine. that you possess the common lot of mortality do you desire the order of nature to be reversed that. you may enjoy. happiness above the reach of mortals. truly yours is a complaint over which this assembly can have no cognizance much less posses the power to redress! Stop Sir! Stop what would you say to a poor labouring man who should at your bar demand justice upon a rich but avaricious employer. who having stipulated with this man that he upon performing for him a certain amount of labour should from him receive a certain amount of wages yet should. upon the work being done and the man. appearing to receive those wages. refuse him the slightest

---

9   This speech is preceded by a canceled half column of Rougue's speech, a false start that Branwell was not satisfied with.

remuneration for his thankless toil? would you not decree to that poor man sevenfold compensation for his <sevenfold> injuries.? now what he would complain of we complain of. and. can you deny to a nation. the justice you would grant to an individual.? for what was it that we suffered ourselves to be conveyed from our paternal country and carried through a thousand perils and dangers over a thousand trackless seas for what did we permit ouselves to be settled at length under a burning sky and. in a country to us unknown amidst people alike unknown for what did we consent to spend our brightest days and our nobliest energies in toils the most severe and in conflicts the most deadly? It Sir was that WE MIGHT BECOME A NATION AND AS A NATION BECOME FREE![10] to this intent we looked round for assistance in our endeavor and we beheld. those men called. the TWELVE'S to them we applied. and in effect they promised to aid us. if we would make them kings and give them kingdoms this Sir who can deny that we did? yes we. made them all Monarchs. and performed beyond their utmost wish our part of the compact. But behold when laying their crowns before them we desired the recompense for our mighty labours they who had sat down twelve lenient. masters rose up 12 bloody tyrants. the[y] placed their feet on our heads. and. added us to the number of their already countless slaves. because we had laboured for them hitherto they condemned us to labour for them hearafter alike cheerless and. alike unrewarded Long stunned. and heart stricken we lay under this load of injustice and injury. but human endurance cannot last for ever. and at length. we have awaked! yes Sir from the mouths of the Gambia to the mouths of the Niger from. the. Jibbel Kumri to the Atlantic Sea we have risen with one voice to demand the long retarded justice. Ancient Rome to gain her. freedom desolated countries and. oppressed others. Greece when overwhelmed by a mighty host of barbarians who slaves themselves . . . [*line of MS. rubbed and undecipherable*] preserved her freedom also by scattering round her blood. and misery But we: to gain our Liberty what have we done? have we destroyed the liberty of less peaceful nations have we destroyed the happiness of. still less powerful familys? have we deluged the earth with blood and filled it with crime? No Sir we worked for our freedom we raised others to raise ourselves we made the earth smile that we might. smile. and behold! though Greece though Rome though America though a hundred other Nations. risen in <injustice> have prospered and have enjoyed. that for which they fought we. alone risen in justice are denied that for which we laboured O the blindness of Fortune! the blindness of the Genii But. now there shall be an end of this, Liberty we will have must have shall have and arms must decide our cause were other aid has proved vain. I am fearful sir of falling into rapsody shoulld I apostrophise those cruel tyrants who now reign over us I will therefore only tell them. that that reign "is over over now" if 12 men can overcome twelve millions if wrong can prevail over right if evil can overpower good then they may hope to continue as they have hitherto been but if other

---

10 Branwell initially wrote "WE MIGHT BECOME A NATION AND BE FREE!," then revised the sentence to achieve greater rhetorical balance.

wise. let them set their houses in order. for the day of retribution draws nigh. now in conclusion will I turn to you. my fellow sufferers my fellow labourers my fellow countrymen. work yet a little while and your efforts will [be] crowned with sucess you have gained your city of refuge[11] you are just turning round youre goal (here Rougue paused. as the clock struck the hour he continued). You here that clock it has just struck. eleven there remains now but one short hour and. this day being ended the night must turn and another morning rise apply this circumstance to your own case. the great clock of time is even now striking eleven. and also in an hour in one little period. your day of suffering must end. and our day of reward must dawn. rise then exert yourselves while exertion will prove of avail slacken not in sight of the goal come on companions one step come on and. VICTORY AND LIBERTY ARE OURS. (Rougue here bowed to his hearers and paused. a mighty shout from every hall and passage and street announced the feeling with which the speech was received One burst of applause rose on another and each louder than the one before while the speaker stood with flashing eyes and compress[ed] lips waiting till silence should be restored The cheers having in time subsided. he continued turning feircely to the astonished assembly.) Now Gentlemen you have heard. the voice of a mighty nation. and that voice. will you dare to withstand. listen while I. rehearse to you the terms upon which they will receive their liberty and then. if you dare. you may refuse them Behold "A Bill for establishing the freedom of the Glasstown countrys now and for ever. clause first.

The the 12 men now cheif rulers of these nations and more particularly the 4 men called cheif kings of the Glasstowns. shall. hereby be deprived of their present priveleges and. banished for ever to the Isles of Monkcay Stumpes. Mauns Isles and. If counquered Frenchiland. there to abide. and to rule. those regions being ceded to them and theirs for ever.

clause second. that all feudal distinctions all titles. and ranks be abolished. and that the two assemblys of the Lords and commons shall immediatly after the passing of this bill be dissolved.

Clause Third. that the 5 present. kingdoms of the Glasstown—Sneakys Wellingtons Parrys and Rosses Lands[12] be instantly joined and united into one nation with. the same laws and liberties. and. the G Glasstown their capital.

Clause Fourth. That upon the passing of this bill. a provisional Government be formed in this city with a president at their head to frame. for the new Nation new laws and a new constitution.
Now gentlemen, pass this bill this night and. you officers open all the doors that the people may overlook. the. progress of their new. birthright.

Scarce was this uttered when. a mighty multitude all armed rushed through door and window filling the whole mighty hall and with the most outrageous threats and cries attempting to force the passage of the bill in vain the president and others rose and attempted to supress the disorder. swords were

---

[11] See Numbers, chapter 35; Deuteronomy, chapter 19; Joshua, chapter 20.
[12] Branwell changed "four" to "5," but lists only four kingdoms.

raised muskets levelled and they were overwhelmed . . . [*Manuscript torn, a small portion being lost.*] midst of this wild tumult Rogue put the question to the vote. his followers with loud vociferations cried "aye aye." many others dismayed by. the mob. voted with them. The Marquis of Douro the 12s sons and a few other dauntless and upright members cried no no and attempted to show the meeting a sense of their duty. but. finding madness to rule in every one they amid the most deafning cries and the most bloody execrations. with sword in hand forced their way out of the hall when in a body the[y] repaired to the. hall of peers to aquaint them with these dreadul proceedings these being departed Rougue again put the question which was received with the most horrid yells of "aye aye." he then in defiance of all law. and justice declared. the bill carried through that house and. dissolved the commons till the 1st of May when. he intended to bring it before the house of. Lords. this tumultous and ominous meeting then dispersed amid the most deafning cheers Rougue was drawn in process[ion] through the city to his own. residence on their way the multitude in passing the house of peers greeted it with the most ferocious yells and curses. these scenes continued through out the whole night. in the Morn the Kings having called out large bodies of troops. Order was in a slight degree restored.

LEADING ARTICLE

The vast press of matter in this our first paper prevents us from. introducing a Leading article properly so called but. we beleive our readers will perceive the state of affairs without one we need not call. their attention to the scenes last night. The[y] are but the begining of the end. What the[y] will lead to in the first instance all may guess how they will conclude. none can tell as we are obliged to go this instant to press. we must conclude. our next paper will contain we fear even more momentous intelligence than this[13]

ROUGE IN PUBLIC
AND—
ROUGE in PRIVATE.
By the—
author of Letters from
an Englishman
[ornamental figure]

One of my first visits on my first arrival in this city was lately to the residence. of. Col Grenville the great Merchant. and almost my only acquaintance. in the Glass town while seated conversing with him in his splendid. parlour. it being

---

[13] No further numbers are known to have existed.

the evening the usual time for visiting in this capital. carriages soon began to arrive and company to enter in a short time. a numerous and select party had collected among whom I could. perceive there were many men of vigorous minds and cultivated understanding conversation both. lively and agreeable was soon. begun. when a commanding knock and an officious bustle at the door announced. the arrival of a distinguished visitor the door opened and there entered a single man tall. and. thin. dressed in a handsome dark full dress. he entered with a careless. air. glanced at the company and. after a few words to our host sat down in silence. many among the visitors I preceived. gazed at him as if he were something superiour to the general run my attention was most powerfully. arrested toward him and I watched his motions for a long time thinking whom he might be. there foremost. at the table. his elbow resting on it and his head leaning on his hand eyes large and exceedingly [*Manuscript torn; two lines missing*][14] abstraction only once did he seem to pay any attention to what was doing around him the conversation had turned. upon politics and the meeting of parliament one. person remarked that the campaign was likely to be severe but he hoped it would end in the defeat of the present rage for false. freedom" the new visitor starting up and looking at him with the keenest glance I ever beheld. only said "do you sir?" the man seemed confounded and was fain to gulp down his words in silence. the to me unknown. then. pulling out of his pocket book a pencil and paper wrote something in it. folded it up and ringing a bell. commanded it to be delivered to some one whose name I could not hear. but I remarked. that. the man who uttered the words before mentioned. turned very pale. and soon rising in evident agitation withdrew from the company as he departed the strange visitor. smiled faintly but many of the company. shook their heads. But a new train of thought now seemed to enter his mind he could no longer continue in his old position but. getting up he began to pace round the room in silence his bright eyes flashing under his pale high forehead with amazing brilliancy. Stopping short and turning to the company he said "Grenville Grenville in the name of wonder. when are you going to bring out the wine? Oh when you please my lord he answered and the servants were ordered to bring in the refreshments. this being done the visitor. sitting down with the rest to table. began pouring out glass after glass. in such quantitys as few whom I have seen could possibly bear up under. he continued drinking untill he had worked himself up to the proper pitch and then. turning to that gentleman who at. the time. happened to be speaking he said. "Flower what are you talking about?" "Oh my lord we are speaking about. the scenery of the upper country and debating whether Elymbos or Aornos be the higher Mountain. "have you seen both" "Yes my lord but some of us hav'nt." "I think so" answered the Nobleman "I think none of you. have either been able to see or judge of what you could see. why who in the name of the world would. think for a moment of perfering the sun. to the moon. now you dogs. because Aornos. is near to your

---

[14] The SHB Misc I version reads: "exceedingly melancholy and full of abstraction" (p. 196).

own city because he is the highest mountain of his range because he overlooks. a country much spoken of. in your annals. you must needs cheep out. that its the finest mountain in the world I suppose now, (addressing himself to me) that you Sir. in your city (London). fancy primrose or Richmond Hill the grandest height in Europe because it looks on London now both of you think whith equal wisdom and found your. arguments upon equal grounds

Elymbos is just as superior to. Aornos as. Snowden to primrose hill.[15] both you havent aimed your height yet my dogs. If you think that Elymbos is the finest height. we possess. you are about on a par with those who. call Snowden the finest height in Europe. Now go to. your Alps to your Mont Blanc at once. climb to the fountain. head. why now once. I. about eighteen years ago was. taking a ride about my lawful buisnes (eh lawful?) over the great hills in the north of Sneakys Land a number of the Dogs we were hunting had slipped. of to the North. west I with a party were following them Ill catch myself just when in the grey of the morning. we were winding up a great pass in the Branii hills. now Englishman there when I speak of hills dont think. I mean risings of 8 or 900 feet in height no. these were ranges of 8000 or 9000. my man. Well we had nearly gained the summit. of this pass I was first. urging my hors[e] to gain a look at what was beyond. I gained the height. I said before it was just dawn. the sky was covered with grey sleeping clouds. thick and dark before us. rolling mists. wavered under our feet. I found I could see nothing save the rocks around me. Looking about much dissapointed. my notice was attracted to two great red lights up in the sky. they only just seemed to glimmer through the clouds like why like the. the. yellow of a[n] egg through the shell. I thought now these were two of the cheif Genii. and therefore began cursing them from the bottom of my soul, but. the morning winds were rising the clouds began to roll of from. the landscape and before I. could say Jack Robinson. the peaks of two. prodigious mountains rose high in the. twilight but flaming. with. a crimson sunshine. there they stood Oh I can see them now rising far before us their mighty bases veiled in darkness thier sides thrusting above the clouds rock over rock. in rival mightiness. gradually enlightened first with a faint then a brighter dawn till. just at the limits of the eternal snows the sunbeams burst on them. and. their towering cones looked. like. why I just fancied them to be the two beacons for the Legions of Genii when wandering over the world all of us had now gained. the ridge. and each man as he. did gain it reined in his horse. and. stood fronting the wondrous. scene the mists were rolling away from our feet. the sides of the. Branii hills seemed to rush down down through mist and cloud and darkness. to the shore of a vast pale shadowy Lake. which stretched. on through the morning without. bound or shore. but beyond its unseen banks. yet seeming close at hand rose. a hundred grey ridges and. snowy peaks: each eger to

---

15 Richmond Hill, near London's Kew Gardens, is a small rise of about 135 feet; Primrose Hill, in Regents Park in the West End of London, stands not much higher at approximately 190 feet. Mount Snowden in Wales, the highest summit of England and Wales, measures over 3500 feet.

catch the first beam of morning. high high above these rose those two rivals
GENII'S THRONES. blazing in exclusive. sunshine. and. shooting far into the
skies" In this manner did he continue talking while all the rest in profound.
silence gathered closer round. him him listening with the most undivided
attention I was perfectly. abstracted from myself. he continued speaking on
different subjects in the same strain enlightning every thing he touched. on. and
showing the most extensive knowledge and the finest imagination in speaking
he seemed wrapt up in his subject his fore head almost shone with light his eyes
flashed. [his hands] sometimes clenched or clasped together extended when. in a
subject which pleased him. he from time to time took immense draughts of the
most fiery spirits. which yet seemed to produce little effect upon his evidently
Iron constitution. but in the midst of one of his loftiest descriptions he suddenly
swallowing down a vast draught of claret. started up. and said Well "Gents I
must off fate calls and I obey. good night." then wraping his cloack round him
he with a polite bow. departed from the room. various expressions of. wonder
and admiration burst from each. visitor. when he had gone. Old Luckyman. said.
"he is a chap is yon Rougue" this unravelled the mistery. it was Alexander
ROUGUE Lord Elrington. I now scarce wondered at what I had heard. Grenville
seeing my admiration and guessing that I would like to see more of this
astonishing man said He has gone direct from this to the commons parliament
where he is expected to make a rare speech. this night were all going there will
you accompany us." of course I gladly assented and we repaired to the Senate
house appropriated to the Commons were Grenville took his seat as President I
sat in the Gallery with. my freind and countryman. Mr Bellingham who from his
long residence in the City and his exclusive acquaintance with everything
relating to it. was admirabley fitted to. explain and elucidate to me what I should
see. when we had taken our seats. the magnificent hall. was fast filling with
members and spectators Grenville took his seat on the. rostrum. and buisness in
a short time would commence. meanwhile I amused myself with surveying the.
character and countenances of the different members & I was particularly struck
with the firm figures and noble bearing of most of the members. they looked to
be worthy of the country and their fame. I observed several old men with white
beards and hair. who possesed shoulders and chests of the most. astonishing
breadth. remarking this to Bellinghame. he said that these were some of the
second 12s who came over. with Wellington after the great war and that they
were among the Patriaarchs of the country of course I did not. see. any of the
Kings or first 12s they being in the upper house. or the house of Lords. but the
President having taken his seat buisness now commenced. and a member rose to
address the House by his lofty stature expansive forehead and flashing eye I
instantly knew it to be ROUGUE everyone was hushed in expectation. but the
moment it was know[n] that he had risen a tremendous shout from the populace
at the doors echoed. and reechoed. from every street and wall. announced in a
manner not to be mistaken his formidable popularity. For a moment he smiled
at this unexpected tribute. but. instantly relapsing into his former stern
expression he advanced into the middle of the hall and. elevating one hand while
the other. grasped his note paper he began in a low but clear tone of voice. and.

with. little or no gesture. as extending his arm and turning to the tribunal. he began with an appeal to their feeling upon the state of his country his voice was low and solemn and his expression. grave and mournful. I knew that what he was going to utter would be the most flimsy sophistry and the most glaring falshood. yet before he had proceeded many sentences I felt that I was about to be born down by his eloquence and carried along like a feather in the wind when he detailed the lengthened course of injustice the frauds and the miseries produced. by the twelves and laid on the glasstown when he besought the assembly to hear him on behalf of their country as they would hear him appeal to them for their own Fathers and at last when with a lightning eye and thrilling voice he. cried "Of what do we complain of what do all men in misery complain of what when condemned unheard and unjustly sentenced when torn from his home and family and doomed to the damp misery of a dungeon when deprived of every earthly friend and. surrounded by every earthly enimy of what does the chained captive complain. then. I say though [I] know all he said to be false and rotten. I could not resist. joining the burst of applause which followed the concluding sentence. pausing till the cheers subsided he again began and. in a clear and rapid flow of eloquence filled with sparkling an[t]itheses and flashing epithets. led everyone on. winding round them with consummate art the net of his supprassing sophistry never perhaps had I heard. such distortion of facts never such. supression of truth such. daring falshood and such flimsy argument. yet notwithstanding all his thundring eloquence his exquisite art his. passionate declamation. the utter throwing of himself into his subject so wound us <u>all</u> up to his own pitch that truth and reason. might have thrown themselves from the windows and were never missed. when he began I said his voice was. calm. and his manner in-active but as he proceeded. his face became flushed his eyes flashed brighter and. the little paper he held in his hand. after undergoing various twirlings and transformations was haff torn in peices thrown by wich extending both his hands to the tribunal he with loud thrilling voice and. advanced foot (the clock then chiming 12) cried that as they heard it strike the last hour of the earthly day so even then over their heads the great clock of time was in like manner. striking the last hour of the tyrant reign. here he stopped and forth burst such a yell of applause from in the house and out of it as I never have heard and never may again. time upon time was it taken. up and. note after note swelled to heaven till in one loud clear long drawn yell it seemed to die of on the farthest hills of Jibbel Kumrii. but here I must conclude were I to relate the scene which followed the atrocious measure attempted to be passed the threats the yells the confusion the mob. all the proceedings of that. eventful night, day would end before my pen could stop. suffice it to say that I was borne to my home from the scene in a true English swoon.

SONG applicable to the present crisis
By. Young Soult the Ryhmer.

A cloud is rolling oer us
 A bloody cloud of war
Dark looms its shade before us
 Cast forword from afar

How long hath it been gathering
 And wherefore doth it come[16]
From whither rolls it fold on fold
 With fast increasing gloom

It comes from kumriis Mountains
 From Hylles misty main
From Niger's infant fountains
 From. Gambia's watery plain

It comes full charged with thunder
 With stormy winds and rain
It come[s] in desolation
 Nor shall destroy in vain

Red Genii fly. around it.
 Before the furies ride
Mars frowns in vengeance oer it
 With death portending pride

Eearth earth the rod of chastisement
 Must now upon thee fall
Long have we slept in quietness
 Within each guardless wall

Long mindless of the Genii
 We have seen our days pass on
Careless of future weal or woe
 Of crimes. unavenged done

But Now in dreadful ordeal
 We must abide the storm
Must sink from our proud pinnacle
 And. seek our kindred worm

YOUNG SOULT

PB Bronte.   April. 26. 1833.

---

[16] The line originally read: "From whither doth it roar."

REAL LIFE IN VERDOPOLIS.
A TALE
By Captain John Flower. MP. FRS &c
.IN. II VOL'S
.VOL, I.

CHAPTER .I.[1]

I DURING the latter end of April. in the midst of those forewarnings which seemed to forbode to our General country. another. dreadful and. protacted. struggle. like those from which she has lately escaped. from and. raised. to by the same means. A Trial came on in the Great Public hall of the Glasstown which. from the strange secrets it was expected to disclose and the manner in wich it was expected to involve. several of the principal mob Leaders and thus perhaps quashing the incipient rebellion. create[d] the greatest intrest ever at such a political period. Five[2] fellows distinguished by the cognomens of. Dick Nose'em[3] Tom Catchem. Frank. Twitchem. and Ned. Stinguishem had been convicted. of. Robbing in the most daring manner a Government Courier on the road to Wellingtons Land laden with large sums of money and several. important. dispatches. The intent of these fellows with regard to the "Blunty"[4] as well as the use the[y] might make of it was very apparent. and readily explained. But when it was understood that their first exclamation on flooring the Courier was "have at the papers" "Mind the flimsys" and moreover when pursued that they dropped the gold. yet retained to the last the higher prized. Dispatches, Men began to suspect that something more than met the eye. was concealed in this business. For why. in the name of every thing thats reasonable

---

[1] A manuscript of 36 pages (1 blank, 11.5 x 18 cm) that has been disassembled and each leaf set into a blank sheet, in the Brotherton Collection, University of Leeds. Because Branwell filled the page from top to bottom and side to side, the top and bottom lines and words at the margins are frequently wholly or partially obliterated because of the mounting of the pages. Although no covers have been preserved, all other manuscripts through 1833 have covers and were stitched together, so it is likely that this manuscript was also originally stitched with covers. Under "CHAPTER I," in longhand, appear the words "Lord < >" and in the bottom right hand corner of the first page "September September."
[2] Only four are actually identified here and in subsequent references.
[3] According to the *Dictionary of Modern Slang, Cant, & Vulgar Words* of 1859, "Nose Em" was a slang term for "fogus" or tobacco ("fogo" meaning stench). More generally, it identifies "nose" as slang usage for a thief turned informer or King's evidence.
[4] "Blunty": probably a variant of the slang term "blunt," meaning ready money. Compare Alexander CB, II, Part I, 19.

should four such ragamuffins as these were feel any desire for. aught except Gold
or "plunder" unless directed from higher qua[r]ters and actuated by hopes of
reward. Feeling the weight of this argument and desirous perhaps in the present
crisis of criminating the Mob Leaders if possible since so doing would.
contribute to quell the approaching commotion the Judge the jury and the
Goverment advocate in the case determined. to pump the prisoners and at the
approaching trial to get from them by every means of coxing the supposed
important secret.

This Trial from whose result so much was expect[ed] and whose advent was
so anxiously waited for came on at length on the. 27.th of April. on that day.
the Public Hall was filled. crammed. choked with. spectators of all classes and
every opinion. JOHN GIFFORD. took his seat as Judge And. Seargent Bud.
acted as advocate for the Government. The Counsel. for the prisoners was a keen
thourough bred Laweyer well known in our city by the title of Lawyer Tweezy
of great repute for ability though Honesty had never once been mentioned in
conjunction with his name Proceedings opened by the crown Advocate stating
the nature of the case to be tried. its criminality. and the punishment which
would rest on its authors. he next hinted somthing of the suspicions afloat
respecting the affair. and then proceeded to question the prisoners who stood at
the dock perfectly unmoved. by all that could be thought said or done respecting
them. His first question was. What were youre motives for the action you have
committed." 'Stinguishem. answered. "Now if wer'e to be treated in sich a
fashion as this Ise—Ise—Ise. Oh. you end of the tail A Bull head you Cod Fish.
you hide of a frog. what do you mean by Motive and haction—you rare dog
you!" Bud "come now my man remember where you are." Stinguish. "I
remember well enough were we are were next door to a roar-ing pothouse and we
cant our heads get[5] in to it we're just forenent a beggerly swipe stakes and we
cant. get our knives into him" BUD. well well that[s] not what I mean now my
rare men. you'll have a chance of getting into the pot house and me to if you
like, If youll just bolt out why you played this plisky[6] what you thought. of the
papers and who told you to lift them eh?
TWITCHEM. Now my rare dog. if you set a squeezing us in this gate why well
just bolt thats all."
BUD come come my hogs[7]. this isnt—.
All the prisoners at this moment cried. "hogs hogs does the catsflesh call us
hogs if things is coming on in this fashion we'll see what we can do oh my rare
ape. if were to be called hogs'—they here all burst out in a fit of crying for it is
well know[n]. these rare lads cannot bear to be called by a name which they are
unused to. had Bud called them apes "end of the tail of a louse" or names yet
more grotesque but to which they had been acustomed they would have past it
over but as it was that unfortunate word. had ruined the proceedings of the whole

---

5   Clearly "get" should be placed before "our heads."
6   "Plisky": a term from Scottish dialect, meaning trick.
7   Originally written as "dogs," with the "h" written over the "d."

evening Bud saw this and turning to the Judge he said "My lord we can make nothing more of these men this night They had better be remanded." Here Lawyer Tweezy rose up and said "My Lord at a proper time and place I shall enter my protest against this mode of proceeding. I am well aware of the suspicions which are afloat respecting this buisness but never were suspicions more wretchedly. founded. These men have informed me that their reasons for appearing so eager about the papers arose from an idea they entertained that they were Bank Notes and as the[y] naturally supposed that some dozens of the notes would containned more value than a box of soveriegns they naturaly upon being warmly pursued. flung the Latter away rather than the former this my lord explains the whole of this formidable mystery."—

A very plausible explanation said Gifford. but however let these men be remanded for the present till something more is brought to light. Officers take the prisoners back in to custody." This order was promptly obeyed. and the prisoners having departed the Hall soon began to pour forth its vast multititudes and in a short [time]. remain[ed] empty gloomy in the decaying evening. One figure alone that of TWEEZY remained pacing its shadowy pavement. he constantly kept looking at his watch and when the hand pointed to the hour of 10. he hurried out of the building and with hasty footsteps bent his course toward the great jail. after threading a multitude of dark alleys and darker passages he arrived in front of the outer portal of this Mighty building He paused not to survey its vast proportions nor the sublime appearance of its shadowy <wall> rising black and indistinct against the starry sky but knocked loudly at the gate The porter opened an aged man of the old days he held in his hand a lighted <lamp> the beams of wich fell concentrated on his ashy locks and stern time worn visage and on the more insidious lurking count[en]ance of the Laweyr. Tweezy desired to be admitted to the four prisoners in the tower. The porter shook his head and said "The time is past. my man for sich as you my orders are against it Tweezy drew him toward a corner and began to converse with him in an ernest tone of voice. for some time at the conclusion of the dialogue the porter casting a hasty look round silently unlocked a small postern in the wall and <they> both entered. with noiseless footsteps they glided through many dark passages and up a steep staircase. till stopped by a small Iron door this the porter opened and Tweezy having entered. he left the lamp he descended and dissapeared. The room. in which the Lawyer stood was the cell [of] the prisoners it was low damp and dark but [from] all appearance the hardy fellows it contained.[cared] little about all its inconveniences they lay on the floor in different postures but all sound asleep TWEEZY advancing toward them awakned them one after another and. when after many yawns execrations and grumblings they became conscious who was speaking to them he said. "Now my rare apes. stick fast. your trial comes on again tomorrow say what you like but dont reveal your secret" "ay" replied Stinguish we will say what we like my rare man weve all made up our minds upon that matter. but as to not revealing our secret. thats a different case. listen my rare ape. we'se determinated. whatsomever comes of it if you. dont. help us out of this dog hole. this very night. why we'll balk we'll let out ivry thing our minds made up. so no more speaking will you or wont yo relase us?" from the determined look of these fellows the Lawyer's searching eyes saw that there was no reply except one. For a moment he stood thunderstruck but at once as if he recollected something he replied "Courage my rare men. Ill let you out this very night One o'clock One o clock be ready." Then stepping out he closed the door after him and descended the steps at the landing place he was met by the porter who silently conducted him back to the great gate. There Tweezy turning round said hast[i]ly. "Tom is your time out by one o clock? the porter answered "Ay my rare lad if thats what you trust to youre lost. im just. going now to deliver the keys to the next watch" Tweezy again seemed petrified he hastily <said> could you think your next watch might he—. "Oh no" said the porter cutting him short. "Oh My rare men he's Ned Standfast. an's been a se[r]vant to the Duke of Wellington" "Oh then" replied Tweezy thats over <now> Well we'll try some other way. Good night Jack." The lawyer stepped out the porter shut the gate and each departed on his way.

CHAPTER. IId. May 20 1833

That Night as Lady ZENOBIA Elrington was seated allone in her splendid Saloon. deeply engaged in the descussion of Senecas Epistles[8] in the original the door opened and her Husband entered the room. he advanced to her sofa and laying his hand on the back of. it stood a little while musing in silence he first broke it by saying "Madam you must neither go to or rec[e]ive any parties or persons here this evening" "What my lord" she answered. what do you command. you may give way to your humours as you like but do not expect me to do the same let me see I shall receive three parties and go <to> 2. five in the whole my lord" "Do you dare to disobey me?" replied ROUGE in that calm deep voice which. with. him. is the sign. of. utter determination Zenobia started at the tone and started still more when on looking at him she observed. the paleness of his countenance and the deadly and even awful gleam of his eyes she knew this was neither time for condradiction or reply and remained silent. "You here me" he continued in the same calm unaltered voice. "yes" my lord" she replied rather fain<t>ly for his expression and manner convinced her who so well knew him that there was "something dreadful in the gale" He nodded and withdrew That night the splendid square of Elrington place seemed deserted The ceasless roaring of carriages the cracking of whips and the dismount<ing> of countless multitudes was silent and the heavy golden knockers rung not with the incessant annunciations of visitors it seemed that the lord of the Mansion was lying dead in its apartments But this was not the case ROUGUE Viscount

---

8   Seneca the Younger (4 BC-65 AD), a Roman philosopher, orator, statesman, and tragedian, was educated in the Stoic school of philosophy. He authored the *Epistulae morales*, a series of 124 essays dealing with a range of moral problems, after retiring from active political life under the emperors Caligula, Claudius, and Nero.

Elrington. was seated alone in his study silent<ly> reading a volume of Lucians Dialogues the cold athiestic sentiments the the continual sneering at humanity and human life,[9] agreed well with his disposition and ser[v]ed for a while to fix his attention but cares and thoughts to mighty to be driven long away soon seemed again to press on his mind he laid the book down and rising began to pace around the apartment. several times he turned to the window and looked out upon the vast city spread below. him. it[s] mighty Edifices its various streets its crowds of houses and. Mills and. palaces all sweeping away in the darkness like black clouds on a midnight sky while the million lights twinkling and glanceing appearing and dissapearing below him. seemed like the stars in a reflected heaven. but if there were stars below there were none above for the sky was covered with moist rainy clouds like his own soul all looked dark and comfortless But Meditation and Contemplation were not the attributes for which ROUGUE was famous he soon turned from this scene to a rose wood cupboard in the corner of the apartment and. taking therefrom. a bottle and Glass sat down. in his accustomed seat here he remained drinking silently but constantly glass after glass of pure undiluted brandy. But just as the clock struck 11 he heard a gentle quiet tap at his door he cried "Come in" it opened. and there entered with slow insidous footstep Lawyer Tweezy. Rougue starting exlaimed[10] "Ha! dog you here! well! what news? quick." Tweezy first taking a chair and giving an affectionate hugg to the bottle replied by stating what had happened. in court with regard to the 5. prisoners. his pilgrimage to the jail and his interview with them. in concluding he said "The porter or Watch Sir is now changed. The men at present watching are not to be tampered. with and for my part I am at a loss intirely how to act. To have the secret divulged would be dreadful to attempt To liberate them would be no less so" "For your part? Fool what should you know look at that straw on the carpet? to you I suppose to let it remain there would be dreadful to take it up not less so? Rougue with his usual penetration and energy had while Tweezy was speaking contrived and determined upon a scheme. which however required more resolution to act upon than skill to invent. he shoved away bottles and glasses from him and opening a desk began to write. he soon indited four or five letters which after sealing and directing he gave into the hands of Tweezy "Now" he said "go instantly and take these letters each to the man for whom they are intended. For your better expidition. you may take a horse from my stables. in default of speed your life shall be the forfeit Tweezy I swear it."

---

[9] Lucian (120-180 AD), a rhetorician, pamphleteer, and satirist, produced about eighty critical and satirical essays on Cynic themes, written in the form of Platonic dialogues or in imitation of Menippean satire. Most notable among these are *Dialogues of the Gods* and *Dialogues of the Dead*. Typically, his works critque the shams and follies of the literature and philosophy of his day, targeting imposters and hypocrites in particular, especially philosphers who fail to practice what they preach.

[10] The next dozen lines of text in the manuscript are written over a faint background sketch.

The Lawyer to well knew his patrons temper and spirit to disobey his injunction he gave a last kiss to the bottle jumped. up and. taking with him the letters left the room, Rougue listened till he heard his horses feet. leaving the square. all weight of care then seemed dismissed from his mind instead of the cold sneering Misanthropy which had hitherto seemed to pervade his countenance, his eyes now flashed fire and his aspect. seemed filled with the ardour which he allways displays on the eve of some great crisis. He rung the bell for his valet who appearing soon attired him in a strong travelling suit. he then seized his hat and sword. and first ordering his fleetest horse hastened to the apartment of Lady Zenobia she had thrown by her reading and was now engaged in writing Rougue as he entered smiled. "Active Active. well I like that. Its better than to be like some Ladies whom I know who when. without company die through ennui. and with it. die through fatigue." The more than usually cordial tone of this speech did not. as it would from any common person please Lady Zenobia but alarmed her she knew well enough that her Lord seldom used words so kind but when on the eve of some great enterprise some awful plunge. his firy eye and his travelling dress increased her fears. she said. hastily "Rougue where are you going what will you do?" "Never mind Zenobia, I hope Im not going home." replied Rougue pointing downwards, he he continued "but listen I have to go a journey now you say as little of it. as you can. keep all things as they are till I come back. Good night Good bye" he turned rond and left the room. descending the stairs he hastened to the yard where his horse stood ready saddled. he mounted cast one look at his vast Mansion rising gloomily in the Midnight sky. and then putting spurs to his steed dissapeared in the darkness.

That Night between the hours of eleven and 12 o clock. The dark desolate alleys lying on the north side of and shadowed by the lofty towers of the General prison exhibited a scene of bustle and animation unusual to them. in general their high crumbling buildings and narrow forsaken pavements at this hour only echoed to the solitary footsteps of some drunken rare lad. or frenchy going to or reeling from the rotten doors of of the low pot house whose red light glinting through a thousand chinks and crannies in wall and window was the only on[e] that broke the doleful gloom. perhaps too at such times it might be the lot of him who chooses to explore these dangerous recesses to stumble over something soft and yeilding which per[c]hance upon his comeing in to contact with it. he might perceive to be a human being gashed over with wounds and rotting in the air. But whatever might in general be the appearance of these places it was widely different. now The light from a hundered torches glared upon each huge decaying wall or fell in wild confusion upon the ferocious and upturned faces of the Multitudes crowding the space below, all present seemed to come together by one consent but not one seemed to know for what he came they were agreed upon only 2 points to be here present and all to have arms. every where Muskets rifles Knives and bludgeons flourished in profusion all waiting for general employment. in the mean time to pass a-way the period till the grand plot should open many a little episode was. acted through the multitudes to an Englishman to a stranger it would have seemed as if two rival and savage armies were combating together for life or death. but. in reality the case was otherwise

though the report of guns was incessant though Knives were every where
brandished though numbers fell dead & wounded the "rare fellows" were "nobbutt
spreeing a bit till ROUGE should appear" a general shout through every lane
and alley in the neighbour hood soon hailed the advent of this distinguished
personage [he] appeared. advancing on horse back pistol in one hand and his
sword in the other tightning the reins of his steed he halted and. pointing with
his sword to the immense walls of the jails which rose above them in the
darkness like a band of formless Genii "Said in his usual loud clear voice "freinds
I beleive that you all see yon towers before us and I beleive that you <all> know
what they are. (a genearal yell) very well. it is you must know very essential to
our general liberty that several men there confined should this Night be liberated.
(a-nother yell louder than the first) the reasons I have given to your leaders
Naughty Lawless Carey and the rest that is sufficient they may deliberate you
must act. have you gott all your arms in order (loud howels of assent) very well
form into three lines (this was accomplished amid direful howlings. thrusting
fighting and eclipsing of the torches) well again now you Torch bearers come in
front. Naughty you head one rank. Carey you another. Lawless take the third.
and Ill. head you all hurra ROUGE for ever! the jail and Victory! A horrid and
tyger like yell followed this speech ROUGE. spurring his horse. galloped on
in a direction opposite to the Prison for the purpose of disentangling himself
from the narrow lanes and. attacking it in front. the armed Multitude of many
thousands of men followed him in due order scouring the streets from side to side
threatning shouting and constantly firing their Muskets as the[y] rolled on their
numbers increased. so that when arrived at the grand Market place the crowd be
came truely alarming the whole area was filled with the blaze of torches and
ringing with their confused uproar by this time a report had spread through that
quarter of the city that some great popular commotion was on the eve of
breaking out and hundered tongued fame magnified it to an attempt at a
revolution, the Government. anxious not to give the Mob one. instance of
"showing fight" hastily assembled as large a body of troops and Military as
could be got to-gether at such an unfavourable hour But where to place them was
the question? for an hour on this point all was uncertainty but from the
continued crys of the advancing Mob "the jail the jail down with the prison" this
doubt was soon put to rest 3 regiments of Cavalry and a large body of police
were instantly dispatched under the command of John Sneaky to guard that
important building and to block up every avenue leading to it. this they did and
haveing surrounded the place waited with fixed arms the approach of the Mob at
this moment the scene was solemn and even sublime it was night <&> over the
huge building the black clouds rolled. thick and gloomily. opening now and then
to show the cold silent Moon which for a moment made visible the mighty City
the summit of the Tower of Nations and the vast buttress of the threatened walls.
its pale light. gleamed fit[f]uly on the long lines of armour which surrounded the
gates and then all rolled ba<ck> in their former gloom. in a short while above
the general hum of the city distinctly rose the distant yet advancing crys of the
Mob. they rose hoarse & discordant as the wind swept past. and wakned the
soldiers to double ardour in a while vast shoals of boys nondiscripts and all the

usual shoals of Idlers attending a popular commotion began to pour forward into the square. and suddenly through the darkness at the opening of a distant street one vast blaze of torch light flashed forward upon all, Now the word of command past quickly from rank to rank. with short shrill screams the boys haild the approaching contest. The Mob were coming! All down the street in long and tumultous array poured the resistless torrent. The lights though in such vast numbers though they glared on all round. with a crimson blaze yet could not dissipate any where the utter darkness and the wild ferocious features of the rioters crowded on in black masses toward. their gloomy goal. First in the front on his noble horse which had borne him safe through a hundered conflicts advanced the leader ROUGUE his gigantic spirit raised now to the highest pitch of which it was capable this was his sport his pastime the scences around. him. were the only ones which could light a glow of pleasure on his noble countenance in the Gambling house in the Senate in private however elated. he might be his features always preserved their iron sternness and cold sarcastic smile but in the heat of a midnight conflict all reserve was thrown by and he gave his fiery spirit full liberty to revel in the darkness and dangers of battle But enough of this, to our narrative. Before the Officers could utter the word "Fire" before the men could prepare their Muskets had the whole body of rioters percipitated themselves pell mell among them.

Among the Glasstowners in such cases it is scarcly cutomary to read the riot act or to fire blank cartridges. for such a proceeding our tempers are neither sufficiently patient or phlegmatic, Here with bayonet and sword with Musket and bludgeon did both parties at once "join issue" Now so long as the numbers on each sid[e] continued pretty equal the More regular and better trained body of Military had greatly the advantage as fast as their antagonists rushed in the[y] heaped them dying before them Once indeed they had rolled the whole torrent backward. and obtained space to pour upon their black and congregated masses a well directed and destructive fire of Musketry but as the smoke rolled of and the echoes of the guns rattled upon the vast walls before them and thundered among the wilderness of buildings darkning behind them it seemed the knell of these brave soldiers to a glasstowner the smell and sound of Gunpowder is indeed "dear as the nut[11] to which his soul conforms. And therefore the moment that the volley ceased. the Mob impetous again rushed forward Rougue seemed guarded by supernatural aid for though allways in the very front of the firing he remainded untouched unwounded. but now new masses of men joined the Mob their numbers swelled as if the earth was restoring its dead around them. Rougue but cried "Now for the jail and Victory"[12] and with with one tyger shout over soldiers walls and bulwarks was hurled onward one blazing mass of men where are the Military now no trace of them is to be seen. Oh yes under the mob there

---

11 Nut: a slang term for head.
12 The following episode, an assault on the prison of Verdopolis which culminates in armed conflict between political factions, invites reading as a parody of the assault on the Bastille at the outbreak of the French Revolution.

is a dreadful heaving and soon the middle of the crowd breaks open and armed men are seen fighting for life with desperate engergy but all this is lost here new shoals of men rushing from every street percipitate themselves over their Fellows and rushing forward. hide every remnant of the gallant regiments Now the great postern of the Gateway is surrounded by the formost rioters Rougue and Naughty like furies rage before its huge iron bound frame

> "There Rougue" among the foremost deals his blows
> And with his axe repeated strokes bestows
> On the strong doors then all their shoulder ply
> Till from the posts the brazen hinges fly
> Dryden[13]

Doubled and trebled were the blows from pikaxe and. crow bar and bludgeon. incessant were the heavings from gigantic and brawny shoulders and at length it gave a crash burst inwards and fell back in the gloom now the great yard was in a moment filled choked with armed men. and the hissing firebrands threw their strong lurid light high up on the buttress's of the assaulted prison here it stood before them in all its gloomy majesty but how where they to enter here every door and there were many was framed of solid iron. but they were not long in deliberation bring fire cried Rougue in his loudest and clearest voice. "I could ken it amang a thousand" the words were scarcly spoken when a thousand torches were bent forward toward him beams barrels every thing combustible rose rapidly in an immense pile before the principal doorway black smoke rose hissing from the heap. in in a few minutes a clear red sheet of flame. rose high in the darkness. a loud and long continued yell announced this gratful. event a yell which was from time to time renewed as. one bright flake upon another burst against the fast blackning walls. the shining sparks and splinters like stars whirled and shot over head and the dense clouds of smoke "blocking" up the air prouduced feeling much akin to suffocation. at length over the astounding tumult three loud cracks in the fire announced the vast door had given way and in an instant over every obstacle like an army of Locusts[14] extinguishing the fire. in poured the resistless mob an hour ago and nothing could be more dark more silent than the interior of this mighty building. nothing could be heard [but] the keys creaking in the doors as the jailors before retiring went round to ascertain that all was safe but now in a moment every endless passage every winding avenue. flamed and thundered to the footsteps and torches of the entering rioters hundereds were heard rather than seen racing along these passages. the lights glancing like like falling meotors every cell door was torn open and the late

---

13 From Book II of Dryden's translation of the *Aeneid*. In the Brontë's copy of *The Works of Virgil, Translated into English Verse, By John Dryden* (London, printed for C&J Rivington, and the other proprietors, 1824), the passage occurs on p. 164, with "Himself" in place of "There Rougue."

14 The eighth plague of Egypt, sent by God when Pharoah refused to release the Israelites from slavery, was a plague of locusts—see Exodus 10:4.

chained inmates joined the mob swelling it like the rivulets to a mighty stream up the strong wooden stairs rushed the resistless multitude and with loud yells and shouting preformed the same kind office to those above. Stinguishem Twitchem Catchem and Nosem were seen now free among the thickest of the uproar. The walls seemed to split with the clamor and high over head the roofs echoed like peals of thunder. now the awful voice of their leader cried. Fire the prison. this was in unison with the most heartfelt wishes of the "rare lads" every heart bent itself to the "sport" every torch was put in requisition. all being cleared from the upper stories. the lower rooms were filled with vast beams rafters piles of wool anything that would flame. torches were scattered among them. then all living rushed from the building and at a respectful distance with groans yells and shouting waited. The breaking forth of the conflagration For some time an incessant hissing in the building was the only thing that told what was going on then the thick smoke began to curl out from the gaping doors quickly it came out blacker thicker and intermingled with sparks. then. tongues or red flame darted forth from the front windows and all knew that the fire had arisen and was devouring all within The flames now came out thick and fast. all were gazing on them when with. a mighty and astounding crack the roof gave way. above, many slates and blazing beams burst into the area. while the main mass hissing and blazing chrashing into the interior tore through. ceilings and floors to the lowest "bed of Flame"[15] now as from a mighty furnace the smoke rolled red and wavering from the gaping building the fires streamed upward to the sky. cast their light through the whole frighted city. the front towers and walls stood black and shattered against the glowing light but every moment portions of them would burst into the blaze and be seen no more. But howere another scene now presented itself which turned the thoughts of the rioters away from. this sublime but terrific spectacle. The streets seemed to shake and tremble behind them. and ere they were aware a vast body of cavalry bloody with spurring fiery hot with haste. headed by the Marquis of Douro dashed boldly in among them. The Government had become aware of their movement and. had sent. 6000 men to disperse them. Now among the suprised rioters nothing was to be seen but utter consternation the horse-men had dashed in among them and where hacking them down by hundreds with frantic fury. they. threw themselves over the walls among burning ruins. burst in a thousand columns down every lane and alley burst impetously in thousands all down the grand street and in an hour had all evaporated. in the general mass of this mighty capital. when the first crimson light of Morning began to stretch through the darkness over the sea. no trace remained of the insurrection. but. the vast heaps of dead bodies covering the feild of fight the thousand peices of armour scattered through the city the houses standing with torn walls and glassless windows round the bloody area. and high over all in the dusky twi<light> the vast. blackned shattered pile

---

[15] Compare "Will be a Bed of Flames, that never can expire," Daniel Baker, "Judith," (1697) l. 147.

of towers and wall "the jail" torn riven. smoking and flaming like. a bursting volcanoe.[16]

CHAPTER. THE, IIId.   May 23, 1833

Reader let us escape from these bloody scenes and. stand here with me, We are in the open country the white mists of morning are softly and coolly rolling back into the stainless blue. and are beginning to fleck the sky with light fluffy. clouds. as these vapours ascend upward. they unveil the landscape before us and what is this Landscape. "it is the Glasstown VALLEY yes. backward and backward sweeps a wide a magnificent sea of verdure golden cornfeilds and hedges of glowing green intermixed with a hundered stately parks and a thousand statley Mansions <standing> white in the morning sun. each side of this plain undulating at first softly then bends up into a ridge of majestic and luxuriant hills long and high yet gentle and cultivated they sweep away through the sunshine toward the p<urp>led and golden horizon through this mighty and fertile valley winds statly on what at first looks like an arm of the sea but its pure glassy surface and the lofty palms and oaks intermingled feathering down to its margin at once destroy that likness it is a vast river it is the NIGER. rolling to the Glass town the collected waters of Africa, through this noble Valley and "at the sweet hour of dawn" the morning after the events recorded in our last chapter. their proceeded from the great Metropolis up the grand Northern road a man mounted on horseback. the reins were thrown loosley over the arched Neck of his steed whose appearance together with the costly equipments and above all the lofty and gracefull bearing of his rider betoken *both* each in his way to be of the "Salt of the land"[17] the mind of that rider seemed taken up intirely with something of great intrest and importance he neither looked around nor seemed to know wether it was night or morn fine or foull his aristocratic features bore impressed on them the marks of stern care and also I must add of deep dissipation no other expression hovered over them except what might be contained in one cold sarcastic smile which he gave as at one point of the road he turned his horse and. stopped to survey the city he had left. That city the Glasstown. lay about 13 miles behind him wrapped in <a> thick cloud of smoke and vapour which stretched along brown and murky over the whole southern horizon through its hazy curtain only 3 or 4 objects showed themselves such as the glorious tower of Nations and far far inward the Huge dome of St Michaels Cathedral.[18] but

---

[16] This incident may have its source in the reform riots of 1831 and the "Peterloo" massacre in Manchester, 1819. Compare Alexander CB, II, Part I, 98-99.

[17] "The salt of the land": proverbially the perfect, the best, the elect. Christ told his disciples they were "the salt of the earth" (Matthew 5: 13).

[18] The Rev. Mr. Brontë's church in Haworth was St.Michael's and All Angels.

what most attracted the attention of our Cavalier was the now fading now blackning piles of smoke which wreathing heavily through the haze denoted the spot where stood the yet consuming JAIL. he looked stead<ily> upon this for a moment and then with that bitter smile turned round his steed and went on his way. after proceeding several miles further through this Magnificent Valley he stopped at the splendid gat[e]way of an exstensive park which for a great distance lined the grand Northern road this gate was opened with wonderful alacrity by the bowing porters and he galloped swiftly up the sunny lawns and shady avenues. till he reached the front of a splendid modern Mansion here springing from his horse he desired of the servants to be shewn into the prescence of their master he was accordingly conducted through a gorgeous suite of apartments to the door of an extensive Library he entered at the upper end was seated at a table surrounded by immersed in piles of books papers and writing materials. the owner of all he saw, He was a man. of about 40 years old. gigantic in size firmly built and evincing vast muscular power. his hair of which he had a considerable quantity was even grey with study and hung wildly down over an immense. and knotty pile of forehead his eye was keen and restless shewing the true fire of Ambition his whole countenance was cast in the sternest mold. energetic harsh and repulsive shattered like his visitor by marks of deep dissipation The moment his guest entered he started up. and looked at him with great astonishment. "what Rougue" he said "you here too" "aye" replied Rougue for he it was whom we have followed on his journey "Aye Montmorency I am here but what mean you by saying too?" saying this he threw himself. languidly on the rich Indian sofa. Mr Montmorency[19] replied Oh why only. Ned Sydney." "Ned who?" asked Rougue starting up "Ned Sydney. the new member for Freetown". a frown of blackest and most tremendous appearance darkened the whole visage of Rougue as he replied. "Hang that viper and has he too started up to cross me!" "Oh" said Montmorency "dont take on so. the more difficultys encountered the more glorious our victory <why"> (with a strange smile) I could crush that one. with a word or too." "Not so" said Rougue the frown however passing of like Majic and giving place to his usual heartless sneer. "you havent seen the toads maiden speech made 2 nights ago you dont know his keeness. he's not like you Montmorency in body but he's something like you in soul."[20] His Host returned "Now there is nothing Elrington which I detest more than cant. and just now you seem about to fall into it. eh?" Rougue answered. "Stop. you saw smoke on the Horizon this morning well. the jail is on fire now. the 5 prisoners. threatened "They'd peach" an' we didn't "lause" <"em">. youll guess what followed" Montmorency at this hint started and his face assumed a yet darker expression "Well Rougue if it does get to light its all up with me." Rougue replied. "Now Mont to prevent undue disclosures would it not be best to make off with these fellows. Tweezy and the 5. I you know am going to our

---

[19] Scott's *Life of Napoleon*, VIII, 176 mentions a Montmorency among the French Royalist leaders after the capture of Paris in 1841.
[20] See Charlotte's "The Foundling," Alexander CB, II, Part I, 73-76.

firm in the Mountains Therefore Ill just leave you to supreintend all that buisness. you're going to the city. to light your lamp. so you can also attend at the same time to our bit of an affair. likewise eh? "I will My Man. but. let us see wether I've got anything in my cellar." answered Montmorency. and rung for the waiter his domestic appearing was ordered to bring forward. a large measure of. Wine and Brandy &c &c, in the interval these to Heros continued talking together in a strain so obscure and technical. that it would be usless to repeat their sayings. the "Spiritual Waters" having made their appearance in the form of 2 vast jars of brandy with several dozens of "the weaker brethren." Rougue and Montmorency by mutual consent set in to profound drinking. for a long time they continued to pour down amazing quantities of the "lush"[21] in perfect silence but in a while their faces became flushed their eyes flashed. and Montmorency first broke silence by uttering in a sotto voce tone. the words "dog dog" This expression Rougue understood as applied to himself. and he therfore first turning down. a glass of Brandy. cried in a rather louder voice "you hound you villain" Montmorency in return swallowed his drink with the words "Beast wretch scavenger" his guest answered him with a loud execration and then both together amid repeated draughts of brandy continued roars of imprecation and incessant shouts of cursing beheld the table floor & at length the whole room whirling about them. like a top till after dropping inumerable bottles and glasses and catching hold of everything around them they grappling with each other in a dying frenzy descended onto the floor amid. the "crash and tumult of tables and chairs hurled above them in promiscuos confusion. The Domestics who well knew what was likely to happen. in a while entered the apartment and conveyed each of these "Nobles of Nature" away to their quiet beds.

Here we shall leave them till the following morning at which time just as the Sun was rising over the glorious valley we behold Rougue mounting his horse at the hall doors with a firmness of step and brightness of eye which showed that such scenes as the one we have been describing were quite trivial with him. Montmorency stood by him to whom Rougue on taking his leave said. "Now Mont' my dove. you know my mind in this matter the upshot of our course conscerns yourself as much as me Therefore youll just do as I told you respecting. Our Gentlemen yonder Now you know were Im going and what I intend to do. And I say should I when I return find that youve played the oaf and slackened your wayes. Ill. why you shant have one farthing of our proceeds." "Wont I." returned Montmorency "you shall see wither I wont. but howsoever. that be. Ill do the thing to a toucher[22] If I light my own Lamp be sure Ill quench theirs. Adeiu my sweet one!" "Farewell My Darling" answerered Rougue as he turned his horses head and cantered merrily down the avenue.

He still continued his course toward. the North & up the glass town valley but he passed the splendid scenes which continualy met his eye without even once looking upon them or if he did it was with the vacant gaze which shows a

---

21 A slang term meaning "strong drink."
22 A slang term meaning "exactly."

mind concentrated upon some overwhelming theme within. in the evening he
arrived at Freetown. from which early next morning he started to proceed on his
journey. This day the scenery began to show symptoms of a speedy change.
First he left the greate vale for wide sunny fertile plain covered with feilds of
gold and trees of gold and fruits of gold then that plain began to raise itself into
long low wavy undulations like the billows of a rolling sea. and just as the sun
rested its flaming disk on the north west horizon takeing one look ere it left this
fairy scene and flinging its level rays all round the sky. Rougues peircing sight
perceived the summit of a long and distant range of mountains beneath the very
centre of the flaming light his stern features at the sight lit up with a freindly
smile for with no very refined feelings he yet adored and reverenced. the hills and
mountains. all other scenes but those of moors and wastes and rocks he with his
usual heat. and. decisiveness contemned and despised. But now so eager was he
to reach his beloved hills that all that night did he ride on without stop or rest.
and had not he and his horse both possessed a more than common share of
strength they would neither have found themselves as they did. when Morning
dawned on a wild. rocky heathy flat. elevated far above the smiling plains of
Ashantee which like a sea stretched back in the hazy behind them. while before
for many miles huge dull swells of heath rose one after the other in monotonous
succsession yet this speceis of scenery Rougue admired above any other. he had
long left the grand north road and striking on to a mountain path. prusued his
way along its unfrequented track. at every turn plunging farther and farther into
the mazes of the wilderness. But all these moors and turns were perfectly well
known to him and even to his horse. who with the reins suspended on its neck
while its master indulged in his reveries continued to trott on in the safest and
indeed the only path. This the fourth evening from his set out from the
glasstown. beheld him gain the summit of on[e] of the long swelling
Hummocks and the sight he saw from it was one which none could grudge
fatigue to veiw.[23]

far down before him swept the side of that hill. black with heath and mottled
with rock. no path. not even a solitary sheepwalk stretching over its face. it[s]
base was washed by the waters of a large and rapid brook. which after running
with a hundered turns through the rushy and marshy plain beyond dissapeared
among deep gorges and <a> confused heap of heathy hillocks. over this chaos
stretched moor after moor lying in mighty terraces one over the other and all
sloping on each side to the plain forming a wide and dark valley for the bed of
some great stream whose broad surface could be observed shining at intervals
amid the waste. Thus far the scene possest sublimity—more from its vast extent
its utter desolation than from any other quality but look forward and see what it
is that casts such a shade over this hill and landscape. The clouds are all rolling
of. into the sky. and gradually unveil first the skirts then the sides of a ridge of
enormous. mountains which sweep forward first and then far far backward. over

---

[23] Several words that are not part of the text appear in the bottom right-hand
corner of the MS page.

the whole extent of veiw. their height alone is terrible but much more <so> are their terrific chasms their white and hoary rocks their precipisces towering a thousand feet into the sky and their vast heads capt. with grey clouds and shining snow these alpine mountains are the "Robbers towers" and that great stream is "The Red River." Ah these scenes Rougue was well aquainted with. his past life had laid many of its acts among them. and every foot track could he trace amid their recesses were all as dark as the "Last night of Coomassiee"[24] but it is high time to return to our story. Rogue stopped a short time to veiw the vast piles before him and then descended the steep. it gave him small uneasiness to veiw the depth of the torrent before him he dashed fearlessly in. and after some hard struggles gained the opposite bank. and continued his way through the marsh amid sloughs and pools where had he not been accuratly aquainted with the place both he and his horse might have found sure stabling and a lasting home. soon he neared the wild raging waters of that King of hill streams—the red river and. here he stopped. for these were not waves to be passed. by a child no nor man either for with that red colour from which the stream is named they rushed onward. one over another. foaming and chafing the rocks and steeps beside them one would think that this opposed an effectual barrier to our travellers journey but it was not so he directed his steed a little way down the bank to the mouth of what seemed a gigantic badger hole or Otters den here he alighted and holding his horse by the bridle entered the gloomy cavity and dissapeared down ward not many minutes had elapsed when he again emerged on the other side. and continued his journey this hole ran along under the whole bed of the stream and ended like a tunel in an entrance or exit on the opposite bank. but. few knew of so great a convenience. when Rougue had arrived among the afore mentioned chaos of rocks and heath and hillocks lying at the bases of the Robbers Towers he halted his wearied steed. and gave a loud shrill whistle but who was their to answer the call all looked the extreme of desolation. a human foot seemed never to have trode or a human voice to have sounded amid this gloomy wild. Oh never mind for this. Rougue had scarcely ceased his whistle when it was answered by another from among the rocks and rubbish. shortly 2 men. armed at all points rushed toward Rougue. from. their hiding place when they. saw him distinctly nothing could exceed the astonishment. which seemed to overcome them. but he forbade speech and commanded them to take his horse to the stables they did this. with the utmost obsequience Rougue himself passed forward among the chaos. till he came before the entrance of [a] huge cavern. black as death. but scarcly <so> silent for from its inmost recesses came forth distant shouts and screams. and. peals of laughter Rougue walked still forward with the air of one well aquainted with every secret of this wild den. in a while. after threading many intricate passages. flashes of red light burst through the gloom and he speedily had his hand on the lock of a great iron door wich he opened quietly and silently. entering the apartment to which it led. stood unobserved a

---

24 Probably a reference to the poem "The Fate of Coomassie" listed on p. 332. There is, however, no evidence that Branwell actually composed this poem.

witness of the proceedings therein that apartment was a huge inner cavern of
great length and height the sides damp rock and the floor black clay at the
farthest end of this apartment roared up, a sort of chimney a huge bright red fire
of peat. which cast a crimsoned and unsteady light through the whole room
nearly from that fire to the door stretched a long oak table. covered with and
groaning beneath. immense dishes and covered <with> roast and boiled beef
mutton deer hares birds piles of bread and mighty jugs and casks and bottles of
Brandy rum whisky arrack, and beer. round this noble fare flashed a hundred
knives and daggers assaulting with eager fury its noblest bulwarks and brandished
by the brawny arms of. as many stern iron looking men of the rare lad. species.
with here and their a northern highlander interspersed these fellows beseiged the
bottom and sides of this table but the top was <governed> by men of different
appearance in the midst sat. a wretched withered feindish looking old man. little
in stature. dirty and clothed in [a] shabby tattered blanket this old wretch seemed
lord of this ample feast. at his right and left hands their sat about a dozen of tall
gentlemenly and officerlike men. dashingly dressed. but of sinister and recless
aspect evidently given up to the vilest dissapation. and prehaps the most lawless
courses for huge pistols were seen sticking in every belt. the knives all used.
were short poinards. and muskets bayonets swords and heaps of packages boxes
carpet with inumerable etceteras lay in wild confusion round the floors. while
Rougue stood concealed behind the door. a hundered conversations from high and
low. produced. the wildest disorder till the scarecrow at the head of the table. by
repeated knocks on the table and vast exertion of his screech owl voice produced
<a> slight cessation of this din. addressing one of those gentlemen on
<over> the fire place was printed in large characters "grand office of Rogue
< >[25] his right hand he said "now Carey. where do you intend to slump to
morrow" "Nowhere replied he "While I can see an ounce of meat or a stoup of
wine in this doghole of ours" "I fancied" said his superior grinning "that
Rougue set you such a spot of work to do while he was of as that if you left it
undone my but he vowed he'd blow your brains out." "let him hang it if I care
provided hell just fill the brain pan with a pint of whiskey. howsoever Ill not
stir from hence for you Sdeath. or that sour dog either" "listen gents" said a
second Gentleman on the left. one of a most deadly and ferocious aspect. "I say
supposing next time the whole rascal shows his face among us we all rise up at
once and each man aims. his. pistol at him till he blows up into the roof like a
foot balls you Sdeath would then be cheif. and I—". "I say" answered Carey
"supposing to practice *in* this pretty sport we now shall all rise and aim our
pistols at yourself O Connor till you smack into the earth like a leaden coffin."
Oh Carey" answered Sdeath. "you should say in a leaden coffin" Nay" answered
another "but we all-ways put our leaden coffins in to the man and not the man
into them." a roar of laughter followed this exquisite joke but O Connor was not
to be pacified by a jest. he first swallowing [a] draught of brandy started up and

---

[25] Because the page has been set in, the bottom line has been largely
obliterated.

clenching his sword cried. "Carey I say? what in the name of murder did you tell them to practise on me for why you thourough bloodhound I'd have you to know that for any such insolent jests Ill sliver you in peices like a turnip. draw you villain". Carey needed not that command but ere anyone could hold him he grasped his sword and dashed over the table at. his antagonist both were slashing and hacking at each other while the crowds stood round laughing fighting cursing and enjoying the fun. when Rougue. steped from his conc[e]alment and. advancing toward the antagonists. cried suddenly. "stop. there" that awful well known tone rung through the cavern recoiling on the hearts of all present and. the huge confusion in an instant ceased every man was amazed. and frightened Old Sdeath ran cowering into a corner and the 2 duellists each. opposite to the other stood. with. flashing eyes and bloody faces but not daring to continue their conflict. Rougue stepped up to the chair vacated by Sdeath. and. after taking a long long pull at a bottle of claret. called out "you Connor fo[r] Mutiny attempted against your leader and you Carey for creating disturbance in our community I here condemn and order to each of you straight way 500 strokes with a cart whip. such dirty conduct deserves a degraded punishment Lawless. and. Scroven do your office" These 2 gigantic executors of the Demagogues will came forward and bore their 2 sullen and determined culprits from the room to the place of punishment. Rougue meanwhile casting round him an eye of fire cried. "Sdeath I say where's Sdeath. the dog. the rascal. come here this moment." Sdeath appeared crouching and fawning upon his incensed superior. "Now" said Rougue "Why in the name of robbery have you in this manner disobeyed my orders. I told you I believe to send these villain[s] each upon his errand and yourself to go immediatly to the great seat of filth the Glasstown. you'll be wanted there sir I assure you." Sdeath replied. "what eh how what secret divulged oh. Ill go I'm of good day you'll serve my turn no more and that be the case." Rougue repiled by a dreadful kick which sent the old vermin yelling to his accustomed corner. But now "The night drave on wi sangs and clatter."[26] Rougue umpire of the feast poured down his throat torrents of the most fiery liquors. his Satellites followed faithfuly his example their inferiors lacked not in keeping up with them. barrels upon barrels were rolled into the hall and their being staved were at once emptied of the contents and incessant storm of conversation rung through the room intermixed with blows curses threats and execrations. the whole seasonably varied by a dozen or two of pistol shots stabs &c by which several men were killed or wounded. the morning had begun to dawn over the huge Robbers towers ere silence and sleep could obtain the ascendancy over those wild and ferocious men.

CHAPTER. THE, IVth.   July. 10. 1833

---

26 Robert Burns, "Tam O'Shanter," l. 45.

The sun was already blazing high over the hills of Sneakysland. ere Lord Elrington. awoke from his deep dead sleep. The fatigues and harrasing which he had undergone since the Night of the attack on the jail would have unhinged the frame of an ordinary man but on him they only produced an impression obliterated by. a single sound sleep. he arose. this day. stern strong and calm as ever. his mind filled with new projects and fresh schemes of iniquity

After conferring a while in private with Sdeath Carey Connor Dorn and Co. he took his gun and walked out to stroll in search of game among the banks and braes of the Robbers towers while wandering on the sides of these desolate hills observed at the distance of a musket shot from him a "rare ape" with "summat ur his back". From his tallness and the agility with which he moved Rougue conjectured that it was Ned Laury. he called him to him. Ned bounded forward and stood before him to receive his commands. "what in the name of Robbery have you got on your back". inquired Rougue ere Ned could speak his burden (but a light one.) lifted up a round rouguish face and a head of curly hair. and cried out. "Oh Rougue Im the Rev Peter Poundtext flying from the face of John Balfour of Burley[27] who is enshrined in the carcase of Arthur Marquis of Douro." "hem you little fool. when did you leave the city." asked Rougue with some earnestness. a few days ago the evening after the jail was tuk" replied. Lord Charles Albert Florian Wellesly!" "Oh replied Rougue you must come with me. to. our counting house. Ned you may locate yourself. by a brandy cask" Ned. bowed most obseqiously and. the three wended their path to the cave. on their road Charlie pulled from Neds pocket an octavo volumn and handed it to Rougue. "telling him to peruse it carefully for it was of his doing. and. he would see why he was flying from the sour puritanical milk sop his brother." Rougue opened the volumn it was the celebrated "Something about Arthur"[28] then just published. with great satisfaction for Rougue hated the Marquis of Douro did he read the mischeivous exposè theirin contained of several of that Young Noblemans earlier scrapes and frolic[s] so causticly told by his impish <brother On arriving at the cavern Rogue sent Ned> to the promised Brandy cask beconed Charlie. into an apartment where shutting the door. and offering him fruit &c he commanded him to relate the news of the City. Charlie though rather awed finding him self before so stern dark and dangerous a Nobleman. as Lord Elrington. began in his usual light mischeivous <chatter.> "Eh Rougue what a scrape youll get yourselfe into. Why my book came out the morning after the jail was burnt so that being engaged with my publisher in important buisness which you Rougue will not understand I had little time to inquire into the passing politics of an hour. however after breakfasting upon an onion. and 3 grey peas. I strolled to Ned Sydneys. I found him immersed in papers and newspapers sayd I to him sayd I. "Sydney my <nose> <isnt> blue this morning Im not cold to day. what a fire there is up by yonder <the kiln's> in a [b]low I am given to understand eh." Sydney cocked his eye and said some unutterable

---

27   See Sir Walter Scott's *Old Mortality*.
28   See Alexander CB, II, Part 1, 7-40.

nonsense about feindish rebellion. execrable treason bloodshed and so forth also cheeping much of Government secrets. quash the demagogue have hold on his nose. pull him where we like and much to that effect which has leaked through my memory Thereupon I arose and rode upon a wheelless chariot[29] to Elrington hall. intending to converse literarily with her ladyship. but her I found to much bound to affairs of the nether world. to listen unto my celestial language her words ran upon the actions of a certain person who shall be nameless. I remarked <suavely> that I cogitated he was hot enough himself. not [to] set ablaze the whole "urbs" or city in the vernacular. I affirmed that he scarcly possessed a "mens et animus"[30] <or> in the as the vulgate renders it. that he was a red mad Bedlamite. I remarked suavely that he ran much danger from his wild courses. and she being inclined <to> weep and lament so beautifuly pictured I the effigies of impeachments gallows bloody bodies bodiless heads. &c. that I. kindly hinted that one who was not a hundered miles from her possesed influence even in the highest quarters and that that influence he would use for the alleviation of punishments &c &c thence I departed to parade the city. For the purpose of seeing how my book worked and "Thus passed the day till evening fell. at which time I again honoured the paperworm Sydney with my prescence I beheld him now giving adieu to Lawyer Bud and a-nother Gentleman whom by his shovel hat lean figure keen visage and musty smell I calculated to be of the same proffession they all upon one casual glance by me vouchsafed to them. appeared to be conversing on political subjects The strange Lawyer more than once aye or twice either mentioned your name sir—and on the whole much of the confab seemed to turn upon your reputable procedures. But now at the witching hour of night when taking a turn through the street hearing the opinion of my opus. or in the received edition my book. mine orbs beheld. Arthur a tramping a stones cast distance. now his visual organs seemed so contracted and obverted and twisted. with feindish fury that though he beheld not me I for fear of co[n]sequences. called out to Ned Laury who I knew was departing for the far off Mountains of Sneakys land. to lend me hoist on his back bone for 2 or 300 miles or so & thou O Wretch knowest. the end.

Rougue could not resist laughing at the conclusion of this doughty speech but. he ceasing suddenly asked but with perfect calmness. what <likeness> was that Lawyer whom he saw with Sydney. "Oh a middle sized middle aged man hooked nose. brown face douce pate and <lean> carcase." Very well replied Rougue. now go to the rare apes in the Hall yonder amuse them with your chatter you may stay here till the storm has blow[n] over" So saying he led him to the hall. and as he himself turned back again he called. out. "Sdeath Carey Connor Dorn here this Instant" those celebrated personages followed him back to the little cavern. half drunk. and reeling from wall to wall. all being entered he shut the door "Haye" said Sdeath "What now. oh I see black as blood blown up divulged. Im off." "Silence" cried Rougue "Sdeath how are your shoes" "Why

---

29 i.e. his feet
30 Mind and spirit.

pretty well I think considering their with out bottoms" "Oh they'll do for that matter. but you know the road to the Glass Town" "Aye and you have a bottle with you" "Aye" "and a sharp knife" "Aye Aye" Well you old wretch. I fancy Tweezy has been or is about to let out now you've a heavy plan of preventing that. pass. this night tramp for the glass town. and—" "a feindish light gleam[ed] from the old wretches eye as he touched the haft of a Huge Knife which stuck in his belt he replied with a hateful chuckle. "Oh. my knife wants scouring its been to long in the sheath Ill give it some rust ointment. heh. but howsomdever the winds up and Sdeaths a cold.[31] Ill take. a draft or so just afore I tramp" Thus speaking he began to smell about the room with his twisted nose. and soon. scented a large Barrel of spirits from a corner he crept to it and with a strength far above its appearance rolled it into the middle of the floor. Connor Carey and Dorn whom thirst had kept silent now rushed in to share the spoil. and when Whisky had given them tongues began to volley forth oaths. and execrations sometimes. upon the liquor sometimes each other and often on their freinds in the far off city. Rougue standing above them poured down huge draughts in silence looking with his usual sarcastic smile upon his lieutenant and minions round him the darkness had come on and the clock was chiming ten when Rougue lent Sdeath a tremendous kick which hurled him to the farthest corner of the room and drove the good liquor out of his head. "Sdeath thou villian its time. Of tramp use your shuffle and that too with good effect. Sdeath got up took his hat and without seeming to give a thought to the length and fatigue of his journey went maundering and groping to the door of the cavern & then climbed his way up the hill side and was lost in the darkness. He being gone Rougue and his Satellites adjourned to the <great> cavern or Hall where around an ample Mountain Feast were ranged. as I have before related. the hundred inmates of this suspicious dwelling. after eating and drinking till a late or rather an early hour Rougue started up. and cried out "Now my lads lets have a little sword play let Fifty go to this side and Fifty to that. and then well begin.—But I must here leave our hero and his gang in the enjoyment of the fiery and dangerous sport.

CHAPTER Vth.   PBB. August 5th[32]

The early dawn of another morning beheld the dwellers in this mysterious cavern assembld on the tongue of land formed by a bend in the river and attentivly listening to the commands of their leader who standing on the summit of an emptied beer barrel thus addressed them "Gentlemen we have been to long idle. and must pay for that sloth with intrest O Connor take 10 men. you know where

---

[31] An echo of Poor Tom's lament in *King Lear*, Act III, Sc. iv, l. 55.

[32] This manuscript page is written over various small sketches, including rivers, a castle on a hill, a country scene of hills, fields and a gateway, and a leg projecting from the left side of the page.

Carnac[33] lies return in two days Dorn with 10 of you march in to the south and back in the same time Carey with your 10 take this letter of instruction open it on the second day from hence march you allong the confines of this country down from the Nevada to Parrys Glass town. you'll see what must be done there and now let 20 men the quickest sighted among you. take post upon the heights just yonder. in differnt spots keep hid observe attentivly communicate your observations faithfuly for the rest this our receiving day. and we expect news from various quarters therefore we must remain in the halls. now away to your posts"—thus speaking Rougue dismounted from his eminence and entered his room while his minions each prepared their troops and well armed but with little provision set out upon their different mercantile expidations. in an hour or two. a messenger arrived on horse back from the south. he was ushered into Rougues apartment. where he continued some time. this man was followed by partys and posts from a hundred different quarters but all from seemingly a great distance. in fact the whole of this day Rougue neither had nor allowed himself to have. a minutes rest from his toils of office. and ere supper time his room was crammed with the huge heaps of papers boxes and dispatches and. the glasstown publications the latter class of parcels he did not open untill having declared that he would not sup in the hall he had sat down a little freed from his press of buisness before his writing desk. and a flask of powerful brandy. with his usual supercilious sneer he drew toward him those bales marked "from the G G town" and opened them one after another, displaying their literary treasures before him he first eagerly seized upon the Glass town or Monthly Iintelligencer[34] dated just after he had escaped from the city and burnt the jail with a sneer thrice refined he looked over its account of that catastrophe. and perused its puzzled expressions of doubt and uncertainty as to the reasons of the arch demagogue for this atrocious act. from this portion of the news his eyes glanced to a letter signed "J T—y. and which ran as follows

Sir I would advise the public to look closely to that seat of vice and villainy Elrington hall Circumstances will shortly perhaps transpire that may make clear the reasons for this my advice

Yrs J— T—y.

This letter was short and indefinate but Rougue read it over a second and third time and then slowly taking from his pocket a little black book with steel clasps he marked in it with a pencil "John Tweezy—death" and proceeded calmly to look over the other paragraphs in the paper. till his eye rested on the notice of "Lord Ronan" the new poem from the pen of Marquis Douro.[35] he hastily opened the packet marked books and fling[ing] out heaps of Phamphlets tracts and volums all published during the few days of his abscence from the glasstown he at length lit upon the work he sought for holding it by the leaves

---

33 Carnac, a small village in the Bretagne region, western France, is famous as the site of more than 3,000 prehistoric stone monuments.

34 See p. 250 above.

35 See the list of publications on p. 332 below, and Neufeldt PCB, 106.

at arms length he surveyed with a bitter sneer it[s] gilt leaves embossed cover
and the name on the back he then opend it and rapidly looked over its glorious
pages now and then stopping at particular passages which he read twice or thrice
over upon laying down the book he exclaimed "very well this wont do" and rung
the bell violently. a minion entered to whom he said get my horse ready by
midnight and be gone you hog" the man departed Rougue for a while paced up
and down the room in deep thought and then by an effort set himself at his desk
to close up as he termed it our arrears. and to answer the thousand letters received
that day and now lying beside him the answers were most remarkable for their
astonishingly laconic expression for instance to a letter requesting to be informed
when the writer should "lead his clerks" to the firm. at W. GT.[36] and when to
the Sierra Nevade. Rougue merely answered.

> Grand Firm
> for <S.L.>
> M— 33:

Sir
WGT—May 21.
S—N—June 3.

> Rougue. C.

To another letter from "Off Fidena wishing to know when Rougue would visit
that "Office" he merely answered by. a scolloped line intimating that it would be
doubtful when he should come for such were the symbols used by this
mysterious and suspicious trading company. In fact to cut all short the directions
of these letters were allway[s] longer than the letter itself. yet with all this speed
and. brevity it was long past Midnight ere Rougue had concluded his
voluminous correspondence he arose then and. ordered minions to see that they
were dispatched <immediately> and anticipating mishap . . . he swallowed some
food[37] together with a pint bottle of Brandy he without further preparation
mounted his horse and. by the light of the early dawn. ascended the hills and
galloped out of sight.

CHAPTER. VI.   August 6th. <1833>

The stranger who on a summers day passes through one of the principal streets
of the Great Glass town. upon observing the mighty crowds and shoals of
carriages horses foot passengers and persons of every clime and character all
'mingling & blending together. flying and running and riding first this way than
that crossing and recrossing jostling sidling retreating and advancing in a

---

[36] Wellington's Glass Town.
[37] Again much of the top line of the page has been obliterated.

thousand different places and a thousand seperate ways each among the inumerable countenances lighted up by a <different> passion and all at once speaking and shouting and cursing in Babylonic chaos. that person I say would upon coming unawares upon this astonishing spectacle would did he not himself become confused to think. fancy that. one. mighty spell. from the. assembled Genii had. brought all the inhabitants of the world together struck at once by fatal and frantic madness. I myself have often stood wondering admiring and speculating upon the enormous groups. thus daily exhibited. yet always. after a little thought and observation I have found each person whom I saw pursuing his own distinct and definite aim Come here to day and observe with me. look for instance at that magnificent young Noble Man who so truly bears out his rank dashing in his gorgeous chariot through the crowd of plebiens and scattering them like mud on every side. his object is first to exhibit himself to the eyes of a wondering people secondly to make haste to his publishers shop and thirdly to keep within the hour his appointment at. "M". Eat him up stoop and roops"[38] new Elysium. for Gentlemen who love to moult. the superflous" next veiw that shoal of. fragments from this principal block. a hundered chariots guided by a hundred sprigs of Nobility. each directing his eye <to>their great Original and and copying from him their every move and motion. leaving out the affair of [the] publisher these young Nobles have the same decisive end in view as him. next see that slow corpulent Gentleman. on horseback. lo how he hastens on his way how he turns up his nose in to the air as if he smelled his quarry from afar This one is going to a grand dinner to feed upon fat and flattery. Then. see that knot of men on foot pacing with knitted brows. and compressed mouths along <the path> way. each copying the motions of. that youth before them upon whose visage care and study [h]as placed every wrinkle <often> these are states men politcians men who hold the affairs of Africa at their tongue and fingers end. Their road lies toward a cabinet council or to the house of parliament— following the same road look at those three men walking arm in arm tall and military. The middlemost. firm and strong and of searching aspect the right hand. one taller but more stooped marked by age and of a cautious and a sarcastic appearance the left hand one. much like this save. more upright and of a franker aspect these three are Kings[39] and it scarce behoves us to speak of their motions. Then interspersed among all these whom I have sketched you see soldiers and officers in full uniform racing and galloping about helter skelter. yet each on an aim some to late on parade. some to early from parade others agoing to Elysium others again going to a different <speices> of Elysium this one riding to a meeting and those are hasting as seconds to the same meeting then veiw the plebains the crowds of poachers and Rare Apes. with movements

---

[38]   An adverbial phrase in Scottish and Northern dialects, meaning "completely" or "entirely," e. g. in Scott's *Black Dwarf*, "we are ruined stoop and roop." See also Alexander CB, II, Part II, 106.

[39]   Three of the four kings whose kingdoms constitute the Verdopolitan Confederacy.

eccentric as those of so many comets yet each attracted or repelled by his peculiar sun. one <party> with stern and ferocious aspect about to assault a mill[40]. others looking gaily toward the country and cocking the guns for the far off moors. thinking while in the streets of "Regina" of the Heath cock now crowing in the pride of power on the wild steeps of Aornus[41]. or the heaths of the Robbers towers but <soon> doomed to lay his anointed head as low as death before the unerring shot of a Scroven or a Naughty. but Reader he with whom we have most at present to do with is yon. young man walking by himself along the path. he is well aye dashingly dressed and seemling aged not much above 20. his unbronzed cheeks. accomodating manners and the want of that fiery eagerness in the eye which carachterizes our young Nobility proclaim him perhaps but latley returned from the Philosophers Isle but the manner in which he stops to reconnoitre through his eyeglass every "stand up" "pausing toss" or "dashing chariot race" pending in the streets. shew that he is game and will ere long be a passable glass[42] town youngster. But to return to our narrative this promising young fire worshipper passing through several streets and turning down a dark lane at length stopped before the corner door of a range of old mean looking houses dark damp and dirty that door was worn and rotten yet strange to relate during the few minutes during which he had stood by it no less than 9 or 10 persons had entered all of whom from the outward man seemed to belong to the very elite of the city. in a little while. an old man little mean and of shabby attire stepped up and motioning to our hero opened the door and entered the house he followed this guide through a multitude of dark musty passages and cold windowless rooms untill the[y] reached not a poor unfurnished apartment but a very large and lofty hall paved with marble and decrorated with furniture of old and shining oak. round this room were placed rows of hat stands whose fruit. for its abundance amazed our uninitiated hero. but he had only time to notice that but one wax taper illuminated. this this spacious hall and that its doors and walls were so thickly coated with matting that sound from another room how ever loud could never penetrate here. when he was lead by his elfish guide to a door at one end to which the old dog applied a key from his pocket it instantly flew open and shuch a blaze of glory burst upon their eyes as for a moment caused the young nobleman to start back in astonishment but his companion more accustomed to the sight urged him forward and himself entering closed the portal. They were on the threshold of a vast and gorgeous room. with-out windows but lighted by a long range of splendid chandeliers whose branches and drops sparkled like diamond and gold the floor was covered by the richest carpets the wall hung with crimson and purple. velvet sofas rosewood and ebony tables luxurious and yeiding ottomans were placed round the room and down the middle. from top to

---

[40] A reference to the Luddite attacks in the early nineteenth century.

[41] See p. 193, n. 3.

[42] Between "glass" and "town" are eight canceled lines, which are almost identical with the first eight lines of p. 5 of the manuscript, suggesting Branwell is using a page on which he had made an earlier false start.

bottom was ranged two long long tables. with on each side a corresponding side board. on these side board[s] were heaped bottles goblets glasses fruit confectionary gold silver chrystal in magnificent confusion round the tables were seated or standing crowds of MEN. in appearance and carriage worthy the name vast in their numbers. of the highest ranks judging from their appearance. none of them past the middle age. they were head over ears engaged in deep play. Flushed already by the splendour and excitement of the scene our hero turned to his companion. and asked was this a public or private dwelling "its no dwelling at all you yong foal. answered the old wretch in gruff snarling tone. as if envying the gaiety life and manliness he saw around him. but his voice was heard at the tables and in an instant a hundred heads were turned to the door "Sdeath you here what have you got there?" asked a hundred voices "Sdeath in the name of murder cried a stern deep voice and Montmorency rushed from the table toward him. they spoke together for a few minutes in an under tone and then Montmorency laying his iron hand on the arm of the young nobleman and. drawing toward the tables said "Gents. ho. waiter a glass of. something Gentlemen. a young sprig here latly sprouted. wants to be planted in the gardens of Paradise. another glass I say Im murdered with thirst. youll admit him into Elysium.[43] Ive no doubt. grand pluck. 20,000 per ann. hem hem Volo if you laugh Lofty Ill smash your brain pan.". "his Name" asked A tall young Man. of an Eagle aspect who was seated. at the head of one of the tables "Out with it you blockhead." cried Montmorency "Fork it you scurvy lumbering degenerate loathsome dirty—" here his volley of imprecations was stopped by a stunning blow on the mouth from the fist of our yong hero. who. though flustered and shy at first began to show evident tokens of "pluck" upon being called in this manner. a roar of laughter from. the. lofty bystanders. made him however relapse again in to his former bashfulness. "Well done capital youve got it Monty a dog this. something decent here" was ejaculated by. the gentlemen round and the tables were deserted in order to veiw the "young dove give play" "Gentlemen. said our hero. gazing upon the crowds of stern supercilious countenances. gazing at him "I am here unknown and unaccquainted with your proceeding or society. but I must say that the manner in which I have been treated would be disgraceful if used to the lowest and most degraded Inhabitit of our city. I declare to you that. if anyone among you intend to amuse yourself at my expense he must do it armed. and out of range of my pistols shot! as he said this drawing out at the same time a brace of firearms. the laughter was redoubled. and that officer like Gentleman who asked his [name] pushing back the crowd laid hold of his arm and said "young man we see that you possess pluck. Follow me and we'll initiate you." So saying and at the same time. in spite of his resistance.

---

[43] A secret male club in Verdopolis, presided over by the Marquis of Duoro and Lord Elrington—see the Glossary. The "Noctes Ambrosianae" in *Blackwood's Magazine* took place in Ambrose's Tavern, Elysium. Ironically, in Greek mythology the name refers to the abode of the blessed. For further information on Branwell's interest in secret societies, see Barker Brontës, 192.

wrestling from him his pistols with an ease which showed his muscular strength. this Nobleman hurried our hero through the room to a door on the opposite end which was opened and they entered a small apartment fitted up like a Chapel with the most costly decorations the gallerys pews and so forth were rosewood and the Altar was ornamented with the most gorgeous gold and velvet to this altar they lead him. and the lofty Nobleman before mentioned ascending the Steps. said. "Young Man what is your Name.?" "My Name is Viscount Castlereagh."[44] "Your age." "21" "You I have no doubt can guess some of the purposes of this society but others you can not. however they will appear in time therefore I need scarce detail them here. This society is called the "Elysium or Paradise of Souls" and here are our rooms of assembly. no one can enter unless he prove himself above the age of 18 are you so"? "I am". perfect in limbs and without deformity. Are you so" "I am" one who has once in his life slain a man have you?" "I have". "Worth at least 5000 a year. are you so" "I am". born a glasstowner are you so "I am" Very well then <Connor. . . to him>[45] that you will never under any pretence whatsoever violate the rules of this society abscond from or disclose the least matter connected with it." "I swear." "rise then Frederic Viscount Castlereagh. a member of the Elyisium or Paradise of Souls. you. Montmorency. write down the entry in our book. and now sir before we go in to the hall I will tell. you the Officers of our bo<dy>

President. Alexander Rougue Viscount Elrington.
Vice president Myself. who am Arthur Wellesly Marquis of Douro
Treasurer. Edward Lofty. Viscount Lofty.
Secretary. Hector Matthias Mirabeau Montmorency. Esq[r]

---

[44] Robert Stewart (1769-1822), Viscount Castlereagh and the Marquess of Londonderry from 1821, was the son of an Anglo-Irish landowner who, elected to the Irish parliament of 1790, embarked on a controversial political career. His tenure coincided with two important events in Irish history: the 1798 Irish rebellion which, as chief secretary for Ireland (succeeding Thomas Pelham), Castlereagh quelled through the use of military force, and the union of Ireland with England which he engineered in 1800. On joining the British War Department after Ireland's political union with England, Castlereagh, as Secretary of War, then Foreign Secretary, reorganized the regular, reserve, and militia forces, thus providing Britain with a more efficient army for overseas operations against Napoleon, and secondly secured the command of his countryman Arthur Wellesley for the Peninsular expedition. In 1812, upon Perceval's assassination, Castlereagh became leader of the House of Commons, and as such was identified with the repressive policies of 1815-19, for which he was attacked by liberal Romantics such as Byron and Shelley, most notably in Shelley's "The Masque of Anarchy." Clearly, Branwell's representation of Castlereagh is less harsh than that of other contemporaries.
[45] Part of the top line of the manuscript page has been obliterated.

Under Secretary. George Charles Gordon. Esq^{r46}
Officer of the Houshold. John Flower. Esqr
Usher. Robert Patrick. Sdeath.

Champions
Richard Naughty. First
Edward Laury. Second.
Jean Pigtail. Third
Thomas Scroven Fourth

:Council for A D 1833
James. Marquis of Abercorn.
Robert Henry. Viscount Molineux.
Richard Carey Esqr
Arthur O Connor. Esqr
Edward Geoffrey Stanley Sydney Esqr

The assembled multitude now rushed from the chapel into the hall where they saluted each other with cries of "whats to be done to night." "Stake" replied the Marquis of Douro who presided in the abscence of Rougue. crowds instantly collected round the table while others sauntered about the splendid room conversing turning over portfolios. or through the glasses quizzing the company several of the political cast were diligently perusing news papers or quaffing large draughts from the side board. the Marquis was playing. Hazard[47] with Castlereagh. for 1 or 2 guinea. points. but the Hawklike glance with which he now and then looked at him. boded ill to the luckless pigeon. Montmorency had drawn Sdeath to a corner of the side board here they were deeply engaged in stirring two stiff rummer[s] of punch. "Sdeath" said Montmorency "I though[t] my dear that you were off at the firm" "No you fool I have been but dye think Ill keep. there all.—" "Silence your grumbling I say Sdeath were endangered. does Rougue know of it. Oh there are 2 fellows at yon board the eagle and the wren whom I could crush crush. hah. and. Ill will crush. them yet. but what do you think. our Law—" "Hush you hound" muttered the old wretch Sdeath "look ye here." and so saying with the usual gleam of cold grey eyes he touched with his withered. finger a dagger protruding from his waistcoat pocket. "thats the mission Rougue sent me on" with a feindish laugh he. drunk off his tumbler and. retired from the room. Montmorency was not puzzled at Sdeaths broken sentences he grinned took a pinch of snuff and walked to the back of a Noblemans chair. from whence he could veiw at leisure the hundred striking countenances ranged round the table. here were no women faces no vapid fashionable. lounging visages. true there were hansome ones in plenty but all

---

[46] George Gordon were Lord Byron's Christian names.
[47] A game of chance played with dice.

presented stern corrugated. brows keen eyes and mouths with endlessly varied expression. Montmorency turned his eye to where stood the magnificent form of the Marquis of Douro. who risen from his <chair was> attentively watching the progress of a stake with Arthur O Connor <often he> passed his hand across his lofty forehead. and over his aching eyes. for not only to night was he involved in. the whirl of passion but for nights before had he been engaged in the house of parliament combating all most unaided the assaults of a bitter and formidable faction. or involved in a wide whirlpool of politics. fashion and dissipation." Montmorency thought as he bent upon him his stern searching eyes. "Ha that youngster moust slacken it wont do to run on at this pace the sword will wear out its scabbard I wish. it would I do" "by the Marquis was seated O Connor whose form and countenance presented the wrecks of a mind. and person originally of the highest order but. now worn & harrassed by the <warring> passions degraded by. the use of everything mean and low. from him Montmorency glanced to a figure at another end of the table. <slightly girlish> and seemingly of small account in life. but. ah Montmorency knew <the mind> the talents the vast Ambition the determined spirit which dwelt in his antagonist. Edward Sydney then he passed his eye over the hansome and fashionable figure of Lord Lofty the. wild dissipated forms of Abercorn and Molineaux. and the dark gloomy countenance of. Secretary Gordon. last he took a long keen look at young Castlereagh. and as he surveyed him. over and over he muttered "hah. Ill have that youngster yet he too shall not fall to the share of that cursed omnipotent." at this moment two men started from the table. and tottered to a side board. where one of them took vast draughts of brandy but the other with trembling hand snatched a pistol and blew his brains out all present at the report turned their heads round but most of them with a scornful laugh turned again to their absorbing employment the Marquis of Douro cried "off with him" and two gentlemen. took up this lamentable victim. to. gambling. and hauling him on the shoulders dissapeared through a dark passage Castlereagh laid down his cards and shuddred he looked at the hundreds round him but not in one could he see an emotion answering to his own all were absorbed in the hopes fears or desparars of their tremendous occupation. & <saw> the Marquis of Douro scrape together with a smile of joy. a huge heap of gold the produce of a nights winnings from O Connor. who said with the utmost nonchalance as he rose from his chair heres my last farthing the last ounce of 70 or 80000£ but I'll. off for a day or so and then return with—" so saying he took his hat and strode out of the room. at this moment the door opened and. there entered a man of lofty stature who strode into the apartment. dashed his hat onto the floor and emptied at a draught a whole bottle of brandy. Montmorency started back the whole company rose aghast it was Alexander Rougue. he seemed raised to an appalling passion his hand shook. his eyes. flashed. and his hair was wild and disordered as if returned from some long and harrassing journey The moment he saw the Marquis of Douro. w[h]o stood gazing at him with a Wellingtonian smile. he advanced toward him elevated his Iron Fist and dashed it into the Marquis face who. fell back with violence his countenance covered with blood. the whole apartment rose in an uproar but. Arthur rising pushed back the crowd and threw his coat to Sydney charging him to stand by as second Rougue. cast of his coat and threw it to the first Bystander who happened to be. Castlereagh. to him Rougue said. "now. young man. you're my second. Mont. my love. hold the bottle." Montmorency obeyed. the bystanders cried out laughing and joking a ring a ring. it was formed. and every one gathered round in the highest expectation to see their President and his vice. "stick it into one another like men of the real stamp." in the whole city there were not known two men who for blood. mettle and science could. in the slightest compete with these 2 renowned Noblemen.[48] they scarcly needed the preparations for the fight but the moment that. their arms were free. and shirts sleeves turned up they put themselves in attitude. and set too. the Marquis had the advantage of the Lord in youth and vigour and his well compacted and supple frame promised well contrasted with the shattered. and decayed. nerves of his Antagonist but. Elrington was the taller the more seasoned of the 2. their arms were epitomes of themselves. the Marquis of Douro's well made fleshy. a fine display of round muscles. and light as a bird in action. Lord Elrington made bare 2. long bony arms devoid of muscle or flesh. but sinewy and nervous to an amazing degree hard as oak. and garnished with fists that scarce needed the aid of gauntlets dead silence was observed you might have heard a pin drop. when Rougue. with a quick glance of caution. darted at the Marquis. a tremendous. facer. which however Arthur beautifully parried and like lightning popped Rougue a dig at the ribs which made them sing like a bell. Rougue staggered but threw his shot. right and left. ending with a blow upon Arthurs. collar that dashed him onto the ground with the victor over him. Arthur. scorned this and began round second. by a cautious guard of his person and. a toucher on Rougues smeller which brought out a beautiful stream of claret. first blood was cried. for the Marquis and. the Odds for him were 3 to 2 Rougue with much malice aimed allways at Arthurs face which malice was returned by his Antagonist with intrest. soon their eyes became black as the Midnight their lips red as coral. their cheeks like those of a Milkmaid. Rougues. face made less show than that of his enimy for the extreme dryness and scantiness of flesh could not bring much blood or bruise but after the 1st hour and the 30 round. he began to shew evident signs of exhaustion. while the vigour and youth of the Marquis. bore the fight in an exquisite manner. the battle displayed perfect sience. and vast powers of endurance. yet after the second hour. fatigue and dissipation began to tell visibly upon the shattered powers of Lord Elrington his falls were more frequent. he was generally undermost. and. the heat and passion with which he had entered the ring. did him damage contrasted with the Wellingtonian coolness of the Marquis. but now neither could stand unless in active fight. they seemed unconscious. of. what they were doing and only to continue the combat from the instinct of surprassing courage. and in the 3d hour of the combat and the 91st round. Arthur opening his eyes or at least one eyes. gave Elrington a hit on the. "cellar door" that dashed him back onto the ground with the Marquis sensless above him both

---

[48] For Branwell's love of boxing, see p. 178, n. 11 above.

were taken up by their seconds quite lifeless and laid on two sofa's "My eyes" said Montmorency. "they must have been mad to choose such seconds look how Castlereagh trembles and as to that hound volo."[49] he rushed up to him. and inflicted upon the young member Sydney such a kick as. hurled him across the room. "ho" cried Lord Lofty "sits the wind in this quarter." and. he snatched a pistol from the sidboard with the intent to set Mont asleep. in an instant. a scene of confusion followed which it would be in vain to describe. our yong hero Castlereagh albeit he enjoyed such work amazingly felt the weakness of unpractised nerves and was tossed about with the combat. stunned and bewildered. untill the bell of St Michaels tolled Four in the morning and. this being the hour. for departing. by the rules of the society. an universal rush commenced out of the room through the long long passages and into the street. Castlereagh was borne foremost and ere he knew anything of the matter he found himself. propelled into a mighty square. in the raw fresh dawn of returning daylight.

Capt Flower[50]

END OF THE..\·
IST VOL.

[ornamental figure]

P B Brontë
Aug. 17. 1833.

---

[49] Volo: an exclamation regularly used by Branwell's male characters, possibly deriving from the Latin *volo* ("I am willing"). Alternatively, "volo" may be a contracted expression of motion—"Let's fly" or "Let's go."
[50] Both this signature and Branwell's below are in longhand.

REAL LIFE IN VERDOPOLIS.

A TALE.

By Captain John Flower Mp. &c.

IN TWO VOLs.

∴ VOL. IId.

PB Brontē
Aug. 17th
CHAPTER. I. α   AD 1833

BEFORE we proceed farther with our tale. we must endeavour to recapitulate sundry political events of the day and to retie the thread of our narrative It was evident that in the fact of Rougue being a declared robber. there was more than met the eye. he either carried on his operations in a different way or upon a different scale than men generaly suppossed. and our readers must have seen. that he scarce wished his actions to be scrutinized or known. how it was for fear of undue disclosures that he. liberated the 5 prisoners and burnt the jail. but this maneuver being contrary to law he was forced to fly from it to the "Office in Sneakland. of "The Firm of ROUGUE Montmorency Sdeath and Co" or in plain terms the den for recieving the goods stolen by the worthies above mentioned. here he remained. till sundry hints in the papers convinced him that his Emissarys in the city were scarcely playing him fair. and. till he read the poem "Lord Ronan" by the Marquis of Douro.[1] a peice directed against him. these things put Rougue into a flame he left his mountain cavern. rode post haste to the Glass town and. entered. the moment he alighted. the rooms of that Society of which he was president. here he saw the Marquis of Douro whom unable to contain his fury. he violently assaulted a battle was the consequence and our readers know the result. Now with relation to the political posture of present affairs we must observe that the Great Glass towne. countriey are and were divided into t[w]o grand parties the ARISTOCRATS. consisting of all men of Rank wealth. and standing headed by the 12s. and the DEMOCRATS. consisting of the lower orders poachers rare apes and &c with various Dissipated. broken or Ambitious men. soured by merited mishaps and burning against all those. whose luck was fairer than their own This party was headed by Alexander Rougue Viscount Elrington and in spite of its worthless materials comprised much. Energy talent. and. firmness compresed in the persons of its Leader, Montmorency. Gordon O Connor Carey and several others. to counterbalance which the other party brought in. the Marquis of Douro Mr Sydney. Lord Lofty. Capt Flower. Capt Goat and many other men of powerful and active talent. at the period. of which I write. these two parties were in active array against each

---

[1] See p. 286.

other and the height to which political feeling had risen boded. mighty and. lasting evils to the state and and country But after making these necessary explanations we must return to our tale.

CASTLEREAH upon finding himself thrown from the mouth of this volcano in to the midst of the open city. paused to take breath and recover his stunned senses. when he looked round he found himself in the midst of a mighty square. in heaven the night was just retiring from the day and while over head the stars peeped. out and the clouds look[ed] black cold and night like in the horizon the red and yellow lines stretching and fadeing round the sky betokened that Morning was now near at hand. in the city no smoke yet curleing above the houses. announced the busy hour of Dawn. But the countless buildings of Verdopolis all stood. cold and raw. with their dark outlines standing out from the crimsoned sky. The mighty palaces round him frowned aloft in sombre shadow. and the rising wind swept round their walls and howled down the long deserted streets. Castlereagh knew that his Hotel was yet locked up and that there [he] could scarce gain admittance he therefore paced down the street. starting at the distinct ehoe of his footsteps and stopped on the parapet of the great Bridge. to survey the gradual unfolding of another day. as the clocks of the city chimed 4 and 5 Mortals began to rouse from their beds First there appeared the. Rare apes going forth with their guns on their shoulders to their early sports and employments then the Naval men with all connected with shipping moving toward the quays and harbours. then the windows of the houses gradualy opened the shops unfolded like flouers a horse or two pattered along the streets a troop or two of cavalry a file of infantry going to a parade. in a while the hum became louder the smoke curled across the city and Castlereagh when he reflected upon the late darkness and silence. could not help feeling astonished to veiw. the rapidity with which the sun blazed out in heaven. the shadows dissapeared and the whole city glistened and thundered. and shook with life light and. the bustle of its millions of inhabitants an hour ago and not a living be[i]ng had passed across the darkened bridge now as the sun glinted over its parapets what thousands of carts and horses carriages and. chariots foot passengers and merchandise of every clime and country teemed incessantly over its expanding arches. it now seemed as if soomer[2] mighty the vast waves below him cease to flowe forward than the tide ov Mortal above. dissapear and be still. Castlereagh yawning frequently for the night had to him been a rough and sleepless one. returned to his hotel and passed his time dozing on the sofa untill breakfast was announced. During that day he remained principaly indoors untill toward Evening a Note arrived addressed to him and datied "Sydenham Hotell. Georges Street. GGT."[3] and was from the pen of Mr H M M Montmorenci in its purpo[r]t it requested him nay commanded him to. dine at. his house that Evening. Castlereagh. ordered his carriage and. drove of to the Hotel. upon his announcing himself he was shown by a footman into a Library furnished. in the highest

---

2   "as if sooner the mighty" probably intended.
3   Great Glass Town.

style of Elegance and which was the study of of its farfamed. Owner no one was
in the room. but the open desk loaded table and. instrument of writing showed.
[th]at it had but just been vacated. Castlereagh curious to see the line of reading.
prusued by Montmorency approached this table. and examined the books thereon.
the first he took up was a Greek copy of "Lucians Dialogues" finly bound and.
bore on the flyleaf the words written. "Alex. Elrington. to. Hector Montmorency
<read> this book mark learn and inwardly digest. Ap. 1. 1830."[4] under this lay
odd volumns of Voltaire Rousseau.[5] the 2 vols of Humes History containing the
English Revolution 1630. to 60. Mignets & Thierry's French Revolution[6] Leafs

---

[4]   See p. 270, n. 9.
[5]   Voltaire (1694-1778) achieved fame as a "philosophe" who crusaded against
tyranny, bigotry, and cruelty, especially religious intolerance and persecution. He
was an early member of the free-thinking society, The Temple; was imprisoned
for one year in the Bastille for mocking the Duc d'Orléans; and spent two years
in England (1726-28), patronized by the court of Queen Anne and political and
literary figures of the day. On his return to Paris in 1729, Voltaire turned to the
relatively new literary genre of history, and over the course of his life, in
addition to writing plays and philosophical tracts, wrote the *Histoire de Charles
XII (1731)*, *Essay sur les Moeurs* (1740), *Le Siècle de Louis XIV* (1751), *Précis
du sièle de Louis XV* (1768), and the *Philosophie de l'histoire* (1765). Toward
the end of his life he was attacked by the followers of Rousseau who decried the
rational philosophy of the "Philosophes." During the century following his
death, his radical ideas were held to have been largely responsible for the French
Revolution.

Jean-Jacques Rousseau (1712-1778) propelled political and ethical thinking
into new channels. In urging parents to regard and educate children differently,
and to give scope to the expression of emotion over polite restraint in works
such as *Émile* (1762) and *Confessions* (1782-89), his philosophies mark the
emergence of Romantic thought. His main tenet that people's natural goodness
is corrupted by external forces—the demands of civilization—is developed in
such works as *Discourse on the Origin of Inequality* (1755) and *The Social
Contract* (1762). This latter work, beginning with its powerful opening
sentence, "Man was born free, but he is everywhere in chains," proposes a
radically alternative basis for a new social order grounded in political and
personal liberties.

[6]   David Hume (1711-1776), the Scottish empiricist philosopher, historian,
and economist, wrote the *History of England (1754-62)*, a survey extending
from Caesar's invasion to the Civil War. While attempting new standards of
"impartiality," this history was also remarkable for offering, more than simply
an account of the deeds of kings and statesmen, a map of Britain's intellectual
and cultural development. Hume's history gained a wide readership, with at least
fifty editions being published between the time of his death and 1894. During
the 1760's, Hume was also passionately engaged in the debate over the
authenticity of James Macpherson's *Ossian*.

Wars with the Genii. several Vols relating to.the Roman Commonwealth. from Gracchus to Marius and Sylla.[7] well fingered and opened one or two other books but what gave. our visitor the most striking notion of the vast cares anxietys weight[s]. delights and. labour attendant [on] Montmorencys present high station in politics was the enormous piles of new political phamphlets Newspapers. parliamentary papers. Circulars. and all the tremendous et cetara obliged <to be> ready[8] by a parliamentary Leader. lastly to complete this literary survey there glittered on the Desk. a half full decantere of Brandy and a tumbler. drained to the

---

Branwell's spelling leads to some confusion over precisely which French historian—Thiers or Thierry—he is referring to. François Mignet (1796-1884) was an historian, archivist, and political journalist who, with his friend Adolphe Thiers (1797-1877), the future President of the Third Republic (1871-3), worked for the *Courrier Française,* a journal opposed to the restoration of the monarchy. Later in 1830, he and Thiers founded *Le National,* a newspaper which was instrumental in precipitating the July revolution overthrowing Charles X. Thiers and Mignet together wrote a two-volume *Histoire de la révolution française* which was published in 1824; but this project was later extended by Thiers to 10 volumes, which he completed in 1827.

Jacques-Nicolas Thierry (1795-1856), a follower of, and later secretary to, the radical Saint-Simon, earned a high reputation as a "Romantic historian" dealing with the gradual ascent of nations towards free government, and was particularly noted for presenting history in picturesque and dramatic terms. However, it does not appear that Thierry wrote a history of the French Revolution.

7   Gaius Sempronius Gracchus (160-120 BC) came from one of Rome's most powerful political and military families. After lengthy military service he returned to Rome unsummoned in order to quash intrigues against him, was elected tribune, and proceeded to enact reforms to lessen the power of the senatorial nobility. But although he was criticized by conservatives who saw this as an attempt to destroy the aristocracy, his purpose was not specifically democratic. Rather, it was an attempt to broaden the base of political power to include the wealthy upper-classes of landowners and traders outside the Senate. Gracchus's second most influential policy concerned the enlargement of the Roman state by incorporating Italian allies as full citizens of Rome (a highly unpopular move with Romans of all classes). However, most of his legislation survived, and his policies in fact formed the basis of virtually all reforms enacted during the last century of the republic.

Sylla, a consul of Rome, was ousted from his "ex-officio" right to lead Rome in the Mithridatic war (88 BC) by his rival, Marius. On Sylla's hasty return to Rome, Marius fled, and Sylla, reinstated, pursued the war to victory. Back in Rome, he massacred his opponents, leaving approximately 7,000 soldiers and 5,000 citizens dead. Their goods and properties were distributed among his own partisans, and Sylla himself was named "Perpetual Dictator."

8   "read" obviously intended.

bottom. Further research was here interrupted by the entrance of the. stern Herculean figure of Montmorency Himself who casting a searching look at. the young Nobleman said. "Well my Lord short Aquaintance is oft surest. you acted as Second to Elrington last Night and its decent that your Services should be repaid. by an acknowledgement. I have invited you to spend this evening with us. here of course you'll be easy. there are only. few at dinner but be quick or theyll pass off. I'll usher you in to the dining hall. an[d] once I get this into me he stepped to the Decanter. poured all the contents down his throat and followed by Montmorency[9] left the room. they entered the dining room. an apartment presenting the most Aristocratic attention to <grace> and ornament. at the dinner table were seated three persons. the first a stately Old. Lady. advanced in years tall in person. and bearing a most majestic and almost regal deportment. She was introduced to. our hero as the Dowager Countess Elrington. Mother of Rougue himself. (by the way she was the only person to whom that Arch Demagogue showed the least glimmer of respect and affection the only one who could. controul his smallest action) the other two. were. given as Harriet and Julia Montmorenci the daughters of the stern statesman. 2 exceedingly graceful and Elegant young Ladys of. 17 or 18. from their appeara[n]ce. but latly. arrived at the Glasstown. and possessing all the elegance without any of the frivolity of the highest circles of fashion. Harriet the eldest was taller than her sister & of a rather Italian appearance. and it was strange to see the resemblance she and even both bore to. their tremendous Father albeit their features were so finly and. fairly chisselled and his so feirce. shattered and so exaggerated by energetic and conflicting passions. however Castlereagh. being a young Nobleman of Elegant manners and prepossessing address a complete hero in short. with to use the cant language. much light hair fair complexion. blue eyes. vivacity and. spirit in conversation. and a decent desire to show off in the prescence of Ladies. he. and they soon. entered into. conversation the statly old Countess bearing her part with a shew of Mind and dignity befitting the Mother of ELRINGTON dinner being over and. the evening being as cool & Mild as ever closed a summer day. the Countess proposed a walk in the ground[s] which was acceded to and. Castlereagh taking her arm. they. proceed[ed] down the ample walks of this Noble Mansion. deep shadow had settled on all around. and the full. moon. was rising over. the towers and domes of St Michaels Cathedral. the vast palaces and Hotels as. the rented houses of the Nobility are termed were ranged along the river in lines of dazzling light. but there was one. which flung forth such superior radiance whose windows blazed out with such uncommon lustre that. Castlereagh remarking the circumstance begged to know to whom it belonged. "Lady Julia replied it was the Hotel of Lord Thornton Wilckinn Sneaky latly arrived at the city and who had sworn in the most public square of the city that he would make such a rattle in Verdopolis as only himself should be spoken of for months to come. Lady Julia. (by the bye her title had descended from her mother) spoke of his character and of. the character of. many others in the city in

---

[9] Should read "Castlereagh."

such a manner as shewed the most acute preception and the most lively fund of imagination. and the unsophisticated manners both of her and her sister threw such a charm of Naiveté over their conversation that Castlereagh. felt far enough from pleased when. the stern voice of Montmorency. from the window desired him to attend him to the study Castlereagh reluctantly left his fair companions and followed Montmorency to the room. as he entered a blazing fire threw its light over the Apartment candles were placed on the table and. on a sofa reclined the figure of a tall Man. his head bound up and his face swollen and bloodless. it was Lord Elrington Ha Mont" he said to their host as he entered with our hero "you villain. look at the bottles." Montmorency removed a large quantity of emptied decanters and from a secret reccess procured an astounding number of bottles. of wines and spirits "Why volo" he said. "you'll drink. off a mans income." but you villain heres Castlereagh your Second." "I see him" answered. Rougue not deigning to take another glance at the visitor. "I say Mont. the moment it strikes 10 I must go is the carriage ready." Yes. But in the name of murder can you possibly sustain this work. just think you were. thrashed and battered senseless last night. the moment you recovered your reason. (hem he-em I mean your want of reason) you ordered yourself to be born to a pothouse where you drank yourself into a state of bestial intoxication. here I found you I ordered the carrion to my own house I again supplied you. (and my self to "taking a vast draught of wine)" with most firery spirits untill you again drank yourself senseless. you then slept an hour and now that you have awakened. you mean to intoxicate yourself a third time. then to. go to the house of parliament. to rise up in your present state of frightful weakness to speak. perhaps against a first rate orator certainly against astounding opposition. for hours on end. your subject matter unthought of. un prepared and. attacked on all sides. truly you horse-leech. an you bear that youll bear everything." "Ill bear that and ten times more Mont you best pass the bottle to that young man. Sir. you'll accompany us to the house.?" Castlereagh was about to decine but Rougue laid his hand. on his pistols in a manner which showed that refusal. might not be safe besides in fact Castlereagh. had the most. intense curiosity to see how Rougue could bear this fiery trial. Montmorency in the meantime. stood at the table filled. himself Glass after glass of the. most ardent spirits untill his eyes began to flash with. intoxication. Rougue and he looked at each other with such incomprehensible sneers of. hatred. contempt and. seeming astonishment. of their respective powers of mind and body. that the impression they produced on Castlereagh was deep and singular. "What mean you to do" said Rougue to his fellow labourer. "I told you." Mont answered in a deep determined tone. "Ha right—good—kill them. weary them out worry them to death." Oh" he continued starting to his feet with a strength produced by. his extreme. fire and emotion "Oh. what a glorious Ministry they will soon be how they will stalk into the house night after night. Pale haggard worn to specters. and how Elrington and Montmorency and Connor and Gordon and Carey and Dorn"—here he stopped a moment for want of strength—"Oh how those glories will rise up the moment they enter and blaze out with such unwearied sarcasm such life destroying taunts and abuse and. invective as shall make them shrink shrink. wither within. themselves how by

my glorious goad that toad that villain that hateful Leopard the Marquis of
Douro shall exasperated to agony start up. and defend himself his Kings his
country the Ministry untill Nature tired exhausted. spent shall refuse him
strength for utterance. Oh. how glorious to see his place vacant. himself raging
with fever and the whole weight of the lower house fallen. on the shoulders of
Lofty or—or—that that—hatful spider Sydney. to see him—him the wretch.
spitting out his burning venom. retaliating the a thousand time urged attacks of
thee Montmorency. confuting thee. harrassing thee yet still himself confuted
harrassed overpressed by the mighty forces of Connor or Gordon or Carey or
Dorn. then—he stopped again—then the report will go [out]. Douro is dead
Sydney has cutt his throat. Flower is absconded. the Ministry is—is broken is
dissolved. the house of Lords wearied with opposing—the Kings—oh. then
come on with full forces. the Mob the rare Lads. storming. attacking rising en
masse. Oh. Rougue—Rougue. Revolution and Vict—here Elrington sank down
in a swoon overpowered by weakness contending with energy. Montmorency
who during this description had lighted up like fire. laughed with delight of
anticipation "to night we'll begin" he muttered and proceeded to lift Rougue from
the floor. who slowly opening his eyes. snatched a pint bottle of brandy and
drank it off at a draught. for a moment he sunk back as if shot and then starting
from his seat while the blood rushed to his face he said the clock has struck. now
we'll go. Montmorency seized his hat. poured of. a tumbler and they left the
room followed by Lord Castlereagh who stunned and appalled. by the scenes the
sentiments he had heard and seen. scarc felt concious of what he was doing they.
all three mounted the chariot and it drove of to the house of parliament. on their
way they were joined by the carriages of Gordon O Connor and many others of
the most influential demagogues so that on arriving at their destination Rougue.
marched up the stairs. into the house followed by a troop of 90 or 100 of the
most resolute and daring members. all warmly attached to his intrest. He took
his seat on the opposition benches with his minions gathered round. him. and
here let me describe A NIGHT IN PARLIAMENT. The vast hall was not yet
lighted up for comparitivly few of the members had yet arrived. the the. crowds
of Members trooping in and moving across the hall like shadows in the darkness
passing from one to another conversing assuming their seats the <maceers>
hustling about to keep [order] and a hundred other et cetera. connected with the
scene. was striking and. enough. shortly after Rogue entered the chandeliers one
by one lit up cast their light through the room. and. the increasing influx of
Members pronounced the hour of buisness near. the Ministers seats were yet
vacant and to them. Rougue and Montmorency directed an anxious eye and into
what a sneer of hatred did they distort their features when their entered a pale. care
worn young statesman. who moved quickly to the table and arranged theron.
sundry heaps of papers. necessary to the buisness of the day. then as hastily
retiring. settled on to his bench with an anxious look round the crowding house.
"Sydney's in rare trim for worrying to night I guess. cried Gordon to

Montmorency. in a short while the pay Master General entered. Capt. Flower.[10] whose firm. < > frame and unwrinkled forhead. no betrayed[11] signs of vigils and watching behind him came the Secretary of State. Marq. Douro. pale shattered. and scarce to be known by those who viewed him as he usually appears. the benches of the Ministry were filled up by. Goat of the War Office John Sneaky of. the. foreign department. Lofty and the other ministers of the lower house. "What sort of a Night <think> you." asked Sydney of the Marquis. "Rough I believe" was the answer. <they muster> black under those windows. but I only fear. for myself physicaly. for our numbers are beyond the risk of defeat." "is not Lord Thornton Wilkin." asked Lofty of Sneaky "to be presented as a new member to Night." "I believe he is but little indeed do I trouble myself with. his motions". at this moment the loud. well know[n] voice of Rougue was heard addressing the house.

"Viscount Thornton[12] Wilkin Sneaky. in consequence of an illness brough[t] on by a too violent exertion of the corporeal functions (loud laughter) begs to be excused from to night presenting himself before you. as Member for Sneakys Glasstown. in room. of. Col Arthur. dead-" Ha" said John.[13] "that young blade—" "Stop" cried Douro. "remark the singular circumstance of. a son of the 12s intrusting his excuse to such a man as Rougue to his party indeed. John I scarce knew. this turn in the politics of our freind." "Indeed Douro" replied the prince "Nor I either but I expected something odd from him however if my Father hears of this good day to Wilkin Sneaky." But at this moment. Col Grenville the speaker entered and upon his taking the chair the regular buisness began. I can scarce call it regular however for for some hours it consisted in ceasless and vexatious attacks made by Montmorency. Gordon and the Democrats in general upon [a] minute affair. relating to expenditure foreign missions &c and directed against [the] Ministers the motion Rougue always persisted in bringing to a division. though the result nearly allway came to the same. thing 100 against Ministers. 600 or 700. for them. Sydney rose and protested against this vexatious mode of proceeding. "What!" said Montmorency in reply will you Sir dare you Sir (order order) Silence Fools. will you attempt to draw a veil over your actions & over actions in the remotest degree connected with you? Why the very sound of. Mr Sydney spoke in favour of this motion. would cast a doubt over any motion or bill let me tell you. that in the whole of these four Kingdoms united there is not a man so much distrusted as yourself the time is come and I must speak. Out. If. the present Minister of Finance remain another month in office it will shake the Ministry in their seats. (cheers and hisses) What right I ask had the Government at a

---

[10] Branwell seems to have forgotten that Flower is the author and narrator.
[11] Obviously these two words should have been in reverse order.
[12] Sir William Thornton (1779-1840) was an officer with Wellington in the Peninsular War, then in the USA where he was wounded at the Battles of Bladensburgh and New Orleans.
[13] John Sneaky, first Duke of Fidena.

moments warning to place in full controul over the persons of millions of their majestys subjects a young man (eh man?) (laughter and loud dissaprobation) a young. man. totaly unknown. untried. untrusted. nay who I shoud say was known but known only for. peculation. (dreadful uproar which continued for some minutes but over which the herculean tones of the Orator rose like thunder.) know[n] only for weakness known only for baseness known only for. bribery for corru[p]tion in his Election for slavery for grovelling. after his Election now. playing the king and tyrant over the people again playing the slave and flatterer to a King. truly such a man neither! neither ought to have a voice in the representation of his country. much less a voice in its government. what party what class of men I ask does this man represent. in parliament.? Not the Aristocracy surely? as sur[e]ly not the rare lads the democracy, neither the merchants. nor the Military. proffession or the liter[ar]y proffession, and what then" ("The mental proffession sir. the Intellect of the country" replied the Marquis of Douro. loud and long cheering) the what proffession does he say. the rental proffession. by him who never knew a rent in his life? The Mental proffession then? ho ho. mind must seek. a higher a worthier representative here. yourself my lord Marquis my noble colleague beside me aye myself even for any one rather than him the gentleman represents in this house of of parliament. the slavery the trickery the poltroonery the. united grovelling habits of 4 mighty Nations and I ask can we not dispense with such representatives here?

Montmorency here sat down amidst thunders of applause from his own party. and the most deafning marks of dissaprobation from the majority of the house. Sydney hastily getting up said.

"Gentlemen however mean and base is the attack just made upon me however worthless the character of the attacker I yet seeing from so considerable a portion of your house his speech so warmly applauded. cannot refrain from rising to confute his aspersions. I know Gentlemen that I am unknown. young little tried I know that I may be eager [to] be involved in that unfortunate pursuit politics but is this a fit reason why an individuall should persume to attack me before you. now far be it from me to attempt replieng to his aspersions in detail you all know of what I am the representative. I am the representative of the populous bouroagh of Freetown in this country where I was elected by an overwhelming majority of Electors. and My Noble freind. the. Secretary of State. has arrogated. for me too high an honour in stating me the representative of your mind an[d] intellect. Mr Montmorency has been pleased to taunt me with respect to my personall appearance. but let me tell him If I am like a woman he is like a deamon and of the two which is the worst.? (loud cheers) Sir too much time has been already taken up. with my. affair I shall now then. scorning alike <the person>. and the character of my attacker sit down (loud cheering) much talking an[d] recrimination now. commenced between the different parties. and some trifling motion respecting custom duties was brought forward by Mr Sydney and Flower. for the Marquis seemed to much shattered by his late victory to speak much. This motion was carried of course by a large majority. at the conclusion. Rougue started. up. and began to adress his utter weakness radically.

however covered by the fumes of brandy shewed itself at first he leant against the bench for support and. spoke in a hoarse low hollow tone but as he proceeded his face lightened up his voice became more distinct and. snatching his arm from its support he advanced for-ward a few steps. with all his usual overpowering tone and attitude. "again and again" he said have the country or part of it asked what right have you to attack the ministry to oppose them to endeavour to unseat them Wh[a]t right have we? say you what right has the. torn stag. to turn on its pursuers what right has the. persecuted outlaw to turn on his country what right has the. armed soldier to fight and slaughter for that country. they have the right Sir of Self preservation the right of the. first and greatest impulse planted in our nature. The present Ministry by virtue of their Office. rule over and govern this vast country they have a mighty share in the. administration of justice throughout this country. and this gift this power placed in their hands the[y] do all in their power to. twist and distort. they were placed there for the good of the many they act for the benifit of the few they were placed to have a single eye toward justice. and they. judge and punish without the slightest reflecting or if reflecting only to the end will it. benifit or injure *us* they were placed there to. hold an equitable jurisdiction over. the laws lives libertys of the subject to. obey these laws to protect these lives and to insure these libertys to repeal taxes not to lay them on to pardon not to slay. to soften not. to. make hard. But alas all these precepts these commands have they most wretchedly and willfully violated and trampled down. Upon the present occasion it is not. my object to lay fully open. their thousand crimes and flagrancys. this. my freind I will do when tomorrow night with your permission I bring forward a bill. for the ejection from Office of all the present Ministers and for the better securing of the Laws and libertys of their Majestys subjects in the appointing of all future Ministers."

Here while his own party were vociferously cheering and. the opposite. one still more loudly deprecating this Eloquent invective Rougue who had slipt behind several of his freinds fell back fainting from his seat a ring gathered round him and he was born off to his carriage by. Montmorency Gordon and several others but now the morning having begun to appear and the nights buisness being got through. the house after a few broken words from the Marquis of Douro whose exhaustion had rendered him incapable of taking an active part in the nights debates. seperated and adjourned.

CHAPTER IId.   Aug 20.
                                               AD 1833

Lady Zenobia that night sat alone in her splendid saloon in Elrington Hall. For more than a fortnight ever since indeed the beggining of our work. she had never heard the slightest intelligence of her Lord. he had departed in an ominous manner and at an ominous period nor could any conjectures avail respecting his return. She now sat. at her table. her head leaning on her hand when she was started by a thundering knock at the Great door. as a carrage was heard drawing up before it. much bustle was heard. in the hall below. and ere long. her room door opened. and. several footmen entered. bearing Lord Elrington. they laid him. on the sofa and left the room. all this transacted as it was in a few moments. seemed to Lady Zenobia like a thunderstroke. and it was some time ere she could advance toward the sofa. where he lay extended without motion, speech almost without breathing, she bent over him. striving to recall her sensations scattered by so strange a circumstance. she saw the proud figure of. Alexander Elrington stretched there. rigid and motionless his. lofty forehead wrinkled with care and. his face sunken ghastly and deadly pale <yet>. she shuddered as she saw the demonic expression of hatred moulded on his features she saw no clue to to the reason of this situation he was in true his head was bound up and a lock of bloody hair strayed from under the bandage. his hands. too were swelled and scared. but these wounds had evidently been made a day or 2 before and utterly unknown to her was the reason of this. Atrophy. seeing no sign of breathing she believed him dying or dead. and stern and unsocial as was this man. fearful and cruel as was his character he yet possessed too many noble qualities and those qualitys were too much in union with her own. to make he[r] careless of his death she might have once feared even detested him but at such an hour in such a time old feeling Old associations return and now leaning over him she wept bitterly But Rougue was not dead. his constitution yet triumphed over his frightful exertions. she saw him move his hand. then. drawing it from hers raise it to his forehead. his eyes opened and. he attempted to sit up but immediatly fell back. through miserable. exhaustion "he muttered." oh. Monty dove. alls up with us we'r defeated—dont back out Mont.—I say sweet I shall kick up. toss off. and. Ill leave thee a legacy. Zenobia. Fire I say. Zenobia. dog (for Rougue had a dim conciousness of her being in the room.) give me that knife now Mont kneel down and Ill create thee a baronet. kneel hound.—and and—die!" Rougue in his eagerness for the death of his friend. started up. which motion. seemed to revive him considerably. he leant against the back of the sofa. and looked slowly round the room seeing Lady Zenobia standing by him he exclaimed "Hey where am I. you here Zenobia. what are you doing. Its a long time scince Ive seen you do you know what Ive been doing eh? tell me.—out this moment. tell me at once youve casting at her a bewildered. look) youve pois—poisoned me you wretch yo murderer ho Sdeath there. old wizard feind take this woman and.—and. (he stopped here. and then continued but in an altered tone) eh no this wont pass Zenobia what have I been doing Its sadly up with me. however was I fighting Arthur. just now. eh. that feind. no. (feeling his head) that wont pass its some time I think. how you were carried here from [your] chariot my Lord. by your Servants. and—." "what Zenobia. by who by my my servant they dared to— bring them here this moment "ring that bell." Lady Zenobia was going to very reluctantly obey for she knew that some either ridiculous or horrid scene whould take place were they to enter when the door opened. and Mr Montmorency was announced. "IN with him said Rougue and this second Mirabeau[14] entered the

---

[14] Honoré-Gabriel Riqueti, Comte de Mirabeau (1749-1791), a French adventurer, sometime secret agent, politician, and orator, was one of the greatest

room. not seeing Rougue he asked Lady Elrington joyfuly. "is he dead. eh.?"
"No. Sir" replied she indignantly. for she liked not such a tone in such a
question. Montmorencys face fell immediatly. but advancing to the sofa. he said.
"Well you scavenger I'd thought you were as gone as a herring" "where did My
husband faint" demanded Lady Zenobia. "IN the parliament house. Madam."
Zenobia sighed for she guessed the scenes that had taken place. the exertions. of
him before her. she shortly left the room. leaving these two statesmen to
themselves. Montmorency knowing how to treat the. illness of his freind poured
down his throat a bottle of mixed gin and brandy. which draught. mightyly
revived the Nobleman he sat upright and took another. tumbler and a third of
wine that effectualy strengthend. him (for the time we mean for our readers may
think of the exhaustion which must follow such a cure) "Now" he said "Now
Mont dove. I want to speak of that young [man] visiting at your house."
Rougue <grinned> as he said this a demoniacal smile Montmorency. put his
finger to his nose "[hes] there still. Ive got it out of him that he's worth. 20000
a year." "Thats well" but we also must have him for a tool. Sir. he's a lord
Mont. and. a Lord doesnt sound ill in our ranks eh? does he take." "Grandly!
Rougue hell come to like murder. noly[15] give him pleasure and hell give you in
return body and soul. I know that If I told him so now it would shock him like
death! but. Volo by degrees. by degrees." "dont teach me Mont" "teach thee!
thourt past teaching." At this moment several carriages drew up and visitors were
announced. they came storming and swearing up the stairs and into the apartment
proving to be. Gordon Connor Carey and old Sdeath. vast quantities of wine and
spirits were brought forth. but as the aristocratical. splendour of the Apartment
did not suit their plebian stomachs they all agreed to adjourn to the nearest
pothouse. Rougue. he who so lately had been brought <in> to the house. dead to
all appearance. cold and still now but an hour after was seen reeling out. cursing
swearing. with his glorious Lieutenant. Montmorency and a <hot> band. of.
followers shouting fighting and disturbing the Neighbourhood as they went
along they all soon turning down a lane. dissapeared in its shadow to some
frightful den of their dissipated Orgies where amid. crowds of rare lads of degraded
Frenchmen and women no less degraded. sat. the. Greatest Orator of Africa
mounted upon [a] taptub and giving laws to his devoted subjects.

Meantime Lord Castlereagh. had emerged from the house of parliament his
soul inspired by the exciting and stormy scenes he had witnessed longing to be

---

figures in the National Assembly which governed France during the early phases
of the French Revolution. He vehemently denounced the privileged classes in a
series of oratorical triumphs (1790)—but remained a firm supporter of the
monarchy and became secret counsellor to Louis XVI and Marie Antoinette. This
position of conflict might have led to a political downfall, but prolonged illness
and early death saved him from this fate. However, when his ministrations to
Louis XVI were exposed after his death, his remains were dislodged from the
Panthéon by order of the Convention.

[15] "only" obviously intended.

one distinguished in the same station. and ready to catch at any means of becoming so. Montmorency. saw this pressed him to a longer stay. at his house and asked him what he thought of a statesmans life. Castlereagh said something warmly admiring it Montmorency whispered. "Theres a bourough in our intrest <just vacant>" set him down at Montmorenci hall and drove of himself to Elrington palace. with Castlereagh meanwhile the hours passed pleasantly on. the soft but spritly manners of his fair entertainers. afforded a striking contrast. to the <stern> highly wound and. ferocious characters of his late associates. and Ladys H and J Montmorenci accustomed. being but lately. arrived at the city. only to the society if it might be termed by that name of their Father and his dark associates. felt a most pleasing contrast in the elegant manners of the young Nobleman.

At dinner Montmorency himself appeared. just returned from his orgeis. where he told Castlereagh he had left. Elrington "in the thick of it" he bore an invitation to them all. to attend. a. grand entertainment to be given that evening. By Lord Elrington. to the principal Nobility. and. fashionables in the the Glass town. at the hour. for setting off. the carriages were ordered. and. Montmorency. with the Dowager Countess Elrington taking one and. Castlereagh with the. two younger Ladies. taking the other they drove off. to. the statly buildings. possessed by the arch Demagogue. On reaching the square of which it forms one side. they found it almost blocked up by the countless multitude of splendid Equipages driving up to the doors of the kingly Mansion disembarking. their crowds of dashing fashionables and. then wheeled round the open space by their respective coachmen each eager to shew of. the beuty of respective horses. Montmorency pointed. out. to his daughters. quite new to the scene. the dashing carriage and. Magnificent horses of the Marquis of Douro. the which shone like gems amid the crowd. of. quadrupeds. the comfortable <wealthy> looking equipages of Col Grenville. and. Mr Bellingham. the neat buisness like barouche of Seargt Tree. and young Bud. and the other hundreds of splendid vehicles of rank and fashion. among which his own 2 carriages shone preeminent for their costly appearance. while looking on this gay and stirring scene all eyes were directed to. a Gorgeous chariot which dashed through the crowd and recklessly. thundring through the crowd drew. proudly up before the doors its sides and. top. of. shining glossy green its cast light wheels of polished brass &c. &c. blood horses. red. and glossy. tossed their heads snorting and pawing the grounds as if conscious of the magnificent. carriage they drew. "whose that?" "what. goes there" who does that belong to." burst from the crowd. of. gazers various guesses were made. but <none> satisfied till as a single person. dismounted and entered the hall. the gazers. cried. "its Lord Thornton." Lord who? lord Thornton Wilkin Sneaky the riddle was explained. Montmorencys carraiges which had been hitherto <detained> by the press of visitors now took their places before the door amid an admiring throng. and the inmates dismounting were ushered through a vast vaulted marble passage. of. classic plainness. into the great Hall its huge Rose wood folding doors were wide open to admit. the constant stream of visitors. in the opening stood the servants to announce the names. and beyond stretched. the mighty apartment. its vast airy roof raised high over head. its grand velvet curtains flowing from thence to the ground. its Light and lofty windows opening onto the wide river and distant harbour. now darkning in the shades of Evening the blaze of a hundred dazzling chandeliers the. furniture of such. wondrous cost and value and above all the crowds of Nobility rank and beauty thronging its ample extent absolutly blazing with costly ornament presented to the eye a picture of overwhelming brilliancy. Near the entrance stood to welcome the visitors the statly forms of the Lord and Lady of the mansion. Both of commanding height of. Noble figures. and. of extreme loftiness of manner well beseemed. their splendid Mansion. Lady Zenobia. was attired in a robe of velvet her usual plume of ostrich feather surmounting the curls of her raven hair and her Italian physignomy lighted up with smiles of courteus welcome. As to Lord Elrington those who could have seen him that morning intoxicated. harrased swearing and grovelling. among the most despicable society those who did see him last night. battered. bound up. hollow storming in parliament. pushing forward his democratic faction levelling his atrocious falshoods at a dignified Ministry or worn with his exertion laid down on the Floor of the house livid and lifeless. would be and were indeed astounded to behold him now. erect and statly free from signs of fight. pale indeed but of composed and. lofty expression looking around him with such an aristocratic expression. as if he would have scorned to mention such society as that in which he was that morning engaged— such as saw him now might beleive him a a dark and wicked man for such was always the expression of his curled lip and treacherous eye. but still would they believe him an honourable Aristocratic Nobleman. he and his lady of course made no ceremony in receiving His Mother Montmorency. and. the 2 young ladies Castlereagh he. warmly and condescendingly shook by the hand. the company still kept pouring in in vast numbers. name after name was announced and. person behind person was introduced. till late in the evening when the arrivals ceased and. Elrington with his lady. led their guests in to the the. grand ball rooms. where. dancing was commenced by Elrington himself. leading out. Lady Julia Montmorenci. a high honour which he confered to oblige her. Father. her beauty elegant manners. and above all the fact of. her being a. new arrival. instantly attracted the attention of all and the elderly Ladies above all. indulged themselves in eternal guessing respecting her. But upon her returning from the dance. a young Nobleman presented himself before her soliciting the promise of her hand at some future period of the evening. She answered "she was engaged to another". "Well well but you are not for the whole evening. surely Madam." "It is scarcely proper for a yong person I think to appear thrice in the same evening" "Volo put off your. engagment to oblige me." "to oblige you Sir!" she answered and turned haughtily away. Castlereagh noticed this young man. and felt a hatred to him at first sight—more than he could distinctly account for. He was apparently. rather under than above the middle size. was firmly and strongly built. possessed red hair light quick eyes. and a whole countenance naturaly of a frank. open. determined character boyant and cheerful. under any circumstances. but some how this pleasant character seemed changed. the frankness and determination. to effrontery. the cheerfulness. to. recklessness. and the whole openness of countenance only expressed a determination. to do. as he wished a conciousness that his wishes were wrong but. a. carelessness as to that wrong. he walked through the room with a free dashing air not coxcombical nor dandyish. but still scarcly. like a true gentleman or nobleman, Castlereagh. prsued him with eyes expressing. hatred and contempt. strongly mixed aye probably. wholly caused by a latent jealousy.[16] he stepped up to. a. tall statly. person far past the middle age. who stood aloof from. the company. eyeing them with. a frozen smile. and eyed by them with. much mingled awe and. dislike. to this. elevated old gentleman Castlereagh. asked. "May I ask sir who. is that young man. who has just passed." "What sir?" was the scornful answer "Sir. I shall not submit to be treated with contempt. who is that sinister looking young fellow I ask." "Do you know who I am." "No Sir. save that your an. impu—" "in the name of. murder what are you at." asked Rougue coming. up. and then turning. to the statly Old. Aristocrat he said. "Your Majesty must pardon this. young. person. he. does not know you" "Of course." said the 12. for such it seemed he was. and. elevating his stern voice he called for his carraige to be drawn. up. immediatly." half a dozen servants ran to execute his bidding. . and he. walking down the room. with an exclusively fridgid. air. turn[ed] to the company who had obsequiously made way for him and with. a. "good. evening. Ladies and gentlemen." bowing coldly left. the room. the host and his lady. attended him to his carriage. "Oh Oh." said the young man. so much. hated by Castlereagh. "Dad is as snap as gingerbread to night. im up with him however.". "how stiff and cold." remarked the Marchioness of Douro. to Lady Julia M. "Sneaky is." "is he always so" "Yes. nearly. but I observed him speaking. scornfully to that yong Nobleman who handed you from the carraiage perhaps it. may. have. contributed to. to." "to starch him. eh." interrupted. the. arrogant young Noble. so often mentioned. "My lady Marchioness the favour of your hand. to night.? eh?." "Engaged. Sir." "pon my soul. tart. as. lemon! put off." "No Sir I cannot." "Volo wont you" he replied and turned abruptly away. Castlereagh. now begged Lady Julia. she accepted and he led. her out. directly. The elegance and grace of the both the dancers attracted. the attention of the company and while. all were gazing on them. in admiration. the arrogant young Nobleman cried out. taking a cigar from his mouth. "eh. what perjured forsworn. eh" and pointed to Lady Julia. "Thornton how can you" exclaimed. 20 voices round him. "Why shes broke her promise." "Whose broke her promise" asked. Ca[s]tlereagh breaking from his partner and stepping furiously up. "Sir. who are you." "One at a time. Your partners broke her promise with me. and Im Lord Thornton Wilkin Sneaky." "then let me tell you your name disgraces you. Sir.

---

16   Four canceled lines follow:
     Stepping up to Lord Lofty. [a] Stately old man who stood by himself he asked. 'who is that young man 'What young man. 'The one with red hair. 'What he's not so very young is Rougue. No my Lord you. know t who I mean. Yes I do kiddy. but let me tell you. that I'm not. the person. of whom to ask idle questions. its Lord...'

we must meet another time." "Nay Nay now not so warmly lad." "Mr Montmorency." called out Castlereagh. "here sir transact buisness with this person he is unworthy another word." "hey. what" cried Montmorency. reeling from the sideboard. "Wheres Elrington a duel order order". "Elringtons off." exclaimed. O Connor. from the table giving a. significant. touch to his nose. "Oh I guess" replied Montmorency. Lord Thornton. cried. "well well Ill accept. but. Connor youll do the needful for me. tomorrow. 2. pm. Scavengers pothouse. pistols. alls settled and now." raising his voice. "Now Ladies and Gentlemen. hear me. I invite all this company. to a grand. fete to be given. at Thornton place. tomorrow. evening. I ask all. all freinds and foes. and if I should chance not to appear through the evening owing to unavoidable accidents (bowing to Castlereagh) Why Volo. you you must. share out my goods chattels and. furniture. among while you are. there. you must." Further. conversation was her[e] broken. by an outrageous din heard in the square below as if. 100 cats were fighting. as many duels. all ran to the windows to reconnoitre.[17] and by the blaze. of. light flung from the windows of the illuminated. Mansion all perceived a huddle of of Mortals in the middle of the square thrown about as if in a mortal. combat. cursing swearing and venting showers of execration one voice. was distinctly heard over the rest. many started Lady Elrington cried. "what voices is that. Mont—" but Montmorency with many of his freinds had sallied out in the square. for they smelt the matter directly. there was Lord Elrington the owner of this kingly. mansion the giver of this splendid feast. him lately so proud. so Noble so. Aristocratic in the last stage of intoxication. reeling through. the square. his hat dashed from his head. kicking along with his whole. force Old Sdeath. his leiutenant. who. sprawled at every. hit. gasping and yelling. for mercy. Rougue himself. often fell flat on his face but then rising. with his countenance blackened by dirt and blood. he vented forth a torrent. of Oaths and execrations laying round. him. his kicks with frantic vehemence. and striking to the ground all who ventured to oppose him. all this. paroxism. arose perhaps upon some most trivial. occasion. for he had drunk himself. to a pitch of absolute frenzy. so that when Montmorency. and his freinds. rushed down to lay hold on him. laughing however at the joke as they termed it he. felled the foremost with a loud. oath and rushed up the stepps to the hall. he stumbled against them and fell rolling to the bottom of the. flight wounding his head. till it streamed with blood. this only. raised him above all <bounds> he. bolted into the house. & made his way. toward the. grand hall in which the company were assembled. as. his deamoniacal figure. rushed through the folding doors. the Ladies screamed the Gentlemen drew their swords but. he not heeding them. rushed through the room and taking a desperate leap. flung himself. headlong

---

17 Four canceled lines follow:
   it was dark outside but. plainly could the[y] hear. the sounds of swearing cursing and execrations. they were not long in doubt. for as the square nosie attracted. crowds from the. adjacent streets. lamps were brought < > and. the. light from'.

into the blazing fire. a cry of horror ran through. the assembly he was drawn
out. by Montmorency and his freinds who throughout shewed far less surprise
than. an[y] others. owing to the no[t] uncommon occurence of these freaks
among. them when extricated he was quite senseless and his face streaming with
blood. the company thouroughly startled only waited till. surgeons had arrived.
when he was conveyed to his room. an[d] then departed. Lady Zenobia. took
leave of them firmly and without seeming emotion but. she looked. pale. and
extremely faint. she was too lofty to shew her feelings openly. but. for all that
they[y] were not less acute.

CHAPTER. IIId											PBB.—

"Well." said Montmorency to Castlereagh. so soon as they had alighted at
Montmorenci hotel. "Our freind. Elrington has drunk himself. up too it to night
I. think. the Fool when such important matters were to have been. brought out
[he] might have had the decency not to knock himself. on the head in this
manner. Ill cut. him Ill—Volo." so saying the Senator seizing by the ears a
large bottle of brandy. retired to his study. Castlereagh remained behind. He felt
hot and feverish. Therefore. seeing the morning. cool. and fresh he. stepped out
from the sashwindow. and paced to and fro through the grounds. the lights. as
the dawn increased were fast fading. in the splendid Mansions ranged along the
river. But. one still remained blazing out as if to insult the. returning day.
"Arrogant wretch." muttered Castlereagh too himself. "But either I tame him this
day. or.—". new thoughts and feeling[s] Castlereagh was aware. had risen. in his
heart. since last morning. or at any rate old feelings were concentrated upon. one
new object for. the young Viscount was not raw. in any thing. but. now
however the fact was plain—he was of course in love. and for that. love was. in
a few hours about to fight a duel <a> very romantic situation and one of course
in which. the "ars poetica"[18] must descend upon one. were he as dull as
Morpheus.[19] he stepped into the room. and taking <from> thence a lute he. sat
himself. down beneath the window. of. Lady Julia's apartment <performing>
with a practised hand and a mellow. voice. the following serenade.

A SERENADE.[20]

---

[18] i.e. the art of poetry.
[19] Ovid's name for the son of Sleep and god of dreams.
[20] "A SERENADE" is preceded by twenty-one canceled lines of verse:
    The eve is darkning down on heaven.
    Black stormy clouds. oer the skys have driven
        And dark /dull/ the shades creep down.
    With peircing sleet with drenching rain.
    With cold blasts howling from the main.
    Now rolling back, now poured again.

The guardian is old and the castle is dreary
Fair was the Maiden and fond is the swain
But the tempest is high and the night is uncheery
And. ne'er may she see her true lover again

The morn on her marriage must gloomily lighten.
Mid. tempests and torrent and glittering rain.
And her Guardian has told her
A Noble must hold her.
Who own round his castle hill valley and plain

Oh to that Maiden fair
Ocean and earth and air
All seem resolved her destruction to claim
But love will ne'er cower
To tempest or shower
And Natures worst madness its bright beams can tame

The Niger is broad and its waters unruffled.
Far through broad Afric its waves wind along
A thousand wide Kingdoms it[s] billows have watered
In history renowned and immortal in song

Rage then O Ocean and hurl thy white billows
high oer the rocks of this desolate shore
Drive shower on shower oer temple and tower
And down each dark valley thy sleety storm pour

Plains may be flooded and roads may be broken
And torrents may burst oer the travellers way

Oer hill and tower and town.
Each streamlet ~~by~~ to a torrent's force.
Is swelled by ceaseless rain.
And. bursting through its. downward course.
roars raging round the plain
The banks ~~are broke by~~ have slided down the stream
The uncertain paths in evenings beam.
Lead to some. darke deep precipices
or. wind above. some vast abyss.
Or stretched along the Moor
lead. to some. quaking black~~xxx~~ morrass
or ~~through~~ oer some mighty summit pass.
Where ~~it~~ shrieking from the shore.
Howls the loud blast with furious tone
Both on the clouds of mist and rain . . .

> But Never O Never
> Can Nigers vast river
> Fall. like. a roadbank. or rise like a sea.

> There then fair Maiden thy boat lies at anchor
> There the rough sailors recline on the oar
> There thy true lover beneath thy proud castle
> But waits thy forth-coming to. sail from the shore

The last notes had scarcly dyed from the lute and Castlereagh had arisen to depart. when. he heard from the trees near at hand. another voice and an other instrument begin a tune in reply to his own. he started but that voice was that of a man. deep. but mellow. it sung as follows.

> Why dost thy pine fair Maiden
> Within thy castle tower.
> Why does the tempest chain thee there.
> Or Oceans driving shower.

> What recks it. if the Night be dark.
> Or. roughly roars the sea.
> What. needs it that. a. feeble bark.
> Shall bear thee far away.

> There are gates enow within this wall.
> And posterns. safe an sure.
> Then rise. awake. command thy page.
> To unbar the hostile door
> Why need we fly oer Nigers. stream.
> Or wander through the storm.
> When I may enter. quickly here.
> And clasp thee in my arm.

The. free. ideas and the bold ready. voice of the singer could not be mistaken. Castlereagh. snatched his pistol. and dashed among the trees. he gazed round with eyes of fire but the singer and the lute were gone. and. had left no sign. Castlereagh. moved heaven and earth but. he would obtain revenge. he return[ed] to the house. threw himself on a sofa. and. tossed their untill. the. sun had risen over the city. Lady Julia met him at the breakfast table with a silent greeting. I must here remark to my readers. that. duels were to common among the Glasstowners for the Ladies. to shewe any very great. distress upon the approach. of. one. for did they weep. on such occasion I could scarce insure them a dry eye through the year therefore though Lady Julia. guessed the one pending that day. she was 'carce less cheerful. or lively than usual. after Breakfast. Montmorenci appeared his hat in his hand and. 2 horses saddled at the door. after cursing every thing rou l him he. exclaimed. "Castlereagh come to your dimner" putting his

finger to his nose. "Castlereagh do you like black pudding." Castlereagh arose
and. with him left the room. they rode through the. street. untill the[y] reached a
dirty. dark lane down which they turned. and. stopped at the. door of a wretched
old. damp. pile of building[s]. the very appearance of which would. damp a mans
soul their horses were held by that old feind Sdeath and they both entered the
building. it was a pot house of. the very lowest order. dark a real Tavern dark
low rotten corrupting within and without. the roof. rotten. the walls rotting the
floor. covered with rotting substances. and all presenting the smell & aspect of a
charnel house. though unlike it it was furnished with. a. rousing fire 2 or three
rotting forms. and severel tubs. and vessels of spirits and ale No one appeared in
the room. but a powerful steam. of whiskey from an inner [area] announced the
occupants to be engaged. at. a still. somewhere about. Castlereagh who be it
remembered was only a novice in glasstown life. shuddered as he surv[ey]ed this
wretched scene and. ask[ed]. his companion. who. was emptieng out from a can.
a measure of "life." "and whom are we to see in this miserable hole" "Pho its
what I call a grand. place. why Connor and Thornton. and Rogue"—"Rogue!
why Sir! remember where we left him how we left him" "aye and see where is he
now." exclaimed a voice. from behind the heaps of cans and barrels they ran to
look. Castlereagh started back. Montmorency. laughed loudly, it was actualy
Elrington himself. yes there lay. that. lofty Nobleman. grovelling in a black
musty hole behind a heap of. casks. &c. drunk miserably drunk his head.
wounded in last nights revel. now bound up. his face pale and ghastly. and.
himself so. weak as to be unable to lift himself or sit upright. "Well done
Elrington" cried Montmorency "my darling. has done it however. why man how
will you get on at this rate." "Oh dear I dont know I am weak. heave me up
Mont onto that. cask by the fire." Montmorency. did as he desired. The
Nobleman. leant his head against the fireplace but did not speak. he presented an
appalling spectacle as he sat there. his forehead white absolutly as. ivory save
where spotted with blood. and shining with cold persperation his hair appearing
in bloody curls. beneath its bandages. his. sunk. but yet lightning eyes flashing
their fire his pale hollow cheeks and his lips and hands trembling. with
nervousness. in fact. the mere exertion of. sitting up. was to much for his
shattered frame. he gazed languidly round the apartment. smiled with a ghastly
expression. and would have fallen back senseless had not Montmorency caught
him in his arms and—laughing all the while. poured down his throat a draught
of hot brandy it revived him slightly. Castlereagh. startled at. the spectacle. said.
"What on earth Sir has his Lordship been doing." "Oh. naught extra. you know
what work he had. the Night before last. all yesterday. he was writing. reading
and forming and executing his s[c]heme for tomorrows vengeance. (here
Montmorenci grinned horribly a ghastly smile) in the evening. he presided at the
feast. The night he presided at—humph you may yet see where. all this morning
hes been laid. up. this day. he has worked so hard. in politics besides other little
matters. that just now he is clean. done up.—but howsoever Thornton will be
here presently and ill just sitt abit till he comes. come Castlereagh. sitt on the
other side of. this barrel. noble cards you dogs—ho what sirrah. cards I say "not
come volo dog beast hound calvestail feind." here the Senator strode from the

apartment into the still. returning soon a flask of spirit under one arm. and. a wretched ghastly Frenchman under the other. "produce your c-s or my teeth!" the startled Monseiur. with a trembling hand pointed to a pack in the corner. Mont seized them. and. hurled the Fr— out of the room. he made Castlereagh be seated at one end of the barrel placed himself at the other. and. the[y] began a light. game to pass away the time. but. before many minutes. Rougue motioned. them to come nearer him and give him a hand. the barrel was drawn before him and. after steadying. himself with. a draught of brandy he. entered in to a rubber of whist. for. a. few guineas. but they had not. proceeded far in their game before. a series of thundering kicks at the door announced the entrance of. Thornton and his second O Connor. they entered the filthy hole. singing and swearing in great glee. "Come" said Thornton. "lets make it up. casty. and gang wi me to my doghole out by <Thornton> "Make it. up Sir.! cried Castl[e]reagh and. took out his pistol. "hump[h]<its bone>." exclaimed. Thornton. admiringly. and took his place at one end of the. room. "your in the dark there lad." "well rouse the fire." a barrel was instantly flung. onto the coals and a blaze soon shot up which made them hot to suffocation. preliminarys were settled. the word was given "fire". instantly flashes succeeded. and all were enveloped in dense smoke. when it had cleared. away the 2 combatants were found standing. Wilkin with his arm shot through and. Castl sans a portion of the ear. all. here burst out a laughing. "Fair hits but clumsily missed somehow." "ho Castlereagh. beg. pardon sir. never do so no more cried. Wilkin.. Castlereagh stared at such ungentlemanly conduct the rest laughed. "Well done. Sneak a prime one." Lord Thornton then inviting them all to. his. house that night. retired with his second. as he passed by to the door Castlereagh staring at his disgraceful conduct just. lifted. his foot and fairly. kicked him out of the tavern. Lord Thornton. as soon as he had. gained. firm ground arose but still laughing heartily. ran off as fast as he well could. a disgraceful scoundrel. exclaimed. Castlereagh. a capital young fellow replied Mont isnt he Rougue." I neither care for him or you. you vile scoundrel. get out of my sight this instant. peice of impudent folly and presumption great gross leather headed Jacobin" "Ill report Rougue an you go on in this way. volo I will. you feind. you— Mont. help me to the carriage." "I. Rougue" thus saying all three left the. pothouse. "Oh" asked Montmorency. on their way home. "Castlereagh. our games not out. lets finish it. here before we go home." he pointed to the door of the Elyisium the Nobleman. hesitated. for he was not far enough drawn into. the Maze of dissipation to treat. this matter so lightly. but. Elrington and Montmorency. winking at each other pervailed on him to assent. they dismounted stepped in and that Night between. O Connor and the Marquis of. Douro Castlereagh lost. a thousand pounds "Dear play." remarked Montmorency. as they drove home but Ill teach. you to morrow. how to. handle it better.[21]

[ornamental figure]

---

[21] The last nine lines are written over a faint, undecipherable sketch.

CHAPTER. IVth.   Sept. 18. PBB
AD 1833.

Two or Three weeks. I must now pass over with. short notice only breifly remarking the events transacted during this space of time That. mysterious but urgent buisness. relating to the "great firms" which at the end of our First volumn had called. Rougue so hastily to the glass town seemed now to be entirely hushed up if we might. guess. from the perfect silence maintained upon the subject. Parliament. too. had. been prorogued and the members were a little time released from their overpowering cares and. labour. This proved of the highest consequence to Lord Elrington. who as we have seen could not have born long with his own policy. but. was fast breaking up and reducing himself to the. doors of death. now however. he relaxed a little and his. Iron constitution began slowly to recover its wonted spring do not however imagine him to be idle. no all this time of general holiday he was actively energeticaly preparing to meet. another campaign. forming his. coadjutors and. associated into a hundered revolutionary clubs. bribing and persuading. to his party every. straying spirit with whom he could. meet. supporting and causing to be. written. a hundred newspapers. phamplets &c. calculated to poison the foundations of society. and finaly. he was exerting. himself to the utmost. to raise also his own private affairs to shine out amongst the Nobility. to seek funds for supplying his boundless expenses. the style in which. he. was living. far exceeded. the bounds. [of] even the most ample. fortune. and would swallow up hundreds of thousands half. a dozen. splendid dwellings in town and country. a. palace almost equal to those of our noble kings feasts balls. and. entertainments day after. day. se[r]vants equipages. horses without number. to support. and worst of all a constaint stream of. perfect bloodsuckers associates. tools. engines. spies. bribers to. pacify and supply. add to this that. his passion for gaming was insatiable. that he strove with all his energies to. be the leader in the race course the ring. the paradise. nay also in the. Halls of Philosopy. as patron of Music of the fine arts. in short he hungered. to be preeminent in every thing. little or great good or evil in which preminence could be attainable. now this mention of. such a boundless ocean of expense. leads one to ask. how in the world he could find funds for the slightest indulgence in them. I dont know. Some things however will come. out. this curious Mercantile concern several times mentioned seemed. a good. reservoir. but what was. it. we dont know. but however. the question leads us to bring forward again My Lord Viscount Castlereagh. who was one. means to defray a few expenses. now. our Readers must see that. somehowe Rougue. and Mr Montmorency proffessed a wondrous freindship for this young person. the truth was. he was possessed of 30000£ a year. these two. Satan and Belial.[22] instantly. fixed their eyes on him as one admirably calculated. to serve

---

22 "Satan" in Hebrew means adversary or enemy and is traditionally applied to the Devil, the personification of evil. Milton alludes to this etymology in *Paradise Lost*: "the Arch-enemy/ And thence in heaven called Satan" (1: 81). In

two [that] end they determined to. draw him over to their party and too fleece him of all his property then to cast him off. and if he proved refractory too Rougue said emphaticaly "get rid of him" now Castlereagh was like most of our young Noblemen wild and thoughtless he liked pleasure & excitment and heeded little how he obtained it the Commanding Spirit of H Montmorency first seized on him. made him beleive himself. his freind. invited him to his house instructed him in the ways of life. initiated him into the Mysterys of. the Elyisium &c. and. finaly. presented. him. a powerful of object of attraction in his daughter Lady. Julia M. then lest this should fail. in effect this vi[c]tim was brought under. the talons of. the great Elrington himself. whose. vast. ability. enchanting powers of conversation. splendid entertainments. and. presiding genius. so enchained him that though he (having naturaly enough sense) distinctly. saw the dangerous nature of the men among whom he was placed. yet it was vain for him to attempt. to free. himself from their Schacles. to all Rougues entertainments he was ever invited. he constantly appeared with him Montmorenci &c. so that as every one instan[t]ly began to regard him as a confirmed. Anarchist. he himself. slipped gradualy into the error. and ere he knew found himself among the meshes of a ferocius Faction. of course his name became enrolled among their club. Rougue offered him. a seat in his intrest and he becam[e] to. a mark in the. Elysiums races. &c. for. the Most Noble Arthur. Marquis of Douro. and his followers to practise upon and destroy. Now at the begining of the 3 weeks we have passed over so lightly. Castlereagh. felt many twinges of conscience. had many sleepless nights. and little liked the race he was just about to run. at the end. though his sleepless nights were not abated yet his spirit had become metal and why his metal. had also become spirit. for he felt himself. minus 80 or 90000£. this seems a tremendous amount. but it was not destined to satisfy. the treacherous and. inexorable. E. and M. They. it must be remarked never won from him. no they advised him to leave off play they. lent him large sums. to free himself from immediate embarasment it was. O Connor. it was. WITKIN. it was Douro. that. fleeced him and. bled him so. the last named gentleman of course they had no control over. he. worked on his own ground. not. in. their intrest and. here they from their souls whished Castlereagh to win. but. sad to say of his money. Douro had pocketed some odd. 9 or 10000£. Lofty &c. 4 or 5 then for the remainder 75000, Wilkin. had. 30000. Connor 25000 and. Carey 15000. of which they by special. agrement made with R. and M. were to refund: 4. 5ths. to these two grand. springs of this conspiricy. But as yet much was to be done. C's property yet exceeded. 4000<00>

Now leaving this miserable mass of treachery. and. feindishness. we must mention. the state of Lord C. with regard to. Lady Julia. his sensations here had ripened into silent but ardent love. To her and. loud. and <burning> hatred to his rival. Lord Thornton W. Sneaky. who with persevering effrontery continued his adresess to. the person of Lady Julia & the purse of Castlereagh. however the Lady. disgusted with his arrogance. and presumption. (for strange to say. though so high in rank and <title> Lord Thornton contrived to seem presuming even to those far in those respects below him) she would have little to say to him. the fine animated. countenance genteel appearance elegant manners and still good estimation of Lord Castlereagh. far far more inclined to her to that quarter. in fact. she could not deny. that her intrest in him had not decreased. on aquaintance. To the usual. attentions. in fashionable society. Castlereagh posse[sse]d. a high skill in music she here could participate. with him. a fine taste in litrature. a large acuaintance. with books and nature here. they agreed. here he could and did also instruct her. But now to go on we are about to describe an account of. the manner in which Castlereagh. spent <his> day concluding the third week of our "passover." it will serve as a specimen.

CHAPTER Vth..   AD. 1833

P B B—tē

Sept. 18

About 12 o clock. Castlereagh who still resided at. Montmorenci house awoke from sleep. not over refreshed nor of an over serene mind. after an hour occupied in dressing he descended. in to the breakfast room where he found Lady Julia. alone. she was standing before the window. and. her handkercheif was in her hand. her eyes glistened it was plain she had been weeping. and Castlereagh knew that it was plain too. she had. heard. from some. hint or other given by her. father. how last Night at. a. great meeting on. the "North ground where a trial took place between. Douro's. Black. Horse "Eagle"[23] and Abercorns bay colt. "Blow it." Castlereagh had sustained. serious. and. heavy. losses in fact he had disbursed. to the tune of. 13. or 14000£ after the usual salutation on his part made. made with embarrassment. she asked him "My lord what. do you see. before you.". "an angel." he answered. "No my Lord. I mean in Life." "Ah. he replied rather starting. "but it matters not. reproach Julia. I know. well enough what will befall. but you should see a way. to get out off it. and. see wether I wont accept it." "you know. the Man who made such a show. on the course last Night." "Yes the Marquis." "very well. from what my father mentioned of your proceedings there I should. scarc. have supposed. that Nobleman poss[ess]ed of many merits or good qualities. I should have thought him worthless. and broken so it is not. he is. secure in fortune. in the estimation of the world <what> is it owing too now. "Ah. good. fortune. I. fear." "No I do not think so he has firmness he knows when to stop. look at him copy him. and. "Yes. yes. Julia. but your are scarcly ignorant of those two. Men with whom I am so much entangled. Elrington and.—" "My Father. you could say. I know.—" she seemed

---

[23]   See the first item in volume II of this edition or Neufeldt PBB, 334.

afraid to say what was on her tongue Castlereagh. began to think. for yesterday had staggered. him. and [he] was <near at > once. for. a month to come forswearing the course. and. Elysium then. the stern harsh voice. of. Montmorency was heard in the passage he entered. shook. Castlereagh warmly by the hand. and relaxing the frightful expression of. ferocious cunning impressed on his countenance. intoo a peaceful serpent like sneer. he said. "Hey! well what now. Castle. what Volo! in the suds. down cast. murder this wont do.! what man. greive for a trifling matter of. 10000! <It> shant. pass look you. Elrington came up to me this morning half smashed. he was. and. he said that if. a matter. of a few <ciphers> could. startle. you why. he would just. forkit at once for you John. bring the desk. now. I'm commissioned. to give you over. My! volo lets see. 1.2.3.4-5-6. what a long purse Elrington keeps 7-8-9-10-11000£. in good bank bills. endorsed Bellingham & Co[24] now what say you to that eh? And. Listen we dont require bonds. We will do with your word. my Hound. but the grandest peice of news is to come yet. this afternoon. at. Astleys course we shall have a real turn up. between. "Swasher" and Clinker And then. Volo in Astleys. rooms.—it is rumoured. there will be. aye more than rumoured. a real turn up. between. the Marquis and. Lord TW. Sneaky quite a treat. but private strictly private none but the first grade will be present and of them all Now if you dont go. why. Volo. you must pass a step lower. thats all but Im. cursedly dry. Ho. Hang your tea Julia I. shall take. a glass or so in my study. Hear. me—there's a general card of invitation to. to the Fetè at Waterloo.

---

24 Here follow twenty canceled lines of verse, with the text continuing in both margins.

Rattles. the Hail like ~~shower~~ storms of stone.
Then pass down bellying oer the plain.
~~Thou mayst not~~/Fair Maiden in such/drear/hour. ~~as this~~
Thou mayst not from thy castle tower
    Flee o'er the waste with me.
But, Oh the. sullen rolling main.
What heeds it storms of sleet. and rain?
Behold thou its. dark. silent plain.
    That huge Atlantic sea.
Our boat is ready on the Shore.
Our sailors rest beside the oar.
Not such light wind as. wailing now.
Covers with sleet. the Kumriis brow.
Can. raise. the ~~sullen wave~~/billow dull
Not such vain storms, though cold they blow
Though earth they hide in clouds of snow.
Can hurl the billows round our prow
Or. rock our. sturdy hull.
Then ~~come with me~~/dancing free upon the sea.
Oh Maiden, fly from. thy fate with me.

palace this night. But come Castlereagh. into the study. we must settle. the.
Bond and then. off." Montmorenci led the way out of the room. Castlereagh
folowed looking back on Lady Julia with a shake of the head. and a melancholy
smile. after. Mont had. remained. sitting in the study opposite to Castlereagh.
fortifying his inner works with a. drink or so of B. R. and Y. or. O.D.V.[25] for
half an hour. a servant entered. and visitors were announced. they came in the
half frank half arrogant figure. of Lord Thornton. the. sinister Belial. O Connor.
the. mean filthy wretch. Old Sdeath and a whole host. of. dark Spirits. men only
to be known by. deeds of villainy. they cried out. "Come M. and C. alls ready.
rare. rare sport. my Masters to day. Rougues waiting for us. at. Elrington hall to
meet. him." Montmorenci looked black. "Could not he have come with you."
"Oh no. hes over high for. that." with a few curses. and execrations. M. led the
way out of the room they mounted their horses and rode off. Castlereagh
however looking much cast down. which they all observed and set upon him
with their bitterest. ridicule. so that on dismounting before the proud. porch of
Elrington hall. he strove. with all his might to shake of this inconvenient
shame. and this troublesome. knave conscience. the party moved forward with
songs and curses into the study of Rougue. and on the door opening there they
saw him fronting them. standing behind. a table. his hands. upon. an open book.
and his high. forehead. showing forth an aspect of the deepest solemnity. "Hey
muttered Montmorency. "What moon stroke now." "Shame." cried Rougue.
with an affected. twang. through his nose. "Shame that. upon the dawn of so
glorious an outpouring men should. be. found. so little. carried forward by a
spirit of. reviving. grace. open your tongues fools for some other purpose than
to. vent your ungodly execrations. and join with me in a little savoury. rising of
the spirit. and a psalm of pleasant thanksgiving. for. the awakening flowers
about. to appear. among the dunghills of a carnal self seeking world.

> Raise your triumphant songs
> To an immortal tune
> Let the wide earth resound the. deeds
> A saving grace has done.
>
> Now sinners dry your tears
> Let. hopeless sorrow cease
> Bow to the. signs of saving grace
> And take—"[26]

here a roar of laughter for some time. suppressed burst from the edifying[27]
assembly. "My heart Rougue does go it" "is he mad." "Aye mad. as the wind"

---

25 Brandy and eau-de-vie
26 Stanzas one and five of Hymn 104 in Isaac Watts' *Hymns and Spiritual
Songs*. Differences from Watts' text in ll. 4 and 7 suggest Branwell is quoting
from memory.
27 The next few lines are written over an undecipherable sketch. This is the
first of a series of ironical imitations by Rougue of dissenting ministers, an

"Ill stick my knife into you an another word" [such]were the expressions of his auditors. for Himself. he closed the book and. standing with his hands clenched. uttered forth such a volley of the hugest oaths curses and execrations as must have startled even some of his hardened hearers then calling for his horse. he led the way. to the square. and as they. all mounted. he said. calmly "Now what number expect you shall we amass." "37. men." "Oh. well just by way of sport. I intend that if we meet. any. of. the. Aristoc—s. we'll just have a row. on the course." a laugh of approbation burst from the assembled and they rode on through the streets.[28] to the place of meeting. one well know[n] to many of my readers. there they found assembled. all the elite of the spirit and fashion of the city. they trooped into the rooms till the race should begin. it was broad Noonday. but here in the halls of misery. thick stone walls shut out every ray of day light. and its abscence was supplied by the red lurid glow of the hundred lamps within. Here as entered. Rougues party. his Antagonist Douro. withdrew to the other [side] untill the desire of betting impelled them to join. the others. and soon the crys of. "2. to 1. on Swasher." "5. to 1. on Clinker" taken. "6. to 1." "7. to 1." all taken. "ho Clinkers the favourite." the Marquis of Douros. firm voice "8. to 1. on Swasher." Castlereagh who had inquired and inspected minutely the points of the horses. "taken" "is it." replied the voice of the Marquis. 'Come with me Sir." Castlereagh retired. with him to a sideboard. Aye asked Lofty of the Marquis "pigeon." "Why. a cropper." "but. Sir. what are your stakes. on the subject." Nay your lordship shall lay them." the Marquis scanned. him over with his keen eye. saying lowly. "20 Castlereagh started but. instantly. cried. "done." the Marquis turned to seek more game. he met Rougue. "humph. a stiff one. winked Lord Lofty." <Eh> Douro." said Elrington "I am willing to risk. heavy. for. Clinker." "A broken winded trump." said Lofty contemptously. Rougue fixed his fiery eye on him. "Well Sir. Since he is so you'll not refuse. a layer." Lofty was caught. "Elrington pressed him. hard. Lofty took bait to the amount of several thousands. Montmorency. eying. poor Sydney in the crowd instanty bribed a man to go up. and. praise the abilities of. Clinker. to him with all his heart. the man. did so and. prevailed. intirely on the simple statesman. to bet any thing in favour of Clinker. Montmorenci. then stepped up and. giving. Swasher a doubtful preference. he. offered 10000£ pounds upon. him. this Sydney accepted. though terribly startled. the officers soon came to say that the horses were ready. all rushed onto the grand stand as the room was cleared in an instant. but in this room will we. remain. till the race is over. we have seen too much of such work to find the detail of it particularly novel. an hour has elapsed and you may hear by the noise that the race is over. the betters return. headlong into the rooms. there is the Marquis his countenance

---

indication, Barker suggests, of Branwell's growing disgust at religious hypocrisy (Brontës, 206-7). See also pp. 325-27; 442 below.

[28] A canceled line follows:

> galloping tossing their hats and fighting with each other. in a manner most disgraceful

illuminated by. a. satisfied. smile. Rougue cool but dissatisfied. Castlereagh pale. as death. Sydney perfectly bewildered Montmorency. venting his laughter sneers jokes <ire> on all round him. crying to Sydney "cash up cash up" till a great blow from an unseen hand. hinted him to be quiet. he. scratched his head and looked dismayed. it was miserable. to veiw Castlereagh giving out 20000£! to the hands of the Marquis who stood over him with a most. provoking good humoured smile. as Arthur glanced round the room he perceived. Sydney. doling out. with hands as blue as steel his 10000£ to the iron Montmorenci, his eyes instantly flashed. he flung the. parcel of Bills onto the table and. with a great exclamation. rushed up to Sydney. "What in the world was the ass <doing> did I not tell you. not to lay. one guinea without my advice." "Oh he's thought better on it." exclaimed Mont. Douro glancing at him a look of blackness. retired with his inconsiderate freind. But the hour. was now drawing on to the promised fight. and the two champions. Douro and Thornton retired to the <dressing> rooms to prepare. the favoured ones who were to veiw the fight. trooped into the. Sanctum Sanctorum the inner betting room in awhile it prepared to commence the 2. sons of <Kings> (humph if their fathers knew it). were placed opposite to one another. Elrington was. Thorntons second. Lofty. the Marquis's. bets were immediatly given and taken to immense amount. our hero Castlereagh. who hated Thornton Wilkin though he was of his own faction determined not to back him but. bet on the Marquis of Douro. the champions were true blood first raters. and in the highest condition for breadth and bone. Thornton had it for height and. experience the Marquis. they began the battle was long and tough to the last. 60 rounds were fought. with equal success till at the end. Wilkin began to fail and some exquisite hits on the part of the Marquis brought [him] to the ground senseless. they were both carried of by their seconds in a weak condition blood was let and. the surgeons required. but[29] the Marquis was declared winner. of the fight. various were the fortunes of the betters but for Castlereagh he won. 6000£. which in some degree aleviated his terrible losses before. the crowd now began to seperate and depart. Elrington. Mont. Castle— and others. rode together too Braveys Inn one the command of the former who swore that. they should not go home. as they ought to be. at Waterloo palace. in the evening. he however. ordered servants to be sent round to their respective residences too. fetch their carriages to the Hotel. Here in the Refectory. they sat down to dinner among several hundred persons. Elrington with the utmost ease. walked to the head of. the vast common table. took. a chair. and. after emptying glases of strong waters. cryed. "Now. Dogs. Look up to me for direction I believe I am your superior.". under the direction of such a president. the bottle was not wanting in circulation. those present soon became outrageous. several English Gentlemen were present. Rougue <with his> usual inclination to evil. pointed them out as objects for sport. the diners. like true Glasstowners set upon them. and committed the most atrocious injury to their persons and effects. Elrington

---

[29] The following six lines are written over sketches of what appear to be birds in flight.

incited all round to drink. and when the waiters entered with their bills our Unlucky. young Nobleman Castlereagh felt. such a buzzing in his brain. that. it was with difficulty he paid his reckoning. Evening now drew on and by the time that he with Rougue Montmorenci and. so forth mounted their chariots for the feast. at. Waterloo Palace. his. dizzyness. had in some degree abated. it. was night when they reach the front. of this Noble Mansion of the Duke of Wellington. crowded. with Equipages blazing with splendour. Elringtons possession did not here forsake him. he boldly. walked up the steps to the Hall. his followers behind him. and was received. by their Host the Duke. a (by the by very respectable. Gentleman. in black. with a pleasnt smile. keen eye and Eagle Nose) with becoming courtesy. the vast crowd entering here. broke one person from another and mingled all in one mass Castlereagh. with whom we have most to do thus seperated from his seeming freinds walked up to the upper end of this Magnificent saloon and looked on the scene before him its stir glory and gorgeousness I need not describe, but this was a usual entertainment given by a Mighty Monarch. No Duchess of Wellington was here but she who officiated as Lady of the Feast. though simple as a may day maiden yet well beseemed. her high rank and station. she was the Marchioness Douro. Castlereagh saw. her. surrounded by. a bright and. glowing circle of beauty and fashion among whom he easily. discerned the proud lofty Lady Elrington the. gay sparkling Lady Sydney. & the. fair form of L. Julia Montmorenci But what distinguished this fete above others in the city yet more than its magnificence was the 5 or 6. men whom he saw standing together alone. at the upper fireplace. conversing together as too high to notice. much around them These were some of the 12s. the. First founders of our mighty kingdom and who could only in the feasts of the nobility be found singly. or. dropping in occasionaly for a moment to shed a lustre. over a whole feast. yet in appearance were they far from sunlike. on the contrary there. stood. a little broad stout. elderly man. stiff and. upright as his own cane. smelling suspiciously of the times of old. His Majesty Stumps. of Stumps Land. a still broader stouter but younger one with red cheeks and frank aspect. His Majesty of Ross'sland. a great. corpulent bluff. carbuncled. rosy nosed. drunken Ox. Bravey the big Burly Brawny brutish. Herculean. armed Bady. the tall straight Scottish unamiable. Monarch of Parrydise. the still taller. far more unamiable. Bald. headed. elderly. sinister. cold blooded polite old Gentleman of the North. These formed that Nucleus of Planets round which crowded. all the boldest and brightest of the Glasstown And to these. Castlereagh could not help directing much of his. gaze.

But we must pass over. much of this feast. for our space permits us not to enlarge. let it be enough to state. that it contained more than the usual portion of. stir variety and splendour. when. the company. had adjourned to the. great saloons there commenced the usual flow of brilliant and varied conversation such as one might. listen to for hours. with highest enjoyment. and here the garrulity and. egotism of the proffessed talkers and authors was finely awed and counterbalanced by the Military gentlemen among whom they stood. Gifford Bud Tree. young Soult. Goat &c. were counterbalanced by. Elrington Douro Montmorenci Lofty. Cavendish Abercorn Sneaky. and a host of spirits of the same stamp. But amid this feast of reason and flow of soul. up rose Elrington and taking a little volumn from his pocket. he mounted a table. and then with his loudest voice commanded silence. a hundred swords were half unsheathed to repress his audacity but curiosity returned them back. as for Rougue rolling his eyes round the assembly and pressing his hand to his forehead. he began. "Oh vain oh foolish Generation wise I know in your own conceit. aye wise as the dust the stones you tread upon. Do not Now. I intreat you continue your path through this so long travelled so weary wilderness. the darkness of this Night just passed may well excuse you from thus far <stumbling> into it and wandering over it. but No farther Childeren No farther look up now O Sons of Men. look behold. What is it you see in the heavens. I see a light rising in the morning a light not of a natural sun. but. the great overwhelming all changing light which. is destined now to rise. hereafter to shine eternaly freinds you have never seen the plains of. parrisland. from Mt Elymbos you have never seen the Natural resemblance. of a spiritual world. yet the frightful wastes of that haughty hill are above those far of golden plains. In nature the hideus. chaos of a carnal world lies deep deep below the heaven of a coming grace. But Oh. how vainly do I speak and am I then tinged with a touch of of earthly. carnal. thoughts vain un godly images. pass of now all of you and vis[i]t me no more. Oh that I could emulate the men of hold[30] and arise. in spiritual strength declaring unto you the thing[s] which are to come. Oh might the mantle of those mighty worthies descend here on me. in this the most waste most unprofitable Vineyard man ever laboured in.[31] It needs indeed a noble faith to believe Morning at hand when we walking in darkness. cannot see even the pitchy sky. but hope against hope have faith in the wildest danger. yes and I have and having it I feel raised above this earth above you. all.

> Faith is the brightest evidence
>   Of things beyond our sight
> Breaks through the clouds of flesh and sense
>   And dwells in heavenly light
> IT sets times past in present view
>   Brings distant prospects home
> Of things a thousand years ago
>   And thousand years to come[32]

Hah children by faith I beleive that morning come by faith I believe Myself its Messenger by faith I believe. this world. was formed by faith I believe it now reforming. Oh Men of this world Ho carnal selfseeking ungodly souls.[33] howl

---

[30] "old" obviously intended.
[31] See, for example, Deuteronomy, chapter 25; Isaiah, chapter 5; Matthew, chapter 21; Mark, chapter 12; Luke, chapter 20.
[32] The first two stanzas of Hymn 120 by Isaac Watts in *Hymns and Spiritual Songs.*
[33] This whole page is written over an undecipherable sketch.

gnash now for your time is at an end Look backward. children of light upon this
Night of darkness. look back upon your original fall look see your natures
dashed and broken fallen in the fall of your fathers. rising with your rising sons.
sons! no more shall we have sons no more daughters no more Fathers or
Mothers I tell you All All are alike now no one is over another. none oppresseth
another. Hah long have I laboured to remove opression but lo it is smote away
by other hand[s] than mine and faith and grace and the spirits and. a continual
Godly savour of the incense of thanksgiving shall rise instead and rule. Howl I
say ye Men of dust and ashes howl aye ungodly lukewarm feeders of my childern
howl Man of Belial Howl thou of false Gravity. Aye Howl thou Old Man thou
fulll of days behold. thy days are done and thy <acts> as nothing before me.
(here the preacher became sensible that he had gone too far by a simultaneous
movement among his hearers and a pistol shot or two fired at him) Vanity of
vanities (he shouted) all all is vanity[34] down upon your knees ye men of pomp
pride power down to the earth. ye unholy pomps and gauditys. down to that dust
from when<ce> ye sprung from wich ye shall not cannot rise. Ha what is this I
see riding on clouds. this the heavenly sun of regeneration this the sweet
harbinger of reviving grace lift up your head Oh all ye <ages> bend down
mountains bend down that grace and godliness may enter in. Now now let me
close my eyes let me die since I here behold the crown of all my hopes the sum
of all my joys Now we all can read our titles clear now we all can see our
heavenly Mansions.[35] and <now> in like manner let us bid farewell to all fears
and short comings and doubts and relapsings. enter enter my childeren into the
morning of light and life of saving grace and eternal joy!!! Heh. Connor there or
you Thornton fetch me that bottle of claret and help me of this table. its like
<Adams desk> your grace. it has my footmarks on. Oh. My Lord Marquis I say
I would intreat. a few moments—but stop a while.—realy now I am so thrashed
<but> this claret seems <worth fashionless. hey> Old Elrington Old Scoundrel
are you at the cordial waters eh? give me a toss. Now (pulling out his watch) I
would just hint to all gentlemen concerned here. it is near time to go <there ye
ken> where. Im presed ye ken Oh what dancing eh. Now My dear Lady
Marchioness Douro I beg I intreat of you the honour of your hand. then shall be
accomplished the saying which was written the lion shall lie down with the kid
I mean the wolf and the lamb.[36] —never mind. dont refuse me Lady or I shall
break my heart." the Marchioness one of the most astounded during the whole of

---

[34] See the first chapter of Ecclesiastes: "The words of the Preacher, the son of
David, king in Jerusalem. Vanity of vanities, saith the Preacher, vanity of
vanities; all is vanity."
[35] Compare "When I can read my title clear/ To mansions in the skies," Hymn
65 in *Hymns and Spiritual Songs*, by Isaac Watts.
[36] See Isaiah 11:6: "The wolf also shall dwell with the lamb, and the leopard
shall lie down with the kid; and the calf and the young lion and the fatling
together; and a little child shall lead them"; and Isaiah 65: 25: "The wolf and the
lamb shall feed together, and the lion shall eat straw like the bullock."

this extraordinary speech for to her these exhibitions were uncommon. was
startled. to find so near a request made to her by the great Actor in this late
extrordinary scene. however he stood by half intreating but with a menacing eye.
she could not refuse. Elrington led her out. with much satisfaction. the company
had seldom seen such a contrast as was here presented to them. her slender
fairylike figure <her face> of such elegance sweetness and innocence his
overbearing stature the haughty glance of his triumphing eye the mixed and
extravagant passions displayed in his face. formed an odd <curious> sight. The
Marquis of Douro looked on gloomily. during the dance and when finished.
instantly beckoned his Lady beside him. All this while Castlereagh had been
looking on with vast intrest. admiring the spreeching of Elrington the figures of
the. fair dancers but. on a pause <being> made. when these last had. retired his
soul relapsed into itself and became the seat of bitter and gloomy reflections on
his future life the. men among whom he had cast his lot. his losses that day his
probable losses that night how could he meet Lady Julia.—here he was roused
by hearing that hateful arrogant. voice. wellknow[n] as the voice of his rival. he
looked up there was Lord Thornton standing before Lady Julia Montmorenci
with "Volo your hand Maam" "it is engaged my lord" "Now fire murder Ill be
be cut off no longer I demand—" Castlereagh had stole beside him unobserved.
he seized Thornton by the collar and catching a cane from Old Lofty he. dragged.
Thornton into the middle of the room and gave it him over the sholders in the
most handsome style "Now here I. declare before all men that this is the only
reproof of avail on the degraded shameless arrogant. scoundrel" so saying he
flung both the cane and the culprit from him with the utmost contempt. the
company stood amazed at this spectacle many laughed outright all tittered. a
smile was even seen to steal over the fridgid aristocratic features of Old Sneaky
as for his worthy son Thornton he upon recovering his breath clapped his hands
to his sides and. burst into a uncontrollable fit of laughter "flat as a fluke broad
as a pancake. he. has <herculeanized> my shoulders they were broad afore they
are. twic[e] it now oh. I ach[e] I ache pathetically didnt. I. ladies look unco
grace—stop waiter hand me that glass of spirits. I assure you I am thirsty Ladies
and Gents your health. Yours too Castle — Oh. Sir I want to speak to you." he
called to a tall elderly Fridgid proud looking Nobleman. who stepped up to him
they retired to a corner and continued whispering too each other. all the time
looking frequently to Castlereagh. in the midst of this Elrington took out a
peculiar little iron whistle from his pocket. blew one shrill call and bidding a
graceful adeiu to His Grace. and the visitors withdrew. in about. a quarter of an
hour. not only his own followers but the Marquis Lofty. Abercorn Cavendish.
and dozens of young Noblemen also withdrew from the rooms.

[ornamental figure]

CHAPTER. VI.   P B B—te
                                               Sept. 21. 33

We shall rejoin the Gentlemen whom we left. departing from the palace. at the rooms of the Great Elysium. or Pandemonium. same night at 12 pm there are as usual congregated. amid a blaze of lurid light. and midnight splendour the brightest and darkest spirits of Verdopolis Elrington is seated at the head of that long long rosewood table. there are hundreds of Noble countenances all darkened with doubt. pale with. despair. flushed. with hope or. in joy standing with native coolness. Our Hero Castlereagh is standing opposite the Elderly. Crafty Nobleman. mentioned before as conversing so eagerly with Thornton. Douro holds the stakes. Rougue looks on with. a strange wink at. the Nobleman who was. it may be time to state. the celebrated Lord Caversham. enshrined in equine and monumental memory the game was brought to a conclusion "Lost." said Castlereagh. "Here my Lord. Count them" "Aye. 5-10-15000£ very well. for a night." said Caversham and stalked away from the table to the sideboard.. Castlereaghs hands trembled violently he. too walked to the sideboard. and poured down his throat large draughts of claret and. brandy.—But a thought strikes me it were better reader for us to step to the street door of this awful dwelling and there wait till four o clock. pm. then that door flew open and there rushed[37] out a wild multitude of men. actuated by the strongest most different passions and feelings among them came Castlereagh. he in spite of the various calls of his freinds (eh freinds?). rushed from the crowd. ran through the dark silent streets. and only. stoped on the. great Bridge which spans the noble Niger. he stopped here and gazed. wildly round it was as usual a raw solemn morning dark and dreary. "Here" he said after a long silence "here I. stood. before. first meeting [th]at accursed Montmorenci Oh what changes have visited me since then then I was worth 400000 now indebted 40000 all through him but save once I will never darken his doors again." he turned down a street hastily and dissapeared.

Montmorency that day. at noon was seated in his handsome study—At one side. of an ample fire. Elrington on the other as croose and canny as twa auld freinds bottles and glasses before them and. the floor and table piled with papers letters books &c. "humph well Mont. hes proved true pluck anyhow lets see. how stand the accounts

Connor has gained from him --------------13000£
Carey from him ----------------------16000£
Sdeath from him ---------------------- 1600£
Caversham from him --------------26000£
Gordon from him --------------------31500£

78100 to Elringtons share.

Dorn. £ gained from him ----------11000
Thornton ---------------------------41000
Eagleton------------------------------3800

55800 to Montmorencis share

---

[37] From here to the bottom of this page the lines are written over an undecipherable sketch along the right-hand margin.

Total of both. 127900£.[38] From Douro Lofty &c he has lost it seems. 60. or 70000£. which lack a day is also lost to us. but however we've made a bright job of it Mont Volo Well let it pass I say Mont. now weve blown him next cut him cut him out and here me. Ill hire. some desperate fellows to shoot him Aye some night in the street. Mont dead mans blood never cries." "Why Rougue if it did your ears would seldom be of <stretch>"[39] "right Mont right hand me the bottle whisht who'se here." a servant entered with a bundle of Newspapers proclamations and so forth. laid them on the table and departed Mont took up the first it was a proclamation for the calling together parliament that Evening for the more fit discussion of several important questions on hand. he looked at it and without speaking handed it to Elrington who soon laid it on the table. the two worthies gazed a while on each other in mute astonishment and then each burst out into a fit of laughter. this paroxism ended. "by my soul" said Elrington in his darkest tone. "out with your speeches convene the clubs. set the machinery agoing. have at them woe to the slackest. dont talk. Ill off this moment. They have found all out. Hang the cursed the thrice despicable scoundrels." here A servant again entered. announcing Viscount Castlereagh. "IN with him" cried Mont The young Nobleman entered. without bowing he walked up to Mont he was pale dressed in black and habited for a journey "Sir he said we must part without regret on your part of course. without either regret or pleasure on mine. Sir I will not reproach you—May I be permitted to speak an hour with Lady Julia". "with Julia my freind she is gone. gone to be married. why Thornton asked her of me this morning." "In reward for merited services" interrupted Rougue "Aye < > and so knowing that between cup and lip you guess the proverb Why we ordered the carriage. volo a kings son is something. though she scarce. thought so however. hah hah hah." "Where is she gone Sir?" asked Castlereagh calmly. "Oh that[s] neither here nor there." replied Mont I tell you sir look here. by my soul. you shall have it begone out of my house and never darken these doors again." Castlereagh turned round. he could not <[b]reathe>. his brain was on fire. he dashed down stairs. while as he went. the loud bursts of feindish laughter from his two betrayers above seemed to scald. his ears. he threw himself on his horse. and with whirling brain. galloped through the streets stopping as by instinct. at. the residence of. Lord Thornton Wilkin Sneaky. as he gazed on the front of that splendid Hotel a pang of anguish stole over him when he reflected on the. sum which he had squandered only on its hat[e]ful owner. he feircly demanded of a servant. "Is your Master within." "No my Lord. gone of in the carriage this morning" "Which road.?" "that to Sneakys Glasstown" "Castlereagh turned his horse and rode furiously off.

That Evening at sunset. on the Great North road there was seen galloping forward. a young Cavaleir mounted and spurring in hot hast[e]. his hat. struck over his eyes. and urging his lived steed to its utmost force. as he gained sight of a carriage rolling along with outriders at a distance. a little behind this carriage

---

[38] The actual totals are 88,100; 55,8000; and 143,900.
[39] Slang usage indicating "relief from fatigue."

there. was a single horseman. toward him this Cavalier who was Lord Castlereagh furiously rode and. as he. came up to him he cried. "draw villian or die." the Horseman looked hastily around. and. then crieng out "ho John, Sdeath, push forward for life dont wait for life I say" he turned to Castlereagh saying "What what now Sir." "Lord Thornton draw" was the only answer as Castlereagh rushed on him bore him to the ground and plunged a sword into his body, it scarce. hit fairly. Thornton drew grappled with his adversary and by his superior strength had got him under and prepared to run him through when Castlereagh drawing out a pistol fired it at him Thornton fell Castlereagh jumped up. spurned him with his foot. and ran into a cottage on the road side. there he called out. "ho is Scroven here." "Aye lad. I am I seed you play that pliskit just now what in the—" "Scroven no questions help me to drag him in to your cottage." they both ran to the road. lifted up the bleeding Thornton and conveyed him into the hut. when he was set down Castlereagh said. "Scroven. you have companions here Ill trust you with the carrion I must ride back to Glasstown for assistance to rescue her contained in that carriage which some time ago passed by. Keep him till I return." he mounted his horse and dashed back to the city. here he arrived. in a several hours it was dawn of morning he had ridden during the Night. as he passed through the streets he. beheld. a vast confusion reigning through them. prodigious considering this early hour even his anxiety and fever of mind. could not. prevail on him to pass on <till> he had inquired the nature of this disturbance. "Parliament is broke up for the night" was the answer "and. the moment they met last evening up got the Marquis of Douro. he. declared that all the robberys and plunder committed through the whole countries. for some time passed. were without a single exception the result. of. one grand united concerted. system of wholscale plunder headed and directed by a few Individuals. who. had established firms and depots throughout the whole country in secret for the reception of the spoil and the organisation of plots and schemes of robbery and for paying the subordinate agents their allowance of profit. that the only Heads of this frightful body. were Alex Rougue Lord Elrington. Lord Thornton W Sneaky Mr. H M M Montmorency. R P Sdeath L Gordon A O Connor Carey M'Dorn. &c&c. and that. the. burning of the Jail. a month ago. was owing to the fact that in it were confined 5 under Agents. of this conspiracy. who were taken up simply for it was thought a common robbery and who had threatened to their employers to divulge the whole secret of the combination. if they did not liberate them that Elrington had had recourse to that desperate measure of storming the jail for this purpose.= farther that this. combination was first discovered to the Government. by one Lawyer Tweezy and. that since then they had been employed in ascertaining the truth. of it. that now they moved that. Lord Elrington Montmorenci Wilkin &c should be impeached for their share in this frightful transaction and that warrants should be issued for. the detention of all the other agents of the <combination> the moment the Marquis had spoken up rose Elrington Mont &c and after a torrent of execration and abuse. the[y] with their followers rushed forward and made a desperate struggle to attain the doors. but they were strongly guarded. the government foreseeing the likely hood of an attempt of this sort. most of them were caught and secured but Elringto[n] Mont Connor and one or two more by dint of desperate valour made their way. through and dissapeared in the darkness. The bill was instantly passed. and they are now hunting after Elrington Montmorency and Thornton for the detention and. presenting of any of whom dead or alive the Government offer a reward of 50000£" "do they" replied Castlereagh. "I can answer for the last one any how" and he rode forward to the Office. of the Home department here he found Sneaky. Douro. and Sydney. he explained to them that with proper officers he could engage to secure Lord T W Sneaky. but wether dead or alive uncertain. Sneaky the culprits father instantly ordered. Horsees and carriages to be got ready and officers to be procured. the[y] followed Castlereagh who. urged them out of the city along the North road for many miles with breathless haste. to. Scrovens cottage. there entering with hand cuffs the officers found Thornton stretched on a settee wounded indeed. but wounderously recovered indeed that shot had not prove[d] at all fatal. he cried out when they had explained why. they were conveying him off. "Oh Castle. I say. Ill give up my Lady Julia if youll engage to free me. eh boy?" "Villain where have they conveyed her." "off to Freetown. 20 miles forward." "If I find her and bring her home unharmed thou mayst hope for thy wretched life if not. woe to thee." So soon as Castlereagh had. seen Thornton lifted into the chaise and conveyed back toward the city he prevailed on a party of the officers to accompany him. to Freetown in search of the. fair prisoner. they drew up at the. Northern Hotel. the officers rushed into the yard and secured. Old Sdeath and his escort. Castlereagh flew into the parlour. there welcome sight he saw Lady Julia Montmorenci in tears in-deed. and. dejected in the extreme. I cannot and need not describe their welcome and cordial meeting. the joy and. rapture on both sides they. mounted the chariot and it rolled backward to the Glasstown. when arrived there. Castlereagh accuainted the Government with the success of his journey and. informed them Thornton at least was secure. The Marquis of Douro informed him that. He for his part through the whole of his short and adverse aquaintance with him had seen and marked. his spirit his mind and accomplishments and had. mourned the evil men among whom he was fallen. of course he could not restore him the money he had gained from him but he was happy to state that government had on his representation declared for his services the highly advantageous post of Secretary of the Foreign Office at his disposal and intreated him to accept it.

Of course Castlereagh did not refuse. he was sick of his late faction convinced of his errors. this post with the 50 000£ restored him to former station repaid his losses. and. after sojourning two weeks at the Marquis of Douro's his marriage with Lady Julia Montmorenci was solemnized before his New and illustrious frends of the Wellesly Sneaky and Lofty family the bride was given away by his Grace of Wellington.

Of Thornton Wilkin we can only say that. his part in the Robbery scheme was found. very. slight rather. indeed suggested by the general indifference of his character he was released as a 12s son and dashes about as usual. the other rascals secured are about to undergo trial the Ringleaders Elrington and Montmorenci still remain hidden, and I fears they will first work in secret. and then come forth again to inspire dread and create confusion

    Lord Viscount Castlereagh and his Bride. have gone with the Marquis and Marchioness of Douro to spend the Honeymoon in the country.

End of the 2d volumn

P B Brontë.
: September 21st
.A D 1833.

═══════════════

Books. published. this
Season.
By. Seargent Tree. GGT.
No 587. G.S.[40]
Lord Ronan. a poem by the Marquis of Douro
I Vol. Oct. 12s.
Something about. Arthur By. Ld C^s Wellesly.
II. Vols. Oct. 20s.
The fate of Coomassie. a poem by Young Soult.[41]
.I Vol Quarto 2$^£$-0^s-0^d.
The Foundling a Tale by Captain Tree.
I Vol Oct. 1$^£$-0^s-0^d
The Green Dwarf a tale. by Ld C^s Wellesly.
:I Vol. Quart. 12s.
Real Life in Verdopolis a tale by Capt Flower
II. Vols Oct. 30s.

═══════════

NB. The. tales intitled. Something about Arthur and the Green Dwarf may also be had. of Seargt Badenough. neatly stitched in. from 12. to 24 NOS price. one penny each.

Seargt Badenough
Pothouse Alley=
G G town

P B Brontë Sept 22 A D 1833

---

[40] Branwell reproduces the formalities of publishing procedure, here presenting the Glass Town Stationer's volume-registration number.

[41] There is no evidence that Branwell actually composed such a poem.

THE POLITICS. OF.

VERDOPOLIS.

A Tale By. Captain John Flower MP. In I. Vol.[1]

CHAP. Ist ∴

From the title I have chosen one would expect the First chapter of this Tale to place its scenes in Verdopolis the seat of politics in the House of parliament amid steam noise and. turbulence. in the. Jacobin club[2] amid. its. darkness. muttering and treachery or. in the cabinet council. amid. Flattery sheeming and. discord. But reader I shall not so place my scene. I whish you to look to a spot different indeed from any of those. just mentioned. Spot than which none could be more removed from the turmoils of political life. The Woodlands 20 miles east of. Wellingtons Glass town

The afternoon of. the. 1st September. in this present year shone brightly. over the noble parks. of. a majestic residence of. ancient date. seated amid the forest grounds of Wellingtons land. The Sun amid a blue. and golden sky. was hanging over the Western Horizon. his upper beams sheding a splendid light upon the few fleecy clouds collecting round his resting place. The lower rays glancing and blazing among the leaves and boughs of. the noble Oaks wich feathered over the smooth shaven lawns. These forest trees began to to spread long shadows over the park. and amid the intervals. of shade. The ground seemed covered with broad lines of golden and glowing light above the great groupe of trees. which at the upper end of the park. stood dark against the sun. rose the several black stacks of chimneys. and the many pointed gables of. an ancient and noble old Hall. with its well known accompanyments of curling smoke and. weather cock above. walks verdure. and. sportive deer below This was. altogether. a most serene and. delightful. sight. and it filled the beholder with

---

1   Hand-sewn booklet with grey paper covers (11.5 x 18.5 cm) of 18 pages in BPM: Bon 141. The covers contain no wording, but on the inside of the covers appears "by Red Rover/ Lynn coach./ Thursday Night./ March 6. 1834/ To be delivered as/ soon as possible./ carriage Paid./ 1^S/ 0$^{d''}$ (originally 2^d but changed to 0).

2   The Jacobin Club was the most famous and the most powerful political club of the French Revolution. Officially called the "Société des Jacobins, Amis de la Liberté et de l'Egalité," it became a loyal supporter of the revolutionary government, its select members being united by common fears of aristocratic conspiracy. It was the Jacobin Club which launched the Terror, setting up a "dictatorship of opinion."

soothing pleasure to turn his eyes toward the sun and follow up that golden lawn those deep shadows those mighty trees. up even to the <gr>ey hills appearing behind the alleys and the bright gloryious heavens beyond. little breeze could be felt in the balmy air but over all things was diffused. the calm spirit of evening. and. though all this was in the wild burning land of Africa yet nothing gave sign of its being any other than a venerable English hall in a fair English Evening

But what I cheifly want to introduce to my reader is a small retired spot surrounded. by vast leafy Elms. save on one side were the. scene look[s] down. on. [an] ivy mantled little church and its. undulating churchyard. This small spot. seemed from its perfect serenity and seclusion. the very Gem of the whole scene. in the middle of the grassy. turf. was placed a. simple elevated. Tablet and urn of white glistning Marble. which bore on its side this simple inscription.

This stone is raised.
Over the grave of.
MARY HENRIETTA.
PERCY[3]
who died May. 1st. ∴
AD. 1815.
Aged. twenty one years.
By Her Husband:
Alexander R Percy.

The wild flower twining round this unstained Monument the one beam of. bright light. which fell on it through two parting trees. its simple. unflattering inscription. offeres to the eye and mind. the most calm and. pleasing ideas and. the evident extreme care taken to preserve it from all encroachments of time and weather. told more for. the unchanged affection and unforgetting memory of the survivor than could have done the most pomppus monument and. elaborate. eulogium yet had he who then present made those reflections he would have been disposed to hesitate did he know who was that survivor

At this time on the day before named. while all round lay thus. under the brigh[t] beams of an evening sun. the wicket leading from the country to this secluded spot was opened. and. there entered a tall man dressed in black he walked up to the monument and stood silent before it! The appearance of this stranger was extremly striking he was I have said very tall. thin and statly. about 40 years of age. his countenance dark. stern. and. of a peculiar aspect. He seemed not melancholy but thoughtful. deep and his finely formed lips were curled into a

---

3   Percy's first wife. Branwell's first use of "Percy" in connection with Alexander Rougue/Elrington, and his descent from the Northumberland 'Percies of Rayestrack" at Alnwick, home of the Dukes of Northumberland, which Branwell traces in **The Life of Feild Marshal The Right Honourable Alexander Percy** in Volume II of this edition. Charlotte also first makes the connection at this time—see Alexander CB II, Part I, 262-67.

cold. sarcastic smile He laid his gloved hand on the monument. and. looked round. with an expression boding nothing good to whoever might chance. to. be loitering nigh. seeing no one he turned again to the Monument and taking off his hat. laid it on the ground. uncovering a head of curled. auburn hair and a forehead of aristocratic loftiness. ill agreeing with the dissipated sneering character of his face. "Well" he said to himself "I am here again. I dare say changed even since last year I am sure changed since I first stood. before this grave. Ah Mary If you saw me now you could no more know me than I you if you stood. here as you are now earth. in earth ashes to ashes.[4] Well Mary I have walked through a weary world but have never seen one like thee.—I think I never shall. I wonder what you would think of your Alexander. should you see him now. Worn wasted. flying His country for fear of the law. immerssed in a line of—hem-hem—ranting with his mouth of Methodism Calvinism and such stuff. thinking in his mind of—of things as contrary to that as thy tomb to this stone. Speaking of Republics of democracy freedom thinking of Aristocracy titles tyranny As well. Ill shall drive on. my eye is fixed on something which I will join even should I find it not gold but fire.—This is a glorious evening. man—times may change the sky—Nature never. When I was here 18 years since standing over the new covered grave. the mourners being all departed. the sky. the scene wa[s] just as it is now. and the same beam of light fell here but not on this marble urn. no on the. raw black heaped up earth." he stopped here and stood bending over the grave. with [a] strange smile one of an expression yet more singluar than the one he usualy seemed to wear it was partly mournful. bitter and. sarcastic. he took from a black box a small portrait set with briliants. it was the countenance of a young woman. of fair mild aspect. and her large hazel eyes seemed to have a slight touch of sorrow about them which gave to the face. evidently young and beautiful a soft melancholy expression it seemed looking at the. stern dark man in whose hand it was held. He noticed this and went on "Ah. just so you often looked at me when you saw a glimpse of my nature. Mary you never stopped me but you always calmed me. Its Twilight now. I must leave you here Mary in your cold damp house and go forward to mine. I wonder how time passes over your Mary—" He had turned his head and. with that. bitter smile was about to leave the tomb when the gate leading from the park opened and. a young lady entered the enclosure. a spectator would at once have been struck with the resemblance she bore to the portrait just mentioned and the man before her. She was about 17 or 18 years old. slight and slender in stature and figure. her small hands and feet and slender waist suited well with a head of curled. auburn hair. a fair open forehead. and large. hazel. eyes. shining with a mild. sad lustre. her smile was of soft winning character her dress. fashionable. dark. in colour and aristocratic in material. indeed her whole air though full of the sweet sadness suitable to the Old Hall the Old trees and ancient prospects round her. was strongly tinged with pride and distance of he who stood before her To this person as soon as she observed him she hastily ran forward. "My

---

4   See p. 165, n. 44.

Father—" "Well Mary. how are you. child I am here you see. but we will speak of that. Let us return to the House how is. it. Ah. Percy Hall" "he said as taking his daughters arm he walked from the enclosure to the open lawn in veiw of the Mansion "Mary love has all past well since I was last here I hope that servants and all about the Hall here. attended your word." "Oh. yes. had they not I should have written." "you would." "certainly" "like some one". "Well Father I am suprised to see you here but indeed agreeably so. I had begun to wish heartily or. to give over wishing for your arrival. are all you have left well. How is my Lady Elrington. above all how are you. Father yourself. for the others I care little." "Oh. Mary well My Lady is tolerable. I am. as you may guess how. I should not have come so soon. but—its a delightful evening child. Have you been visiting. that you have got that. beaver Hat on. for I suppose you still keep the whole plan of walking through the park without bonnet." "Oh I never visit. I am not so fond of it as to spend in so doing such a fair evening I have been taking my usual walk. with Roland here." as she spoke a huge Dog. came bounding toward. her but observing her father it. gave a yell of joyful recognition leapt round him licked his hands. and jumped into his face. and then set of at once round the park. at full chase. scattering the stags round in all directions. "Dear! Father I wonder you will not oftener delight in this place since all here so joyfully welcome you." said his daughter smiling as she looked up in his face. "Silence Mary—I care for no ones welcome but thine"[5]

CHAPTER IId   Oct. 23.
                                1833.
                                PBB.

Next morning rose over Percy Hall as fair as the Evening had sank. and And every feild park wood and tower of this. English like country was. white with dew and golden with the beams. of the morning sun. The Honourable Miss Percy according to her usual unsophisticated custom. had arisen early to walk through the park and up the sequestered. lanes of this pastoral region Her usual guard. Roland.[6] a huge deer hound followed. gaily in the steps of his young mistress. and under his protecton she walked shurely along. A large Hat shaded the sun from her. face and well set of her brown hair. expressive eyes and sunny smile. From the mild cordial manner and sweet voice. with [which] she addressed the country "apes" and "rare lads" who crossed the path. and the. joyful. hearty deference with which they obsequiously saluted her. could directly be seen the admiration she was held in by her Fathers numerous tenantry. in our lands a young lady cannot. find a single opportunity for alms giving distribution [of] tracts soup or blankets and such condescening et coetera. and. the only way to

---

5   The chapter ends with five canceled lines.
6   Named after, suggests Christine Alexander, the most famous of Charlemagne's paladins, the protagonist of the "Chanson de Roland."

secure. the favour of. the surrounding people is by a free. cheerful. look and. kind sentence spoken in passing farther than this they. neither wish nor need And thus by her fairy shape. gentle voice and. perfect cheerfulness. the young Lady of "the Hall." gained the warmest. affection in these feirce. rough Irish like. Gentry. should a shower come on in her walk. twenty bullet headed lads were. off like lightning for the carriage. from the Hall. among her Fathers servants also from the Houskeeper to the mere servant wench. from the Steward to the gardeners boy. just the same feeling reigned.

But among the gentry the the opulent. people. and the inhabitants of Wellingtons glass town. she showed a different. character. her high station her rank. and. her fathers wealth power and. vast consequence. raised her above those who are considered the principal persons of the country Glass towns. for be it remembered. that. the Kings their familys and. the great Nobility all reside in the. Mighty Verdopolis here she was looked up to paid deference to invited as the queen of their parties. and considered the standard of taste for the youuth of the city. but all these attentions were in vain. if she chose to be present at a party which choice was seldom indeed she was here alltogether unapproachable. by a cold. distant pride. not shown in haughtyness arrogance or in an offensive manner. but by her short stay Silence. quiet assumption of the principal place and cold. bows to those who would fain be thought most intimate aqquaintances. The splendour of her carriage and equipage was equalled by many. but the unrecognising manner with which she passed through a crowd of silks and satins to enter it. and the air with which her chariot drove of. could by none be approached and what added to. all. was that while she. took. leave of all entertainers with. a single word and a silent nod. she perhaps turned from them too step in to the carriage with a a kind. cheerful familiar sentence to her coach man or footman. and a display of. smiles and and alacrity on their part most laughably. contrasting with the silent deference and. eager assumption of the slightest shake of the hand. by their superiors. now. all her conduct in these cases though so cold and distance. was I have said preserved from being disagreeable by. her unsophisticated looks and. a manner perfectly free from haughtiness. when any one entered a party who was or whished to be considered. of vast consequence any lady blazing in satin and jewells. of course the Hostess would introduce to her. The Honourable Mary Percy. but while that Fashionable Lady. sailed to her and greeted her with perfecty appearance of equality. perhaps of superiority. this said Honourable Mary Percy would look at. her with. an unobservant turn of her hazel eyes. hold out her hand. and after a single sentence retire. back. as if she had not seen. her. now reader this manner was. <just> the same to the untitled as to the titled. and she affected not in the least to give one more word. to a velvet robe than to a silk gown though she would give twenty to ruddy cheeks and a <russet> stuff. We all know that her father filled as he is with the most relentless contempt and. hatred of Mankind extends not these sentiments to Women. yet he swears that if he sees any Woman excersising airs. striving to sit in the place of Man arrogating a fancied superiority. affecting contempt of. her Lords. By. the Heart of Sylla.[7] he would cut of her head with his own hand. Now his daughter possessed the sentim[ent][8]

Now though Lord Elrington. stood aloof from freindship with any one though He. could look with a smile on no one. though he. drove from his house his two sons and. threatened. the most tremendous vengeance should they dare to molest him and look on his face again. Yet save the. uncertain gleams of sunshine bestowed now and then on his Lady. all the light of his favour was bestowed on this child of Nature and Aristocracy she must want nothing All her wishes must be gratified. and wo[e] be to the man woman or child who should dare to slight. her. to the servant who should dare to neglect her word Our Readers must not suppose that he often when absent deigned to think of her or that he ever dropt a tear. on thinking of her. or that he over frequently wrote to her or saw. her. But when he did think or write or visit his Daughter. it was with a pleasant feeling and a. relaxation of his cynical smile. She in fact was the only creature on whom he with pleasure bestowed a smile favour or kindly word. and in whom he felt. pleasure and pride. Now though by him she was thus petted and indulged. Yet had she dared to contradict. him. or thwart him in any thing the severest punishment if he were pressent an unsparing blow. would have been the instant effect of her disobedience But she never did or would disobey him Her father was with Mary Percy. all in all. and the slightest word said in her prescence against him would. make her eyes flash and her glow with instant anger. never more might that person hope to regain her favour She was aware of the Life of Elrington his tremendous character his ferocious and unrelenting disposition his constant endeavour to light the flame of discord and to plunge his country in the convulsions of revolution and war. [h]is dissipation. and recklessness were. all or partialy known to her. but in her mind. it mattered little what he said or did. it was if not right at least. half justifiable by circumstances at all events it was great. showed his vast power and ability. it was done by. Her Father. he to whom she looked. up with mingled fear affection. and. awe.

I have diggressed much concerning the Honb[le] Miss M. Percy But it is right my readers should understand. her character We left her walking with her Dog. through the. parks of her Fathers Hall. in a delightful Autumn morning Lord Elrington soon joined her. he had his gloves on his hands. "Mary I intend to ride. the City this morning. the carriage is ready. you may accompany me. get ready child." "I am ready I believe Father." "What you dont spend an hour. or 2 in dressing then when you go out." "No I go exactly as I happen to be. it is not worth while to dress." "Say rather child for I detect cant. that you think yourself always fine enough." "yes I do. go home Roland. Now Father I am ready. Ned. (speaking to a stout. ape. who was going by.) take Roland back to the Hall— here's something to drink. my Fathers return with." She dropt into his hand a sovereign smiling. The sturdy youth. scratched his head. "As how. Ise—Ise.

---

7 In Greek legend, Scylla is a female sea monster who seized and devoured mariners as they sailed past its cave in the Straits of Messina.

8 Three and a half canceled lines follow.

drink it my Lady and yours too as long as it lasts I will." The Carriage now drove up. they both mounted and the aristocratic vehicle rolled away with well oiled. wheels along the smooth road to the city. Miss Percy. broke a short silence with "Father from the works lately published. which I have received from the Great Glass town I have taken the strongest desire to visit. it. when will you take me." "Do you realy wish to see it." Yes I do indeed." "Well you shall go then when I return." "I would thank you Father only it is needless." "I gueuss you will be pleased but remember Mary you must behave civilly to you[r] step Mother. you have not seen her. she will behave coldly But. Ive cautioned her. against. disrespect or haughtyness to you. in terms she will not forget. But child if you go I must buy you a new carriage and poneys and augment your cash accounts." "No. I—." "Silence I know very well what you must have. you now receive from me 500£ per ann[um] I shall augment it to 5000£. so long as you continue in the City. you would not like to be behind the other Ladies of the Capital." "But surely Father none of them possess that sum yearly. I shall scarcely know what to do I shall indeed feel the incumbrance of riches." "Oh never fear. it will melt. But come were in the city. and a handsome on[e] it seems to be. Yet how far below. the great Verdopolis. Why its not above one 20$^{th.}$ of its size." They soon entered the great street stretching through the city and. as they rolled along in their sumptous chariot attracting the instant Attention of all passengers for not to mention the young Lady herself. Lord Elrington was no common or uninteresting object. in this. western capital. He alighted at a splendid hotel. and then leaving his carriage and servants. crossed the street with his daughter on his arm. and a footman behind them. This attendant stepped up before them to the Door of a Majestic Mansion. and knocked authoritativly. announcing to the porter Lord Elrington and Miss Percy. They who without further. notice. walked into a splendid apartment. and while she was carelessly adjusting her hat at a vast mirror (not taking it off) the Master of the House entered with evident marks of suprise on his countenance. he was a thin anxious looking man of middle age and Gentlemanly manners. in one hand he held a newpaper. with the other he shook that. of Elrington who looking at him with a direful squint cried. Ha Caversham. well what do you stare for I am here flying from the furys of that infernal ministry. Sir my Lord. I must relax a little you know at my country seat "yes my Lord." replied this noted Nobleman. "But have you seen this mornings papers? "No what in the name of earth is stirring" "Heres ones of them the Verdopolitan Intelligencer published 5 days since arrived here this morning" Elrington seized the paper threw himself onto the sopha. then wandered with searching glance through its columns Caversham stood over him leaning on the back of the sopha. twisting his keen eye toward him. and smiling at the black expression of his countenance Miss Percy looked at her father with fear and hesitation. for she saw that no little thing discomposed him. on a sudden 2. splendid chariots. but splashed up to the windows. Thundered up to the front door. the gallant horses as the[y] were reined in snorting tossing and curvetting back on their very haunches. Rougue hastily glanced to the window. and. cried. "In the name of Belial. Those are Great Glass

towners." then turning to his Daughter Mary Love. you must ride back to the
Hall. come [I'll] hand you to the chariot. I shall return perhaps to Night. good
morning child." His Daughter bowed to Lord Caversham. mounted the chariot
and. it rolled of wheeling round the corner and was out of sight. the folding doors
of the parlour of this Mansion flew back. His new visitors 4 or 5 in number
dismounted and entered one behind. another into the room The First was a tall.
dark man. The second a not so tall but still darker looking man. The third was
[a] Gentleman of. lofty stature. and. noble deportment who wore his hat. pulled
firmly down over his forehead. leaving only seen beneath a fine crop of curled.
whiskers and Black mustachios. Behind him followed. 2 or 3 Gentry of grim and
<lifeless> aspect. emissarys seemingly of the very crew of darkness[9]
"Hah Connor and Gordon." cried Elrington stepping forward for. for Caversham
before his master though that assumed. a lower place. "What in the name of
wonder are you here for. Sit down Gentlemen. Caversham order the bottles stay
Ill ring. Here Butler Out with your best. Now who is this. My noble freind. my
dear aborigine.[10] take your place. and rehearse to me your reasons for this flight
from. the city. The third Gentleman to whom the latter portion of this speech
was adressed. took his hat of and displayed a countenance of the darkest copper.
he was a perfect Othello. seemed nearly 30 years of age. and po[sse]ssed a
majestic deportment. noble forehead and an eye like a young Eagle. "Reasons
enough of them." he muttered. and. sat down in silence "Come Gentlemen."
cried Rougue "we must speak of this buisness sir Hang it you know that. those.
infernal Ministers knowing us to be at present scattered Lambs. have at once
hoping to find us unprepared. seized this opportunity to dissolve parliament. and
to order a new election.[11] Now please fate they shall not find us unprepared. we
must arm sirs and be doing of course I shall. find means to return a host of.
Gentry for other places but at present we have most to do. with the City the
strong hold. of the Constitution. Sir. (rising with animation) I will defeat them
By the bones of Sylla. I'll bring forward two members for this Wellingtons
Glass town and Ill carry them through. Quashia I have made up my mind and
you shall stand for one. Sir you know The African interrupted Elrington with

---

[9] Branwell is once again associating Elrington and his followers with the
Miltonic Satan. In the bottom right-hand corner of the manuscript page is a
sketch of a fortress-like building linked by a bridge to other buildings—see
Alexander & Sellars, 305. In the left-hand margin are two columns of numbers.

[10] Quamina Quashia, the only son of Sai Too Too Quamina. Quashia was
adopted by the Duke of Wellington—see Alexander CB II, Part I, 3, 178-79—
echoing the historical Duke of Wellington's adoption of the four-year-old Salabut
Khan, whom he had rescued from the battlefield during the Mahratta Wars in
India.

[11] The election campaign described here is inspired by the agitation throughout
the United Kingdom over the Reform Bill of 1832, and may reflect Branwell's
personal experience of electioneering in the previous year—see Barker Brontës,
199.

"My Lord. no. one can command me. and—" "Stuff. silence I say that since you are the Duke's adopted son. my heart. but youre best representative of his adopted city. Quashia Quashia. funds. are in my purse draw Sir at your need and draw freely." "I consent Elrington. but rouse and commence operations who shall be collegue." "Volo—come to the Hall. all of you to Morrow to breakfast. and Ill tell you." He stopt a moment. the others were about to speak. "No words" he interrupted "No voice Sirs. ho Caversham give me. yon desk. and while I write. be silent." He. strode to the Desk and sitting down began to write. vehemently for [a] quarter of an hour and them rising re commenced. "Now Sirs. I have given your—stop. hand me that glass of Claret. hah—good—well I have given you at once the draught of a Handbill. for circulation. the plan for a comittee and. a note or two on the subject. Now first."

"To the Freinds of freedom to all Glasstowners to the Electors of the Metropolis of Wellingtons Land.

Freinds and Fellow country men. A great crises has arrived and. a vast struggle will now ensue. Tyranny corruption and the. Ancients wish to retain. Freedom justice. and the present wish to partake. upon yourselves my freinds lies the option either to groan and pine the slaves of. Despotism or to rise and flourish the. lords of Africa. undoubtedly. you wish for nothing save the last. but your chains are on you and you see no hope of release. you are placed in the stronghold of the. 12. governed by their laws throught their minions. bridled by your monarch and threatened by his vengeance. no people possess more sense than you none than you see farther into the folly of our present Government. none more wish to reform it. But you say. our. chains lie heavy round us. and we dare not stir. Well then here I stand. Glasstowners I. am free and my arms shall be employed to release you I understand. that the 12. frightened at the aspect of their affairs have dissolved parliament and. have proclaimed a new Election. undoubtedly they will strive again to saddle. you with 2 members. But. if our strength and justice avails us they shall not.!

Electors of Wellingtons Glass town. we offer two you. two men to represent you[r] noble city in our common parliament one the broad basis of justice to yourselves justice to all. at present I shall not say further. save to tell you. that. on the Afternoon of Monday. 4 September they will. occupy the front of the Western Hotel there to show you their persons their principles the plan for your welfare. meet them there my Freinds and there judge them. Till then. I remain you[r] ardent welwisher A Elrington—dated. Caversham House. Sept. 2d Now for my second affair.

"It being determined that. Mr. ------ and. Mr------ (blank for the Names to be filled up). shall stand for the representation of Wellingtons glass town in parliament. on the principle of thour[ou]gh Reformation. it is agreed to that a committee be immediatly formed. for the purpose. of watching over and promoting their return. This Comittee to Hold its meetings every Evening (beginning with Sept. 3d.) at. 6. pm. in the Western Hotel. untill the conclusion of the. Election.   A Elrington.
Paper third.

"The following Noblemen and gentlemen are requested to form the Comittee for Promoting the return to Parliament for Wellingtons Glasstown of ——— and. ———.

> Alexander. Viscount Elrington M.P.
> -Arthur O Connor Esqr M P.
> -George Charles Gordon Esqr M P.
> Frederic Viscount Caversham. M.P.
> Captain. John. MacArthur
> Richard. Wareham. Esqr
> Colonel. James Fitzherbert.
> Thorncliffe Eversham Gordon Esqr.
> Captain Juilius Gordon.
> St. John Richard Streighton Esqr
>
> A Elrington.

Paper Fourth.
Copy of. a circular to be adressed to the. principal. Newspapers of the City.

"Sir. Not doubting. that. you will instantly take up the side of justice the Comittee for the return of two Liberal Members for this city. request you to accept of the enclosed Bill of. 1000£ to meet your expenses in the cause of civil & religious freedom. should you return a note. stating your determination to advance that cause to. the utte[r]most. you will in directing it to the Comittees rooms Western Hotel. have your Bill. doubled in amount.

> A Elrington.

Paper Fifth.
Copy of a circular to be addressed to all the Inns and Public Houses and places of Entertainment in the City.

Sir upon sending a note to the Committee. for the return of two liberal members for Wellingtons Glasstown. stating your cordial determination to support. any reforming Candidate. you will be requested to. throw your house open to all persons for what they may demand. and. at the conclusion of the Election you will direct your account to the Comittee which account will be punctually paid. meanwhile aas a surety of their honourable dealing they beg your acceptance of the enclosed note of 100£.

> A Elrington.

Paper Sixth. a letter
Enclosing the above 5 papers. and addressed to Seargent W J. Despard. Bookseller. Wellingtons street Wellingtons Glass town.

Sir. The Commitee for the return of 2 Liberal Candidates for this city. request you. to print of. instantly of the first numbered paper herein enclosed. 5000 copies. of the second 500. copies of the third 500 copies of the fourth. 20 copies of the 5th 500 copies—after printing you must instantly forward them to Elrington Hall. your Bill. you will please to. place to the account of the comittee enclosed you will find. a note of 1000£ pounds. for trouble &c requesting your ardent support in the regeneration of your country I remain

> A Elrington.

"Now Gentlemen." continued. Rougue with energy after he had read these papers. and folded them in a sealed wrapper. "What think you of my speed and animation go on like me and. rest assured you'll. gain. Here Footman. take this parcel. this moment too the Bookseller. Despard. and heres a guinea for your pains. now Go. quickly.—well sirs Now to speak of money matters vast sums will be ready to carry our candidates through. but courage we will speak of that to morrow. when you must. Gentlemen meet me at. the Great Western Hotel. Good Morning. I must. go and call on the other members of the unborn commitee to make them enter. on the work.".

Elrington. bowed to his friends. and ordering his carriage strode from the apartment. his companions when the door was shut gazed at each other in mute surprise. Caversham first broke [the] silence with "on my Soul. He's Energy. why he'll carry all before him. did any one ever hear of anything so audacious. elect democrats here beard the lion in his den oppose to the Duke. you my rare prince. on my soul it beats. any thing ever before done. well. we shall gain to your glasses Gents. Connor that corkscrew." They drew their chairs to the table. and at the bottles we shall leave them.

CHAPTER. III

PBB. Nov. 5th 1833.

On the Evening of this day. The Hon Miss Percy. in the noble Supper room of Percy Hall. sat. on a sofa. in perfect ease amid the gorgeous splendour of all around her. she seemed a very picture of indulged aristocracy on the splendid ottoman. reclining before the glow of Chandeliers and Fire. with books. drawings and a hundred et cetera's strewed round her and the huge dog Roland lying gazing up at her Face. and. licking the small hand. so condescendingly held out to him. yet in spite of this. Africa. held not a Heart so. freed from sophistry [than] that of the daughter of Lord Elrington. A footman. entered "John here. do place those books in order. I have thrown them round me most wickedly." "Yes my lady I will. Theres an old Gentleman in the Hall. who wishes to see my Lord. I said. he was not at home. but he wont. go. he wished to see you." "Who is he what is he like." "I cant say just for that. but as how hes stuck on the topp of as decent a peice of Horse flesh as a body could see." "Well John. show him in. but mind you stay here behind my sofa. stay Thomas you. show the Gentleman in here." a Lad ran to obey his Mistresses command. the visitor appeared. at the door the momen[t] the young Lady saw him she turned to her footman and whispered "Oh John. I am Glad. I told you to stay" "I for that matter I am." The visitor a. little. withered. Old man. covered with a brown great coat and. slouched hat which he did not take. of. tramped readily from door to fireplace. Which as he stood before he first spit in and then poked with his stick then scratching his head he began turning to his offended hostess. "I cant but zay. Maam. bud I'm as how Ise come fra the Glasstown. to speake to Rougue. on. a buisness or so. as how. Sdeaths a cold." [12] he continued rubbing his withered palms over the fire. and then elegantly blowing his nose with them. "As how Maam. iv you're—my Lords—hum—haw daugh—I mean. Honble Miss Percy. Youd happen tell un when he'd be in. haw" squirting into the fire a quid of tobbacco. Miss Percy just stared. then looked frightened then. tried to look grave and lastly laughed out right at the conclusion of this doughty speech. "John John take him in to the Hall. give him beer and. refreshment. My Father will be Here shortly you shall then see him. take him in John. and give him.—" "Aye Aye Ise go. Im agoing youll do as she tells you and get me somut. haw. Sdeaths a hungry." so saying he spit out a third quid and taking his staff followed the servant out of the room. he being gone Miss Percy had not time to recover from her suprise. when a carriage was heard driving up. the door opened and her father entered. "Oh Father I am glad your here I suppose from the Newspapers this morning there has been. a dissolution of parliament and have you been all day. active[e] respecting it." "Yes Mary I have. but I am both cold and thirsty." "You look so" "I dare say. seeing I have he eaten to day. but here is not supper nearly ready.?." Yes it is But Father there has just been here the strangest old man I ever saw. he wanted you I could not make any—" Is he in child. show him in Sdeath by my life. show him in child. leave the room. "But you will take supper." "Stuff no. in with him. good night Mary. "Good night Father." she. departed and Sdeath entered "Well you scoundrel" cried Elrington "what now" "The carriage is waiting." answered. Sdeath. "Volo another word on that subject and Ill cleave your scull to the chin "Will you. as how weve had grand doings in our town Rougue and the Governmenters think they'll smash all before em. The dogs. haw. hem but as how we'd a meeting of th' club and Mont an tothers ha sent me to you. sixteen hundred mile and better to speak on how we must fill. the house and pile the courats with the slain. as how I mean the reforming members." "Stop villian Ill write a list of the principal[s] sit down" "I theres a bottle here". Elrington took pen and paper wrote hastily and shortly. delivered to Sdeath the following paper. "Sweet Mont. Gordon. for Denard. Connor. Seldon. Carey. Silsden[13] Dorn Fidena. Quashia and some other fellow. This city. Sdeath!!!!!! Sneakystown Caversham Rosstown Thyself. Parrystown Myself Glasstown McCarthy Harlaw. so much for the principals. secondarys 13. to my 13 bouroughs. 23 to their private ones. 4. to thy 4 burroughs. or seats. 2. to Cavershams couple of seats 1 to Careys 3 to Dorns. 50 or 60. to try where they can. best hit and at the old sure places. 16. total. 134 or perhaps 150 in the mainland for stumps 11. for Monkeys 21. grand total. 166. make up if possible 200. or 250. members in all. and for cash from 150 to 200 000£ of my own is at comand. our struggles monty must be violent. tremendous good day.

A Elrington.

---

12 See p. 285, n. 31.
13 A village in West Yorkshire.

here Sdeath I am frothed up with writing.—How was Mont when you left and what did the city look like." "Mont was as mich <activ> as you are the City was like in a bit of a confusion the Ministers as aye rapping from one anothers offices like mad On I could a wished to stick one or two I could." here this worthy wiping his mouth. with the sleeve of his coat gave a deep sigh. "Rougue Rougue I zay if you are at a loss for a second member here I can show you one." "Can you—where" "I az I was a trotting here foregathered about 9. miles off with like a gentleman. on horsback. he seemed rather fresh in our ways but we began to talk abit and. I found him to be. a bright un a real leader disposed Rougue. to take any way to gain a name." here Sdeath got up. Rougues eyes were bent on him with an eagle look. he continued vehemently. "Rougue Elrington take my word Sir. he's one will rise I could see that directly. why though as raw as blood in these countrys of ours he did shew sich eagerness in every thing about un. sich cautiousness in talking that by Sdeaths heart. I felt him a stiff un Rougue think no more ont but. take him at once." Rougue look[ed] for a minute thoughtfully on the fire and then turning to the desk. drew out a sheet of paper upon which writing he then read as follows

     "Sir

          I earnestly request the Honour of your company at Percy Hall. about 6 or 7 o clock. to morrow morning apologising for the abruptness on the score of haste I remain. your. &c

                                                                 A Elrington.

Sdeath Sdeath whats his name." "Its I got it out on him though he was sharp. "Sir Robert Weever Pelham. of. English. Hotel in this city he is building a house called Tamsworth Hall a few miles off" Rougue wrote the direction sealed it and. rung a bell a servant appeared. "James. take a horse and. carry this instantly to the place mentioned on the direction. off. man" The servant dissappeared and they soon. heard him clattering down the avenue. But now a second. servant entered. with a very large parcel. which he laid beside his Lordship stating it to have come from the bookseller Despard. "Ha well give the bearer his skinfull go" Rougue the cutting open the parcel. took out a specimen from each printed paper and handing them to Sdeath said "Here hound fold in the letter to Mont these 5 it will show him how to get on now. go go to the Hall there rumble thy belly ful spit fire begone I must write all night. next morning thou must receive some more letters which I must write then to thy ain het hame again."[14] Sdeath chuckled a laugh and departed Elrington. walked to a cupboard. concealed in the wall and from thence taking forth a bottle of brandy and glass placed it by him then giving vent to a few oaths and curses wound his watch and sat down to write the whole. night through First he took. the. Hand bills and filled up the blanks for the members names. with the names of. the two whom he wished to be member[s]. Zerayda. Quamina Quashia. and. Robert Weever Pelham. but ere he had done he. violently rung the bell a servant

---

[14] Compare Robert Burns, "The Holy Fair," ll. 107-08: "To 's ain het hame had sent him/ Wi' fright that day."

appeared. "Ho call in my secretary go." This person soon appeared "Shut the door Mr Seaton. take your implements fill up these blanks with those two names indorse the. papers of this pile with the names of the Editors of our newpapers Those of this with the different Inns. then. fold and seal them all and afterward tell me." The man sat down to his work in silence Elrington then set to writing hasty Letters too his different tools and. fellow labourers through our country. directing their notions offering money. adjuring to exertion. and. dilating on the tremendous crisis approaching all this occupied his Lordship till. 5 o clock in the morning when he flung his pile of work to his secretary and after telling him to direct and seal. he threw himself onto the sofa and fell into a feverish sleep. an hour had not elapsed ere his Secretary awoke him. by stating that he had. finished his work. Elrington told him then to leave the room. and he being gone the Nobleman gott up. extinguished the sickly and fading candles. and undrew the curtains of the ample window he looked out with a weary smile. The sun had arisen all the park and the distant hills were rolling away the dew. and seemed filled with life and song. his Daughter. was walking in the lawn. he strode to the table emptied the half finished bottle and raising the window sash stepped out into the grass. Miss Percy advanced to him. "Oh Father have you not slept to night. I see you have not. now take a walk through the country" "I cant Mary I cant. I must sleep still less. for a while yet." They were stopped by. a Horseman who rode up and as he drew near dismounted he seemed. a tall gentlemanly person. about 30 years of age. with light hair and hansome features composed into an expression of the most stern and guarded solemnity. He advanced to Rougue and after bowing politely to Miss Percy. spoke. "Lord Elrington I believe" "I am. and I hope I may address you. as. Sir R Pelham" "Certainly my Lord." Oh come then sir into my Library. I wish to speak. to you." The gentleman followed his Lordship into the room. where he being seated Elrington stood opposite his pale countenance and feirce eye gleaming with light. "Sir. you know though perhaps you are a new comer. the state of our nation. you see what a convulsion is arising oh. Sir Robert. he who wishes to rise must strive now. and since I hear. of your talent and. ability from sure sources I do offer you. the post of candidate. for. this city. Sir Robert we must have little speech upon it you know my. principles proffess them. Sir if only for a time and them be sure of. success look at these papers just printed see my movements." he stood looking anxiously on the Baronet who with a composed but. peircing glance first surveyed his host then the papers. "My Lord I realy proffess liberal opinions I see. nothing to object to here but of course should I stand for the representation of this City. you. will. leave my own course?" "Yes. Sir" "before and after" "we will" "I stand then" "Right Sir Robert." They now began to talk together of. the political affairs of our nation Elrington bent his powers to extract. the weight of his visitors ability who though he showed a vast fund. of cold cautious calculation. yet. exhibited. as much. cool clear judgement. taste and fluency both of thought and language. he seemed well learned in the mysterys of politics there was a strange. sinister expression and a deceitful smile in his otherwise fine countenance which though it would repulse most men yet. gave Elrington a still better opinion of him. He seemed during

the conversation also to be measuring the. character of that wonderful Nobleman
They parted on mutual terms of seeming satisfaction mutual agreement and
internal. cautiousness of each other Rougue adjuring Pelham to. be present two
hours hence at. the Western hotel. and pelham. consenting wished Elrington
good morning and rode off. This gentleman had scarcely gone when. a carriage
drove up to the door out off which leaped. Connor Gordon and Quashia. They.
walked into Rougues study and. after the usual allowances of. mutual cursing.
Connor exclaimed Elrington we have. not only arrived to accompany you to the
meeting but to tell you a disagreeable peice of news. That cursed. villain Capt
Flower with another Gentleman. called. I think. Morley. accompanied by. the
Dukes Agent and Steward. Messrs. Maxwell. and Evans. have arrived. in the
City hot from the Glasstown and whats worse. Earl St Clair the feind incarnate
is. on his way here behind them they affirmed that he will arrive. toward noon.
Volo. Elrington we shall have hot work of it. but youve got energy. my Heart
they say that. the two. first Morley and Flower will be proposed as candidates."
"Well Connor and whose Morley." "Why he is. they say a young fellow. stuffed
with Reading and politics a dab at speaking too Volo. my—" "Well. I shall
match him." "Rougue interrupted. Gordon "We met a hound riding down from
the avenue whom we. did not like. know. a rum stiff un he bowed coldly to us
and stared at Quashia's black phiz—" Hold your toungue brute. yes he did but Ill
have his blood I—" exclaimed the ireful. African. "fool" cried. Elrington. "Why
he is your Colleage Sir he is Sir Robert Weever Pelham." Quashia stood silent
but scarcely appeased he broke out "I hate him." "Stuff. Quashia but Sir I want
to register your. promise made to me. before I consented to open a seat for you."
Zoreyda. Quamina Quashia promises to Alex. Viscount Elrington that upon his
gaining him a seat in parliament he. will should Elringtons party on any great
convulsion need his assistance bring down from the interior of Africa. any
number of. native troops commanded by himself. not exceeding 30 000 men. as
witness our hands." now Ive put my name. then Qua[s]hia put your name and
you two scoundrels as witnesses add yours." The three did as commanded
Rougue. muttered to Quashia now remember. and taking first a glass each of
brandy. and next their hats they. sallied out mounted their carriage and drove off
Rougue followed them. in his Chariot and ere long they alighted. in the heart of
the city at. the Grant Western Hotel.

CHAPTER.IV.   Novr. 6.th
                                     AD 1833.
                                     PB B—te

Sir Robert Weever Pelham. was by birth an Englishman. The fact of his not having been educated on the philosophers Island[15] debared him from the privileges of a thourough Glasstowner. He was born in Lancashire England. where His father originally poor and of no note. had raised himself. by. injenuity and perseverance to vast wealth and a Baronets title. which on his death he Bequeathed to his son. Sir Robert. who finding himself. unfettered and aware of his own great ability and knowledge. looked about for some place some method. by which. to signalise himself exert his ambition and employ his mind. but Alas England affords no feild for such he saw that and. determind to embark for the widly celebrated and magnificent regions of Africa. where he felt that his talent would find its way. He therefore instantly converted a property of 1100 000£ into ready money and set sail for Wellingtons Glass town. where so soon as he had arrived he bought a splendid estate and. Mansion called Tamworth Hall.[16] Now. he applied himself. most ardently to the Study of the History and politics of our strange and. mightty country. in secret. perfecting himself. so that. he could contrive. to emerge from his. situation it might [seem] as. the. newly fixed Butterfly. The age of this Gentleman was about 30. his person we have termed Handsome. and extremly cold and. proud. his character was like it. cautious. plausible. and even at times deceitful. alway[s] alert for politics and well versed. in their labyrinthe. just now after settling in this country we see that the Parliament was dissolved and. the Elections commenced Sir Robert was looking round for a bourough. when he came in contact with Elrington whose keen searching glance saw in a moment. his vast ability. he fixed him he thought to his side and. showed him the road to power. We left Sir Robert. parting with Elrington. he. turned his Horses head toward the city. and. mused for a while in silence at last. soliloquizing to Himself. thus "Well I have seen the great Elrington so soon after my landing truely an unexpected. aquaintance.—I certainly could wish my step to parliament had been on the other side but. I shall. be content as it is it shall not hurt. me. He is a great man. and cannot sink." While thus musing. a carriage dashed up from behind. it was the one containing Elrington Quashia and the two others. who from the slow pace at which Pelham moved had overtaken him. Elrington called out. "Well Sir Robert. we are all bound on the same destination. let me introduce to you first your colleague. Z. Q Quashia. son of the former monarch of Africa. next to my worthy and excellent freinds. Messrs. Connor and Gordon." The first. Quashia bowed to Pelham. stiffly. the other two. eagerly and greedily. Pelham returned it gentlemanly. and all rode on together—on alighting at the Hotel they found there. assembled. all those. gentlemen. mentioned before as to compose the Comittee after mutual introductions. wine was called for. Elrington took the

---

[15] See "Philosophers Island" in the Glossary. Thomas Pelham (1756-1826) served under Pitt in various ministries, including Irish Secretary (1783) and Home Secretary (1801).

[16] Sir Robert Peel (1788-1850) became Member of Parliament for Tamworth in Staffordshire in 1830.

chair and buisness was entered on. "Money makes the mare to go." This was therefore the first thing debated. on. Quashia offered. 40 000£. Pelham 50 000£. The rest. 20 000£. Elrington at once offered 80 000£ thus making a totle. of. 190 000£. an immense sum which Elrington remarked must carry weight. The formid[ab]le nature of the opposition likely to be met with was talked over. shemes were promptly formed. for by bribery &c. getting over as large a number as possible of Rare Apes &c. who were to have arms placed in their hands. and. placed at the. meetings to awe and overpower honest voters. a large sum was voted. for. bribes to Electors. and every means however unjust were laid hold. of to ensure sucess. Pelham sat amazed at. the reckless an[d] iniquitous nature. of the proceedings but he wisely looked on winked and said nothing a[f]ter arranging matters for the speechifying and. showing forth of the candidates to morrow. The meeting separted. Elrington inviting them all to dinner that Evening at Elrington Hall.

IN the Meantime the Handbills during the Night had been posted up in all parts of this great Metropolis. The morning Newspapers appeared with long commentarys and speculations on the approaching struggle and its probable consequence too many of them evincing. palpable appearance of the Ass laden with gold[17] having vis[i]ted their Editors. All the Inns were open. the scarlet flag was every where flying and. shoals of. rascals about the streets were shouting Elrington and Liberty Democrats for ever. Public feeling was wound up very high. and this scene only presented an image of what was just now going on through the whole kingdoms. True the master spirit worked here. But his agents were active everywhere.

IN the mean time. the opposite and hitherto reining party were far from being idle. The Government of the Great Glasstown anxious to secure this City had prepared means for instantly seizing the representation. and as we have said. on this morning there arrived 2 or 3 carraiges. containing the intended <afore mentioned > candidates Mr Morley myself. (ie Capt Flower) and. the Dukes two agents with 3 or 4 other Gentlemen to forward. the Election. we saw at once on arriving that. the most energetic. measures must be had recourse to to keep pace with our formidable. though new sprung antagonists. placards letters Handbills prepared at Verdopolis were instantly promulgated stating our arrival. motives for action and day of presentation. to bribery we disdained to have recourse. we knew that our party was strong. enough without this aid

Sir Robert Pelham. having left. the Hotel. after the conclusion of the meeting. took his horse and proceeded. along the noble banks. of the. Gambia toward Percy Hall. musing within himself upon. the strange and awkward situation he was thrown into. for his politics and private. opinions it could easily be seen were. scarce so extreme. as. those of [the] strange men. among

---

[17] Midas, the legendary king of Phrygia, had his request that everything he touch be turned into gold granted by the gods; according to other legends, he was also endowed with a pair of ass's ears by Apollo after favoring Pan over Apollo in a musical contest.

whom he had. pitched for a time his tent. But however He; at least however raw in actual politics was no novice in theory no man easily daunted. his cool and searching intellect. saw paths for escape. where to others all seem thick. rock and prison. wall. and his sly wily accomodating temper enabled him to worm through them with ease. peculiar to himself.

Sir Robert after riding 2 or 3 miles. entered the splendid avenue. leading to Percy Hall. He gave his Horse to a porter and. stepped into the park. desirous to see it. before. entering the Mansion. or rather to have an opportunity of finishing his speculations on. his political prospects. But the beauty of the scenery around him. often diverted his attention from these weightier matters. He was standing upon an eminence admiring the noble trees. which stood above him. the green lawn. spread far below him. the old. Hall lifting its grey chimneys over the dark. foliage before him. and the aierial peaks of Africa stretching in the sunlight in the clear calm heaven beyond him. While thus gazing. but with a mind perhaps rather. occupied with other feelings than those of. pure scenic admiration. A young Lady. whom Sir Robert instantly recognized as Miss M Percy turning round a corner appeared before him. She knew not. of the vicinity of any one. and happened to be reading. She looked up. But bowed. without. any confussion. Sir Robert. could not. use his usual stiffness toward one so. young and fair. he. returned her morning salute or rather (for he had made his first) after mentioning the. reasons for his arrival remarked. I have several times Madam been mistaken in. my notions of this country. I had supposed. Africa to afford no prospect. so fair and English. as the one I here see. and give me leave to remark. that I did not. suppose the poet whose works you. hold. in your hand. had been so much as heard of here." "Sir. in the latter case I believe you are right. or nearly so. eastward of these mountains this work is scarcly know[n]. will you not give me credit for superior knowledge. I. have lived nearer to your Island. and. on looking over this book have scarcly found it. so mean as. England ought to produce. What does your Nation think of Lord Byron."[18] "My Nation. Madam are frightened at him they could not understand him he was to much. of. a—a Glasstowner for our comprehension. for my self I knew him. and could. appreciate him." Miss Percys eye lighted up rather when she found. that Sir Robert had been personaly acquainted with one whose works she admired. Did you know him. Sir? My Father has once or twice. on looking at. his works affirmed that he was born for our country. and died. because he did not stand in his natural soil. you are too proud. of. your poet Sir. look at this one." Miss Percy gave to him an exquisitly bound. little doudecimo. printed in a superlative stile upon. paper like Ivory. The fly leaf. bore "June.—1824. A. Percy. R. to his daughter M. H. Percy." it was a volumn of the poems of. Arthur Marquis of

---

18 Lord Byron, famous for constructing the poetic persona of the outlaw hero, much like Branwell's fictional hero-villain, was both reviled and lionized by English society.

Douro.[19] "Hah. Madam. I know we must bow to this one. He is above us. Byron Himself—" "must. fail before him you would say. yes. yet they are like each other. But. Sir you must walk forward to the Hall My Father e pects you soon. Good morning or evening." She stepped into a side walk. and. dissapeared among the trees. Sir Robert took his road to the Hall. where he stepped into the saloon and introduced himself with his usual staid formality There soon entered. his worthy fellow candidate. Quashia. and their supporters and committee men to the number of a couple of Dozens. Dinner was served up as usual in splendid style—Miss Percy presided. at the Head of the Table and in spite of her general. shyness. of manner with the greatest ease and elegance. Elrington opened his vast store of. brilliant languge and varied information. he strove to please all and. his endeavour was not in vain. All his Guests though men. of. in general the most dark and treacherous character for not one save Pelham was present who would have scrupled. to. the most infamous means to gain an end.—were yet. Gentlemen. and. knew much. The cloth being drawn. Bottles and. glasses were brought forth. The chairs were drawn closer. Eyes. looked brighter and. with glass upon glass tumbler over tumbler. bottle on bottle. there came out the full tide of Glass town language Glasstown politics and the momentous affair upon which they were. then met. Pelham who wished to present an unspotted character took care though. he took a decent quantity not. to exceed the bounds of moderation. and his smooth. ready flow. of gliding language kept his hearers from noticing his slower circuit of the bottle. Elrington poured down a bottle of spirits as a matter of every day occurence. Quashia. half a dozen of wine as a thing. of extemeest pleasure. ere 10 or 11. at night. the Company separated. many. in a state. of intoxication all pleasantly exhilirated. all too intending to meet. again on the morrow. on the hustings. of Wellingtons Glasstown.

CHAPTER. Vth.   Nov^r—.
                                        the. 14th
                                        AD 1833.
                                        PB B—te

The Morning for the presentation of the 4 candiates on the Hustings at length arose. and even ere the first reddning of the Horizon. thousands were astir through the City. upon this all important buisness. A grand Husting capable. of Holding 2 or 300. persons had been erected in the great square in front of the City Hall. 2 companys were drawn up on each side. armed. to prevent if possible the almost certain riots. every street of the city flamed with placards and and handbills of. brilliant. Red (the Democratic) and Green (the. Constitutional)

---

[19] Charlotte's earliest known manuscript dates from 1826. Branwell may be referring to **THE VIOLET A POEM WITH SEVERAL SMALLER PIECES BY THE MARQUIS OF DUORO**, dated November 14, 1830.

colours. innumerable flags and banners of the same Hues. preceded the different
bodys of Electors pouring into the city from every point. while. Bands of Music.
clashing of bells and. peals of shouting roaring and sounding at one and the same
time. all tended to exhilirate and. to heighten the scene.

I shall pass over the constant rows and fighting of this morning the
Drinki[n]g and bribeing and threat[n]ing and. extortion. these things every body
can picture. but not so easily can my readers conceive. when the sun hung in his
Meridian over this noble city all that vast Wellington square. crammed close
with 200 000. men. every house and building bearing to one their roof windows
and chimnies. their countless numbers. The crowd was wedged to suffocation all
round the Hustings then hung round thickly throgh the extremity of the square.
and at every opening and vista of a receding street. still appearing still pouring
forward. with band and banner for each favourite candidate. Green and red red and
green. waved from spire. window and Flagstaff v:.hout ceasing. The Hustings as
yet was empty but about noon. a loud and overwnelming shout from a distant
street taken up continued and increased to a tremendous roar. up to the ve[r]y
town Hall announced the arrival of the Candidates. the storm of music rose
higher. the Banners floated thicker forwards and the crowds opened an long
lane—to admit the. 2. splendid lines of noble carriages. which dashed. dust and
foam spattered up to the hustings. the. noble horses were reined in. First Mr
Maxwell. stepped out and took his station in the middle on an elevated seat. as
the representative of the Duke. absent. and High Sheriff of the meeting. then.
alighted from their row of chariots amid the exclamations of their freinds. the 2
constitutional candidates Mr Babbicome Morley[20] Myself. (Capt Flower) with
my supporters and Backers in this ardous struggle. these took station on the
Sheriffs right Hand. Then like wise amid the cries of their Favourers came up
The tall form of Viscount Elrington who though no candidate was considered by
all of course prime mover of the opposition followed by His candidates Sir R
Pelham. Q Quamina. and the Hosts of Cavershams Gordons Streightons
Connors and that dark revolutionary Fry A small degree of silence having been
obtained the Sheriff in a short speech. explained the reasons for their being called
together. the Motives on which they ought to act and. in conclusion called upon
the Constitutional candidates to appear. and. show themselves—His Highness.
TRACKY Duke of Nevada. stood forward and the assembled multitudes took of
Hat and cap in reverence save the dark looking group on the sheriffs left. he in a
short and most condescending speech introduced. to their notice. Myself as
candidate for the office of representing in Parliament this vast and mighty city. I
advanced admid. tremendous cheering and still greater opposition in fact. between
the one and the other I could not through my whole speech be heard beyond the
platform in the crowd below many were the blows given and taken many the
broken heads and legs. to be laid to my account on that day. it was long before
silence could be restored. and not then without military force. The Right

[20] Possibly based on John Parker, Earl of Morley (1772-1840) who supported
the Catholic Emancipation Bill.

Honble. Thomas Beresford Bobbadil.[21] Major General. of the Army. of W's
Land advanced And in a very short. and scarc[e]ly gracious speech. introduced. to
the Pekin[22] Thomas Babbicome Morley. This young Gentleman came forth.
amid the same wild and uprorarious tumult as myself. But his loud and trumpet
toned voice soon commanded attention. kept up by his short squat. figure and.
Broad. glimmering countenance. but however unprepossessing in look. his
overpowring voice. his readiness in speaking the distinct arangement of his.
ideas and. the eloquence the weight the sparkling antithesis of every sentence.
carried on in spite of every other hindrance. Elrington bent his keen eye on him
following him out throgh his speech. with unmixed intrest and when he
concluded. with "And Now Gentlmen though placed in this strange dilemma of
Right and Bigotry opposed to. Wrong and liberty. yet let us not. at all despair.
there is to man a body and a soul the first soon in the lapse perhaps of a few
seasons must wear out decay and pass in to. annihilation the last shall survive
the loss of this companion shall rise up to endure. in unending in eternal
Existence. So though now in all our arguments and contest[s] wrong is so
strangly opposed to wrong right opposed to right. all mixed and warring in vain
confusion yet wait. the time. when that wrong shall rot of and vanish and leave
the right to join. its once. seperate parts and endure in an existance. which
neither the force of Man. can extinguish or the lapse of ages destroy" Then with
this last sentence Elrington joined his powerful voice to the roar of applause.
that range from the hustings to the Horizon mingled through at length with
hissing riot and fighting

Frederic Viscount Caversham in an elegant speech introduced Quashia
Quamina. This strange and furious Gentleman came forward bowed to the
meeting and with lighted eye. stepped back without speaking. affirming to his
astonished freinds. "Will I fawn on the descendants of my Fathers Murderers.
They shall die" Viscount Elrington stepped forward and. taking of his hat.
prepared to introduce the last candidate. the the dissabrobation which ran. through
the crowded square on his first appearance soon. subsided into undisguised intrest
and attention. He began with his well known thrilling voice and unapproached
Majesty of Language. He spoke of the Tyranny of the 12 of their unjustifiable
oppression of the people. he reprobated. the disgraceful. listlestness of that
people in so long enduring their iron yoke. But described the feeling the wish
now. abroad to throw it of spoke of his own efforts. and. losses in the cause of
liberty. showed the means for the nation now soon to gain it. introduced Sir R
Pelham. as one grand. step up the ladder spoke of him in the highest terms as
the only fit person to represent their Noble City. and thus concluded "ON The
death of Louis 14th the Great Monarch of France. the Archbishop Fenelon.[23]

---

21   See pp. 93, n. 5, and 123.
22   A name given by Napoleon's soldiers to civilians—a term of contempt. See
Scott's *Life of Napoleon*, III, 70 and Alexander CB, I, 28.
23   The archbishop Fénelon (1651-1715), French theologian and liberal man of
letters, was appointed tutor to the grandson and heir of Louis XIV in 1689. He

was appointed to preach his funeral sermon. he mounted the pulpit. and cast his eyes first on the huge Cathederal whose pillars windows and roof rose high above him. Then on the mixed and mighty Multitude. which filled choir and nave and Transept beneath him. He saw that. Building. lighted with. the flame of a thousand torches that. assembly. shining. with the lustre of their high splendour there were the Mightiest Nobles of the Mightiest Court of Europe Gathered in full blown pomp and solemnity round that. Coffin resting under its palls and canopies of velvet. and what did Fenelon think that coffin contained. the body of a King? No he knew it held a dead and corrupting carcase. offensive to every sense close shut from Human sight. fast. festering to decay.! It was that this mighty Building was open to admit this vast Multitude assembled to deplore. Fenelon lifted his hands over his hearers and cried out O My Freinds God only is great. Now Glasstowners apply this case to your own circumstances and tell me may I not say when I see That. Old. Rotten withered heap termed Majesty Royalty Loyalty Constitution. and so forth. lying enshrined in the most pompous state Revered. and worshipped by. the greatest Nation on earth and though in its life it had trampled on abused and sacrificed them. and in its death had left them only fetters bondage. and misery. yet they still. feared the corrupting man. still held their chains and slavery. and when. once should come and tell them their time of servitude was expired. should offer to strike the fetters form their feet and. give them a long unknow[n] happiness I say would not you say to such people oh infatuated wretches. oh wretched effects of. Depotism will you not let me cry. oh My Freinds Liberty alone is Great! Now then is not this case your own. yes it is Here (pointing to himself) stands Fenelon. There (pointing to The Constitutional Candidates) there lies the rotten Royalty. Here too in the person. of. Sir Rober[t] Pelham stands. your. paredon your salvation." A Roar of Applause burst from the. mighty Audience. Sir R. Pelham came forth his. fine figure. Gentlemanly adress and finely toned voice. received its due attention. he entered on his speech without hesitation. but. with an affectation of Modesty. in calm dignified well balanced Language fin[e]ly glossed smoothly reasoned argument unmoved features and statuelike attitude. The consequence was that on his speech being finished. though every man present stood convinced of his hollowness insincerity and political trickery yet charmed by his plausibilty Gentlemanlyness. and ability. the sense of the meeting did most certainly run toward him. Now the High Sheriff after a few words in conclusion ordered the poll to be opened. The Hustings was cleared and that momentous part of the buisness was begun upon with the wildest and most outrageous uproar fighting and even bloodshed.

---

enjoyed various national honors before falling under the Pope's disfavor in 1697, which resulted in Fénelon being exiled to his diocese.

CHAPTER. VI.   Nov 14
                                1833.
                                PBB.

ON the Evening of the Day following that described in our last chapter. while Miss Percy was. cross questioning her. attendants on the probable fate of the Election. the well known[n] carriage Dashed up. and Lord Elrington entered the room. he looked. quite exhausted. "Oh Child I am quite knocked up. I have never slept or rested since I left this house." He threw himself on the sopha. "Do order Tea or supper or what else it may be Mary. Do you want to no the end of the Election its over. look at this paper" His daughter took it and read.

> For Pelham --------4958.
> For Morley --------3132.   D-7059.
> For Flower---------3011.   C-6143.
> For Quashia ------2101. (total votes 13202)

Returned. Sir Robert Weever Pelham (Democrat) and. Thomas Babbicome Morley (Constitutionalist) His daughter was about to speak when a thundering knock was heard at the Door Elrington motioned her to leave the room Quashia entered he seemed the picture of Rage and stood before Elrington with doubled fist and flahing eyes Il never stand again Is this the way in which I am to be made a fool of. speak." "Why my Dear Q. what has come over you." "Why Ill go back to Africa and you may find your 40 000 men just where you. can." "Quashia think are there not a hundred places besides to try at—for Instance Northtown—Quashia sat down for a while in moody silence. soon he started up Elrington give me you Daughter in marriage. and Ill promise you to return an MP. and empowered to bring down 70 000." Elrington looked as if he did not know whether to knock. his brains out. however. he directly put on an obliging smile. and said. I promise on those condiditions." "Hah but Ill have paper writen outs" "Well Here ring the bell." 2 servants entered. Elrington wrote down the promise. He and Qu- signed. and the servants. put their names as witnesses Qu snatched it up putt it into his memorandum book. and after saying "Rogue now your safe. I intend to go to Northtown. The Member is returned for this place but. (touching a pistol) this and Sdeath. Hah. you understand I shall set off today. Good Evening Elrington." He turned. strode from the room and. His carriage was soon heard. whirling of from the Hall. He had scarcely gone when Elrington burst into a loud laugh. "I give Mary Percy to such a wildfire scoundrel. I throw her away on an outlawed blackamoor.—never. Hah in spite of his promises. Ive got him. killing a member to obtain his seat he and his promise shall smoke for it." A servant Here announced Sir R W Pelham. MP. As that Gentleman entered Elrington rose up shook him warmly by the hands congratulated. him most affectionatly. upon his sucess. and rung the bell for His Daughter. on her appearing he introduced Sir Robert to her as. an MP. for her native city. and Her to him as. Mistress of Percy Hall. for said he "I must set of by daybreak to morrow morning for my own. affair not that I shall go to the

Great City my seat there is so secure that I shall hold it by proxy. but to other stations and. Elections to aid my minions as I have done here. And Now Sir R. your Tamworth Hall. is you know only now rebuilding I swear by the Bones of Sylla that you shall make. this Hall your Home till. I come back which will be in 8 or 10 days Not another word on it. Curse your pride and stiffness. Good Night. to you both. I shall not see you again. to morrow Sir Robert here are your instructions and advice written out and sealed for you till I come back. Elrington bowed to the Baronet and left. the room before he could answer a single word. Sir Robert was about to remonstrate on this arrangement but. Miss Percy rose and. said that it could not harm him. Her Father wished it. she must request it. The Baronet bowed. politly. and they sat down to supper.

Elrington set off next morning. Sir Robert remained shut up all day in the Library. on the day following he appeared at Breakfast [and] Dinner but. during the remainder of the time. was in the city. On the third morning he relaxed his ungracious conduct. ordered his carriage and entreated. Miss Percy to accompany him to visit. Tamworth Hall. she was as proud as himself but when she knew. that. on one of his character. unbending it was time enough. for her to do so to she gladly consented He as gladly accepted They drove of in a glorious exhilirating sunrise. along a pleasant rural road for several miles spent in. delightful conversation for the highly informed mind of both. could well afford means of supply. Sir Robert spoke much of England Europe. of Litrateur scenery. she supplied him with knowledge of our own noble country Tamworth Hall soon appeared in sight. an unfinished but extensive and majestic edifice surrounded by Grounds laid out upon such a scale of tast[e] and magnificence as could not but impress the beholder with the most exalted idea of Pelhams. wealth. fine taste. and judgement They returned to Percy Hall. through the fair lawn like woodland district. and the courteous manner. fine voice. flowing language and varied information of the titled MP. made time fly on cheerily. with his yong and beautiful Hostess—as to his person—but it didnt matter—

Next Morning while. Honbl^e Miss Percys maid was arranging the inextricable curls of Her Misstress auburn hair The confidant as usual ran on in the general chat of those. priveliged gentle women of her station. "They say that Sir Robert Weever Pelham I loves to give folk. the right name. They say he is a fine man and a proud man. and a rich man and I am sure he is a handsome man to be. certain he is. a little bit high seldom speaks to one but when he does he's got. such a voice. oh His Lordships. was never like it I think. though his was not the tone one can always hear. Have you seen his new house that he is building young Ned. Havealem took me and one or two besides the day before yesterday. to see it. and its as fine as this almost Im sure." "Come Jani have done". said her Mistress. but this corageous confidant was not to be. silenced Thus she ran on upon Sir Robert his house and the Election. untill a late Breakfast. waited for her indulgant Mistress. for a week. Sir Robert. continued to reside at the Hall his pride and haughtiness was only exercised on those most used to it. the Groom. footman and. such other divinities. He continued himself to admire his position and his Hostess more and more. Let not the reader

suppose him taken by surprise. in this matter the moment Pelham first entered
the Hall his cool. searching mind had forseen that. his admiration of Miss Percy
on further aquaintance would certainly increase to fair love. and devotion but he
prepared for all this. As for Mary Henrietta Percy she was completly taken by
suprise. she could not help admiring one of his character at first light and
appearance appearance. that goes for much. a tall gentlemanly figure fine statly
handsome countenance. proud reasured. eye. and a slight but expresssive smile.
go as far as one the one hand. as a small slender form. fairy hands and feet.
Bright curled Auburn ringlets Large Hazel eyes. little finely shaped Nose and. a
mouth with an inimitable. smile. with manners so unsophisticated so natural yet
so curiously capricous and reserved. and proud to her either realy equals or to
those who whished. to be thought so and. what strange to say made everyone
like here the more was the great similtude she bore in features to her tremendous
and. awful father the same hand the same nose. the same hair when angry a look
and flash of the eye by no means dissimilar. This I say. went far enough with.
Sir R Pelham. But enough of this let it be enough to say. that on the middle of
the second. week of Sir Roberts stay at Percy Hall. when through the boles and
foliage of vast umbrageous elms the sinking sun scattered dazzling and golden
light. upon the grassy summer lawn Miss Percy stood beside. the tomb of her
mother. And Pelham. there with his usual calm distinct meliflous voice declared
his feeling respecting her made an offer of himself. possesions and Head and
hand. He concluded by saying that he did not wish to trifle or be trifled with.
Miss Percy first turning red then white. said that she dared not speak till her
father returned. This was enough for both.

Next Morning Elrington arrived from his long and harrasing journey as
usual exhausted in body by vigourous in mind. Sir Robert had a long
conversation with him in private. after which. when they had entered. the
Breakfast Room. Elrington called his Daughter to him. and said "Mary you
know that when I hated everything living that hatred never extended to you. and
that I have not left you without any thing you wished that I could supply. you
are aware that though I expelled.[24]—hem let it pass you know however that you
have been and are now the creature on which I spred my sympathy. I have been
made aware of the feeling you have entertained. to each other. during my
abscene. I am pleased. my words shall be few. Sir Robert. will you take Marys
hand?" "I will my Lord" was the prompt reply. "Mary. will you accept Sir R
Pelham's hand" "I will father" was the as decisive answer. "Very well in the
Great Glasstown a month hence.—Lord Elrington was going to say more but the
door unfolded and Quashia entered in a travelling dress. a glance at the two
figures of Sir R and Miss P standing in such confusion opposite! their hands
clasped in each other and the stern countenance of Rougue. with a smile

---

[24] Percy ordered that his sons Edward, William and Henry be killed. The first
two were saved by Sdeath's disobedience of those orders, but Henry was
murdered. See p. 338 above, **The Wool is Rising** in volume II of this
edition, and Alexander CB II, Part I, 262, n. 120..

struggling in his dark. treacherous expression convinced the quick thoughted African how the case stood "villain" he roared "Elrington by the Bones of my fathers." "Ho Quashia glad to see you step this way with me." Elrington "frowning dreadfully drew the ci devant prince into the next room there he made out his resolution to keep his promise and averred the scene with Pelham. only a farce "To keep him. to him. you know" Quasia left the house. half dissatisfied notwithstanding his Lordships persuasion. Elrington then drew Pelham aside and. explained to him promise with Quashia the reasons for it &c he then said Now should he turn realize I have got him by the nose he has just attained a seat in parliament by causing to be assasinated the representative of a certain town now I have an excellent witness Mr Sdeath who was present. to prove the fact. I shall deliver him up to Government who will indeed be glad to have him."

Next Morning Elrington signified. his intention of Leaving Percy Hall for the G Glasstown. with his Daughter. and retinue. Sir R Pelham. also intended to set of on the same route. with him. Quashia. Caversham. and many other Leaders of the Democrats who had been getting elected to seats. in the country. would directly follow

In two or 3 days they all set. off.

CHAPTER. VII.   Nov 15.
1833.
PBB.

─────────────

This scene is to be laid in. that vast. emporium of all the universe the Great Glasstown. in a splendid Apartment of Elrington Hall. gorgeously fitted up. and lighted. with noble chandeliers. sat one evening on [a] sopha. on one side of the fire. A Magnificent looking young Man in a half Military costume. opposite to him on the other sopha a tall statly. Majestic Lady. with fine Italian features. and. robed in splendid velvet. The Viscountess Elrington. Wife of the Awful Nobleman. as this was his Verdopolitan residence. "So Zenobia" said the young Officer. "you expect His Lordship to day. Ill certainly stop to see him. Fine work he's made for Government this sessions I am positivly dying to behold him. and Miss Percy too. By the Bye did you ever see the young Lady" "No my lord Marquis I have not." "Do you expect. with him. that Gentleman. who has so fearlessly seized hold. of. a seat in my fathers City. We have heard much of him." "I believe he will be here. and I should like to see him Elrington in his letters mentions his Ability and Information he is rich and proud." "Eh Zenobia what did I hear. hem there they are. as he spoke they heard the sound of many carriages Dashing up and stopping before the Grand steps of the great Entrance. Lady Zenobia was going to go out to meet her Husband but as she and her visitor arose. the Doors flew open. and the well known form of Lord Elrington entered. a beautiful girl splendidly dressed. leaning on his arm. from under her large Gypsy. Hat beamed the thickly curled Auburn hair large bright eyes. and aristocratic look of. Miss Percy. Elrington directly introduced her to his Lady with a look. well understood by Zenobia who received Her step daughter with the utmost courtesy and kindness mingled with the pride and distance which Miss Percy was not slow to return. Then Lord Elrington turned to the splendid looking person before mentioned "Ha' well done good and theres you here to wellcome. me. Ive settled you well. Marquis heres. my. Daughter Mary Henrietta. and child here. is the Marquis of Douro." Miss Percy had. read this young Noblemans glorious works until he himself though she had never seen him. fixed as firmly in her mind. as tha[t] of her own Father. her admiration of him was unbounded and. being quite unsophisticated. and unused to disguise her feelings kindly or unkindly she warmly took his offered hand and with lighted eye and enthusiastic smile. was ere three minutes. firmly aquainted with him. he Admired her enthusiam language and appearance. said he was determined on a splendid party at Wellesly House to morrow. Evening and. warmly invited Elrington His Lady. Miss Percy. and also he begged leave to add. Sir R Pelham. to it. They assented. willingly.

Next day. after Dinner. the Marchioness of Douro. in her sitting room in Wellesly House sat with. her three intimate freinds. Lady Julia Sydney. Lady Castlereagh and. Lady M. Sneachy. who as invited by her had arrived. several hours before the. usual Time to the grand. Fete that night to be given. "Well. Marian" said the sprightly Lady Sydney to the Marchioness. "Im. burning to see. this new comer a daughter of Lord Elrington forsooth. not an ordinary. creature you know. from what I have heard she must be a little petted proud conceited thing who will speak to no body. or—but. Ill tame her. Marian." "Oh Julia how you rattle But the Marquis saw her yesterday evening." "did he did he" exclaimed The Ladys. all in a breath. "yes" replied the Marchioness "and he quite admires her. she is enthusiastic. warm hearted. polished as—much as you Julia. and 10 times as natural." "Stuff. Marian we shall see. the Marquis's conceit leads him to believe that everybody admires him we shall hate her But then theres Sir Robert—Robert—what. Oh Sir Robert Weever Pelham too another wonder. I dare say he will be something decent. now" "I said Lady Castlereagh "saw him this morning at my fathers." The Ladies lighted up anew. "He. is quite a Gentleman. looks like a born and bread Glasstowner & is tall and handsome. but oh I could not trust. him." "eh a theif." cried Lady Sydney. "No No. But he looks so incincere. so. smooth and his eye." "Ah. eye you know he's a Rougueite and they must have eyes."—"Come now said the Marchioness. I believe the Company are arriving cease your slandering do and. come. in to the saloons. her three fashionable freinds arose. and in their splendid. and dazzling attire followed the elegant little Marchioness. into the gorgeous saloon where the Company were fast assembling. Ladys Sydney. Sneachy. Castlereagh and. 1 or 2 others of high rank beauty and fashion seated themselves apart to reconnoitre and make observation on the fast entering visitors Julia using her eye glass. with vast effect. "Eh. look at. Edward. (Mr Sydney). Hes been just. so ever since the Elections Commencede do condole with me I cannot tell what to do with him there he. is. hands stuck in his pockets. and I veryly believe he holds his eyesight in them for his eyes are staring about as if they saw nothing he is quite blue and white and sucks in his cheeks like. a dried bladder" "Julia have the decency to spare—" "to spare. who pray. Ha theres the Duke my uncle. how pleasant he looks I admire him. so nicely dressed in black with such keen eyes and such a recognising smile. eh theres my Father." The lively Lady dropt her Glass and sat down with an expression so. inimitably demure that. her freinds and fellow criticisers. could not help bursting into unsupressed laughter. The Marquis of Wellesly who supported on his cane wrapt in 5 several coats. splendidly decked out and looking blue with cold had entered the room. noticed. their laughing and seeing his daughter among the laughers. fidgetted up the room turned bluer than indigo. and. adressed those about him in a voice so snappish as to startle all round. "And theres my Father" exclaimed. Lady M Sneaky as. a very tall statly old. Gentlemen. (or King rather) stalked up the apartment. bowed coldly to those round him. and after adressing afew words to the Duke of Wellington again left the rooms "Come" said Julia. "we can see nothing. here do come to the windows. and see the carriages draw up." The other Ladies followed her. as she sailed majesticaly across the room throwing killing glances to every side round her. "Eh whisht whose that now." she said as a loud. familiar voice was heard on the stair. directly. among the entering throng appeared. a firm set. red haired frank. arrogant. looking young Gentleman handsomly attired in uncoxcomical black. with white gloves and. leading by the hand. a well known little. fellow 8 years old perhaps with a curly head and a roguish smile. who dressed in handsome. black satin swung from the hand of his. conductor. stopping instead of going forward. twisting round talking and laughing with all he met and. ocassioning considerable. inconvenience to the dashing Gentleman who led him "Eh" cried Julia "Thornton I declare and got up again too Old Girnington dead look how Charlie troubles him. Ah. My. old freind Thornton how dye do." This well know[n] personage stepped fearlessly up. to the Ladies "Well and how are you all. you My Lady Julia. you. My Lady Castlereagh. you. Sister and you and you. Ha. I'm well Girnington's kicked the bucket. 70 000£ a year. a decent personable. figure If any Lady would think it would suit. I cant say but Im ready Ive quite go over my Reumatism dye know nought but a slight head Going to fit out Thornton Hotel in such a style. dash away. come have you seen my new coach. here. look at. it." he drew them to the window where amid the crowd of carriages he pointed out his own. a splendid new mourning coach. of the finest appearance. "Lady Julia cried "Ah Now. look. they are coming." Three or 4 noble carriages were seen dashing up. emblazoned with the arms of Elrington. but as they drew up the crowd prevented. them from seeing those who alighted Julia and her accompanying freinds turned their heads to the door and waited. patiently soon there entered. Viscount Elrington His Lady and the observed of all observers. His Daughter who was attired in plain unornamented. but fashionable. Dark. coloured satin not a jewel not an ornament in her. hair the strange Elrington cast of her countenance. all yet so sweet. and animated by such. unaffected. grace interested at once the company in her favour. Quite otherwise than many. Julia and her freinds among the Number. instead of looking hurried out of place. and ignorant among so vast new and splendid a company. stood by her Father quite composed without a smile on her face. but with a silent obervant glance at the Company round she bore her introductions with such reserve and shyness and yet with such grace as was. quite new and agreeable. The Marchioness of Douro introduced her to Lady Julia Sydney. and. the Ladies about her. Julia began to rattle tried to bring her to talk. laughed ridiculed the Company. pointed out characters to her but it would scarce do. she was so cautious in coming out that. at. length. Julia wispered to Lady Sneachy. "is her tongue cut out" Miss Percy heard. her. her eyes lighted up with all the fire of her Fathers War and bloodshed might have been the consequence had not. the Marquis of Douro stepped up with. Young Soult. "Well Miss Percy" he said glancing at the same time a frown to Lady Julia. "I am glad indeed to see you here you from your expressions yesterday evening I believe you will be pleased to have an opportunity of forming accquaintance with. my best freind Alexander Soult—Soult. Honble Miss Percy. Miss Percy instead of behaving with the shyness. Lady Julia was looking for instantly entered into animated conversation with Young Soult. which that agreeable and. eloquent young man. returned with his usual enthusiasm She showed Lady Julia here that her tongue was not. cut out and the Marquis seemed quite pleased with. her fine taste. quick fancy and highly informed mind. They moved of to where The Duke of Wellington was conversing with. Sir R W Pelham. who had just entered. with Lord Caversham. "Well" said Julia. "the thing has got a tongue but. oh I detest—"Nay stop Julia." said Lady Castlereagh. "you are far too severe. She is proud and shy but it looks. pleasant with her and she is very pretty. see how well she looks. but. whose that Gentleman standing by her talking so to the Duke and Marquis Julia. lift your glass." Lady Julia obeyed like lightning. "Lord. Harriet it is. Sir R Pelham. well he is a fine looking man. look how he smiles. what an abortive attempt. it is indeed a wooden smile. The Duke and Marquis seem pleased with him and now there is a broad. short. coarse ill dressed plebian sandy haired. young fellow with great glimmering grey eyes come up to them with. poor Edward who looks. for all the world like a drowned rat." Julia spare your own—" "Oh. Harriet dont advise me why look at yours. see he has just spit into the fire how. he swashes about in his dan[d]yish dress and. with his coxcombical hairs. Oh Castlereagh." the young Nobleman came up. "Well my Lady I am glad indeed to see you we've quite a new turn out today." "Well and what do you think of our Heroine." Pretty very pretty. Beautiful. shy as. a winter moorcock. but she conversed with the Marquis and me till. we forced her to smile." "I dare say." said Julia. "Theres Sir Robert Pelham. My Lady Julia—never saw such a man. hes as smooth as oil and as hollow as a gun barrel." "Very <poetical> Castlereagh proceed." His Grace has taken him mightily and the Marquis quite admires him. they. say he's quite a lover of Miss Percy" "Who the Marquis. Ah Marian—" "No No Sir Robert Ha Ha Ha But Have you seen Thornton. He's come out in such style. but I see Abercorn and Lofty there Good evening—" Castlereagh skipped away with the ease of a Noble Dandy. "The coxcomb." said Julia The Company were now ushered into the Ball room. and matters were soon arranged for dancing. The orchestra. was filled. and. the first Couples led out. Miss Percys hand. was asked for by a Dozen. She refused all till. the Marquis of Douro asked her. she looked at Sir R Pelham he nodded. and the Marquis led her out with his usual perfect ease and gracefulness. while she on hers shewed. the same to a degree that left not a shadow for envy to rest on. Sir R Pelham advanced to Lady Julia and completely won her favour by leading her for[th]. to waltz. Lord Elrington took Marchioness Fidena and when Thornton swaggered up and asked. her afterward he received such a sly. and well given hit from the Marquis Fidena that he retired back clapping his hands to his side and groaning. Mr Sydney took Lady Castlereagh. the Marquis of Fidena took. Marchioness of Douro. Myself had the Honour of leading out. Lady Z Elrington. As for Miss Percy she had found a treasure. On sitting down at a sofa. to rest she observed. a little wild looking creature with curly pale wild blue eyes and a ludicrous expression on its round laughing face. creeping about the sopha chairs and tables dreadfully annoying a little dapper gentleman in blue and white. she called this strange creature to her. it came forward. a thought struck her she hastily asked it "are you Lord Charles Wellesly." "I have that supreme honour and who may you be." "Mary Percy." "Mary Percy and whose Mary Percy." the little monkey went on. Miss Percy was quite. delighted she had read the works of this exsquiatic author 20 times. she admired them inexpressible And now she found the thing itself who had written them in speaking to him of course she intirely laid aside her. shy distant manner and assumed her natural cheerful gay laughing temper. one rarely exercised. she took the small Monster up lifted him onto the sofa. where he twisted about. chattering laughing talking to her. and as he expressed it. "not over and above ill pleased with her manners considering" she kept him in a good temper. but found it utterly impossible to controul his wilful movements she asked him how he liked his noble Brother. He exclaimed. "Brother the stuck *pig* ninny no brother of mine Thornton. says and Emii[25] to says that I am to make away with him by. a neckerchef tightly twisted. round his craig." This Language Miss Percy could scarcely understand. but notwithstanding she and Charlie scraped a handsome acquaintance. Many Ladies and some of the Gentlemen had. gathered round the back of her sofa. and heard her gay. cheerful conversation with the "whelp of sin" as the Marquis of Douro had termed him during the Evening But when she saw herself beggining to be observed. she gradualy relapsed into first. plain staid speaking and then silence. nor could the imps winding about laying hold of her hands. looking into her face. sharp critisisms on the company. laughable observations regarding herself antics or any other of his movements extract from her more than a smile. stroke of the head. (at which it was highly indignant.) or perhaps a single word or two. spoken to it. The Duke of Wellington came up. and. entered into conversation with her. His Grace Miss Percy admired above all men almost and in speaking to him all her reserve vanished in an instant she was one too whom his Grace. liked. and the special smile and voice which he can so well assume. now ornamented his stern. but. kindly countenance. But Morning had now begun to rise and The company. was breaking up carriages were put in requisition and The Square before Wellesly House again became a sene of bustle and. tumult. Almost every one in departing bowed and. took Their farewells of Miss Percy and she received inumerable

---

[25] Chief Genius Emii—i.e. Emily.

invitations. all these salutations she returned. by a bow or single word. save those of persons she liked. to whom she bid warm adeiu or at once accepted. their invitations. And when her Father and Lady Elrington departed. the Marquis of Douro led her to the door and the Duke of Wellington himself handed her into the carriage

CHAPTER. VIII   Novr 15— 1833 PBB—

Next Morning the Duke of Wellington His noble son the Marquis of Douro and Mr Secretary Sydney. were seated together in the room of the Home Office talking on the aspect of politics or on. the fete of last night "Well said the Duke Rougue has gained a real accession to his party. But I question. that too for I fancy it is a very insecure. one Sir R. Pelham is certainly a man of most extensive abilitys. But as slippery as. diving a statesman. as. I have ever been able to see." His information said the Marquis of Douro "is remarkably extensive and. his language is so extemly meliflous. I admire him Father But what do you think of The Honourable Mary Henrietta Percy. Elringtons Daughter" "Why Arthur? I dont think Ive often seen a young Lady whom I liked Better. She is I see at times uncommonly. shy. though." "Not to your Grace Im sure but. My wife alias Lady Julia is taken with such fits about now of Hatred and then forced to like Im sure—" "Now Sydney. But she will be admired in our city. They say that she is about to be married to Sir Robert Weever Pelham. and if so as I believe is the case it will. tie him strongly to Elringtons party" "Never fear Arthur. she. I can see will always go with her father. as. she adores him. but in our country I am glad to say however our Ladies take a wholesome and healthful intrest in politics they do not. think of intermedling or trying to stay the course of that wild and stormy current. and moreover Pelham I can see is not one to be tied by any one. You will see he can run creep walk. swim fly. dive or remain still just as suits his ambition or intrests. those lye with the constitutionalists and to us. ere long he will cast an eye." Here conversation was stopped by a clerk. announcing Lord Elrington and Mr Sdeath. The Duke and the others smiled with suprise but. they were introduced. Elrington after nodding to all present. began at once with a suitable oath. and execration to affirm that he was wearied of that African traitor Q Quamina that he was injuring him sadly and that he had made a resolution. to deliver him up. to Government. for that the Scoundrel. had. killed Col Ashton MP for Northtown. (whose death had excited from its sudden and singular nature such rumors in the papers) that by doing so he should mount to the seat which he did. that Mr Sdeath there worthy man. was present at the assassination he was not prepared to state in what capacity. and that he could prove anything requisite." the Duke stared and winked with wonder but. willingly consented. to seize the dangerous African who Elrington affirmed was at present in a gambling house he named. Officers were immediatly sent of to apprehend him. and Elrington departed. the Marquis of Douro stept out after him. to gain a true account of what seemed on Elringtons part so strange an action. Elrington at once told him that. Quashia had refused him what he immensly stood in need of unless he gave. him Miss Percy in marriage that he to keep him to him promised her that. upon. Pelham declaring his attachment to her and hers to him. he without hesitation agreed to their marriage since he considered Pelham as. a lofty. wealthy able man and since he was certain that Miss Percy both wished the union and would find it the best she could ever have. upon knowing this Quashia made a vast uproar. produced Elringtons written promise to him and determined to strive by law how to obtain fullfillment. that He (Elrington) of course upon this considered how he might put the black rascal out of the way. that he. fixed upon this. as the most just. and defensible (for the assasination &c was a fact. as He and the Marquis. were speaking together Quashia was seen brought past to the prisons. in chains foaming swearing by his Gods. on the in the height of anger He was safely lodged in stone walls.

    Miss Percy Has been eagerly received into all the great interhabimente All the city speak of Her. admire her for her. beauty Nature pride reserve cheerfulness gaity. freedom from sophistication and. elegant mind. Sir Robert Weever Pelham by the sheer force of his abilty. has at once seated himself as a principal Glasstowner His approaching marriage with. His Mary Henrietta Percy. is publicly known. and vast preparations are making to celebrate it in a style of splendour worthy. Himself and Her Great Father. The Marquis of Douro will give the Bride away. and two souls more fitly framed to unite together were never formed than those of Robert Weeve[r] Pelham and Mary Henrietta Percy. NB highly important Lord Charles Wellesly has condescended to say "she is one whom I can say I am pleased."[26]—End.   PB Bronte Nov 15.th AD 1833.

---

[26] See Matthew 3:17; 17:5.

AN HISTORICAL NARRATIVE.

of.

THE "WAR OF ENCROACHMENT."

FROM. NOV.EMBER. FIRST.
AD 1833.
TO.

NOV 18.

IN   VOLS.—BY SIR JOHN FLOWER.   PB B—te

1833.

—VOL I—[1]

Before I commence my narritive I believe it will be necessary at once to. give the names and offices of our Ministers at the commencement of this. war. on. November 1st. the old ministry was remodled. The Marquis of Douro Lord Lofty and one or two interior members having resigned. It. on Nov 14. stood as follows.

Earl St Clair.[2] ----------Prime Minister &. Leader in the Lords.
EGS Sydney-------------Home Secretary &. Leader in the Commons.
John Bud ---------------Secretary of the Board of Trade.
T B Morley-------------Colonial Secretary.
John Flower------------Secretary of the War Office.
Marquis of Fidena------Foreign Secretary.
Colonel Grenville------Speaker of the House of Commons.

Together. with. 10 other Gentlemen to fill up minor offices act as under Secretarys &c All together forming a consolidated. cabinet on. a Highly Constitutional and Conservative plan of action. and Strongly Governned by Their Majestys. Sneachie & Parry. The Marquis of Wellesly and. His Hig[h]ness Gravey. Primate of Africa

The Condition of the Empire of Frenc[h]yLand. has long been known to the world. and The pitch of insanity to which this singular people in the course of the present year. had arrived. threatened to all clear seeing eyes. either. a total overthrow or a speedy change Not in one House perhaps throughout all Paris was a single fire lighted. or a single peice of furniture used. or one duty or office

---

1   Hand-sewn booklet in brown paper covers (11.5 x 18.5 cm) of 16 pages in HL: MS Eng 869. There is no lettering on the covers. The absence of a terminal date and the blank for the number of volumes suggest Branwell was unsure how many he would produce.
2   Probably based on James St.Clair Erskine, Lord Rosslyn, (1762-1837), a member of the noble Scottish St.Clairs—the St.Clairs of Roslin—from Scott's *The Lay of the Last Minstrel.*

of social life ever entered into The one grand object which employed. the minds of every Frenchman was. what singular and unheard of death he could find out for himself and others out much arsenic and. prussic acid he could contrive to swallow at the command of every one who met him how much of these delicious articles he could distribute to them. and. the accomplishment of a hundred such figments and crotchets continualy. flitting across. his whirling Brain. Now amid all this lamentable Frenzy which actuated the French Nation scarcly one man could be found so free from it as to. give one word of advice one. Law to check. it. Their Mighty Emporer the Once great Napoleon himself yielded to none in frensied madness. Leaning from. a window of the Thuilleries[3] his constant exclamation upon the luckless fools who passed below was. "To the Bastille with them instantly."[4] Such now was the condition of France But. in the Heart of this hideous Bedlam[5] a few dark. determined spirits still. found abode. untainted. by much of the. countrys folley. but in secret. plotting and. executing the overthrow of the Government. (if they had any) and the Emperor. These Men under the Name of. the Faction Du Manege.[6] and headed by Bernadotte[7] Moreau[8] Barras[9] Jourdan.[10] and others of name and ability. were

---

[3]   See p. 13, n. 6.

[4]   Originally a fortress built in Paris in 1369, the Bastille became a state prison during the seventeenth century. With prisoners interred by "lettre de cachet"—a direct order of the king from which there was no recourse—the Bastille came to stand as a symbol of the despotism of the Bourbons. It was stormed and destroyed by an armed mob on July 14, 1789, during the opening days of the French Revolution.

[5]   The hospital of St. Mary of Bethlehem in London was given to the City of London in 1547 by Henry VIII as an asylum for the insane, but by the nineteenth century it had became infamous for the brutal ill-treatment of its inmates.

[6]   See p. 16, n. 13.

[7]   Bernadotte was the name of the royal dynasty of Sweden from 1818. In 1810, John Julian Baptiste Bernadotte, a celebrated Marshal of France under Napoleon, was elected Crown Prince of Sweden, and in 1818 became king of Sweden.

[8]   Jean Victor Moreau (1763-1813), a leading general of the French Revolutionary Wars (1792-99), helped to conquer the Austrian Netherlands and was subsequently given command of the Army of the North (Rhine and Moselle). He played a minor role in the military coup d'état of 18 Brumaire (November 1799) that brought Napoleon to power, but was later banished by Napoleon for allegedly taking part in a counterplot to overthrow him. Moreau returned to France in 1813 by invitation of French royalists and joined the allied forces against Napoleon, only to be killed at the Battle of Dresden in 1813.

[9]   Paul Francoise Barras (1755-1829), a Provençal nobleman who joined the Jacobin Club, emerged as one of the most powerful members of the Directory during the French Revolution, casting his vote for the death of the king. As

encouraged in their proceedings and. assisted in money by. a large faction in our own city which I need not name. and were now gradualy ripening their schemes for open revolt.

In this state of things the daily mails which should have arrived from Paris. ON the Morning of the 10 of November failed. to make their appearance at the usual hour 1.2.3.4. and 5 o clock passed by and Government had not received. their usual despatches. and letters. strange rumours were. afloat through Verdopolis respecting the reasons for the nonarrival of these Coaches. but. though no care was given to such vague reports of the hour. matters looked odd enough. for. the premeir to call a Cabinet council at which Mr Sydney Marquis Fidena. Col. Grenville. Mr Morley. and Myself with. His Majesty Parry and. Marquis Wellesly attended. These instantly determined upon sending off Couriers. that night to France for. no sign was visible. of. Mail or News But while they were sitting in deliberation at the Colonial Office. A Gentleman alighted from a splashed and travell stained. equipage and introduced himself. as. direct from France He was a tall man with a pale thoughtful cast of features and. polite adress. He gave in his card as General Moreau. and. without much further speech opened a packet and. while he was. taking from it his despatches he said. addressing the premeir "My Lord. the state of France has long called for remedy. his Hig[h]ness Bernadotte has laboured. to procure that cure. inspired by his sentiments Paris. has risen dethroned Napoleon her grand evil. and. elected. by arms. Bernadotte as Cheif. Consul. His Highness. instantly. upon his accession called out the. members of his Faction Du Manege. placed them at the head of a force. and. after seizing the person of the late Emperor he liberated the prisoners in the Bastille supressed at once. the sale and distribution of white bread and prussian butter.[11] ordered all found killing themselves or instigating others. to

---

Commissar in the French Army of Italy, Barras was instrumental in liberating Nice, Toulon, and the Var from royalist forces. Later, however, he also acted as a key figure in the overthrow of the Jacobin leader, Robespierre, and, as Commander of the Army of the Interior, helped crush the revolt of the Parisian populace. He fell from power in Napoleon's coup of 18 Brumaire (November 1799), and was exiled until the restoration of the Bourbons in 1815.

[10] Jean Baptise Jourdan (1762-1833), although a member of the French nobility, actively supported the Revolution. During the revolutionary regime, he was one of the first sponsors of military conscription, and later under Napoleon became one of the Marshals of the empire. Jourdan was particularly noted for his military method, employing Lazare Carnot's new strategy of concentrating troops and artillery at points of attack. This strategy won him a decisive victory at Hainaut and led to the complete collapse of the Austrian resistance. In 1813, however, after failing to control his troops at the Battle of Vittoria, he was dismissed from his command. In 1814, he favored Napoleon's abdication, and on switching loyalties to Louis XVIII was made head of the Army of the Rhine. In 1816 he was named count and in 1819 made a peer of France.

[11] See p. 20, n. 17.

that act. to be instantly shot. and enforced a few such. salutary regulations. By which means. Paris and af[t]er it the (I hope whole country) has. shaken off its shackles of madness and is. now in a great measure restored to reason. I am deputed from the new Government to demand from these countrys an instant. rec[o]gnition of our right. and lawful authority over the new Republic of Frenchy land." Moreau here. delivered to St Clair sundry papers &c. from the rebel confirming and enlarging upon what he had. said. and threatning the instant commencement of Hostilitys should the Government refuse.—Now though France certainly needed nothing more than a change of Government though. that change just made had evidently been entirely for the better though. though we owed. no sort of obligation to the late Emperor. yet on the other hand. the New Government was composed of turbulent seditious men was perfectly democratic in principle and was one fostered and. encouraged by a most dangerous party at home besides bearing on its very front the stigma of Rebellion and the Subversion of an established. Authority and King. Taking all the considerations into the account Earl St Clair said to Moreau. he felt himself fully justified in at once declaring that. the 4 Governments of the Glasstown could not possibly agree. to recognize the new and upstart Government of France. That. should. war chance. we. would firmly meet it and abide by the consequences. With this decided declaration after once or twice. endeavoring to extort something more satisfactory General Moreau. took his leave and departed post haste to France. Earl St Clair and the different. ministers who had attended the Cabinet set of directly to inform the Kings and their fellow ministers of these strange and eventful feelings. Mr Sydney and Myself were commissioned. to repair to the Home Office there to set about ascertaining the force of the Army and ord[i]nance. departments with the sums of money which could be available at the present crisis and. the amount to which the troops might directly be increased. as we alighted in front of the Office vast crowds of Gentlemen had collected. to ascertain from us immediatly the truth or falsity of the rumours which like wildfire. had flown through the city immediatly upon. the. knowledge. being gained of General Moreau. having alighted at the Treasury Office. After. shortly satisfieng their enquirys we both commenced our ardous. duty and toiling through a long night and morning amid yawning and over worked clerks it was 12 <o clock at> noon on the following day ere we could arise. from our desks. Mr Sydney then departed. to The Treasury office to communicate the hitherto result of our Labours I. to Braveys Hotel. were should they arrive. the French Mails would. draw up and. where from Newspapers and Individuals I should be. able to discover. the state of feeling amid our Nation. But I had scarcely mounted. the Grand steps. when. a Government Messenger arrived breathless after me requiring my instant attendance at the Cabinet Council at the Treasury Office I set off for it. wondering all the while what could be the cause. of this urgent requirance. But. on my opening the Door and entering the apartment. I cannot describe the feelings which came over me. There struck my eyes at once. the silver locks. stooped figure high forhead and calm pale saintly look of.

TALLYRAND.[12] He noticed my petrified look upon entering the room. and. handed over to me his despatches and papers hastily I ran them over their contents were astonishing. While Moreau was with us. Napoleon Soult[13] and several. Others had Broken from the Bastille had. presented themselves to the. soldiers where. Bonaparte as is with him ever the case was welcomed at once with the hearty shout. of Vive Le Emperor. He. placed himself at the Head of about 6000 troops who rushed to the Thuilleries seized the persons of Bernadotte Barras Moulins[14] and others of the principal Rebels immured them in the grand. state prison. drew the so[l]diers round the palace. and proclaimed. the Emperor through the Streets of paris By this energy the Emperor found himself firmly again seated in power. He therefore seeing a fine army at his disposal (just levied by Bernadotte.) after having proved his sanity by ratif[y]ing that Gentlemans. decrees respecting White Bread. killing &c. &c. caused a paper to be drawn up to the Governments of our Countrys of the following singular purport.== "That. firstly. seeing that in the Old Times. 50 years back the Cheif Genii decreed that none but Frenchmen should Inhabit Sneachies Land. therefore. it being supposed. a decree of the Geniis could never fall to the ground. so. Sneachies Land must then have. been about that. time. given in to the hands of the French. and as M[r] Le Emperor is the undoubted King of the French. Sneachies Land must without any delay be intirely given up to him

Secondly that as the Manns and Wamons Isles ly just off the coast of Frenchy land and evidently by nature do belong to the Glasstown Governments are instantly. required to sanction the. occupation of them by French Forces in the Name of the Emperor. If both these. demands are not directly complied. with. the Emperor will at once. commence Hostiliitys against all the 4 Kingdoms of the Glasstowns. and their dependancies.

---

12 See p. 242 n. 6.

13 Nicolas-Jean Soult (1769-1851), one of Napoleon's most famous Marshals, earned a reputation both for personal courage and method, as well as opportunism in political dealings. Enlisted in the infantry at the outbreak of the French Revolution, he was later put in charge of the southern part of Naples by Napoleon, and in 1804 made a Marshal of France. Sent to Spain in 1808 after orchestrating a series of victories against Austria, he was soon put in charge of all French armies involved in the Peninsular War, where he was opposed by the English under Arthur Wellesley. Soult remained in Spain for five years, but with his troops outnumbered he was eventually forced to retreat, and was defeated at Toulouse in 1814, four days after Napoleon's abdication. During the First Restoration (1814), Soult declared himself a royalist; but during Napoleon's Hundred Days, he again supported Napoleon, acting as his chief of staff at Waterloo. Subsequently exiled at the start of the Second Restoration (1815-30), he was recalled in 1819, and served under three ministries, as minister of war and president of the council. See also p. 13, n. 7.

14 See p. 366 above.

The moment I had finished. this glorious. paper I dropt. it on the table and. could not forebear breaking out into a real. guffaw. The greater part of the Ministers. joined. me. and Talleyrand. himself vouchsafed. a benignant smile. which was however changed to a Blacker expression when four officers entered the Room arrested him in the name of the Four Kings and. having placed him in a carriage. received orders to lo[d]ge him in the Great State prison. as one who mocked the Great Kingdoms of Verdopolis a Courier was then despatched to Paris. to. announce. to the Emperor our instant declaration of War. A Grand Cabinet Council was then called. for that Evening at the Duke of Wellingtons. residence Waterloo Palace I attended and found Their Majestys Wellington Sneachi and Parry. and almost all the Ministers in close consultation upon. the Subject of. what force should be employed what number. under what Generals and. where to direct their operations. after a consultation of the deepest intrest which lasted Nine hours. the following paper was agreed on.
"That. The

1st. Rejimint. Horseguards Colonel. Marquis of Douro
9th Reg^t Horseguards Colonel Viscount Elrington
11th Reg^t Sneachies Dragoons Colonel Viscount Lofty
21st Reg^t Sneachies Dragoons Colonel Viscount Caversham
18th Reg^t Northern Greys. Colonel. T Mac Arthur.[15]

Placed Under the Immediate Command. of Brigadeir General Elrington

1.1 1st 4.6.13.46.47. regiments of Foot

Placed under the Immediate command of Brigadier General. Bobbadil.

1.2.3.4.5.6.7.8.9. regiments. Northern Foot.

Placed under the Immediate command of Major General Fergusson.[16]

16.17.18.48.49.62.63.64.65.72. Reg$^{ts.}$ Foot.

Placed under the immediate command. of. Major General. Hardinge.[17]

---

[15] Possibly based on John McArthur (1755-1840), co-author of *The Life of Lord Nelson* (1809) and author of "A translation from the Italian of the Abbé Ceasarotti's Historical and Critical Dissertation respecting the Controversy on the Authenticity of Ossian's Poems," 1806.

[16] Sir James Ferguson (1787-1865) served under Wellesley in the Peninsular War 1808-14, with distinction, rising to the rank of Lieutenant Colonel by 1814.

[17] Henry Hardinge (1785-1856), a British soldier and statesman, served with distinction as staff officer in the Peninsular War. He acted as brigadier general with the Prussian Army at the Battle of Ligny, where he lost an arm in 1815. Between 1820-44, he twice served as Secretary of War, then as governor-general in India, 1844-48, where he was involved in the first Sikh War, 1845-46. In 1852 he succeeded Wellington as commander in chief of the British Army, and was promoted to Field Marshal in 1855. See also "An Echo from an Indian Cannon," Neufeldt PBB, 278.

These five corps. composing in the whole a force of. 31.000 men. to be placed under the. command of. the Major General Marquis of Fidena. and. to move. to the north East. toward. Angria Hilltown and Morayton.
    That the.

3^d Regiments of Horseguards	Colonel Streighten,
11th Regiment of Dragoons	Colonel Stafford.
41st Regiment of Dragoons	Colonel Fizherbert.
64th Regiment of Dragoons	Colonel J Bud.
65th Regiment of North Greys	Colonel H Elrington.
66th Regiment of North Greys	Colonel. Mackinnon.[18]

Be placed under command of. Brigadier General Moray.[19]
    23 101.102.103.104.105.106.107.108.109.110.111.112.113. foot
Be placed under command of. Major General. Harrison
    21 36.37.39.41.42.73.74.75.76.77.78.79.80.81.82. foot
Be placed under command of. Major General Hill[20]
Be all placed. in. 3 corps under the sole command of. Major General Thomas Grenville. in all 36000 men and destined. as a Southern Force to move. upon. Mouthton Davenham and Olympian."
    This paper. was at once promulgated and. published through the whole City. It was indeed inspiriting to see. the enthusiasm and activity of all men in meeting and seconding the whishes of Government. vast members applyed for admittance into the army it was soon collected and ere Monday the different Regiments were rapidly concentring from their diferent. cantonments into the Grand Focus of the great Barracks. of Verdopolis. Troops and companys of Horse and Foot. were constantly observed Filing through every street with long strings of Cavalry Horses trooping to their destination. On Monday. morning the. Baggage and Amunition waggons with the greater part of the Artillery commenced. their route to Seaton. on the North and Rochester[21] on the South the places destined as the first stages of the different forces. I delighted to see the trains of Waggons and cannon and Horses pouring from the city into the wide champaign country.
    ON Monday afternoon Nov 18. a Cabinet council was held. at the War Office. On which occasion I had the Honour of Being promoted to the rank. of Colonel of Foot and destined as the principal Staff Officer. of General the Marquis of Fidena. besides being destined to act. as the principal. Government.

---

[18] Possibly based on Henry Mackinnon, a major general killed in 1812, and author of "A Journal of the Campaign in Portugal and Spain," 1812.
[19] Thomas Randolph, Earl of Moray, military commander under King Robert the Bruce, captured Edinburgh, defeated the English at Bannockburn, and played a major role in negotiating Scotland's independence.
[20] Probably based on Rowland Hill (1772-1842), a distinguished military commander with Wellington in the Peninsular Campaign and at Waterloo.
[21] Davenham, Seaton, and Rochester are British place-names.

agent. for his Army. A second resolution of this Cabinet showed itself that day by the vast bustle and. increased preperation observed through the City. that exciting day. This was an order. issued for. all the Forces to assemble. in the Great Square fronting Waterloo. palace. upon 8 o clock. Tuesday evening there to. set off at once upon their march. Every Officer was required to hold himself in readiness.

For 3 days past Every Evening a vast number of the most splendid Entertainments. Had been given in all parts of the city by the principal Members of Government and the Great Officers of the forces about to depart. The Lion of Sunday Evening. was the Fete at. Elrington Hall given by Colonel Viscount Elrington that of Tuesday the one at Wellesly House by. Colonel the Marquis of Douro. But on Monday the. very night of our departure was prepared. the most splendid of all. given by His Grace of Wellington at Waterloo palace. Here I arrived. at. 5 o clock pm. as I passed through the Square doomed as the place of our departure I. saw. the quantity of Double Drums. Bugles Trumpets French Horns and Clarionets and. other Instruments of the Military Bands <constantly> shoaling by. grand rows of stands had been erected round the square and the mixed Solemnity and animation every where visible plainly foretold some approaching great event In the Interior of the Palace 8 vast saloons were most splendidly decorated. for the entertainment. and were now rapidly filling with Company. I was Myself. Dressed in Military Costume and had during the whole day previous been winding up my affairs before entering upon the coming war. and now with excited heart. prepared. This. Evening to depart The Company. At length mustured. between 900 and. 1000. amid which shone preemine[n]t 5 Kings and. 150 or 200 distinguished Noblemen. It was curious to see. the Number of full dress Military Uniforms glittering. amid the throng And the titled and celebrated Persons who bore them. added. to the extreme intrest of the scene I stepped up to where the Marquis of Douro and. Lord Elrington. were conversing together. The tall. statley. but. wasted figure of the last and. the. youthful. Noble and well compacted frame of the first. Both inveloped in the same scarlet white and Silver. "Well" I said "The hour at last has come on and. ere 10 o clock. we shall be on our march to the north. "To Death." answered Elrington "Who ever heard of a Government sending out. troops raw and unexperienced. with for a First March. a Raw cold gusty Night like this will be. Volo" "Elrington Colonel is quite down in the mouth he believes that this work will kill him and so all his enthusiasm has died away and withered. he cannot see the dashing warlike appearance. of a night along a muddy road through a wild stormy country as I can." replied the Noble Marquis. Castlereagh Here joined us. who had been strutting round the room. to show off his Hansome shape. and Military accoutrements. "Eh when will we set off." "Not yet Irishman." "Aye you know my descent is Irish. But. realy I am glad my Lord Marquis of this Night work it will impress. the. City. with an idea. of what war is." "Begone Puppy" said Elrington As we stood here together a knot soon gathered round us of those who shape their course by the actions of the two great stars of fashion Douro and Elrington and of Ladies who wished as Lady Sydney said to extract sense from all the[y] could. these at once began to criticise the appearance of the different Militairs in the room. "Theres Thornton. Captain Thornton and a smart figure he looks remarked the Marquis "He's compact. straight and. sets of. his Scarlet and blue. with a much better air than you do Elrington." "Aye Arthur." said Lady Sydney "and look at Lord Caversham theres as good a man as yourself. For all your airs of consequence see how smart and Noble. 'pon my word you all look three times as well in your. Military dress. as in your usual vile Black blue or brown. Well My Lord Castlereagh you want a kind word or so for yourself. What do you command man." "A file of Bayonets my Lady. as do Molineux and Abercorn" "Eh what and no men too them." "we hope too have some behind them. Hah." "Have done Castlereagh" said Elrington "Here are the Generals however." As he spoke. the conversation ceased and Ill warrant some hearts beat quicker and. more hurried. when the grand. folding doors opened. And His Grace of Wellington with Generals Fidena and Grenville. and a long. train of. Generals Ministers &c. entered the room. "Gentlemen said his Grace. "I am sorry to announce the conclusion of. the entertainment time wears late it is 8 o clock. and the troops are assembling." ==when his Grace ceased speaking all could here outside the windows. which looked on the grand square. the gradually increasing noise of. vast crowds arriving and filling it up. with a slow swelling uncertain sound which became even painful. to the Silent listners in these mighty Saloons. Knots of freinds began. to form farewells and. last words to be given. the Eyes of Ladies. to glisten with a tear those of the Gentlemen to glitter with animation. and when a sudden swell of martial Music broke up at once outside in the Square. and the loud wail of trumpet Bugle and Horn broke in on the stillness of Night. and adeiu. I. cannot answer for the feeling of those. concerned in this eventful. expedition for the feelings of those left behind. "Gentlemen" said the Duke. while even his stern eye. sparkled a with the spirit of other years "Gentlemen are you ready." A gradual movement was made to the doors and file after file. in long succesion of. the Noblest and Greatest and. most famous Glasstowners poured our of the Magnificent Saloons. behind them followed a splendid train of their Ladies of Our City. who hastened to take their stations in the grand Balconies erected. outside to command a full view of. the armies and their departure. I was delayed a little while in speaking to a Minister and did not follow till the vast Apartments in all their brightness and splendour stood nearly empty and. even echoed to the voice. and foots[t]ep then I. walked out into the square which presented an appearance. splendid and warlike in the highest degree. it was dark. perfect Night. and blank clouds covered the sky. the whole of the immense square shone in a blaze of torch and gas light. and every window of every house and palace round it lent its bright. glow to the. splendour. the. whole vast area below was filled with the tossing and waving lines of Military whose bright arms steel Caps and plumes of feathers. undulated along glittering to the light far forward up a long long line. of Streets till lost in partail darkness. Eleven Noble Rejiments of Cavalry snorted pranced and curvetted. in front along the face of Waterloo palace and. there was indeed mounting in hot haste. for every Officer after the shakes of the hand. single words and nods of parting was flying to his steed. and many now seated. were prepared for instant departure. The two Commanders in cheif. with splendid staffs. were ranged before the grand parties and surrounded by a splendid throng of Kings and Nobles. a glittering crowd of Ladies filled the vast Balcony erected along the front of the palace. Grenvilles forces had begun to move off and a storm of Military Music swelling and. bursting along the lines Accompanied the compact Regiments as they shoaled away out of the square down the great sweeping street and. out of sight mingling in the crowds and darkness General Grenvilles loud. stately voice then ordered his Cavalry off. and 6000 mounted soldiers. were at once in motion rattling. over the stones. and choking up the streets before us. The Marquis of Fidena. now gave orders for his van to pass onward and ere I was aware I. was mounted on my Horse at the head of my Regiment and fast in motion from this gorgeous scene of. stirring grandness. The Marquis of Douro and Viscount Elrington rode beside me. heading their Rejments and we formed the advanced Horse guard of Fidenas army. I saw no more of the departure.[22] and. the square. the Glasstown was a blank hence forward and after. the filing through an endless line of half lighted labyrinthine streets we at 1 o clock in the morning found ourselves riding out of the great gate of the Angria Road. The Mighty and animated city behind us and a dead wild waste of dark Midnigh[t] country flat marshes muddy roads and. a rough stormy champaign before us. yet in this was there a vast deal to excite and warm the mind. to its stern Military duties.

In darkness of Night the van of the army filed over the Bridge across the Noble Guadima. and. marched hastily forward. to their morrows station. 20 miles beyond I rode beside two of the noblest and most. able officers of our Army though owing to circumstances. they. had only attained. the rank of Colonel.—The Marquis of Douro. and Viscount Elrington. In the company of these and. situated as we were conversation never flaged. and spite of the rain the darkness the great press upon the roads. every Hour seemed to pass swiftly by untill. the red. light over toward the east. gradualy bursting in to dawn and daylight. shewing the great undulated. plain the marshes rivers and roads clearing up from rain in the cold raw morning light. about 10 o clock. pm. we arrived at. the Villiage of Hillburn Foot. the days station for the main body of the army. Here we mustered. present 17000 men. 3000 of whom composed of Cavalry under. Douro Elrington. and Lofty received orders to march. under Gen Elrington. to. Seaton. as soon as the Horses. had. rested an hour or two. This they did and. I saw them winding from the villiage up the North road at 1 o clock pm. at Hillburn Foot. we found the greater part of the Baggage. and Amunition which had been sent out during the week Blocking up in their huge carts and waggons every street and lane of the little place and every moment long lines moving off on their destination I dont know what the villiage looked like Sometimes it seemed a grand. Market or fair so immense were the Packs of

---

[22] Branwell's account of the festivities associated with military departure, while somewhat extravagant, is not unhistorical. "The Subaltern—A Journal of the Peninsular Campaign" which appeared in *Blackwood's Magazine*, xvii (March 1825), 284, records that "the whole town of Dover" came out to cheer the army's departure for the Spanish Peninsular War.

waggons and amunition so thick the droves of cattle Horses &c. again it was turned in to the rendezvous of an army when file after file and troop behind troop of. Scarlet and Armed Soldiers. swept over the streets on their way "To Fight the French" Brave fellows all of them but. going to a stormy death. I believe. that ere 2 o clock pm. on Wednesday. as I sat at the window of the Inn I. had seen 18000 soldiers file by. at that Hour the[y] came in thicker. and. instead of going forward Halted. and drew up in the market place. where a Military Band was drawn out. which began to play the usual strains of Martial Music. I was wondering what this should augur when the. rapid arrival of. Military Servants and. the vast bustle through the Inn below announced it to be the. presage of the arrival of. Our Commander in cheif Marquis Fidena. He arrived at dusk attended by a numerous staff to which I belonged and. took up his residence in the villiage INN. I was called for to attend him. upon entering the room. I found him standing at the fire wrapt in Military cloak. and possessing his usual commanding and polished air of. dignified. Solemnity. He is young being only. 28. but his. admirable coolness and wisdom waived all considerations of that sort and placed him at once in command of a difficult and dangerous enterprise. Maps were spread before him upon which he was gazing but on my entering he stepped forward "Well Flower how are you. when did the advance of Cavalry pass through this place." "6 hours since. My Lord. and since that time. the main body has also been filing through in excellent order." "Thats right Flower. 17000 men have passed I. hope. and. must have now arrived at Seaton. where they will halt to night. the 3 regiments of advanced cavalry. will march forward. to Angria the great head quarters of the enterprise. 4000 men are in this villiage. 10000. under Bobbadil are behind. me. I shall sleep here this night to morrow we must go forward. good night Flower" I. departed. and retired to rest. sleeping most soundly untill the Bugles in the stre[e]t Below roused me up at early dawn. I was dressed mounted. and out shivering in the rough wild Blast. almost ere I was aware. But the noble sound of the trumpets and the. stir and. arms around me soon roused up my spirit to delight and Enthusiasm. The Troops had been passing on before us while I slept soundly and Now the General was ready for following in fact the rear guard under Bobbadil. of 10000 men. were just marching up the villiage hill and their sh[r]ill fi[f]es and rolling drums could. well be heard by us. The Marquis Mounted his Carriage the Staff. gathered round him and we set off at a full gallop. for the City of Angria. Evening was sinking beyond. the long lines of Black. sharp. eminences that marked a town when. the towers of. the Cathedral first rose up before us. on entering we alighted at the Great Hotel which had been prepared for the Commander. This city was filled with. 13000 troops. and presented the usual Martial aspect of Baggage Waggons. Artillery and. Soldiers with the wail of Bugles and the swell of Military music. I attended the Marquis when he fully explained to me the project of the champaign which I shall here simply detail.

The plan of the French Emperor. was found out to be thus. two armies. the first of 40000 the last of 30000 men. were assembled. the larger placed under the

Command of Massena.[23] the smaller under Marmont.[24] Marmont was to pass over the grand bridge. to Doverham. 100 miles South of Verdopolis. here he was to strive not. for victory but merely to keep a footing on the coast. untill Massena could come up who was ordered to cross over to the east coast of Africa. then make a bold march Northward through the great desert east of the Olympian Hall up into the country. Northwest of Angria and. nearly 200 miles north of Verdopolis. there he was to divide his force into 3. parts each placed opposite to one of the great passes Southward. and. instead of attacking in deatail but simultaneously the 3 forces which under the Glasstowners would most probably be placed to protect and command those passes. Massena was on a sudden to concentrate his forces into one. and bear down in overwhelming numbers upon one. of those passes then throw that Glasstown force in a complete route on the second and all upon the third. which would carry them allong before him in a mixed and melted heap. down to the Great Glasstown where he would leave the scattered remnant. and. pushing down toward Marmont unite himself to that struggling general. and destroy Grenville who would be

---

[23] André Masséna, Prince d'Essling (1758-1817) was a leading French general of the Revolutionary and Napoleonic wars, demonstrating a particular genius for maneuvering forces over difficult terrain. As Napoleon's most trusted lieutenant, nominated "Enfant de la Fortune," the "beloved child of fortune," he won a key victory in the Battle of Rivoli during the Italian campaign of 1796-7. Although his troops mutinied after the fall of Rome (1798) forcing his recall to Paris, he was made commander of the French army in Switzerland, and there defeated Russian forces, preventing their march into Italy and thus saving France from imminent invasion. In 1806, he reconquered Calibri from the British, but three months later, in command of French forces fighting the British in Portugal, he was severely defeated by Wellesley and subsequently relieved of command. Although he was in Paris in 1815, he took no part in the Hundred Days of Napoleon and instead supported restoration of the monarchy.

[24] August-Frédéric Marmont (1774-1852), having entered the artillery in 1792, was noticed by Napoleon at the Seige of Toulon and made an aide-de-camp. So prominent were his actions in the Italian campaign that he was made Colonel at the age of 22, appointed General in 1798, and made Governor of Dalmatia in 1806. Here he forced the Russians to lift the seige of Ragusa, thereby securing control of the Adriatic coast for the French. However, he had little success against the British when called to command the French army in Portugal. Marmont's military career took a dramatic turn in 1814 when, as Napoleon's Chief Lieutenant in the battle under the walls of Paris, he surrendered the city and took his troops to the Allied lines. For this, he was called traitor and Judas by Napoleon and his supporters. However, with the restoration of Louis XVIII, Marmont was rewarded for his desertion of Napoleon and made a peer of France. But in the Revolution of 1830, when his troops once again failed to hold Paris, this time for Charles X, he was again accused of treachery, had his name stricken from the list of marshals, and went into exile. See also p. 52, n. 12.

opposed to him. The Great Road to Verdopolis would then by this masterly movement be laid open and Napoleon meant then to pour forward. on the City a vast army. headed by himself.

ON the other hand the Glasstown Government formed a plan to counteract this one Firstly Grenville with 38000 was to be sent down to. the South to keep Marmont in check and. The Marquis of Fidena with 31000 men. was to march to the North to oppose Massena. he was as Massena wished to divide his Army into. 3 divisions which were to occupy those towns which the French reckoned upon. Angria below them being the general Head quarters and great Key to the City Now these towns which Massena ment one by one to attack. are seated around. the outskirsts of a long ridge of Isolated mountains extending 50 miles NW and SE and called the Warner Hills. These hold. a wild and inacessible tract of Moorland in their bosoms. to which every division of. the Glasstowners might in case of need retreat and. to which. if as was highly probable Massena with his combination should press hard. on them they were to all retreat concentrating themselves at Howard a villiage in. the midst of that wild tract. and. when the French having gained the Verdopolitan Road should press forward to Verdopolis the. retreated Army of the Marquis of Fidena. should wait till these French had. got. before them and then pour down at once in three great divisions attack. them in rear and. dissipate them ere they reached the city of Angria. By that time the Ministry at the City would have had time to levy. adittional forces. werewith to overwhelm Marmont and. aid Grenville to complete his destruction.

Having thus explained the plan of this Campaign I must go on with my Narrative At the conclusion of my interveiw with the Marquis he said. "General Elrington with the advance. or rather with. the force destined to occupy the grand pass of. Warner. has. I find acording to my orders passed. on. long before us. with 3000 Horse under. Douro Elrington and Lofty and. as many Infantry. now Flower this is the principal pass and to this I am certain Massena will direct his attention. Flower take horse and ride forward to Warner and I shall follow with the Staff. in an hour or two hence. with. 3 or 4000. more troops.". Fidena then gave orders to Bobbadil to set forward with. 8000 men. for Howard and Boulshill. the middle pass. amid the Warner Mountains and. for Fergusson with. 6000. for. Pendlham[25] the southern pass. Col Mac Arthur. was to remain at Angria with the principal Baggage &c. and a reserve of. 7000. men. while all the troops were in a tumult and. bustle preparing to execute these movements. I took my Horse and with a Servant set off for. Lit Warner the Northern pass where the Commander in cheif intended. to follow. My journey had lasted 20 miles. along a trampled miry road. in the dusk. of evening and in wet boisterous weather when just as on the hilltops before us. the lights and watchfires of the advance rose on veiw at the distance of 5 miles I all at once distinctly heard the sound of firing born on the wind which blew toward me. the Dull. continued. roll. left no doubt of its being cannonry and I set spurrs to my horse eagre to get

---

[25] Boulsworth Hill is near Haworth and Pendle Hill stands between Colne and Citheroe in Lancashire.

on. As I. rode up the hill on which Warner is seated. I. Heard. fully the. rattle and blatter of Musketry and the deep discharges of artillery and cries shouts and all manner of sounds rushed on my ear while entering the half deserted villiage. on gaining the top of it. the scene of action became visible through the darkness on the other side.—The villiage there sloped. down steeply northward. too a large Beck filled with rapid water. a rough steep bank opposite was topped By a Battery of ten peices of Artillery manned by 600 French Infantry and which poured upon the villiage an incessant storm of heavy shot. on this side the beck. Elringtons regiment of Dragoons were feircly engaged with a corps of French and Castlereaghs Infantry were drawn up to protect the town The Marquis of Douros Horseguards. had been attempting to charge the Battery 3 times successivly and just. then were recoiling back over the Rivulet and on the villiage under the tormenting fire of the Enimy.[26] The Darkness and drizzling rain was though so inconvenient scarce heeded here and. a Moon. which had arisen though unseen through its clouds. served to show objects where the fierce flashes of fire did not. give their sudden light. I gallopped across the feild to Gen Elrington. "How goes the night General" "Ho Flower you here—well I believe—if I could only gain the Battery Douro does what man. can do. Ho! Horseguards charge again." This command was obeyed. The broken ranks. of Douros Troops rallyed. and broke down the bank. through the Beck and under their Noble Colonel. made the most furious attempts to storm the opposite steep. but it was evident Murat[27] the great French Cavalier was above with a large force which However could scarce bee seen through the. Dark night and thick smoke of the Battery. Douro at last. seemed about to gain the. eminence And the General commanded. Captain Thornton W Sneaky of the. 1st. Infantry to charge with a detachment of 300 Foot. up the bank and drive the Enimy back with the point of the Bayonet. This young Officer. in spite of his innate lowness. and vulgarity of mind when. in the Great City. now proved himself. a beautiful Officer. at a charge his strength. immpenetrability and. senselessness of Danger was combined with a quickness of observation. and an attention to the wants and. wishes of his Men. Truely admirable He here formed at once. took instant advantage of a wall. in his descent to sheild himself from the Battery. and after crossing the Beck. made a steady unshaken charge up the great Bank. opposite. He. steadily pushed forward amid the smoke and darkness. and heading his men with consummate coolness. Burst through the smoke and firing full upon the Enymys battery slew or took all the. Artillery men. and with a loud shout proclaimed that formidable position captured. Murat who had with a Regiment of French Horse been engaged in a

---

[26] Compare Scott's *Life of Napoleon*, VII, 361-67.

[27] Joachim Murat (1767-1815), one of Napoleon's most celebrated marshals, was a particularly daring leader of cavalry forces. During the Italian campaign of 1796-97, his contribution in bringing up the cannonry won him his place as aide-de-camp to Napoleon. In 1800, Murat helped win the decisive battle of Marengo, and in 1805, played a conspicuous role in the successful Austerlitz campaign. See also p. 22, n. 4, and p. 52, n. 12.

tremendous but extremly doubtful conflict with Douro's troops. now disengaged himself from that Heroic Officer and burst upon Thornton with uplifted sabre before his gallant Horse men. The sturdy young captain turned from a pint of Ale which he had been drinking and confronted the Beau Sabreur with extended Bayonet. which in a twinkling was buried in the chest of the Horsemans Charger. Murat. disengaged himself from the fallen animal and mounted another but just then Douro rushed up at the front of his men and. drove back. in huge waves the fiery cavalry. of the enimy. that could not bear his assault but recoiled back. man over horse horse over man down the hillside and into a meadow oposite where the darkness and shower was yet undisturbed by Battle. Castlereagh with the remainder of our Infantry. ascended the Hill secured the position. and the French retired. on all hands. Elrington who down in the valley had been repelling them with his usual science and coolness. now followed on their lines harrassed them and returned with 50 or 60 prisoners which without consulting the General. he formed. into a hollow square and. after. a few rounds of musketry and a succession of. stabs among the heap with Bayonet. all those fine fellows. lay mangled and dead. before him.[28] But this cold blooded and truely Rougueite action was obliterated and gloased over by his admirable conduct during the action. As for the Noble. Marquis of Douro. and the Gallant Castlereagh and the realy excellent and. active Captain Thornton they acquitted themselves. above all praise. The Numbers engaged. killed and wounded &c stand as follows.

Action at. Little Warner.
the first in this war.

Number of. G Glasstowners --------------------3000.		
Probable No. of French————————4500		
Killed. .G GTowners-------------------------------163	} .total—loss. 374.	
Wounded Do-------------------------------------211		
Killed French---201	} .total loss—	$\frac{661}{1035}$
Wounded Do-------------------------------------391		
Prisoners Do (killed)----------------------------071		

This engagement was warm indeed and the advantage lay wholly [with] us. But now except the Force destined. to p[r]otect the newly acquired battery. the. troops were drawn upon the Hills and villaige to Biavouac. when rattling up the street came. the Commander in cheif with his staff and behind him the strong force of 7000 men. destined to form the force to command this grand pass. Fidena. repaired to the Inn his head quarters and sent for the General Elrington. after learning the. details of the action. he. desired me to seek those officers who had distinguished themselves. that he might in person congratulate and thank them for their actions I rode to the feild of action where I found. Elrington Douro Lofty Caversham Castlereagh and. Thornton. conversing with each other. to

---

[28] See p. 199, n. 10 below.

these I mentioned the wishes of the general but in return I found myself scarcly treated by these feirce officers with the common decency due to me. it seems that on my visiting the feild in the midst. of the conflict. before. my arrangement of my boots or some such matter had given offence to the strange and rude soldiery or "rare apes" and now those distinguished Officers encouraged them to insult me. However I smothered my feelings and prevailed on them to accompany me. when we arrived at the Generals head quarters. while the Marquis was complementing them on their efforts. an orderly man of Douro's by name Edward Laury. entered and said a person without desired to speak with me. I walked to the door of the public house where he and 4 or 5 of his comrades seized me and. personally and grossly insulted. me The noise made by their conduct. brought those within to the door. and so soon as the cause was discovered the Marquis of Fidena ordered the privates engaged in it to be. seized and confined untill punishment could be given for abusing a Colonel in the army. But Lo up started Douro and Elrington and. the latter clapping his hand to his Pistol they both declared. that were. any of the Soldiers laid hands on they would at once. move of their regiments and. leave the Army Viscount Castlereagh. Lofty and. Capt Thornton. instantly ranged themselves beside these two and spoke to the same effect.—Every body started. at this frightful movement. truly the room presented a singular spectacle at that moment it was night and dark butt the fire blazed up brightly and cast a red light through the room. at one end. stood the Marquis of Fidena. Gen Elrington and myself. all amazed at. what was passing Fidena on his legs. and with an anxious look gazing on the. figures opposite the fire. there. stood. the tall Noble form and pale sarcastic countenance of the Great Elrington his eyes looking furiously at his commander and. his hand on. his side to alleviate his incessant coughing by him was the fine military figure of the Marquis of Douro his magnificent features wearing a trancendent expression of pride and anger. a little behind. them could be seen the hansome faces of. Lofty and Cast[l]ereagh and the square turned Thornton his. frank countenance. wearing an expression of. Brazen and sunburnt impudence. In the darkness at the out door stood. the 4 feirce soldiers whose insolence. their Officers seemed so bent to protect. "Gentlemen you are mad" said Fidena calmly. "John. we cannot have our. best Fellows shot for playing with a half Englishman" said Douro. "Order these 5 Officers into custody" answered his Commander. but while. several men were reluctantly moving to obey the command. out of the room. into the street rushed the impetous Douro and ere a minute had elapsed he re entered. at the head. of a file of fellows who. planting their boots and heavy muskets on the floor made the whole howse ring. under cover of these. the whole 5 officers trooped from the. inn ran to their several Rejiments and moved. them all at once through the town acrosse the beck. and onto the Hill of the Battery which. they promptly turned upon the villiage. and stood in readiness. placing two or 3 cannon to command a road by which to obtain supplys. Thus by one mad action had. mutin[i]ed 2 regiments of Horse and one of Foot the three best in the whole army and separating from it had become perfectly useless to the enterprise. to add to our distresses an. Orderly. man. entered hastily and said a long row of bright fires was observed on the horizon in the east. Fidena hastily mounted an eminence. and took a veiw of the country. it was evident at once that Massena's troops in an overwhelming mass. were coming rapidly down upon us. and might be now distant 6 miles. Fidena returning instantly called a council of war the principal remaining officers attended Fidena. said "Gentlemen we are placed in alarming circumstances. Deprived by an unheard of mutiny of our best and bravest forces. what can we do with them. frightful as it would be to my own feelings I would order the five leaders to be instantly bound and. carried to the great Glasstown but should I do so not only these 3000 men but all this Brigade would mutiny. and to pass over what has been done no one can think of.—and here besides we have. Massena with probably 20000 troops full upon us while we can owing to this lamentable incident only muster. 7000 men. without. a single troop of cavalry. had not this mutiny happened. we with. 8000 foot & 2000 noble horse. should of course either repulsed the enimy or according to the plans laid down have made an excellent junction amid the Hills with the rest of our army. But now Gentlemen as matters stand I am sorry indeed to say that Nothing remains for us. but. to. evacuate this place directly and fall back this night upon Angria. avoiding the French as we would a Tyger Messengers must be sent to the passes of Boulshill and Pendleham telling the forces there to fall back upon Angria and thus with out fighting without being beaten we shall be forced to retrograde. from 20 to 30 miles and submit to be cooped up in a fortified City. For the rest. a courier shall be instantly despatched to the City to receive from Government orders how to manage those. mutineers wether to come to terms to attack them or. what other plan to pursue. now Gentlemen humiliating as it must be prepare to fall back directly to Fidena. the meeting broke up the troops were assembled in the utmost haste and ere another hour had elapsed we were in Full retreat. in a wild stormy and boisterous night down for the City of Angria the Mutineers remaining behind on the Hilltops. we arrived at Angria early on Friday morning. dreadfully harrassed by the night march in so wild and stormy weather upon learning our ill fate. all Angria was in tumult and consternation the. French were pouring down upon us. That great pass. had been got over and now. come evil or good. a miserable step backward. was forced to be taken by the army while a courier. rode of with all speed possible to the Glasstown. to aquaint the Ministry and Kings with our alarming state. and to request their advice concerning the mutiny The Marquis of Fidena after snatching a disturbed sleep of an hour formed the bold resolution to ride of. to Howard. a town amid the Warner Hills and. there. bring down himself. Bobbadils Brigade of 8000 men to the relief of Angria. Howard was 25 miles of it was yet Night dark and stormy but the case wa[s] immenet the carriage was got in readiness and. Fidena. Myself and. Col Mac Arthur set off on this perilous journey. leaving the City under Gen Elrington. after a tempestous Journey. we alighted at Howard. a wild villiage. seated amid barren uncultivated Hills. about. Noon of Friday and. on learning that Bobbadil was at Warner Hall. A messenger was dispatched to him to meet us at our quarters in the Inn. Bobbadil soon arrived. in vast astonishment. which upon the events of yesterday being told him was agumented to distress like ours. while he. hurried to prepare his troops for instant departure for. Angria. Fidena determined

to take the Invitation sent by Bobbadil from Warner Hall to honour the owner of
that Mansion with his company untill we should set of. taking myself and Mac
Arthur with him we set out for. that place. This Gentleman whom we were
about to visit was I must inform my readers A Country Glasstowner. and the
principal person of the whole provinces of Angria or Paquena or Norhshire. His
name was Warner Howard Warner. Esqr. of Warner Hall. He is descended from an
antient and distinguished family.[29] and is himself possessed of property worth
the enormous sum of 290000£ a year!!! all the wild. Warner Hills & the towns
around. and. cheif. part of Angria. belonged to him. The Glasstown and the
fashionable circles however. were not accuainted with him for—from pride or
distaste for fashionable life he had kept so much aloof from citys that we had
scarcly ever heard of him before. we now reached the Hall huge and splendid pile
of Old Buildings calculated in appearance to give a vast idea of the owners
power. and. wealth on alighting we were ushered through a Hall. filled with
trophies of the chase. into a large and mostly nobly furnished Apartment.[30] the
hanging of whose walls depicted. the different varieties of sports. and mountain
pastimes. at the Noble fire lay. 6 or 7 huge Dogs. of. extremly feirce appearance.
and of the wolf and. deerhound breed. being seated the Marquis. on a raised sopha
prepared for him. Mr Warner was announced we impatiently waited to see the
strange man but instead of finding as we expected. A Huge old Glasstowner. of
bygone times enter from in size and appearance—we heard a light step. and
slight cough. the great door opened and a Gentleman between 20 and 30 years of
age. 5 feet 5 inches high. slightly and slenderly formed. with fair flaxen hair. of
flaxen texture breshed over an open forehead. small nose. and a feminine
unhardened cast of countenance. his whole face was still and. without expression
save what reigned in his bright kindled eye. which roamed. hastily rond the room
as he entered. with the utmost ease and. a strange assumption of dignified
equality he. bowed and saluted the Marquis and ourselves. walked to the fire. and
after quieting his rejoicing crowd of Dogs entered into conversation with perfect
politness courtesy. and mildness of manner and a voice singular[l]y soft and
melodious but all this was so strangly counterbalanced. by those bright

---

29 Howard is the name of an influential Yorkshire family related to the Dukes
of Norfolk and the Earls of Carlisle. Between 1738-48, Sir Charles Howard was
the Colonel of the Yorkshire Regiment (known today as "the Green Howards").
In 1778, his descendant, Sir Frederick Howard, headed a commission sent to
America by the British Government to treat with the Rebels. On his return, he
became Lord Lieutenant of the East Riding of Yorkshire (1786), devoting
himself to local Yorkshire politics, as well as the famous family residence,
Castle Howard. One of the Howard sons was killed at the Battle of Waterloo
(1815).
30 Castle Howard, a Yorkshire landmark thirteen miles northeast of York, was
designed in part by Vanbrugh and Hawksmoor. The residence of the Howard
family since the seventeenth century, Castle Howard contains an extensive
collection of art from the Flemish, Dutch, and Italian schools.

wandering kindled blue eyes which peirced through all he looked on at his slightest word a host of retainers appeared who looked on him with perfect deference. and at once executed his bidding "My Lord My Lord". he said with that strange diff[er]ence in the soft tone and feirce. emphasis "I have heard from my tenantry of your mishap last nigh[t] 10 miles off. I sincerly regret it. I. fear its consequences. But my Lord. be of good cheer. matters shall end well. my. Horses are ready I will attend you to Angria. But. My Lord. I must remain neuter for myself for the present I will not resist I will not assist the French. you look suprised astonished. you dont know me. my Hills are my own they are inacessible I have 4000 armed devoted tenantry. and have power. may the Genii continue it to keep my own. I will not assist you actualy till I see the time proper. My Lord you Gentlemen. dinner is waiting for you I shall conduct. you." He rose. and shewed the way to the Dining Hall The Marquis he. pointed first to enter himself next we last. Fidena and ourselves. all the while inwardly cogitating on this curious doctrine. of. independence and on the utterer of that doctrine. sitting down to the. splendid dinner he continued. his strange ideas. and said. "If Massena does not. give me full compensation for the injurys he has done to my country. He shall not return back through it. so far as I know I have or can have 12000. men under arms these shall stop the passes of my mountains and even with his 40000. I defy him to defeat me. as for you I perceive you to be in a falling state and. I cannot afford to give my powers to ruin I will not help you now. But intend. to. form a corps of observation. of. 1800 men with which to hover round the flanks of your army and Massena—in your retreat. yes My Lord retreat dont shake look at it in its worst light and you will have the satisfaction of knowing that you have seen your evil—Money Fidena I am willing to advance you. upon promise from your Government of full repayment. men Sir you shall not see till more encouraging times.". All this Mr Warner spoke with. mild. equal voice and unconcerned manner. but as for the Marquis and we who were with him it first. ran in our minds to. seize him and send him to preach his doctrine to the Government. But this plan we soon found. not feasible W H Warner Esq[r]. certainly held immense power indeed absolute power through the whole Province of Angria. was in possesion. of. at least 3800000£ worth of property and held at his beck. 12000 armed men. he could do us vast good or incalculable evil.—his Ideas indeed were such as Government in an ordinary case could never countenance. But now we saw them expedient and determined to bow to circumstances

We now received intelligence that. Bobbadils troops were on their march to Angria. The Marquis and we mounted. the carriage. Mr Warner who had determined to go to Angria to look on his intrests as he said—mounted a horse. and notwithstanding the wild stormy weather. accompanied us. without carriage or great coat. (which but I forget. the Glasstowners wont wear the latter conve[n]ience). or other shelter. and on alighting at the Grand Hotel doors in Angria. on the carriage doors. being thrown open there he stood below his steed smoking beside him. waiting with calm face and unquiet eye to hand the Marquis out of his carriage. His slender figure. beaten and. drenched with the wind and rain of almost 30 miles. we could see at a glance. the. respect he was held in by the Angrians for these stubborn. provincials on passing obsequiously took of their hats and caps to him where they refused that homage to the Marquis an heir to a throne. Here Mr Warner left us as he said with the utmost ease to go and. speak with the french. our forces from. Howard were now all arrived in the city and. it was full time for Massena. from all sides was bearing down on Angria devastating all around him. and amid all the tempest as evening sank down fires from more than one burning villiage burst up in the <level> plain country below. on the Marquis of Fidena Mc Arthur and Myself arriving at head quarters. we learned the delightful intelligence. that. during our abscence. the Mutineers had appeared in full force upon the heights above the town that they had. seized the Batterys commanding the east and now occupied them determined. if molested. to use them. on stepping out. we had full confirmation of this. report in seeing the long lines of watch fires crowning the Beacon Hill. But while we were gazing in gloomy silence upon this heart rending sight to carriages thundered past and alighted at the Hotel beyond. we turned to see them. Two Gentlemen alighted from them and walked up to us The Earl St Clair and Sir R W Pelham. we eagerly met them. "Few and short were the words we said."[31] They two (Sir R just being enstalled as Secretary of War) had. on the receipt of intelligence of the Mutiny had by command. of their Majestys. the Kings. ridden post haste to Angria. to settle matters. and bring this frightful scene to a close. Messengers were sent up immediatly to know from the Mutineers wether. the Premeir War Secretary their General and. the Government Agent. could be admitted to a conference answer was returned permitting us. we all walked up the hill and. reached the encamp[m]ent. it was their a black howling night where wind and sleet swept over the hill without staying. large fires all round us threw light and heat. upon the long ranks of stern soldiers. ranged with fixed Bayonet before 3 hideous pieces of black Battering Cannon. whose ominous mouths gaped full upon the city below. we were conducted to a large fire in the midst. surrounde[d] by. trampling horses and piles of amunition. here we recognized. the principal. Officers of the Mutiny. Lofty leaning. his head on his hand in silent melancholy. Castlereagh dressing his hair at a steel cap. for mirror. Thornton tossing cheese. at the fire. Douro and Elrington the principal leaders conversing with faces turned to the. flames. Upon our introduction they both turned. and each noble countenance. became suffused with. a sneer of disdain. Elrington so soon as he saw Sir R. Pelham. a member of the Ministry. turned as black as death. said. "Douro youll transact. buisness" and. sat down cursing at the fire. Douro did transact the buisness. and after a long conversation. he agreed in the name and with the consent of his colleagues to the following conditions.

"1stly that the 1st and 2d Regiments Horseguards. Col^S. Douro and Elrington. and the 13th Regiment infantry Col. Viscount Castlereagh.

---

31   Charles Wolfe, *The Burial of Sir John Moore*, Stanza 4—"Few and short were the prayers we said."

do lay down their arms and surrender themselves to their General Marquis of Fidena.

II^dly that upon so doing they. be not proceeded against in anywise. for late offences but. stand exactly upon the footing they did before the mutiny

IIIdly that should hereafter. any man or number of men. in these 3 Regiments commit any offence whatever against military law they shall not be protected or sheilded by their officers but. delivered ove[r] immediatly to. justice.

Signed. upon the part of Government.

<u>facsimile's</u>

	Ministers	L	{	St Clair R Pelham J Flower

Splendid Writers
one and all[32]

	Mutineers	S	{	Duoro Elrington Castlereagh Thornton

Chris Dobson. Clerk.   General in cheif Fidena

The Genii be praised! This frightful buisness was now over Elrington Douro Lofty and Castlereagh. returned back to the Great Hotel. with. Fidena. Clair Pelham Myself —where we spent a pleasant evening and. at 1 in the morning. the premier and War Secretary. again set. off for Verdopolis. The three mutinous Regiments evacuated the Hill and entering the city ranged themselves under their old Generals.—I. retired to rest and closed my eyes with a spirit lightened by the events of the evening and a body fatigued indeed with the toils of the day.

Eearly indeed upon the morning. of November 24. Saturday. I hastily arose and after dressing. drew back the curtains of my window. I know not how dismally I felt upon seeing the wide wrack of Nature around us. Stormy as the proceeding days had proved. this morning arose yet wilder and more severe. and the whriling eddies of wind. the. clouds of Rain which swept by howling along the streets. and bursting over the champaign country beyond. proved. most deadning and disheartning to the mind. amid the wind on opening the window. I fancied I could hear a sustained thundering sound. from afar of. which to me. seemed the roaring of artillery. But not being able to. certify its nature. I. stepped down. into Fidenas breakfast room. where he with. Generals Elrington and Douro. were standing. at a table. in silence looking over many maps and plans and papers without the usual Mornings greeting Douro pointed me to the. Daily papers of yesterday morning just received from Verdopolis. upon taking

---

32   Written in longhand.

them up my eyes were blasted with the. intelligence that "IN Grenvilles troops which in the south were. vigourously carr[y]ing on hostilitys with Marmont upon the receipt there of news of the mutiny at Little Warner. several officers of bad character and turbulent. opinions had seized the opportunity to create fatal dissensions. and. 3 Colonels. O Connor Carey and Dorn. well known names in our City. with 6 officers of lower rank from other regiments had at once withdrawn. from the main body of the army and. taking with them. 4300 men had encamped upon. some eminences near. Doverham. where having amunition and. artillery they had commenced levying contributions on and shamefully plundering the country round them That. Grenvilles forces at once being thrown into confusion by this unexpected deffection. had. been unable to. withstand a charge from all points made upon them by the whole of Marmonts forces. (who knew of the mutiny.) and had therefore been forced. 30 miles back into the country giving the french overwhelming advantages over them in numbers. position and vicinity to Verdopolis. the officers of the Mutiny now commenced. a negotiation with. Marmont. by which they stipulated. that. on each being raised a degree high[er] in the french service. than in their present. state and on receiving each 7500£. they. would. deliver all their troops 4300 men into the hands of the french. Marmont eagerly seized upon this offer but the men drawn into the mutiny by the voice of these renegade officers could not bear the idea of. going over to the french. and rose up against their commanders. But upon. Marmonts sending upon them Regnier with. 9000 bayonets. they were forced to fly after an obstinate resistance. toward Grenvilles retreating army. while Marmont after receiving into his camp the renegade officers. pushed. column after column in pusuit of the repentant fugitives and. at last threw them. in perfect confusion. upon the rear of Grenvilles forces. Now the French General. saw his time was come and Bringing up once again the whole force of his Army he assailed. the confused and weakened Force of the Glasstowners with such repeated and desperate charges that Grenville was obliged. to retreat at once to within 30 miles of Verdopolis where he took up his positions. having in the course of this short and miserable campaign. lost the object of their expedition. dreadfully damaged that of our expidition as will be shown. and. lost 3000 prisoners. and 6700 killed and wounded. all through the mutiny of 9 officers of infamous and dishonest character. Now as for Marmont he after having pushed matters forward in a manner worthy of his Great Master. now made the Bold determination to leave. in his rear the baffled enymy and make a bold march northward to join and. strengthen the forces of Massena. and accomplish the ruin he had set out therefore and by these last despatches. was advanced up the very road by which we. had. come toward us. having in his command. 28000 soldiers and. 130 heavy artillery." This was the substance of the horrible news which I glanced over. Ere I could. find utterance to answer Fidena spoke. "Well Flower" he said. in a voice of fixed. agony. "You see there is only one way left us. Massena. already possesing a force. greatly superior to our own. is drawn round this city and rapidly nearing its gates the weather is wild and stormy in the highest degree. Massena will be it seems directly reinforced. up to. 60000 men! No way Sir No way Gentlemen can remain but this day amid this weather to.

commence a retreat from this city not. southward to our great Home but. North Western. over the Hills. 150 miles to. Freetown on the Niger you start. but there we shall. have good quarters and I can have open communication with the City. by the Niger and by the great road. The March I know will be tremendous. But Gentlemen we must endure it and I shall now give orders for matters to be begun." While Fidena yet spoke the. trembling of the windows without any particular sound heard above the roaring of the wind announced to experienced. ears that a cannonading must have somewhere begun we all stepped out to the street door. and on gaining the open air the long stormy. rumbling sound mixing with the tempest. soon assured us of the fact. in truth Massena's advanced guard of 6000 men was vigourously atackking Fergussons division of a similar number. who was acoording to the instructions given when we retreated from Warner now endeavouring to concentrate his forces. from his station of Pendleham. to this City but the French had discovered him and now seemed from their exertions. to endeavour to annihilate him. Fidena. ordered 2 Regiments of Horse. to be. got ready and to proceed under. Col Viscount Elrington to the scene of action which lay about 3 miles South east of Angria. I accompanied this reinforcement and. amid. a terrific storm of wind and rain we arrived at 10 o clock upon the feild. where their rear resting on a large rivulet the wearied and exhausted troops of Fergusson were striving to sustain themselves against a force at first only of their own amount but now. rapidly increasing and bearing down on them. Here I saw 12000 men in close combat. upon a day. which might have served Borodino.[33] Elrington with his own vigour and energy dashed forward with his 2000 Calvary and made a determined charge upon the french lines for a moment it rolled. them back. in confusion over the marshy and. deluged feilds back on their batterys and encampments. But Murat. with 4000 horse soon came up on the french lines and commenced again a terrific struggle with the tygerlike Elrington This Man never weakened himself or strengthened himself by ardour or enthusiastic chivalry. but with Bloodless face. and cold peircing eye. he could. advance under a galling fire upon. a force 3 times his number could attack. them murder them. seize his advantage. and gain that advantage or he could without. a change of look or feeling recoil back. pass his position retreat and. leave the feild to the victors but still ready and alert to wring himself through the slightest hole to ruin them and. if he could gain that end to destroy them. delight at the valour of others pity and. anguish on seeing brave heroic men born down trampled under horses. lacerated by sabres or mowed down

---

[33] The Battle of Borodino (1812) took place during Napoleon's invasion of Russia between 130,000 French and 120,000 Russian troops. The battle was fought after the Russian General, Kutuzov, managed to stay the retreat of his troops at the town of Borodino and build hasty fortifications to block the French advance on Moscow. However, with the loss of 30,000 soldiers on the French side and 45,000 on the Russian side, Napoleon gained a narrow victory which allowed him to occupy Moscow for a brief period before being driven out of Russia.

by a galling fire never so much as entered his mind. he would willingly have seen Murat dying at the back of a dyke by a stone flung from a wall top. However while disasters pressed heavily upon him. while his own and Fergussons forces of 8000 men were almost in vain striving to keep gro[u]nd against a storm of wind and rain a worse storm of Balls and 9 or 10000 Frenchmen new reinforcements burst on them. under a man different indeed from himself. I saw through that wild waste of Battle and tempest. 1500 Cavalry thunder up. over the feilds and break down the lanes and roads full into the midst of the scene of action. Their well known Leader the Marquis of Douro at their head fired with his noble impetuosity his chivalric and. high wrought Courage. dashing foremost on the french lines confronting the smoking Battery and charging time after time over the lines and piles of slain 22000 men were perhaps now engaged. and the carnage became dreadful but. all was in vain the french fast increasing were under their glorious Horsemen. imperceptibly driving us back by the weight of numbers and. the fire of their Batterys. and at Noon. Aids de camp. arrived. from Angria communicating the distressing intelligence that we must fall back upon that city immediatly to cover and in the end follow the retreat of the army. westward. Now then after making a front to intercept the french the rear of the troops engaged began to pour off. along ever[y] opening for the city. I was required. at head quarters and setting spurrs to my horse soon arrived at the Head quarters of the Hotel. Here all things were in the wild confusion[34] attendant upon a removal and it was 2 hours. ere I could speak with our General mean while. the artillery waggons and baggage. with the van of the army under Gen Elrington were streaming in long files through the streets toward the western road and. blocked up with inextricable confusion. the openings and. paths. of their road. From the south long files of wounded. and. flying men covered with rain and mud and. gory. with battle. seemed pushing in with the same. disorder. and the peal of the nearer artillery from Massena's lines some of whose balls actually now fell in the streets did not tend to quiet the tumult I passed the day in a whirl of opposite sensations untill in the evening I round went to see the Marquis Fidena. he was in a room ready equipped for travelling and walking through the apartment with a steady step but hurried eye. The slender form and calm. feminine features of W,H, Warner. Esqr. stood. at the fire. his feirce eyes alone lighted with the enthusiasm natural to his strangely complicated character while his voice maintained its calm and. equal tone without a single quaver. "Oh. My lord" he said as I entered. "I suppose your wounded. will. be found of a vast number I should think 5000. these it will be utterly impossible to take with you 5 miles believe me it will. Now on the other hand should Massena. take them the gibbet and. cannon will be the softest words with him. But this city belongs to me these. people in it are mine. with

---

34 Branwell's description of the "wild confusion" of military engagement parallels the indescribable "confusion and dismay" recorded in such eyewitness accounts of the Napoleonic wars as "The Subaltern—A Journal of the Peninsular Campaign," *Blackwood's Magazine*, xvii (June 1825), 719.

Massena I am not at enmity and now I can do you a service. I will engage to
take all the wounded under my care to prevent Massena from destroying them.
and to supply them. with all necessarys at my own expense. provided the
Government. will remunerate me at the rate of 1.s. per head per day. Sir every
wounded man while I have them under my care. averaging probably. 1785£ every
week. I shall require a note signed by yourself. securing prompt and. full
payment from your government. Now My Lord." Now however revolting the
tone of this offer however illegal the manner in which it was put. it was not one
to be slighted or thrown aside. Willingly indeed. did. Fidena seize it and. having
written the note assuring Mr. Warner of remuneration. he gave into his hands all
the wounded then in the City or hereafter coming in. Mr Warner himself. rode of
to Massena's lines to aquaint him with the settlement. and its terms. probably.
also to bribe that able but avaricious General into prompt acquiescence.

But we must return to a more disagreeable narrative. Evening was fast
drawing on its shadows rendered yet darker and far more dreadful. by the storm of
wind and rain which never ceasing through the whole day seemed now
redoubling in violence. From the western outlets of the City for many hours
cannon baggage and long columns of men had been filing out on their retreat.
and now the General only waited. for the arrival of Colonels Douro and
Elrington with the horse. which had been engaged in protecting the retiring
corps of Fergusson from the Battle. in the plain. The constant stream of.
shattered Battalions covered with blood drenched in mud and rain which from
that quarter passing down the great street were filing on to the Westward. along
with the troops of wounded. creeping in all directions and stumbling about like
men intoxicated scarce able to gain the Hospitals sufficiently indicated the
terrible nature. of the previous struggle when at last the two noble defenders of
our rear amid their broken and. weakened Regiments alighted at the Door of the
Hotel they were scarce able to give a higher notion of the conflict than we had
received before. "Well Elrington and Douro" said our General as these two
entered. the room "you have nobly distinguished yourselves this day promotion
follows close upon such conduct." Douro his countenance brightend and flushed
by the noble enthusiasm. which marks his character Answered "Oh Fidena for
ourselves we have done what we could but it is to our men to our soldiers we
owe safty and. life. 18000 to 9000 is odds indeed. It bitterly greives me to know
our destination this night. and in spite.—but come. I—we shall wind up for the
worst." Elrington did not speak but. walking to the fire with the help of chairs
and tables. he threw himself on to a sofa in exhaustion. all the splendid actions
which he had done and seen that day failed to inspire him with a spark of
Enthusiasm. at last he said. "Oh I. cannot enjoy those scenes as I once could
when your age Douro. but. I can eat if not relish." he smiled. slightly and then
sunk into his usual state of moody abstraction.

Shortly. the kettle drums and trumpets under the window. struck up the
signal for marching Douro and Elrington hastily rose and. seizing their swords.
hastned to the street their Rejiments directly after. rattled off westward. 3000
men now only remained in the city. Therefor the Marquis Fidena. Gen Elrington
Col Mac Arthur and myself. with the staff. Officers. all mounted. and. rode off

in deep silence to accompany the retreat. protected by those 3000 Infantry under. Castlereagh. we soon gained the Great Bridge and the escort swept over. into the wide dark and stormy champaign. After half an hours hard riding we came up with several divisions of the army moving along harrassed with fatigue beaten by the storm and. confused by the darkness to the last degree. as we pressed forward amid the wild throng of men arms horse. and artillery. we heard. something sounding incessantly above the wind. and. holdi[n]g forth a long unmodulated roar. we could not be mistaken this was that Guadima which we were about to cross and. which we could all pass over before the arrival of the French we might by breaking up the Bridges interpose as a bar to all further molestation

So we thought. But the Genii had not here decreed an end to our misfortunes. Ere we had advanced much farther a pressing back amid the crowds instead. of going forward. wild cries coming from the yet distant banks of the river. and. echo[e]d and swelled By all around us. gave distinct information of some unhappy event. what was it it could not be an attack of the french. for that maneurvre could not wring such a despairing howl from a Glasstown soldier were he assailed. by 10000. another conjecture which shot through our minds. seemed nearer the truth. was the Bridge swept away. by rains. I believe though from the darkness I could not see it that every face turned pale at such a supposition. and I know that the Marquis and our staff. after a moments silence broke furiously through the thick pressed multitude and. not halting till they had arrived on the Banks. there cast one hasty glance and said simultaneously. "Then it is" of a certain. there the <bright> light from a moon unseen amid the thick and stormy heaven disclosed to us a huge River surging onward. 200 yards broad. bursting down from the north in black waves rolling over each other chafing the Banks and swelled. to a mighty height. Two large <a[r]ches> and a shattered half. carried the road. about. 60 feet across the torrent all farther was a wide. raging waste of stormy water. A Noble Bridge Had. here existed ere the unpredecented rains of the last. 2 weeks swelling the swift Guadima to a hitherto almost unknown height and fury had torn it from its very foundations and carried. every stone to the sea.

No situation could be worse than ours then was and my hand trembles at this moment in writing it. a Retreating army of. 23000 men. with a huge attendance of Cannon Baggage Amunition and. etc. was thus stayed inevitabley. in the wildest and most inextricable confusion. upon. feilds and roads. where they sunk. knee deep at every step in mud and water. a dark Night above them and a tremendous tempest of rain and wind incessantly beating upon them. Before them an unbridged and rapid river over which they could not fly. Behind. them and rapidly approaching a vast & victorious army. with whom they could never fight. I know not what supported Fidena in this frightful scence certainly his manner and voice was calm and. steady but the tones hollow indeed. A wooden Bridge. not yet swept away. existed about a mile to the northward. This we knew of and to this all seemed determined to proceed. We rode foremost to the place while the army now almost a huge heap of confusion rolled on by instinct. bewildered and. struck as if by lightning I saw Douro and Elrington in rain amid the tumult and darkness endeavouring to restore some slight appearance of order. when we had gained this wooden Bridge what was it. a frail wretched structure about 8 feet broad.

Men instantly Began to push over in files of 4 deep mixed. with Artillery and Baggage And a noble stream of caps. and Bayonets poured forward into the darkness with something like returning order. in 2 hours Fergussons division of 7000. had. gained with their Artillery and amunition the other side But by this time. for it was yet far from morning light the wildness of the storm the incessant pouring of cold drenching rain had almost exhausted the spirit of the troops cries and murmurs began to spread frightfully and. at length by a sudden impulse one universal rush was made on the frail wooden structure. wave over wave of mixed and. mingled. soldiers pushed each other along. The Bridge groaned and cracked. horribly. Oh how my ears were strained and tortured to hear that sound which came ere long a stunning and deafning chrash a loud yell of horror. and. splashing into the foaming water. down broke hopes and Bridge and. 600 men. overwhelmed. amid. the. surging torrent Below.[35] all further sound all dying shreiks and gaspings were hushed by. the sudden roar of Cannonry which burst upon our rear. Here at last the french were upon. us. "Gentlemen" cried Fidena "to your ranks Douro. Elrington advance check them. Castlereagh support the charge. Now for the rest of you the river must be trusted to. Gentlemen follow me. he spurred his charger to the. Bank. plunged in and dissapearing for a moment in the rushing water was seen directly struggling forward amid the waves hundreds followed at once after him. and. intense looks were fixed. upon them in hopes they would gain the opposite Banks. The river was wider and smoother than down below and. 50 out of the 80 staff. reached the shore encouraged by this others dashed. in. horses and men sometimes sinking at other times beings swept away or struggling toward shore now filled this unhappy river. and directly long files of foot with the most desperate intrepidity plunged in and buffeted the Billows on their way. But while this was transacting in front. the Loud crash of Artillery <pusled> up with trebled thunder in our rear. and the thick flashes of fire. burst out from the French Batteries along the whole of our harrassed line. by gigantic efforts Elrington Douro and Castlereagh. managed to present something like a front to the impetous charges of cavalry which Massena hurled on them in thickly compacted masses. the wildest havoc. was made among us by the french cannonry and nothing but suprasssing courage could have born the oppressing load of enimies. all gave the feeling excited in a horrid Nightmare of our struggling in vain against a. supernatural load. pressed for ever upon us. The wind and rain. rendered our muskets nearly uncervicable Bayonet and sabre was our recourse against Bullet and Cannon ball and what was worse than all. incessant showers of Grape and Cannister shot. in a while Douro's force of cavalry was called. away from us and

---

[35] Compare with the description of the bridge collapse and disastrous river crossing during Napoleon's retreat from Moscow in Scott's *Life of Napoleon*, VII, 377-84 and 587-90.

that splendid Officer after driving back. a force of french in one desperate charge recoiled on to the River and. plunged in. Elrington in a little while farther. was forced to drop off the huge River received him. and. here were left behind not quite 3000 infantry to make head against. a van of 13000 french. the plan laid down was to oppose constantly a front to the enimy while the rear dropt of by degrees into the River and gained the Banks beyond. ere many minutes had elapsed the Gallant Colonel young Lord Castlereagh. was struck down by a grape shot. a file closed round him and he was born. off to the River the command then devolved upon Captain Thornton (or more properly I should say. Viscount Thornton Wilkin Sneachi) this young man. had all along beheaved with a steadiness Bravery and coolness above all praise and now ordering 1000 men to fall Back and over the River without any more. delay he formed. seized his Bayonet. and. with a loud shout burst forward at the head of his men dashed full on the thundering Batterys broke through fire and smoke. and rolled the whole French van back from the feild. then reforming his gallant line he conducted them steadily on to the river banks plunged in and. struggled to the opposite shore. with a shattered and lessened troop he made a forced march of 9 miles and at length joined the rear of our retreat. at. Burnfoot. amid the Hills. daylight Here broke upon a wild and haggard group of men streaming along over the scarce passable roads and pathways at every yard droping cannon waggons horses and men. all drowned in rain famished with hunger. yet still retaining the highest and most invincible courage and firmness. This day the weather continued. so wild and stormy that save in this our extremity. nothing could have been attempted. in war. we pushed on in 3 pararell Columns over the country on our flank along the Hills marched. 1800 men forming corps of observation tentantry of Mr Warner who proffessing strict neutrality led this body. to hang upon either army and observe their movements. through this strange man we were releived of some of our countless wounded. and sometimes supplied with a drove or 2 of. mountain cattle. But frightful as were the sufferings of the main army so was our rear of 5000 men under General Elrington. Day after day their whole course. was one continued Battle against a force which eternally surrounded. overwhelmed and cut them ere long the General Elrington. received. a horrid wound. in the jaw which seemed. sufficient to destroy him he. was instantly conveyed. to the main body of the army then the command devolved upon. Lord Elrington but directly. fatigue combined with Bodily and mental. irritation and weakness. reduced him to temporary delusion. at Length the weight fell upon the shoulders of the Marquis of Douro. He did what man could do.

But Reader I will not. enter into any details of this unhappy retreat. it presented only one wild scene of storm and confusion in the elements and misery and ferocity in man. I will only say that in 8 days. from the evacuation of Angria. we having marched over 150 miles of country reach[ed] the long whished for hills. looking down upon Freetown and the Vale of Verdopolis this march we began with a force of 23000 men and. ended with. one of 13000. our loss might. be—3000 killed. 5000 wounded. 2000 Prisoners. in men. 130 pieces of artillery. left behind. and. 1800 horses destroyed. The Evening was wild and stormy as the troops harrassed. and. exhausted. climbed the rough. heights of Velino. and upon reaching the summits. there appeared not a the huge swell of landscape sweeping down on the other side into a mighty and fertile valley and overlooking a Glorious river and noble City. no. all round us lay flat elevated marshes and moorlands. untracked by pathways and. delugged with water. beyond and on their sides rose wet moorlands. heights of no striking elevation above. these uncultivated table lands but far indeed above the level of the Sea. over all the clouds of Evening seemed to hang down and rest themselves upon the heavey air below. in many places rolling along the ground half cloud half rain. This was the wild rough station appointed for that nights rest of the army. sheer fatigue. compelled us to rest. without proceeding down the other side to Freetown. which lay 11 miles westward. The Marquis of Fidena. with his staff. proceeded toward the little villiage of Velino. 3 miles beyond us. where also the Baggage and sick. were about to be conveyed The skeleton of our army in three divisions was drawn far round this villiage over the expanse of the moors. The north division of 2000 men under Fergusson the middle under Douro of 3000. and the. South. under Elrington of the same number. a reserve of. 5000 under the Marquis himself. occupied the villiage. in the rear. on the direct North the hills of Velino rising above the marshes. blazed with the fires of. Warner's neutral corps. which had uunder their strange commander. followed us. through the whole retreat. as the Advance of Massena's forces were rapidly pushing forward to the attack. and as it was <not> known <how> soon their van might be upon us. all the troops were ordered to lie in rank and in their arms. But I will venture to assert the prospect of at length a fair open Battle lightened the hearts and trebled the courage of all around me.

For myself I must state that as this account pretends to little more than a personal narrative of my own experience in this eventful war. the reader must follow me. in my own. feelings and. adventure. and I must confine myself to what I felt and what I saw. my pillow that night was like many an other. on the wet wild heather. And between cold and excitement I could not close my eyes to sleep. but lay listning to the dying sounds of encampment and to the troops. all. marching to their resting ground. when deep night had settled over us all noise abated and. wrapping my cloak closer round me. I turned my eyes up to the stormy expanse of heaven above. it hung over me heavy dark and. covered with clouds through which at intervals the Moon looked out upon us and. then hurr[y]ing overhead. was lost again in the chaotic masses. a wild and delightful feeling came over me. when I. thought and gazed on. the scenes before me. Battle was expected and my ears at the slightest sound far off. stretched to hear the awakening Bugles. But only the monotonous sugh of the midnight wind. swept across the heaths of Velino. About Midnight when I had almost composed myself to sleep with. rousing and. depressing thoughts. I heard some one speak. not far of the voice was soft. and solemn. and recited. with repressed feeling the following lines.[36]

1   I see through heaven with raven wings
           A funeral Angel fly
      The Trumpet in his dusky hands
           Wails wild and. drearily

2   Beside him on her midnight path
           The Moon glides through the sky
      And far beneath her chilly face.
           The silent waters lie.

3   Around me not the acustomed sight
           Of Hill and vale I veiw.
      Wide meadows bathed. in cheerless light.
           Dark woods in Midnight hue.

4   No all the earth behind before
           Seems one wide waste of graves
      And round each trench so dark dark and drear.

      The black earth stands like waves
These are not common graves of men
Where when their lifes short hour is done
Neath the old. yew trees waving by
They peacefully and silent lie
      These seem as if a torrents force
           Had rent its sudden way.
      They seem as if the channel course
           Of some tremendous sea
Aye these are graves of armies where
Foeman and Freind and horse and spear
Bloody and cold together thrust.
         Together must consume
And. rotting in their native dust.
         Their dark and narrow tomb.
Oh God and what shall this betide
Why does that Funeral Angel fly
Why does yon moon so solemn ride

---

[36] The poem is preceded by a canceled version of the first stanza which is identical, except that l. 3 reads "sinful hands." For a similar description of the night before battle, see "The Subaltern—A Journal of the Peninsular Campaign," *Blackwood's Magazine*, xvii (June 1825), 719-20.

Across this dark and stormy sky
Why does my spirit chilled and drear
In this dark vision linger here.
Behold upon that midnight heath
    A Mighty Army lie
Hushed in deep sleep each warriors breath
    Fast closed each lion eye.
The Moon from heaven upon each face
    With saddest lustre shines
And glitters on the untrampled grass
    Between the long drawn lines.
Are ye the tenants of that tomb
    Oh ist for you these graves are made
And shall ye in that narrow room.
      Be silent laid.
Oh God avert the avenging sword.
    And turn thy wrath away   13
Pass of ye hungry yawning toombs   4
    ARise all cheering day.   52

I looked hastily round when this wild and solemn measure ceased my minds was saddened and superstitious feeling crept over me. a dark figure stood near I called out "Who are you" Mr Warner advanced it was him I started up and And. shaking his hand we both for a moment in silence. looked on the dark scene around us. "You will fight to night." said Warner in his usual soft solemn tone. "I know it and as the scene of a great Battle shall I say a great Victory. I hope so I hope so. you are almost in despair and despair gives surety of hope But 13000 to. 26000 is odds indeed—how solemn the night is. it is fit to usher in a battle." He c[e]ased for 2 or 3 figures were seen walking toward us. we advanced they proved to be the Marquis of Douro Lord Elrington and Viscount Lofty. Elrington looked stern and cold. his face wore a damping and sarcastic smile. Douro whose eye glanced with more than its accustomed light was. endeavouring to r[o]use to cheerfulness. his freind Lofty whose handsome features. bore an. air of steady and fixed Melancholy while he with a forced smile was endeavouring to meet the expressions of his Noble Friend. Warner for a moment fixed his keen glance upon him and then turning to me he said in a whisper "Believe me that youngs mans days are out he. knows his death. this night"—The three new comers now came up and we all entered into conversation looking upon the heaths and shading with our hands our faces from the rain. while wide round us the vast moor twinkled with the light of the watchfires. All at once the roll of drums struck. our ears followed. by a loud burst of Martial Music. straight from the north. The Blood shot into our faces "Here they are cried" Douro "We must off to our divisions" Elrington took his cane under his arm and coolly and calmly walked away toward his post. about a mile of. Douro mounted his Horse and with Lofty galloped quickly toward his post. Mr Warner. I lost in the darkness. For myself I stood still a moment. the scene which so late. had seemed so solemn and silent now. shook with the thunder of the drums. the bursts of Trumpets. and the shouts of. men. single soldiers and small bodies of men hurried by me to their posts without cursing and. I knew that it was time for me to hurry down to the villiage to my General. therefor calling for my Horse I mounted him and. rode back over the. moorside to the wild Little villiage of Velino the head quarters of Fidena. The Moonlight had. struggled forth with rather more light. at that time and shewed me all the reserves of 5000 men under arms ranged. in the street and. road and mooredge. quite ready for action. Fidena was. attending at that moment the dying General Elrington. But. ere long he appeared. spoke a few words to me. ordered his staff. and mounted. "Flower" he said "we cannot stand. the french charges in our shattered state. my only way is to. ascertain their position Bring up the front and rear and advance my whole Force without a moments delay—a sudden impression is the only plan for. 13000 against 30000. Forward gentlemen." as he spoke. he spurred his horse. and. the skeleton of his staff. with myself among them pushed on to the coming engagement. ere. we had gained the marshes however. the stunning uproar and. cracks like thunder. repeated without ceasing announced. the French to have placed their Artillery and to have begun. I. gained my late silent resting place. now not a vestige of the fire appeared. it was covered with Thorntons detachment of Bayonets and. torn up by the constant discharges of a battery close by. toward. the north. I could observe amid the darkness. the well known Murat charging with a noble body of cavalry the Horseguards of Douro. at the back. Warners watchfires still twinkled on the Hill. allmost every thing else was lost in mist and darkness. I was here obliged at once to join Fidena. he. rode up to the Marquis of Douro. who called to him "for Heavens sake Fidena let us charge. I cannot bear to let Murat. cut us up. without hindrance." "Soon Douro soon". next we pressed up to Elrington he was standing by the Body of his Horse just killed. and. on. a great rock. seemed scarcely conscious of the storm around him. "My lord" said Fidena. The nobleman looked up and. calmly said. "My lord Marquis. give me. a company of bayonets to charge that Battery." "Do it yourself. Elrington said Fidena rather suprised. "No! replied. this strange man with the same impenetrability. "I wont myself. I dont like sabre work." Fidena gazed in astonishement. "Surely <u>you</u>! are not a coward." broke from his lips. but he saw that impulse was groundless. For as a ball struck. the earth at Elringtons feet and. dashed round a cloud. of mud and earth. all stepped back save. that Nobleman. who though covered with earth. stood. quite unconcerned. Fidena. knew his character saw this. peculiarity and determined not to oppose him. he therefore dispatched me to bring up Major Thornton with part of Castlereaghs Rejiment. I. soon by the flashes of fire found this Gallant Officer standing with his men and his whole soul employed upon eating a peice of Bread and cheese I communicated my orders he swallowed a huge mouthful. wiped his mouth with a hand[k]ercheif and saying "Now my lads we've a peice of stiff work but at the Frenchmen and eat them". he placed his peice and. led his hearty fellows on to the attack. They dashed through the smoke and fire. when shortly a hearty cheer announced. them sucessful. Massena it was evident had. now brought a great front to oppose us but. it was best to charge ere he could bring up a still greater. the reserves were coming up. Fidena. rode rapidly along the uneven fronts of battle. placing in order Douros and Loftys Regiments. in the midst. Elringtons in the south with Thornton and he then passed up the line toward the immediate foot of. the hills where. Fergusson was hotly engaged with Lannes Grenadiers. I did accompany him there but was attached to Douros noble Regiment. who upon command being given for the whole line to charge. flew forward. galloping with his men over the ground bursting upon Murats Cavalry and rolling them. man and horse over each other back. onto the rear of the French army. Elrington did not execute his charge with this splendid brilliancy but with almost equal effect. for he. with his accustomed cold science and descision. wedged. between two French divisions. and cutting one from the other took prisoners 6 or 700 men. these he had. drawn up in a hollow square and after his usual ferocity and unsparing character. he caused the battery he had taken to be directed upon the unhappy men and ceased not firing till every soul of them had perished. then he prosecuted with the utmost coolness this great advantage and. attacked with the utmost vigour the retreating enimy. But Douro in Murat had. to encounter a most dauntless and congenial enimy. and for a while. nothing passed there but mutual charges and. dreadful but indecisive combat. The darkness (for no flashes of musketry or cannon brightened here.) combined with the increasing storm. wrapt all up in a double horror. Yet I saw that. noble. scion of the House of Wellington. engaging in the teeth of the overpowering numbers the. greatest cavalier of Africa. and. by degrees. pushing his forces back wards and backward through the. irresistible impetouosity of his charges. In these not even the Marquis more distinguished. himself than did Lord Viscount Lofty he seemed bent upon wiping out with either glory or blood the stains which have so needlessly stuck. to his character from the ridiculous transactions mentioned in a manner so lively in. "Arthuriana." by Lord. Chas Wellesly".[37] In my eyes a double and more melancholy intrest this night afixed to this Young Nobleman. for whenever I veiwed him amid the storm and darkness burst through the thickest flash of sabres and armors the wildest chaos of fighting and flying men. I could not help feeling a cloud come over my minds eye on reflecting on the solemn words of Mr Warner so lately spoken. and Now at midnight when the tide of Battle seemed on every front turning at last in our favour. Lord Lofty mounted a fresh Horse. and. while Douro his freind. charged. not far off. he. rallied his forces and. rushed headlong full against a wild. chaos of cavalry broke through them and found himself almost surrounded. amid the rearguard of Massena's huge army. then he faceed round. and accompanied by his few followers. boldly slashed against even the staff of the Great French General overthrew all who opposed his progress. and by his lionlike conduct even shook. the whole. body of enimies. just as he was spurring his. horse forward. to the staff. of Massena. a shot struck his horse it fell. and he fell with it. ere he could. regain his feet a blow from a sabre made the Blood stream down his face.

---

[37]   See Alexander CB, II, Part I, 207.

yet he still grappled with his adversary and. found space to despatch a messenger to Douro for help meanwhile he. with his sword. dealt terrible blows around him. yet. what. could one arm do against a hundred. a musket bullet. struck him in the Breast he fell backward. and. ere his eyes closed on life. Douro with several hundred horse dashed up to where he lay. the Marquis flung himself from his steed seized the hand of his freind and knelt beside him Lofty returned his grasp. opened his eyes and smiled faintly. "Fare well Douro. fare well remember me to—to the princess—the Lady Edith.—" he would have. said. more but. his eyes closed. a convulsive shiver passed. over his noble features and he sank. back in the arms of his freind dead shot through the heart. Douro gazed at him without speaking. for a moment then regaining his steed. dashed. in an agony of greif full upon. the stern line of Bayonets before him. the weight of his charge could not be withstood. he hove all things before him and rolled the French back upon their very rearmost line. Now while matters stood thus the rerserve of our forces amounting to 3000 advanced. up the Marquis of Fidena at their head. These were the North highlanders destined for a final charge "forward" said Fidena. "forward. you defend your country". and with a loud shout the whole body rushed. upon the already confused enimy Fidena gazed steadfastly after them. At once I veiwed him fall from his horse on to the ground I and a hundred other officers rushed up to him he was sitting still gazing upon the splendid advance. with unaltered countenance. we hoped to heaven he was not wounded. But alas a cannon ball had struck. him on the shoulder it was horridly shattered. and as. the Marquis of Douro and. Gen Fergusson and myself lifted him into a military cloak. he swooned away. In silence we bore him to the rear of the. fight. and then I with several Officers being left in charge of him the rest were forced to hurry back to their stern duty. while I looked over the slowly recovering General. the. thunder of the Battle. sounded backward. and. all things showed marks of a successful charge and descided victory. But I. now. assisted to convey our Noble commander over the heath toward the villiage. where we placed him in the small Inn used as head quarters. here. the loud tumult of conflict roared and surged in the increasing distance. He. slowly began to recover his speech and. to every one who entered. his inqury was. "How is the Battle." all the answers returned were favourable. In a while music was heard without mixed. with the sound of vast moving multitudes. The Door opened and. Douro Elrington. Fergusson and several others entered Fidena. smiled and held out his hand. "I—I am rejoiced to see. you. how is the Battle." "Gained gained your Lordship." said Fergusson "I have done all for the best.—the retreat has proved disastrous. I hope. my country will be satisfied I hope my country will do me justice.—have you escaped un hurt.—where is Lofty I. saw him behave nobly is he here." all round looked sadly on Douro. who repressing his feelings said calmly. "My Lord. Lofty. is Dead." Fidena groaned. and th[r]ough exhaustion sank back. The surgeons now entered and after examining the wound pronounced it though not exactly mortal. extremely dangerous. As for myself. I. from pure exhaustion. now retired to rest. and I worn out with anxiety for the fate of my General. for the fate of my country. as I was aware this victory could be only a transient <moment> I. fell into a profound sleep.

When I. awoke and had finished dressing it was. morning. but. on looking from The windows of my room I. saw. the same wild. melancholy scene as heretofore the wind. and the rain were rushing down the street and rattling against my windowpanes.

On calling for my servant he told me that. the army had been. marching down through the villiage the whole of last night and that. now there was only. Mac Arthurs rejiment of 600. foot in it who were just preparing to depart. for Freetown the grand. Goal of our hopes. and wishes. I upon hearing this arose at once. mounted my horse. and pursued the road to that fine. and populous City. of my journey I can give no account. For beaten and exhausted by the storm I. had to encounter. the streets of this town I saw. filled with. halfdrowned. exhausted and fatigued soldiers. who were slowly. moving to their different consignments. After visiting our General whom I found. much weakened and exhausted. I. repaired to my own apartments to write out. an account of the late battle and a summary of the champaign for our Ministers The list of gains and losses I shall here give.

Total amount of the whole Northern Army.

on the arrival at Angria ————	31000.
Loss at. the. Battle of Little Warner ————	374
Loss at the Battle of Angria ————	4846
Loss at the Bridge of Guadima ————	2131
Loss in the retreat ————	9100
Loss of Baggage. &c. in value 81600£	
Loss of Cannon. One hundred and eleven	
Loss at. the Battle of Veleno————	1549
Total of the Army. which arrived at Freetown.—	13000
Total loss killed. ————	7500
Ditto wounded. ————	10500
Ditto sick. ————	4000
Grand Total of loss.————	18000

We had now then after a retreat never suprassed. at last gained Freetown but what was our situation there. with an effective army of only 9000 men. Burthened with 4000 sick and wounded. destitute of accoutrements cavalry. or. cannon— commanded by. an almost dying General we. were cooped up. in a scarcly fortified town By an overwhelming force of French. commanded by [an] able General and well supplied with all the muniments of war fare. and that force now amounting to. 22000 men. And by the arrival of Marmont. whose conquering forces had reached. Angria and were fast. marching forward. just about. to be increased to more than. FIFTY THOUSAND. and upwards. while it was understood that a vast force perhaps fourscore thousand Africans were hovering about the whole eastern frontier and just about to descend. This veiw was dismaying and disheartning in the extreme

There were only two things which at all counterbalanced. it and. these were first the fact of our army withered and shattered. as it was. containing many. of the finest soldiers and the most. admirable Officers in Africa. or the World. among whom shone pre[e]minent. the Marquis of Douro. Lord Viscount

Elrington. Col. Viscount Castlereagh. Major Thornton W Sneachi and a hundred others. The second. beam of sunshine was that. taking things all in all no place could be found better than Freetown as a shelter for our. shattered forces. the place it self though scarcly fortified was large and healthy. and above all. it stood directly upon the grand means of communication between. Wellingtons and Sneachi's Glasstowns and. Verdopolis itself from which it was distant. 170 miles and the noble Niger flowing under its walls. gave. as well as the Great Road. an uninterrupted. channel of communicating with the vast parent city. indeed any one who looks at the map. must be convinced of the immense importance of Freetown in time of war for if you lost it. if your enimys gained it they could. at pleasure. stop and command. the direct path to. the west and the north. to the Glasstowns & the course of the Niger. gain Freetown. and. the road to Verdopolis is easy. Government knowing this at once sent orders for us to remain at all events—to defend and keep that town. arms. and amunition were forwarded to us up the Niger and promises made of succor. and reinforcements in the amount of. 30000 men.[38]

But to continue my narrative. I upon. the Second day after the Battle was dispatched. to Verdopolis. to confer with Government upon the state of affairs. I left Freetown. on the morning of December 5. 1833. the weather proving still wild and stormy to the hig[h]est degree. I rode over the well known streets of Verdopolis. upon the evening of the sixth. after an abscence from it of. Twenty days. The first thing I did was to. call at the residence. of Earl St Clair our Premeir I received notice that he was at present at a Cabinet Council. at Waterloo Palace. Thither I directly went and on being announced was ushered into the Apartment. on entering I at once. recognized the well known. features of my. superiors and brethern of. the Government. there was his Grace of Wellington. standing by the fire and looking on the great table and its occupants with his usual. and. never to be forgotten. Countenance exhibiting. that mixture so harmonized of inflexible sternness and hearty socialty. of. even lofty and military bearing with. a sort of. fireside. "auld acquaintance." smile. (if I may so term it) behind him. at the very Hobb. or "luddend." sat. Old. Sir A Hume Bady. his soul wrapt up in himself. a pipe in his cheek and his eyes glinting with the accustomed twinkle. upon the frothing pint which stood to warm on the stove. The Marquis of Wellesly. wrapt. in. 5 or 6 great coats paced rapidly up and down the apartment. fuming and fretting himself at. he scarcly. could tell what. Earl St Clair. stood at the table. gazing with cold and offended severity upon Mr T. B Morley who. having fast hold of his button was delivering forth his. flowing tide of broad sentences. and laboured axioms. Their Majestys Sneachi and Parry. stood at a great window apart and far retired conversing upon the democracy of the times round the table it self covered and loaded with Maps and papers sat. Sydney Goat Bud Pelham. and several other ministers. All these different persons with various degrees of cordiality welcomed me upon my

---

[38]   In the midst of the text of this paragraph appear two sets of numbers, related to Branwell's calculations of losses above.

entrance. "Well Flower said his Grace. of Wellington. "Bring out breifly your news of the Army." I did so and when I had detailed all our proceedings my commissions orders &c. a vast variety of conversations. sprung up upon what I had shown forth. His Grace the Duke said "Now My Lords and Gentlemen. will you vote liberally. Arms. and men. for your country." "Arms and men" cried. Wellesly. "Why realy Arthur. how can you. ask for men do you not see at once the folly of spending money upon what we lose directly" "Money." repeated His Majesty Parry. "Money. how can any one speak. of it. certain I am that. such sums have been already spent. as must shame. sense. And decency." "Oh my country" broke in faint voice of Mr Sydney. "Well. My. Lords. ye are. going clean wrong clean." wrong" interrupted the trumpet tones of Morley. "all I can tell you is the fact that. money must be saved and the war must be carried on there are. two kinds of perdicaments the oon. pleasant the tither. unpleasant. and I must say this is. "—Silence" cried Sneachi "Really" snapped Wellesly. "For decencys sake." slid. in Pelham. "for the sake. of. appearances do preserve. your tempers." "Tempers." shouted. Bravey shaking the table with his fist "Tempers. The worst room of my public cant shew you such a scene. if we just take our pipe and pint like my Brother there and sit down to crack a bit like old freinds. why I should see something in it. come. now. I go with the Duke.". "And I." said Bud "And I." said Goat. "On conditions" said Pelham "Hang Conditions again shouted Bravey. "Let us depart." said. Sneachi—"shut th' door. Bravey." roared Ross—the Duke of Wellington. laughed aloud. and then seeing the confusion almost shameful his Grace fairly. cursed them. all in good round oaths for a set of. insane and incorrigible puppys whose heads were so stuffed with figments and crotchets as to admit neither sense or reason. I agreed indeed with his Grace and could not help saying "Oh your Majesty ruin must follow this course.—In a little while dinner was announced to be ready and this mortifying scene of Cabinet Harmony was stopped for a moment by. the welcome. annunciation. The Duke presided at the table. and. around him sat the illustrious crowd of Majesty rank and. title All were about to settle into calm and. cool discussion of the tremendous events just about probably to pass over the stage of. time. when in an. evil hour. His Majesty Ross sent a waiter. for. a slice of Roast Beef. "No"—spoke the boisterous voice of His Highness Bravey. "He shant have it. Ive taken the Beef to myself." "Here goes then for the plum pudding" cried. Ross in wrath. "Oh hold your filthy language realy I can not eat my rice curry in peace." peevishly exclaimed Marquis of Wellesly—"A little of the breast of a chicken" faintly asked. Mr Sydney "The chicken's for me." uttered the shrill voice. of. Mannikin Mussel. "Eh what is. partition the order of the day." asked. Bud. "Then this goose is doomed for me." Sneachi cried "Sirs this venison realy is mine." No Your Majesty." cried. St Clair "I took it" "dont you see my Lord its near. me." "Yes But—" "Silence." exclaimed Parry. Thay forcocks. mann be mine.". "Oh Scotchman!" "you you penniless. Lanchashire" This hit was intended for Sneachi but unfortunatly Pelham took it. "What. who wert called me. Lonkshire. ist thee tha—Ned o Tims!" "Gentlemen. this pork is for none but. me and. I can pruve it above ye firstly—" "Hang you Morley with your. firstlys "Gentlemen I beseech silence. and that porter and also for there are two kinds. of liquors that Ale. and."—"Well Done Morley" interrupted his Grace. who stood apalled at the scene. "Thats right take it all.—But be Silent be Silent I wished you to meet here to take into consideration the state of our country. while we are doing nothing. the French Emperor. [h]as. lodged 60000 men under two able Generals in the heart of our country. is bring[ing] forward. from the east. 80000 Africans upon us and has now on the coast of France 60000 french in reserve just about to land on our southern shore. mean while we. have by our miserable penury and inertness suffered 2 fine armies to be wrecked and dissipated. and though thus threatened by a force of. 190,000 soldiers. we play and. quarrel out our precious time. but believe me Arthur and Alexander. time is indeed precious and. [we] do nothing to stop. this mighty evil now more than threatings[39] us without another word I do. directly propose that to save our Kingdoms for which we ourselves must answer.

Firstly—36000000£ must at once be raised.

50000 horses be procured.

1000 peices of cannon parked.

and a force of—100000 men be directly formed.

To be in one weeks yes in one weeks time. made ready for active operations against the enimy.

Then for. without. excellent Generals all this will prove. useless and. without encouraging the deserving we cannot procure excellent generals I move That secondly.

The Marquis of Fidena. be removed to Verdopolis.

General Mackinnon be appointed. to command. of the forces of Angria. which must directly be raised to 20000 men.—Sir H Hardinge with the remains of the. present force those agmented to 20000 to move on Angria

That. Colonel Lord Viscount Elrington be raised to the rank of Leiut General

That Colonel. The Marquis of Douro be raised to the rank. of Lieut General.

That. General Fergusson with. 20000 men. be appointed. to move. on Pequena

That Sir H Hardinge with 20000 men move on Angria. after driving the French from Freetown

That. General Bobbadil move with. 20000. men. on. Seaton.

That. General Grenville move with 20000 on. "the Hill"

That. General Harrison move with. 20000 on Rochester.

And Thus my lord besides the Freetown Garrison. having as I hope we shall do. driven the french back eastward we shall be enabled. to present a noble line of immediate defence in five divisions of. 100000 men extending from. Pequena to Rochester. a distance of 200 miles and forming a straight bar. opposed between the french and Verdopolis. meanwhile we in. City must relax no endeavours

---

[39] "threatening" obviously intended.

augment and raise. very large additional forces to. rise up and. joining these 5 posts to act on the Offensive. and drive the French back into their own country. No time must be lost. My lords those. who. agree with me pass over to this side" immediatly. upon the conclusion of this admirable explanation of as admirable a plan of action. Pelham Bravey Ross Bud Morley Sydney Mussel. Goat. and Myself followed his Grace to one end of the room. leaving. Sneachi Parry and St Clair in a melancholy minority at the dinner table Directly His Graces plan was written out. a copy was given to me. with signed papers containing the. grant of Generalships to those Noble. Officers. the dark Elrington and the bright Douro these I was to carry direct to Freetown Sir H Hardinge following me as soon as possible. with Gen Mackinnon. and. the 27000. men necessary to. make up the garrison of Velino. and the corps to march upon Angria.—meanwhile the money was to be raised. the troops mustered and under the Generals. to march off to their five respective stations.

I left the. Cabinet Council highly elated at the sucess of my mission and. early next morning I set off for Freetown. wither passing through the usual stormy weathe[r] I arrived again. on. December 8. meeting on my way. a detachment and carriages. containing our lamented General. the Marquis of Fidena whom they were already removing to Verdopolis—he was dreadfully weak and. shattered When I. entered Freetown it seemed a sad scene of. riot and confusion <truly> it wanted a head. fever and. fatigue had begun to tell on the troops but the news I brought served to rouse up an[d] inflame. all round me. I entered the apartment of the Inn where sat the Marquis of Douro and Lord Elrington. to them I directly communicated. the fact of their al[t]eration to the ranks of Lieutenant Generals. instead of like common men receiving it with joy and gratitude. Elrington who lay languidly on a sofa deigned. just to lift. his eyes. with the words "Pho. only a lieutenant curse their souls." "Douro. who was examining his pistols at the table." Just nodded with. "Well. forced from them I dare say." However in civility they bid me be seated. I entered. into social conversation which happened to turn upon carriages. and the comforts while I was explaining the advantages of padded chariots—my two Noble listners exchanged. strange glances with each other I felt ill at ease and my words for they came forth mechanicly. seemed to choke me I yet endeavoured to gulp down my fright when suddenly Douro whose eyes had been gathering perfect flashes of fires. called on his servant. and on a stout. soldier entering bid him seize and hold me while. [he] proceeded with the most unfeeling brutality to force. down my throat some wool and butter. mixed. Elrington lay on the sofa looking on with feindish sneer laughing and coughing alternatly. after vast struggle I burst from these strange men and. escaped to my Hotel half dead with my fright. Thither I was ere long however. again dragged back to the dread rooms of these Officers by 2 huge soldiers their servants. on the door being opened my heart died within me there were collected shouting swearing and laughing a whole host of. reckless iron hearted and wild blooded young Officers. Castlereagh Aberco[r]n Thornton Morpeth. Molineux S Elrington Sdeath &c. headed by their great leaders Elrington and Douro.

Here I neither hoped mercy nor received any. after being. suffocated in putrid water crammed with Fullers soap[40] made to swallow suds. and <musty> bacon and tossed in a blanket. untill exhausted Nature. threw off. the filt[h]y food—I swooned. and when after a long space I. recovered my sense found my self in bed in my own hotel. dreadfully injured by my bloody and brutal treatment—I must pass over with few words the whole of this disgraceful transaction for several days I. remained on the verge of life and death. constantly. afflicted by most violent fits of reaching and vomiting increased I. firmly believe by the malice of my persecutors on the 11th. I. at last was able to rise and wrapt in great coats and comforters by the aid of servants to walk to the street door here while standing shivering in the breeze. I saw a sight of which I dare scarcly speak. so low so. ridiculous was it amid a huge crowd of soldiers and people and amid deafning shouts of laughter I saw The Marquis of Douro moving along bearing on his shoulders Lord Caversham and in his arms old Mr Sdeath he staggered and. tottered neath His load to the end of the street. and then. with. no gentle hand throwing off his burthen he gave Caversham a violent series of kicks which brought the blood from his mouth and nose and rendered him sensless.

Of the causes and ends of this strange scene I dare not and cannot speak but must pass forward. Gen Mackinnon now arrived with Sir H Hardinge and. the 27000 men so prompt had been the Government on learning this the french Army who remaining on the hills had all along blockaded us. now fell back over the whole country and joined Marmont at. Angria 120 miles eastward. Sir H Hardinge then with. the old remains of the Army and his new corps. altogether 20000 men leaving Mackinnon garrisoning Freetown commenced. on the. 13 a forced march over the hills toward Angria his force. being divided into two divisions of 10000 men each. under Elrington and Douro we after a wild march reached. Angria on the 15 of December. and. after a sharp action in which the Elrington and Douro nobly distinguished themselves. we drove the french still 50 miles farther eastward full on the African muster.

Here at Angria we now on December. 16. still remain. and by His Grace of Wellingtons exquisite. managements. the whole of the posts of Pequena this City. Seaton Hill and Rochester. are now occupied by the respective divisions appointed by him for their defence now musters are making in the Glasstown & activity is rising every where. all our affairs look better and more hopeful through the exertions of Wellingtons genius

Yet still if the war now presents a better face much much indeed remains to be done. vast difficultys to encounter mighty enimys to overcome. Massena and. Marmont lie straight east of us on the confines. with 50000 fiery soldiers the Africans muster. north east 80000. ready for a descent and on the south east bank of the Calabar. news has arrived that the Emperor. Napoleon has just made a lodgement under Soult of 60000 men. He himself is just ready to pass over to lead this mighty army and combined in one grand movement to attempt and attack on Verdopolis.

---

[40] Probably a reference to Fuller's earth, used to cleanse cloth.

> The crisis is tremendous
> The struggle is tremendous
> May the Genii defend. us
> > Farewell
> > > John Flower
> > > Angria Dec. 17th
> > > > AD. 1833.

P B Brontë. Dec. 17. 1833.
PS. I have to acknowledge my thanks to my Gover[n]ment. they Have created
me a Baronet by an order from council.
> > > John Flower.
> > > Angria. Dec. 17.th

P B Brontë. Dec. 17. 1833.

69	
89	
301	
323	19.
	_8_
32	20
32	_8_
_32_	80
96	_10_
	00
	_80_
	800[41]

---

[41] Branwell's numbers.

AN. HISTORICAL NARRATIVE OF. THE WAR OF. AGGRESSION.[1]

In my last Volumn I concluded. with Observations upon the present state of affairs. in the middle of December. and on the whole. found them upon a cursory veiw To be encouraging to all. those combating in defence of Africa.

I say I found them encouraging in a cursory veiw. for the french were driven Back. and upon their mustering again in vast and overpowering numbers. Government at Verdopolis seemed at once upon the representations of his Majesty of the west. to rouse themselves from their stupor and meet the encresing danger with encresing energy to follow up at once the advantageous step which they had just gained by the. retreat of the french from Freetown to Angria and from thence. to the New Rhone.[2] and lastly to place. upon the while[3] line of fortresses. defending the great city a noble force of 100000 men. opposing the french on every point. But my readers will ask. how could this force oppose the french whom it was well known were just descending under Napoleon the great. with double that number of. men? stop reader His Grace of Wellington foresaw all this. and in his accepted plan of operation he was far from intending that those 100000 placed in different points should bear up. against and defeat 200000 concentered on one point. he only intended. that these. forces should. present. a descicive strik[e] on the enimy untill an additional. army of the same amount could upon being directly raised and equipped. by Government. march up join and decivsivly operate with them. and thus combining the advantages of equal numbers freindly country and. better position effectualy crush and beat. the isolated army of Napoleon.

Now all this was very well. the plan was excellent. judicious and. open to every comprehension. the first part. the retreat of the french had been gained the second part. the occupation of Pequena. Angria. Seaton the Hill and. Rochester. by 100000 men. was directly gained also. for these men these stores. were just gathered and ready for action But Reader. the third part. the. instant raising and equipping of. a second hundred thousand. the moving them also forward. this the last the most important act that without which all the others would prove useless nay worse than useless. for without it all the other forces must perish. This I say at the outset. was peremptorily negatived quashed silenced!.

---

[1]   Hand-sewn booklet in brown paper covers (11.5 x 18.5 cm) of 18 pages (1 blank) in HL: MS Eng 869. The covers contain no lettering on the outside, but on the inside appears "Mr. W. C. Atkins (Robemaker) next the Hoop Inn, Cambridge

[2]   The Rhône-Alps region of east central France, famous for its wines, has Lyon as its capital. Branwell's naming of "New Rhone" reflects common colonial practice—transporting names from the old country to the newly settled world.

[3]   "whole" obviously intended.

How! you will ask. Where were those fools to be found. who could thus so
badly betray their country could. prohibit its salvation. What. cause what reason
could they alledge for an act so base and. idiotic.

Hush! the persons who thus acted. were the Government of the Glasstown
country Their resons for thus acting--the reson of saving. The Government of
Verdopolis was. at this time and for a long period had been. divided into three
parties. The first. Exclusively Aristocratic Haughty and. Frigidly proud eager of
place and rapacious of pension. men whose whole souls were. embodied for the
one sole desire of. aggraneissement of self. and. accumulation of MONEY. This
faction consisted of. "The Aristocrats"

	I	His Majesty Alexander King of. Sneachis land.
	2	His Majesty. Edward William King of Parry's land.
	3	His Majesty. Moncay. King of Moncays land.
	— 4	His Highness. W Gravey.------Arch-primate of Africa.
Aristocrats.	5	His Hig[h]ness. Traccy. Duke of Movena.
	— 6	The Most Noble Marquis of Wellesly.
	— 7	The Most Noble the Marquis of Fidena.---Commander. in Cheif
	— 8	The Right Honble. Earl St Clair.-----Prime Minister
	— 9	E G S Sydney. Esqr.--------------Home-Secretary.

The second party though of course each highly Aristocratic for under this
distinction was comprehended all those not under the Faction of Elrington
Montmorenci and the democrats—were by no means so bigoted and exclusive as
the first. would sometimes listen to reson. sometimes were swayed by prejudice.
and oftenest stood with the first party This if it might be called a party. consisted
of. "The Vacillators"

	1	His. Majesty. John King of Rosses land.
	2	His Majesty Stumps. King of. Stumps land.
Vacillators	— 3	Lord Viscount. Musselburgh.-----Chancellor of Exchequer
	— 4	Lord Viscount Macara. Lofty.----Quarter Master General
	— 5	John James Goat. Esqr.----------Under Home Secretary

The third and last party. and the one (for the second was nothing). which
strongly was opposed and which constantly clashed. against the first consisted.
of Conservative Constitutional men of cool heads and unpredjudiced minds who
saw both what was right and what was expedient. who looked to the general well
fare of the Glasstown countrys and not to the narrow questions of Aristocracy
and. money. this consisted of. "The Rationals."

	1	His Majesty. Arthur. King of Wellingtons land.
	2	His High[n]ess. the Duke Bravey
	3	His High[n]ess. the Duke Sir. A H Bady.
Rationals	— 4	Sir R W Pelham. Bart----Foreign Secretary
	— 5	Sir John Flower. Bart-------Agent for the forces

— 6   Colonel Thomas Grenville.---Speaker of the Commons

— 7   John Bud Esqr.----------------Secretary of the Board [of] trade

8   T D Morley. Esqr.-------------Colonial Secretary

It will now at once be seen that. the Aristocrats of first faction. of the Ministry taking with. them. their frequent allies. the Vacillators. mustered by far the strongest party in rank and numbers comprehending. 5 Kings. and. 7. Noblemen with. 2 distinguished Gentlemen in all 14. men--the other faction. the Constitutional Rationals mustered only. 1 King 2 Noblemen. and 5 Gentlemen. in the. Ministry. Thus the 1st. party Here obtained in numbers an immense preponderance. But the last. as to talent ability and. a leader. rose far above their pennywise competitors. Their Leader the Duke of Wellington was a host in himself.

Yet Now. in that vital organ of the body politic the actual ministry. of the country. the fountain head in which must rise and from which must flow all the measures and plans either to agument the prosperity or to bring on the ruin of a country. the first faction of Aristocrats. possesed and maintained a decided. preeminence. and though constant Heart rending and shameful were the quarrels and. disputes in the Government. this faction invariably. withstood all reason and kept the rule. By choosing his opportunity and forcibly representing the Frightful urgency of the case we have just seen that the Duke of Wellington extorted from them. agreement to his plan for action and. a gift of 100000 men with distinct Promise of supporting that 100000 and adding so soon as it could be raised. a second 100000. having gained this delightful. aquisition and se[c]ured all as we thought I was instantly despathched with the news to the army the. forces were put in possession of the fortresses and. as I sanguinly hoped all was going on properously.

ON the. 16 of December. I was sitting in my room in the great Hotel of Angria listening while sitting by the fire to the music of the bands outside the street and thinking upon the approaching Sessions of Parliament when. a servant entered. with a letter for me. stating that a courier had. brought it post hast[e] and only waited for an. answer. I. hastily took it it was from. Sir R Pelham. and contained these words.

Verdopolis Dec 15
1833.

"Dear Flower.

The Aristocrats have turned restive. have. refused further concurrence in. the Dukes plan. ruin threatens us. haste at once to Verdopolis. meet me at my house. in haste I remain &c.

R W Pelham.

I with trembling hand answered. and despathched my answer this was miserable news. just that afternoon I had been a hearer of the joy of the army at the receipt of the Dukes plan. and their determination to aid him by all means Now all looked again dark and gloomy. <again> I departed for Verdopolis where I. arrived. on the following evening Dec. 17 and. repaired to the house of Sir R Pelham. on entering his apartment. I found him seated with. J. Bud and T Morley. firm freinds. and active ministers. concern sat on all their faces and with[out] even. a ruflle upon his unyeilding visage. the Baronet told me. that. the Government at this moment were assembling at. the Sneachi Palace. and that they were just about to join this We all. got up and departed for that. Majestic abode of majesty. on entering the council room the of late usual scene. presented itself. to us. the. Rationals and their leader the Duke standing at one table. Sneachi Parry and. their adherents at another. we in silence. the former. Sneachi was just saying as we entered. "My Lords you Arthur. I distinctly repeat. that placed. in the positions I have mentioned. 100000 men are able to encounter and to beat back exactly 200000!!! my knowledge of the art of Engineering gives me. (a titter among several. members) And if it come to this will a government scorn its sovereign will you trample under foot your. King divide--divide directly upon the question shall we or shall we not spend. 1000000£ upon the. raising of a second army of. 100000 men"

I ought not to insult my reader by telling him that this insane party of. the Exclusives carried their point by a majority of 6 voices in the. loftiest most enlightened Ministry in the world. with a hearty curse the Duke of Wellington strode from the Apartment. We his followers shortly too left. overwhelmed with sorrow at the mad folley of our allies.

The second evening after this Dec. 19. I. again slowly entered the room of distraction and viewed the usual scene. Oh what would Napoleon have given to ensure the state of things. now taking place Parliament was to meet. to morrow. a mighty opposition had organized against the Govermment determined to overthrow it and its leaders. and all this at a time when a tremendous Enimy was just thundering at our gates. I found this evening that. as an episode in the. great drama of Destruction the party of the Aristocrat penurists had come to a vote. to. disposses. Lord Wilkin Thornton Sneachi youngest son of. His Majesty Sneachi of his rank and title. it was his father who suggested. this proposal. and all only because this son had not the principals of exclusive Nobility possessed by his father. I was just representing How the army with whom. Lord Thornton was a decided. and. meritorious favorite would. hate and. execerate. this resolution that they were already not well disposed to Government and that. a single other ill office would fairly exasperate—here a Courier from Angria was announced. with despatches. he. entered with breathless haste. Edward Laury. the noted servant of the Marquis of Douro These Despatches were not addressed to the Government but to the Duke of Wellington the principal one. was from the. hand of. Viscount Elrington and stood as follows.

Your Majesty.

I proceed according to orders to inform you of the state of Affairs in Angria on. December. 14. all things I believe in all the stations stood well and right it was conjectured that the Emperor Napolein would. concenter his forces upon Pequena. in this case our General Sir H Hardinge. had so ordered his arrangements as to be able to bring up a large force to their assistance if requisite. On Dec. 15. Sir H H— received. further intelligence. that the Emperor was. rapidly moving for ward at the head. of 90000 men. and that. Massena would. be despatched with a few thousands upon Angria to keep us employed. that we might not interfere with the attack upon Pequena. This Sir H had provided it made. no difference in his arrangements. Dec.16. we this morning did not hear but saw a vast collection of forces. occupying every rood and eminence eastward of the city. this was clearly not the Division of Massena. here was the Emperor and Massena. had been sent upon Pequena. Sir H held a council of war. I advised him to. collect all his 20000 men leave Angria defencless and the road to the Glasstown. open to the enimy. make one days forced march north to Pequena. unite with the 20000 under. Gen Fergusson. then even perhaps retreating still north we should. let the Emperor with his whole force. push full. down on your City and. gathering what force we could. from the. country combining also. a promised aid of 17000 men from a wealthy and influential gentleman here Mr Warner by name we should over whelm the Emper from the north fall on his rear distract disperse and dissipate him. ere he reached you.

My Lord. Sir H Hardinge. is a Martinet a formalist. and though urged by the whole powers of my Noble freind The Marquis of. Douro though powerfully enticed too by my own complaints and threatnings &c. He could not bear to think of Napoleon turning his flank and. the[re]fore. He resolved. to retreat at once from Angria to Seaton. where he could gain Gen Bobbadils 20000 upon the. following morning. . Dec 17. My Lord. Duke this morning the forces commenced. their retreat. information having been obtained of an action at Pequena between Fergusson and. Massena. in which we lost. the cooperation of the whole north division my Lord. Duke. Fergusson is prisoner with 17000 men. I curse our Ministry for this work. For ourselves we commenced our retreat. Douro and I. defended the rear. and it had need of our defence my Lord. The attacks made on us by Napoleon were severe and uninterrupted. this. day. Sir H Hardinge. received a severe wound in the Head. he—curse him was conveyed directly too. the south of the forces the command of which now devolvd. upon Douro and myself. our work. was warm. the retreat continued. this evening we reached Seaton. thus forming a junction with Gen. Bobbadil. and how mustering joined forces of. 40000 men. opposed my Lord To 90000. Dec. 18. this Morning we received the following wretched letter. Hang your Government. for it and its consequences.

To. Lieut Genl^S. Douro Elrington and. Bobbadil.
"The Hill." Dec. 16. 1833.
Fellow workers I may say in affliction.

From the Rio Calabar. east and opposite to my post have just made their appearance. a corps of 60000 French. under Massena. They march full against my 20000. and as it would be vain to withstand them. I shall. ere long join your retreat. mine is even now begun— with sorrow I remain yours

Tho^S Grenville.

My Lord could this please us. I tell you we. were now in a state of Hatred to our
Country and Government. This day the French pushed. so vigourously forward
that. we were forced to oppose a front and fight for our passage. Major Thornton.
conducted. the charges. of infantry with his usual spirit and Gallantry. I greive to
tell you that we have sustained a mighty loss but. I hope only a temprary one.
in leading an attack upon a French Rejiment the Marquis of Douro received. a
severe wound in the left side He was born to the rear The command has now
devolved upon me. Had my legacys been always like this I should not have. been
now alive. I succeeded in freeing my self from the French ran with a loss of
3000 men. I am continuing my retreat. toward you. to morrow I expect. a
reinforcement of. 20000. men the. retreating force of Grenville. we shall then
muster nearly 60000 but. sire the French Napoleon will receive at that moment a
reinforcement. of. just the number of our whole army. He will. then bear down
with 150000—a miserable sorrow hangs over me at this moment and it will not
clear away.

I conclude this. letter my Lord Duke with the assurance that all this chaos of
disaster owes its. origin. to. the cursed and infatuated. conduct of of our
Gover[n]ment they have refuse[d] us. forces and. we could not stand. your plan
sire was perfect theirs—but My Lord. the Army will decide their conduct. a paper
is just now being drawn up and. the Officers will put their names to it it.
speaks of their feelings toward our Monarchs and. our ministry.

I remain my Lord Duke.

your. constant. servant in war.

Elrington.

PS. The wound of Sir H Hardinge is under the supereintendance of French Army
Surgeons. they. may. Bulletin if they please on him.

The Marquis of Douro bears up against Death with I think distinguished success.
Elrington.

This letter closed the lips of. all who heard it and. our hearts fell dead at.
the. account it gave us. the wording of it is characteristic of its writer. The Duke
of Wellington first broke silence. "Now then you Have accomplished the ruin of
as fine an army as. ever. march forward. My Lords. the Commons. to morrow
night will demand. a heavy reckoning for this." The Duke. with a stern look left
the room. So soon as the[y] could. find utterance the 5 kings and their followers.
began to strengthen one another in their way of madness. I was so disgu[s]ted to
hear them that. I with Sir R Pelham. Mr Bud Mr Morley. and. Bravey. left the
Council room. directly.

We left the Marquis of Wellesly croaking with spite and revenge.

Next morning Dec. 20. opened up to us. the beggining of a stormy and
eventful scene Parliament was this day to open. Political parties met in all parts
of the city. all the Newspapers appeared disclosing the events of this retreat
speculating upon the march of Napoleon. upon the coming Evening. thundering
forth anathema's against our Ministry. The Noblemen and House of Peers I
greive to say. all seemed obstinatly bent on supporting the. Aristocrats. in the
afternoon I attended. a secret meeting of our party at Waterloo palace. then I

retired Home to think and recover my bewildered brain. When the Darkness came on and the lights were blazing in the streets. My Carriage stodd ready to convey me to the House of commons. On entering the house I took my seat beside. Sir R Pelham and Col Bud. two ministers but to rational and wellingtonian onces few members had yet arrived. and. the. House was yet only in progress of being lighted up. "Well" said I."Gentlemen what do you think will be this nights proceedings." Bad enough for our country any way." said Bud. "Bickering among ourselves or a union if it be for a foolish end. are almost alike dangerous I think But however I apprehend the matter has got into other hands than ours and the army. will. have little softness in a purgation. I say nothing but from what I know of. the. 2. self. imposed Leaders. I fancy they will help us whether we will or not." "We are truely interrupted Sir Robert."placed under embarrasing circumstance. we form part of a ministry whose proceedings it cannot be expedient to hold. and we scarcely can part from. them or agree with them I certainly am inclined to think that. the interference of the military will not conduce to aid us in these untoward circumstances." "Sir Robert." bawled the voice of Mr Morley. "you speak as one in confusion and. It is my unasked—I mean my. unpriced opinion that as true knowledge and liberal opinions now lie at the bottom of the well a commotion and. tumult among the waters may peradventure stir knowledge. aye use ful knowlege up even to the top."

Further conversation was stopped by the rapid entrance of members and the chandeliers soon cast their light not upon bare boards and benches but upon one vast. uneven crowd of various heads. swelling up from the area to the gallerys and from thence toward the roof. At a glance all saw the decided superiority in numbers possessed by the adherents of the army over those of the Ministry and a settled gloom semed to hang upon every countenance. in that intrest. for the part of myself Sir R Pelham Col Bud and. Mr Morley. we were in a most peculiar and disagreeable perdicament ministers in name yet agreeing in no sense with ministers. in name the enimies of the army in effect. among its warmest wellwishers.

In a little while the doors leading from the House of peers were opened. and the officers appeared requesting the attendance of the Commons House at the floor of the House of Peers. There to hear the speech of Chrashey from the throne. At once the members rose and made their tumultous exit from Bench and gallery toward the entrance to the Lords. Mesars Sydney Goat Bud. Morley. Lds Lofty and Musselburgh. Sir R Pelham and myself. leading the way as Ministers. We advanced or rather were impelled into the Area of the upper house and so soon as I found breath I took a glance at the chill Aristocratic scene round me sorrow I confess I felt when my eyes beheld amid that mighty assemblage of the great and noble scarce one single man. whom I could account. liberal and reasonable. in opinions. On every face above me lowered. a cold haughty pride and stern unbending bigotry And on at least every second face around me. stood a yet stern courage. a yet more determined boldness. Crashey our Venerable Patriarch was not present and. the speech which he ought to have spoken was delivered by Earl St Clair our prime minster. it was short. and ambiguous. little inference could be drawn from it. and that little was. unfavourable and to the army almost insulting. upon its conclusion the House of Commons again poured back to their old seats and on Sydney the Home Secretary taking the speakers chair in abscence of Grenville. Buisness. began. amid the setling noise and clamour. up started a Gentleman. whose slight shape. quiet features and restless eye. showed at once to me the unexpected figure of. Warner Howard Warner. He waited not an instant. no not to catch the speakers eye. but commenced in a low rapid unhesitating voice.

"Sir. Sir a better man than I see before me should have occupied that chair and I do greive that the last tie is. broken which could bind me to office or ministry. I wont address my speech to a minion of injustice but I turn round. and speak to you to my Fellow members and fellow countrymen. (vast uproar from the ministerial benches.)

Gentlemen. No sorrow ever oppressed me so overwhelming as that which I now. feel. When I look. around me and above me. and in the. heavy and. thickning cloud which hangs over my country. I cannot rest my eye upon a single assured opening for a single ray of light. I see old and experienced. men before me in this assembly and I ask them. Have they ever seen or known. so melancholy a prospect as the one now lying so gloomily before them. I could spend this whole night in venting bitter and. unavailing recrimination on those unhappy men who have brought us to this state. of. misery but. other feeling[s] and other duties stern and solemn as they are. have power to draw me from this more grateful task. (cheers and. dissaprobation) Gentlemen I propose to myself. to. first distinctly to show to you the state and nature of our affairs next the. probable. consequences of this state and. last the means for altering and improving. it is now I think. two months since the French Empror. (here Mr. Morley firstly looked very uneasy and then started. up "Sir yere wrong. may I beg leave to interrupt one month and. 21 days preceesly"). Sir who is that who dares interrupt me. well. then so long is it since Napoleon. having quashed a rebellion roused himself and his country from a state of certain insanity and gained possession [of] a noble and imposing force of men. employed his newly recovered. intellect in. searching for room in which to stretch himself. for means in which to exert his mind. and at once he hit upon a shceme. which bid fair to employ all his vast forces to exerst all his capabilitys to hazard all his fortune but if successful to render him all powerful. he fixed upon the Country of the Glasstowns as the enimy with whom to fight the Prize for which to contend. and after picking up a slight and sophistical ground for dispute he began by declaring open hostilitys with us and continued by setting a foot and secretly landing upon the coast of. Africa. an army of. 70000. men. Now what should our Government the Kings of the Ministry of Verdopolis. do upon this occasion.—why. push forward to oppose the french their whole disposable force. set afloat means for raising another. force and instantly convene Parliament. that it might in this emergency assist their operations and supply them with means. Sir they did not do so they did not act thus. no they calculated. that as the french forces mustered. 70000 men. it would just be fair to oppose to them and equal force of. the same number. that to bring out a single man in addition would be a useless waste of the Kings money that to call parliament would be like. relying upon Plebians.

that these in short would do and if not why they would then look out for more. leave time to reflect time to act. (here Montmorenci roared out from his bench Aye. and they did leave Time both to reflect and act for Volo they did none of it themselves loud laughter and Hisses) Well. Well. true. But. I must proceed. Sir. Gentlemen. These. forces of. 70000 Glasstowners. marched out to oppose the French. headed by. the sons the minions of Aristocracy. while the. freinds of. their country the men of ability marched. behind and did their bidding. the hands directed and the heads worked. (Montmorenci again "Volo & dies Man. cant ye. say it at once. they marched on their head. with their heels uppermost." roars of laughter. from all sides.) Sir Gentlemen. very well—right.—I appeal to you against such interruptions. Sir such a fools. Banner flaunts ill against so black and stormy a heaven. I proceed. with bitter sorrow I tell it that owing to this vain mode of proceeding our two armies of the north and the south. each. the moment it was attacked fell in peices. dissipated and fled. Well. Cabinet Ministers do I know the miserys you have. brought upon your soldiers ("Aye." cried Montmerency. "and your shoulders too I think. Man") Silence I will demand silence no one shall thus interrupt me with impunity—Gentlemen I saw that fatal retreat from Angria and. if beholding its effects was not enough I felt them too. Yes I felt them. and the. loss of property on my part amounting to 300000£ will long be felt and must yet be atoned for (coughing on the part of several northern members) Why do I. thus spend my time in recapitulating the miserys of this unhappy war I must pass hastily over that retreat to Freetown the dissipation of. Grenvilles forces. the lodgement of 60000 Frenchmen in the heart of our territory the arrival of another 60000. upon its shores. the threatened irruption of. 80000 Barbarians from its mountains. I must pass over all this to speak of the far more. frightful and overwhelming evil. of blindness and discord. and madness among its. protectors and defenders. Oh Verdopolitans whereever this fatal calamity has broken out in a city. beseiged. the beseigers. may sit down and feast themselves in peace. They may rest assured that city must fall. May the Genii grant that thus may not the end of. Verdopolis. be. to them only do I look for hope. now that. unjust man is both. mad and triumphant while just man though so wise. is so shackled. and bound (loud cheers and dissaprobation.) When his Grace of Wellington beheld matters in the state I have described. He though alas<Hevenles>has not helped. him. yet. lent. his shoulder to the wheel. and had his plan. of. placing a hundred thousand men upon the towns round Verdopolis with a second hundred thousand. just behind in an inward chain. thus opposing an effectual barrier to the Enimy untill fresh forces could be raised to set upon the offensive. Had this plan been followed all would. yet have been well. but it is here Sir it is here Gentlemen where I do. cry out against. the hideous blindness the willfull insanity of our unhappy Government. Oh 30000 french. soldiers under the command of Napoleon himself. might hourly be drawing nearer. constantly edging them in yet would they not move one finger to support their country to save themselves. and. after having basely pushed forward 100000 soldiers. in to their hands they basely betray them by refusing the aid. which just before they had solemnly promised. And Now Gentlemen what is the prospect which this frightful road has brought into our veiw why. northward we

see. only 100 miles distant. fourscore thousand Africans. Hurrying down from
the Gordon Mountains. devastating a fertile country. but bent eagerly upon this
long hated city. eastward and. perhaps 50 miles. distant. 160000. French under
Napoleon. in like manner push forward upon this given point. and drive like
sheep before them our gallant and martyred Army. Southward the Sea and the
opposite coasts of France are covered with reserves just launching for our
destruction Below us around us you Gentlemen know. what you see and. in the
distance far before us. the Glass of reason and reflection shall show. you. all
these mighty armies concentered. in Verdopolis. her Kings. her Nobles paying
their penalty or flying for their lives. her sons and her childern. falling and dying
beneath the rough hands of the foreeign oppressor—I wont say any more I am
disgusted at the scene I wished to describe. and time flys so fast that nothing
now remains to me save to. shows you. the one only road left of safty and
honour. Now Gentlemen are you in a disposition to here me. tell you. your
remedy. you are assembled here in deliberation to act as the guardians and.
Fathers of your country as a check upon that Ministry those Noblemen. who
have placed you in your present melancholy situation as I lay all the curses all
the miserys all the faileurs of this war [t]herefore upon there heads so if you do
not act as I wish you I will those hereafter upon yours. You have heard that
speech delivered. by our premeir this night. as if from the lips of our glorious
Patriarch. that speech to all intents mocks and derides you now. refuse this night
to return your usual answer to that. Address you see those men in Office.[4] you
see them sitting upon these benches. now.
Gentlemen isolate yourselves from these your tyrants. refuse to accede to a
single measure they propose. and purpose yourselves every measure wich they
will not acede to. regard them as leprous as unclean persons. and. in condemning
them I am sorry to say. you must also condemn the house of peers Now upon
going forward in this manner you of course will. hurl from office the whole
present Ministry then. seize your opportunity thrust in to office. your own
minstry let the touch stone of. fitness be. the activity with which the candidates
have hurled out the predecessors. then grasp the hand of the army. then—but I
wont insult you by speaking any more you will know your duty. I am tired of
speaking and. must conclude my countrymen by. moving that this house. do.
this night. enter upon their minutes a refusal to answer the adress. just read to
them by their Prime Minister. a refusal to consider it the adress of their
Patriarch. and that a copy of this refusal be addressed to the house of peers.
Gentlemen do this do it without fear the. Army relies upon you for salvation.
and with safty may you rely upon it for protection."

   Mr W H Warner concluded this maiden speech amid perfect roars of the most
deafning applause. and feeble indeed were the marks of dissaprobation which were
intermingled Our fellow ministers looked at one another. with countenance
expressing blank and horror. stricken amazement. Mr Warners ability and
powers. had struck. them like a thunder bolt. Mr Sydney after a while true to his

---

4   Four and one-half canceled lines follow at this point.

post and his superiors. attempted to rise in answer. But up sprung Hector
Matthias Mirabeu Montmorenci and erecting his stern head and brawny shoulders
he. drowned all opposition in the overpowering thunder of his well know[n]
voice.

"Well done thou good and faithful servant[5] —Oh Pysician thou dost deserve
thy fee. I say Mr Warner. you have my thanks for this usable work. but Man
you have only prepared the physic for your patient I will administer it. and volo
if he refuses it.—Now Gentlemen. for I follow the plan of my. predecessor and
address the Building in preference. to its furniture. the house. in preference to a
chair. (loud laughter in which the speaker joined) I say Gentlemen. let us
proceed. to buisness and as Mr Warner has. pointed out a general plan for your
future. action I will submit to your consideration a few particulars. The grand
point for which we move is just how to oust the present Government. and to
Night let us conmence our work As the Honourable Member who has. just
spoken said do I now say. You see before you upon yon lines of Benches.
walking sitting standing lying deformed creation. Look at them Look at those
fellows. their countrys blood dripping from every hair of their atrocious heads.
(huge and continued uproar) hey. hey what now come bairns. be quiet. you see
them sitting upon those benches—Volo! now the moment one of them rises to
speak. down with him Hiss him down cough him down cry him down down
with. him if you can peaceably but at all events I say down with him!!!
(prodigious cheering mingled with strong marks of dissatisfaction) Now. I shall
be over whelmed with your flattery. I havent much to say to you to Night except
just how to make a seat uneasy. put pins in it man—put pins in it. if you do its
occupant will rise up and stand since there certainly is not another. chair in our
room. Speaking of chairs I ask. what of that I see there and wheres the speaker
and wheres Col Grenville and wheres decorum and wheres decency and wheres.—
why and. wheres the use. of mocking and reproaching your president by thus
tacitly declaring his best representative by his abscence to be chicken bones and
Napkins mop slates. dipped. in whitewash! (Oh Oh and cries of Order.) Order
Aye as poor Rogue used to say I will indeed call you to order. my Heart. is this
your game Get out. of that seat thou impertinent puppy begone. thou Addle egg.
Scoundrel. quit evacuate and leave room for men!"

Here Poor Mr Sydeney the object of all this abuse. could bear no longer he
rose in a frenzy of agitation.

"Gentlemen. I appeal to this house. ("Appeal to your spouse. shes got the
upper hand of you." "Oh mont". "go it Hector." "Order" "for shame" "pull
him. down"). Oh my freinds. are you insane. are your senses bewildered by the.
trash just now. whelmed upon you. I appeal. not to you not as. hearers of a
mountebank. but as the. rulers of Verdopolis against.—(Montmonency. "Now
what hearken to Him for. when I have just told you down him fell. him you
need. only use your tongues. hell pop of with a puff of wind Mr Sydney. strove
to make himself heard amid this wild confusion but it was in vain and amid a

---

5   See "the Parable of the Ten Talents," Matthew 25: 21, and p. 443 below.

constant and varied roar of. groans yells and hisses. the words "Gentlemen." I intreat" "I Beseech". "Hearken." "listen. "Gentlemen." "My Country." were every now and then heard. like the words in a catch. till at last amid the increasing dissaprobation this unhappy member of the Cabinet folded his arms. and. sat down in an agony of despair Hereupon Mr Montmorency. broke out again upon his series of blasting abuse.

"There he is there let him be. and. as he has fared so may all like him fare. So may our Premeir so may our ministers and Government fare. But I did not rise. up to box with a spider and now let me turn to the buisness of the night. easy it is to see. the condition of. this House and when. I behold. the vast number of the true and steady supporters of rational and. patriotic. energy thus. numerous and triumphant. I do argue well yet for our honour our Army ourselves and our country. Mr Warner sat down proposing as a motion that. a refusal to answer the base and unworthy address called Chrasheys speech. be entered upon our minutes and notified to the peers. I do here with all my heart. mind. soul head. and bottle second that motion. Speaker scoundrel take the sense of the house."

(Mr Sydney the speaker) "No I will not."
For a moment upon this announcement delivered as it was in a firm steady tone. the members seemed all. struck dumb with amazement.—then. ere. a second had elapsed the chair was surrounded by a tumultious crowd of members. the. speaker was virtually pulled from his seat and hurried back onto the crowd. Mr Montmorency seized the chair Mr Warner pulled out his pistols commanded his followers to do the same And he heading them they closed round the chair and with loud cries threatened to shoot any one who should lift a finger against them. a most riotous and tumultous vote was them passed by about 400 of the members present. carrying Mr Warners motion. who was deputed to present to morrow night this refusal to the house of peers.—Directly Mr Sydney Mr Goat Lord M Lofty and Lord J. Musselburgh[6] accompanied by perhaps 60 members took their hats and withdrew from the House.

A quarter of an hour further was spent in tumult and altercation. and then Mr Montmorency. vacating the chair declared the house adjourned. the Members rapidly left the Hall.

Upon arriving at my own house I had scarcly time to sit down a moment. and reflect upon these terrible symptoms. of approaching. internal convulsion. even now that a deadly enimy was so close upon our gates when just as the clock. chimed. 4 in the morning and I was. preparing to retire to a hasty rest a servant entered. bearing a note for me. I found it to be a summons from Sir R Pelham. entreating my prescence at the Cabinet Council just then holding at Waterloo palace. I ordered my carriage and instantly drove to the grand square fronting that noble edifice. on my way groaning to see at this dead Hour of night the swollen and troubled appearance of the City upon alighting in the court of the palace the vast crowds of the Equipages. livery servants and torches told me.

---

6   Musselburgh is a city in Scotland.

that. the Kings. must have attended. and from. this I argued but slender good. in fact my mind was fully prepared for the melancholy scene. which greeted my entrance. there they were. in that noble room crow[d]ed round the table. Kings and Nobles and Honourables. all without the least decorum or decency talking. and. threatning at the top of their voices. "Oh Flower" said Bud advancing to me. "This Night has done it we are ruined. the countenance they have received from the peers. has confirmed them in their blindness while the awful check. just given from the commons has. shattered their senses and look what still more. confuses and distracts them. read that Flower."—Bud pointed to a long roll of. parchment lying upon the great table. and. extending to the floor. I stept up and surveyed it. On the top My eye recognized the well known hurried hand of Lord Elrington and. one glance. showed me the nature of its contents. its was a Manifesto Adressed to those Men calling themselves the Government of Verdopolis. Stating that. the Army of the East. in all its divisions unaminously and positivly renounced all further dependance upon or. connection with the Kings. or Ministry. refused. to address another despatch to them to. receive another order from them. But declaring that. all their directions. hereafter should proceed from the "Commons Parliament of. Africa" that. that House they would serve and. that house defend but should it prove. refractory in any part. other measures must be looked. to the paper powerfully enumerated. the many greivances sustained both by the country and the Army. and. denounced. their Majestys Sneachi Parry. Ross Moncey Stumphs. and the Ministry as the direct cause. of all This. Remonstrance. was dated. Seaton 40 miles from Verdopolis. and was signed. By. Generals Elrington Douro. Fergusson Bobbadil Harrison with 700 Commissioned Officers. My whole mind on perusing it recoiled back upon the. pretorian Bands The Imperial Guards[7] the Stern Soldiery of Oliver Cromwell.[8] and the thoughts of 90000. armed warriors headed by all the. pride. Ability and Revenge. of Percy and Wellesly. crowded thick upon my Imagination.

---

[7]   The Praetorian Guard, a select body of the best Roman troops, functioned as a bodyguard for the commander (or "praetor") of the Roman army. Later, as instituted by Augustus, it became an Imperial bodyguard attending the Emperor.

In 1804, Napoleon instituted his own Imperial Guard to function as a personal bodyguard and as a loyal and stable core of the French armies. By the time of the Russian Campaign of 1812, the Imperial Guard numbered 55,000 men and had become the most prestigious military formation of the Napoleonic armies.

[8]   Oliver Cromwell (1599-1658), military leader of the parliamentarians during the Civil War and later lord protector of England (1653-58), was raised with a strict Calvinist faith, and insisted that the men who served the parliamentarian army should be carefully chosen and trained. He not only demanded good treatment and regular payment for his troops, but also exercised and expected strict discipline in his ranks. Soldiers were fined for swearing or put in the stocks if found drunk.

My Readers will ask. me Why when the House of Commons and the Army stood so firmly forward in support of reason did Not the Duke of Wellington and the Rational Ministers instantly secede from the Main Body of Government. and join ostensibly to effect a total change in it. for all must see how shackled. they were now.? To this natural question I answer. the Duke of Wellington Bravey and Bady. formed a direct integral portion of the confederacy of the 12. and could never seperate from that confederacy without temporarily at least dissolving that Mighty Body. The foundation of all our prosperity and our. constitution And However disstressing an union. with. men who were fast bringing things on to a revolution—yet to dissolve that union involved consequences. almost as disstressing and till His Grace and his coadjutors could see a distinct and decisive good. to be gained. by that step it could not be safly practised. But Now at last this Night when all saw that without it there would be a certain commotion with it only a probable. His Grace the Duke as our leader. wound up his firm mind to the trial.—stepping up to the Table where I stood lost in reveries upon. the paper above mentioned. the Duke. spoke thus in his cool stern voice. so distinctly heard. by all.

"Your Majestys My Lords. I. this Night cut off. the Kingdom of. Wellingtons Land from the. confederation of the 12. and. declare myself and it no longer. members of that Body Their High[n]essess. Bravey and Badey. likewise. have determined upon my course. we are now no longer. Members of this Ministry. All who will follow me in my declaration. step to this side."

His Grace. Bady and Bravy. coolly paced across the room. "And I will" cried Bud. "And I" cried myself. "Certainly. But. conditionaly." said Pelham. "Upon the Strength of my argument." Bawled Morly—thus. 7 men where ranged struck off at once. from the Government of Verdopolis

The opposite Party upon seeing this maneuver after a porten[t]ious Silence broke all at once into the most violent threats and reproaches. "Abominable. slaves." "Disgraceful Scoundrels" Traitors to Monarchy." "Liars." "Plackless Beggars" "Begone you. Blood thirsty wretches" and a thousand. such expression[s] burst from every mouth in the most shocking confusion. in the midst of it the Duke. accompanied by us the 6. seceders. all left the. room. His Grace. Pelham Morley Bud and Bravey. in another Apartment. sat to consult upon this frightful emergency. I being considerably exhausted. and worn out. with fatigue. drove home to snatch a short and hasty repose. I foresaw the Tempest of the rising day.

When I awoke Dec. 21. it was broad day light. and. the busy hum of men could well be heard in the city below I hastily arose and descended to my Breakfast room. here upon the table lay. the Newspapers of the day. all damp from the printing press. Eagerly I snatched them up and dipped in to their leaders one after another. for by the tone of the Newspapers we may allways learn the feelings of the people. they who write to please mankind will not willing incure its resentment. the Topics for disscussion in them were the state of the Army. the Remonstrance to the Government the proceedings of that Government. and. the. First Night of Parliament. by 6 of these papers. the Government was characterised. as the basest and most infernal tyranny ever invented. their destruction was pronounced. at hand and even the Monarchs were indirectly threatened the commons were supported and. a revolution was prophesied. 4 Papers endeavoured to uphold the. Ministry. abused the Army and declared the french defeated. in all. the tone taken up was bitter and threatning The most important peice of "NEWS." contained in these papers. consisted in the declarations concocted by the Council last night after we had separated from them. these were to the following effect.

Ist. that. Major. Wilkin Thornton Sneachi be dissposed of his rank and Title as Viscount and. son of a King

IIdly that. Generals Viscount Elrington and the Marquis of Douro Be declared outlaws and traitors to the Kingdom.

IIIdly. that the forces now retreating from the french should upon Their arrival before the city. bivouack in the villiages around it and that not a Man. from among them should enter Verdopolis without express leave from Government.

IV.thly. that Major General. the Marquis of Fidena. be recieved by the Army as its commander upon its arrival.

These insane decrees. did indeed persage an approaching downfall. Moreover a Second highly important peice of news was that. at length. this Morning 3 o clock the van of the retreat had made its appearance. in compact order and was now occupieng the villiages and suburbs east of the city. More disagreeable than. any thing else was the fact. that 46000. Highlanders under the orders of the Premeir. had entered Verdopolis from the North and were now garrisoning and covering the. House of peers. Barracks and citadel.

Such is an abstract of the overwhelming news of the Day. While I sat. in a reverie. the paper in one hand the teacup in the other. Sir R Pelham was announced gladly I received him. and eagerly I began to question him.

"Oh Sir Robert. we are in a deplorable state.!"

"Certainly. we are situated among untoward events."

"Whats to be done Sir Robert."

"Ah Flower that cry is frequent. now."

"Madness. cant you. look at a thing with warmth."

"Certainly. Sir. I can so do. when. circumstances call for such a look."

"Were you ever. situated as now"

"Why the question cannot be answered. decidedly. but I should think scarcly."

"Sir Robert speak out. now leaving every other consideration aside are not We. we the Secceders from the Ministry now placed. in a most frightful situation. you see. on the one hand we have cast of the Nobility and the Nobility have cast of us. on the other. the Democracy the Parliament. and Army. have not moved to take us in and we cannot move to enter. we are isolated Sir. and. belong to no continent. amid this approaching uproar. what are we to do. our leader the Duke thro[u]gh his whole life has been accustomed to command and who can think he will suffer himself to be commanded now.—And we all know whether the Marquis of Douro and Lord Elrington like to receive orders or not. No Sir I cannot. tell who we can join. and our numbers are to small to raise a party to ourselves. unless indeed we become the Heads of the Middle men."

"Hem. I should think. that. such a position would be scarcly expedient
"Truely Pelham. Then what do you think of the. DECLARATIONS. the.
46000. The approach of the Army."

"Hem why all these thing[s] look untoward enough but a statesman must
accustom himself to difficultys.

"But the country—Verdopolis."

"Of course the country will face the ill effects of the inconvenient line of
politics the Kings have chosen to adopt. In fact I sh[o]uld [think] that we all
have a rather unpleasant prospect of confusion and bloodshed. The Heads of the
Aristocracy are I might say even obstinant. and. retentive. The Heads of the
Movement. are. impetous and. inveterate. at le[a]st. appearances warrant my
saying so. In fact I do not know a character. which so ill can bear scrutiny as
that of Lord Elrington. He is cold. blooded. tyrannical and. rapacious The
Marquis of Douro is Hotheaded. headstrong and. overbearing. Mr Montmorency
is Merceneray Brutish. and Bullying. Mr Warner. is proud predjudiced &
passionate. These Flower are direful heads. for a faction. dangerous rulers of a
revolution. And when for their subordinat agents you find. such men as. Col.
Thornton. Cool Courageous and Hardy. Viscount Castlereagh. Dashing obedient
and noisy Y M Naughty. Bold Ambitious. and. undaunted. Edward Laury. Frank
Generous and vain minded. Thomas Scroven. quick cunning and Malignant.
Robert Sdeath cruel creeping and. detestable. There are the men Sir these are the
men for embroiling a Nation for seizing the Helm and for directing the vessel to
perdition."

"Well done Sir Robert it is not often you speak out when you do you clench
it but alas What you say is I fear too true. yet let us in like manner review our
troops. the Rationals and see what they will prove. As Leaders behold the Duke
of Wellington Comprehensive indefatigable and infallible. Colonel Grenville.
Sober. Solid and substantial. Bravey. obstinate Blunt and well meaning. Badey
selfwilled sottish. and stupid. Mr Bud. Learned. sagacious and. crotchetty. Sir
Robert Weever Pelham. Sir plausible imperturable. and. sophistical. Mr Morley.
obstrepulous. ready tongued. and. thrifty Sir John Flower why ahem. a
goodmeaning. plaindealing acter up.[to] now I think these men. backed by. Sir H
Hardinge. Formal straightforward. and. fiery. General Bobbadil stolid. exact and
clockwork. General Fergusson. Bold hearted. strong handed. and unflinching.
These I think should be able to effect something. should they not Sir?"

"Perhaps So. Flower well since you have taken up my beggining I will
continue them. let us take the faction of the Aristocrats and look at their Leaders.
look at Alexander of Sneachis Land. proud griping and deceitful. Wm Edward of.
Parrysland. Stiff. obstinate and. meandealing John of Ross's land. Frank. nearly
and. nose lead.—William of Moncey's land. whale bone. old fashioned and
narrow minded—Frederic of Stumps land. short souled short bodied. and mulish.
His High[n]ess Gravey Solemn sedate and prudish. His Highness Tracky cold
stern and biggoted. Marquis Wellesly. Despotic snappish and drivelling Earl St
Clair. jaundiced. hot tempered. and pride swollen. The Marquis of Fidena. shy
reserved and. unyeilding E G S Sydney. narrow carping and. fretful J J. Goat
ignorant book learned and. despicable. Lord Lofty. crafty. selfish and. cowardly

Lord Mussleburgh. Atomic schoolboy and. Jack of all trades. take all these
followed By such men as. Old Earl Lofty. Old Earl Elrington Earl. Medford. and
so forth Doting. greiving Biggoted old Aristocrats. Behold them and—but
Flower I hope that is I trust. you have not. within hearing servants or or
malicious. I mean well intentioned who yet would misrepresent and.—
    "No fear Pelham no fear. Ah I thought this fit of. boldness would not last."
At this moment. A messenger entered bearing letters from the Duke of
Wellington and requesting our attendance at the palace.
    The remainder of the day passed off amid distrust fears and alarms. the
elements of society seemed about to dissolve and each man stood looking to
himself. or at his neighbour it was understood that different corps of the
retreating Army were rapidly entering the villiages and suburbs east of the city
and it was even rumoured that the two great. Leaders Douro and Elrington either
had arrived there or were this day expected. This event by all freinds to peace and
order was a thing not alt all to be wished for should these men intermeddle with
the present state of politics. Bloodshed and Despotism must ensue. we all knew
Lord Elrington. and with his. remorseless principals. bitter feelings and
unbending energy. aided by the Admired Intellect. great influence. and. eager.
spirits of. His freind. the Marquis Douro what might not the Army be capable
off. Such reflections as these occupied the minds of all sober reflecting men.
mixed with sorrow extreme at the Obstinate Bigotry of the Aristocrats. untill
Evening drew on and then. All men in suspense prepared to listen to that nights
deliberations in Parliament.
    After I had finished my tea. and when Evening drew on. I ordered my
carriage And accompanied by Col Bud. drove to the House of Commons.
remarking as we passsed the excited appearance of the whole City. as we
ascended the vast steps of. the House of Commons. we beheld Mr W H Warner.
accompanied by 23 members. all his Relations. dependants and devoted
followers. all too firm Adherents of the Army. troop up before us. Bud
remarked. "How filled for stormy water is that. Man Warner it is in public
tempests that such as he arise. Elrington first appeared. in the. troubles of the
successions." At the Doors of the House the crowd of persons was so extremely
dense that I and my freind found the greatest difficulty in wedging through them
at last however we attained our seats and looked round us. the house was full the
Lamps lighted and in the thousand Faces. turned up to the light. what a vast
variety what an intense eagerness of expression was visible. Mr Montmorency
was on his legs speaking vehemently and rapidly and leveling his accustomed
thunder against the Ministry with even more than his accustomed violence. The
occupants of the Government Benches turned toward him. Faces wearing the
expression of Trouble anger and anxiety. and among them. there was a constant
wiping of the foreheads. and convulsive twitches toward one another. The
Opposition Benches showed us head over head great rows of countenances.
frowning with. sympathetic scorn. Eyes glittering with triumph and mouths just
opened for the ready cheer. The seats upon the cross Benches were this night I
was suprised to find. remarkably full. in fact many. cool and judicious men.
seeing the turn things were taking and alertted at the violence of the two great

factions seemed now determined to take a middle line and. be. ready to cast the balance where justice should dictate. upon these Benches amid these men. I. Sir R Pelham. Mr Bud. and. others late Ministers now took our seats.

As for the Speaker. Mr Montmorency. upon our entry. stood in his place erecting his. huge Black. figure. knotty forehead and red. whiskers. His chest displayed his Arms folded. as in all the joy of conscious. power. He turned his stern features. to the unhappy Ministers. and. shook the house with his Tones of thunder

"Aye. so then I find you in your places. Right. Ba[i]rns. you have come to be flogged. as Mammy told you. well now. that Mammy Montmorency is standing over you. mind to repeat to yourselves at every lash. For how can I keep dinning it into you. "This will save us from being hanged. Yes childern the Gallows knows not a more. inveterate enimy than the rod. and. the Hangman dislikes the Birch far more than the Pulpit. Listen to me. I am the rod. and as the Childern of Israel. while. dying amid the horrors of. the Desert. But gazed. upon that Rod and Serpent. and. received life and health again[9] so. do you But look on and listen to me. and. you will find your benifts no whit inferior. Well Gentlemen. so far right enough but. Volo! If I am the rod. the Army is the Gallows. and if you run from me. you must inevitably. run to that. Now make your choice. will you be flogged or be hanged will you listen to what I say to what Mr Warner Mr Morley Mr[10] <   > and a hundred such like say will you take our advice. cast off the Ministers. shackle the Kings cripple the Lords. and raise a power of our own. or will you. wait the arrival of the Army in fright receive its Officers. be crushed despised and set to nought. dragged. out into an empty square ranged all in a hollow ring. stand fixed like post[s]. or Targets [by] the Army be fired at and DIE. (loud cheering and hisses). There is no other way no middle course you cannot cry. Oh. we will judge from ourselves we will take a penny from one man and a halfpenny from another. a cake of Bread from this one and a pint of Drink from that. We will go Begging for ourselves and let others drink alone. "No. No I say you cant do this. you cannot and dare not. Just listen quietly to me. then listen quietly to Mr Warner then. turn out the Ministers. increase the forces. remonstrate to the Kings. spit at the peers. take me in to the Government and. nobly you'll thrive. Now Ill turn to you to you the actual Minister[s] present in this house. there you sit. let me see. one, two, three, four five. yes and 6 and 7. Faugh get up with you. Nay kneel down Aye kneel down. and pray. Oh Sirs look I beseech you to another world. For in this your time is like to be short. indeed. and Earth to Earth ashes to ashes. dust to dust.[11] off you sweep from the stage of Human existence. dont think that I or any off. us feel at all more exasperated at you conduct. yesterday in preparing that abominabl[e] declaration. For had you spent the time occupied in concocting that <meal of uncleaness.> in penning a full and distinct.

---

9 See Numbers, chapter 21.
10 "Grenville" crossed out but no alternative provided.
11 See p. 165, n. 44.

confession a clear and explicit. prayer of Pardon for all and off all the crimes you have committed. dont think I say that. all this or more than this. could alter for a moment your fixed and inevitable doom. sooner may my voice bring down that dome in ruins around me than. your cries avert the sword. from descending upon you. the Army <process> your Fate. and to dust you shall descend as from dust you came"

Mr Montmorency sat down amid a dreadful uproar of Applause remonstrance and. dissaprobation. next up rose. a Gentleman from the middle benches.

Sir Markham. Howard.

"Gentlemen I must protest against. such violent language as that which you have just heard from the Honourable. Gentleman. who spoke before me. Certainly that language is calculated to bring on the crisis it declaims against and once more I pray (violent commotion prevent[ed] the member for some seconds from proceeding). Gentlemen I intreat. (renewed and double Interruption.) I appeal to the Law."

Mr. Montmorency. "Pull him down."

Mr Warner. "Shoot the scoundrel"

Hereupon a violent assault was made upon the liberal Member. he sank amid the crowd around him. But as he fell. Mr Sydney roar[ed].

"Gentlemen. are you mad. are you distracted. What frightful calamity threatens us that our noblest assembly should. (cries and hisses) Oh. in the name of justice of mercy. in the name of our common country I beseech you. (Mr Montmorency. "to get you hanged")

Hereupon a frightful assault was made upon Mr Sydney. by the Martialists This assault the Ministerials and. Moderates both for the honour of justice united to repell and after a dreadful clamour of praying cursing and threatning mixed with actual violence. those parties headed by Marquis Fidena suceeded in obtaining a disturbed and. broken hearing by the Honourable Member. He went on to defend himself and the Government. not daring to speak against the army with considerable vehemence and eloquence. for half an hour.

While he was speaking I. got up and stepped. to the window meaning to take a glance at the City below. But to my extreme astonishment instead of. the great lighted square. crowded with. people and equipages. appearing before me I saw nothing the window [w]as dark and the rain beat heavily against it. the gas lights. had been all quenched. just around the house. for they yet twinkled in the distant line of streets and houses. In the square below I could hear though not see and the result of my hearing proved to me that. however dark. this square was by no means. devoid of people. a sullen sound as of great numbers. intermixed with. clashing and trampling but all voice [h]ushed and stiffled. proclaimed an unusual state of things.

However ere I could express my astonishment. as I turned back to my seat Two tall Gentlemen wrapt. in cloaks entered walked up the house and after composedly taking off those cloaks and hanging them on a seat calmly sat down on the Front opposition Benches side by side. all look[ed] at them There was no mistaking them. The pale harrassed and. unquiet countenance of Lord. Elrington the high proud and martial features of the young Marquis of Douro. were known to all

"Hah" said Sydney gathering strength from the shock he recieved "Hah is it thus and. do you dare to break thus the laws of your country."

Douro glanced upon him a look of intense scorn. Elrington hastily rose and striking his hand on his forehead cried. angrily

"What now! take him off."!!

A hundred Members rushed to obey his orders Sydney was silenced. directly

Lord Elrington stood forward and. in a voice at first hoarse and broken and then clear loud and. emphatic entered upon his buisness of terror. and coercion.

"Go" he said "And tell the world that Verdopolis hesitated wether it should. hang or drown itself. wether it should perish like a halfpenny wick or a farthing rush light."

This was spoken with his well known bitterness and acrimony. indeed he seemed. ashy pale with rage. while He spoke. My ears caught sounds from the Hall of Entrance which I did scarcly like. The stifled mutter of voices the thud as of muskets upon the floor the now and then short note sounded upon. clarionet or Bugle. told. unutterable tales as did too the. constant and fiery glances bestowed by the Marquis of Douro upon that quarter just mentioned. Elrington spoke. on.

"Now silence Sirs. you are. you all. ready to sign this paper it is a plain declaration. adressed to the country that you. the Commons of Verdopolis will no longer suffer Ministry or Peers or Monarchs to trample upon you. Here lies the paper I place upon the table come each Member and sign he who refuses He who refuses. My Heart that man shall die. Douro Hah."

The Marquis of Douro hastily rose and with a bitter laugh walked out off the House. The members guessed somewhat of the reason many I saw tremble many strove to gulp down their agony. Mutterings of treason. treachery tyranny. were heard in many a place. The click of pistols. struck through my heart. even the lights seemed to burn faint and sickly Elrington the ruler and director of this scene and such scenes—stood. aloof with. folded arms. and glittering eyes. casting glances of peculiar me[a]ning first to his folowers Mont. &c. then to the unhappy and devoted Ministerialists at. once the. Great Door flew open The Marquis of Douro reentered behind him tramped. in. a Double. Row. of Grenadeirs. Headed By. Major Thornton their high caps and bayonets glittering. in the lights These stern. Military. ranged themselves in an ominous mass along the lower benches the Doors and at the tables. Behind. at the Great Entrance appeared. a new company of soldiers. with Col. Vis Castlereagh. fading back into the Darkness. at once. the. Bugles Trumpets Clarionets and Trombones. burst up shrill and deep and. loud and clear. and the. inspiring   music <of the>[12] Elrington thrilled through passage and. apartments. and was answered according to my private. guess. by Drums Trumpets &c. from the square without. The Noble storm of music fired the whole souls of the Martialists and

---

[12]   Part of the bottom of the page has been torn away.

struck a lead sickness through those of. the. Ministers. The. agreeing Members pressed in crowds to sign the paper. then came the time for the other[s] a pause of. dead silence ensued none came forward. a second pause still they kept. back. movements and mutterings ensued. "Silence." shouted Elrington "will you sign.".—"Hah. by. the bones.". "Up Soldiers." cried Douro as he sprung on to a Bench seized the Home Secretary and dragged him onto the floor. Thornton and the soldiers. rushed forward. Down were hurled tables benches and lamps and men. a storm of confusion rose such as I have never seen equalled Members were hurried by soldiers from their seats. dragged to sign or in case of refusal directly born headlong from the Hall. were judging from the confusion outside a rough reception awaited them. Pistol shots soon were heard in the hall swords clashed and I saw a member fall stabbed by a bayonet. The Marquis of Fidena drew a brace of Pistols and declared that should a man lay a finger on him he would shoot him dead on the spot. Douro. strode up with eyes on fire. "lower your Arms Fidena "No." "Then I. will." "Do and I will shoot you.". "No you will not." Yes. Douro I must." "I ll try." The Marquis stepped. up his tall form and plumed cap. towering above the. interested gazers "In the name of God Douro stand off" "Fidena. are you mad" he stepped. on. Fidena raised his pistol a soldier reached out a pole axe and struck his arm up. the pistol went of. the ball. struck through the heart. Mr Philip Warner. he fell. then Douro sprung on Fidena. and. bore him down the Hall rose in renewed. confusion but. the. soldiers arrived in thicker bodies the area was choked with plumes and bayonets The refractory Members were born down directly. and I well remember—or rather I do not remember being hurried out breathless by <those> <energit[i]c> works of a factions will and ere I could gain my senses I was standing out on the out door steps. around me the. Martial Members of the commons. Below the. rows of bound and pinioned members. beyond. great black and bright. masses of Infantry and. swaying strampling Cavalry the Gaslights again blazing and the great Military Bands Bursting forth with the fifes shrill notes and the Drums thundering roll. the Clarionets burst of sound. and the long wail of the Bugles. The Great Verdopolitan. slow march Elrington Douro and Castlereagh and Thornton ruled the uproar. at. once two soldiers by the command of the first mentioned Nobleman seized me and placing me on horseback hurried me. along the streets to my house enjoining me not to stir out. for fear of what may happen as I alighted I beheld vast lines of Cavalry and Infantry sweeping away toward the House of Peers and rows of pinioned Members hurried back through the square by their. <military> jailors Thus closed my experience of that tremendous night.[13]

Early next morning December 22. Sunday. I arose as from a feverish Dream and hastened. to obtain from the city accurate information of what last night I had first heard and seen. On entering the streets their troubled state. the. determined or cowed and broken aspect of the populace. and above all the. thick

---

13 Compare with Scott's description of Napoleon forcibly dissolving the Council of 500 with troops, *Life of Napoleon*, IV, 182-89.

squads of Military dispersed in every direction and the. vast shoals of cannon and baggages waggons moving up the streets leading from the east convinced me that the 2 great leaders of the Movement had brought the army into the city in spite of the Government. what they intended to do with the captured and refractory Commons I could not tell.

As I moved hastily and excited. toward the region of. Parliament Square. the crowds both of civilians and military increased. amazingly and the openings before that Noble Building presented one dense mass of Hats plumes and. Bayonets. Through these I pushed forward. till on a sudden I. entered onto a wid[e] space in front of the steps. surrounded by lines of Military the Band playing with muffled drums. and. a black flag displayed over the cornice of the House of Commons In a few minutes their issued from the House. 2 or 3 Gentlemen in Black followed by 12. armed Musqueteers ranged. 10 paces opposite. the other two persons stood at one side. the isolated man A tall Noble looking person. in deep mourning I knew at once to be. the Earl of St Clair. our prime Ministry. he was led forth and their placed to die. it was Montmorenci and Warner who stood by him. the stern features of the first in a snear of hatred the angelic countenance of the second composed in to an aspect of solemn resolution the. first considered the buisness as one. to gratify his. long burning hatred the last. as a matter of stern necessity for the good of the country and I know not which countenance looked more pitiless. Warners I think. As. for St Clair my Eyes dimmed in gazing upon. my unhappy freind superior and prime Minister. brought alas to such an end. by such. mournful blindness and to be slain by such bloody hands. He stood. pale indeed and solemn. but otherwise calm and unmoved. in appearance. looking upon his destroyers with an air of contemptous unconcern. Montmorenci in his accustomed blood thirsty manner. strove to embitter his death by taunts. sneers and. reproaches. but. all without effect. save when he said Aye my man the Kings will meet their fate were wound up. and as for your squad of Highlanders My. I—the trench and quick lime. will be the word for them. 40000 heads. Ah. Marat.[14] would have liked that." Then indeed. St.

---

[14]   Jean-Paul Marat (1743-93), radical, editor, and Montagnard deputy to the National Convention, was one of the foremost radicals of the revolution. He moved to Great Britain (1765), became a prosperous physician and writer of philisophical treatises, but then returned to Paris in 1777. In 1789, he was pursued by police for inciting the insurrection of 5-6 October and forced to hide, then fled to England in January 1790. Marat was vocal in his demands for executions, declaring anywhere from 500 to 100,000 heads needed to be cut off in order to save millions of lives. He was unique in his early and frequent calls for a dictator. Marat initially favored a limited monarchy, but when France became a republic in 1792, he became a republican. Marat was a leading Montagnard and the object of violent attacks by the Girondins. He played an important role in the insurrection of 31 May-2 June 1793, in which he obtained his revenge on the Girondins. When Marat was assassinated by a woman, C. Corday, on 13 July 1793, he was already dying from lung and skin diseases and

Clair glanced upon him one look of concentered disdain. "My Lord" said Mr Warner

"My Lord. you must die—think of your end. Shall we send for Gravey. He though bound can come. we must do this if at all quickly for Elrington is soon to arrive.

"Sir silence I wish not the primates feelings to be embittered. more than I know they now are. I will die alone. If die I must."

"Yes Die you must. but though the act be necessary cruelty is not. and I am willing to afford every consolation. to one about for ever to pass from this world."

"Silence Sir."

"No. My Lord. and will you not. think upon your late actions think upon what you have done.

"Aye Warner and what he's undone

Mr Montmorenci this is scarcly time for joking. And My lord your injustice and blindness having"----

Here. Mr Warner received. a tap on the shoulder he turned round in his usual seriousness at a poke. There. stood behind him Lord Elrington whose horse from which he had. just alighted. stood. held by a page beyond This great Nobleman. came forward to St Clair. with an expression of fridgid indefference upon his. features Clair received. him as fridgidly as himself. but. detestation at one who seemed about to throw a country in to blood and destruction mingled in the Prime Ministers countenance. Elrington did not attempt to insult him did not seem to triumph. over him to reproach. him But with a keen anxious eye to buisness. hurried forward matters to a conclusion. and here I noticed the difference between this man and his coadjutor in the revolution. the Marquis of Douro if he brought himself to kill Lord St Clair or any other lofty and distinguished person would have. conducted their death. with a full consciousness of the great character and real moment of the deed. he would have given the word. with a flushed brow a kindled eye and too probably a look of triumphant and unrepressed hatred. Lord Elrington Just seemed. in a hurry for some other important. transaction whised for fear of obstruction to get this over. never thought of the deed as the death of a fellow creature. he stood there a tall figure dressed in deep black. his yellow cane under one arm. his black gloves in his left hand his. white Handkercheif for the signal in the other. he gave [a] keen look at the 12 soldiers "Men you are too distant. step a pace nearer. stop how are your muskets.—Mont look at the mens arms." This worthy steped round. to examine the locks. "Well enough Rougue. but this peice"—"Hah. its bad I see it here soldier. take this pistol of mine its surer." He. coolly pulled from his pocket a

---

his death ironically hastened the Terror and the Revolutionary government. While at first he was "Pantheonized" and his embalmed heart hung from the ceiling of the Cordeliers Club, his reputation was denigrated in the Anti-Terrorist wave after Thermidore, and his body removed from the Pantheon in February 1795. However, the term *maratisme* became synonomous with ultra-terrorism, reaffirming Marat's ambiguous legacy.

handsome. pistol. presented it to the soldier. first cocking it himself. "Now then
let me get it over stand to your paces present. when I throw this
Hand[k]ercheif.—" Mr Warner interrupted. him "Elrington stop Lord St Clair. do
you wish to communicate. anything before"—Here a flash of Elringtons
slumpering inpetuosity broke forth. "Death and! Furies. curse. his
communications. stand St Clair! fire dogs. fire at him! Volo!" he rudly pushed
the unfortunate Nobleman into his place. flung his Handcercheif. and. the great
crack struck on our ears and rattled from the buildings around I pressed my hands
to my eyes a sensation of sickness came over me. when I looked again the.
crowd round had rushed before me. and I only saw Lord Elrington. fling himself.
onto his horse and. asking loudly "is he quite dead." he is A Seargent answered.
"quite dead" He with a "very well" struck his hat over his forehead and galloped.
away down the street.[15]

This bloody deed the manner. in which it was executed. the probability of
further executions. filled my mind that day I continued my excursion through the
city but it was with a dizzy feeling that I saw the immense walls of the state
prisons which I knew contained so many great and noble though misguided men.
the vast numbers the daring words the evident power of the Army now all
concentered upon Verdopolis struck me with awe. Lord Elrington Marquis of
Douro. Lord Castlereagh General Thornton (as he was now dubbed) Mr
Montmorenci and Mr Warner. had evidently seized upon all power and authority I
must proceed breifly but more distinctly to recapitulate the course of events
which led to this state of things

"Yesterday Morning December. 21. The rear and principal officers of the
Retreating Army had arrived in the villiages round Verdopolis. instantly on that
arrival though the Government had published an express prohibition of their
communication with or entry into the city they opened a direct association with
Montmorenci Warner and the Opposition Members of the Commons (intirely
leaving us the dissentieus ex ministers though so much their freinds out of the
question) with these men they conceited a plan for that evening while. the
Ministers in Parliament were worried and badgered by this opposition the Army
in 3 great columns of. 30000 each should move upon the City concenter in the
middle. and. that a strong body of troops surrounding the two houses of
Parliament. Generals Elrington Douro Thornton and Castlereagh should enter.
force the Peers and Commons to an agreement with their plans. seized their
antagonist the Ministers. and convey them in the state prisons. and in
conjunction with the commons opposition they should seize the helm and take
all power into their hands this great movement the[y] proceeded to place into
execution at Nightfall. all the eastern streets of the City were choked by an
irresistible flood of Military horse and foot. pouring down every opening toward
the center of Verdopolis Here at Midnight the van with the Leaders arrived. both
houses of Parliament were perfectly surrounded. Elrington Douro and Thornton

---

[15] Spencer Perceval, shot dead by John Bellingham on 11 May 1812, is the
only British prime minister to have been assassinated.

entered first the Commons their proceedings in which I have above full[y]
described. they at the muskets muzzles forced the Members to sign their own
destruction seized the refractory amounting to 83 men and. with the Members of
the Ministry. averaging 12 they threw them bound into the state prison of
Verdopolis after the execution of this tremendous deed of daring despotism they
entered by force the house of peers acted as before in the commons. forced. as
many as force could compell to agree to their usurpation. then laid hold upon.
THE KINGS.! yes actually all the Kings excepting the one of Wellingtons land.
laid hold on them and. hurrying them into their carriages. drove them of to the
Citadel. where they were placed by the Military in strict and. iorn confinement
the Aristocratic Peers 209. they. also threw into the same. stern building. This
Frightful Change being completed. the leaders of it broke up all the
Government. and. after consigning all power civil and military into the hands.
of. a council. of 6 men. consisting of

Lord Viscount Elrington
The Marquis of Duoro.
Lord Viscount Castlereagh
General. Thornton.
M M Montmorenci Esqr
W H Warner Esqr

They drew the Army into the whole city quartered it in vast masses through
every suspicious part. filled Citidal. Barracks. and all the strongholds with
regiments of trusty servants. awed the populace into instant submittion.
Bloodily slew. the late Prime Minister Earl St Clair. laid an instant hold over all
the suspicious Newspapers levied contributions upon the inhabitants of
Verdopolis—and Now having thus by one act of unparrarelled. boldness and
energy. secured their power and Authority of same. they. the Leaders of this
mighty Movement. turned sternly to the Eastern storm and prepared. if possible
to arrest the progress of the overpowering forces of Napoleon the Great.

From December 22d to December 29. a whole week passed away in the City
without any visible alteration in our affairs the Army had seized the reins and
they seemed determined to keep them. The 46000 Highlanders had after a few.
movements of insurrection and a few fatal skirmishes—at length by means of
force and bribery incorporated themselves under General Fergusson. with the
main Army and its intrest This last Hope of the Kings and Aristocracy being.
thus gone. they. all remained with the refractory commons in close and. illegal
confinement. certainly. their wants were attended to. and no insult was offered to
them certainly too they had deserved a check and punishment for the rash and
iniquitous measures they lately had drawn themselves into. yet still the fact
could never be denied. Here were 5 Kings. 200 Noblemen. 20 ministers and. 80
commons. seized placed in prison and their detained without trial or form of that
without. law. and in defiance of law. by their own subjects and fellow
countrymen.

Thus stood the case yet let no one think that the rulers of the Army cared for it. The injustice might have been ten times more glaring yet it would have never moved the hearts of these inflexible men.

In the city during this week. the people were at the beck of a red coat and Helmet all the Newspapers were either suppressed or came forth under their auspices. No man if he uttered a word against this new authority dared to call His life his own and innumberable were the instances in which through Verdopolis. people were suddenly seized & hurried of to prison or barracks by Monts notorious minister of. Despotism. Thorntons Bayonets or Elringtons or Douro's Dragoons. In one instance I know of a Manufactorer. who seeing the disastrous turn of affairs felt that trade had no longer any security and determined. to resign his buisness. that night a Colonel and. 10. infantry. entered his. counting house. showed him a warrant from the grand Council and told him that unless he carried on trade to prison he must go The Manufacturer had no alternative but to proceed in his ruinous buisness. It was by such measures on the part of the Army that. Trade and commerce shattered by the want of. credits. were forced to go on.

That Grand Council the list of whose Members I have before given. met. every Night at. either the. Home office or Elrington Hall and it was here amid 6 men that the destin[i]es of. 7 Kingdoms were. marked and decided. Their deliberations were so strictly private that not a breath of. their intentions ever escaped to the public untill those intentions were put in practisce. As for us. the Rational Members of the Late Cabinet the armys firmest freinds in times of the greatest difficulty were were frowned on silenced and discarded. The Duke of Wellington alone the only King not imprisoned. was admitted into the secrets and deliberations of these Lords Military. in fact he formed a 7.th councillor. Still. Lord Elrington and the Marquis of Douro were by all known as the Heads of the Movement and present Kings of our Empire. and to two more. able dangerous and tyrannous despots no kingdom could ever be entrusted. what they might now have done in Verdopolis the Genii only know. had not circumstances occured which. compelled them to other courses. during this last week in December. the French our tremendous Enimy so long amid Domestic quarrels kept from sight. had been under the Mighty Emporer concentrating and augmenting their forces along the whole line of country east of Verdopolis and now. 150000 French men and 80000. Africans. were in 3 great Bodies from NE··E··and··SE··quickly and irresistibly sweeping on upon Verdopolis.

The Army at home were not ignorant of this.

On Monday. December. 29. a Notice was posted up in all parts of the City of Verdopolis to the following Effect.

".The Forces of the Army. will evacuate Verdopolis to morrow Dec 30

"They with the Offices of the Government and. the prisoners of State. will. will.

"Fix their Head quarters at. Alnwick. 50 miles West. of this City

"From thence. hereafter for some time the decrees of council will be issued."

signed $\left\{\begin{array}{l}\text{Elrington}\\ \text{Duoro presidents of Council}\end{array}\right.$

Elrington Hall. Dec. 29. 1833. -------------------　　E D.

The dismay and Horror which this Notice excited exceed description. through the whole of this day. all mouths were filled with smothered. execrations upon the authors of so base and treacherous. a paper. It was evident that the Army. were that concious of the superior strength of the Emperor. to leave Verdopolis to him as the bait. which the man flings to the dog to worry while he himself prepares his blow. And however. energetic wise and necessary such a course. and certainly this plan was all three. yet it struck the ears of the. offended citizens. as such cold calculating parricide and treachery that certainly they could scarce contain themselves. All this the Army regarded not. It was easily seen who was the Author of many of these tryannical though Politic measures. And the mingled degrees of. coolness and energy. cruelty and wisdom. combined with the attention to an knowledge of Civil warfare and commotion the constant inattention to all generous and patriotic feeling combined with much right just and. necessary conduct. made up a mental chaos. which only one man could have been proved possessed of. Douro was too youthful too impetous. to design the evacuation of the city. to proud too inexperienced to meddle with the forced. credit in the commerce. his Heat and imperiousness of temper would have failed him in these cold calculating transactions. Montmorenci possessed much experience in such affairs but he had not the influence with the Army or the impenetrable coldness to carry him through. Thornton all knew to be incapable of taking that political and extended view of affair[s] which the late measures prepsupposed in the author. Warner was too irritable. and thought the measures for maintai[n]ing commerce. and money matters. in a fictitious height might have suited him yet the means for carrying these measures into effect. the traitorous desertion of the city He dared not have calculated upon. The Duke it was evident kept himself clear of all these hazardous adventures. the one remaining Member of the council was by all pointed out as the detested author of much of this illegal misery. and Lord Elringtons constant attendance at the Offices and Army his keen scowling glances in passing through the city his thoughtful abstractedness of manner. and. evident alacrity in every thing tending on a revolution. all too plainly indicated too whom we were to owe our flourishing Army suspended country and dying commerce. on this day when the Dreadful Notice was promulgated I beheld Lord Elrington pacing along the street in the direction of his huge plunder built　Hall. dressed in his accustomed funeral black which not even. War itself. could for any length of time displace. his cane under his arm his eyes bent on the ground. and his pale countenance unexcited by the huge tumult of the streets the constant trooping forward of cavalry and infantry or by the aspect of his own great <white > placards flaming from every wall around him. I look[ed] at him with attention and then at the Marquis of Douro whom I saw advancing toward him from another street. The Marquis was on horseback but. when he. saw the Nobleman. before him he

flung himself. from his steed gave the reins to a page and. advanced with nodding
plume and elastic step. toward. his coadjutor. They met. cordialy shaking hands.
and stopped to converse on the pavement. The Marquis Martial. and Heroic
Figure. quick eye and. animated though. haughty countenance. contrasted
curiously with the. equally tall form the civilian apparel. the treacherous eye and.
inexpressive smile. of the. Lucifer Like Elrington. The former stood erect
unsupported and gazing with evident. pleasure upon the. warlike sights around.
him and. the Huge Dark classic buildings above him. the latter stood not erect.
leaning on his cane his gloves half pulled from his hands in the eagerness of
talking and. a saffron hue of earnest and anxious feeling overspreading his else
mild composed features

    "Well Elrington as usual this Morning.—I dont like the plan."

"What plan Douro"

"That of leaving the city."

"Oh a patriot I suppose" with a suppressed yawn.

"Hem If all patriots were as I am!! Elrington this city may be harred 20
times over and save over my own goods and chattels a sigh shall not escape
me No. but. give up one step and you give up. two.

"Proverbial eh"

"Yes—perfect Solomon."[16]

I doubt it"

IT is you who are proverbs. with your exquisitely laconic sentences" But
Elrington the Army is numerous. it musters you know. 130000 men. The
City is strong the French why true the French too are strong but this is not
the first time Glasstowners have beaten numbers."

"Nor the first time Glasstowners have been beaten by numbers. the retreat
from Angria runs too strong in my head to make me scorn the. uneven.
number.

"Oh you are Nervous. and I affirm. that were it not to use another proverb
Elrington that Division is destruction I could seperate my forces from yours
and abide my time myself.

"Eh your proverbs are needful to save you from the charge of Idiocy

"Come Elrington clear up. draw out the forces. place them allong the
suburbs. Advance charge in columns on the French lines. dash into them
and end All."

"Aye end all"

"Sloth mole. creeper. Ill leave you. to your sickly fancies."

"Stay. Douro wheres your Policy. this is weak this is boyish this is
Enthusiasm Ardour Generosity. Oh are you not above them. we must be
conquered to conquer we must die to live. Thou fool dost thou not know
that which thou sowest is not quickened except it die. thou sowest Grain it

---

[16] The biblical King Solomon was proverbial for his sagacity: "And
Solomon's wisdom excelled the wisdom of all the children of the east country,
and all the wisdom of Egypt. For he was wiser than all men" (I Kings 4: 30-1).

may be wheat or some other grain. the earth covers it and. it perisheth yet to every seed God giveth. a body and to each seed its own body. why for that matter to each seed. a dozen bodys.—The ressurection man death and the Ressurection dont you believe in the ressurection.—Eh the Army is the seed we are just going to sow it It shall grow and the fruit thereof is Victory."[17] The Marquis of Douro turned round and with an impatient laugh sprung on to his steed and followed by his page Galloped quickly away Elrington with a cough and. curse took up his limbs and paced slowly on. a crowd of persons tradesmen shopkeepers and what. Douro would call fellows of the baser sort. really. honest men ruined and dejected by the courses of the Army had gathered. round. the two Noblemen while conversing and now with their eyes followed the Latter as he walked. slowly on. a mutter of impatient despair escaped several. when they saw him pass. by so unobservant of their ruin and misery and quickly this murmur. increased. and became louder. some one mischeivously threw a stone a spark among gunpowder could not have produced this effect instantly whatever came nearest was seized on and stones cats rats sticks and Hats were hurled. in a shower of curses on the head of the. Haughty Nobleman. The Mob thickened round him and closed him in among them. he was not looking up and evidently was unconcious of the tempest untill a Brickbat struck his hat from his head. and. a Dead Cat smacked against his face. He looked hastily up and drawing two Pistols from his pocket he with uncovered head and. eyes flashing lightning turned short round and rushed. full upon his assailants. The Lion was an over match for the wolves and as the smoke of the discharged pistols enveloped him in dusky cloud. the Mob first. wavered then turned. and in an instant fled scattering of in all directions. Elringtons fiery temperament was excited to its utmost and. coming against the rear of an hindmost rioter he. he gave him such an emphatic kick as hurled the poor fellow flat against the wall of an opposite House. Elrington stood up. and in his loudest vociferated. for soldiers—a party of Cavalry were just passing their Officer in the. uncovered Hair bloodless lip and excited eye of his. General saw tokens not to be. uncared for he drew his sabre and at the head of his men thundered down the street. hacking and slashing amid the. flying and Howling Multitude. Elrington looked on for a moment and then spleeinfully kicking his hat from him he with almost a shout of cursing hurriedly strode up the great steps of Elrington Hall.

For my part I hurried home and seeing that Verdopolis was about to be given up to the fury of the Enimy I in common with thousands of others spent the whole of that day in directing my affairs to be closed up and preparing to set out for my residence. at Ross's Glasstown. All the familys of the Cheifs of the Army were departing or had departed. to the country. Rumours of the french were thickning and darkning round us. and it was the Army alone this terrible Army which could save us.

January the First A D. 1834. had now Dawned upon us. and how different was its rising from the January of 1833. who could have believed it had it been

---

[17] See I Corinthians 15:36-8, and p. 442 below.

told them then that this year succeding should thus open upon Africa and Verdopolis. that Newyears Day. 1834. should be astir not with feasting and revelry but with the departure of its Defenders from Verdopolis and the abandonment of our Capital. to the French our Enimys yet so it was and when this morning at dawn amid the the struggling twilight of morning the sound of instrumental music in the street below impressed my. half sleepy senses with the belief that this was Christmas Morning and that that was the Christmas Hymn. for a moment I yeilded to the fancy but the thrilling notes and. rolling drums. the. stir and confusion without did not strenghten the idea of a calm Christmas morn I hastily rose and looked from the window it was raw red dawn over the house roofs. The dark street was crowded with. people ranged on each side a great Band playing in the middle and before and behind stretching till lost amid other streets shoaled on long broad bristling lines of marching soldiers after dressing I [s]tood. upon the great steps to view this martial but melancholy marching. this street was the great thouroghfare of the Niger in to the West and here was passing the principal van of the First Division of the Army in their retreat from Verdopolis. Infantry. 12. broad with advanced Bayonets. went sweeping by. the. Colours of the Rejiments. fluttering overhead in the morning wind. and the great Rolling Drums and. fifes and. trumpets timing their footsteps. as each Rejiment passed on fresh ones succeded and Banner behind banner rose over their heads in the distance. untill those countless crimson flags. seemed doomed. never to end. one swept in to the foreground instantly another rose in the background and then another and another untill counting became confusion. I in a while returned into the House and while sitting at Breakfast I could still hear the sweeping tread of footmen and the continual Music of the Bands. Ere I arose again however the sound had lost that majestic sameness and had become. tortured. crashing and confused. I guessed the cause and stepped to the window this was the Cavalry. and it being about to conclude was now mixed with Cannon and waggons in almost inextricable confusion. the dregs and refuse of the march. Shouting and cursing and. blows and kicking and neighing and railling echoed through the place in a perfect chaos of sounds and when I left the Street at noon all the tumult had not in the least subsided

From my house I passed to Braveys Hotel. it was filled with Gentlemen taking the. Coaches to the 3 great Capitals. Sneachis Parrys and Rosses Glasstowns and. in short every cheif Inhabitant of Verdopolis was hurrying from the devoted city as soon and as quickly as he could. consternation and. anger seemed to pervade every mind. And the Trade commerce and. Buisness of every kind in spite of all the Elrington proclamations at length had come to a dead. still stand.

During all the Day the forces continued to evacuate the city. and at Night fall all it was understood. 70000 men were full on the Road for Alnwick and the west country. where Pro Tempore the seat of Government was to be fixed.

Jan 2. 1834. Still Did the course of the Government continue. this Morning Douro. departed. at the head of his Division and. Thornton. only waited with 30000 men untill the Council and State prisoners should remove that he might cover the rear. all the western roads are choked. with. Troops Cannon waggons proceeding to their Alnwick quarters. Carriages Equipage Tresure and people flying from the Approaching Tempest. The Great Families are all lodged in their farthest country Houses. This Afternoon I saw long. lines of Carriages Rolling down the western streets containing under a powerful guard of Cavalry the persons and suites of the Kings Minsters and Aristocrat Noblemen. All the council had left save Lord Elrington who remained alone to superintend the closing of this Second Act of our Tremendous Tradgedy. and truely his capacious and Experienced Mind was exerted. to its utmost to calm manage and reconcile the horrid chaos of confusion into which his country and Faction were falling The City was fast lapsing into a state of dissolution and stealing robberys and riots. had crowded thick. upon us during this week.

At. 10 o clock. at night Elringtons Carriage drove off. and General Thornton with the rearguards of the Army and an immense. crowd of. Inhabitants with their Effects began to leave the city. I. myself I should have informed my Readers though an Officer in the Army had recieved so many discouraging hints as to taking my place with my Rejiment that I felt myself bound. to protect my own intrests and therefore. this Night. I accompanied by my family and household. also left Verdopolis for my seat. near Ross's Town. Left it to be. a prey to the. ruthless Spoiler.!

On January. 4.th. I with a crowd of other noble and. respectable. Fugitives. arrived At Rosses Glasstown and calmly sat down to watch the turn events should take. I must here breifly describe the present state of our Affairs.

In the large town of Alnwick.[18] and in the country all around it. lying from 50 to 60 miles West of Verdopolis. lay quartered. as it were under arms about. 130000 soldiers. forming what has so often been called the Army of Verdopolis. and here too was established. the Temporary Government of the Six omnipotent usurpers. along with their Noble and Kingly prisoners. All waiting till the Dog should seize the bone and till they could seize their stick.

IN Verdopolis and in the. suburbs all round. it. lay. firmly holding on. The French Emperor Napoleon. with his Army of 230000. men. resting for a moment in the splendour of the Regent of Africa untill they should be ready to march follow up the blow they had given. and quash intirely the forces of the Glasstowners. Over all Verdopolis these bloodsuckers. the French Commanders

---

[18] Alnwick, a parish town in the county of Northumberland, is dominated by Alnwick Castle, a walled fort of Norman origin. Alnwick Castle became the principal seat of the Percy family (the Dukes of Northumberland) according to the legend which Sir Walter Scott both recounts and refutes in *Tales of a Grandfather*. According to this legend, when Malcolm III of Scotland invaded England, Robert de Mowbray brought him the keys of Alnwick Castle suspended on his lance. Handing them from the wall, he thrust his lance into the King's eye, whence he received the honorary name "Pierce-eye."

For Branwell's history of Alexander Percy, Earl of Northangerland, see **The Life of Field Marshal, The Right Honourable Alexander Percy**, in Volume II.

had. spread their talons and. griping extortion threats and. cruelty. was exerted to the utmost on the defenceless citizens.

As for myself being not a spectator as heretofore of the scenes and Actions for some time to come I shall just proceed briefly and historically to discribe these in order as they came on.

While the French with their Emperor were fastening on the vitals of the Devoted city the Council of Six. exerted themselves to their utmost. to. conciliate their sovereigns to raise the Glasstowncountrys and. bring to bear an overpowering and irresistible weight of Numbers. To this End they in the first place by what means I am not fully aware. after earnest deliberation. brought the Kings over to the side of Energy. And their Majestys seeing the necessitys of their common country consented to <waive> for a while all cause of distrust and quarrel. and agreed in common with the <reviled> Nobles to do their utmost to aid the cause of the Army and. the country To this End while His Grace of Wellington stayed at Alnwick to aid. the forces. there. Sneachi departed for his land Parry His and Ross for his there to raise instant reinforcements and despatch them to Alnwick. while. the other Kings collected their rousing people. Ross. I myself saw enter His city and from that Hour. the public departments were put in motion activity prevailed every where Drums beat Recruiets poured in and ere a weeks end. 40000 men were dispatched under Prince Admiral Tut. Ross to the general Head quarters. The other states were acting in the same manner and I understood that the Alnwick country was one huge Barracks of Military and Baggage.

Here let me speak a few words upon the state of the people the inhabitants of Verdopolis And the Glasstown countrys they may have appeared under a wrong light to some of my readers they may have seemed like the people of other countrys cowardly passive sluggish and selfish The Glasstowners are not so. they through the whole of this war showed that. voicless courage scorn of suffering which they have always shown. but with these qualitys were mingled. a blind adherance to respective factions a neglect of general welfare. in seeking. party aggrandizement. and a disposition to let injuries pass to harbour up a competent revenge. True In the East and in the City they were now like Europeans. trampled on threatened. and Extorted from by their Enimy. and true they suffered it and seemed as if they could not save themselves. true also that it required active measures to rouse them in the provinces and countrys I grant all this but I declare that the reson for their conduct was. that. being determined each soul to adhere to his faction not to stir without it an unhappy hesitation came over and possessed them. and when the french Emperor had overwhelmed. squeezed and. scattered them. their minds were drowned. in the one sole thought of coming revenge Then and not till then would the Army look to the Aristocrats or Moderates or the Aristocrats and Moderates strive to aid the Army. but when they did all consent to pull together we shall see the effect they produced.

To proceed. Elrington Douro and the Council still though the Kings and Noblemen were now freed and reinstated kept a firm hold on their power and resolutely refused the reinstal[at]ion of a Ministry all Matters were yet transacted by them all power of the soldiers was lodged in their Hands. Night and day they were engaged in issuing orders demanding Money. forcing loans and receiving soldiers and like the store of a Miser the troops were gradually swelling up to a tremendous number. Matters were preparing to commence the march on Verdopolis and. to let loose the floodgates. for the stream On January. 8th. The liberated Marquis of Fidena received the command of. 50000 men and instantly commenced a forced. march North East to his fathers Territorys to repell the attacks which the great masses of Barbarians acting in conjunction with Napoleon were menacing on the Frontiers.

On the same Day I at length received orders instantly to join my Rejment stationed at Alnwick. With joy and eagerness I obeyed the proposal I was anxio[u]s indeed to observe the aspect of things in that quarter. And. after taking leave of Ross Town I. mounted my Horse and followed by a trusty servant. hurried to join my Rejment. during the whole of my rapid journey. of 300 miles. the roads were filled with evidences of war and Arms. but it was not till Noon of the 3^d Day of my Set out that. I. entered upon. this "Theatre of accumulation" as Mr Warner termed it Then. we had gained the sumit of a long cultivated swell which looks down from the great height upon all the great cultivated. field of. Alnwick. that flourishing town lay. about 10 miles before me on the Horizon. and from it to me streched wide lawn Feilds woods. slopes and. hills. all undulating along. up to the ridge over which my pathway lay. the district is populous and villiages and houses. spotted ever[y] road and. direction of the country the houses and parks of the <North> Glasstowners ornamented the scene in many points and above. all. that Great Building of Alnwick Hall with its immense and overwhelming grounds. spread out along the whole side of a slope plain and. the outskirts of the town announced. the Noble second country residence of. Lord Viscount Elrington. In that huge Hall were collected the 6 Omnipotents the Duke of Wellington and the Family of his Lordship. of Elrington Square. toward it I lent my course. and. the feilds trampled and perfectly destitute of cattle. the potatoes. clean torn from the ground the hedges cut down for firewood. the thousand footprints on the roads the. crowds of cannon and Baggages. the. doors of every cottage. showing a scarlet coat and. the glittering of arms the crowds of soldiers filling the street of every hamlet and villiage. the rooms of every little Inn crowded with redcoats the stables filled with horses the. numbers. of little boys with rush caps. thornstick swords and ragged uniforms. the. blast of Bugle from every market place. the. air when you stopped for a moment. coming charged with distant music and reports of fire arms. all these and a thousand such incidents spoke strongly of war and. confusion. only an Army present could have created the confusion I now beheld.

We continued our road. untill evening then we had advanced as far as Chillburn. were we were blocked up for half an hour. by the march of 9000. recruits from Sneachis land. a stirring spectacle. as these succession of Rejments blazing in new uniform tired and harrassed though they were pushed. on toward the town and rendezvous.

Darkness soon drew on and then a new spectacle. presented itself. at once round the horizon every common and. eminence glittered with the light of a hundred lines of Bivouack fires and. from every point of Heaven the red haze glared ominously benea[t]h the sky of Night. I. avoided Alnwick itself through which on account. of the. blocked. up state of the streets owing to the pressure of Military I understood it would be next to impossible to pass. I therefore s[t]ruck up one of the park gates of Alnwick Hall. and arrived at the Building about. 10 at Night this seat was perfectly crow[d]ed with. Officers and Generals and. the capacious stables hardly afforded space for our two solitary Horses. I was shown on alighting into the. Great Hall. which burst upon [me] like. a vast mass of. lights and purple and scarlet and gold. there were present his Grace of Wellington. Lord Elrington THE Marquis (par excellence) Mr Warner. and a crowd of Generals and Officers. with. Lady. Percy. Lady Elrington Honble Miss Percy. and. 1 or 2 distinguished visitors from some of the Noble Residences round. from some converstion I had with Elrington and Douro. I found that round Alnwick there was now collected. a force of. 190000 men. I had been st[r]uck on entering the Hall with its unusual splendour and the high aspect of the entertainment. I happened to ask his Lordship. "When will the forces march forward.". "To morrow. this is the farewell feast. Sir John to morrow." I felt cold enough the crisis was. drawing nigh.

Next morning at earliest Dawn of light. I was on horseback. and at the head of my Rejment. galloping over the roads. on our way to Verdopolis the van of the Army in which I was. left. the Alnwick. country about Noon so that I did not see the. wild uproar of confusion which must have heralded the exit of of. 200000 men from its towns and villiages. we the van under. General Castlereagh pushed on till nightfall to. Warden.[19] 30 miles from Verdopolis. Here a message arrived requiring us to Halt immediatly and quarter.

Next day. Jan. 14.th the usual tones of martial music. awoke me from my slumber. Elringtons Divishion were passing through the town. to the attack of Verdopolis 60000 strong His Lordship was himself there and. by his impatience and threatning the men were pushed on at a prodigious rate. He alighted at my Inn where I had to receive him. he said "I intend to charge through the streets myself. I must bear the heavey shot as well as I can. Douro has urged me to it he would have had this buisness himself but the Duke convinced him it would not suit his inexperience—Im. quite knocked up—why these soldiers they dont move at all (he was looking from the window. the men were crowding on as quick as the[y] could do) Hang them I must go and hasten them." He left the room I could shortly after hear his imperious voice raised amid the storm of confusion without. I did not see him any more. at Evening his servants in Hall the Inn with his horses &c.

For 2 days till. Jan. 16[th.] we stayed in Warden witnessing the filing through Army untill the evening of this day the rear. under Gen Thornton as well as and accompanied by His Grace the Duke of Wellington arrived. and

---

[19] A town in Northumberland.

quartered in the country round. At midnight while I was at my supper. I heard the church Bells clang out a ringing a great Band burst playing and. shots and volleys cracked through the town as if all there were seized with madness. in the Inn there was no one to accquaint me with the reason of this I hurried to the Dukes headquarters there I learnt that that morning Lord Elrington and the Marquis of Douro had. made their entry into Verdopolis. they had brought out all their forces drawn them toward the city and begun battering in real <grim> ernest hereupon Napoleon who had prepared for such a movement as he liked not Verdopolis for fighting ground had withdrawn his troops on to the east country and firmly concentrated himself there. Elrington and. Douro's troops charged forward in to the city with little resistance. seized 2000 prisoners but little cannon or stores this the emperor had. conveyed away. Still though a great step was gained this event was no defeat of Napoleon

The Drums in Warden beat to arms and. ere two hours elapsed I was with my rejment and the whole rear of the Army comprehending his Grace and General Thornton full on our way for Verdopolis.

Here I arrived on the morning of Jan 17. I directly repaired to my House. in Western Square. the French had visited it it was clean gutted

Jan. 18. this morning the Council had a secret meeting After which. Thornton's Division. 90000 men. were. all got under arms and commenced their march out of the City there was no time for public rejoicings or feasting in Verdopolis on the return of our Army Every man was too closly engaged. in looking to himself. the troops to warmly buisied in the tremendous buisness of combat to spend a thought upon minor considerations. All understood that these gallant Fellows on their exit from the city were to plunge into instant. battle. their General was about to proceed with them their object was to force the french a league or two back to give all free scope for the great game about to be played. I saw them passing along the streets and till evening heard nothing farther.

About six o clock I was riding along a street. near the Bridge over the. Guadima and about 2 miles from the eastern walls. the wind blew from that quarter and on passing a street opening up in that direction at once the thunder of. cannonry struck on my ear. it was. perhaps. 6 miles distant was hoarse and continued. and among the thousands who stood listning to its dreadful thunder. not a soul but prayed for the defeat of. its producers.

When after an hour or two I returned. through the. stripped. and gutted streets to the center of the city I was met by Mr Montmorenci who requested me to accompany him to a meeting of the council gladly I acceded and we repaired to the Home Office where we found standing at a great table. Warner Castlereagh. Fergusson Harrison. and several other. Generals the Duke of Wellington stood at a window Elrington and Douro. walked together conversing round the room. Every one seemed engaged about. his own buisness. and the papers &c piled on the table were intirely unattended to till. at last a General was announced. General Thornton entered covered with dust. but. looking <hearty> and Homemade as ever. all eagerly greeted him. Elrington and Douro. walked up to Him the Duke turned round from the window to him. He himself. Took of his

Hat passed his Coat Cuff over it and. after wiping his forehead with his
Handcercheif began.

"Hay well I thought I never should get back again we had what I call now
desperate work. howsever my lads. and me. did it bravely. why. we just marched
on along 3 roads. at a quickish jig or so till. we came up with an advancing
corps of french under some of them. villainous <elusive> scoundrels they gave
fire I made no more ado but. clapped my Bayonet and we lead forward. why then
they did the same and we fairly came to a <tug> afore we guessed ought at all.
now. this was scarce fair and it cost us some. brave lads and some. precious line
why after 3 charges and. the matter of happen. 1500. killed or so it was as much
as we could do to hurry them off over the feilds and on to ward the main of the
of the Frenchmen. now My Lads and myself. why we you know formed a great
semicircle of the matter of a mile or more just as you adivised us and chalked out
for us we kept advancing steadily. under a hellish pop of fire from many bushes
and walls and the like as the country could afford we had our work out Ill
promise you." (Elrington) "Cut short Thornton"—

I we were cut short. but how'sever we made on till we came to the French
lines about Dusk. and then it got to clear killing amang us. The French let out
all along their front such a storm of shot as forced us back on to our pos[i]tion.
before. hand. and then as if this would do we had to bear up against such a charge
of Cavalry as. I never yet heard rattle over ground but howsever me. and General.
Bobbadil and General. Ghraham and tothers we stood our ground like so many.
lads. as we were. why we kept place then. and for aught I think weve got it now.
Were making out lists of the. killed and so on I should think. they come up near
to. the matter of 4000. I left Bobbadil in command. at Girnington. the quarters
and have come back myself. just. to tell truely whate happened."

Wellington "Well done General."!

Douro "A Brave Lad Thornton."!

Montmorenci "O Rare Witkin."!

Warner "Hes done well."

Elrington "To long. too long" Thornton wheres. Bobbadil."

"Why at. Girnington."

"Castlereagh go. and see how things stand take horse."

"As to that My Lord. I must first consult.—"

"Castlereagh take horse."

Castlereagh. spit into the fire. sipped his wine and danced out of the Apartment.

Douro "Well Elrington whats taken you now."

"Douro mind your own affairs. He has not done enough."

Omnes "Elrington! not enough."—

"He. should have driven them farther.—it was not my plan."

Wellington   "Well my lord if you expect to much I pity you!
dissapointment must ensue"

"The troops ought to push out to night. they should. strike on the french
and butcher them all"

Warner "what Sir and without consideration—I wont"

"Who said I wont"

I did"
"Did you what do you mean.?"
Douro. "Upon my honour this wont do. Elrington are you crazy.?"
Molineaux. "Realy pray now.!"
"Aye Ive a good mind to pray now"
Douro "Do pray." with a twang.
"Shall I."
S'death. "Eees." from a corner.
"Volo I will."
This singular Nobleman instanty knelt down at a chair turned his eyes to heaven clasped his hands and <while> a heavenly pensiveness. at once diffused itself over his stern. countenance he began with a doleful low and. melodious twang
"Oh—may we be saved.—may we all be saved. (Sdeath—may we be saved). saved to life everlasting saved to ever lasting life. (Mont. just so) Oh Grace.—oh Grace. come down upon us. (S. come.) (Mont come) Oh Grace come down upon us give me the Spirit give me thy Spirit grant that my soul my heart my mind. may be centered. all in thee. Oh. we are dark. (M. we are) we are dark. enlighten us enlighten us. set us on fire. inflame our Souls our reason—our sense.—give us faith. faith to remove mountains give us love—love a holy a godly love. and godly zeal and godly fervour and. a happy living and a triumphant dying we are dead now oh. we are dead now. (Sdeath. we are dead now). Oh save us. save us. revive us raise us. oh. save us. save thy lambs save thy sheep. save they lambs. (Thornton. "It would be better If he told you how to save. your Hams") Sinner come down Sinner come down down on your knees pray pray. consume oh consume consume in the hottest flames. of refinement of purifying. Oh. come forth come forth thrice refined. come then bride of the lamb. come. my spirit sayeth come. (S & M. Come) May we be saved may we be all saved. (M. Aye.). all saved. Oh. weare. saved we are all saved. (S. just so) May. thy blessing descend on us. we are now free. Sin no more no you cannot sin. You may sin but in you it shall be imputed righteousness." (rising standing erect and his Eyes flashing.") We are lighted in dreadful times for now my freinds wickedness is turned thrice wicked. and Godliness is. turned thrisce that The lamb did I say the lamb. the light goeth about you like a roaring lion[20] (Douro He's wrong there") yes the light is not a beam that cheereth it is a flame that burneth I tell ye that this world and yourselfes and myself and. Heaven and Hell and Earth and all around them and within them must shortly die. For how can ye. live except ye die. and how can the grain grow except to perish and where is the ressurection save in the death of the body and where Oh were is the. Heaven save with the death of the soul.[21] I will say more of this at present my time is short. to morrow Morning. 3 o clock at dawn I will exhort ye aye as ye love yourselves I will teach ye at the villiage of Girnington. I will teach ye how to die.!"

---

[20] See 1 Peter 5:8
[21] See p. 434, n. 17.

Elrington hastily turned away and left the room. all present burst out in to a fit of. laughter.

Wellington "Madness."

Warner "Blasphemy."

Montmorency. "The Old Way"

Thornton "nought and waur nor nought"

Douro. "Well done thou good and faithful servant.[22] well Ill hear him Ill go to him now. Ill hear him at Girnington."

The Marquis half. smiling half serious also left the room.

For 3 day farther untill. January. 21. little of importance was done. For believe it postievely during the whole of this while. the two greatest leaders of the Army. Elrington and Douro. the first cleanly mad. the last half so. were going about. through city and country preaching and praying and exhorting untill the whole city began to be furious the whole Army distracted Montmorency with Old Sdeath accompanied them in their. frantic howlings. But. meanwhile the Duke of Wellington Gen Thornton and Mr Warner were forced to take matters into their own hands. the Army was fast concentrating eastward of the city and now. If any one. as thousands did. stepped up the hight of the towers of St Michiels he would see. East of him. Two vast semicircular lines of fires extending. parrarell to each other. along the whole Horizon from North to South. The inner one. that of the Glasstown Armys—running N. and S. from Scarton to Girnington 13 miles. the outer. from. Northangerland. to Zamorna. 23 miles. and constantly the bright light of Rockets the flash of Cannonry. broke on the. Fixedness the. crack of Musketry and. long echoing roll of Artillery on the silence of these. anxious nights. At last January. 22. Douro and Elrington seemed to wake from their madness. after a long and anxious conference with their coadjutors and. a hurried survey of Affairs. they ordered from the city all the forces remaining in the city out—at noon that day left it themselves.

Now then. all Hearts beat all ears waited. at length had dawned the great the important day. and now on the feilds of Zamorna and Northangerland was to be decided the fate of Africa. For myself I declare I will not give a general account of. movements and operations but only a particular one of those things I felt and saw.—All this day Verdopolis was in an uproar. at Evening I left it being by Elrington peremptorily ordered to my Rejment. (I rep[e]at I will only relate what I saw) I found this Rejment at Girnington in the centre. of our line. it was dusk. and night was drawing. a message arrive[d] from Lord Elrington and my. corps was instanty marched forward on to a common in the vicinity of the french this we took possession of and Bivouacked upon. the evacuated villiage was filled with <cold> troops. I wrapt in my watch coat. lay down at a fire on the wide common. the fires of my soldiers round me in the foreground those of the french. spread along before me in the Background. over head in the black blue sky the great golden Moon marched calmly and coldly our. there was a frosty feeling in the air and its coldness and keenness. carried distinctly all. the numerous sounds.

---

[22] See p. 416, n. 5.

which eternally broke on the ear of night. what to me aided the solemnity of the scene was the mystery in which the operations of the army were to me wrapt up in and the uncertainty attending my ignorance of them. I was about the center of our line and. could command a good view of matters as they went on though great part of each forces. were at rest yet still from the sounds I heard it was evident in some places a hot combat was being carried on Here underneath this moon and with in a space. of 10 miles square lay. 400000. armed men and 2000 peices of Artillery about to scatter round the death and horror on the coming morn. the greatest Generals the Mightiest Abilitys the noblest soldiers on earth. were just about to try their mutual force and power. Our Forces mustered perhaps. 180000 men and were divided into two grand divisions the south opposed. to. Zamorna under the Marquis of Douro the North opposed to Northangerland. under Lord Elrington to this I belonged. around me this night all seemed quiet but the. constant beat and swelling roar. of cannonry announced that all was not so. elsewhere. all that night did that hoarse thunder. keep up its note now in the south then in the north then near then far off. yet still. unceasing. and. the same. about Dawn my fellows and myself were <roused> by an advancing and. sweeping sound behind us. directly therre. passed by long columns of armed men trains of Artilery and great bodies of Cavalry Elrington was there mounted on Horseback. hatted and gloved as usual The Division passed on full to the front onto the plain country befor the French. They were intended for a charge. they might number 40000 men while they were passing. a tremendous sound broke up on the the South and crack over crack. burst over burst. spoke loudly of the. stern fire of the Marquis of Douro most probably he had charged. at once upon the French on getting his troops on the ground the sounds of his onset waxed louder but were almost drowned in the pouring by of the troops around me. I remained with my men on the common untill orders came from Lord Elrington then. I was. instead of being ordered forward commanded back to my old position in the rearward villiage of Girnington my men. sullenly obeyed this command. during that day though I was farther removed from the scene of actual warfare. the sounds of it were stronger. and sterner all the country seemed in an earthquake. in a while. crowds of wounded and fugitives. began to arrive at my station. and. the. streets and feilds were choked with horses and carts and wounded. and. exhaustied men.

At length. this afternoon I received orders to join Elrington on the scene of action. this was a stirring moment for me. our Kettle Drums sounded to horse. we hurried on amid a wild labyrinth of counter marching troop till we reached at length the very feild of combat. I hurriedly cast my eyes. around. there were. stretched the stern lines of military the great rows of cannon and. heaps of killed wounded. Horsemen stores arms. and. Artillery. covered the space between us. and the French who occupying all the opposite space of feilds and ground. were wrapped in a constant cloud of smoke from their batterys. Elrington I saw on horseback. at a little distance cooly conversing with a circle of his staff. I direc[t]ly received. sufficient hints of my dangerous situation the balls flew thick around me. and two horses and a man fell just by my side. A staff officer. came up. "Flower you are to charge" I obeyed. off we galloped. along the grou[n]d

over every obstacle swords waving men huzzaing around. me. grim faces looking
bayonets fixed smoke bursting before me.—some of my after experience is lost
in the wild uproar and hideous dangers of actual combat—the charge which I
made did not prove effectual. fresh troops were brought up. fresh advances made.
But to me all was lost. in the. terrific thunder of the surrounding guns. At length
as Night fell on I. saw Elrington dismount from his steed spring on to a fresh
one. draw two pistols and turning round becon to the black crowds of cavalry
ranged away in the smoke behind him He s[t]ruck his spurrs into his horse. of
they flew and. with the shock of an Earthquake broke upon the stern ridges of the
foe. amid the firing shouting hacking and charging I could see the French give
way and when at 9 at night General Thornton arrived on the feild with a
reinforcement of Bayonet and charged unhesitatingly upon the Enimy they fairly
gave way and were rolled back in hideous rout and confusion.

At this moment just as Lord Elrington was entering by s[t]orm the villiage
of Northanger land—A messenger arrived from Douro demanding instant
reinforcement. Several Rejments of Cavalry were dispatched To Zamorna mine
among the number. we reached that feild of Battle. at midnight but between
moon. and firelight there was light in plenty all Zamorna was in a blaze and
shells were bursting an[d] cannon roaring everywhere round it. amid the storm of
confusion my Eyes fixed at once on the Marquis of Douro. mounted on a
splendid charger.[23] Decorated with. Helmet plume and. all the gorgeous
ornaments of war. seeming himself from his flashing eye and. triumphant
countenance the Genius of the scene around him. his sabre he held in his hand
unsheathed that it had often found use. that. day and Elringtons pistols [were]
<found> more smoky than it was bloody. when I saw him he was conversing
with Mr Warner who mounted on a gallant hunter was leading on his followers
to the Attack. "Oh Douro this work is dreadful." "Yes Warner. Napoleon keeps
[firm] and from grasp but I have him another charge and <thus> lead your Foot
Gentlemen (turning gracefully and bowing to the Cavalry around.) "Gentlemen.
follow me. straight for Zamorna. He waved his Sabre and was lost to me amid
the onpouring of a thousand resistless horses. I was amid the hindmost rejements
and there long had to halt. for I could not get on there was evidently a terrific
combat before me and No discharge of firearms was heard it was all charging
clashing desperate and silent fighting our hind Horses we had. so strong was the
press to rein backward and backward till I feared we were going to fly. at once
then A tremendous shout arose in front all were hurled forward and the way was
clear. The French were in rout in clean rout. and through the Blazing Zamorna.
the Marquis of Douro. thundred with his troops resistlessly upon their rear. over
roads and feilds and Rivulets and marshes. He bore them fighting or flying in a
certain overthrow. There is no safty for the French now. and. all are blent. in a
great mass of confusion none can turn to combat for

---

23 See Branwell's poem, "To the horse black Eagle," in Volume II and in
Neufeldt PBB, 334.

"who fights finds death and death finds him who fly"[24]

There never was a scene as dreadful. positivly Douro alowed nothing to remain behind. him. I happened to stopp. to gaze at the scene when he who had for moment been delayed at the villiage passed by. He saw me still seized hold of my Horse reins and with a "Forward Sir" a[f]ter striking me with his sabre tore away himself. Far before me.

My Rejment soon being fatigued out. returned from the retreat to their quarters around the first lines of Girnington. and gradually the forces of Lord Elrington. came on returning. from the Battle while those of the Marquis of Douro were still pursuing the flying and routed French. we had gained a complete Victory along the whole of that extended Line. and the stern blow of Percy. the firey. dart of Wellesly had effectualy. struck and. shattered 200000. men.

---

[24] Dryden's translation of the *Aeneid*, Book II, p. 159 in the copy owned by the Brontës. See p. 274, n. 13.

Glossary of Glass Town/Angria Persons and Place-names

Abercorn, James, Marquis of: A member of the Council of Elysium, Rougue's secret society. He also sees military action during the War of Encroachment under command of Elrington and Douro, being recognized, along with Molineaux, as a "reckless, iron hearted wild bloodied young office[r]."

Acrofcroomb: A city and province of Ashantee, home to a tribe of cannibals ruled by ten brothers. After its inhabitants attack Glass Town, the city is razed by the Twelves in an act of revenge.

Alnwick: A large town about fifty miles west of Verdopolis which becomes the temporarary seat of Government after Verdopolis is evacuated during the final stages of the War of Encroachment.

Alnwick Hall: The "Noble second country residence" of Rougue Elrington in Sneachiesland, this "huge Hall" becomes home to the Council of Six during their evacuation from Verdopolis in the War of Encroachment. It is the ancestral home of the Percy family and the Earl of Northangerland.

Ancient Britons: According to tradition, "some thousands of years" before the Twelves arrived in Ashantee (West Africa), twelve men of gigantic size from Britain, and twelve from Gaul came to the area, but after years of continual war, they returned to their respective countries.

Aornos: A tall mountain near Glass Town, reputedly home to the Genii and therefore regarded as the "Olympus" of the Glass Town Confederacy.

Aristocrats: A political party, also known as the Exclusives, "consisting of all men of Rank wealth and standing headed by the 12s." It counts among its supporters the old Earl of Elrington and the Marquis of Fidena. Although the ruling party of Glass Town, it represents only the interests "of money." During the War of Encroachment, when it refuses to lend financial support to the army, thereby exposing the Glass Town Confederacy to the threat of military defeat, it is ousted by force, and replaced by "the Council of 6."

Ashantee: Located on the African Gold Coast, identified with Guinea; Ashantee consists of a series of countries extending 1700 miles from east to west, and 500 miles from north to south. To the east of Ashantee lies the desert; to the west the Atlantic; to the south the Gulf of Guinea; and to the north the Gibbel Kumri Mountains (the Mountains of the Moon). It has been chosen by the Chief Genii to be "the seat of all Grandeur Fame and Glory."

Badey (Bady) Dr. Alexander Hume: One of the Twelves. A large "exceedingly ugly" man who dissects corpses stolen by his accomplices, but an excellent surgeon; father-in-law to Douro.

Barras: A leading member of the "Faction du Manege" who works to bring about the downfall of the Emperor Napoleon. He is later imprisoned in the French State Prison by Napoleon for his part in the attempted coup d'état.

Bellingham, James: A "rich English banker" who travels through the Glass Town territories with the Marquis of Douro, Charles Wellesly, and Young Soult, and whose escapades during Glass Town's revolutionary times are narrated in **Letters From An Englishman.** As a result of approving a £13 million loan to the Glass Town government, intended to finance its counter-revolutionary effort, he is imprisoned and threatened with death by the leader of the insurrectionary forces, Rougue. He later plays an important role in Zamorna's Angrian Wars, supporting him in the way that the Rothchilds supported Wellington's Peninsular Wars. See Alexander CB, I, Part I, 213.

Bernadotte: Insurrectionist against the Emperor Napoleon, and one of the leading members of the "Faction du Manege." After successfully (but only temporarily) ousting Napoleon from office, he is elected Chief Consul of France, and assumes the title of His Highness of the New Republic of Frenchyland. Upon Napoleon's successful counterattack, he is imprisoned in the State Prison.

Bobbadil, Thomas Beresford: As Major General of the Army of Wellingtonsland, he maintains order at the Hustings during the heated Glass Town elections. During the War of Encroachment he serves as Brigadier General, placed in charge of 8,000 men.

Branii Hills: A vast mountain range to the north of Sneaky's Land, "savage and barren"; home to the Highlanders.

Bravey's Inn (later Hotel): named after William Bravey, its corpulent landlord and one of the original Twelves, it is an important meeting place for the Young Men and for Glass Town politicians and literati.

Bud, Captain John: An eminent Glass Town political writer and historian, author of **The History of the Young Men** and other works, the greatest prose writer of early Glass Town; a pseudonym of Branwell, and a friend of Lord Charles Wellesley. See Alexander CB, I, 126-27.

Bud, Sergeant: Son of Captain Bud, "a sharp thin Lawyer like looking young man," sometime publisher and bookseller, who executes a writ on behalf of the Duke of Wellington requesting the presence of Alexander Rougue before the court of Admiralty to answer charges of piracy. He also acts as Government prosecutor in the Glass Town trial of five men convicted of robbing a Government courier of certain Government Dispatches. See Alexander CB, I, 128.

Carey: A member of the Council of Elysium, Rougue's secret society. He is entrusted by Rougue with minor charges, participates in the fleecing of Castlereagh, and brawls with O'Connor.

Cashna Quamina: The king of the Ashantees at the time of the Twelves' arrival. A "mild old king" who trades and communicates "amicably" with the new Glass Town settlers until his death, he is succeeded by his son, Sai Tootoo Quamina.

Castlereagh, Frederic (Viscount Castlereagh): A young and wealthy visitor to Verdopolis from Ireland, he is initiated into the secret society, Elysium. Although he believes himself the political protégé of Rougue and Montmorency, their real intention is "to fleece him of all his property then cast him off." Castlereagh loses his estate in gambling debts, but when he subsequently rescues Lady Julia Montmorenci from an unwelcome marriage to Lord Thornton Wilkin Sneaky, he is granted the post of Secretary of the Foreign Office (worth £50,000) by the Marquis of Douro, and subsequently marries Lady Julia. He later takes an active part in the War of Encroachment, distinguishes himself in battle, becomes a member of the Council of Six and subsequently an Angrian minister and close friend of Zamorna.

Caversham, Viscount (later Baron) Frederic: A Colonel in the Dragoons during the War of Encroachment, and an associate of Alexander Percy, who murdered Caversham's father in a duel at Percy Hall.

Cheeky, Alexander: One of the Twelves; a surgeon on board the "Invincible" and one of the founders of Glass Town. He is renowned for his courage: "the most stout hearted man in the ship."

Coomassie: The Ashantee capital, located by "a deep and rapid river" near Rossendale Hill. The city of 500,000 inhabitants is destroyed in an attack by the Twelves. Later visited by the author of **Letters from an Englishman**, it is described as a majestic ruin, "desolate and inhabited by tigers and owls."

Crashey, Captain Butter: One of the Twelves, and Captain of the "Invincible." One hundred and forty years old, he is a "mighty and venerable patriarch," the oldest and wisest of the Twelves and Glass Town arbiter, possessed of benevolence and "more than mortal wisdom." It is Crashey who first advises the Twelves to elect a king in order to "attain unity" of vision and purpose through effective leadership.

De Lisle, Sir Edward: An eminent Glass Town portrait painter patronized by both Earl St Clair and the Marquis of Douro.

Democrats: Glass Town's revolutionary political faction, headed by Alexander Rougue, and "consisting of the lower orders poachers rare apes and &c with various Dissipated broken or Ambitious men."

Dundee, George (later Sir John Martin Dundee): A popular artist of "the sublime," associated with the nineteenth-century painter, John Martin.

Elrington, Dowager Countess: The mother of Rougue. A "stately Old Lady" with a "Most majestic and almost regal deportment." She is one of the few persons to command "the least glimmer of respect and attention" from Rougue.

Elrington Hall: The Percy family residence in Verdopolis.

Elrington, Lady Zenobia: The proud, haughty daughter of the old Earl of Elrington, she is first attracted to the Marquis of Douro; their relationship is a complex one: they admire each other's mental and physical abilities, but when she tries to become a rival for Marian Hume, their relationship cools. But this "Majestic Lady with fine Italian features" is also admired by Rougue/Percy who, after capturing her on his pirate ship, marries her. Although largely excluded from her husband's illicit activities, she maintains a prestigious Salon, and devotes much of her time to reading classical authors "in the original," engaging in literary discussions, and writing letters. She is also known for her pride and choler, and her dress indicative of a decadent background—see Alexander CB, I, 286, n. 2.

Elysium or "Paradise of Souls": A Secret Society in Verdopolis (also known as "Pandemonium"). Members must be worth over £5000 a year, be over the age of fifteen, and must have slain a man. Rougue serves as its President, and the Marquis of Douro as its vice-president; its champions include Pigtail; and its members include Montmorency, John Flower, Castlereagh, and others. The club's main activities appear to consist of drinking, gambling, and brawling.

Faction du Manege: A secret society in France dedicated to the overthrow of the Emperor Napoleon. The Society is given financial support by an unamed faction in Glass Town, presumably Rougue's.

Fidena: A "noble city" of "tall monuments and shining domes" and capital of Sneachiesland, which Rougue targets as a strategic key to victory in the Revolutionary War: "Gain Fidena and you will gain Africa."

Fidena, Marquis of: See Sneaky, John Augustus.

Flower, Captain John (later Viscount Richton and Verdopolitan Ambassador to Angria): An eminent scholar in Verdopolis, author of **The Politics of Verdopolis, Real Life in Verdopolis** and other works. Loyal to the Twelves, he stands as a Constitutional candidate, is later appointed Secretary of the War Office, and subsequently plays an active role in the War of Encroachment when he is promoted to the rank of Colonel of Foot Soldiers, and principal Staff Officer to General the Marquis of Fidena. One of Branwell's pseudonyms from 1831-34.

Freetown: A large town of strategic importance during the War of Encroachment: "Gain Freetown," states Sir John Flower, and "the road to Verdopolis is easy."

Gambia: River on which Glass Town is situated.

Genii: The presiding spirits of Ashantee, who assume various guises, and exhibit supernatural powers. The Chief Genii are Talli (Charlotte), Branni (Branwell), Emmi (Emily), and Anni (Anne). Guardians and protectors of the Twelves, they use powers of shape-shifting and transformation to aid the Twelves in times of crisis.

Gifford, John (Professor, R.A.S.): Lawyer and antiquarian, and later Chief Judge of Glass Town; a learned historian whose research aids Captain Bud in writing **The History of the Young Men.**

Glass Town: A confederacy of four kingdoms—Wellingtonsland, Sneachiesland, Parrysland, Rossesland—formed by the Young Men in Ashantee. Its capital is the Great Glass Town, later Verdopolis.

Glasstown Valley: Traversed by the River Niger, the valley consists of "mighty and Fertile" plains which house vast cornfields and "a hundred stately parks and a thousand stately Mansions."

Goat, John James, Esq.: The Under Home Secretary in St Clair's cabinet during the War of Encroachment.

Gordon Mountains: Located one hundred miles from Verdopolis, these mountains are home to "fourscore thousand Africans" who threaten to join forces with the Emperor of France against the Confederacy.

Grenville, Thomas: Speaker in the House of Commons, member of St Clair's Cabinet, and a Major General in the War of Encroachment, taking command of 38,000 men to serve as a force against Marmont's French division.

Guadima: River which flows over the plains of Dahomey and on which Verdopolis is built, site of a great loss of life during the War of Encroachment. Probably based on the River Guadiana in Spain, scene of much action during the Peninsular War.

Guelph, Frederick (King Frederick I): One of the Twelves, he is also the second son of George III of England, the Duke of York. He is later elected first king of Glass Town.

Highlanders: "[D]ark, gigantic savage beings," the Highlanders are descendents of the 42 Regiment of Highlanders who came to Ashantee with the Duke of Wellington. Dressed in plaids, bearskins, and eagle feathers, and wielding "vast clubs" and bows, 70,000 Highlanders descend from the mountains to join Rougue's forces in the revolutionary war. However, because they have no cause but "the sake of fighting," they eventually turn against Rougue's own forces and contribute to the defeat of his army.

Hume, Marian: Daughter of Alexander Hume Bady, first wife of the Marquis of Douro, always presented as "an angel" and an ideal heroine.

Kumriis: Gibbel Kumri or Mountains of the Moon; see Ashantees.

Laury, Ned: Glass Town villain, poacher, and body snatcher; rival of Young Man Naughty; "noted servant of the Marquis of Douro."

Lawyer Tweezy: Counsel for Dick Nose'em etc.; "a keen thorough bred Lawyer . . . of great repute for ability though Honesty had never once been mentioned in conjuction with his name." He is a tool of Rougue Elrington, but after writing a letter to the newspapers hinting at Rougue's illegal activities, he is marked for death by Rougue.

Leaf, John: The Glass Town Thucydides, originally sent from England by Pitt's ministry in 1782 to sue for assistance from the Twelves in the war against Napoleon. He subsequently becomes one of the first historians of Glass Town, keeping records, transcribing speeches, and writing "The Acts of the Twelves." Unfortunately, his history is "much mutilated."

Lofty, Viscount Frederic, Earl of Arundel: a close friend of the Marquis of Douro, an accomplished horseman, and a highly popular General.

Manns and Wamons Isles: A pair of islands "just off the coast of Frenchyland" which belong to the Glass Town Governments. Possession of these islands is demanded by the newly armed Emperor of France, and the War of Encroachment ensues.

Marmont: The French Commander of 30,000 troops which are to move "100 miles south of Verdopolis" in order to keep a footing on the coast, and eventually join forces with the French commander, Massena, in a final push toward Verdopolis.

Massena: Commander of a large French force of 40,000 men which, according to the French plan of action, is to move "nearly 200 miles north of Verdopolis," and from thence attack southward, eventually joining forces with Marmont in a final push against Verdopolis.

Molineaux: A member of the Council of Elysium, Rougue's secret society, and a patron of the boxing ring, who is described as "wild dissipated." Under the command of Elrington and Douro during the War of Encroachment, he is recognized, along with Abercorn, as a "reckless, iron hearted and wild blooded young office[r]."

Montmorency, Hector Matthias Mirabeau: A Verdopolitan nobleman, banker, and "familiar" of Alexander Rougue. He has two daughters, Julia and Harriet. He wishes to arrange a politically advantageous match between Julia and Lord Thornton Wilkin Sneaky, but his daughter eventually marries Castlereagh. He later takes an active role in ousting the ruling Aristocrats during the War of Encroachment, and becomes one of the Council of Six replacing the ousted Ministry.

Montmorency, Lady Julia: A young lady "of 17 or 18" of lively disposition, she is, with her sister, Harriet, a new arrival to Verdopolis. Her father wishes to arrange her marriage with Lord Thornton Wilkin Sneaky, but she is rescued from this fate by Castlereagh who fights a duel on her behalf. She subsequently marries Castlereagh.

Moreau: A General of France, as well as a leading member of the "Faction du Manege," Moreau takes part in the overthrow of the Emperor Napoleon. He visits the Glass Town government, which is impressed with his "pale thoughtful cast of features," but refuses to countenance his demand that the Glass Town government formally recognize the new government of France. Because of this diplomatic trip, he is absent from France when Napoleon regains power, and thus, unlike his co-conspiritors, stays out of prison.

Morely, Thomas Babbicome: Returned as a Constitutional Candidate for Glass Town; he is later made Colonial Secretary; is loyal to the Twelves.

Moulins: A leading member of the "faction du Manege," Moulins is imprisoned along with the faction's other leaders for his part in the unsuccessful overthrow of the Emperor Napoleon.

Murat: During the War of Encroachment, Murat leads a regiment of French horsemen at the Battle of Little Warner against Douro's troops, but despite engaging in courageous personal combat with Thornton, he and his regiment are repulsed. He is killed by a stray rock thrown during the turmoil of battle.

Musselburgh, Lord Viscount: Politically affiliated with the Vacillators, he is also Chancellor of the Exchequer in St Clair's government during the War of Encroachment, and therefore indirectly responsible for the government's withholding of funds from the military during this crisis.

Naughty, "Young Man": Glass Town villain and body snatcher, as well as "champion of the poachers." Of gigantic stature, cruel and ruthless disposition, he is a follower of Rougue Elrington, being entrusted with the command of rebel troops during the revolutionary wars.

O Connor, Arthur: A member of the Council of Elysium, Rougue's secret society, he is also one of Rougue's Colonels. Described as "a mind and person originally of the highest order," he has, however, been "degraded by the use of everything mean and low." His fate is sealed when, in command of Rougue's rebel army, and contrary to Rougue's instructions, he orders a retreat while in a drunken rage, thereby causing the deaths of 30,000 men. Although he attempts to take his own life rather than face a dishonourable execution, he is strung up on the gallows by Rougue's order.

Parry, William Edward: One of the Twelves and King of Parrysland.

Pequena: A strategic location for the defence of Glass Town during the War of Encroachment. It becomes the focus of attack by Napoleon's force of 90,000, and is the site of action between Fergusson and Massena.

Percy Hall: The Percy family residence in Wellington's Glass Town, located in a pastoral region twenty miles east of the city.

Percy, The Honourable Miss Mary Henrietta: The daughter of Rougue Elrington and Lady Mary Henrietta Percy, she has inherited her mother's gentle manners, and is much beloved by her father, Rougue, as well as by the tenantry and local peasants. In addition, she is courted by Glass Town's high society owing to her father's "wealth power and vast consequence," but does not relish this kind of attention, preferring, instead, to discourse with thoughtful souls on literary and philosophical matters. She marries Sir Robert Weever Pelham, like herself, a lover of books and in particular of Byron.

Percy, Lady Mary (Maria): The soft spirit who charmed Percy/Rougue away from his evil genius; after her death Percy becomes a desolate man, his "life and motives utterly perverted."

Pelham, Sir Robert Weever: Coming to Verdopolis from Lancashire, England, after having inherited "vast wealth," he contributes £50,000 to Rougue's political activities, and is returned as a member of Rougue's Democrats party. Upon marriage to Mary Henrietta Percy, he establishes himself as "a principal Glasstowner."

Philosophers Isle: Where the young nobility of Glass Town receive their early schooling and training. Manfred is President of the University on the island.

Pigtail: Champion of the French; 7-9 feet high and very ugly; cattle thief; arrested for selling "white bread" (a mould of arsenic and oil of vitriol) and "Prussian Butter" (Prussic acid made up to look like butter); picks up stray children to sell to the mills or for torture for public entertainment.

Quashia Quamina: A great Ashantee chief and brother to King Sai Tootoo Quamina. He slays King Frederick during the Battle of Rossendale Hill, after which he is immediately killed by a volley of shots from the remaining Twelves. See also Zerayda Quamina Quashia.

Rare Apes: A generic name for Rougue's "low life" companions—petty thieves, poachers, and brawlers.

Rationals: Glass Town's "opposition" political party, consisting of Conservative Constitutionalists, "men of cool heads and unprejudiced minds who saw both what was right and what was expedient," and who "looked to the general well fare of the Glass Town countrys and not to the narrow questions of Aristocracy and money." Its members include the Duke of Wellington, Sir Robert Weever Pelham, Sir John Flower, and John Bud Esq. The Rationals support the overthrow of the government by Rougue and the Marquis of Douro during the War of Encroachment.

Red River: The "king of hill streams" which rushes through the Robbers Towers. Its course is diverted by the Twelves against the oncoming Coomassiee army.

Robbers Towers: Rugged and inhospitable Alpine mountains to the north of Glass Town in which Rougue and his accomplices have constructed a cavernous but lavishly furnished hideaway that serves to house a "hundred inmates."

Rougue, Alexander (Viscount Elrington): The villain-hero of the Glass Town saga, stern, dissipated and ruthless; motivated to action by the "true fire of ambition" coupled with a "relentless contempt and. hatred of Mankind." His marriage to the gentle Mary Henrietta Percy, which produces one daughter, the honourable Miss Mary Percy, charms him away from his evil genius, but heartbroken upon her death he returns to his former ways. While a pirate, he seizes Lady Zenobia Elrington and her father from their ship, abruptly woos and marries her, and returns to Verdopolis as Lord Elrington. Operating principally as a gambler, robber baron and political agitator, he works against the ruling Aristocrats, repeatedly inciting the mob to revolutionary ferment, and the army to mutiny. During the War of Encroachment, he assists the Marquis of Douro against the French, but propels the downfall of the Glass Town government when it withholds support from the army, and personally executes the Prime Minister, Earl St Clair.

Ross, John: One of the Twelves; "frank open, honest" and brave; he is killed on Ascension Island, but later magically restored. He is one of the founders of Glass Town and King of Ross's Land.

Rossendale Hill: "[A]bout the size of Pendle hill in England," and located on the outskirts of Coomassie, it is the site of the Battle of Rossendale which Captain Bud calls the Twelves' "battle of Marathon." Here King Frederick I meets his death at the hands of Quashia Quamina. Subsequently, a small temple, which eventually becomes a pilgrimage site, is erected to commemorate these events.

Sai Quarenqua: The eldest of ten brothers ruling the region of Acrofcroomb. He is defeated and killed after mustering an attack on Glass Town.

Sai Tootoo Quamina: Son and successor of King Cashna Quamina. "[Y]oung headstrong and vengeful," he instigates a series of battles against the Twelves. Although his armies are defeated, Sai Tootoo survives.

Scroven, Tom: One of the "Rare Apes,"a poacher of intimidating mien: "8 feet high, bony, haggard and lean," with a "sinister, malignant expression," companion of Ned Laury and Young Man Naughty.

Scrovey's Cottage: Home of Tom Scroven, located in an isolated heathy region frequented by poachers and thieves; the place to which Lord Thornton Wilkin Sneaky is carried after he is shot during a duel with Castlereagh. It also offers shelter to James Bellingham and his companions during their travels.

Sdeath, Robert Patrick: A pirate and murderer—according to Captain Flower, a "little hideous bloody old man"—his name is derived from the oath "God's death." He is the "usher" of Elysium, and acts as partner and servant of Rougue. He possesses supernatural powers, for although capable of being wounded, it seems he cannot be killed.

Sneaky (Sneachie), Alexander: King of Sneachiesland.

Sneaky (Sneachie), John Augustus: Duke of Fidena, eldest son of Alexander Sneachie; one of Douro's most respected and trusted friends. Foreign Secretary and later Major General and Commander-in-Chief during the War of Encroachment.

Sneaky, Lord Thornton Wilkin (later Captain Thornton): Son of the King of Sneachiesland. Although he is unsuccessful in his bid to marry Lady Julia Montmorency, and humiliated when he is wounded in a duel with his rival, Castlereagh, and although his Parliamentary career is jeopardized when he is named as one of Rougue's criminal conspiritors, he later exonerates himself during the War of Encroachment by distinguished action on the battlefield, and becomes a member of the Council of Six.

Soult, Alexander: Son of Marshal Soult, he is the "celebrated poet" of Glass Town, unconventional, bohemian, "hair-brained." He accompanies James Bellingham, the Marquis of Douro, and Charles Wellesly on their tour of Glass Town; is wounded upon being captured by Rougue's forces during the revolutionary wars. As "Young Soult the Rhymer," a pseudonym used by Branwell, Charlotte recognizes that his "beginnings are small" but believes "his end will be great."

St Clair, Earl: Prime Minister and Leader in the House of Lords during the War of Encroachment. He is executed by Rougue after he and his party, the Arisocrats, withhold financial support from the army.

St Michaels Cathedral: Like the Tower of All Nations, a landmark of Glass Town, visible from afar. Its great dome gives a view of the entire spread of the city.

Standfast, Ned: Formerly in service to the Duke of Wellington, he is an honest night guard in the gaol where Dick Nose'em and his companions are being held. Because he cannot be bribed to release the five prisoners, Rougue is driven to muster a mob which effects the release of the five prisoners when they attack and destroy the prison.

Sydney, Lady Julia: Niece of the Duke, and wife of Edward Sydney, Lady Julia belongs to a circle of ladies "of high rank, beauty and fashion" who regularly attend society events in Glass Town.

Sydney, Edward, Geoffrey Stanley: Initially a Member for the populous borough of Freetown, his successful political bid earns him the hatred of Rougue. Although he enters Parliament "unknown young [and] little tried," he makes a spirited speech opposing Rougue's attempt to bring division and discord into parliamentary proceedings. He marries Lady Julia, the niece of the Duke of

Wellington, and by the time of the War of Encroachment, fills the office of Home Secretary and Leader in the Commons.

Stumps, Frederic (King Frederic II): The thirteenth crew member of the "Invincible," and the crew's first casualty. He is killed on Ascension Island but is miraculously restored to life, and later appears to the Twelves after the death of Frederick I. He is nominated king and duly crowned King Frederic II.

Tamworth Hall: A "splendid estate" built by Sir Robert Weever Pelham on his arrival at Wellington's Glass Town.

Tower of All Nations: Landmark in Glass Town, modeled on the Tower of Babel or Babylon, it rises 6,000 feet and is the home of Crashey, the great patriarch.

Tree, Captain: Famous Glass Town prose writer and pseudonym of Charlotte.

Tree, Sergeant: Glass Town's chief publisher, printer, bookseller, a "clever lawyer and a great liar."

Twelves, The: Originally Branwell's toy soldiers; they become the discoverers, explorers, and settlers of Ashantee, forming the Glass Town Confederacy. The original Twelves who board the "Invincible" for Ashantee in 1770 consist of: Butter Crashey, the Captain, aged 140 years; Alexander Cheeky, the surgeon, aged 20 years; Arthur Wellesly, a trumpeter, aged 12 years; William Edward Parry, a trumpeter, aged 15 years; Alexander Sneaky, a sailor aged 17 years; John Ross, the Lieutenant; William Bravey, a Sailor, aged 27 years; Edward Gravey, a sailor, aged 17 years; Frederick Guelph (the Duke of York), a sailor, aged 27 years; Stumps, a midshipman; Monkey, a midshipman, aged 11; Trackey, a midshipman, aged 10 years; and Crackey, a midshipman, aged 5 years. The first Twelves later form the House of Lords of Glass Town; the second Twelves form the House of Commons; four of them—Arthur Wellesly, Sneaky, Parry and Ross became kings of their respective countries: Wellingtonsland, Sneachiesland, Parrysland and Rossesland.

Vacillators: Glass Town's third political party, aligned for the most part with the Aristocrats. Unlike the Aristocrats, however, who operate largely from principles of "obstinate bigotry," the Vacillators, though "sometimes swayed by prejudice," "would sometimes listen to reason."

Velino: A range of hills outside of Vedopolis, and close to Freetown, housing a small village of the same name. This "wild Little" village affords a retreat to Fidena's army and becomes the general's new headquaters during the War of Encroachment..

Verdopolis: Capital of the Glass Town Confederacy—first called Glass Town, then Verreopolis, then Verdopolis; on the river Guadima; center for government, "high life," and commerce; "a splendid city rising with such graceful haughtiness from the green realm of Neptune," with walls, battlements, a cathedral, the domed Bravey's hotel, the Great Tower, and many fine streets with fine shops. It is later sacked by the French army during the War of Encroachment. See also Glass Town.

Warner Hall: Residence of the millionaire, Warner Howard Warner Esq.

Warner Hills: A long ridge of isolated mountains north of Verdopolis; site of the first military engagement in the War of Encroachment, and of a subsequent mutiny in the Glass Town army by its "three best" regiments, which is henceforth known as "the Mutiny at Little Warner."

Warner, Mr. Warner Howard: A reclusive millionaire "from an ancient and distinguished family" whose property includes a significant "part of Angria." He commands "4000 armed devoted tenantry," and an additional body of 8,000 men. On condition of full repayment, he offers the Glass Town Government troops and financing during the War of Encroachment, as well as full hospitalities to the 5,000 casualities of the Battle of Little Warner. He also makes a decisive speech in Parliament castigating the ruling Aristocrats for their "hideous blindness" and "willfull insanity" in refusing to support the army, and calling upon members to "hurl from office the whole present Ministry." He subsequently becomes a member of the Council of Six. Credited with the gift of second sight.

Waterloo Palace: The "Noble Mansion" of the Duke of Wellington. Branwell may be thinking of the case of John Churchill, the Duke of Marlborough, whose reputation for military skill was unrivalled until Napoleon. In gratitude for his victory over the French at the Battle of Blenheim in Germany (1704), the English parliament had Blenheim Palace built as part of the nation's gift to Marlborough for services rendered to the country. Designed by John Vanbrugh, Blenheim Palace offers one of the finest examples of Baroque architecture in Britain.

Wellesly, Arthur: One of the Twelves (originally a trumpeter aboard the "Invincible"), and a co-founder of Glass Town. "Ardent for all military glory and fame," he is chosen by the Genii to return to England to help in the war against Napoleon. He becomes the "champion of Europe," and is awarded "the title of DUKE OF WELLINGTON." Upon returning with 3,000 of his "brave soldiers" to Glass Town, Frederic II relinquishes his crown in favour of Wellesly who is "formally installed 'King and ruler of the 12s town and of all its inhabitants.'" Later, however, with the refusal of the ruling Ministry to support the army during the War of Encroachment, he secedes his kingdom, Wellingtonsland, from the Confederation of the Twelves, thus "dissolving that Mighty Body". Upon the forcible removal of the Ministry, he, "form[s] a 7th. councillor" to the Grand Council of Six. He is the father of the Marquis of Douro and Lord Charles Wellesly.

Wellesly, Arthur Augustus Adrian (Marquis of Douro): Eldest "noble son" of the Duke of Wellington. A distinguished warrior and leader on the battlefield; and in the city, a respected minor poet; friend and rival of Rougue Elrington. He is Rougue's opponent during the latter's War of Insurrection, but joins forces with Elrington in the War of Encroachment. In return for his war efforts, conciliating "a divided army," and shoring up "a shattered government," he demands the territories of Angria, Calabar, Northangerland and Gordon, "to be yeilded up to me unconditionally and immediately, in just right to myself and my heirs and successors in due and rightful sovereignity."

Wellesly, Lady Julia: Cousin of the Marquis of Douro.

Wellesly, Lord Charles Albert Florian: Precocious son of Arthur Wellesly, Duke of Wellington, and brother to the Marquis of Douro (whom he despises as a "sour puritanical milk sop"). As the young author of various literary libels and tracts, including "Something about Arthur," he is the subject of Captain Bud's **The Liar Detected** in which he is "unmasked" as "a Boy uterly destitute of all common understanding Foolish and Inconsiderate in the extreme But with a few small marks of some sort of a genius." While travelling with his brother, Young Soult and James Bellingham, he is captured by Rougue during the revolutionary insurrections, and wounded although not fatally.

Wellesly House: Residence of the Marquis of Douro.

Zerayda Quamina Quashia: The "son of the former monarch of Africa," and later "the Duke's adopted son." Dedicated to revenging "my Fathers Murderers," he lends his support to Rougue Elrington's political intrigues, but after failing to win a seat as a member of Elrington's Liberty Democrats party, he demands the hand of Elrington's daughter, Mary Percy, as a political liaison, and later, with the aid of Sdeath, kills Col. Ashton, the member for Northtown in order to obtain his seat. He is yielded up to the Government by Elrington, and imprisoned.

INDEX OF FIRST LINES AND TITLES

As some titles have been derived from the first lines, neither titles nor first lines have been inverted, so definite and indefinite articles have been treated as keywords in alphabetization and occur at the beginning of lines.

Titles of manuscript volumes and of stories and poems have been printed in italics. First lines of stories and poems, including poems that occur within stories, are printed in roman type in quotation marks. Titles in italics and quotations marks indicate story titles derived from the first line of text.

When there are several installments of one story, these have been placed in chronologial order. Dates have been included in square brackets where necessary to distinguish two or more items with the same titles.